P9-AOR-104

In the Reading Gaol

In the Reading Gaol

Postmodernity, Texts, and History

Valentine Cunningham

B
BLACKWELL
Oxford UK & Cambridge USA

First published 1994

Blackwell Publishers
108 Cowley Road
Oxford   OX4 1JF
UK

238 Main Street
Cambridge, Massachusetts 02142
USA

British Library Cataloguing in Publication Data
A CIP catalogue record for this book is available from the British Library.

Library of Congress Cataloging-in-Publication Data
Cunningham, Valentine.
In the reading gaol : postmodernity, texts, and history /
Valentine Cunningham.
p.   cm.
Includes bibliographical references (p.   ) and index.
ISBN 0–631–13133–7. — ISBN 0–631–15198–2 (pbk.)
1. Criticism.   2. Postmodernism (Literature)   3. English
fiction—19th century—History and criticism.   4. English
fiction—20th century—History and criticism.   I. Title.
PN81.C86   1994
801'.95'0904—dc20
93–26399
CIP

Typeset in 10$\frac{1}{2}$ on 12 pt Garamond
by Graphicraft Typesetters Ltd, Hong Kong
Printed in Great Britain by Hartnolls Ltd, Bodmin

This book is printed on acid-free paper

Contents

Reading, Reading, and Reading Gaol: a Short Paratext on This Book's Title (or Paratext)

Much of the most influential reading theory and practice of our time – variously known as postmodernist, deconstructionist, or just theorist (though always bearing the implicit claim of advanced, progressive, non-fuddy-duddy, latest new-technological) – would confine texts to themselves, locking them up in 'the prison-house of language'. Language is proposed as self-referring, and so are texts. So history, the world of things and people, the varied outside of texts, gets deferred, waived, put off as no longer central to what matters in reading games. Reading is reading. By contrast, the argument in this book is that reading can never be simply reading. Reading is, for example, also Reading.

Reading / reading: the same word, but also different words; different words, individual, separate, but also inseparable, identical. And the identity and difference really come home to the reader at, say, Reading railway station. There signs tell you, provokingly, that you're at Reading. In the text of those station signs, word-stuff (this word 'Reading'; there for your reading) and world-stuff (the place, the station, the town of Reading in Berkshire) converge with agitating power. And it's this doubling of reading matter and more than reading matter – that is, Reading matter – that this book is adopting as a main metaphor for its continual interest in the simultaneous connection, and difference, between text and context, literature and history, words and things, signs and places, the textual and the human.

Reading. Is it reading or Reading? It is, of course, both. The word on the station sign looks homophonous with reading. And so it is. The place's written name can indeed rhyme with reading, the activity that the station signs induce. Unsuspecting foreign travellers often pronounce it so. But, of course, the place-name, while accepting the reading-rhyme, also, you learn very quickly, quite rejects it. *In loco* – among the locomotives – Reading, the place-name, is allowed to recall reading only as a faint para-rhyme, a distant pun or paronomasia. Walter Redfern, the doyen of the pun who's a professor at Reading University, has undoubtedly thought of this one. We know that Victorian dons, on their railway to Oxford from London, chuckled over it. But in Reading your average citizen will readily disabuse the foreigner. To mix up Reading and reading would be just a mistake of pronunciation.

But the pun won't go away. The reading potential of Reading will intrude. The curiously many bookish associations of the town do rather bring it home. Dickens, for example, has the orphaned girl-narrator of *Bleak House* sent to school at Reading. The HQ of Britnuc, the dubious nuclear energy company in Fay Weldon's novel *The Cloning of Joanna May* (1989), is in Reading. En route to Oxford by bus and train from Heathrow airport, Jacques Derrida catches a train at Reading, and his entranced reading of his bus ticket that reads 'to Reading Station → Oxford' gets into *La Carte postale*. Less entranced, T. E. Lawrence left a massive draft of *The Seven Pillars of Wisdom* at Reading station, and never got it back.

Such literary encounters assert the sorts of reading connection any place might have, even a humdrum English town. And, after all, all places are reading matters, if only because what we do with any name, including place-names, is read them. But still, for a reminder of the necessary convergence between places, naming and reading, Reading does rather beat the band. And just how much reading matters can interact with apparently non-reading ones, one famous British writer learned to his cost precisely at Reading.

On his way from Oxford to London – a journey also reported in *La Carte postale* – 'près de Reading', Derrida recalled, as any bookish traveller might, Oscar Wilde, and meditated on literary 'inversion', mindful no doubt of the sexual activities that had landed Wilde so cruelly inside Reading Gaol. Carl May, the quite literate boss of Weldon's Britnuc, quotes from Wilde's *Ballad of Reading Gaol*. The Gaol is still visible from the train at Reading. It was not a quarter of a mile from the Britnuc offices. But neither Carl May nor Jacques Derrida reflected, as Edward Said would in his fine book *The World, the Text, and the Critic*, that Wilde was in Reading Gaol precisely because he foolishly imagined (or so he said) that a letter, an epistle, a piece of private reading matter, could be just that, a piece of art, or text, merely for art's, for text's sake. Misplaced faith in the prison-house of language, the reading gaol, landed Wilde in the Reading Gaol. Wilde suffered, so to say, at the insistence of a careless proto-postmodernist notion of reading that failed to appreciate what the homophony and pun of reading might spell in terms of Reading, a theory of texts that never spotted until too late the way that Reading, as it were, policed the act of reading.

This book argues that the convergence of writing and worldliness, text and context, literature and history, as exemplified in the interlocking of reading with Reading, is as important for every reader, theorist, and theory of reading as it was for poor Saint Oscar. Joseph Conrad was one great writer, I will suggest, who caught on to this, and exemplarily so, when he put a biscuit-tin from Reading – a Huntley & Palmers biscuit-tin, a piece of merchandise manufactured in the great sprawl of buildings adjacent to Wilde's Reading Gaol, buildings that were in Conrad's time even more visible from the train than was the Gaol, and whose sweet biscuits Wilde had upsetting acquaintance with – when he put such a tin into the heart of Africa in *Heart of Darkness*.

The biscuit-tin from Reading that Conrad offers for our reading and digestion in *Heart of Darkness* (curiously ignored by all readers of this text until now) occurs, of course, in a metaphor. But this too is exemplary. A main contention here is that history and tropes are inseparable, with all the inseparability of Reading and reading. Deconstruction, as defined by Paul de Man and his disciples, has influentially dictated otherwise. For that party the 'problem of reading' consists in the resistance that literary work, text-making, rhetoric, troping, offer to history. It's the kept-up argument of this book that the literary evidence says quite differently, and that the problem of reading is always inextricably woven into the problem, so to say, of Reading, the problem of what Reading's Gaol, not to mention its biscuit manufactory, are all about.

1

Word and World: The Wor(l)d of Mrs Woolf

So lebt das Tier *unhistorisch* . . . / It's the brute beast that lives thus *unhistorically*. . . .

Nietzsche, 'Vom Nutzen und Nachteil der Historie für das Leben'/
'On the Advantages and Disadvantages of History for Life' (1874)

'You all remember,' said the Controller, in his strong deep voice, 'you all remember, I suppose, that beautiful and inspired saying of Our Ford's: History is bunk. History', he repeated slowly, 'is bunk.'

Aldous Huxley, *Brave New World* (1932)

At the mid-point of the twentieth century, on what was to become a rather famous critical occasion, René Wellek and Austin Warren raised what they described as an 'extremely difficult epistemological question', namely that 'of the "mode of existence" or the "ontological situs" of a literary work of art'.[1] The question was not new, though their book put it thus with particular force – like so much else in their book – on the map of the post-war English-speaking world. Nor has the question gone away. The issue of this 'ontological situs' is still with us, still vexed, still unanswered with any finality, half a century later. 'What is a text?' is still a key question. Roland Barthes is only one of the influential putters of it. Cannily, though, he supplemented it: 'What is a text, for current opinion?'[2]

Barthes's was a canny recasting because current opinion is horribly current, fluid, even shifty in this matter. So the question itself, let alone any answer to it, depends greatly upon who's asking. But the asking, the challenge to the nature of text and textuality, continues unabated. *Text* has become *the* terminological football of recent criticism. Books and articles with *text* in their title have spawned in multitudes. Text preoccupies us. It's become the cant term of cant terms. Text and its sprawling cousinhood of related terms – texture, textural, context, metatext, *hors-texte*, *avant-texte*, pre-text, *après-texte*, subtext, inter-text, hyper-text, social text – slip and slide in an extraordinary frenzy, an ecstatic mob, across the Western critical scene. We live, according to America's favourite folksy hopalong pragmatist philosopher Richard Rorty, in an era of *textualists* and *textualism*. For the French, ours is the time of *textologie*. *Texting* is what writers and critics are all about nowadays.[3] In some (post)structuralist opinion, texting or textualizing is what every individual, every institution, every society, certainly every movement of thought does, simply.[4] *To text* – *texter* in French – was, according to Derrida, a necessary coinage: the times demanded it.[5] The *textual* is what really excites our critics; it rhymes so pointedly, of course, with *sexual*.[6]

Once upon a time people asked *What is Art?* (with Tolstoy), *What is Literature?* (with Sartre), *What is Poetry?* (with Roman Jabokson to name but one).[7] Now they ask 'What is a Text?' with Barthes, and Paul Ricoeur,[8] and Harold Bloom, and Jacques Derrida, and . . . and . . . . It's only late on in his career when he's seeking with extreme vehemence to undo some of the critical crimes done in his name, that Derrida reverts, challengingly, to the older mode of the question – though it remains, even in the French and English versions of his essay, provokingly cloaked in the Italian of the first occasion of his asking it: *Ch'e cos'è la poesia?*[9] The Italian denotes, for French as for English readers, the calculatedly unmodish and estranged. For it's *text* and its ways that keep on stirring us, *The Question of Textuality*. 'What is the meaning of a text?' is what we still demand to know.[10] And the more we search, the more, as ever, texts and their meanings simply elude us – like mirages in the desert.

'Is There A Text in This Class?' demanded Stanley Fish, playing the big bad textual Wolf-Man who'd huff and puff until he blew all your textual confidences down. But the pose of Bad Guy in the Saloon has stuck, and Fish's scepticism about textual objects and recognizing a poem 'when you see one' has gone on mounting.[11] Feminists, not least among politicizing critics, have rushed in with ideological sticking-plaster – 'Is There A Woman in This Text?' was Mary Jacobus's stern supplement to the Fish enquiry – but they have not managed to put an end to Fish's kind of demand.[12] The answer to 'What is a Text?' is now vaguer than ever before. 'We are specialists in . . . texts,' declared Derrida in 1984, addressing an audience of critics; but he added, 'texts, of all sorts'. At the time, he was talking about the 'text' of modern warfare, the discourse, the stories, fictions, arguments, fantasies, predictions, and so on, to do with nuclear conflict.[13] Barthes's question 'What is a text for current opinion?' has now become, awesomely, Just What is a Text for Current Criticism?

For the textual scene has indeed gone nuclear. It's a scene of dissolution, a vertiginous help-yourself canteen, a dizzyingly liberal *bricolage*, a great stirring melting-pot where the old canons of 'literature' are invaded by textual stuff from psychology, philosophy, law, medicine, geography, and the old generic boundaries are down, and the distinction between 'literary' and 'non-literary' goes, and old minor or marginal texts (authors' jottings, essays, fragments, versions, foul papers, say) cease to lurk in the supplementary shadows and come busily in from the margin and the cold to receive equal treatment with what were once thought of as the main objects of concern, the poems and novels and plays, the published stuff, the final versions, and so on.[14] 'Le texte n'existe pas,' in fact, certainly not in any old familiar sense.[15] It goes without saying – which does not stop it being said repeatedly – that the days of Matthew (Seeing the Object as in Itself It Really Is) Arnold and of F. R. (Great Tradition) Leavis are past. But, of course, the collapse of old critical confidences and the welcome afforded to our postmodernist chaos make the question of the nature of text more, rather than less, urgent. And central to the issue is, still, the question of where texts – any texts, but in particular 'literary' texts, 'literary' words – stand in relation to the world that frames them and their utterers. And, of course, the troubled Sartrean question of what the 'literary' is – a question that the commandeering modern preference for the 'textual' has sought without conviction to bypass in acts of re-naming, re-defining, re-locating – remains, still, at the very heart of the matter. ' "What is literature?" or "Where does literature come from?" "What should we do with literature?" ' – that they raise these Sartrean questions is precisely, for Derrida, what makes the work of his favourite modernists, Blanchot, Ponge, Celan, Joyce, Artaud, Jabès, and Kafka so important.[16]

A 'literary' person, or at least the published version of her diary, rather wittily, if unwittingly, provides us with a very nice clue, I think, to the relationship of word and world, granting us a word, or sign, to frame my discussion of the framing of signs. This potent word is to be found in a crime story in the Virginia Woolf diaries. It's about a Christmas shopping expedition that went terribly wrong, involving three coats, three or four women, a male detective, and a purloined handbag. The story got aired a couple of times, first in Virginia Woolf's diary, in the entry for 23 December 1930, and then, on Christmas Day itself, in a letter that's a kind of Christmas box or gift (a supplementary gift, as it turns out) to be sent through the post to her sister Vanessa.

Here's the diary entry, followed by the letter, which is a kind of footnote or supplement to it (and a reinforcement, of course, of the conventionally provoking 'literary' supplementarity of diaries, as opposed, say, to novels):

Tuesday 23 December

I will make this hasty note about being robbed. I put my bag under my coat at Marshall & Snelgrove's. I turned; & felt, before I looked 'It is gone'. So it was. Then began questions & futile messages. Then the detective came. He stopped a respectable elderly woman apparently shopping. They exchanged remarks about 'the usual one – no she's not here today. Its a young woman in brown fur.' Meanwhile I was ravaged, of course, with my own futile wishes – how I had thought, as I put down my bag, this is foolish. I was admitted to the underworld. I imagined the brown young woman peeping, pouncing. And it was gone my 6 pounds – my two brooches – all because of that moment. They throw the bags away, said the detective. These dreadful women come here – but not so much as to some of the Oxford St. shops. Fluster, regret, humiliation, curiosity, something frustrated, foolish, something jarred, by this underworld – a foggy evening – going home, penniless – thinking of my green bag – imagining the woman rifling it – her home – her husband – Now to Rodmell in the fog.[17]

Monks House, [Rodmell, Sussex]

Xmas day [1930]
Dearest Dolphin

I rang you up on Tuesday, but you were out. It was only to say that we sent you a black coat; and that if you hate, it, or it doesn't fit, you can change it. I thought it might come in useful in the evening; anyhow keep you warm in the country.

. . . I had a queer adventure by the way, the day I got your coat at Marshall and Snelgroves. I was given £6 to buy Xmas presents; I put my bag under my moleskin, and turned, for one moment, to try on your coat. Then I thought I ought not to leave the bag, so turned to get it – and behold – in that second a thief had snatched it! There was then a great hue and cry, and a detective appeared, and they said a woman in brown fur had been seen; but of course they could not catch her; so there I was, penniless, without key, spectacles, cigarette case or handkerchief. Marshall's refused to lend me a penny as they said I was not on their books; but the detective gave me 10/- of his own. Later that night the bag was found, thrown in a drain; and marvellously, though the £6 were gone, the thief had left my spectacles, keys, and one old earring. I had just bought two for a present. So didn't do as badly as I might.[18]

As with much modernist writing – indeed, with much fiction – we are here in the presence of a story of a crime, a transgressive exchange between people. The diary paragraph, which concerns me most, has much of the shape and polish of a short story. Notably it is a very self-conscious piece of writing, like so many of Mrs Woolf's diary entries. These writings know themselves as writing, as *écriture*. They repeatedly meditate upon their own writtenness, on their mode of production as writing, on the pens and ink they've been composed with, and so on. 'I will make this hasty note.' The opening sentence announces that this is a text self-consciously aware of its status as a piece of text. Here, right at the start, are words about words, text upon text. This is not least a metatextual encounter for the reader. And the note, so conscious, as it were, of being written, at the very moment of its writing, comes embedded in, framed by, an astonishing array of quotations from and references to other texts, to writings off-stage, outside and around this bit of writing in the journal. The whole sequence of Virginia Woolf's daily jottings is writing about writing about writing, and so on and on. Here is intertextuality with a vengeance.

Hereabouts in the diary, in an effort to give 'continuity' to 'this book' (though which book, the diary itself or a 'book of criticism' that she was thinking of writing when she'd finished doing *The Waves*, we simply cannot tell), she was copying headlines from daily newspapers into her diary.[19] 'Horror death of Douglas: Indian Conference. Fog. Intermittent. Weather to be colder', ran the sampled quotations the day before the handbag case, Monday 22 December. The entry of that day was otherwise devoted, as other entries are at this point in the diary, to how she would end Bernard's final speech in *The Waves* and so bring to an end the novel she was currently writing. 'It occurred to me last night while listening to a Beethoven quartet that I would merge all the interjected passages into Bernard's final speech, & end with the words O Solitude.'[20] She eventually settled for 'O Death' a few weeks later, on Saturday 7 February 1931.[21] Clearly, Mrs Woolf's mind was greatly taken up, as ever, with words about death. And, as often, specifically with death by drowning in gloomy waters. The 'Horror death of Douglas' was the recent drowning of the English cricketer J. W. H. T. Douglas when the steamer *Oberon* sank in a collision with the *Arcturus* – a Shakespearian Fairy Prince clashing with a bright Greek star – in the Danish waters of the Kattegat on the night of 19 December. Virginia Woolf had recently been reading Dante, and on the opposite page of her journal, as a kind of classic literary parallel to the horrible drowning of the cricketer and forty-one other passengers, she copied out in Italian the nine lines from Dante's *Inferno*, canto xxvi, 94–102, part of the moving story which Ulysses tells of his drowning at sea – interestingly, in fact, the section of Dante's poem that was Tennyson's major inspiration for his poem *Ulysses*:

> Ma misi me per l'alto more aperto
> Sol con un legno e con quella compagna
> Picciola, dalla qual non fui deserto.

Forth I sail'd
Into the deep illimitable main,
With but one bark, and the small faithful band
That yet cleav'd to me.[22]

Words about words, text upon text upon text. This bit of diary-writing could scarcely be more thoroughly steeped in its own condition of writtenness. You could hardly expect to find anywhere a more energetically copious example of the notorious *mise en abyme*, the ultra-formalist plunge down into the dark backward and abysm of textuality, of the kind that postmodernist criticism and modernist and postmodernist fiction offer us as the necessary and normal state of writing. This is, of course, the repeated condition or siting of Virginia Woolf's fiction: the place at which the reader finds her- or himself on the opening page of, say, *Jacob's Room* (1922) – inside a hyper-written condition, inside double quotation marks as it were, within a piece of a writing that is a letter by Mrs Flanders (' "So of course", wrote Betty Flanders, pressing her heels rather deeper in the sand, "there was nothing for it but to leave" '), in a text whose initial, initiating subject is a pen and ink and the marks on paper that they make: 'Slowly welling from the point of her gold nib, pale blue ink dissolved the full stop.' This is the place – inside a story, inside a story inside a text inside a text, a discourse within a discourse, in the presence of a 'Once upon a time' that is repeating, quoting an already given or uttered 'Once upon a time' – where *A Portrait of the Artist as a Young Man* dramatically locates us: 'Once upon a time . . . His father told him that story.'

And openings like this are consciously, deliberately repudiations of the supposedly simpler condition that old-fashioned realist novels thought they were delivering the reader into. That messy drop of ink in the opening paragraphs of *Jacob's Room* must recall the rather precise drop of ink that George Eliot's *Adam Bede* (1859) opens with:

> With a single drop of ink for a mirror, the Egyptian sorcerer undertakes to reveal to any chance comer far-reaching visions of the past. This is what I undertake to do for you, reader. With this drop of ink at the end of my pen, I will show you the roomy workshop of Mr Jonathan Burge, carpenter and builder in the village of Hayslope, as it appeared on the eighteenth of June, in the year of our Lord 1799.

The drop of ink at the end of George Eliot's pen is offered to us as a mirror of the real, historical, given world; the drop of ink at the end of Virginia Woolf's pen is in the first place a mirror only of the drop of ink at the end of Mrs Flanders's pen. George Eliot's pen generates a world, a time, a place, a scene of work realistically conceived – carpentry, Hayslope, 1799 – a mirror, no less, of the world, and a world that Marian Evans's friends and relations were able to decode easily as *their* world, and so to recognize Marian Evans's as the actual pen-wielding hand behind 'George Eliot'. Virginia Woolf's pen, for its part, gives birth to more pens and ink. And, bringing the case still more dramatically home to the reader, not just to pens and ink, but also to paintbrush and paint, for Mrs Flanders is not simply a persona-as-writer; she turns out to be the focus of a painting being painted by a Mr Charles Steele. She's a dab of paint. 'Here was that woman moving – actually going to get up – confound her! He struck the canvas a hasty violet-black dab. For the landscape needed it.' 'Steele frowned: but was pleased by the effect of the black – it was just *that* note which brought the rest together.' The text's black widow is a piece of black pigment.

But all this is by no means, of course, the whole story. Even though at this stage of *Jacob's Room* there is obviously no intrusive authorial 'I' in the old-fashioned fashion of *Adam Bede*, there is already an implicit hand and pen behind the hand and pen of Mrs Flanders, an implied writer behind that writer, an implied external source of discourse behind that supplied discourse (the novel and Mrs Flanders's letter within the novel), an implied framer outside the framing painting by Charles Steele. This outside source is, naturally enough, the writer who wrote the words 'wrote Betty Flanders'. It is the speaker who later intrudes several times in *Jacob's Room*, *in*, or in something like, *propria voce* and *persona* ('Either we are men, or we are women . . . In any case life is but a procession of shadows, and God knows why it is that we embrace them so eagerly,' and so on), much to the consternation of many current readers who regard such reminders of a worldly, extra-textual, authorial presence behind the text as a scandalous throwback to the simplistic practices and assumptions of George Eliot's time.

There is, however, no getting away from the authorial hand and voice *avant la lettre*, outside the text, and particularly not in the detective story in the diary. The repeated 'I . . . I . . . I . . . I . . .' of Virginia Woolf thrusts that worldly presence upon us. This is, emphatically, a text that knows itself as text, but it is *also* a text about the world of London shops, London fog, Christmas shopping, female shoplifters, male and female store-detectives – shop-walkers as they were called. It's about a brown fur coat, a green handbag, six English pounds, a couple of brooches.

And the key word in that last paragraph is *also*. For this text is a curious, arresting, even puzzling amalgam of word-stuff and world-stuff. It is certainly neither all of the word nor all of the world. And it is the argument of this book that this amalgamation of word and world is the condition not just of Virginia Woolf's writing but of all writing. It is the condition of all language, and so of all things made out of language. And this little narrative – at once so strikingly a writing, about text, and sited so vividly in a context of text and texts, but also so emphatically about the knowable, touchable world of city streets, shops, country houses, possession, persons who exist outside of narrative, that is the Real World of Alex Zwerdling's title – grants us a key word for the doubling, ambivalent, even duplicitous condition of its so mixed existence, its very fraught ontology.[23]

The Woolf Woman's Magic Word

For, describing her unaccustomed, bruising *entrée* into the world of the thieving underclass, the criminal underworld – 'I was admitted to the underworld'; 'something jarred, by this underworld' – Virginia Woolf did not actually write, in either of those two phrases, the word *underworld* but – arrestingly! – *underword*. But what a wonderfully illuminating Freudian slip that was! For, of course, in her writing about the episode, the *underworld* had become words about the underworld, comprising an *underword* condition. And for us, the readers, access to this particular bit of the underworld is only to be effected through contact with Virginia Woolf's words about it – what we might label her *underwords*. But the underwords of this text are also about, of, even in, the underworld. The words about the underworld are vividly present, but through them, so is the underworld they bring to us. In the hands of this powerful writer, the underwords are a means of making vividly present – recalling, recounting, re-enacting – the underworld. Both – words *and* world – are present. And neither's presence is possible without the presence of the other: no underwords, no underworld for us; no underworld on this occasion, no underwords about it in the diary or for us. Both items in this reading–writing transaction, the word and the world, exist only by courtesy of each other, because both consist, for the reader, in each other. They are coterminous, coextensive, coexistent. So that the textual emendation by the *Diary*'s editors at this point, their solution to the problem of their author's having written *underword* when she 'meant' *underworld*, is entirely, indeed brilliantly, happy. *Underwor(l)d* is what actually appears in the published *Diary*. All at once, it registers the *wordiness* of what Virginia Woolf wrote, it acknowledges the *wordliness* that the words encounter and inscribe, and it produces a new nonce-word, a very *bon mot* indeed, to register the awkward and persistent duality of language – made of both wordy and worldly things and not absolutely either the one or the other. *Wor(l)d*: the word is mightily expressive for my purposes, a very apt sign for what I'm arguing is the continual co-presence of world and word, word and world, at every moment, in any text whatsoever, however extremely it might at first appear that a particular writing had been able to shed the one and consist only of the other.

That this place where words and worlds converge is a risky place is acknowledged by many texts of Virginia Woolf, as it is by her life. In this particular pre-Christmas encounter with criminality, accumulating words of distress signal huge dismay: *futile* (twice), *foolish* (twice), *ravaged*, *frustrated*, *jarred*, *penniless*; *Fluster*, *regret*, *humiliation*. The violation of a portable piece of property, the handbag, is like a violation of the self. Virginia Woolf, and not just her bag, is the object of alien *peeping*, *pouncing*, *rifling*. Her imagination ('I imagined the brown young woman peeping, pouncing'; 'imagining the woman rifling') is as offended as her portable self-extension, the bag. The store-detective used the phrase 'These dreadful women'. Virginia Woolf repeats it and clearly shares the hostility. Seemingly, her feminist feeling of sisterly solidarity has also had a jarring. And what happens in this underwor(l)d is all one with what happens in the texts that surround this account in the diary: horrors at sea in newspapers and in Dante, mortality in *The Waves*. This textual border site where words and world abut and overlap is evidently a dangerous frontier, threshold, marginal place – the 'dangerous edge' that Browning's Bishop Blougram, speaking perhaps for most writers, declares that his 'interest' is 'on'. It's difficult to keep your equilibrium there, says Browning's Bishop – the 'giddy line midway': take 'one step aside' and you're 'done with'. The prospect of being done with, or done for, is what Mrs Flanders experiences as she sits writing and weeping on her Cornish beach, that margin between land and sea: the ink-blot and the tear-drop converge on her troubled page as the bay quivers, the lighthouse wobbles and the mast of Mr Connor's yacht bends. 'Accidents were awful things.'

When Mrs Dalloway stands at her particular domestic-textual border, at her own front doorstep in a posh quarter of London, and on the opening page of the novel that bears her name, she doesn't appear like a candidate for trouble. Her party is coming off soon; the morning is 'fresh as if issued to children on a beach'. 'What a lark! What a plunge!' But thoughts of the Mrs Flanders kind, of weeping, accidents, death on beaches, will not be held at bay for long: the promising 'flap' and 'kiss of a wave' turn, in a moment, 'chill and sharp'. Clearly you have to watch your step on doorsteps. Doors and windows may look like places of regular and easy exit and entrance, barriers that can readily be coped with. 'The doors would be taken off their hinges; Rumpelmayer's men were coming.' But in the meantime the hinges still squeak, and that squeaking alerts us to some lurking problem or other, whether at Clarissa Dalloway's childhood home Bourton, now again in Bloomsbury, or in Bloomsbury's favourite novel, *Tristram Shandy*. The entrance-exit, the doorway, the window, the place where insides and outsides, presence and absence, meaning and unmeaning, life and death, articulation and disarticulation (hinge-work), converge is indeed most disconcerting. At Bourton, at the open window there, Clarissa felt 'that something awful was about to happen'. She feels it again now. Her thoughts turn to dull Peter Walsh and his pocket-knife and to mothers who've lost sons in the Great War. She hears the *leaden, irrevocable* boom of Big Ben. She 'stiffened a little on the kerb': Durtnall's van might run her over. The stage is set for Peter Walsh's weeping, for the intrusive self-slaughter of shell-shocked Septimus Warren Smith, for the sky-writing that pithers away into unreadable alphabetical blur ('But what letters? A C was it? an E, then an L? . . . a K, and E, a Y perhaps?'), for the leaden passage of time, the grim arrival of death.

When words meet worlds, when writing occurs, when readers leave the world to enter a text, 'the stakes' – to borrow Paul de Man's words to J. Hillis Miller – 'are enormous'.[24] The quest for meaning is like the desire for life, presence, survival, against the threatening encroachments of death, absence, annihilation. What Virginia Woolf feels at the moment of that encounter, what she has her characters feel, especially at the initiatory, introductory, prefacing moments of her fictions, and so also what she has her readers feeling as they step across the text's threshold into the text, negotiating the emblematic doorsteps, beaches, window-sills that cluster there (*To The Lighthouse* begins at a window) may all be extreme. Of course, Virginia Woolf's sense of danger hereabouts is heightened as it is inflected by her terrible personal proneness to fearful visions, horrid spectres of death. If ever anyone was specially possessed by death and saw the skull beneath the skin with a particularly frightful intensity, she did. Terror abounds in every motion – and slip – of the tongue as she contemplates initiating the textual, word–world encounter. 'When you asked me to write a preface to a book which you had collected of papers by working women', she wrote in her 'Introductory Letter to Margaret Llewellyn Davies', published at the beginning of *Life As We Have Known It By Co-operative Working Women*, 'I replied that I would be drowned rather than write a preface to any book whatsoever.'[25] But, I would argue, the extremity of Mrs Woolf's sense of what's at stake is only a heightened case that brings vividly home the normal anxieties.

What threatens in the Marshall and Snelgrove encounter – it's typical of Virginia Woolf's writings, and, I'd allege, typical *mutatis mutandis* of writing as such – is emptiness, absence, loss, bewilderment, frustration, the threat of anarchy and meaninglessness, the failure of good-will and desire, the abortion of attempts at family and social rituals (this buying of a Christmas present), and the helplessness of detectives and other agencies for order, moral regulation, meaning, to make sense and to curb hurtful, aggressive, disruptive behaviour. These are the characteristic issues and problems of story. Traditionally fiction has been supposed to take on these forces of darkness and to enact ritual affirmations of meaning, presence, order, fulfilled desire, to affirm the success of language and story in the creation of sense and of moral and civic order, and to do this particularly in the repeated recreation of successful detective stories. Detective-type stories – they go all the way back in the Western traditions of narrative – are those in which some keen moral agent, reliable narrator, substantive hero or heroine, will resolve problems, solve crimes, apportion final praise and blame, set moral chaos to rights, restore damaged selves and lives to order – in other words, behave like God at the apocalyptic Last Day of the Christian end of the world. Twentieth-century fiction has become increasingly sceptical as to these finalizing, closing, detective possibilities. The implication of most accounts of modernist or postmodernist fiction is that the turn to openness, the advent of modern and postmodern scepticism, have successfully and finally routed earlier naïve faith in the possibility of story any longer achieving all those old desires convincingly for us. We have become, it's supposed, adults, and we've put away all those old childish things.[26]

Much modern criticism, summing up the old cravings for meaning, closure, truth, certainty, as dubiously founded, centred in some doubtful *locus standi* (phallocentrism, logocentrism, phallogocentrism, theologocentrism: all the logo–Lego building blocks of the House of Criticism), is confidently dismissive. But what, among other things, is wrong with these recent critical assumptions is that it is by no means clear that the traditional story was ever as confident in the solutions it suggested or sought as some of its modern critics would claim. Nor is it at all certain that modern fictions and criticism have between them done away with or negated what can be summed up as logocentrism. This book will constantly seek to illustrate the impossibility, naïvety even, of both these assumptions, the one about the nature of past texts, the other about the nature of current ones. Which is why Virginia Woolf's underwor(l)d shopping expedition is so exemplary, whether considered as story in general or modernist story in particular.

In one sense, here is your usual modernist sceptical reversal of traditional labyrinth-solving tales, a variant, it might be, on Conrad's *Heart of Darkness* or Alain Robbe-Grillet's *Les Gommes* (1953) or his *Dans le labyrinthe* (1959). The handbag is stolen, the detective is frustrated, the victim ends up penniless, the thief escapes. It is as if the Minotaur had vanquished Theseus, or Ariadne Woolf had been clueless. We thus come uncomfortably close to the disturbing conclusions engineered by the moral and narrative reversals of Conrad's Marlow, the narrator-friend of the villain Kurtz, or to the criminality of Robbe-Grillet's detective Wallas, the crime-buster who's found finally committing the very murder he investigates. In other senses, though, at least in Act Two of the Woolf drama, in the supplementary epistolary narrative, there is a kind of traditional success. The detective comes to the victim's aid with 'ten shillings of his own'; the stolen bag is restored; £6 have disappeared, alright, but 'my spectacles, keys, and one old earring' return. Act Two, then, is supplement as counter-vailer. What's more, the mixture in this narrated incident of failure and success, of anti-detection and detection, is pertinent to Virginia Woolf's fiction generally. The mast of the yacht in *Jacob's Room* wobbles awfully, but also straightens out. Death is rampant around Mrs Dalloway, but 'there', at the end of her novel, she 'was'. And this blend is perceptible too in numerous contemporary fictions. Stephen Dedalus both loses himself and finds himself in what his text describes as the 'maze' of Dublin: he is the hero confoundingly reduced to Minotaur ('howling like a beast' as he prowls the filthy latrines and transgressive streets of the city's Jewish-brothel quarter), but also the free-flying poet. We do, indeed, at the end of her novel, wonder precisely *What Maisie Knew*, but we have been convinced too that her precocious grasp of events has been extraordinary. Clearly, too, this same paradoxical mixture can be detected in traditional stories of detection. (And if, like Matthew Arnold, we think that in, say, *Hamlet*, 'modern problems' have already presented themselves, we are really making the same argument against a radical ancient/modern split.) Certainly, it would be absurd to read *Bleak House* as a total and simply exemplary triumph of detective work, illustrating Dickensian or Victorian or earlier Christian confidences in the novel-as-moral-police-force. *Per contra*, although Dickens's Inspector Bucket is in many ways an extremely successful and highly admired epistemological and hermeneutical scout, a deft winkler-out of secrets and difficult truths, a useful and necessary exposer of transgression, he still fails to save Lady Dedlock's life. His bucket of deductions and knowledge is, as it were, all at once full and not full enough.

Which is much like Virginia Woolf's green handbag, and the odd array of coats in her Marshall and Snelgrove story. And here, I'd argue, we are closer still to the heart of this Woolfian narrative's status as exemplum. Those many coats (and the wearing and buying of coats obsess Virginia Woolf's diary in the run-up to this episode): there's a brown fur coat which is so closely identified with its wearer that she becomes 'the brown young woman', Virginia Woolf's own moleskin, and the coat for Vanessa that's the origin of all the trouble. The brown fur, fully occupied, a full sign, a complete emblem of its otherwise anonymous wearer, the mask, or persona, of a criminal. Mrs Woolf's moleskin, worn, taken off, put back on again – that is, now occupied and full, now emptied, now occupied again, but in the interlude of emptiedness a temporary cover for the green bag, but only temporary, for that occupation or fullness was only momentary before the bag was stolen, leaving the coat, at least for a short time, fully emptied. And Vanessa's black coat: empty on the shop rail, tried on – that is, filled – by Virginia Woolf who happens to be more or less her sister's size, emptied again, and then parcelled off to Vanessa to try on, with the possibility of further coats, a vista of further emptyings, fillings, puttings on and off ('if you hate it, or it doesn't fit, you can change it'). It's a complex series of fullnesses and emptinesses, presences and absences (arrestingly vague at a key moment: what, the £6 gone, did the black coat get purchased with?), that frames the crucial play of fullness and emptiness, presence and absence, with the handbag. Now the bag is there; now it's gone; now it's found again. It's there present, but concealed invisibly, encrypted, beneath a coat. It's found, but in a conduit for emptying waste waters away, a drain. It's full, but with £6 that are about to be spent; it's empty of £6, two brooches, a cigarette case, but it still holds spectacles, keys, one old earring, and (?) a handkerchief. Virginia Woolf goes home penniless; but actually armed with ten shillings. The present was purchased, despite the absence of the present money. The two earrings 'bought . . . for a present' are absent; or is the 'one old earring' that's still present in the bag one of those that were intended to be a present? The undecidability of the question is pertinent to the general contradictory *mélange* of empty–full coats, and the full–empty, present–absent–present handbag. The overlap and convergence that the diary piece arranges between word and world, the siting of its meanings at a curious border composed of word-stuff and world-stuff – a betweenness that is neither completely all one thing nor all another but an indissoluble, duplicitous blend of the two – come to seem like a master trope, a master metaphor for all the contradictory margins, the paradoxical plays, the doubled meanings, that occupy this Woolfian text and its supplement.

Infelix Culpa

That much literary criticism in the twentieth century, from I. A. Richards's Practical Criticism to the American New Criticism, from structuralism to poststructuralism and deconstruction, from modernism to postmodernism, has been theoretically formalistic, turning its back, in principle at least, on the worldly side of textual life, is a curious phenomenon that has naturally attracted the attention of many sceptical commentators, particularly those of a Marxist bent. That so many professional readers of books should have made the world, the context, history, such a shibboleth is indeed a thing to marvel at. Explanations need to be sought; blame, even, attached. And without doubt, much of the blame for the more recent popularity of this very arrestingly

odd rejection or side-lining of the worldly connection of language and writing attaches to how post-war critics responded to the Swiss philologist
Ferdinand de Saussure. The genesis – a real genesis, or a *fons et origo* happily
siezed on after the event as a kind of adoptive, or step, father – of what is
at best an unhappy and at worst a disastrous set of preferences for word at
the expense of world in textual discussion and theory is to be found in the
popularization of certain readings, misreadings, invented readings, of Saussure's
Cours de linguistique générale (published posthumously in 1916), notions
usually acquired in poor translation, often at second hand through popularizing
guides and handbooks or, worse, through garbled third-hand seminar-room
gossip. Not the least convenient effect of the widespread poststructuralist
fashion for demeaning an inspection of origins – conducted in terms of a
despising of authors, fathers, authorities, historical and biographical criticism, intentionalism, and so forth – is to deflect attention from the funny-
peculiar roots of this and other often unhappy sets of critical ideas. Critical
theory has always been self-serving, but never so much as it is nowadays, and
not least in this declaring the question of origins off limits. But a reminder
of what is at stake in the now terribly skewed legacy of Saussure, some
realization of what went wrong in the post-war spread of versions
of his linguistic thought, is necessary even to begin clearing up the extraordinary murk and confusion that have reigned in criticism ever since American
and English critics came to his notions, his allegations – and allegation upon
allegation about his allegations – so insultingly late in the day.

All structuralist and poststructuralist criticism begins in encounters with
Saussure's lectures on general linguistics given in Geneva before the First
World War. And from the beginning, an immense original contradiction in
those lectures has bedevilled, bedazzled, and confused all the critical approaches
growing out of them. On the one hand there was the repeated and carefully
elaborated declaration that language – and hence, it may be assumed, everything textual, everything semiotic, all sign-systems, all texts – is a set of
indissoluble, necessarily yoked binary units, of which the combination of
word-stuff and world-stuff is the overarching or basic instance. On the other
hand, there has been the cheerful readiness within Saussure's scrappy
methodology precisely to drive a wedge between these binaries, and from
time to time to shelve, ignore, or deprive of momentousness one whole part
of the combination, usually the worldly side of the union. Saussure's *Cours*
attempts to have things both ways. It announces the union of word and
world in the linguistic sign (the object of linguistic study 'is the social
product stored in the brain, the language itself'[27]); it is immensely preoccupied with language in history, in society, in its geographical aspects; it
even anticipates a science of 'signs as part of social life', that is, semiology

or semiotics; it advocates, we may say, wor(l)ds. But it also proceeds on the steady assumption that language, and language stuff, arrange a hierarchy in which word is more important than world. This is contradictory and illogical, certainly, but it has been for literary critics in our time immensely attractive.

Saussure – it's an old story, but like all great genesis myths it's one worth repeating – argued with revolutionary power that the Verbal *sign* consists of both *signifiant* and *signifié*, signifier and signified: a verbal sound in the mouth or a mark on the page, and also a meaning, something signified, the accompanying mental concept of a something the sign refers to, out there in the world; and these two elements are indissolubly one, like two sides of one sheet of paper; they're as essential to each other's make-up as hydrogen and oxygen are to the composition of water. Just so, language is a necessary combination of *langue*, the system or store of language possibilities, there ready, as it were, laid up, systematically, in the linguistic granary or recipe-book, a great *potentia* for language-users; and of *parole*, actual speech acts, discourse, as it were the practical linguistic cooking and eating. Again, in another of Saussure's powerfully formulated binaries, linguistic states are always dual, chronologically considered: words exist always in a dual time zone, at once *synchronic* – that is in the given contemporary state of a language system – and also *diachronic* – that is, possessed of a history, a philological past, an archaeology or geology or dendrology: they're marked by the traces and scars of past existence, their passage through history, rather as trees have tell-tale age-marks or rings. But, crucially for much of our recent critical theory, at the same time as insisting on the indissolubility of his systems of linguistic binaries – as necessarily yoked together as pairs of railway lines, or *binari*, as the Italians and the trilingual Swiss call them – Saussure also dissolved his binaries, prized apart his *binari*, or at least declared the possibility of their separation, even suggesting that for the purposes of any *wissenschaftlich* linguistic analysis it was necessary to dissolve them, and thus gave rise to the idea that linguistic and textual analysis could simply and for ever park or bypass the signified and *parole* and diachrony, and consist, or mainly consist, of signifiers, *langue*, synchrony. In consequence of which, word got about in critical circles that Linguistics had thus demoted reference, the world, actual language-users, real speech acts, the historicity of language, the history of language; had successfully and in the name of science put these things on the back-burner, not only despising them, but demoting and down-grading them, putting them without question beyond worthy or first-rate critical consideration.

Of course, Saussure's promotion of synchronic linguistics came as a distinct refreshment at the end of the great philologically orientated nineteenth century – it coincided more or less with Nietzsche's powerful attack on the

German obsession with history in the essay from which I take the first of this chapter's epigraphs – a century in which historical linguistics had dominated language study and Saussure as a Professor of Sanskrit had been compelled to steep himself only or mainly in the pastness of languages.[28] But the *Cours* is still full of diachronic linguistics (as its careful readers know full well).[29] It is true that the *Cours* did indicate that semiology would belong with social psychology and that Linguistics 'is only one branch of this general science'. And Saussure declares that semiology must be preceded by a study of 'language in itself', thus implying a gap between language as such and language in society.[30] And, to be sure, the *Cours* has little to say about reference. But nowhere does it envisage the life of signs as in the end practically separable from social and historical life. Nowhere in the *Cours* is the casual modern assumption by literary critics (of various stripes) that signifiers are verbal entities ultimately capable of being kept apart from signifieds ever finally sanctioned. Saussure had been in enough trains to realize that they normally need two *binari* to run on.

'If Saussure had not existed,' declares Roy Harris, 'it would have been necessary to invent him,' given the wide current of structuralist thought he inspired. Then he adds in a footnote, 'In a sense he was invented,' referring to the way the *Cours* was cobbled together posthumously from students' notes.[31] It's clear from even the briefest acquaintance with the *Cours* that the inventing didn't stop with Saussure's students, but has carried on busily right to this day. And those who happily pursue their fictionalized Saussure down the path of linguistic a-worldliness draw support from two grand principles of the *Cours* which have enjoyed truly momentous effect among literary critics: the *arbitrariness of the sign* and *difference*.

Saussure's great (and vexed) 'first principle' of the 'nature of the linguistic sign', insisted on repeatedly in the *Cours*, is that '*le signe linguistique est arbitraire*'. One of those furry miaowing creatures with four legs and a tail could be named anything: *cat* is an arbitrary label; the name has an arbitrary, or unmotivated, non-determined relation to the thing it signifies. And put like that, the notion is innocuous and fairly incontestable. As Saussure has it: 'Le principe de l'arbitraire du signe n'est contesté par personne' (which is no longer absolutely true, but still nearly so).[32] The second great principle is that *langue* is a system of differences without positive terms: '*dans la langue il n'y a que des différences . . . sans termes positifs.*'[33] That is, the word or sign *cat* is recognizable as itself only because it exists in a field of different terms having related but different sounds. It's in a group of differential phonemic relationships associating it with, but also distinguishing it from, enabling it to have a distinctive life of its own separate from, the likes of *rat, fat, fart, faint*, or *cit, cut, cur*, or *cop, cope, come, cant, cunt*, and so on. Again, put like that, unexceptionable. What goes wrong (and what went wrong) is when the proposition that signs are arbitrary and thus the relation between the linguistic entity and the worldly entity it refers to is arbitrary as well – that is, the sign considered as a phonemic entity, a set merely of sounds or of marks on paper – gets extended, glibly and strangely, to deny that signs are related to the world at all and to suggest that languages, and so texts, exist quite cut off from the things and the world that they seem to refer to. This is the fallacy of extrapolating wildly from the system of *phonemic* differences that comprise *langue* to the level of *semantics* and *semantic* operation.

It's one thing to perceive that the separate linguistic existence of the sign *cat* hinges on its not being the sign *fat* or *spat*, and that a main linguistic essence of *cat* is that *c* has a separate significance insofar as it's not *f* or *sp*. But this is worlds away from proposing that the meaning of the word *cat* consists only in its place in a linguistic field or table which has reference solely to a roster of other signs, *fat*, *spat*, and so forth. That's just silly, though its silliness has not prevented many literary critics from solemnly declaring such things. The word *cat* also leads us, if it does anything at all, to the variegated world of pets – actual creatures, not just concepts of creatures – and to the particular animals that the English-speaking world everywhere knows by the term *cat*. In other words, *deixis* occurs inevitably in language use. Words point to things – even invisible things, like God or toothache or epistemology. In other words, again, semantics are as important as phonemics in the totality of language use – in fact, far more important in the quotidian world we all use language in. After all, most speakers of English have no call whatever to be mindful of the phonemic breakdown of *cat*. Nor do most readers. What's at issue in speech or writing, the world of actual discourse, is the capacity to connect the word cat to the world of miaowing furriness (and so also beyond that to the metaphorical and other extensions of the term: catty, cattiness, cat-like, Cat-woman, big cats, and so on). Language refers to the world we know. Isn't it odd, as Raymond Tallis puts it, that sentences like 'The dog is barking' occur a lot, ones like 'The dog is quacking' appear scarcely ever, and that the sentence 'The dog is reading [Derrida's] *Of Grammatology* with pleasure and profit' had never occurred until he set it down.[34] The well-known playground riddle puts the point of the necessity of reference with great force. Smart-ass question: What's the difference between an elephant and a post-box? Puzzled reply: I don't know. Triumphant put-down: Then I shan't ever send *you* to post a letter. Or if kiddy riddles seem too child-like to move a mountain of post-Saussurean assumption, take Ora Avni's lovely use of the French *fabliau*, about the sexually inexperienced peasant who was fully equipped with a set of words for sexual congress (*foutre*, *con*, etc.) but had no idea of their physical reference and so got tricked by a cunning wife and her mother into thinking *cunt* signified *mouse*, for a more grown-up demonstration of the mistake of assuming that verbal systems are independent of what they point to.[35] But then, of course, these objections pertain to the world of *parole*, words in operation among real speakers, and that got itself shelved temporarily for purposes of analysis. But *parole* simply won't accept being shelved when it comes, as it quickly must, to the real linguistic world of telegrams and anger, of actual texts and actual readers, of keen seekers after the truth of the word *con* who aren't going to be fobbed off long with mousey substitutes. But, of course, again, the theory indeed said that *parole* couldn't really be put on one side: it is, after all, the other side of the *langage* coin, for ever inseparable from its co-equal partner in the language business, *langue*.

Try as one might, two sides of a coin cannot be separated and yet remain legal currency. Normal trains indeed need two *binari* to run on. And though it might appear to be able to do so, the principle of linguistic difference simply cannot exclude or debar linguistic reference. Reference, or as older linguists used to call it, the *signatum* of the sign, is necessary to both the theory and the practice of signs. As long ago as 1939 Émile Benveniste argued most convincingly that the very example Saussure produced as a demonstration of the arbitrariness of the sign in fact proved that signs were necessarily related to the reality-situation of the world. (And it is one of the scandals of post-war literary criticism that in all its enthusiasm for certain aspects of Saussure's work it either ignored or simply was ignorant of the classically elegant meditations by Benveniste on the Saussurean problems of general linguistics.) Take the *Cours* on sister/*soeur* and cow/*boeuf*/*Ochs* (in a standard US translation): 'The idea of "sister" is not linked by any inner relationship to the succession of sounds *s-ö-r* which serves as its signifier in French; that it could be represented equally by just any other sequence is proved by differences among languages and by the very existence of different languages: the signified "ox" has as its signifier *b-ö-f* on one side of the border and *o-k-s* (*Ochs*) on the other.'[36] But, as Benveniste powerfully puts it, this frontier crossing-point where *boeuf* abuts onto *Ochs* also comprises another frontier, where both of these signs encounter their signified, and their signifed in the flesh (their *signatum*), the mooing creature that they denote. And, as Benveniste explains, the arbitrariness of *boeuf*/*Ochs* may only be alleged by

recours inconscient et subreptice à un troisième terme, qui n'était pas compris dans la définition initiale. Ce troisième terme est la chose même, la réalité. . . . Quand il parle de la différence entre *b-ö-f* et *o-k-s*, il se réfère malgré lui au fait que ces deux termes s'appliquent à la même *réalité*. Voilà donc *la chose*, expressément exclue d'abord de la définition du signe, qui s'y introduit par un détour et qui y installe en permanence la contradiction. . . . Or c'est seulement

si l'on pense à l'animal 'boeuf' dans sa particularité concrète et 'substantielle'
que l'on est fondé à juger 'arbitraire' la relation entre *böf* d'une part, *oks* de l'autre,
à une même réalité. Il y a donc contradiction entre la manière dont Saussure
définit le signe linguistique et la nature fondamentale qu'il lui attribue.

And, of course, as Benveniste goes on to argue, once a sign is in place, in use,
the relationship between signifier and signified becomes a necessary one:
boeuf/Ochs/cow are necessarily, ungluably, attached to the mooing creatures
they from then on denote:

> Entre le signifiant et le signifié, le lien n'est pas arbitraire; au contraire, il est
> *nécessaire*. Le concept ('signifié') 'boeuf' est forcément identique dans ma con-
> science à l'ensemble phonique ('signifiant') *böf*. Comment en serait-il autrement?
> Ensemble les deux ont été imprimés dans mon esprit; ensemble ils s'évoquent
> en toute circonstance. Il y a entre eux symbiose si étroite que le concept 'boeuf'
> est comme l'âme de l'image acoustique *böf*.

'L'esprit ne contient pas de formes vides, de concepts innommés': the human
mind does not hold with empty forms, or concepts without names. 'Pour le
sujet parlant, il y a entre la langue et la réalité adéquation complète: le signe
recouvre et commande la réalité; mieux il *est* cette réalité': as far as the
speaking subject is concerned, there is a complete equation between language
and reality; the sign recuperates and controls reality; or, better still, it *is* that
reality.[37]

Roman Jakobson called this a 'beautiful demonstration', and declared that
Saussure's 'arbitraire' had been a most unfortunate term.[38] Lévi-Strauss was
also convinced by Benveniste, and reformulated the argument most impressively thus: 'the linguistic sign is arbitrary a priori, but ceases to be
arbitrary a posteriori.'[39] But despite these endorsements, and even though
Benveniste's *Problèmes de linguistique générale* got into English in 1971, literary
critics in the English-speaking world have been more or less unaffected by
Benveniste's irresistible supplementation of the arbitrariness discussion.[40] The
alertest critics in the non-francophone world – even Marxists and feminists,
even theologians and other ideologues, who ought surely to have given
themselves longer pause for thought – have preferred the headlong extensions
of Saussure's linguistics that cluster about the name of Jacques Derrida.

Pas de Hors-Texte?

Derrida has vigorously continued Saussure. Where Saussure would sideline
parole for the immediate purposes of linguistic methodology, Derrida goes

much further, showing how *parole*, voice and presence still massively infected Saussure's discussions of *langue*. In his extraordinarily influential *Of
Grammatology* (1967 in French, 1976 in English) Derrida offers the allegedly
more rigorous case that writing and writtenness, *écriture* – that is, the signs
on the page, self-existing quite apart from the presence of speakers or things
– are the main, or most important and truthful, essence of language, or at
least the aspect to concentrate on if we are ever to escape from the delusions
of centuries of Graeco-Christian metaphysics, or logocentrism.[41] Further,
Derrida seeks to reinscribe the Saussurean principle of difference with a kind
of revved-up post-Saussurean vigour. His view of writing appears even more
hostile to reference than the Saussurean specializing concentration on signifiers
was. The traces of the real in the sign must on this view be reckoned as even
more distant from the world than in Saussure's already world-suspicious
signified. Saussure's signified, the meaning that's in the head, the 'social
product stored in the brain', was far too referential, too worldly, for Derrida,
too easily linked with things and meanings 'out there', and so altogether too
metaphysical, too soaked in old Graeco-Christian concepts of the logos, of
words that under God's aegis referred 'transcendentally' beyond themselves.
That's the old 'metaphysics of presence' registered in the concept of the
'transcendental signified'. And so the principle of difference has to be not
only reasserted, but strengthened by playing up the idea of the deferring of
meaning, presence, reference, by bringing out the sense of deferral as also
contained within the French verb to differ, *différer*, from which the French
différence comes. To bring this home, Derrida notoriously produced one of his
key terms, the noun *différance* (one vowel different from its old colleague
différence). *Différance* denotes deferring of meaning as well as difference of
meaning: what Jonathan Culler deferentially christens 'difference-differing-
deferring'.[42]

One major point of the neologism is that the difference between (traditional) *différence* and (new) *différance* appears only in writing and not in speech
(they sound exactly alike), which is intended to underline the essence of the
situation being argued for: namely the pre-eminence of writing, *écriture*, mere
scribing and scriptedness, in what language does, over speaking, inscribing
and inscription, and so reference.[43] But whatever one thinks of the power and
pertinence of Derrida's *différance* – and some of its admirers do seem excessively bowled over by a rather laboured piece of punning – the essence of the
Derridian case is that the meaning of words, writing, text is not ever successfuly
produced, presented, contained on-stage, as it were, so much as perpetually
deferred back into mere linguisticity, into yet more writing. No *mise en scène*;
rather a *mise en abyme*, a plunge into the abysm, or black hole, of mere text.
A ' "text" . . . is . . . a differential network, a fabric of traces referring endlessly

to something other than itself, to other differential traces'. And writing thus viewed absorbs or swallows up everything else. It colonizes all things, turns everything into writing: a 'text overruns all the limits assigned to it . . . all the limits, everything that was to be set up in opposition to writing (speech, life, the world, the real, history, and what not, every field of reference – to body or mind, conscious or unconscious, politics, economics, and so forth).'[44] And thus magisterially – the sweep of the claim quite taking the breath away – the stage, or anti-stage, is set for the most flagrantly exclusive denial of all: '*Il n'y a pas de hors-texte.*'[45]

What does this notorious *pronunciamento* mean? It is of course a French tradition to go in for these magisterial dictates – Derrida offers lots of *il y a* formulations – and it's easy for anglophone readers to forget that they all need to be taken with a pinch of French salt. What's more, the French have *hors-textes* and the English-speaking world does not, so we tend to miss the reference to the prefatory, preliminary material at the beginning of French books that's usually labelled *hors-texte*. Derrida's resistance to *hors-textes* is one with his resistance to the separability of prefaces from texts, his refusal to accept a clear demarcation of 'proper' textual material from 'minor' pre-textual or marginalized textual stuff. But still, how is the phrase to be translated? Gayatri Spivack havers, and properly: 'There is nothing outside of the text [there is no outside-text; *il n'y a pas de hors-texte*]'. Well, which is it? The translation stutters and gives up the ghost, reproducing the difficult French as a last resort. And what, actually, is an *outside-text*? The English language finds it hard to recognize such a creature. The context in *Of Grammatology* suggests, in fact, that everything 'outside the text' is also text and so, I suppose, 'outside-text'. The trouble is, as some commentators recognize, that this would imply there is also 'inside-text', while Derrida is at pains to blur old-fashioned distinctions between what's allegedly inside texts and what's apparently outside them (hence his busy play with that mounting roster of exemplary metaphors for, and textual instances of, the undecidable margin between insides and outsides – *preface, supplement, hymen, parergon, brisure*, and so on). For his part, Derek Attridge revises Spivak: '*There is no outside-the-text*' is his preferred translation, thus avoiding the outside-text problematic, which he sharply recognizes.[46]

Clearly something had to be done about the messiness of the Spivack translation, and not least, Derrida himself felt, because the pronouncement has generally been taken as David Lodge's university lecturer in English chirpily takes it in Lodge's novel *Nice Work* (1988). Twice she declares that 'There is nothing outside the text'. This, the world's reading, and an apparent sanction for literary critics to believe that literature, texts, exclude or suspend reference, history, reality, being, 'real-history-of-the-world', has haunted Derrida ever since 1976. He's been at some pains to rebut it, especially in interviews (speech, incidentally, correcting a writing: so much for the pre-eminence of *écriture*). Rebutting in this particular matter is just one aspect of Derrida's increasing impatience with much of the American deconstructionist thinking done in his name since the late sixties.

In the early seventies Derrida 'turned' to the context, and, obviously vexed by the jeers of Michel Foucault and other old comrades on the Left about the apparent rejection of history, came to adopt a decidedly Foucauldian interest in manifestly historical texts such as are found in archives, and noticeably came round to incorporating Foucauldian thoughts about the textual and other policing functions of the university and the State into his own textual concerns.[47] Moreover, he expresses deep hurt at being taken as intending anything else:

> the concept of text or of context which guides me embraces and does not exclude the world, reality, history. Once again (and this probably makes a thousand times I have had to repeat this, but when will it finally be heard, and why this resistance?): as I understand it . . . the text is not the book, it is not confined in a volume itself confined to the library. It does not suspend reference – to history, to the world, to reality, to being, and especially not to the other, since to say of history, of the world, of reality, that they always appear in an experience, hence in a movement of interpretation which contextualizes them according to a network of differences and hence of referral to the other, is surely to recall that alterity (difference) is irreducible. *Différance* is a reference and vice versa.[48]

But how much of a difference do these pained modifications and clarifications actually make? They certainly alert us to Derrida's actual sense of the historical, especially as a Jew who suffered as such in wartime Algeria.[49] They point us to his continuing radical left-liberal politics (from earlier *Tel Quel* Maoism to later sympathy for Mandela and the rights of French immigrants), to his concerns over nuclear weaponry, his readiness to given a freebie lecture in Oxford in aid of Amnesty International (1992), his political activity in the real world, his appearances on liberationist and egalitarian platforms, his public efforts to help the Mitterand government in promoting philosophy in French education, his notorious brush with the police in 1982 when he visited Communist Prague to offer aid and comfort to beleaguered philosophers (an episode which apparently reconciled Foucault to him), as well as to his later philosophical work on the subjects of grief and mourning, and so on. Still, for all this, *context* remains a textual thing, always mediated, never outside of text: 'What I call "text" implies all the structures called "real", "economic", "historical", socio-institutional, in short: all possible referents. Another way of recalling once again that "there is nothing outside the text".' And, once more, he declares that 'That does not mean that all referents are suspended, denied, or enclosed in a book, as people have claimed, or have been naïve enough to believe and to have accused me of believing'. But, yet once more, he insists that 'it does mean that every referent, all reality has the structure of a differential trace, and that one cannot refer to this "real" except in an interpretive experience. The latter neither yields meaning nor assumes it except in a movement of differential referring. That's all.'[50] Indeed it is. Derrida had just affirmed that the 'entire "real-history-of-the-world" ', or 'context', was limitless and limitlessly textual, and that 'The phrase which for some has become a sort of slogan, in general so badly understood, of deconstruction ('there is nothing outside the text [*il n'y a pas de hors-texte*]) means nothing else: there is nothing outside context.'[51]

So has anything really changed, except the substitution of *context* for *text* and the insistence that difference is reference, from the original place of the no *hors-texte* declaration in the *Grammatology*? There it is insisted that Rousseau and the other characters (the ordinary reader would say *people*) who feature in his *Confessions* are of less interest than the writing that gives us access to them; that 'we have access to their so-called "real" existence only in the text and we have neither any means of altering this, nor any right to neglect this limitation'; that

> in what one calls the real life of these existences 'of flesh and bone', beyond and behind what one believes can be circumscribed as Rousseau's text, there has never been anything but writing; there have never been anything but supplements, substitutive significations which could only come forth in a chain of differential references, the 'real' supervening, and being added only while taking on meaning from a trace and from an invocation of the supplement, etc. And thus to infinity, for we have read, *in the text*, that the absolute present, Nature, that which words like 'real mother' name, have always already escaped, have never existed: that what opens meaning and language is writing as the disappearance of natural presence.[52]

Friends of Derrida agree with him in lamenting that *Il n'y a pas de hors-texte* has so frequently been mistaken,[53] but from first to last it's clear that Derrida believes that text encompasses all. Nature and mother, the history, selfhood, reality, politics, and so forth that Derrida so keenly espouses in his published disavowals of 'misreaders', all appear in inverted commas. Reference is, from the first until now, in fact difference, and 'to infinity'.

So history remains, like presented meaning in general with Derrida, 'under erasure', a *realium* and a reference point, yes, but not really.[54] And thus Lodge's lecturer, cocky Robyn, was not, it would seem, wrong; nor, for all Derrida's rage, are all those dissolvers into text of presence and the subject and history, all the advocates of 'rhetoric' who give it precedence over history or see it as going 'all the way down', and who would look for support in these positions to Derrida and his super-Saussurean retreat from the transcendence, the something-beyond-mere-wordiness, beyond textuality, of the signified. The 'used-up formula', as Derrida called the no *hors-texte* pronouncement in 1989, refuses to become unusable, *inusable*, worn out. It still has its uses for the anti-history school.[55]

What previous linguistic thought labelled the *signatum*, what Saussure for his part, cutting the business of reference back to subjectivity, called the signified, have all been, then, as it were by deconstructive fiat, dramatically wiped out. On this view, nothing that we can know through language, through text – or, simply, nothing – can be known as anything but language, as text. And of course, for all Derrida's protests, the idea of Benveniste's speaking subject, and in particular the idea of the author or writer, is one of the first things to be, in this manoeuvre of thought, vigorously degraded. New (post)structuralism thus chimes in with the old New Criticism's resistance to the so-called Biographical Fallacy. The very idea of authorship, of personal origins for utterance, keeps up, it is alleged, the old metaphysical ideas of divine or quasi-divine creativity, beginnings, authority, which all this foregrounding of linguisticity is designed precisely to subvert. Derrida's master, Heidegger, declared, influentially and in Nietzschean vein, that 'Die Sprache spricht, nicht der Mensch'.[56] Now Roland Barthes could spell it out in his notorious piece on 'The Death of the Author'. As it was for Mallarmé, he said, so 'for us too, it is language which speaks, not the author; to write is . . . to reach that point where only language acts, "performs", and not "me" '.[57] Even Michel Foucault concurred that, since Mallarmé, the 'disappearance of the author' had become an undeniable 'event of our time'.[58]

'What's become of Waring / Since he gave us all the slip?' asked Robert Browning's poem, referring to the self-exile of his friend, the minor poet Alfred Domett. And Anthony Powell would repeat the question in the title of his novel *What's Become of Waring?* (1939). But we're now supposed to think such a question and concern redundant. Waring has not just disappeared; he was, apparently, not really there in the first place. After all, the language, or the writing, is what writes, not some human entity mistakenly known for all these years, deludedly, as the writer. And if he were in some way once there, he's now been wiped away, *épongé* in fact, sponged up, mopped up, in the inevitable postmodernist fate of the French poet Francis Ponge in Derrida's punning anti-biography *Signéponge* or *Signsponge* – Ponge who becomes the representative poststructuralist poet for wiping himself out in the very act of

signing himself (*signé Ponge*). Signing one's name, the ultimate claiming act
of the author, is thus to signify in fact a disappearance of one's title to the
work, the real erasure at the heart of that conventional mode of authorizing,
authority, authorship.[59]

But What Does Become of Waring?

It is, of course, mightily handy that France has a Francis Ponge (if *he* didn't
exist, he'd have to be invented, and as far as most English readers are concerned,
he might well have been). But there is only one Ponge. And spongeing away
a Dickens or a Joyce or a Shakespeare and all the rest isn't to be achieved by
a mere wave of any magic Derridian sponge. As Malcolm Bradbury is driven
to concede, the literary-biography trade flourishes as never before, flying
busily in the face of anti-author theory.[60] And this rift between theory and
practice flourishes at the theoretical centre as well as at the untheorizing
margin where the mere common reader unrepentantly lurks. The Bradbury/
Lodge tribute to *Signéponge*, their spoof account of a French postmodernist
author called Mensonge (Laureate of Absence) in a critico-documentary fiction
entitled *My Strange Quest for Mensonge, Structuralism's Hidden Hero* (1987), is
a natty enough theorists' in-house jest. And the postmodernist analyst Gilbert
Adair's spry novel *The Death of the Author* (1992), in which post-author
theory meets old whodunit, is Barthes boiled down most agreeably to farce.
But more telling than these satirizing encounters so typical of the British
way with big theory is the actual practice of Barthes and Foucault and
Derrida. Foucault, for example, was in practice by no means keen to leave
empty for long the 'space left by the author's disappearance', even if that
'disappearance' had become a marked feature of certain psotmodernist fiction
(he had Beckett very much in mind, apparently).[61] After all, Foucault was a
historian and animated by 'post-historical transformations', eager to ask where
ideas 'come from', how they're 'circulated', who 'controls' them, and so on.
And he was soon busy in his 'What is an Author?' piece analysing the
'author-function' and inspecting 'transdiscursive' authors, people like Homer,
Aristotle, and the Church Fathers, as well as the great nineteenth-century
'initiators of discursive practices', people such as Marx and Freud who 'produced
not only their own work, but the possibility and the rules of formation of
other texts', and so 'established the endless possibility of discourse'.[62] If authors
can disappear, they can, it seems, also, after all, reappear.

They can also come back from the dead. 'Let's hold the tears,' as Foucault
put it in reply to Lucien Goldmann's attack on him on the occasion of the
Author-Disappearance lecture: he didn't believe in the 'death of man', nor in

the 'death of the author'.[63] Nor, in fact, did Roland Barthes. A notable feature of Barthes's later career was his belated stress on the real historical aspects of semiotics, particularly in the moving and captivating book on photography *Le Chambre claire* (*Camera Lucida* in its English version), a text inspired by the death of his mother.[64] And there was the biography of one author that came to interest him a great deal, namely his own. 'Once I produce, once I write, it is the Text itself which (fortunately) disposseses me of my narrative continuity.' But these flannelling denials of *Roland Barthes par Roland Barthes* are predictable and lame. The face of Roland Barthes peers out at you from a majority of this book's photographs. And what the English version keeps conveniently dark is that the book appeared in France in the very extensive *Ecrivains de toujours* series of tomes about writers whose formula is always *X par X* and always built on biographical, autobiographical, historical, author-centred assumptions. In agreeing to appear in this series, Barthes was undoubtedly siezing a chance to try and subvert its going authorly norms; but, try as he might, he had committed himself irreversibly to what his theory had sought to rebut: the high interest that readers have in knowing about the authors of the books they read, and the conventional but proper feeling that knowing about authors' lives does help you get closer to their work. The German translation is quite unblushingly titled: *Roland Barthes Über mich selbst* (About Myself, or On the Subject of Me).[65] And the same authorial presence commands the posthumous collection of Barthes *entretiens, Le Grain de la voix*, both in that book's own ensemble of authorial snapshots and in the text's pervasive 'I', the historiographed self of the famous Parisian intellectual, the author manifestly eager to 'self-explicate' himself, to describe his work-practices, to present himself now pen in hand, now at his typewriter.[66] Barthes's own writing never stopped being I-manual labour. Not a case of Emmanuel, God with us, but its logocentric neighbour, a situation of I-manual: the authorial self continually with and behind and in the text.

In fact, just as the Chicago New Critics could not keep authors out of textual discussion at the same time as keeping up their insistence on the alleged Fallacy of Biography as a critically informative exercise, so structuralism and poststructuralism have been manifestly unsuccessful in their hostile intentions towards authors. Not the least interesting of the many memorable things about, for example, Derrida's *La Carte postale* (1980) is the story in it of how he first came to find the book's originating postcard of a thirteenth-century illustration of Plato and Socrates in the foyer of the Bodleian Library in Oxford on a pedagogic visit to the city, or the repeated presentation of himself having his picture taken in instant-photo booths. And of course Derrida has been as prone to talk about himself to interviewers as ever Barthes was – as, not least, the volumes *Positions* (1972) and *Points de suspension: entretiens* (1992) amply witness. Derrida is, in fact, a non-stop self-testifier. The *Jacques Derrida par Geoffrey Bennington et Jacques Derrida* volume (1991) not only consists in considerable part of a long 'Circonfession', but ends with a 'Curriculum vitae', photographs and all. After *Barthes par Barthes* the family photo album is again a cherished text. And Derrida has even got around to using the word *biography* approvingly (readers 'cannot deny my attention to context, to history, to biography'). That was, of course, in the midst of the defence of Paul de Man ('Biodegradables', 859), which was, as nobody failed to notice, conducted by Derrida and others very much in old-fashioned literary-biographical terms (de Man did, or did not, do this or the other wrong; his texts do or do not reflect this or some other aspect of his life's actions and opinions). But why should this intrusion of even authors such as Barthes or Derrida into their own textual scenes be all that surprising? For it is as impossible for us to imagine a text without an author, or a busy pen or paintbrush without some hand holding it, as it is for a text of any kind to exist without some text-making hand. Texts are not made by machines. Even writing machines need operators and programmers (the *Jacques Derrida* volume just referred to has a photograph of Derrida seated at one, on p. 15). As Derrida puts it wryly: 'a text is not exactly a sausage' ('Biodegradables', 861). That's why the moment in Philip Sidney's *Arcadia* is so terrible – and intentionally so, one guesses – where there's a painter, so 'desirous to see some notable wounds, to be able the more lively' to execute his picture of the Centaurs fighting the Lapiths, that he joins a crowd of uprising rebels, and gets his hands struck off by the sword of one Dorus: 'And so the painter returned, well skilled in wounds, but with never a hand to performe his skill.' It's a terrifyingly bitter as well as cruelly vindictive fate, one to place reprovingly beside Barthes's cheery vision of the author's hand 'cut off from any voice, borne by a pure gesture of inscription'.[67]

It is in practice impossible for us to talk about texts without the presence of a presumed writing hand and of the person the hand belongs to, and (sooner or later) the history, the context, the ideology, the whole matrix of that person, invading the discussion, as these had no doubt previously invaded the text. On an earlier occasion I showed how this incursion takes place willy-nilly in Frank Kermode's bravura discussion of Henry Green's novel *Party Going*, thus undermining an analysis that seeks to set the tone for the presentation in his important poststructuralist book *The Genesis of Secrecy* (1979) of the would-be exemplary text-generating auto-textuality of the the Gospel of Mark.[68] Kermode's dramatic lapse from the self-denying anti-biographical, anti-historical ordinances of the formalism that he was then espousing was by no means difficult to detect, just as, I would argue, it was not easy to avoid. Such lapses from the theoretical stance in question are actually endemic to language-talk. The impossibility, which Benveniste detected, of discussing the nature of *Ochs* and *boeuf* without bringing in real cross-border relations between Germany and France is exemplary. It pervades, and I'd allege naturally pervades, Saussure's *Cours*, and to a degree that really does spill the beans about all language and metalanguage, all text and talk about textual stuff.

The Train now Standing at the Binario

Saussure's famous and attractive illustration involving the 8.45 p.m. express train from Geneva to Paris is just one example among others – lateral and longitudinal sections in tree-trunks, chess-playing, the composition of water atoms, and so forth – of the impossibility of thinking about language apart from the real world of language use. Jonathan Culler glosses this train-spotter's analogy with the spryly boyish looseness that characterizes so many of the Anglo-Saxon world's literary-critical appropriations of Saussure:

> linguistic units have a purely relational identity. . . . Saussure offers a concrete analogy. We are willing to grant that in an important sense the 8.25 Geneva-to-Paris Express is the same train each day, even though the coaches, locomotive, and personnel change from one day to the next. What gives the train its identity is its place in the system of trains, as indicated by the timetable. And note that this relational identity is indeed the determining factor: the train remains the same even if it leaves half an hour late. Indeed, it might always leave late without ceasing to be the 8.25 Geneva-to-Paris Express. What is important is that it be distinguished from, say, the 10.25 Geneva-to-Paris Express, the Geneva-to-Dijon local, etc.[69]

Here, you immediately think, is a critic who would have benefited from a reading of Benveniste. For, obviously, linguistic units hotly deny any 'purely relational identity' in any discussion of them that's built, as this one is, on 'concrete' things like doings at railway stations. Great draughts of scepticism are called for. Even at the simple level of mistranslation. Saussure's 8.45 express has become, oddly, the 8.25. Why? Because Culler – like many another actor who will feature in what Beckett (in *Murphy*) called 'these informations' – is relying in his gloss on a botched American translation (Wade Baskin's). Much more has been lost, though, in the rather silly and rushed paraphrasing of Saussure. 'What is important', for example, if you are a flesh-and-blood traveller rather than a second-hand linguistic theorist, is not just that the 8.45 is not the 10.25 in the timetable, but that the 8.45 does not in fact leave at 10.25 – nor, of course, at 8.25. And how that idle talk of its not mattering too much if the train doesn't leave on time is shown up in all its wrong-headedness if indeed we alter Culler to read 'the train remains the same train even if it leaves twenty minutes early'. For commuters, the folks waiting for the train, the most important thing about the identity of a train such as 'the 8.45' is that it should exist precisely as I'm insisting (and Saussure in his better moments allows) that signs do indeed exist, namely in a convenient and regular convergence between text and world – in this case in the text of timetables being reliably and daily translated into action on Geneva's railway platforms. (As they did, and do, of course, Swiss trains being notoriously reliable: a Saussure could bank on events on Switzerland's *binari* going according to the published plan.)

Saussure himself does, of course, go too far in this illustration of the 'linguistic mechanism'. If all the 'conditions' are the same, he says – the time of departure, the itinerary, the distinguishing circumstances – then you get 'the same entities'. Which is not altogether the case. The 'same' train can exist in its sameness as 'the 8.45' without comprising all 'the same entities', the same rolling stock and so on, every night. But, more crucially, Saussure's argument at this point is not even purporting to do what Culler, and no doubt others with him, believe it's doing.

The name of the train, 'Genève–Paris 8h. 45 du soir', says Saussure, denotes a thing, the train that departs each night, whose identity is indeed a relative one, a matter of difference (it's this train, not that other one; it's 'the 8.45' in the timetable, not 'the 10.45' or 'the 8.25'). The train case is similar to the other example that Saussure weaves into his train paragraph. Demolish a city street and rebuild it. All the materials will be different, but the name of the street remains the same, 'because the entity it consists of is not purely material, it's founded on certain conditions that are alien to the stuff it happens to be made of, for example, its location relative to other streets' – that is its differential relationships in the system of streets, marked on the street-map. But what's particularly important to note in Saussure's text at this point is his repeated rhetoric of *matérielle*. Train-labels in timetables and street-names have necessary *material* manifestations, and, as ever, the names and the *materiality* they denote coexist. The identity of the street 'n'est pas purement matérielle'. Like train-labels, street-names are names, signifiers, arrayed in a system of signifiers – the timetable, the gazetteer. But at the same time these signifiers denote travelling machines which you may board at stated times, pavements you can walk down, houses you may enter. 'Et pourtant', Saussure's paragraph ends – though you would not suppose so from Culler's summary – 'celles-ci [the 'entités' that make up the street or the train] ne sont pas abstraites, puisqu'une rue ou un express ne se conçoivent pas en dehors d'une réalisation matérielle' (these are not abstract entities, since a street or an express are not to be thought of, are inconceivable, outside of – *en dehors de* – a material realization). *Il n'y a pas de hors-text?* Well, Saussure, at least on this occasion, clearly, did not think so. He begins his paragraph on the linguistic relationship between identity and difference, this train paragraph, by appealing precisely to what exists *en dehors du langage*: 'Ce caractère [of language] ressort bien de la comparaison avec quelques faits pris en dehors du langage.'[70] And, following Benveniste, I'd say that the character of language and writing can only ever adequately be thought and talked about and, as in this case, illustrated with reference to what happens 'en dehors du langage', because language never exists independently of some relationship to what's 'out there', beyond the merely linguistic and textual.

Talking Martian

Not to follow Saussure down that particular material street, or aboard that particular material train, is to stick to him at his worst moments. Preferring the line of non-referentiality is to opt rather for the truly dark side of Saussure's imagination, the vision that drove him to spend up to four years filling forty or so notebooks with his efforts to show that certain poetic texts, certain ancient and modern poems, had a secretive anagrammatical content – that is, cryptic, often self-referential meanings (authors' names, for example) seeded deep within them. What he was after was a sort of ultra-formalism, a cryptic punning that would reveal a kind of subconsciousness of language, poetry, text, *per se.* What the long search indicates is a high level of faith in the arbitrary, almost magical self-subsistence of meaning. And it was this idea of a kind of self-assertiveness of language that did not, it appears, allow him instantly to dismiss as ludicrous the Genevan spiritualist medium Mlle Hélène Smith when she was brought to him in his professional capacity as a Professor of Sanskrit to investigate her claim to be inspired by spirit guides to speak Sanskrit. She also, more unusually (for there was a lot of pseudo-Indian mysticism knocking about Europe at the end of the nineteenth century), claimed to speak Martian.[71] Arrestingly, Saussure decided that she probably was uttering bits of Sanskrit, and probably some Martian as well.

The episode should give us considerable pause. For whether he was questing for hidden, possibly random, and unintentional names, words, meanings in a kind of superstructuralist (or cabbalistic) search for the deviously internalized senses of poems, or taking the medium's glossolalic capacities in Sanskrit and Martian seriously enough to delve into her manifestly non-referential utterances, Saussure was only doing, as Tzvetan Todorov has suggested, what he tried to systematize in parts of the *Cours*, namely treating language and text as arbitrary, non-referential, non-symbolic.[72]

Saussure was attending Mlle Smith's séances in 1895–8. The anagrams,
or *hypogrammes*, as Saussure called them, pre-occupied him in 1906–9. The
lectures in the *Cours* took place 1907–11. This chain of events looks oddly
like a progression. Louis-Jean Calvet's argument that the *Cours* was an
attempt by Saussure to provide himself with a general linguistic frame, a
metalanguage, for those earlier, more particular researches into texts and
textuality looks at least plausible.[73] Structuralists, certainly, have seen the
connection between the *Cours* and the anagrams. Calvet records enthusiastic
interest in the anagrammatical quest from Jakobson, Julia Kristeva, and
Michael Riffaterre.[74] To his credit, Saussure eventually developed doubts about
the anagram research, and never published this work.[75] But the merchants of
non-referentiality have had few or none, it seems, of the master's hesitations.
Sylvère Lotringer sees the *Cours* arising out of the repression of the anagram
labours as their true manifestation: it was the anagrams that began the work
of consecrating 'the irruption of the signifier on the scene of writing'.[76] Paul
de Man celebrates 'the Saussure of the anagrams' as a quiet revolutionist, an
explorer glimpsing a possibility for language that was 'potentially disruptive
to the highest degree', but one that terrified him ('a terror glimpsed') so that
he 'backed away from it'. But what he had discovered was 'the New World'
(*terra* – rather than terror – *nova*), a discovery by no means simply to be given
up, an irrecoverable step, rather like the opening or uncovering of the box
of Pandora. Dropping such deep linguistic truth was 'as if Columbus
had decided to keep his discovery of the New World to himself'. And de
Man won't allow that his voyaging predecessor did in fact give up his
anagrammatical discovery (he refers to 'its assumed suppression').[77] 'Discovery'
is, of course, a bit rich for what was an aborted, abandoned set of probes. But
for de Man and his deconstructive crew there seemed no doubt that Saussure
had made a landfall in hermeneutic *terra nova* well worth celebrating. De Man's
pupil Barbara Johnson rejoiced in it with her ship's master and with someone
she believed to be another happy shipmate, Jacques Derrida himself. In her
Translator's Introduction to Derrida's *Dissemination*, Ms Johnson explains
Derrida's interest in the word *pharmakon* in Plato as precisely an 'interven-
tion' along the 'route' of 'Anagrammatical texture'. This, she says, is 'derived
from Saussure's discovery [that hyperbole again] of the anagrammatical
dispersal of certain proper names in Latin poetry'.[78] As Jonathan Culler
observes, the logic of post-structuralist anti-logocentrism demands that the
anagrammatical Saussure be taken seriously as a sort of deconstructionism
avant la lettre.[79] The rhapsodic deconstructionist Vincent B. Leitch is in no
doubt about the matter. He declares that focusing on the meaning of the
anagram work is the way forward for criticism. Saussure's 'Adamic guilt',
his doubts about that work, is now, Leitch opines, 'invariably absent', and,

as far as he's concerned, happily so. He quotes a French enthusiast with enthusiasm. The 'anagram' should be defined as standing for 'une multiplicité infixable, indécidabilité radicale qui défait tous les codes' – an indeterminable multiplicity, a radical undecidability which undoes all the codes.[80]

Come Back History

The anagrams, a more literary or textually regular version of Mlle Smith's glossolalia, are quite clearly a most discomfiting episode in the founding of the movement of thought which Leitch heralds. With such shaky foundations[81] it's small wonder that the critical enterprise variously built on Saussure should have inspired what Paul de Man deplored as Resistance to Theory. This was, with a certain ironic aptness, in the very volume that enthuses so about the anagrammatical 'terror'.[82] In the face of such openly terroristic theory, it's not too difficult to sign up with the Resistance against Paul de Man – much like, you might say, in wartime Belgium, when de Man was also on the side of the party of terror. And, of course, in the wake of poststructuralism's terrorizing claims for textuality, numerous oppositional factions and counter-parties have emerged, variously engaging, claiming to engage, attempting to re-engage, with the extra-textual, with history, philology, ideology – in short, with the context – in defiance, or fear, of what critical fashion did to the critical enterprise when it put on the partial (one can't call it the whole) armour of Saussure. The critical institution, motored by powerful herd instincts though it be, is nonetheless now as fissiparous and segmented into factions as Victorian Plymouth Brethrenism was and revolutionary socialism has more recently been. Old Marxism, Neo-Marxism, followers of Mikhail Bakhtin and his revised Russian Formalism, Feminisms of all shades, Black Criticism, post-colonialist critics, so-called Subaltern Criticism, New Literary History, admirers of Foucault, New Historicism, Cultural Materialists, gender critics, theorists of institutional power, canon formations, and the control of interpretation, the many varieties of Reader Receptionists (including even Stanley Fish, Pragmatist Richard Rorty's favourite critical pragmatist, and his communities of poem-making readers; even Richard Rorty himself with his desire to see a real reader engaged in 'an encounter with an author, character, plot, stanza . . . which has made a difference to the critic's conception of who she is, what she is good for, what she wants to do with herself: an encounter which has rearranged her priorities and responses' – that is, a reader like Rorty himself reporting on the emotional progress he

made going through Nabokov's *Pale Fire*, not excluding the 'But shuckses'
he uttered and all): all these, and many more, have sought, and are seeking,
in the nicely catchy phrase of Edward Said, to link up the world, the text,
and the critic.[83] History, ideology, the multiplex outside relations of literature, will, evidently, not be repressed. History's time will always come, or
come back.

Many readers and critics, of course, have been effectively endorsing Frank
Lentricchia's brisk realism through all the (post)structuralist heyday – 'the
clean distinction between text and history is absolute garbage' – even if they
might deplore his butch Marxist-blokeish way of putting it.[84] Others have,
for various reasons, quite changed their line. At any rate, history is now the
side that lots of critics want to be seen on, a latest form of politico-critical
correctness.

Empson's Charlady

The return of, and to, history does, it has to be confessed, bring its surprises.
It's not the blowing in the critical wind as such that surprises one about
Jonathan Culler. After all, his book *On Deconstruction* (1983) was already holding
open the door of a bolt-hole labelled feminism. But what's specially arresting
about his later collection of essays *Framing the Sign: Criticism and its Institutions* (1988) is the way it responds to what he calls 'The Call to History'
by espousing the importance of William Empson's book from 1951, *The
Structure of Complex Words*. Whoever would have thought, even a decade or
so back, that Empson's animated plain-man reflections on language would
ever make a come-back? Empson the philologist; Empson the lexicographer;
Empson the truculent ideologue forever locked in debate with Milton's God;
Empson the garrulous *homme moyen sensuel*; Empson the Cambridge mandarin
in thirties-fashionable, Leavis-style, open-necked shirt and slangy paragraphs;
Empson of the *neck-beard*; above all, Empson the devotee of *parole*, usage, real
speakers of the English language. It is, Empson declares characteristically,
the business of words 'to be fluid in meaning so that a variety of people can
use them . . . " 'E's what I call thrifty", the charlady will say, with a rich
recognition of the possibilities of using the other word.'[85] When Empson and
his charlady or his 1931 class of Japanese students reading Housman are
pushing their way briskly through the critical turnstile (not to mention the
home-spinning linguistic philosophy of Empson's supervisor I. A. Richards and
of C. K. Ogden, whose *The Meaning of Meaning* (1923) did more than
anything else to keep Saussure out of British and American universities until
well after the Second World War), then things are certainly changing. These

are come-backs as taking-aback as, say, Barbara Johnson's turn-around. Who would have thought (again) that the translator and editor of Derrida, the loyal disciple of Paul de Man, so HMV-positive (her master's voice, in short), would turn so firmly from the world of *différance* to *A World of Difference*, as her title of 1987 has it, leaving 'the realm of linguistic universality or deconstructive allegory' for 'contexts in which difference is very much at issue in the "real world" '; asking for a re-examination of the 'prevalence of the view that "theory" is a turning away from the world'; attempting to link the de Manian concentration on rhetoric, textuality, literariness as mere troping, with that older accent on rhetoric as worldly in orientation, a business of persuasion?

Ms Johnson isn't keen to be caught actually striking her father dead, wholly throwing off Paul de Man, so she declares she's trying to 'recontextualize' rather than displace his 'certain way of reading'. She resists the formula that she's on 'an itinerary that could be labelled "From Deconstruction to Feminism" '. But, of course, she *is* engaged on a process of feminist patricide. Paul de Man would not, presumably, have admired her effort at a politicizing rewrite of deconstruction's internalizing way with rhetorical figures. Metonymy and metaphor get discussed in terms of Black writing, and *apostrophe* and *prosopopoeia* (personification) are linked with the question, so vexed in the USA, of legalized abortion and when foetuses acquire personhood. In the abortion piece Barbara Johnson can't bring herself actually to target Paul de Man; but he's present, in a footnote and in the shadows throughout, a ghostly father having his precious rhetoricity put in its political place. 'Gender Theory' indeed meets 'The Yale School' here. The world of Derrida's white mythology of philosophical texts gives way to the new mythographics of black persons. The one-time enthusiastic practitioner of deconstructive rhetoric has thus acquired a 'human politics' and an ethics (as she put it in an interview published in 1987, all at once adroitly deferring to Paul de Man and also putting him and her de Man period under erasure), an ethics newly magnetized by 'the continuous moral imperative that says that any kind of formalism like deconstruction is, finally, too reductive, too "inside" '.[86]

The year 1987 was a good one for the salutary impact of moral imperatives on readers and a bad time for the excesses of reductive internalizing American deconstructionists; for that was when the scandalous wartime association between Paul de Man, darling of the Yale School of US deconstruction, and wartime Belgian Nazi ideology, especially as manifest in the anti-Semitic and pro-German articles he'd written during the Nazi occupation of his native Low Countries, became widely known in the USA. (It was known in Antwerp, de Man's home town, some time before that. I first heard of it in that city in 1986 on a visit during which I was shown the Antwerp pub that's a shrine to the Belgian SS battalion, a grim place peopled by Fascist skinhead thugs, with German beer mugs lining the bar-rafters, including one from Dachau.) When news of de Man's fascistic youth got out in the USA, there were absurd over-reactions by friends as well as by enemies of deconstruction. Few people behaved seemly. It was silly, or worse, of the friends to try and apply deconstructive techniques to his wartime texts, as Derrida did (notoriously suggesting that anti-Semitic writing could possibly be anti-anti-Semitic writing[87]), and as Shoshana Felman did (asserting, for example, that if the older Paul de Man had owned up to his murky past, he would have aggravated the early Nazi lying, because language can't bear 'straightforward referential witness'[88]). Silly, too, of the opponents, eager for any weapon against views they disliked, to suggest that somehow deconstruction was now proved to be intrinsically flawed by Fascism. Wrong, as well, of the allies to round on the accusers with charges of a totalitarian wish to conduct a neo-Holocaust by ridding the world of de Man's thought,[89] or to suggest that the fascination with presence and the resistance to difference were the real 'fascist tendencies', a linguistic totalitarianism that de Man had been right to confront.[90] But amidst all the panic and the aggravation, the manifest gainer was the sense of the momentousness of history for texts and for criticism, particularly as registered in the horrors of Nazism. The meaning of Auschwitz had come home to roost.

De Man's texts were dredged for signs that he and deconstruction really did take ideology seriously, after all. What such a rereading brought home, said Shoshana Felman, desperately, was a kind of historicist confirmation of deconstruction, a lesson in 'the nonsimplicity of reference in the shadow . . . of contemporary history'.[91] In his responses Derrida came the closest he'd ever got to erasing his customary erasure from history: he and deconstruction dealt with 'things, yes, *things* – real, resistant, historical, political things, in other words, referents'.[92] Hillis Miller was driven to declare (albeit in a mere supplementary footnote to a rereading of Paul de Man reading) 'that the juxtaposition of de Man's early and late writings is a starkly dramatic way to confront the fact that the triumph of Nazi totalitarianism in Germany, the Holocaust, and the Second World War were a decisive transformation of Western culture and even a break in world history. Whatever we say, do, or write, do by writing, thereafter takes place against the background of those events, whether or not we know it or wish it.'[93] Auschwitz had really come home to the rest-home of so-called Post-Histoire, to that zone of American literary criticism whose theme tune had traditionally been 'Don't Know Much About History'.[94]

The European experience that has continued to dominate European fiction and thought – both of them, since the Hitler War, morally belated in relation to the Holocaust; always, as Adorno put it, 'After Auschwitz';[95] locked into an historico-ethical imperative that has characteristically commanded the ethical demands of a Philippe Lacoue-Labarthe[96] and geared the discontents with structuralism of a Julia Kristeva[97] or a Tzvetan Todorov[98] and been distinctly present to those with ears to hear in the texts of Derrida (*La Carte postale* is a good case of his Holocaust concerns) – the inerasable European trauma had forced its way irresistibly on to the American-speaking agenda. It had taken the Paul de Man showdown to bring American literary critics around to the crisis point that American poststructuralist historian Hayden White had been driven to several years earlier. The inventor of post-Saussurean historiography in America, White's influential books – *Metahistory* (1973) and *Tropics of Discourse* (1978) – had powerfully urged historians to see how history was really only history-writing, a textuality utterly commanded by the narratology and rhetoricity it was constructed by and through. But even he had exempted the Holocaust from being a merely rhetorical construct, lest he appear to give succour ('morally offensive . . . intellectually bewildering') to right-wing revisionist historians eager to deny the factuality of the Hitlerite horrors. White had been moved to this concession – a fudging, grudging one, because it is indeed mightily unsettling for his meta-historical theoretical posture – not least by the protests of Pierre Vidal-Nacquet, a Jewish memorialist of the Hitlerite crimes. 'I try', Vidal-Nacquet movingly declared, 'to be a man of memory' – facing up to what Maurice Blanchot (discussing Foucault) referred to as 'what remains in our memory the greatest catastrophe and horror of modern times'. 'One cannot not speak of the scandals of an epoch,' says Hélène Cixous, addressing the question 'How to unite History and text?' – as a 'Jewoman'.[99]

And, of course, the Holocaust was already on the North American critics' agenda, but cryptically, a repressed memory and trace, there in every argumentative turn of Paul de Man's attempt to switch the face of literature and literary critics away from history. Again and again in those magisterial paragraphs steering textuality away from the extra-textually historical connection and the old human (and humanist) purports of literature, de Man had been, it now became abundantly clear, fencing in a coded way with the horrors of the Auschwitz years during which he had been, albeit temporarily, in the camp of the guilty. It's difficult now not to tremble at the seductiveness of his arguments against history and humanity, not to feel relief at the revelations that called his bluff and made sure that his Mephisophelean – or Faustian – game was up. How, you think, could the critical establishment have swallowed, for example, his dismissal of the human connection of language (in opposition to Schiller's equation of language and humanity)? Such a linkage was, de Man said, an illegitimacy, 'since there is, in a very radical sense, no such thing as the human'. 'If one speaks of the inhuman, the fundamental non-human character of language, one also speaks of the fundamental non-definition of the human as such.' All the old humanist talk that pervaded the humanities had better be dissolved in 'the inhuman, dehumanized language of linguistics'. But this was Auschwitz talk, if only we'd known it, a kind of plea-bargaining, the *post hoc* effort of an old anti-Semite at covering his tracks, a making of excuses for old transgressions. Even those in whose gullet such *trahisons de clerc* stuck at the time of the original lecture from which I'm quoting (Neil Hertz and Meyer Abrams) could not bring themselves to voice their objections outright in clear, blunt sentences. Fawningly, they hedged and stuttered, havering politely before the smooth terroristic imperatives of the master.[100]

Happily, though, history had caught up with this morally renegade talk only a year after it was published in *The Resistance to Theory*. And it's now impossible to read those passages without a keen post-Auschwitz mindfulness. Just as we can't now encounter de Man's attempt brusquely *umzukippen* (rudely to overturn or kick over) the historically centred idea of literary reception promoted by the German Hans Robert Jauss and the Konstanz School, in the name of the mere play of signifiers, without attending with freshened wryness to de Man's talk of butchers and butchery. This discussion is in the key chapter 'Reading and History' in *The Resistance to Theory*, and is focused in de Man's corrective rereading of Jauss's reading of Baudelaire's *Spleen* poems. Jauss, says de Man, is lamentably uninterested in, even dismissive of, 'the "play" of the signifier, semantic effects . . . on the level of the letter rather than of the word or sentence'. Jauss did note the poet's word-play by which the name of a painter called *Boucher* (Butcher) is made to rhyme with *débouché* (a bottle of perfume is uncorked; but *débouché* also suggests decapitated), but Jauss dismissed this as too grotesque a piece of verbal playfulness. De Man, though, celebrates this very moment in Baudelaire's poem. It's just the sort of 'frivolous', excessive play on the words that he believes poems to be all about, a superabundance of signifier-work on 'the difficult-to-control borderline' of ludic aesthetics and *Wortwitz*. So de Man butchers Jauss's historic emphases in the name of a verbal game, or *Witz*, about butchers and butchery. Which is an ironic enough advocacy from a man whose one-time party made butchery a chief part of its political game, giving rise to the likes of Klaus Barbie, the Butcher of Lyons. But there's more. In an astonishing subverting reversal of the anti-historical argument (but in a linguistic manoeuvre of the kind that de Man was much given to celebrating in his interpretations of texts) this antagonist of history, this proponent of politico-textual quietism, goes on to celebrate, albeit in the name of 'the rhetorical dimension of language', a shift occurring, as he believes, in

Baudelaire's poem, away from the inwardness of textualized memory and merely literary dissonances to the *literalness* of blood being spilled beyond and outside the confines of the aesthetic. 'This pale and white text of recollection (the first line of the poem is "J'ai plus de souvenirs que si j'avais mille ans") turns red with a brutality that takes us out of the inwardness of memory, the ostensible *theme* of the poem, into a very threatening literality to which an innocent art-term such as "dissonance" hardly does justice.' If a guilty, repressive conscience should be brought unwillingly (as in a scene from *Macbeth* or some other Gothic text or movie) to the point of confession by reminders of past bloodshed, of Auschwitz no less, this, you think, is how it might be done. And this is, in fact, what seems to be happening. A bloody history insists on defying de Man's argument for, and Baudelaire's text of, historicist quietism. Insisting on mere rhetoricity can't keep that bloody history at bay; it's in the rhetoricity itself; and the words of Paul de Man, the very attempt at using the 'play of signifiers' against an historically minded literary analyst, are turned, willy-nilly, Auschwitz-wards (and all the more piquantly given that this is in an argument with a one-time youthful member of the German SS who had not, unlike Paul de Man, covered up his personal tracks, nor called the disavowal of history in aid of such a cover-up, but had repented his past, come to the front of the critical stage with a famous insistence on the historical factor in texts, and, what's more, espoused an alternative democratic historicity in a prominent and active membership of the post-war German SPD). Willy-nilly, de Man's resistance to history had turned him in the very direction from which the recent (Re)turn to History would receive its mightiest push.[101]

Some of the reaction against hypertextualism, the so-called Return to Philology, to use Paul de Man's own phrase, has, naturally, been simply reactionary in the old sense, the survival and recrudescence of old prejudices and practices and tired yearnings for a quiet life. Such nostalgias can be seen in M. H. Abrams and other doughty enemies of deconstructionism who did battle with the likes of Hillis Miller in the pages of *Critical Inquiry* in the later seventies, or among the contributors to Laurence Lerner's *Reconstructing Literature* (1983) – the reconstructors include the knee-jerk right-wing 'philosopher' Roger Scruton, whose presence in the volume rather sets its tone – as well as in a multitude of old grudgers and grousers in common-rooms across the globe. There has been – there always is – a great deal of simple fuddy-duddyism in the face of incoming critical fire. There's a Hogarthian cartoon figure who adorns that page in the satirical magazine *Private Eye* devoted to doings in the British Press: a journalist turned down-and-out wino begging in a gutter in Fleet Street, the 'Street of Shame' that formerly employed him, under a banner reading 'New Technology Baffles

Pissed Old Hack'. He stands, *mutatis mutandis*, for many a professorial reactionary full of self-pity for him- or herself as a victim of the critical wars that
have raged since the mid-sixties. Among such, sighs of relief can be heard
as the old Paradigms look as if they might be about to be Regained, and the
New Literary History turns out to have some nicely recuperable connections
with the old literary history, or the wind is knocked out of the
deconstructionist sails (and sales), and the Yale School scatters, and yet another
gleeful journalistic piece or book such as David Lehmann's *Signs of the Times:
Deconstruction and the Fall of Paul de Man* (1991) puts the boot in. So,
thankfully, that's Another Book – or set of books – To Cross Off Your List,
in the words of F. C. Crews's wonderful parody of Leavis's dismissiveness in
the person of *Winnie the Pooh*-slating Simon Lacerous in *The Pooh Perplex: A
Student Casebook* (1964): you can hear them saying it. But a reaction that
would return simply to reference, history, context, failing to take any account
of the recent years of accumulated attention to the tricksy ways of word,
rhetoric, text, will not, by itself, do. That's only the polar mirror image of
the simple and extreme (post)structuralism that would have nothing to do
with history.[102]

Born Again and Again

Careerism, of course, inflects some of the Return to History. Jonathan Culler
is not the only one with a wind-sock. After all, the Will to Power in the US
university struggle for professional mastery depends on keeping up, never
looking old-fashioned, changing your critical coat promptly to avoid looking
like yesterday's *vieux jeu*. We're all historians nowadays: it's being said with
the same skin-saving fervour as old British aristocrats used to avow being all
working class nowadays (I myself heard Professor Lord David Cecil say it),
and it carries as much weight. The heady extremist rush to ditch presence in
as many of its manifestations as possible – authors, the subject, authority,
certainty, determinacy, fulness of meaning – for its tricksy opposite, in as
many of its manifestations as credible – textual mystique, negativity,
crypticism, Cabbala, black holes, dark backwards and abysms, gaps, *béances*,
woolly pragmatisms old and new – has been matched by the equally Gadarene
haste towards the opposite extreme, to plead the cause of history, context,
politics. And for every Barbara Johnson changing step with a sort of *mea culpa*,
there's an unapologetic Gayatri Chakravorty Spivack – expertly chameleon,
the one-time white-face translator of Derrida's *Of Grammatology*, the most
strident of deconstructionists, now recovering her Indian-ness in the name of
Third World feminism and cultural materialism and what she calls Marxist

deconstructionism, and not troubled enough to hide the full-speed, forever-jotting, always position-shifting suppleness of the successful corporate prof.[103] Shape-changing is a mode of careerist survival. Notoriously, Stanley Fish has urged that the professorial critic is finished, over, if he doesn't retool every eighteen months or so. And his graduate students and any others who want jobs naturally pay heed to the command to become critical fly-paper, just as the now notorious seminar group obeyed their professor when he ordered them to read a group of linguists' names he'd written up on the board as a Metaphysical Poem, he having told them it was one.[104] In some institutional circumstances you toe the party line, or in this case the successive lines, or else. It's a situation George Orwell was thoroughly familiar with.

Uncritical Theory

Whatever you think, however, of the grim scene of institutionalized critical politics in the USA, more generally worrying is the striking thinness of so much of the history or historicism, the actual force of the context, the ideology, the ethics, and so on, that are nowadays being variously let back in, or revived, whether by the tired business-as-usual people or the smart careerist Artful Dodgers, or even by the sincere devotees of the New Historicism and the newly revalued worldly connections of the text. 'Always historicize!' The first words of Fredric Jameson's *The Political Unconscious* (1981) make a bonny motto. They're quoted widely and with approval. Robert Scholes is one of the many who do so: 'One does not have to be a Marxist to endorse. . . .'[105] But historicizing is, to quote the hero of Martin Amis's novel *Money* (1984) on the subject of the hard-ons he fails to achieve, it is, well, hard.

Derrida all unwittingly indicates just how hard history is when in his new or renewed mood of historicity he approaches the shibboleth of the textualized historical date. 'An utterance', he declared, in defiance of what many have believed to be his ahistorical line, 'is always dated.' And he meditates in several politically impressive and historically well-intentioned pages on the preoccupation with historical datedness of the poem 'In Eins' by the Holo-caust-survivor Paul Celan (from *Die Niemandsrose*, 1963). Its first stanza begins 'Dreizenter Feber' (Thirteenth of February), talks of 'an awakened shibboleth' and of being 'with' the people of Paris, apparently in some po-litical activity or demonstration, and ends '*No pasarán*'. As Derrida points out, 13 February 1962 was the day of a funeral for Parisian victims of an OAS (Organisation de l'armée secrète) terror bomb, a demonstration against the right-wing supporters of the French occupation of Derrida's native country, Algeria. But what's the Spanish connection? 'No pasarán': they're the words of the Spanish Republicans of 1936, offering resistance, a military *aporia*, to Franco's Fascists: 'They shall not pass.' And Derrida turns to another February by way of explication: 'February 1936: this is the challenge to the fascists, to Franco's troops, to the Phalange supported by Mussolini's troops and Hitler's Condor Legion: "They shall not pass" is the cry of the Republicans and the International Brigade, what they are writing on their banderoles, just before the Fall of Madrid in February.' And incited by the occurrence of the slogan 'No pasaran' in an earlier poem of Celan's, actually entitled 'Schibboleth' (in *Von Schwelle zu Schwelle*, 1955), which has another reference to an unspecified February as well as to the doubled 'redness' of Vienna and Madrid, Derrida speaks of 'the fall of Vienna and the fall of Madrid in February '36'. But well-intentioned though all this historicizing is, these pre-war dates are a farrago of mistakings. The Viennese leftists fought and lost in February 1934; Madrid fell to Franco at the end of January 1939 – neither date close to 1936. Nor was *No pasarán* a slogan of February 1936. The Franco insurrection didn't occur until *July* of that year; *No pasarán* wasn't a going slogan until at least then; what's more, the International Brigade wasn't formed until some months after that. Whatever 13 February Celan is referring to, it's not the one in 1936. And, to be sure, Derrida is aware that he is guessing ('I am unaware' of 'the so-called "external" date of the poem'). Our confidence in his datings is not, of course, boosted by his insistence that precision in dating both matters and also does not matter ('The more indeterminate the date, the more ample' its possible siting: another example of the *sous rature* tic – now accurate dating is important to deal with, now it's not). But whatever we think of this fast-and-looseness, coping with history, in this case dates in poems, is clearly shown to be as difficult to get right as it was hard for the original Biblical Ephraimites to pronounce the word *shibboleth*. The shibboleth of history is evidently troublesome even for its latest friend. Derrida had run up against an interpretative aporia in more sense than one.[106]

And even for history's traditional literary-critical friends, the historical has proved an awkward shibboleth business. Clamantly history-friendly, in theory at least, Marxists have a terrible practical record in the matter from *Das Kapital* on, when Marx declared that we needn't take the 'prayers' of *Robinson Crusoe* seriously. Georg Lukács's mumbling focus on the more formal technics of Solzhenitsyn's *One Day in the Life of Ivan Denisovich*; Terry Eagleton's rough-and-ready vision of the Brontës' relation to the working-class movements of West Yorkshire or his jokey wrongness about the Elizabethan vocabulary for female pudenda (and so on and on); Anthony Easthope's silly speculations about the 'bourgeois' nature of the iambic pentameter; the Methuen New Accent speakers' misreadings of Dictionary Murray and Murray's *Dictionary*'s relationship to the State; even the Nottingham Theory Group's excitement over 'purchases' in *Heart of Darkness* (of which more later): they are all representatively revelatory of the difficulty of truly encountering the subtleties of contextual presences in texts.[107]

New Historicists – neo-Marxists many of them – have managed, in general, a lot better, particularly in handling Renaissance texts. In fact, New Historicism can be said to have quite resuscitated the flagging corpse of Renaissance studies for end-of-century readers with its particular and insistent repertoire of historico-textual functions – or props, as they've been called:[108] power (above all power), power on display, power stage-managed, ritualized, embodied, transplanted to colonies overseas, power enacted in State sites and institutions – monarchy, church, marriage, the city, the gaol, the lazar-house, the plague hospice. The pressure of Foucault's obsession with the histories of hospitals, asylums, prisons, and the social definitions of illness, madness, crime, sexual deviance, is felt, and praiseworthily, everywhere in this work, ably egged on by the ghost of Mikhail Mikhailovich Bakhtin, especially his revolutionizing story about the revolutionary effects of the carnivalesque in Rabelais – that insurgent, overturning, radical pressure from the lower parts of society, language and the human body.[109]

New Historicists are much drawn, in principle at least, to the necessity of what they admire Clifford Geertz for labelling 'thick description'.[110] Geertz is New Historicism's favourite anthropologist.[111] But nobody achieves thickness of description simply by invoking it. And the New Historicist shopping list of the most important textualized historical features has very rapidly resulted in a rather thin, limited, and limiting menu. Embodiment, Desire, Disclosure, Gender, Power, Others: the chapter headings of a recent book *The Culture of Love* by Stephen Kern[112] indicate how utterly normal now, how totally expected, is the presence of such themes in any half-way respectable historical-textual survey. Hermeneutical correctness demands these particular zones of focus. But they do lose their challenging effect, important as they are, and they get their sharp edges eroded, by endless repetition and clichéd availability. 'I feel so empowered,' declares the fashion model Cindy Crawford in an MTV advertisement for her *Shape Your Body* work-out video, the language of power and empowering absorbed into a clichéd Californian solipsistic body-fetishizing rhetoric that laughably leaves the actual power structures of late capitalist market-place economics – imperialist, exploitative of women – firmly in place (and thus not out of keeping with the favourite New Historicist emphasis on power always in the end containing and limiting subversives and subversion, giving a sense, as Frank Lentricchia put it, that 'there is a kind of monolith of power that crushes and makes irrelevant all intention'). Which way madness lies – and Lentricchia rightly cites *Brazil*, the movie, and Orwell's *Nineteen Eighty-Four*.[113] It's a rhetoric that can leave texts pretty intact too.

To mean powerfully, to be analytically potent keys, power and desire and bodies and otherness, and all the other going concerns of New Historicists, have to be broken down, particularized, granted the singularity of time and place and person. Otherwise they're simply uninspected, if heart-warming, tokens that are being circulated like Hallelujahs at a prayer-meeting, just a kind of politically correct cheer-leading. 'If *1 Henry IV* can be said to be "about" anything, it is about the production of power.'[114] That's the kind of New-Historicizing critical allegation that's now neither new nor really historicizing, and certainly not illuminating beyond the simplest level of interpretative approach-shot. Blunt, it's just blunting. As blunting as to fall into the gravest New-Historicist error of supposing, with deconstructionists and Hayden White (and like Foucault in certain, though by no means all, of his moods), that the context is just (or mainly) another text, more reading matter, only discourse.

At its best, some of the recent contextualizing work undoubtedly rises above the limits of limited New Historicism and triumphantly addresses the convergence of word and world with considerable aplomb and interpretative success. My account of *Heart of Darkness* in chapter 5 is incited, in part, by Edward Said's discussion of Oscar Wilde in his *The World, the Text, and the Critic*, and it should be taken as paying tribute to the strongly informative weld between context and text which Said has achieved, not least in his book *Orientalism* and his (more gently meandering) *Culture and Imperialism*.[115] In this Said (or Said–Foucault) tradition also come the best of the French and American Classicists and the British Cultural Materialists, especially the students of colonialism and of the victims of other kinds of repressive and oppressive ideologies, such as homosexuals.[116] The British Cultural Materialists, all transgressively defiant of theory's artificial barriers between word and world, politically motivated bad boys (Byron: 'The tragic poet of course deals not in your good-boy characters'[117]), Faustian, Mephistophelean, of the Devil's party and knowing it, do certainly have their faults (Alan Sinfield, for instance, is prone to go in for startlingly crude dismissals of the 'human'[118]); but their exemplary virtue is their respect for the twin play of word and world within a steady refusal either to go back to a naïve historiography, one unalert to problems of textuality, of writing, of the story-telling aspects of history, or to rest content with history as merely reflection, story, text, discourse. In Homi Bhabha's pun there's Nation in Narration; in Wole Soyinka's there's an engagement between *langage* (that 'cold typography before the linguist') and *l'engage* (words in their 'socially active meaning'), and the best Cultural Materialists probe usefully at the conjunction.[119]

Of course, as Foucault, not least, has profoundly reminded us, the world is in a continuous state of rhetoricization; the real is never not a matter of rhetoric, writing, story, never not sailing through (and sometimes becalmed in) the tropics of discourse; but still, the historical *realium* is also never not just a construction in a text – not ever, and especially not in the worlds of power and victimization, of colonizing and persecution, where ideology impacts on the body, and bodies are tortured, minds deformed, men and women cut up, maimed, killed, and otherwise subjugated. In brief, not in Conrad's Africa or Auschwitz or Bosnia-Herzegovina. It is indeed necessary and important to engage with the way the real is written, with the perpetual being-writtenness of reality, but in and through our encounters with the Imagining of America and the Writing of Ireland or Spain or Vietnam or Elizabethan England or the Holocaust or whatever, it should never be forgotten that there's raw material there, present in and through and also behind the textual material.[120] The world, things, self, knowledge, are, as Elizabeth Fox-Genovese nicely insists, not simply or only a text or texts. History (and politics and morals) demand that we pay attention to more than texts and their interpretations, and that when we are textually engaged (as New Historicists are) we be alert to the always more than merely textual nature of the texts we're in.[121]

Believing that when you are as a reader 'in' a text you're only in a text is an error that James Young's investigation of Holocaust testimonies, documents, fictions, narrations, and tropes does not make, even if he is mightily compelled by Hayden White's thoughts on the rhetoricity of history. But then his subject is the writing of Auschwitz.[122] But the oversight James Young avoids is one that Stephen Greenblatt, New Historicism's potent father-figure is not unhappy to condone. And, after all, California is, as Dr Johnson might have said, from Auschwitz rather far. Influentially, Greenblatt's characteristic ploy has been to read the canonical texts of Shakespeare not against the *realium* of the world, against some event 'out there', but against another text, a text representing the world alright, but still the world refracted textually. *Representations*, Greenblatt's rightly influential journal is called. But in his demonstrations of how great literary texts work in their contexts, texts do not represent a context as such; rather they represent the context's written re-presentations. 'We need to develop terms', Greenblatt declares,

> to describe the ways in which material – here [he's talking of Norman Mailer's 'true life novel' *The Executioner's Song*, based on the life and death of executed murderer, Gary Gilmore] official documents, private papers, newspaper clippings, and so forth – is transferred from one discursive sphere to another and becomes aesthetic property. It would, I think, be a mistake to regard this

process as uni-directional – from social discourse to aesthetic discourse – not only because the aesthetic discourse in this case is so entirely bound up with capitalist venture [Mailer's own book; and the book *In the Body of the Beast*, the letters of another convict, Jack Abbott, that were published after the Gilmore case got publicized, and which became a stage-play] but because the social discourse is already charged with aesthetic energies [Gilmore was moved by the film version of *One Flew Over the Cuckoo's Nest*, and 'his entire pattern of behavior seems to have been shaped by the characteristic representations of American popular fiction, including Mailer's own'].[123]

It's a plausible circulation of textual effects, but it is just that: from the film of Ken Kesey's novel to Gilmore to Mailer's book to subsequent book and stage-play, all these are transactions between one kind of discourse and another. But the so-called social discourse includes the double murderer Gilmore, executed by firing-squad, and the murderer Abbott, paroled through Mailer's efforts and the book of letters, who stabbed a waiter to death shortly after his release from gaol. Here, clearly, is much much more than discourse, even discourse given a lick of contextual paint as 'social discourse'.[124]

Video Nasty

Uncritical theory, Christopher Norris has quite rightly called this sort of dissolving into mere text of the *realium* of the world of guns and knives as they impinge on the human body. It's what Jean Baudrillard did with the Gulf War, what Derrida has done with nuclear war, what Hillis Miller did with 'all wars and revolutions', what a pair of Oxford feminists have done with the business of sex-murders of women by men.[125] It is, for that matter, what Jean-François Lyotard does with toothache. 'My teeth hurt' may, he says, seem to refer to the physical reality of the body, but the 'body "proper" is a name for the family of ideolects' – it's just a linguistic reality. And as the only feeler of the pain, its exclusive addressee, you cannot 'verify that it is lived experience'. 'It is like the voice of God.' All a case of the 'grammatical remark'. Which is a casting of doubt upon the reality of bodily pain that torturers and warmongers might well find comes in handy by way of excuse. Revealingly, a page or so after this dismissal of the reality of toothache, Lyotard is to be found talking easily of 'the discourse named "Auschwitz"'.[126]

Baudrillard has, of course, been practising this textualization for a long time. Confronted by the great Behemoth of modern consumerism, the commodity fetishism that hawks its offered pleasures nightly across our TV screens, he boiled it all down to a set of arbitrary object-signs, and ones not, as you might have supposed, aimed at impelling us into shops and plunging us into lots of cash-nexuses, but signs involving us merely in a sequence of differential information exchanges. The old story: not reference, but difference. And a whole continent could easily be sent the way of such shopping. For Baudrillard, America becomes, well, Amerika: the capital of 'fiction become reality', a reality, primarily, of film and TV image, of 'the marvellously affectless succession of signs'. In other words, America is for him just like Roland Barthes's famous analysis of the French fashion system, which is in fact only an analysis of a lot of fashion photographs perceived as a Saussurean system of signifiers, signs without extra-textual *signata*. And that's photography on a model which Barthes severely revised, as we've seen, after the painful death of his mother made him come to cherish photographs as records of irrecoverably past times and persons.

That was a revision, though, hotly spurned by some theorists, not least by those unstickably wedded to the idea of the photograph as mere discourse. For such analysts, the Saussurean division between sign and referent, signifier and signified, remains as firmly in place as ever.[127] It's a division that even the 'Always Historicizer' himself, Fredric Jameson, has come more and more happily to embrace, the more his version of postmodernism has come to dominate his thought. Jameson will say that he he wants criticism to break out of the Saussurean prison-house of language into the contiguous zones of politics and context; but in the event he keeps knuckling under to the dictates of post-Saussurean formalism, the authority of 'discourse'. The alleged death of the subject, the loss of an historical sense, the erasure of reference, were once offered by him as (post)modern opinion to be rather deplored; gradually they've slid over into seeming the truth of postmodernism and what is for him postmodernism's essential medium, namely video. They are now presented as the apotheosis of a Saussurean reality of media – a 'realm of language' where the sign is 'disjoined' from the referent:

> Such a disjunction does not completely abolish the referent, or the objective world, or reality, which still continue to entertain a feeble existence on the horizon like a shrunken star or red dwarf. But its great distance from the sign now allows the latter to enter a moment of autonomy, of a relatively free-floating Utopian existence, as over against its former objects. This autonomy of culture, this semiautonomy of language, is the moment of modernism, and of a realm of the aesthetic which redoubles the world without being altogether of it, thereby winning a certain negative or critical power, but also a certain otherworldly futility. Yet the force of reification, which was responsible for this new moment, does not stop there either: in another stage, heightened, a kind of reversal of quantity into quality, reification penetrates the sign itself and disjoins the signifier from the signified. Now reference and reality disappear altogether, and even meaning – the signified – is problematized. We are left with that pure and random play of signifiers that we call postmodernism, which no longer produces monumental works of the modernist type but

ceaselessly reshuffles the fragments of preexistent texts, the building blocks of older cultural and social production in some new and heightened bricolage: metabooks which cannibalize other books, metatexts which collate bits of other texts – such is the logic of postmodernism in general, which finds one of its strongest and most original, authentic forms in the new art of experimental video.[128]

That acceptingness is extraordinary coming as it does from the USA's most famous Marxist critic; but it's symptomatic of the persistence of Saussureanism when even Marxists like Jameson profess broad agreement with it. 'With the work of Martin Heidegger, his student Hans Gadamer, and from another quarter, Hayden White, we need no longer argue that the starting-point of "history" (whether as discipline or referent, the temporal record itself) is necessarily with the act of interpretation and the location of that act within the sociocultural matrix.' That's the Marxist Frank Lentricchia.[129] Notice how the 'act of interpretation' precedes the 'sociocultural matrix', and that 'we need no longer argue' with this 'starting-point'. No wonder Derek Attridge declares that Lentricchia 'must be numbered among Saussure's progeny'.[130] But then, the Saussureans comprise a large tribe indeed, even among those who ought to know better, and among some who think they do.[131] What again and again confronts us – whether among deconstructionists, regenerate and unregenerate, among certain New Historicists and wavering Marxists of the Jameson stamp, among those for whom ethics are reduced largely to the ethics of reading,[132] among the loud utilitarians, the suit-yourself rhetoricians, and the roll-your-own-meaning pragmatists like Fish and Rorty who imagine texts and their meanings are just what you suppose they are, as it suits your convenience,[133] among scholars of the Hayden White meta-history school and the meta-literary-historians (the ones going in for history, but in its softer options as the history of discourse, tropes, rhetoricity and, most popular, the history of the literary critical institution[134]) – all over the shop there is a certain hesitancy, a fudging, a shrinking back, from what Lynn Hunt has called the Scandal of History and Jerome McGann The Scandal of Referentiality: that scandal implicit in all language, texts, sign-systems, discourses, the problematic which, for all of its stubborn refusal to lie down and quietly expire, we still persist in not being able to look squarely in the face.[135]

After the End of History

Deconstructionists and their ilk were, of course, crying wolf even before the Paul de Man scandal really stopped them in their *binari*. History had refused

to throw in the towel, they lamented. It never went away to the extent
that their critics alleged that they'd have wished. Or it returned with too
prompt a vengeance. Lovely post-Saussurean truths had been strangled in
their cradles. 'To judge from various recent publications, the spirit of the
times is not blowing in the direction of formalist and intrinsic criticism.
We . . . continue to hear a great deal about reference, about the nonverbal
"outside" to which language refers, by which it is conditioned, and upon which
it acts.' That was Paul de Man already in 1980.[136] 'The commitment to
[explaining works of literature 'by their political, social, and historical contexts'] as a main focus of literary study, perhaps *the* main responsibility of
literary study, is so widespread today.' That was Hillis Miller in 1987.[137]
And the very regrettable nature of this regressive 'shift to history' and
'resistance to theory' were main themes in Hillis Miller's astonishingly
bad-tempered Presidential Address to the Modern Language Association of
North America in 1986.[138] Critics like him had really wanted, it seems, to
sweep history away, to get rid of the non-verbal 'outside' from critical reckoning, and they were mightily regretful about the return even of the New
Historicism's heavily textualized history. They might be citizens of a profoundly post-colonialist culture, but they were very depressed by history's
interference with their own desired critical imperialism. They had truly wanted
to effect a sort of deconstructionist apocalypse, a revolutionary *Endlösung* or
Final Solution against 'history, the real, man, subjectivity, etc.' and, alas,
here were historical things still stumbling about in the blitzed city on the
day after the final air-raid.

> There have been a number of signs in recent years that we are perhaps
> approaching the end of what has been labeled . . . the 'poststructuralist' phase
> of theory and criticism. The gradual demise (or dispersion) of the so-called
> 'Yale School of Criticism' and its notion of 'deconstruction as literary criticism'
> undoubtedly constitutes the most obvious of these signs . . . A battle is now
> raging on many fronts to impose or reimpose forms of previously challenged
> orthodoxies in order to cut short debate and experimentation and reestablish
> what is [sic] sometimes claimed to be more solid foundations for humanistic
> inquiry: namely, history, the real, man, subjectivity, etc.

That's David Carroll, one of those 'hailed' by Hillis Miller in his Presidential Address as within the pale, inside the *numerus clausus*, on the proper
deconstructionist side of the critical battle-line.[139] Notice that 'debate' and
'experimentation' are all on one side in Carroll's last sentence. No sneers or
presumptions are barred in these discussions.

But at the same time, of course, the wolf-criers have over-egged the pudding, overdone the *Angst*. They may pretend that they're now on the run or down in the Last Bunker with the armies of historicist and politicizing reaction at the door; but in fact things have gone massively their way, even among those they churlishly persist in labelling the enemy. There has been, President Miller declared with some truth, an 'almost universal triumph of theory'. 'The rejection of theory today [he meant of course post-Saussurean theory: it's one of the key argumentative tropes of supporters of that theory to hog the label "theory"] can only take place in the context of the whole history of structuralist and poststructuralist theory – Saussure . . . and the rest.' And he waved once more some of the key flags that I've here had occasion to be sceptical about – 'Saussure on the arbitrariness of the sign', Derrida on Celan and Schibboleth, Paul de Man on Saussure's hypograms.[140] And he was right about the triumphalist spread of the linguistic ideas that he has busily drawn on. When critics wish now to return poetry, say, to the arms of historicity, they do so with considerable defensiveness. Take Frank Kermode, for instance, a critic who has recently nailed his historical colours in a finely principled way to the critical mast. Value, he's sharply declared, taking on the postmodernist pragmatists, is important in texts and, what's more, depends on historicized readings: 'out of history, value'. 'We cannot in the end deal with mere offcuts'. We need the wholeness of history: 'Our treatment of it may be a bit rough and ready, but at its best it is at least sensible, and in any case life [institutional and personal] would be impossible without it.'[141] But even so, seeking after all that to address some 'poems about history', he still feels compelled to go through a series of apologetic little hoops before getting going on his subject: 'This modest enterprise . . . may be seen as an archaism, a reversion to a mode of literary history now finally discredited. But I offer no apology, since something of the kind must happen if we are not to collude with the destruction of certain values not easily attained but too easily lost.'[142] Well said. But the tentativeness ('This modest enterprise') is of course apologetic. 'I offer no apology' – rhetorically the device is *occupatio*, claiming not to say something that you then do say – is usually an apology. And Kermode sets a going tone: historicism is now to be apologized for.

There has indeed been a sea-change in critical orthodoxy, and one not fundamentally shifted by the Return to History and Philology in whatever mood that return has been undertaken, whether unabashed or grudging, whole-hearted, half-hearted, or hard-hearted. Here's a random, a truly random, paragraph. I found it by putting a finger into the pages of *Victorian Studies*, a journal that's never sought to be at the forefront of critical theory.

Contemporary critics, unlike Charlotte Brontë's characters, avoid old-fashioned questions of identity. We do not ask '*Who* is it? *What* is it? Who speaks?' as

Rochester did in his blindness. We ask how the heroines come to act as subjects, how we are to perceive their development, and how they connect, or defy connection, to a cultural and economic nexus. Meanwhile, the homely question of identity has shifted its locus from the text to the metatext. Now we inquire of the critical study, 'Who are you?' and 'Where do you come from?' or skeptically, 'Are you what you claim to be?'[143]

What 'we' do is confidently asserted. 'We' are busy with metatextual questions. 'We' are not interested in people, but in subjects, selves constituted as mere clusters and networks of discourses. The very question of identity is 'homely' – uninstructed, old-fashioned, folksy, what they asked down on the farm before they got to the city and the university. There is, to be sure, a cultural and economic nexus somewhere about, but it's not something people are in, only what subjects might or might not connect with. As far as the cultural and economic go, the connection is highly tangential. And metatextual questions are the real ones now: the issue of identity is now refocused on the critic and the critical text. The identity of the reader and of the reading now matters more than what used to be called in a quaint down-home fashion the 'characters' in the novel. What's more, if you don't think like this, you are asking the wrong questions, redundant questions about disappeared concepts of person and text. You are, in fact, as blind as Rochester. And all this is taken as read at *Victorian Studies*, one of our staidest scholarly journals. No one is expected to object – just as in a Paul de Man or Stanley Fish seminar. Clearly a new set of orthodoxies is firmly in place – and there are many more signs of it in the rest of the review I'm quoting – its cast-iron instatement revealed in the casually throw-away assumption that 'we' all think alike on all these matters. And these casual assumptions are all, of course, rooted in casual assumptions about language that go back to Saussure. Their origin may already be clouded in unknowing, but their power pervades. The authoritarian Paul de Man has gone, but his Saussurean dictates still resonate. 'By an awareness of the arbitrariness of the sign (Saussure) and of literature as an autotelic statement "focussed on the way it is expressed" (Jakobson), the entire question of meaning can be bracketed, thus freeing critical discourse.' 'Semiology', as he put it, has had wonderful 'demystifying power': 'It demonstrated that the perception of the literary dimensions of language is largely obscured if one submits uncritically to the authority of reference.' 'It especially exploded the myth of semantic correspondence between sign and referent, the wishful hope of having it both ways, of being, to paraphrase Marx, a formalist critic in the morning and a communal moralist in the afternoon, of serving both the technique of form and the substance of meaning.'[144]

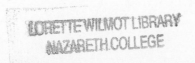

The Black Spot

Says you, might be one response to that typical piece of domineering de
Man-ic assumption. Of course, it was characteristic both of Paul de Man's
thought and of what he helped establish as critical orthodoxy that 'substance
of meaning', 'reference', referents, 'communal moralism' (a nasty phrase that),
could never be banished entirely, even from his own paragraphs (and that's
what his apologists are now very eager to stress about his enterprise). But at
the same time it's also characteristic of his arguments that those externalia
are allowed only grudgingly to enter the picture; they're always going to be
bracketed, marginalized, jeered into submission, handed the critic's version
of the death-sentence in Robert Louis Stevenson's *Treasure Island*, the black
spot. Readers are expected to know precisely which side of the *binari* to come
down on, which way politico-critical correctness lies, if they're to have any
seminar-credibility. The technique of de Man's paragraph is precisely Saussure's
technique, the adroit but also highly manipulative rhetorical strategy of the
whole mode of criticism – which is most of what's currently labelled 'theory'
– schooled by Saussure.

The method floods Hillis Miller's Presidential Address to the Modern
Language Association. The climactic metaphor of his speech, and a very
American trope too, is of critical explorers busy on both sides of 'the apparent
canyon between history and language . . . doing the difficult work of thinking
out the relation between language and history'. But the word 'apparent'
proves to be just a verbal con trick. The canyon's reality emerges in the next
breath in all its true strength as a *realium*, a given. There really is, for this
President, a great gulf fixed between language and history. And as far as he's
concerned, only the explorers on his side of the canyon count. He drew up
lists of opposed names, plainly indicating who was saved and who was damned,
who sheep, who goats: on the one side the history and reference people
(Jackson Bate, not least the great biographer of Dr Johnson; René Wellek,
who had accused contemporary critics of 'philosophising on [their] own';
Eugene Goodheart, author of *The Skeptic Disposition*; John Searle, the philosopher who early on crossed swords with Derrida in the Limited Inc. dispute;
the Marxists Edward Said and Frank Lentricchia; Stephen Greenblatt's New
Historicist journal *Representations* and all it represented), all sadly misguided;
and, on the other, 'my collaborators in a common task', most of them, you
might say, terminal poststructuralists.[145] On such a reading as this, the canyon
is impassable, and President Miller knows which side he's on.

And Miller is the critic who, after all, relegated his Auschwitz acknowledgement to a footnote in an admission as grudging as it was wild (he

suggested that since Paul de Man's later criticism 'also took place against the background' of the Holocaust, he somehow shouldered the moral burden of post-Auschwitz witness: by the same token, so, one supposes, did Dr Mengele's later career).[146] For Miller you may invoke history only if you then somehow squirm away from the impact of its invocation, and it disappears pretty promptly into sign. Miller will talk of 'the evidences of history', but they 'are always one form or another of signs to be read: documents, paintings, films, or "material" artifacts'. Once again, discourse reigns supreme, OK? Notice the quote-marks around 'material'. And this trick, of invoking the other side of the canyon only to have it put down or away, the great post-Saussurean disappearing trick, is one Hillis Miller has practised with considerable dexterity even since he got his new deconstructive religion.

Again and again it has been President Miller's ploy to announce the coexistence of some set of binaries within texts and textuality (what Barbara Johnson suggests we should think of under the rhetorical label *hendiadys*, one thing under two names) – canny and uncanny criticism, two forms of repetition, two kinds of allegory, the tradition of presence and the tradition of difference, metaphysical and anti-metaphysical criticism, and so on – only straightaway to hierarchize one position over the other. Hendiadys, in other words, evoked and revoked in the same paragraphs: spilt hendiadys. And it's the same position that's always given the preferential treatment. What's alleged to predominate, always, is the intrinsic, the formalist, the internal reference or self-reference, difference, puzzle, hermeticism, play, emptiness, absence, rhetoric, metaphor, troping, textuality, metatextuality, even inter-textuality, as opposed to the extrinsic, the contextual, reference, presence, fullness, mirroring, the political, the worldly, the historical, the secular.[147] 'A critic must choose either the tradition of presence or the tradition of "differance", for their assumptions about language, about literature, about history, and about the mind cannot be made compatible,' Miller declared in 1971, in his piece on George Poulet, with all the force of a Calvinist, or Stalinist, or simply American imperialist dogmatism. By 1984 he may have split the likely 'grounds' of literary study into four possibles – social, psychological, linguistic, deconstructionist – but he was more insistently monological and hierarchical than ever: 'People . . . always say, "Can't you combine these?" . . . it appears to me that ultimately you have to choose one, that they are not reconcilable except in a hierarchical way.'[148]

The poststructuralist pairing or oppositions at issue here do, of course, owe a lot to traditional critical oppositions. That writing looks in two directions at once, being comprised of extrinsic and intrinsic reference, is one of our oldest feelings about it. Roland Barthes's opposition of *lisible* and *scriptible*, 'heterogeneity to language' and 'homogeneity to language'; Roman Jakobson's of *metonym* and *metaphor* (greatly popularized by David Lodge); Frank Kermode's of *pleroma* and *kenosis* (fulness and emptiness); Denis Donoghue's of *epi*-writing and *graphi*-writing; Ian Watt's of *heterophoric* and *homeophoric*; Jacques Lacan's of *full* and *empty* words; Hayden White's of *normal* and *absurdist*; Robert Scholes's of *secular* and *hermetic*; even, I suppose, in the end, Paul de Man's of *blindness* and *insight*: these are all versions of the oldest opposition between inside and outside, historicism and formalism, rhetoric and reference, form and content.[149] They are all variations on the Saussurean theme. And like Saussure's binaries they carry, as such, no intrinsic presumption of, or push towards, a choice, let alone a hierarchy or, even worse, the assumption that one set of poles is more progressive, less reactionary, than the other. But like Saussure and Barthes and David Lodge and Frank Kermode (at least in the matter of kenosis and pleroma) and Hayden White, critics do choose, do prioritize, and do assume it's progressive to do so and regressive not to. And thus they succumb to the great Saussurean Original Sin, falling prey to the greatest lapsarian fallacy in twentieth-century letters, the allegation that you not only *may* choose, but that you *must* do so. This is the great Saussurean error, the decisive Fall in the modern linguistic Garden of Eden, criticism's Paradise Lost. And this is no *Felix Culpa*, a lapse proleptic of salvation to come. This *Culpa* is a decidedly *Infelix* one.

A Second Adam

And, of course, this particular Fall in the Garden might not have had the far-reaching effect it has had were it not for a Second Adam appearing, not to undo the work of the first binarist Adam, Saussure, but to reinforce it. This dubious advent took place in 1966, when Jacques Derrida turned up in the USA, a relative unknown, at the conference designed to introduce structuralism to the wider US academy, but which brought European poststructuralism across the Atlantic instead. Derrida announced, with momentous effect, the 'Two Interpretations of Interpretation'. Here, at a stroke, was deconstruction – 'Here or there I have used the word *déconstruction*': what wonderful casualness! This was indeed salvation from Paris, France, arriving with magnificent gallic *éclat*, a super-*nouvelle cuisine* to be swallowed unhesitatingly and whole by all too many, the nourishing supplement to Saussure and all his linguistic works, just what criticism needed to pep up the post-war critical routines that everyone was tiring of.

> There are thus two interpretations of interpretation, of structure, of sign, of freeplay. The one seeks to decipher, dreams of deciphering, a truth or an origin

which is free from freeplay and from the order of the sign, and lives like an exile the necessity of interpretation. The other, which is no longer turned toward the origin, affirms freeplay and tries to pass beyond man and human- ism, the name man being the name of that being who, throughout the history of metaphysics or of ontotheology – in other words, through the history of all of his history – has dreamed of full presence, the reassuring foundation, the origin and the end of the game.[150]

(The reassuring foundation, the origin and end of Hillis Miller's game, becomes instantly clear, of course, in such a paragraph.) Translation of Derrida's French into US-speak helped deconstruction catch on, but skewed his meaning no end. For a start, the French *jeu* is far too freely translated as 'game' or 'freeplay'. 'Freeplay' is not, as the first translators erroneously claimed, the normative meaning of *jeu*; but translating it so sparked the great mistaken belief that Derrida encouraged absolutely free interpretations. Freeplay: how many crimes have been committed in your name! *Jeu* was more accurately rendered as the simple 'play' in the lecture's subsequent retranslation.[151] But the damage had been done. And the casualness of that turning of *jeu* into 'freeplay' was matched by the casualness with which the 'Two Interpretations' were widely read by critics. Here, it was assumed, were two reading poles to choose between, a Saussurean binary for obvious splitting: the one offering the vertiginous Nietzschean excitements of the endless play of signifiers, interpretation unbounded, the other deluded by ancient dreams of knowing for certain and of fixing interpretations, old-fashioned deluded dreams sponsored by boring old humanism, metaphysics, onto-theology.

But just as with Saussure, who never said that analysis could do finally without *parole* and signifieds and diachrony, but only suggested that it might be possible to get along without them *pro tempore*, so here Derrida never actually said that we could ditch the old humanist and metaphysical assumptions. He only said that we should try to do so. In the French and in whatever translation you look at, whether the 'freeplay' or the 'play' one, Derrida is clear. These two interpretative goals are irreducibly different; but we 'live them simul- taneously and reconcile them in an obscure economy'. There is 'no question of *choosing*': 'il n'y ait à *choisir*.' It is not so easy to rinse away logocentricity, the metaphysics of presence, the notion of a referential system: the *history* we all inhabit won't allow us any real choice in the matter. Even if we glimpse another kind of situation that might one day be born, some future 'non- species', 'in the formless, mute, infant and terrifying form of monstrosity' – and Derrida's tone yearns, clearly, for the pre-eminence and success of the Second Interpretation 'to which Nietzsche showed us the way' – we and our language are trapped within the logocentric system that the dualistic play of the Two Interpretations craves to subvert. This repeated burden of the later

Derrida is clearly stated right at this beginning (or American-beginning) moment: 'We have no language – no syntax and no lexicon – which is alien to this history [i.e. the relationship between the history of metaphysics and the destruction of the history of metaphysics]; we cannot utter a single destructive proposition which has not already slipped into the form, the logic, and the implicit postulations of precisely what it seeks to contest.' 'There is', as the available American translations have it, 'no sense in doing without the concepts of metaphysics in order to attack (or shake) metaphysics.' Except that Derrida in fact said 'Il n'y a aucun sens à se passer des concepts de la metaphysique': that is, there is no way of doing without the concepts of metaphysics, there is no route by which to by-pass them. Which is a quite different and more radical impasse than the curiously mistranslated 'no sense' suggests, and one to be impressively supported, with ever more stridency, as time passed and Derrida's impatience with his American fans' mis-takings increased. (The long 1989 interview with Derek Attridge, for example, insists again that the 'metaphysical', the 'transcendent', are not eliminable, are all-pervasive, and are a condition of meaning in our tradition – 'In any case, a text cannot by itself avoid lending itself to a "transcendent" reading. A literature which forbade that transcendence would annul itself.'[152]) But no way of doing without transcendence or not, even no sense or not, critics in the USA and, in their wake, critics in Britain and elsewhere plunged on exuberantly, taking their cue from Derrida's tone, imagining a world of freeplay, decentred texts, dogmatic anti-pleromatics, decentred humanity, anti-ontology, anti-teleology, anti-theology, happy to be part of a monstrous birth that Derrida allowed only a glimpse of, and all with only a shadow of the authority basis they imagined, in the temporary hierarchized polarities of Saussure and the wished-for hierarchy of Derrida.

Derrida, of course, went on providing these ambivalent stimuli. He is, after all, master of the *sous rature* effect, of having your cake and eating it, thus: ~~cake~~. He has gone on vigorously correcting what he emphasizes are lopsided readings – just as on the occasion of his 1968 'Différance' talk and, of course, on the day of his 'Two Interpretations' lecture: 'I didn't say that there was no center, that we could get along without the center. I believe that the center is . . . a reality, but a function. And this function is absolutely indispensable. The subject is absolutely indispensable. I don't destroy the subject; I situate it.'[153] But for all that, he has gone on giving terrific tonal support to the decentred Nietzschean dream of reading, all the while piling up metaphors of duality (margin, supplement, edge, border, *timpan*, hymen, *pharmakon*, preface, parergon, *brisure*, and so forth, all emblems of the double-interpretation position) which have lent themselves to resolution in the lopsided fashion of Hillis Miller and his colleagues. And the hostages to

fortune have kept on coming, aiders and abetters of such slanted under-
standings: *il n'y a pas de hors-texte*, nuclear warfare as discourse, the textual
'outside' as text, and so on. A whole critical generation has simply not had
ears to hear Derrida's cautions about history and reference and the subject
and all, not least because it's been easy not to. It is perhaps no accident that
when the 'Two Interpretations' lecture reappeared in the volume of Derrida
pieces entitled *Writing and Difference*, the amending discussion just quoted
('I didn't say there was no center . . . The subject is absolutely indispensable',
and so forth) had been dropped. In the dozen years between the lecture in
1966 and that volume in 1978 the academy had got used to what it wanted
to hear from the master.

The arguments of this book are, to the contrary, very glad to be able to
endorse the *hendiadys* of Derrida, his strong position on the combined irrec-
oncilability and necessary reconciliation, or co-habitation, of the two interpretations of interpreting, and to endorse the logics of his lexicon of metaphors
for meaning, his linguistics of the margin, his insistence on encrypted
betweenness, or duality, in the sign as in the body, and so in the text. 'On
the borderline between the outside and the inside, itself a system of edges,
the buccal orifice plays this paradigmatic role in introjection only to the
extent that is *first* a silent spot in the body, never totally ceases to be silent,
and only speaks through supplementarity.'[154] 'What counts here is the
in-between-ness of the hymen . . . the logic of the hymen . . . neither desire
nor pleasure but in between the two. Neither future nor present, but between
the two. It is the hymen that desire dreams of piercing, of bursting, in an
act of violence that is (at the same time or somewhere between) love and
murder.' This hymen marks the place of the *antre*, a cave of making (and of
making it), which is always *entre*, between.[155] We should take this as a reflection of the original wisdom of Saussure, the as it were primordial insight
that preceded the (almost simultaneous) Saussurean *lapsus* from it. (Not
dissimilarly, according to some ancient theologians, the Paradise Garden of
Eden lasted only a matter of hours.) 'Linguistics', as Barthes put it at the
same 1966 gathering at which the Two Interpretations were announced,
'asks us to recognise that . . . cultural facts are always double . . . As Benveniste
remarked, the discovery of the "duplicity" of language gives Saussure's reflection all its value.' And the translator's footnote in the Macksey/Donato
volume quotes one of Benveniste's finely magisterial pronouncements: 'Nous
touchons ici à ce qu'il y a de primordial dans la doctrine saussurienne, à un
principe qui présume une intuition totale du langage . . . Ce principe est que
le langage, sous quelque point de vue qu'on l'étudie, *est toujours un object double*,
formé de deux parties dont l'une ne vaut que par l'autre.'[156]

There is no either/or, only a combination, a doubling: the paradoxical,

parasitical dualism contained in the Virginia Woolf *wor(l)d*. 'Art or Society:
Must We Choose?' is the title of a symposium on art criticism in *Representations*
(1985). My argument is that we not only need not choose, but that rigorous
analysis will not allow us to choose: *il n'y a aucun sens* of doing otherwise. The
true Saussurean, the true Derridian, the *linguistic* case is that meaning arises
at that duplicitous, slippery place where apparent opposites apparently conjoin,
so that both of the connecting, opposed sides of that border must inevitably
get taken and be read and interpreted conjointly. This is the logic of the
betweenness of writing, of works of art, that Martin Buber has classically
endorsed: 'Art is neither the impression of natural objectivity nor the expression
of spiritual subjectivity, but it is the work and witness of the relation between the *substantia humana* and the *substantia rerum*, it is the real of 'between'
which has become a form.'[157] Or, as D. H. Lawrence put it, repeatedly, the
business of art, the morality of the novel, the crucial truths of fiction, are all
enacted in a 'between' place:

> When Van Gogh paints sunflowers, he reveals, or achieves, the vivid relation
> between himself, as man, and the sunflower, as sunflower, at that quick mo-
> ment of time ... The vision on the canvas is a third thing ... It is neither
> man-in-the-mirror nor flower-in-the-mirror, neither is it above or below or
> across anything. It is in between everything.[158]

And the fiction of Lawrence, continually striving to occupy this functional,
relational place between character and character, characters and nature,
characters and animals, characters and things, between self, text, word, author, and world, between 'man and his circumambient universe',[159] makes a
rhetoric of *between* absolutely central. 'They knew the intercourse between
heaven and earth ... They mounted their horses, and held life between the
grip of their knees,' as the famous opening chapter of *The Rainbow* describes
the agrarian Brangwens. *Between*. Once you start noticing the centrality of
this marginal, interfacial place in Lawrence, you can't stop noticing it everywhere in his texts. And this is, I'd argue, only the making explicit of something
that is always implicit about writing, the condition precisely of fiction, of
text. The word is always in-between. It is always wor(l)d.

It's apt, I believe, to end this introductory discussion as it began, with a
writer, to conclude with Lawrence as we began with Woolf. For, in the end,
imaginative writers and their writings matter more than mere critics and
their theories about writing. Or, as that distinguished Lawrence-admirer
Philip Larkin put it with his usual blokeish vigour when expressing a distrust of 'theorizing': 'the only worthwhile theories, or statements of belief, are

works of art. All else is just farting Annie Laurie through a keyhole as Gulley Jimson says.'[160] That's going a bit far, of course. But still, it is my book's continual belief that generalizations about language and its uses, theoretical generalizations, are only of use to readers, to criticism, if they can be shown to pertain to the literary case, to literary cases. So all the literary criticism, or *Literaturwissenschaft*, that matters and reveals comes down to practical criticism (in the wide sense). And so the following chapters seek to test the in-betweenness, margin, wor(l)d paradigm on some classic and occasionally not so classic fictions. They do so by looking at fictions which seem to foreground (as people say) certain binary oppositions which have come to seem central in recent criticism – fictional–historical, metonymic–metaphoric, full–empty, present–absent, realistic–playful, candid–hermetic, ideological–scriptural, all of them aspects of the great textual–extra-textual divide that has rifted recent critical thought – and by demonstrating in each case that, even if criticism and critical theory, critical fashion, might wish or attempt to priorize (again as they say) one or other side of the binary coin, the texts in question will simply not allow any dominance by either side, but in fact present meaning as arising precisely in the busy overlap, interaction, clash, between the two. These demonstrations are offered in the belief that in such textual dualities of meaning – meanings perpetually on edge, perpetually in-between – you have, essentially, real enactments of what Saussure perceived as language's 'dualité oppositive'[161] and actualizations of what is really arresting for Derrida in the marginality of textuality, the quintessence (or even, as Henry James might have put it, the dangerous Quint-essence) of the parasitology, or paralogics, that preoccupy Derrida and other members of the deconstructionist family. This is my – or rather, I should say, classic writing's – version of what David Carroll has recently dubbed *paraesthetics*: what is happening in the place of the convergence between aesthetic, textual stuff – which is to say rhetoricity – and a something else – namely the historico-worldly Other beyond the text, out there in the extra-linguistic, heterologic zones of that which is not merely verbal.[162]

NOTES

1   René Wellek and Austin Warren, *Theory of Literature* (Cape, London, 1949), ch. 12; 'The Mode of Existence of a Literary Work of Art'.
2   Roland Barthes, 'Theory of the Text', in *Untying the Text: A Post-Structuralist Reader*, ed. Robert Young (Routledge and Kegan Paul, London, 1981), 32.
3   Richard Rorty, 'Nineteenth-Century Idealism and Twentieth-Century Textualism', in *Consequences of Pragmatism (Essays: 1972–1980)* (Harvester, Brighton,

1982), 139ff. For a wonderful rash of international-French *textualité* terms, see *Avant-texte, texte, après-texte*, ed. Louis Hay and Péter Nagy (Éditions du CNRS, Paris / Akadémiai Kiado, Budapest, 1982), Papers from the Colloque internationale de textologie à Mátrafüred, Hungary. For *hypertext*, see George P. Landow, *Hypertext: The Convergence of Contemporary Theory and Technology* (Johns Hopkins University Press, Baltimore and London, 1992).

4   See e.g. Shari Benstock, *Textualizing the Feminine: On the Limits of Genre* (University of Oklahoma Press, Norman, Okla., 1991).

5   See Jacques Derrida on 'the calculated necessity of this neological usage of the verb *to text* [*texter*]': 'Limited Inc abc . . .', *Glyph*, 2 (1977), 252, n. 1.

6   See e.g. Toril Moi, *Sexual Textual Politics: Feminist Literary Theory* (Methuen New Accents, London, 1985).

7   Leo Tolstoy, *What is Art?*, trans. Aylmer Maude (1899); Jean-Paul Sartre, *Qu-est ce que la littérature?* (Gallimard, Paris, 1948); Roman Jakobson, 'Qu'est que c'est que la poésie?, in *Questions de poétique*, ed. Tzvetan Todorov, (Seuil, Paris, 1973).

8   Paul Ricoeur, 'What is a Text? Explanation and Understanding', ch. 5 in *Hermeneutics and the Human Sciences*, ed. and trans. John B. Thompson (Cambridge University Press / Éditions de la Maison des sciences de l'homme, Paris, 1981).

9   J. Derrida, '*Ch'e cos'è la poesia*', *Poesia*, I, (11 Nov. 1988), and *Po &sie*, 50 (Autumn 1989); in Derrida, *Points de suspension: Entretiens*, ed. E. Weber (Galilée, Paris, 1992), 303–8; also in *A Derrida Reader: Between the Blinds*, ed. Peggy Kamuf (Columbia University Press, New York, 1991), 223–37. Derrida has several times indicated the influence on him of Sartre's book: e.g. 'An Interview with Jacques Derrida', in *Jacques Derrida: Acts of Literature*, ed. Derek Attridge (Routledge, New York and London, 1992), 36. For the sublimation of the question of reading into a question of 'Textuality', see e.g. William V. Spanos, Paul A. Bove, and Daniel O'Hara (eds), *The Question of Textuality: Strategies of Reading in Contemporary American Criticism* (Indiana University Press, Bloomington, 1982).

10 J. Stout, 'What Is the Meaning of a Text?', *New Literary History*, 14 (1982), 1–12. Richard Rorty praises this piece for nicely stating the pragmatist case: Rorty, 'The Pragmatist's Progress', in Umberto Eco, *Interpretation and Overinterpretation*, ed. Stefan Collini (Cambridge University Press, 1992), 89–108, esp. 93, n. 2.

11 'Is There A Text in This Class?', in Stanley Fish, *Is There A Text in This Class?: The Authority of Interpretive Communities* (Harvard University Press, Cambridge, Mass., and London, 1980), 303–21. Cf. the notorious sister-piece 'How to Recognize a Poem When You See One', in ibid., 322–37, and idem, *Doing What Comes Naturally: Change, Rhetoric, and the Practice of Theory in Literary and Legal Studies* (Clarendon Press, Oxford, 1989), *passim*.

12 'Is There a Woman in This Text?', in Mary Jacobus, *Reading Woman: Essays in Feminist Criticism* (Methuen, London, 1986), 83–109. 'What happens when one raises Mary Jacobus's question?' asks Barbara Johnson, good-naturedly

prodding her own earlier book *The Critical Difference* for feminist lapses: 'Gender Theory and the Yale School', in Johnson, *A World of Difference* (Johns Hopkins University Press, Baltimore and London, 1987), 39.

13   Jacques Derrida, 'No Apocalypse, Not Now (Full Speed Ahead, Seven Missiles, Seven Missives)', *diacritics*, 14 (Summer 1984), 22.

14   Paul de Man's influential deconstructionist approach repeatedly challenged the distinction between 'major' and 'minor' texts; see e.g. his use of Wordsworth's 'Essay upon Epitaphs' in 'Autobiography as Defacement', *Modern Language Notes*, 94 (December 1979), 919–30; *The Rhetoric of Romanticism* (Columbia University Press, New York, 1984), ch. 4. Derrida's textual excursions have also set a massive example of eclecticism, always provoking the question, which his practice consciously defies, as to whether he belongs 'properly' to philosophy or literary criticism. For characteristically powerful results of this Derridian mode see e.g. Nicholas Royle, 'Nuclear Piece: Memoires of Hamlet and the Time to Come', reading Harold Jenkins's edition of *Hamlet* against Derrida's *Memoires for Paul de Man*, in *diacritics*, 20 (1990), 39–55; or Royle's *Telepathy and Literature: Essays on the Reading Mind* (Blackwell, Oxford, 1991), ch. 3: 'Cryptaesthesia', reading *Wuthering Heights* against *The Wolf Man's Magic Word: A Cryptonomy*, by Nicholas Abraham and Maria Torok (translated by Nicholas Rand, University of Minneapolis Press, 1986), and Derrida's essay 'Fors' at the beginning of the *Cryptonomy*. New Historicism's notorious practice of reading high-canonical literary texts, e.g. Shakespeare's, against formerly less well-regarded 'secondary' texts and pamphlets and other political, factual, polemical, and so on discourses, unites it in effect with deconstruction's textual habits. See e.g. Richard Helgerson, *Forms of Nationhood: The Elizabethan Writing of England* (University of Chicago Press, Chicago and London, 1992), where Spenser's *Fairie Queene* and Shakespeare's History Plays are put in their place alongside the likes of Coke's *Institutes of the Laws of England*, Camden's *Britannia*, and Hakluyt's *Principal Navigations of the English Nation*. The question of the nature of the literary text in our (post)modernist era is, of course, massively complex and far too obsessively addressed for anything but sketchy documentation here; but see e.g. Stephen Orgel, 'What is a Text?', *Research Opportunities in Renaissance Drama*, 24 (1981), 3–6; Jonathan Goldberg, 'Textual Properties', *Shakespeare Quarterly*, 37 (1986), 216; Jerome J. McGann, '*Ulysses* as a Postmodern Work', in *Social Values and Poetic Acts: The Historical Judgment of Literary Work* (Harvard University Press, Cambridge, Mass., and London, 1988), 173–94.

15   Thus Louis Hay, founder of ITEM (Institut des Textes et Manuscrits Modernes), centre of French textual genetics: ' "Le Texte n'existe pas": Réflexions sur la critique génétique', *Poétique*, no. 62 (April 1985), 147–58. For more on *avant-texte*, see Jean Bellemin-Noël, *Le Texte et l'avant-texte* (Larousse, Paris, 1972). For textual-genetic critique as applied to Joyce, see *Joyce upon the Void: The Genesis of Doubt*, by Derrida's friend Jean-Michel Rabaté (Macmillan, London, 1991).

16   'Interview with Jacques Derrida', *Acts of Literature*, 41.

17   *The Diary of Virginia Woolf, 1925–1930*, ed. Anne Olivier Bell and Andrew McNeillie, vol. III (Hogarth Press, London, 1980), 339–40.

18   *A Reflection of the Other Person: The Letters of Virginia Woolf 1929–31*, ed. Nigel Nicolson and Joanne Trautman (Hogarth Press, London, 1978), 263.

19   Woolf, *Diary*, III. 332 [?11 November].

20   Ibid., 339.

21   Virginia Woolf, *The Waves: The Two Holograph Drafts*, transcribed and ed. J. W. Graham (Toronto University Press / University of Western Ontario, Toronto and Buffalo, 1976), 743.

22   The Revd H. F. Cary's translation – almost certainly the one Tennyson used – *The Vision; or, Hell, Purgatory, and Paradise, of Dante Alighieri* (Chandos Classics, n.d. [1814]), 81.

23   Alex Zwerdling, *Virginia Woolf and the Real World* (University of California Press, Berkeley, 1986).

24   Memorial Service tribute by J. Hillis Miller, in *The Lesson of Paul de Man*, *Yale French Studies*, 69 (1985), 3. The echo of Henry James's title *The Lesson of the Master* is no doubt deliberate.

25   Margaret Llewellyn Davies (ed.), *Life As We Have Known It By Co-operative Working Women* (Hogarth Press, London, 1931; Virago Press, London, 1977), xvii; the piece appears as 'Memories of a Working Women's Guild' in Virginia Woolf, *Collected Essays*, vol. 4 (Hogarth Press, London, 1967), 134ff.

26   See e.g. Patricia Waugh, *Metafiction: The Theory and Practice of Self-Conscious Fiction* (Methuen, London, 1984); Linda Hutcheon, *Narcissistic Narrative: The Metafictional Paradox* (Wilfrid Laurier University Press, Waterloo, Ontario, 1980); Brian McHale, *Postmodernist Fiction* (Methuen, New York, 1987); Christopher Nash, *World Games: The Tradition of Anti-Realist Revolt* (Methuen, London, 1987).

27   Ferdinand de Saussure, *Course in General Linguistics*, trans. and annotated by Roy Harris (Duckworth, London, 1983), 24.

28   Friedrich Nietzsche, 'On the Advantages and Disadvantages of History for Life' / 'Vom Nutzen und Nachteil der Historie für das Leben', in *Untimely Meditations / Unzeitgemässe Betrachtungen*, part 2 (1874).

29   See e.g. Derek Attridge, 'Language as History / History as Language: Saussure and the Romance of Etymology', in *Post-structuralism and the Question of History*, ed. D. Attridge, Geoff Bennington, and Robert Young (Cambridge University Press, 1987), 183–211, and (slightly tinkered with) in D. Attridge, *Peculiar Language: Literature as Difference from the Renaissance to James Joyce* (Methuen, London, 1988), 90–126.

30   Saussure, *Course*, trans. Harris, 16.

31   Roy Harris, *The Language Makers* (Duckworth, London, 1980), 154–5.

32   Ferdinand de Saussure, *Cours de linguistique générale*, critical edn ed. Tullio de Mauro, trans. from Italian into French by Louis-Jean Calvet (Payot, Paris, paperback edn, 1972), 100.

33   Saussure, *Cours*, 166.

34 Raymond Tallis, *Not Saussure: A Critique of Post-Saussurean Literary Theory* (Macmillan, London, 1988), 71.

35 Ora Avni, *The Resistance of Reference: Linguistics, Philosophy and the Literary Text* (Johns Hopkins University Press, Baltimore and London), 1990, 1ff.

36 Saussure, *Course in General Linguistics*, trans. with an introduction by Wade Baskin (McGraw-Hill paperback, New York, 1966), 67–8; *Cours*, ed. Tullio de Mauro, 100.

37 Émile Benveniste, 'Nature du signe linguistique', *Acta Linguistica*, 1 (Copenhagen, 1939); repr. in *Problèmes de linguistique générale* (Gallimard, Paris, 1966), 49ff. A. D. Nuttall comes to a similar conclusion in his *A New Mimesis: Shakespeare and the Representation of Reality* (Methuen, London, 1983), 33, when he argues that Saussure in fact reverses 'the usual doctrine of linguistic arbitrariness': 'by Saussure's doctrine the relation between word and meaning becomes very tight indeed (*fleuve* means 'fleuve' and does not really translate *river*)'.

38 Roman Jakobson, 'Sign and System of Language: A Reassessment of Saussure's Doctrine', a lecture given in East Germany, 2 October 1959. English version in Jakobson, *Verbal Art, Verbal Sign, Verbal Time*, ed. K. Pomovska and S. Rudy (Blackwell, Oxford, 1985), 28–33.

39 Claude Lévi-Strauss, *Structural Anthropology*, trans. C. Jacobson and B. G. Schoepf (Peregrine, Harmondsworth, 1977), 90–1, in a superb post-script worrying at Saussurean propositions, including a sharp discussion of whether *pomme de terre* was an arbitrary name even at its point of origin in French. The issue is clouded, of course, by the loose talk that characterizes so much post-Saussurean discussion. David Lodge's fiction, e.g., has helped popularize the phrase 'arbitrariness of the signifier', which is not a Saussurean concept at all.

40 Émile Benveniste, *Problems in General Linguistics*, trans. Mary E. Meek (University of Miami Press, 1971). Jonathan Culler refers to another essay in the *Problèmes*, but eschews mentioning this one: *Saussure* (Fontana Modern Masters, London, 1976), 125. Even that very sharp commentator on Saussure, Roy Harris, has no dealings with Benveniste: see *The Language Myth* (Duckworth, London, 1981), 44–53, and *Reading Saussure: A Critical Commentary on the Cours de linguistique générale* (Duckworth, London, 1987). It's perverse of Fredric Jameson in *The Prison-House of Language: A Critical Account of Structuralism and Russian Formalism* (Princeton University Press, 1972), 30, n. 26, to play down Benveniste's case as 'true' but 'misleading'. Robert Scholes arrives at a similar position to Benveniste on *boeuf/Ochs* without mentioning Benveniste, in his excellently sceptical chapter 'Reference and Difference', in *Textual Power: Literary Theory and the Teaching of English* (Yale University Press, New Haven, 1985), 90. Leonard Jackson calls on Benveniste twice, in other cases than this one, in *The Poverty of Structuralism: Literature and Structuralist Theory* (Longman, London, 1991); but Benveniste is in nasty company in Jackson's slapdash, boorish, heavily wry tome. Raymond Tallis's happily far funnier *Not Saussure*

drags in Benveniste only to sneer at him as a lapsed structuralist. A pity. Even more of a pity, though, has been the dismissing of Tallis's admirably sceptical and witty hatchet-job on the pervasive misreadings of Saussure by the literary-critical establishment because its author happens to hail from the alien discipline of Geriatric Medicine. Richard Freadman offers some sharp words against arbitrariness, inspired by Wittgenstein: *Eliot, James, and the Fictional Self: A Study in Character and Narration* (Macmillan, London, 1986), 7–11: 'Words and the World: The Case Against Arbitrariness' (and Richard Freadman and Seamus Miller, *Re-Thinking Theory: A Critique of Contemporary Literary Theory and an Alternative Account* (Cambridge University Press, 1992) is worth looking at for its pro-ethics, pro-reference stance and general scepticism, even though some of its targets – Catherine Belsey's *Critical Practice* in particular – aren't big enough for the heavy artillery deployed). For some neat summaries, see 'Arbitrariness', in Oswald Ducrot and Tzvetan Todorov's immensely useful *Encyclopedic Dictionary of the Sciences of Language*, trans. Catherine Porter (Blackwell, Oxford, 1981), 130 –7.

41 Jacques Derrida, *De la grammatologie* (Editions de Minuit, Paris, 1967); *Of Grammatology,* trans. Gayatri Chakravorty Spivack (Johns Hopkins University Press, Baltimore and London, 1976). Derrida remains difficult, even after all these years of assimilation and alleged familiarization. Jonathan Culler's discussions in *On Deconstruction* (Routledge and Kegan Paul, London, 1983) remain admirably clarifying, even if, as is often the case with Culler's work on foreign masters, over-normalizing. See particularly his section 'Writing and Logocentrism', 89–110. Raymond Tallis is rightly critical of Derrida's exaggerated denigration of Saussure on writing: see *Not Saussure*, 169–71, on *Of Grammatology*, 34–5.

42 Culler, *On Deconstruction*, 97.

43 See Derrida, 'Différance' (1968), in *Margins of Philosophy*, trans. Alan Bass (Harvester, Brighton, 1982), 1–27, and *Derrida and 'Différance'*, ed. David Wood and Robert Bernasconi (Parousia Press, Coventry, 1985; Northwestern University Press, Evanston, Ill., 1988).

44 Derrida, 'Living On: Border Lines', in *Deconstruction and Criticism*, preface by Geoffrey Hartman (Routledge and Kegan Paul, London, 1979), 84.

45 Derrida, *Of Grammatology*, 158.

46 Attridge, 'But it is also true that there is no inside-the-text, since this would again imply an inside/outside boundary' (editor's note, *Jacques Derrida: Acts of Literature*, 102, n. 21).

47 For the arrival of context, see Derrida, 'Signature Event Context' (1972), trans. Samuel Weber and Jeffrey Mehlman, *Glyph*, 1 (1977); also trans. Alan Bass in *Margins of Philosophy*. The Marxist Lucien Goldmann's attack on Derridian *différance* for apparently annihilating the subject ('As for Lévi-Strauss, Foucault, Barthes, Althusser, Lacan, Greimas, so for Derrida, there is no subject') occurred after the original *'Différance'* lecture in 1968. So did Derrida's denial, 'I have never said that "there is no subject".' As Goldmann noted, Derrida 'retained praxis', unlike the structuralists he'd named – i.e. he'd remained a

Marxist of sorts – but still contradictorily 'eliminates the subject': *Derrida and 'Différance'*, ed. D. Wood and R. Bernasconi (Northwestern University Press, Evanston, Ill, 1985), 91–2. Foucault's bitter rejection of 'A pedagogy which teaches the pupil that there is nothing outside the text' followed Derrida's scornful critique of Foucault's *Folie et déraison* (1961) (*Madness and Civilization*, 1965) for not being critical enough of the meaning of 'history' or 'archive' and Derrida's insistence that 'archaeology' was primarily textual, 'an organized language . . . a sentence, a syntax' (Derrida, '*Cogito* and the History of Madness' (1963), in *Writing and Difference* (1967), trans. Alan Bass (Routledge and Kegan Paul, London, 1978): Michel Foucault, 'My Body, this Paper, this Fire', *Paideia*, 1971; repr. as appendix to 1972 edn of the *Folie* (now *Histoire de la folie*), trans. in *Oxford Literary Review*, 4, no. 1 (Autumn 1979), 5–28. For Derrida on the University, see e.g. 'The Principle of Reason: The University in the Eyes of its Pupils', *diacritics*, 13 (Fall 1983), 3–20. This Cornell lecture seems to be a version of the Frankfurt lecture that Samuel Weber describes as provoking Jürgen Habermas to amazement: 'That the author of *De la grammatologie*, for whom there was "nothing outside of the text", should now be addressing something as evidently extra-textual as the University. . . .' Weber argues that the 'turn' to the context should not have surprised, it being already implicit in the *Grammatologie*. (Well, it wasn't very clear, and Habermas is not the only one to be surprised.) See S. Weber, Introduction to *Demarcating the Disciplines: Philosophy, Literature, Art, Glyph* Textual Studies, 1 (University of Minnesota Press, Minneapolis, 1986), ix ff. For Derrida on archives and their survival, see e.g. 'No Apocalypse, Not Now'; and 'Sendoffs', in the *Reading the Archive: On Texts and Institutions* issue of *Yale French Studies*, 77 (1990). *La Carte postale: de Socrate à Freud et au-delà* (Flammarion, Paris, 1980); *The Postcard: From Socrates to Freud and Beyond*, trans. Alan Bass (University of Chicago Press, 1987), is filled with concern about what policemen and holocausts do to texts. The articles on Paul de Man's anti-Semitic writings engage in a personal and horrified way with the Holocaust, as well as with the threat to libraries and archives ('nucleo-literary waste'): 'Like the Sound of the Sea Deep within a Shell: Paul de Man's War', trans. Peggy Kamuf, *Critical Inquiry*, 14 (Spring 1988), 590– 652; 'Biodegradables: Seven Diary Fragments', trans. Peggy Kamuf, *Critical Inquiry*, 15 (Summer 1989), 812–73.

48 Derrida, 'Afterword: Toward an Ethic of Discussion', in *Limited Inc* (Northwestern University Press, Evanston, Ill., 1988), 137.

49 See Derrida, 'Biodegradables', 858: 'the *numerus clausus* in force during the Occupation in Algeria, and from which I, along with a few others, did effectively suffer'. For the quarrel and reconciliation with Foucault, see Didier Eribon, *Michel Foucault*, trans. Betsy Wing (Faber, London, 1992), 119 –22.

50 Derrida, 'Afterword: Toward An Ethic of Discussion', 148.

51 Ibid., 136.

52 Derrida, *Of Grammatology*, 158–9.

53 Attridge, Introduction to *Jacques Derrida: Acts of Literature*, 16, n. 21.

54 See Stephen Melville's comments on Derrida's 'simultaneous reliance on and

evasions of "history" and "event" ' – a good example of the Derridian double
bind, his 'words necessarily at war with themselves', i.e. *sous rature* to use the
famous Derrida formula: Stephen W. Melville, *Philosophy Beside Itself: On
Deconstruction and Modernism*, Theory and Literature, 27 (Manchester University
Press, 1986), 3.

55 Derrida, 'Biodegradables', 873. For the rage see ibid., *passim* – as also, 'Limited
Inc abc . . .', his reply to John Searle, the 'aggressivity' of which worried
Derrida later: see 'Afterword: Toward An Ethic of Discussion', 113. 'Come on,
would anyone ever have talked or heard talk of deconstruction for more than
ten minutes if it came down to such derisory dogmas or such stupid monoliths
as these (of the sort: "I don't believe there is any context! There is no authorial
intention! There is no subject! No unified subject! We have to stop paying
attention to these things!")': 'Biodegradables', 827. But they did so talk,
because they thought, with not bad reason, that deconstruction did come
down to such things.

56 Martin Heidegger, *Der Satz der Grund* (Neske Verlag, Pfullingen, 1957), 161.
It's discussed by Colin Falck, *Myth, Truth and Literature: Towards a True Post-
Modernism* (Cambridge University Press, 1989), 100ff.

57 Barthes, 'The Death of the Author' ('La Mort de l'auteur': 1968), in *Image–
Music–Text*, ed. and trans. Stephen Heath (Fontana, London, 1977), 143.

58 Michel Foucault, 'What is an Author?', in *Language, Counter-Memory, Practice:
Selected Essays and Interviews*, ed. with an introduction by Donald F. Bouchard,
trans. Bouchard and Sherry Simon (Blackwell, Oxford, 1977), 120.

59 Jacques Derrida, *Signéponge/Signsponge*, trans. Richard Rand (Columbia University Press, New York, 1984).

60 M. Bradbury, 'The Telling Life: Some Thoughts on Literary Biography', in *The
Troubled Face of Biography*, ed. Eric Homburger and John Charmley (Macmillan,
London, 1988), 131–40.

61 The original lecture 'was based, of course, on Beckett's words: "What does it
matter who speaks, someone said, what does it matter who speaks" ': Eribon,
Michel Foucault, 210.

62 Foucault, 'What is an Author?', 113–38.

63 Eribon, *Michel Foucault*, 210.

64 Barthes, *Camera Lucida: Reflections on Photography* (Cape, London, 1982), Richard
Howard's trans. of *La Chambre claire* (Seuil, Paris, 1980).

65 *Roland Barthes by Roland Barthes* (Macmillan, London, 1977), Richard Howard's
English trans. of *Roland Barthes par Roland Barthes* (Seuil, Paris, 1977). In
German, *Roland Barthes Über mich selbst*, trans. Jürgen Hoch (Matthes und Seitz
Verlag, Munich, 1978).

66 'J'écris toujours mes textes à la main puisque je les rature beaucoup. Ensuite,
il est essentiel que je les transcrive moi-même à la machine à écrire parce que
vient alors une seconde vague de corrections, corrections allant toujours dans
le sens de l'ellipse ou de la suppression. C'est le moment où ce que l'on a écrit,
qui reste très subjectif dans l'apparence graphique de l'écriture manuelle,
s'objective: ce n'est pas encore un livre ou un article mais, grâce aux caractères

de la machine à écrire, il y a déjà une apparence objective du texte et c'est une étape très importante' ('Roland Barthes s'explique', *Lire* (April 1979), in *Le Grain de la voix: entretiens 1962–1980* (Seuil, Paris, 1981), 302).

67   Philip Sidney, *The Countess of Pembroke's Arcadia*, ed. Albert Feuillerat (Cambridge University Press, 1965, book II, ch. 25, p. 313. Roland Barthes, 'The Death of the Author', 146. For a sharply sceptical discussion see Sean Burke, *The Death and Return of the Author: Criticism and Subjectivity in Barthes, Foucault and Derrida* (Edinburgh University Press, 1992).

68   Valentine Cunningham, *British Writers of the Thirties* (Oxford University Press, 1988), 6.

69   Culler, *Saussure*, 27.

70   Saussure, *Cours*, ed. Tullio de Mauro, 151–2. So animated was Saussure by what happened 'en dehors du language' that the train example seems variously to have consisted of 'the 12.50 and 5 a.m. (or 4 a.m.) express for Naples', 'the daily 12.50 express', 'the express that departs every day at 5 for Berne': *Cours*, critical edition ed. Rudolf Engler, 4 Fascicules (Harrassowitz, Wiesbaden, 1967–74), Fasc. 2 (1967), 244–5.

71   On the extraordinary case of the anagrams, see Culler, *Saussure*, 106ff., and Jean Starobinski, *Les Mots sous les mots* (Gallimard, Paris, 1971). On the speaker of Sanskrit and Martian, see 'Saussure's Semiotics', in Tzvetan Todorov, *Theories of the Symbol*, trans. Catherine Porter (Blackwell, Oxford, 1977), and Victor Henry, *Le Langage martien: étude analytique de la genèse d'une langue dans un cas de glossolalia somnambulique* (J. Maisonneuve, Paris, 1901).

72   Todorov, 'Saussure's Semiotics'.

73   Louis-Jean Calvet, *Pour et contre Saussure: vers un linguistique social* (Payot, Paris, 1975).

74   Ibid., 44–5.

75   Saussure, *Cours*, ed. Tullio de Mauro, 350.

76   Sylvère Lotringer, 'The Game of the Name', *diacritics*, 3 (Summer 1973), 2. Cf. 'Here we can glimpse briefly the infinity of language, "the sacred mystery", a textual process without origin since it is caught in a ceaseless play of referral and reverberations, and without end inasmuch as it unfolds itself in a self-referential space, a perpetual refraction in a hall of mirrors where every site is a citation and every citation an *incitation*' (ibid., 4). Lotringer is even patient with Saussure's discovery of the name *Leonora* in a text of Filippo Lippi, supposedly a reference to his mistress – who was actually called *Lucrezia* (ibid., 8).

77   Paul de Man, 'Hypogram and Inscription', in *The Resistance to Theory*, ed. Wlad Godzich, Theory and History of Literature, 33 (Manchester University Press, 1986), 36–7.

78   Jacques Derrida, *Dissemination*, trans. and ed. Barbara Johnson (University of Chicago Press, 1981), xxiv, xxv.

79   Culler, *Saussure*, 110.

80   Vincent B. Leitch, *Deconstructive Criticism: An Advanced Introduction* (Hutchinson, London, 1983), 9–10.

81 'Foundations' is the title of Leitch's first chapter.

82 Paul de Man, 'The Resistance to Theory', *Yale French Studies*, 63 (1982), 3–20; repr. in *Resistance to Theory*, 3–20.

83 Edward Said, *The World, the Text, and the Critic* (Faber, London, 1984). For Rorty on Fish and on readers, see Richard Rorty, 'The Pragmatist's Progress', in Eco, *Interpretation and Overinterpretation*, 89–108, and Rorty, Introduction to Vadimir Nabokov, *Pale Fire* (Everyman Library edn, London, 1992), v–xvii. For some of the many clamant 'post-theory' theoretical possibilities, see Ralph Cohen (ed.), *The Future of Literary Theory* (Routledge, New York and London, 1989).

84 Frank Lentricchia, interview, in *Criticism in Society*, ed. Imré Salusinszky (Methuen, London, 1987), 187. A good example of a wide-ranging critique of the relation between literature's inside and outside from a good old-fashioned Marxist turned neo-Marxist is Tony Bennett, *Outside Literature* (Methuen, London, 1990).

85 William Empson, *The Structure of Complex Words* (Chatto and Windus, London, 1951; repr. Hogarth Press, London, 1985), 30.

86 Johnson, *World of Difference*, 2–4, 6, 32ff. ('Gender Theory and the Yale School'); 155ff ('Metaphor, Metonymy, and Voice in *Their Eyes Were Watching God*': originally in *Black Literature and Literary Theory*, ed. Henry Louis Gates Jr (Methuen, New York and London, 1984); dedicated to Paul de Man); 184ff, n. 47a ('Apostrophe, Animation and Abortion'). Interview, Salusinszky, 165.

87 Derrida, 'Like the Sound of the Sea', 623ff.

88 Shoshana Felman, 'Paul de Man's Silence', *Critical Inquiry*, 15 (Summer 1989), 704–44: an astonishing – and morally sickening – attempt to prove that convenient silence and amnesia are really the most powerful provocation to, and demonstration of, real remembering, at the same time as confirming 'the radical impossibility of witnessing' 'the original' – i.e. the atrocity of Nazism.

89 Derrida, 'Like the Sound of the Sea', 651: to call for 'censoring or burning his books is to reproduce the exterminating gesture which one accuses de Man of not having armed himself against sooner'.

90 Jonathan Culler, letter to the Editor, *London Review of Books*, 21 April 1988, p. 4.

91 Felman, 'Paul de Man's Silence', 743.

92 Derrida, 'Biodegradables', 851.

93 J. Hillis Miller, ' "Reading" Part of a Paragraph in *Allegories of Reading*', in *Theory Now and Then* (Harvester Wheatsheaf, Hemel Hempstead, 1991), 357, n. 7.

94 Cf. Stanley Fish, 'Don't Know Much About the Middle Ages: Posner on Law and Literature', in *Doing What Comes Naturally*, 294ff. The English cartoonist Steve Bell's *If* cartoon memorably featured President Reagan singing versions of the song 'Wonderful World' by Sam Cooke, Herb Alpert, Lou Adler, beginning 'Don't know much about history'. For the role of Henri de Man, Paul de Man's quisling uncle and Marxist renegade, in the promotion of *Post-Histoire* or The End of History, see Lutz Niethammer, *Posthistoire: Ist die Geschichte zu Ende?* (Rowohlts, Reinbeck bei Hamburg, 1989), and Perry Anderson, 'The

Ends of History', in *A Zone of Engagement* (Verso, London, 1992). For a persuasive discussion of parallels between Henri de Man's retreat from Marxism
and Paul de Man's espousal of a melancholy post-political quietism
in his account of Wordsworth ('Wordsworth and Hölderlin'), see Christopher
Norris, *Paul de Man: Deconstruction and the Critique of Aesthetic Ideology* (Routledge,
New York and London, 1988), 20ff.

95 For Adorno and 'After Auschwitz', see his *Negative Dialectics*, trans. E. B. Ashton
(Routledge & Kegan Paul, London, 1973), 361ff. For Jean-François Lyotard
and Auschwitz see *The Differend: Phrases in Dispute* (1983), trans. Georges Van
Den Abbeele (Manchester University Press, 1988), *passim*, esp. sect. 152, pp.
87–8. See also Geoffrey Bennington, *Lyotard: Writing the Event* (Manchester
University Press, 1988), 144ff. ('Auschwitz').

96 Philippe Lacoue-Labarthe, *Heidegger, Art and Politics: The Fiction of the Political*,
trans. Chris Turner (Blackwell, Oxford, 1990), 33, on Heidegger's denial of
'the duty of thought to confront' Auschwitz as phenomenon 'and to seek to
take responsibility for it'.

97 Julia Kristeva, *Desire in Language: A Semiotic Approach to Literature and Art*, ed.
Leon S. Roudiez, trans. T. Gora, A. Jardine, and L. S. Roudiez (Blackwell,
Oxford, 1980), ch. 1: 'The Ethics of Linguistics': versus 'the sterility of theory',
and pro 'the signifying process' not being limited to 'the language system',
because 'there are also speech, discourse, and, within them, a causality other
than linguistic, a heterogeneous, destructive causality' (p. 27).

98 See Tzvetan Todorov on Nazism, Heidegger, De Man, Blanchot, and related
matters (including Richard Rorty's pragmatism), *TLS*, 17–23 June 1988, 676,
684.

99 Hayden White, 'The Politics of Historical Interpretation: Discipline and De-
Sublimation', *Critical Inquiry*, 9, no. 1 (1982): repr. in *The Content of the Form:
Narrative Discourse and Historical Representation* (Johns Hopkins University Press,
Baltimore and London, 1987): see esp. 76ff. Maurice Blanchot, 'Foucault as I
Imagine Him', trans. Jeffrey Mehlman, in *Foucault/Blanchot*, trans. J. Mehlman
and Brian Massumi (Zone Books, New York, 1987), 99. Hélène Cixous, 'From
the Scene of the Unconscious to the Scene of History', trans. Deborah W.
Carpenter, in *The Future of Literary Theory*, ed. Ralph Cohen (Routledge, New
York and London, 1989), 1–18. For one among many outraged historians on
Hayden White (and his Holocaust concession), see Gertrude Himmelfarb,
'Telling It As You Like It: Post-modernist History and the Flight from Fact',
TLS, 16 October 1992, 12–15. The grudging nature of the concession can be
weighed by the use White makes of a Barthesian epigraph for *The Content of
the Form*: 'Le fait n'a jamais qu'une existence linguistique' (the fact/deed never
has anything other than a linguistic existence). But of course the statement is
true only if you translate it 'the word/sign *le fait* only ever exists linguistically'
(and even then this is true only at the merest level of technical linguistic
existence).

100 Paul de Man, 'Walter Benjamin's "The Task of the Translator" ', in *Resistance
to Theory*, 94ff.

101   Paul de Man, 'Reading and History', in *Resistance to Theory*, 65ff.

102   'The Return to Philology': Paul de Man, *Resistance to Theory*, 21–6. Paradigms
      Regained: James L. Battersby, *Paradigms Regained: Pluralism and the Practice of
      Criticism* (University of Pennsylvania Press, Philadelphia, 1991).

103   Gayatri Chakravorty Spivack, 'The New Historicism: Political Commitment
      and the Postmodern Critic', in *The New Historicism*, ed. H. Aram Veeser
      (Routledge, New York and London, 1989), 277–92.

104   Fish, 'How to Recognize a Poem When You See One'.

105   Fredric Jameson, *The Political Unconscious: Narrative as a Socially Symbolic Act*
      (Methuen, London, 1981), 9; Scholes, *Textual Power*, 16.

106   Derrida, 'Shibboleth' (originally a lecture in Seattle, October 1984), in *Midrash
      and Literature*, ed. Geoffrey H. Hartman and Sanford Budick (Yale University
      Press, New Haven and London, 1986), 319ff. (For more dating interest in the
      later Derrida, see *Ulysse Gramophone* (1987): 'Ulysses Gramophone', in *Jacques
      Derrida: Acts of Literature*, ed. Attridge, 259.) For the Celan poems see Paul
      Celan, *Selected Poems*, trans. with an Introduction by Michael Hamburger
      (Penguin, Harmondsworth, 1990), a very useful bilingual edition.

107   Karl Marx, *Das Kapital*, vol 1 (1867), part I, ch. 1, sect. 4: 'The Fetishism of
      the Commodity and its Secret'; *Capital*, vol. 1, Pelican Marx Library, trans.
      Ben Fowkes (Penguin, Harmondsworth, 1976), 169. Georg Lukács, *Solzhenitsyn*,
      trans. William David Graf (Merlin Press, London, 1969). Terry Eagleton,
      Myths of Power: A Marxist Study of the Brontës (Macmillan, London, 1975); *idem*,
      William Shakespeare (Blackwell, Oxford, 1986), 64 and 107, n. 1. Anthony
      Easthope, 'Pentameter and Ideology', in *Poetry as Discourse* (Methuen, London,
      1983), 64ff. For alleged Government funding of the Dictionary (!), see Brian
      Doyle, 'The Hidden History of English Studies', in *Re-Reading English*, ed. Peter
      Widdowson (Methuen, London, 1982), 26. Douglas Tallack (ed.), *Literary Theory
      at Work: Three Texts* (Batsford, London, 1987), 190. See my chapter 5, sect. iii:
      'Reading Biscuits, Reading Gaol'.

108   Alan Liu, 'The Power of Formalism: The New Historicism', *English Literary
      History*, 56, no. 4 (Winter 1989), 721–71.

109   Jonathan Dollimore, 'Introduction: Shakespeare, Cultural Materialism and the
      New Historicism', in *Political Shakespeare: New Essays in Cultural Materialism*,
      ed. Dollimore and Alan Sinfield (Manchester University Press, 1985), 2ff.
      John Stallybrass and Allon White, *The Politics and Poetics of Transgression*
      (Methuen, London, 1986). Terry Castle, *Masquerade and Civilisation: The
      Carnivalesque in Eighteenth-Century English Culture and Fiction* (Stanford Uni-
      versity Press, Stanford, Calif., 1986).

110   Clifford Geertz, 'Thick Description: Toward an Interpretive Theory of Cul-
      ture', in *The Interpretation of Cultures: Selected Essays* (Basic Books, New York,
      1973), 3–30.

111   See e.g. Louis Montrose, 'Professing the Renaissance: The Poetics and Politics
      of Culture', and Elizabeth Fox-Genovese, 'Literary Criticism and the Politics
      of the New Historicism', in *New Historicism*, ed. Veeser, 19 and 213.

112 Stephen Kern, *The Culture of Love: Victorians to Moderns* (Harvard University Press, Cambridge, Mass., and London, 1992).

113 Lentricchia, interview, in Imré Salusinszky ed. *Criticism in Society*, 206, 188. For opposition to the subversion/containment binary, see T. B. Leinwand, 'Negotiation and New Historicism', *Publications of the Modern Language Association of America*, 105 (1990), 477–90. The pervasiveness – and emptiness – of 1990s empowerment talk (*Clinton-speak* as it's sometimes now known) can be measured by the Marriott Hotels advertisement that boasts of its security officers' power to silence noisy kids in neighbouring rooms with boxes of chocolate: 'I believe they call this kind of initiative Empowerment at Marriott hotels' (British Airways's *Business Life* magazine, February 1993).

114 David Scott Kastan, ' "The King Hath Many Marching in His Coats", or, What Did You Do in the War, Daddy?', in *Shakespeare Left and Right*, ed. Ivo Kamps (Routledge, New York and London, 1991), 241–58.

115 Edward Said, *Orientalism* (Routledge and Kegan Paul, London, 1978); *idem*, *Culture and Imperialism* (Chatto and Windus, London, 1993).

116 Good instances include Richard Terdiman, *Discourse/Counter-Discourse: The Theory and Practice of Symbolic Resistance in Nineteenth-Century France* (Cornell University Press, Ithaca and London, 1985); Homi K. Bhabha (ed.), *Nation and Narration* (Routledge, London, 1990); Marcel Detienne and Jean-Pierre Vernant, (eds), *The Cuisine of Sacrifice among the Greeks*, trans. Paula Wissing (University of Chicago Press, 1989); Jonathan Dollimore, *Sexual Dissidence: Augustine to Wilde, Freud to Foucault* (Clarendon Press, Oxford, 1991); David M. Halperin, *One Hundred Years of Sexuality and Other Essays on Greek Love* (Routledge, New York and London, 1990); *idem*, John J. Winkler and Froma I. Zeitlin (eds), *Before Sexuality: The Construction of Erotic Experience in the Ancient World* (Princeton University Press, 1990); Amy Richlin (ed.), *Pornography and Representation in Greece and Rome* (Oxford University Press, New York and Oxford, 1992); Alan Sinfield, *Faultlines: Cultural Materialism and the Politics of Dissident Reading* (Oxford University Press, 1992); David Trotter, *Circulation: Defoe, Dickens and the Economics of the Novel* (Macmillan, London, 1988); Robert Young, *White Mythologies: Writing History and the West* (Routledge, London, 1990). See also Jean E. Howard and Marion F. O'Connor (eds), *Shakespeare Reproduced: The Text in History and Ideology* (Methuen, New York and London, 1987), not only for some good work on political issues, feminist, anti-colonialist themes, etc. in Shakespeare, but also for two surveys of such political-historical work: Walter Cohn, 'Political Criticism of Shakespeare', and Don E. Wayne, 'Power, Politics and the Shakespearian Text: Recent Criticism in England and the United States'.

117 Jonathan Bate (ed.), *The Romantics on Shakespeare* (Penguin, Harmondsworth, 1992), 337. It's thought that Mary Shelley may have written the Byron–Shelley dialogue in which this view appears: *New Monthly Magazine*, n.s. 29, no. 2 (1830), 327–36.

118 Sinfield, *Faultlines*, 10: 'as a cultural materialist I don't believe in common

humanity' (though his appalled and satirical hostility towards violence in this book appeals to a general agreement that political and other violences are inhuman and therefore wrong).

119   Wole Soyinka, 'The Critic and Society: Barthes, Leftocracy and Other My-
       thologies', in *Black Literature and Literary Theory*, ed. Henry Louis Gates Jr
       (Methuen, New York and London, 1984), 27–57.

120   Peter Conrad, *Imagining America* (Routledge and Kegan Paul, London, 1980);
       David Cairns and Shaun Richards, *Writing Ireland: Colonialism, Nationalism and
       Culture* (Manchester University Press, 1988); 'Women Writing Spain', in *Spanish
       Front: Writers on the Civil War*, ed. Valentine Cunningham (Oxford University
       Press, 1986); Michael Anderberg (ed.), *Inventing Vietnam: The War in Film and
       Television* (Temple University Press, Philadelphia, 1991); Helgerson, *Forms of
       Nationhood: The Elizabethan Writing of England*.

121   Fox-Genovese, 'Literary Criticism and the Politics of the New Historicism', in
       New Historicism, ed. Veeser, 213ff.

122   James E. Young, *Writing and Rewriting the Holocaust: Narrative and the Con-
       sequences of Interpretation* (Indiana University Press, Bloomington and Indianapolis,
       1988).

123   Stephen Greenblatt, 'Towards a Poetics of Culture', in *New Historicism*, ed.
       Veeser, 1–14.

124   There are numerous critics of the New Historicism; in addition to those to be
       found in the Veeser volume, *New Historicism*, see e.g. Jean E. Howard, 'The
       New Historicism in Renaissance Studies', *English Literary Renaissance*, 16 (1986)
       13–43; Lynn Hunt (ed.), *The New Cultural History* (University of California
       Press, Berkeley, 1989); Leinwand, 'Negotiation and New Historicism', *PMLA*,
       105, 1990, 447–90; Joseph Litvak, 'Back to the Future: A Review Article on
       the New Historicism, Deconstruction, and Nineteenth-Century Fiction', *TSLL:
       Texas Studies in Literature and Language*, 30, no. 1 (Spring 1988), 120–49; Liu,
       'Power of Formalism'; *ELH*, 56, no. 4 (Winter 1989), 721–771; Edward Pechter,
       'The New Historicism And Its Discontents: Politicizing Renaissance Drama',
       PMLA, 102, no. 1 (January 1987), 292–303; Carolyn Porter, 'Are We Being
       Historical Yet?', *South Atlantic Quarterly*, 87, no. 4 (Fall 1988), 743–86; Brook
       Thomas, *The New Historicism and Other Old-Fashioned Topics* (Princeton Uni-
       versity Press, 1991).

125   Christopher Norris, *Uncritical Theory: Postmodernism, Intellectuals and the Gulf
       War* (Lawrence and Wishart, London, 1992). Derrida, 'No Apocalypse, Not
       Now'. (Norris's *Uncritical Theory* is over-kind to Derrida on this issue.) J. Hillis
       Miller, 'Open Letter to Jan Wiener', in *Theory Now and Then*, 379: 'all wars
       and revolutions are *"textual" through and through*' – which is a big jump
       from Miller's rhetorical question to Wiener: 'you surely do not believe that
       we were in Vietnam for reasons that had nothing to do with words and
       the ideology expressed in "texts".' Deborah Cameron and Elizabeth Frazer,
       The Lust to Kill: A Feminist Investigation of Sex Murder (Polity Press, Cambridge,
       1987).

126   Lyotard, *Differend*, 83f., 86ff.

127 Jean Baudrillard, 'The System of Objects', in *Selected Writings*, ed. Mark Poster (Polity Press, Cambridge, 1987); Baudrillard, *America*, trans. Chris Turner (Verso, London, 1988). Christopher Norris, 'Lost in the Funhouse: Baudrillard and the Politics of Postmodernism', in *What's Wrong with Postmodernism: Critical Theory and the Ends of Philosophy* (Harvester Wheatsheaf, Hemel Hempstead, 1990), 164–93. John Tagg, *The Burden of Representation: Essays on Photographies and Histories* (Macmillan, London, 1988), 1ff.

128 Fredric Jameson, *Postmodernism: Or the Cultural Logic of Late Capitalism* (Verso, London, 1991), 96. Jameson's shift from 'Postmodernism and Consumer Society', in *Postmodern Culture*, ed. Hal Foster (Pluto Press, London, 1985), 111–25, to the revised version of that piece in *Postmodernism and its Discontents: Theories, Practices*, ed. E. Ann Kaplan (Verso, London, 1988), 13–29, to *Postmodernism* is rather marked. Cf. Robert Scholes's scathing look at Jameson's anti-empiricism, *Textual Power*, 84–5.

129 Frank Lentricchia, *Criticism and Social Change* (University of Chicago Press, 1983), 56.

130 In Attridge et al. (eds), *Post-structuralism and the Question of History*, 202.

131 Cf. Alan Sinfield's eclectic and quite contradictory mix of data about Reform Acts, Peterloo, stamp duty, rural labour and Saussurean structuralism, difference and Lacanian self-construction ('Thus language actually constructs the distinctions which it appears to identify in the world'), in his *Tennyson* (Blackwell, Oxford, 1986).

132 See J. Hillis Miller, *The Ethics of Reading* (Columbia University Press, New York, 1987), and *idem*, 'The Ethics of Reading', in *Theory Now and Then*, 329–40.

133 For Stanley Fish being pragmatic about what a poem is, see 'How to Recognize a Poem When You See One'. For a good example of his faith in the all-in rhetorical absolutes of actions and texts and their interpretations, see Fish, 'Withholding the Missing Portion: Power, Meaning and Persuasion in Freud's The Wolf-Man', *TLS*, 29 August 1986; repr. in *The Linguistics of Writing: Arguments between Language and Literature*, ed. N. Fabb, D. Attridge, A Durant, and C. McCabe (Manchester University Press, 1987), 154–72; also repr. in *Doing What Comes Naturally*, 525–54. For the truly astonishing Rorty, see e.g. his 'Philosophy without Principles', in *Against Theory: Literary Studies and the New Pragmatism*, ed. W. J. T. Mitchell (University of Chicago Press 1985), 132–8, where text, meaning, goodness are all defined as what *you* think they are, what it pleases *you* to believe ('the question "What is the meaning of a text?" is as useless as the question "What is the nature of the good?" '). The pragmatist code, according to Rorty, consists of just 'making it useful', and avoids trying to 'get it right': 'The Pragmatist's Progress', in Eco, *Interpretation and Overinterpretation*, 89–108. (It was clearly a mistake for literary critics to believe that Dickens and the other nineteenth-century fictional moralists, who wrote precisely to show the evils of the fashionable utilitarianism of their day, had won the argument hands down, and that after *Hard Times*, *Mary Barton*, and so on, such arguments would not dare to raise their heads again.)

134   Hayden White, *Metahistory: The Historical Imagination in Nineteenth-Century Europe*
(Johns Hopkins University Press, Baltimore and London, 1973); *idem, Tropics
of Discourse: Essays in Cultural Materialism* (Johns Hopkins University Press,
1978); *idem, Content of the Form.* Jonathan Culler, 'Criticism and Institutions:
The American University', in *Post-structuralism and the Question of History*, 82–
98, much adapted and dispersed about Culler's *Framing the Sign: Criticism and
its Institutions* (Blackwell, Oxford, 1988). Gerald Graff has made a career out
of institution history: *Professing Literature: An Institutional History* (Chicago
University Press, 1987); Graff and Michael Warner (eds), *The Origins of Lit-
erary Studies in America: A Documentary Anthology* (Routledge, New York and
London, 1989); Graff, 'The Future of Theory in the Teaching of Literature',
The Future of Literary Theory, ed. Ralph Cohen (Routledge, New York and
London, 1989), 250–67. See also Frank Lentricchia, *After the New Criticism*
(Athlone, London, 1980), and Donald Morton and Mas'ud Zavarzadeh (eds),
Theory/Pedagogy/Politics: Texts for Change (University of Illinois Press, Urbana
and Chicago, 1991). Susan R. Horton is a little more wary than is customary
of this institutional narcissism in 'The Institution of Literature and the Cultural
Community', in *Literary Theory Futures*, ed. Joseph Natoli (University of
Chicago Press, Urbana and Chicago, 1989), 267–320. So are Morton and
Zavarzadeh, in their *Theory, (Post)Modernity, Opposition* (Maisonneuve Press,
Washington, D.C. 1991).

135   Lynn Hunt, 'History as Gesture; or, The Scandal of History', in *Consequences
of Theory, Selected Papers from the English Institute, 1987–8*, n.s. 14, ed. J. Arac
and B. Johnson (Johns Hopkins University Press, Baltimore and London, 1991),
91–107; Jerome McGann, 'The Scandal of Referentiality', in *Social Values and
Poetic Acts, The Historical Judgment of Literary Work* (Harvard University Press,
Cambridge, Mass., 1988), 115–31. (McGann is one of the most lively and
persuasive historicizers around, much inspired by M. M. Bakhtin and P. M.
Medvedev, *The Formal Method in Literary Scholarship: A Critical Introduction to
Sociological Poetics*, trans. A. J. Wehrle (Harvard University Press, Cambridge,
Mass., and London, 1985.) See Jerome McGann, *The Beauty of Inflections: Literary Investigations in Historical Method and Theory* (Clarendon Press, Oxford,
1985), and *idem, The Textual Condition* (Princeton University Press, 1991). On
the (depressing) persistence of the Saussurean anti-historicist frame of thought
cf. Ora Avni:

'Even today, after Poststructuralism and Postmodernism, the framework
of the most vigorous investigations remains unchanged: current approaches that rely on the interplay between culture (or literature) and
social and historical contexts (Marxism, new historicism, feminism, black
studies, etc.) nonetheless rest their views on the unquestioned premise
of cultural constructs akin to *langue* and on the relativity of the ideological systems of thought and signs that they command'. (Avni, *Resistance
of Reference*, 18.)

136   Paul de Man, 'Semiology and Rhetoric', in *Textual Strategies: Perspectives in Post-*

Structuralist Criticism, ed. with an introduction by Josué V. Harari (Methuen, London, 1980), 121.

137 Hillis Miller, *Ethics of Reading*, 5.

138 J. Hillis Miller, 'Presidential Address 1986. The Triumph of Theory, the Resistance to Reading, and the Question of the Material Base', *PMLA*, 102, no. 3 (May 1987), 281–91. Repr. in Miller, *Theory Now and Then*, 309–27.

139 David Carroll, *Paraesthetics: Foucault, Lyotard, Derrida* (Methuen, London, 1987), xi.

140 Miller repeats his point, essentially, in the Preface to *Theory Now and Then*: the 'recent forms of "cultural critique" are more the continuation of deconstruction than its cancellation' (p. x).

141 Frank Kermode, *History and Value* (Clarendon Press, Oxford, 1989), 145–6.

142 Frank Kermode, *Poetry, Narrative, History*, The Bucknell Lectures in Literary Theory (Blackwell, Oxford, 1990), 50.

143 Sue Lonoff, Review of books on the Brontës, *Victorian Studies*, 34, no. 4 (Summer 1991), 502–4.

144 Paul de Man, 'Semiology and Rhetoric', in Harari (ed.), 124.

145 'Criticism becomes philosophizing on one's own': René Wellek, *The Attack on Literature and Other Essays* (Harvester, Brighton, 1983), 85. Eugene Goodheart, *The Skeptic Disposition: Deconstruction, Ideology and Other Matters* (Princeton University Press, 1984); with a new Afterword (Princeton University Press paperback, 1991).

146 Miller, ' "Reading" part of a paragraph', in *Theory Now and Then*, 357, n. 7. Hayden White, having unwillingly granted the Holocaust exemption from the textuality-only view of history/historiography, simply proceeded much as before; see the epigraph to *Content of the Form* (referred to in n. 99 of this chapter), and the essays surrounding the Holocaust discussion in White's volume – which appeared, of course, with certain irony, in the terrible 'Paul de Man' year, 1987.

147 Miller, 'George Poulet's "Criticism of Identification" ', in *The Quest for Imagination*, ed. O. B. Hardison (Cleveland University Press, 1971); *idem*, 'Stevens' Rock and Criticism as Cure, II', *Georgia Review*, 30 (1976), 330–48; *idem*, 'On Edge: The Crossways of Contemporary Criticism', *Bulletin of the American Academy of Arts and Sciences* (January 1979). (All three of these pieces are in *Theory Now and Then*, respectively 31ff., 117ff., 171ff.) *Idem*, 'The Two Allegories', in *Allegory Myth and Symbol*, Harvard English Studies, 9, ed. Morton W. Bloomfield (Harvard University Press, Cambridge, Mass., and London 1981); *idem*, 'Two Forms of Repetition', in Miller, *Fiction and Repetition: Seven English Novels* (Blackwell, Oxford, 1982). For hendiadys, see Johnson, *World of Difference*, ch. 2: 'Rigorous Unreliability', p. 19.

148 J. Hillis Miller, 'The Search for Grounds in Literary Study', and the Symposium on Marxism and Deconstruction, in *Rhetoric and Form: Deconstruction at Yale*, ed. with an introduction by R. C. Davis and R. Schleifer (University of Oklahoma Press, Norman, Okla., 1985), 19–36, 89.

149 Roland Barthes, *S/Z* (1973), trans. Richard Miller (Blackwell, Oxford, 1990), 4–5. *Idem*, 'Theory of the Text', trans. Ian McLeod, in *Untying the Text: A Post-Structuralist Reader*, ed. Robert Young (Routledge, London, 1981), 39. Roman Jakobson, 'Two Aspects of Language and Two Types of Aphasic Disturbances', in Jakobson and Morris Halle, *Fundamentals of Language* (Mouton, The Hague, 1956). David Lodge, *The Modes of Modern Writing: Metaphor, Metonymy, and the Typology of Modern Literature* (Arnold, London, 1977). Frank Kermode, *The Genesis of Secrecy: On the Interpretation of Narrative* (Harvard University Press, Cambridge, Mass., and London, 1979). Denis Donoghue, *Ferocious Alphabets* (Faber, London, 1981). Ian Watt, 'Impression and Symbolism in "Heart of Darkness" ', *Southern Review*, 13, no. 1 (January 1977), 96–113. Jacques Lacan, 'The Empty Word and the Full Word', in *The Language of the Self: The Function of Language in Psychoanalysis*, trans. and ed. Anthony Wilden (Johns Hopkins University Press, Baltimore and London, 1968), 9ff. Hayden White, 'The Absurdist Moment in Contemporary Literary Theory', in *Tropics of Discourse*, 261–83. Scholes, *Textual Power*, 75. Paul de Man, *Blindness and Insight: Essays in the Rhetoric of Contemporary Criticism* (1971), 2nd edn with an introduction by Wlad Godzich (Methuen, London, 1983).

150 J. Derrida, 'Structure, Sign and Play in the Discourse of the Humanities', in *The Languages of Criticism and The Sciences of Man: The Structuralist Controversy*, ed. Richard Macksey and Eugenio Donato (Johns Hopkins University Press, Baltimore and London, 1970; paperback edn 1972), 247–65. Followed by 'Discussion', 265–72.

151 Derrida, 'Structure, Sign and Play', in *Writing and Difference*, trans. and ed. Alan Bass (Routledge and Kegan Paul, London, 1978), 278–93.

152 'An Interview with Jacques Derrida', in *Jacques Derrida: Acts of Literature*, 45, 47, 49.

153 Derrida, in Discussion of 'Structure, Sign and Play', in *Languages of Criticism*, ed. Macksey and Donato, 271.

154 J. Derrida, '*Fors*: The Anglish Words of Nicholas Abraham and Maria Torok', Foreword to Nicholas Abraham and Maria Torok, *The Wolf Man's Magic Word: A Cryptonomy*, trans. Nicholas Rand, Theory and History of Literature, 37 (University of Minnesota Press, Minneapolis, 1986), xxxviii. Cf. Nicholas Rowe, 'Cryptaesthesia: The Case of *Wuthering Heights*', in *Telepathy and Literature: Essays on the Reading Mind* (Blackwell, Oxford, 1991).

155 J. Derrida, 'The Double Session', in *Dissemination*, 212ff.

156 Roland Barthes, 'To Write: An Intransitive Verb', in *Languages of Criticism*, ed. Macksey and Donato, 136. Émile Benveniste, 'Saussure après un demi-siècle', in *Problèmes de linguistique générale*, 40.

157 Quoted by Falck, *Myth, Truth and Literature*, 86.

158 D. H. Lawrence, 'Morality and the Novel', in *Phoenix: The Posthumous Papers of D. H. Lawrence* (Heinemann, London, 1936), 527.

159 Ibid.

160 Philip Larkin to J. B. Sutton, 29 September 1946, in *Selected Letters of Philip Larkin 1940–1985*, ed. Anthony Thwaite (Faber and Faber, London and Boston,

1992), 125. Gulley Jimson is the painter-hero of Joyce Cary's novel *The Horse's Mouth* (1944), whose vigour and resilience Larkin greatly admired.

161 'Là est, me semble-t-il, le centre de la doctrine, le principe d'où procède tout l'appareil de notions et de distinctions qui formera le Cours publié. Tout en effet dans le langage est à définir en termes doubles; tout porte l'empreinte et le sceau de la dualité oppositive': Benveniste, 'Saussure après un demi-siècle' (1963), in *Problèmes* (1966), 40.

162 Carroll, *Paraesthetics*.

2

Textual Stuff

Not fierce *Othello* in so loud a strain
Roar'd for the handkerchief that caus'd his pain.
Alexander Pope, The Rape of the Lock, 1712

Virginia Woolf's little detective story about coats and handbags poses with challenging verve the question of what happens – what is uncovered and what remains covered up – in encounters between textual stuff and worldly stuff. The undisentanglable skein of worldly stuff within the texturality of this narrative's writtenness offers a dual challenge: to any theory that would warp texts away from the world, would deny the world much or any place in the woven warp and woof of the text, and also to that view of literary modernism which would see it as effecting a more or less total retreat into the hermeneutics of mere writing. This modernist detective story simply will not allow itself to sustain the imperialistic negatives assumed in (post)-modernist readings of detective fiction – those negative assumptions which have made Poe's 'The Purloined Letter' such a *locus classicus* of deconstructionist interpretation. In other words, this piece of intense textual self-reflexiveness – peculiarly intense because the bearing of textual witness is done with so much reference to textiles: all those coats – is counter-exemplary for its refusal to allow that we – or texts – can simply say 'Get Stuffed' to the context, the world, the *hors-texte*.

Handkerchief Moody

But that, and defiantly, is what Hillis Miller is still saying in his latest reading of a classic crime story involving a textile, Nathaniel Hawthorne's story 'The Minister's Black Veil' (in *Twice-told Tales*, 1837). This narrative, in which a New England pastor suddenly covers his face with a black crepe veil which he then refuses to remove or explain is taken by Miller as 'a parable of history' – in which 'history' turns out to be only, and absolutely, a set of textualized signs, and signs, like the black veil, which conceal or reveal only a blank. There is no historical face behind the texts of history. Signs on this reading – emblematized in the crepe veil – deface any reference to physicality, materiality, or 'out-there' actuality that they might ordinarily be thought of as laying some claim to. The 'material base', as Miller puts it, provocatively borrowing the old Marxist trope, the materiality that the crepe might be supposed to incorporate into the story, however wryly and lightly, because it is so manifestly a piece of textual stuff, is said to be 'incommensurate with the parabolic meaning it carries'. Stuff – what stuff? And this critical ban extends – naturally enough – to the story behind the story, the historical case invoked by Hawthorne, in a footnote, of the Reverend Mr Joseph Moody – 'Handkerchief Moody' – who veiled his face after accidentally shooting a friend. The relevance of an historical handkerchief behind the minister's veil is precisely what Professor Miller wishes to repudiate. Behind his veil is only a set of blank signs, more veils, a sequence of blank faces or defacements. 'The veil . . . is an enigmatic sign that appears to give access to what it stands for while forbidding the one who confronts it to move behind it by any effort of hermeneutic interpretation. If Hooper's face behind the veil . . . is yet another veil, then it can be said that the real face too is not a valid sign but another de-facement. The face de-faces . . . it.'[1]

Hillis Miller is by no means troubled enough by the troublesome residue of something, some material reference point, within and/or behind the veil, signalled, however minimally in that '. . . it'. His argument roughly brushes aside all of Hawthorne's play with the traditionally delicate questions of Biblical hermeneutics as to what figures are figures of, and attempts to drive a bull right through the china shop of ages-old exegesis as to what the Old Testament story of Moses' veiled face might mean for the Christian interpreter (as in 2 Corinthians 3, for which see my chapter 8: 'The Rabbins Take It Up . . .'). Veils and handkerchiefs are here brusquely stripped of all their enigmatic material force.

That the so-called New Historicism is more provoked by the materialistic suggestiveness of textiles will be one more reason why Hillis Miller is at pains to repudiate its main stance in his Hawthorne discussion. 'Is the text "embedded" in history, as my formulation suggests, or is history "embedded" in the text, as Stephen Greenblatt's way of putting it affirms?'[2] Miller's own answer is clear. But even Stephen Greenblatt, praiseworthily preoccupied though he is with the historical texture of texts, is still, I think, too ready to give up the historicality of, say, the old ecclesiastical clothes that became props on the Elizabethan stage, in deference to their figurality.

Greenblatt is rightly responsive to the charisma of historical textiles, especially those priestly garments commandeered by the Protestant reformers at the Reformation – the gorgeous apparel of the Roman Church, the albs, copes, amices, stoles, and so on – which were flogged off insultingly to the theatrical joint-stock companies. These garments resonate with the wonder that historical textures, the surviving texts and textures of the past, are afforded, and of course properly so, by the New Historicism. They're characteristic of the props that New Historicists get excited over. They get in everywhere. They intrude into Greenblatt's later meditation on Cardinal Wolsey's hat. They preoccupy what has become a foundational piece of New Historicism, his essay 'Shakespeare and the Exorcists'. What, Greenblatt asks, was the force, the status, of the old ecclesiastical wardrobe on stage – given that 'When an actor in a history play took the part of an English bishop, he could conceivably have worn the actual robes of the character he was representing'? Certainly, some sort of 'polemical service' was being rendered. The players were 'signifying that the sanctified vestments were in reality mere trumpery whose proper place was a disreputable world of illusion-mongering'. Surely, too, the players were involved in a paradoxical continuation of the Romanist mana: robed thus, the players 'acquired the tarnished but still potent charisma that clung to the old vestments, charisma that in paradoxical fashion the players at once emptied out and heightened'.[3] But, for all this manifest presence of touchy polemical actualities on-stage, invested in the vestments, a question still – properly – remains as to the mixture of the rhetorical and the realistic present in these textiles within the play-text. Greenblatt settles the dialogue, as New Historicism has tended to do, on the side of the figural or discursive. 'This is less realism than rhetoric.'[4]

Can we, though, afford to be so positive? Surely the mode of existence of those old clothes on the Shakespearean stage is more highly complex than Greenblatt allows.[5] Were not those second-hand textiles actually all at once real enough, material stuff, actual *Stoff*, as well as signs, rhetorical stuff, the stuff of textuality, symbolic, metaphorical? They arrived in the tiring-house already ambivalent – on the one hand, tailor's matter, pins and needles work, mere warp and woof, and on the other hand, 'rags of Rome', desacralized custodians of once sacred meanings, emblems of ecclesiastical and divine unction come down in the world, sites of lost liturgical struggles. And these ambivalences were multiplied on-stage in garments ever tangible and knowable, really there before the audience's very eyes, and yet also part of the stuff of fiction, the non-worldly stage-play world. And so, of course, these particular costumes joined in that curiously mixed existence enjoyed by other components of the stage-play's materiality – actors' real bodies and audible vocalizations, those so-real human presences, spitting and sweating and smelling and stamping about up there on the actual boards of 'the buskined stage', clad in Jonson's learned sock and other actual threads, and sporting actual staves and swords, and bumping into actual bits of stage furniture – manifestly in a fiction, a text, a story, a plot, and yet also physically present, touchable, material, there. This is indeed a challenging, even cautionary, tale for theorists, or *theoroi* – that is, spectators. In the drama, at least, the line between rhetoric and realism is by no means easy to draw. The bodiliness of drama will not allow a materialistic poetics to be wholly swamped by a totally rhetoricized one. Which is one reason, perhaps, why deconstructionists have so little of a practically realist kind to say about the mode of production (if one may borrow a Marxist slogan) of these particular works of art.[6] It is also why *Othello* is so arresting and, I would allege, exemplary.

Handkerchief Othello

Othello is an old crime story in which textiles enjoy a peculiar on-stage prominence. There are the wedding sheets Desdemona is murdered in, the pillow she's commonly stifled with (after the Folio's stage direction *Smothers her*), and, above all, the embroidered handkerchief that Othello gave his wife, the absence of which is built up by Iago into evidence of her adultery with Cassio. Desdemona is killed because of this handkerchief, the only proof Othello ever gets of his wife's alleged unfaithfulness, and she dies in her wedding sheets, stifled (usually) by a pillow. In every way this is a crime story about textiles, involving a crime committed because of and by means of textiles.

But what is revealed – what is veiled, what unveiled – about the status of the crucially evidential piece of cloth in this story of Handkerchief Othello? Othello believes the handkerchief is material evidence; we know it isn't. So is its alleged materiality impugned by its actual immateriality? Does it represent the power – corrupt, perverse, but still power – of the material? Or is it rather a demonstration of the subservience of the material – real stuff, *Stoff*, on-stage – to the inventions, the lies, the story that Iago weaves about it? Are we, in other words, being demonstrated the subordination of the material to the rhetorical? Simply to put the question is to realize that, in fact, the issue between realism and rhetoric is not only right at the heart of Iago's plotting and of Handkerchief *Othello*'s plot, but also that there is no easy answer to it. *Othello* offers no easy interpretation on this or any other question.

Ambivalences are woven into every aspect of the handkerchief's signifying function – as it is exploited by Iago to effect Othello's downfall, as it takes centre-stage in the whole course of the play, as it offers itself for interpretation in the difficult realism–rhetoric debate. The handkerchief is present, there, visible; but it proves most evidential to Othello when it's absent, lost, not there, when Desdemona cannot produce it. The handkerchief is the only material evidence Othello gets; but it is immaterial, worthless evidence; worthless evidence, however, that convinces Othello. The handkerchief is so evidently a physical thing, a piece of textile, 'spotted with strawberries' – embroidered work that Cassio asks the doting Bianca to take out; and yet it is also an utterly magical thing, the stuff of fiction, the object of another of Othello's exotically tall stories. An Egyptian magician, Othello claims, gave it to his mother. It's a piece of extraodinarily magical cloth. There is indeed 'magic in the web of it', if Othello is to be believed:

> A sibyl, that had number'd in the world
> The sun to make two hundred compasses,
> In her prophetic fury sew'd the work;
> The worms were hallow'd that did breed the silk,
> And it was dyed in mummy, which the skilful
> Consult of maidens' hearts.
>
> (*Othello*, III. iv. 68–73)

And this curious concatenation of weird womanly work has magical properties which pertain to the traffic of love and hatred between wives and husbands. It makes husbands love their wives; but if it's lost, it makes men hate their wives.

In the play of significations here, then, paradox layers dramatically upon paradox: love and hatred, material and immaterial, presence and absence, gain and loss, discovering and covering up, and all to be subsumed, perhaps, within the larger paradox of the play of realism and rhetoric. On this reading, the handkerchief dramatically focuses the problem of signification in *Othello* and, by implication, in any text. The handkerchief offers a challenge to any allegation that the rhetorical is only rhetorical, for it represents the convergence, quite central to this play, of the rhetorical and the material. Rhetoric is utterly central to everything that happens in *Othello*, but so also is the inextricable relation of rhetoric to action, bodies, materiality. The connecting of words and materiality – the converging of these twain that so much theory seeks to resist – is what the *Othello* plot *does*.

Othello is a story about Iago's triumph in making a rhetoric come true. His plotting grants his figures, his metaphors, material life. He has a low, bestial, materialistic view of women, and he manages to impose his foul line of thought and talk upon Othello, who then translates it into terrible action. Iago's rhetoric reduces love, marriage, women, to a violent, satirical farrago of the coarsely, animally physical. With him, pillow talk is a matter of sneers about stuffing. Perhaps Othello would like to 'grossly gape on' while Desdemona is *topp'd* or *tupp'd* by Cassio? It's a grotesque drama that Othello can't bear to imagine himself a *supervisor*, or *theoros*, at. 'Death and damnation . . . O!' he exclaims, but already he's theorizing the possibility, which Iago dilates: it would be difficult

> To bring 'em to that prospect, damn 'em then,
> If ever mortal eyes did see them bolster
> More than their own. . . .
>
> (III. iii. 404–7)

Bolster, noun, pillow – a phallic sausage of cloth; *bolster*, verb, to stuff – most materialistic of idioms for sexual intercourse.[7] It's a metaphoric vein that Iago claims to be able to put into Cassio's mouth for Othello to overhear:

> For I will make him tell the tale anew,
> Where, how, how oft, how long ago, and when,
> He has, and is again to cope your wife.
>
> (IV. i. 84–6)

And *cope* embraces a cornucopia of coarsely materializing emphases. *Cope*, noun, is a cloak, a covering garment, especially an ecclesiastical one of the kind the theatres got from the Reformers' purges. As a verb it means to *cover* (a common word for animal intercourse, as well as a roughish-toned one for human love-making) and to *buy* (which turns woman into a marketable, purchasable thing, a commodity, a whore) and to *strike violently against* (sexual congress as acts of violent male aggression against females, envisaged early and late in English as *fucking* and *banging*).

Iago's language is all like this. The play's opening scene sets his tone with its talk of purse, price, debts and credits, provender, Desdemona 'covered' by an Arab stallion, tupped by a goatish Moor, making the beast with two backs with a Black, and of clothes, clothes, clothes ('oft capp'd to him', 'toged consuls', 'trimmed' forms, coats 'lined' with financial advantage, hearts worn on sleeves, 'a flag'). And right from this start, Iago assumes that the rhetoric of Othello is much like his own:

> But he, as loving his own pride and purposes,
> Evades them, with a bombast circumstance,
> Horribly stuff'd with epithets of war.
>
> (I. i. 12–14)

Stuffed: stuffing – in cuisine (stuffing, forced meat, farcing) and sexual congress and tailoring, as well as in texts (farces: bits of texts used to pack out or make more copious certain liturgical and theatrical occasions). *Bombast*: cotton material used for padding and lining. It's also rhetorical padding. Othello's rhetoric is declared to be bombastic, gratuitously padded, and so is primed, made proleptically receptive, to become entirely a rhetoric of gross Iago-esque materiality. Soon Othello will be talking of goats and monkeys and of chopping Desdemona into messes – bits of food, edible stuff, fit for ingestion by a husband and lover who has turned anthropophagus, or cannibal; and soon after that he will be treating her bestially and as a beast – no longer as a transcendent, angelic creature – and will play the cannibal of his own most grotesque traveller's tales, smothering his wife in her wedding sheets, her bed covers, in a grotesque parody of a lover's covering of the beloved. ('What needst thou have more covering than a man': John Donne, Elegy 19.)

Rhetoric, story, metaphor, signs, have, then, this terrible way of materializing in *Othello*. Provokingly, words, rhetoric, achieve here this ghastly materiality. And yet they never shed their equally challenging immateriality. Iago says he 'must show out a flag, and sign of love'. But he adds that this 'flag' will be 'but sign': an immaterial, an empty sign. And then Brabantio appears in what will prove a terribly proleptic 'night-gown' (I. i. 156ff.). Such is *Othello*'s way. It keeps up a profound – and I would say challengingly exemplary – dualism of words and cloth, sign and reference, rhetoric and realism, metaphor and materiality, immaterial and material, as well as of presence and absence, possession and loss, discovering and covering up.

Veiling and Unveiling

And all this is wrapped up in the handkerchief. Which may be one reason why in *Bleak House* (ch. 59) Inspector Bucket, generic detective hero of the modern English novel, recommends Mrs Snagsby to 'Go and see Othello acted. That's the tragedy for you.' Bucket is, of course, primarily mindful of Mrs Snagsby's wifely jealousy. Encountering the terrible results of a spouse's jealousy in Shakespeare's play might go some way towards curing her silly worries about fanciful relations between her husband and other women. But *Bleak House* enjoys larger affinities with *Othello*. Dickens's text is another story of crime that's also greatly preoccupied with love and jealousy and the wronging of a husband that ends in the death of a wife. And in this story too a handkerchief plays a chief – and, once again, an ambivalent – role.

Lady Dedlock is this novel's heart of darkness – the wife with a darkly secretive past involving a lost lover (who travels under the self-annihilating pseudonym of Nemo) and a lost daughter, but who shows a mask of aristocratic aplomb and icy self-control to the world. And her public mask, her *prosopon*, or face, of respectability that's carried through also to her private domain – for her husband is ignorant of her secrets – becomes more than a metaphor when she puts on a veil, to go scouting for news of the dead Nemo (ch. 16) and to run away after being exposed as a transgressor and under a cloud of suspicion that she has murdered the omniscient lawyer Tulkinghorn (ch. 55). She successfully eludes her pursuers, Inspector Bucket and Esther Summerson, in a labyrinthine chase, until the point when it's too late to save her life, by swapping her clothes and her veil for the clothes of Jenny the brickmaker's wife and sending Jenny off as a decoy. Disguised now in a poor woman's garb, she heads for the urban burying ground where Nemo is interred. When Esther Summerson, the lost daughter, arrives there, she supposes that it's Jenny lying slumped across the cemetery threshold: 'I lifted the heavy head, put the long dank hair aside, and turned the face. And it was my mother, cold and dead' (ch. 59). And thus is Lady Dedlock all at once found and yet lost, found out and beyond finding out, unveiled and yet also still in the disguise afforded by Jenny's clothes, a mystery woman who is discovered and who will yet escape public exposure because she's now dead.

This recognition scene at a graveyard threshold, a border place where veiling and unveiling converge and interact as the veil of hair is pulled aside to reveal a face that's now cold in death, this final discovery of one forever lost, is in fact a grim reprise of the earlier scene when Esther Summerson looks at her own face in the mirror for the first time after recovering from smallpox (ch. 36). Her hair, cut off during her illness, has, she tells us, grown again, 'long and thick'; her mirror is covered with a muslin curtain: there is thus a doubled veiling going on. Esther then lets down her hair. She

> shook it out, and went up to the glass upon the dressing-table. There was a little muslin curtain drawn across it. I drew it back: and stood for a moment looking through such a veil of my own hair, that I could see nothing else. Then I put my hair aside, and looked at the reflection in the mirror.

But what's seen after the removal of the doubled veil, the curtain and the hair, is still a kind of veiling, for her complexion has been greatly altered by the pock-marks left by her recent disease. 'I was very much changed – O very, very much.' As she remains looking, her face becomes 'more familiar'; but it is still altered. The face estranged by the veils of muslin and of hair is still an altered, estranged face, a new *prosopon* which is still defamiliarized, unalterably altered ('Very soon it became more familiar, and then I knew the extent of the alteration in it better than I had done at first').

And these plays of veils drawn aside and veils remaining – this persistent doubling of vision and knowledge, a version of the famous Pauline seeing, through a mirror, but still in an enigma (*per speculum in aenigmate*) – get their intensest material focus in a handkerchief. A handkerchief is the means by which Lady Dedlock, the veiled/unveiled lady, is joined to her long-lost, covered-up daughter Esther. It's the same handkerchief that Esther had laid as a compassionate veil over the otherwise naked dead baby of the brickmaker's wife Jenny, the same woman who later helped Lady Dedlock keep up her masking by an exchange of clothes. Jenny had preserved it as a memento; 'a lady with a veil' took it away (ch. 35). So a lost child's handkerchief covers up a dead child, and is the means of a mother and daughter discovering one another. 'I cannot tell in any words what the state of my mind was, when I saw in her hand my handkerchief, with which I had covered the dead baby.' But this uncovering cannot undo the thorough disguising job that the smallpox effected, which gladdens the newly found daughter confronted now with an abased, penitent mother: 'When I saw her at my feet on the bare earth in her great agony of mind, I felt, through all my tumult of emotion, a burst of gratitude to the providence of God that I was so changed as that I never could disgrace her by any trace of likeness; as that nobody could ever look at me, and look at her, and remotely think of any near tie between us' (ch. 36). And the paradox of this little textile continues when Bucket gets his hands on it (ch. 56). He finds it stowed in a secret drawer in Lady Dedlock's boudoir, hidden among gloves. It's marked with the name 'Esther Summerson'. This discovery is added to all the others ('There has been a discovery there, today. Family affairs have come out'). That Bucket can penetrate handkerchiefs as well as veils, we learnt earlier in the novel, in chapter 22, when he and Tulkinghorn got Joe to finger Lady Dedlock. Joe recognizes the veil that these male pursuers of Lady Dedlock have got her maid Hortense to dress up in, but disclaims knowledge of the other's hand and voice: 'that there's the wale [i.e. the veil], the bonnet, and the gownd. It is her and it an't her.' But though the handkerchief is a penetrable little text, it still retains, like the veil Hortense has on, the power to mystify. Bucket takes the potent pocket textile away with him ('carefully puts it up'); but were it 'able, with an enchanted power, to bring before him the place where she found it, and the night landscape near the cottage where it covered the little child, would he descry her there?' And even if he did, he'd only see a 'figure of a woman', one 'miserably dressed'. Even as an enchanted textile, able to provoke telepathic discoveries, the handkerchief would respect Lady Dedlock's disguise. The secret of Lady Dedlock's switch of clothes would remain.

The dualism of the handkerchief and all the other veils in *Bleak House*, these textured agents of simultaneous revelation and concealment, makes them emblems for *Bleak House* in particular, but also, arguably, of texts in general. *Bleak House* celebrates Bucket's extraordinary powers of detection, just as Dickens's *Household Words* articles celebrated London's Inspector Field. No reader came more intelligent than these new detective masters of the urban-criminal labyrinth.[8] 'The velocity and certainty of Mr Bucket's interpreta-tion . . . is little short of miraculous' (ch. 56). Bucket's I Am – 'I am Inspector Bucket' (ch. 56) – is little short of divine. He knows and is the cause of knowledge in others – 'I know, I know, and would I put you wrong, do you think? Inspector Bucket. Now you know me, don't you?' (ch. 57). Like all detective stories, *Bleak House* celebrates the discovery of dark truths, the unveiling of evils and hypocrisies formerly concealed, the solution of mystery and enigma. Like allegories – and not for nothing is the figure of Allegory painted hugely across the ceilings of Mr Tulkinghorn, legalistic master of dark repositories and secret deposits – detective stories are fictions in which the concealed is able to be revealed and undercover meanings are brought to light. At the same time, this detective story is about the preservation of enigma. Lady Dedlock's disguises were not cracked in time to prevent her death; she evaded her pursuers until too late. Nemo was named only after he died. At the heart of all the novel's inter-connected plots stands the gothic mystery of Mr Krook's death by inexplicable and unexplained spontaneous combustion.

And this blend of some mysteries being solved while other enigmas remain puzzling applies to the novel's social themes. *Bleak House* utters dark truths about the underground life of London and its environs, the plague-ridden slums, the beaten wives and dead babies, the illegitimate and unwanted children who are the result of illicit loves and transgressive sexual encounters, as well as uttering dark thoughts about the conduct of respectable lawyers and politicians and of apparently good Christian people all across the reli-gious spectrum, from Mr Chadband to Mrs Jellyby and Mrs Pardiggle. At the same time, this satire stops well short of going the whole hog. As immense pains are taken by Bucket and company to protect the Dedlock name, so the novel goes soft on Sir Leicester, letting him off the hooks duly reserved for his rotten cousins and cronies. Dickens will not follow through the logic of his distaste for the social, legal, and economic machinery that keeps Sir Leicester and his glacially enigmatic wife in place. After all, the good Esther and her good medical husband have, however tangentially, a little mansion reserved for them as part of that very same social system.

So the generic, formal, rhetorical functions of the text intimately mirror the handling of the social ones. The failures and successes of the fiction as fictional stuff – as detective story, as allegory, and so on – correspond pretty precisely to the combined blunting and pointing of the contextual subject, the satirical stuff. And the dual focus – text and city, fiction and history, rhetoric and realism – is, once more, nicely emblematized in a handkerchief that is all at once material stuff, prominent in a busy satirical engagement with contemporary realities of transgression, poverty, orphanage, sexuality, and male power (only respectability and wealth separate Tulkinghorn, who has Lady Dedlock under his foot, and the wife-beating brickmaker), and prominent also in the novel's haunted weave of reflections on the strengths and weaknesses of textuality in the novel's city of so much paper, ink, writing materials, and reading matter.

And, of course, such dualistic play of rhetoric and realism is embarrassing and scandalous to much current criticism. It's why Hillis Miller banishes Handkerchief Moody to a footnote on a footnote in his discussion of Hawthorne's talk about the minister's veiling. But handkerchiefs on stage have long embarrassed certain fine critical noses. Our modern finesse over material stuff in texts is only an updated variant on the sniffy pulling back of French skirts before what was perceived as the sheer indignity of Desdemona's handkerchief.

Getting Up the Gallic Nose

On 24 October 1829, the occasion of the opening night of *Le More de Venise*, his version of *Othello*, Alfred de Vigny boasted of how he had reversed ninety-eight years of French hostility to having a handkerchief on stage. Until then, such a vulgar object was not to be named in polite Gallic theatres. Politer, classier substitutes had been provided for such an offensive item – a letter, it might be, or a diamond tiara. A handkerchief might be mentioned on-stage only in a translation of a play by a foreigner, and a German at that, Schiller's *Maria Stewart*; and even then it was not to be named as such, but only referred to as *cloth* or *gift*. Only in 1829 did a Frenchman, namely Alfred de Vigny, have the temerity to name such a textile in the French theatre, by courtesy of Shakespeare.

> Would you believe it, you English – you who know the language of Shake-speare's tragedies – that the French tragic muse, or Melpomene, took ninety-eight years before she could bring herself to pronounce out loud: *a handkerchief*, she who said, quite straightforwardly, *dog* and *sponge*? . . .
>
> Finally, in 1829, thanks to Shakespeare, she pronounced the great word, to the horror and swooning of the timid, who broke out that day in prolonged and anguished wailing; but to the satisfaction of the public, the majority of whom are in the habit of calling a handkerchief a handkerchief. The word

has made its debut. Ridiculous triumph! Will it always take a century to introduce an ordinary word on stage.[9]

The French theatre's refined reluctance to call a handkerchief a handkerchief might be a model of the reluctance of much recent criticism – including even Greenblatt's New Historicism – to come to terms with the muddy rhetoric–realism paradox, the scandal of materiality's interference in the textual, that disconcerting proclivity of text that causes verbal texture, the *tissu* of narratives, to get mixed up vulgarly with the texture of things such as textiles.

The English tradition, as de Vigny noted, was never embarrassed thus, in particular the tradition of the English novel. *Bleak House* is by no means alone. English fiction is like a great suitcase or trunk just packed with exemplary textiles, not least important, as my later discussions will indicate, the various pairs of galligaskins in *Tristram Shandy* and all the many species of cloth that are yarned about in *Heart of Darkness*. But then, novels in other languages are not too squeamish either. And, in fact, once criticism starts talking about textiles – and recent criticism has been very preoccupied with such stuff – squeamishness of any kind soon gets hard to sustain. 'The hymen is . . . a sort of textile. Its threads should be interwoven with all the veils, gauzes, canvases, fabrics, moires, wings, feathers, all the curtains and fans that hold within their folds all – almost – of the Mallarméan corpus.'[10] Cultures that can talk thus in public have abandoned linguistic squeamishness (try such a discussion in, for example, most Indian lecture-rooms or in fundamentalist Islamic countries). And it's the sheer materiality of all textiles *per se* that is – as the old French bowdlerizers clearly knew – an agent of such vulgarity and an enemy of the linguistically formal and the critically formalist.

Virginia Woolf's wor(l)d – the textual steeped in the worldly banalities of handbags and Oxford Street coats – rules, then, OK? Well, yes, if Julián Ríos's extraordinary novel *Larva: Babel de una Noche de San Juan* (1983), translated into English as *Larva: Midsummer Night's Babel* (1991), is anything to go by. A devotedly massive encyclopedia of very many of the now standard tropes and tricks of postmodernist fiction, a gargantuan Son of Borges, a great intertextural tribute to *Tristram Shandy*, and an extended appropriation of *Finnegans Wake* which translates Joyce's Dublin to a contemporary London, it includes an episode that vividly supplements Virginia Woolf's narratives of crime in an Oxford Street clothing store.

Unfrocked in Oxford Street

Larva is a post-Derridian set of paired text-lines – jottings on right-hand pages supplemented by notes on accompanying left-hand pages – which are in turn supplemented by extended 'Pillow Notes' towards the back of the book. In one of these long notes, number 58, 'Sexy Black of Night', the female character Babelle tells how she went looking for her Midsummer's Eve party frock in a basement store in Oxford Street opposite the Oxford Circus tube station. Down below street level is a 'houri's paradise' of fancy textiles – 'shimmering silks tulles crepes scented sachets sheer satin formals, des soies de soirée!' And she steals a black silk number, stuffing it into her bag. Years of practice stealing books from Foyles bookshop to sell at second-hand shops further down the Charing Cross Road come in handy. 'Do I dare – I don't dare, squeezing it for all it's worth, balling it up, ça serait facile de la glisser dans mon sac, an easy slip into my bag, looking around, barely a handful, I go crazy for a moment, crumpling wadding that little silk ball. And why not? Much easier than the books, to rob a robe . . . .' The echoing of the tones and the inversion of the plot of Virginia Woolf's narration is startling (and impossible to say whether unwitting or no): 'already in the bag! In the blink of an eye I bagged an eyeful! my new evening gown in my old looting bag . . . The robe robbed my foolish five-finger discount.' But a store-detective – 'a female store-dick [Dickless Tracy?]' – has spotted the action:

> Would you mind opening your bag? that mean mannish woman in a tailored tweed suit, at the exit, holding me almost affectionately by the arm. Would you please open it. And I or she or we emptied the bag, froufrousse! that black rag with the bad tag still dangling. You didn't pay for it, did you? very slow and courteous, unfolding the evening gown. No, I haven't paid yet! She asked me to walk with her, all quite discreetly, to the elevator. Then to a messy office, please sit down, where two lackeys filed or shuffled papers. Both joking their stupid private jokes while she called the police.[11]

In keeping with the intensive inversions of detective-story tropes within (post)modernism, the heroine of Ríos's text is now the thief – just as the literal underworld, the basement store, has in fact become a metaphor for the overworld, or simply the world, thus reversing the process by which Virginia Woolf, entering the respectable world of Marshall and Snelgrove found herself suddenly in the underworld. But this place of inverted moral hierarchies is still that dramatic Woolfian interzone of wor(l)d and underwor(l)d. Specifically so, indeed. Earlier in *Larva* (on page 391) we encounter another woman, one of the numerous desired women of this text, an airline stewardess, appearing as the world-knowing, globe-carrying heroine of her airline's advertisements. 'Miss World?' Yes, but also 'Miss Word!', known to her narrator and to us through the newspaper texts she appears in, and so 'Alice in Worderland', desirable subject of the textual and urban labyrinth, 'chased Susanna of Babylondon', and, as the side-note on page 390 describes her, 'La signorina Parola', 'A letter-day saint who . . . carries you further onword . . . this ever-changing kaletterscopic lady'. But as the globe-trotting star of airline advertising texts, she's the exclusive possession neither of world nor of word; and so her (Derridianly *sous-rature*) slogan is 'the wor×d is my dream'. And Babelle is just such another wor(l)dling. Her criminal confession is, of course, self-consciously fictional, and at an extraordinary pitch of self-consciousness brought about by years of Ríos's pumping of (post)modernist iron with Sterne and Joyce and Derrida and all the rest. Her narration knows full well its fictional place: in a supplement to a brief note on an enigmatic mention of an exiguous evening gown at a moment (page 425) where male narrator and female beloved disappear into a Shandyesque square of black printers' ink labelled 'Escape into the dark'. And yet this is also a narrative located – like *Ulysses* and *Finnegans Wake* – in a named, mappable, traceable urban place, this time in Virginia Woolf's London. Oxford Street and Oxford Circus tube station, like Foyles bookshop and the Charing Cross Road and all the other places carefully named in this text are also real ones. *Larva* comes with a street plan of its *mise en scène* which comprises pages simply reproduced from the standard *A-Z* London street guide. What's more, at the end of the book comes 'Babelle's Photo Album', fifty photographs of the novel's major locations: 'Snapshots in alphabetical order of some London sites mentioned in this novel'. The alphabeticism of this text includes the *A-Z* street plan. This fiction's alphabetical ordering is happy to take in a set of documentary photographs alphabetically arranged from Battersea Park, SW11, to the *World's End* pub, SW10.

The photographic supplement to this so intensely textual – and intertextual and metatextual – fiction will be, no doubt, as scandalous to the kind of textual theory that my account has in its hostile sights as Barthes's *Camera Lucida* appears to be. These photographs might seem to stake the kind of realistic claim that is more apt to George Orwell's documentary *The Road to Wigan Pier* (1937), which appeared in its original Left Book Club edition with photographs, than to the high ground of rhetoriciety that *Larva* lays claim to. But they should be no more scandalizing than, for example, the photographs of Vita Sackville-West as 'Orlando' that appeared in the first edition of Virginia Woolf's *Orlando* (1928) or the photos that A. L. Coburn took under the careful direction of Henry James himself for frontispieces to the New York edition of the master modernist's fictions.[12] What's being illustrated in these photographs of real persons and places intended as illustrations of fictions is what Roland Barthes very properly comes around to at the end of his (and his mother's) life: namely, the intermediate nature of signs

and texts, poised between reference inwards and outwards, always stuck with
and between words and the world – nothing less than the troublingly dual
texturality of narratives.

NOTES

1   J. Hillis Miller, 'Defacing It: Hawthorne and History', in *Hawthorne and His-
    tory: Defacing It* (Blackwell, Oxford, 1991), 62ff.; 130–1, n. 9; 94; 117; and
    passim, 46–132.
2   Ibid., 110.
3   Stephen Greenblatt, 'Resonance and Wonder', in *Learning to Curse: Essays in Early
    Modern Culture* (Routledge, New York and London, 1990), 162.
4   Stephen Greenblatt, 'Shakespeare and the Exorcists', in *After Strange Texts: The
    Role of Theory in the Study of Literature*, ed. Gregory S. Jay and David L. Miller
    (University of Alabama Press, Alabama, 1985), 110. Some New Historicist work
    is, of course, neo-New Historicist in refusing to accept 'staging' as simply
    metaphorical or discursive. See e.g. *Staging the Renaissance: Reinterpretations of
    Elizabethan and Jacobean Drama,* ed. David Scott Kastan and Peter Stallybrass
    (Routledge, New York and London, 1991), particularly the editors' introduc-
    tion: 'Staging the Renaissance', 1–14.
5   Though Greenblatt, interestingly, havers in his repeated revisions of this essay.
    When it reappeared in *Shakespeare and the Question of Theory*, ed. Patricia Parker
    and Geoffrey Hartman (Methuen, New York and London, 1985), 163–87, the
    'less realism than rhetoric' had gone, though a polemic against deconstruction
    and 'the abstract purity of autonomous signification' had been added. In the
    still further revised version in Greenblatt's *Shakespearian Negotiations: The Cir-
    culation of Social Energy in Renaissance England* (Clarendon Press, Oxford, 1988),
    94–128, those very polemical additions have disappeared.
6   For a characteristically fluffing case of high deconstructive evasion of stage
    practices, see Jonathan Goldberg, *Voice Terminal Echo: Postmodernism and English
    Renaissance Texts* (Methuen, New York and London, 1986), 3: 'These characters,
    then, are little more than marks on a page assuming their life; they act out a
    version of text, stand for the production of an author engaged in his own
    disappearing act. For although Shakespearian characters embody texts – and
    have voice only in such appropriations (they are appropriated), the text that
    Shakespeare writes exists only in the simulacrum of performance.' *Simulacrum*
    (= deceptive substitute) takes us back to J. L. Austin's idea that stage utterance
    is parasitic upon off-stage talk – which so vexed Derrida. (See the whole debate
    in Jacques Derrida, *Limited Inc* (Northwestern University Press, Evanston, Ill.,
    1988).) Cf. Judd Herbert, *Metatheater: The Example of Shakespeare* (University of
    Nebraska Press Lincoln and London, 1991), an account mired desperately in the
    problematic of performance as infected by rhetorical (Austinian) performativity.
    The best published deconstructive idea about Shakespeare as text and performance,

Patricia Parker's aporetic analysis of *dilation* as both (textual) expansion and also delay in *Othello*, stands quite alone for interpretative power. Recycled – dilated, even – repeatedly (and quite properly so) it seems, though, to have generated few if any like-minded critical offspring. Patricia Parker, 'Shakespeare and Rhetoric: "Dilation" and "Delation" in *Othello*', in *Shakespeare and the Question of Theory*, 54–74; dilated in 'Deferral, Dilation, Différance: Shakespeare, Cervantes, Jonson', in *Literary Theory, Renaissance Texts*, ed. Parker (Johns Hopkins University Press, Baltimore and London, 1986), 182–209; and dilated yet again in Parker, *Literary Fat Ladies: Rhetoric, Gender, Property* (Methuen, London, 1987), esp. ch. 2: 'Literary Fat Ladies and the Generation of Text', 8ff.; and ch. 5: 'Transfigurations: Shakespeare and Rhetoric', esp. 81–5 ('Dilation and Delation by "Circumstance" ').

7   See later discussion of *bolster* in its lexicographical (and Shakespeare-editing) aspects: chapter 5, section i: 'Lexical Fix/Lexical Fics'.

8   See esp. 'On Duty with Inspector Field', *Household Words*, 14 June 1851, 265–70.

9   Alfred de Vigny, 'Desdemona's handkerchief on the French stage: "preface of 1839 to *Le More de Venise*", "letter to Lord——on his opening night of 24 October 1829 and a system of dramatic composition" ', trans. Rosanna Warren, in *Comparative Criticism: An Annual Journal*, ed. E. S. Shaffer (Cambridge University Press), 8 (1986), 244–5.

10 Jacques Derrida, *Dissemination*, trans. Barbara Johnson (University of Chicago Press, 1981), 213.

11 Julián Ríos, *Larva: Midsummer Night's Babel*, trans. Richard Alan Francis, with Suzanne Jill Levine and the author (Quartet Books, London, 1991), 525–9.

12 See Ralph F. Bogardus, *Pictures and Texts, A. L. Coburn, and New Ways of Seeing in Literary Culture*, UMI Research Press Studies in Photography, 2 (UMI Research Press, Ann Arbor, Michi., 1984), esp. ch. 2: 'So Salient a Feature: A Portfolio of the Frontispieces', 23–48.

3

History in Text and Text as History

... the realistic historical novel, about which I shall say nothing ...
Christine Brooke-Rose, 'Palimpsest History', in Umberto Eco, *Interpretation and Overinterpretation* (1992)

The particular scandal of handkerchiefs is part of the large-scale modern scandal of reference – indeed of the very large scandal of historicity. Historiography has become embarrassing. The claims of *Post-Histoire* can be found glibly posted up all over the place. Hayden White's devoted crying up of the embarrassment of traditional historical writing's claims to historicity, to veracity, to a one-to-one relationship with 'what actually happened', has made keen disciples.[1] History, as New Historicist Stephen Greenblatt has nicely put it, has lost its 'epistemological innocence' as a consequence of post-Saussurean theory. 'History cannot be divorced from textuality.'[2] And if old-school historical writings and historians are now embarrassing, how much more so are the historical novels of the past. They now look guilty on so many counts. For a start, they seem to make a dubious genre claim, pretending to special status and to the belief that there's something specially historical about their doings, a historicity that other novels might be entirely or partially without. Worse, though, their pronounced self-labelling as historical seems to deny too much to the rhetoricity of all fiction. Very noticeably, deconstructionist analysts have steered well clear of them, apparently giving them up as a bad job. Christine Brooke-Rose's theoretically cultured abstemiousness is widespread.

There's clearly a large analytical gap to jump if these 'historical' fictions are to be assimilated readily to the Hayden White view that all history-writing is only a kind of fiction production.[3] Still, James Young has taken up the Hayden White challenge with admirable moral as well as historical verve in his inspection of Holocaust writing, including 'documentary fiction'. The Holocaust being, of course, such a sharp test case, Young's argument for

an acknowledgement of the figurativeness of its narratives, alright, but also
of their historicity (Young invokes the ancient Hebrew concept of 'what was
– was') inevitably has things rather easy. And the major examples Young
takes – D. M. Thomas's novel *The White Hotel* (1981) and Peter Weiss's play
about the Auschwitz trials *The Investigation* (English version of *Die Ermittlung*,
(1965), trans. A. Gross, 1966) – do rather make for easy pickings: the one
simply transcribing huge chunks of report from Anatoli Kuznetsov's docu-
ment-novel *Babi Yar*, the other using actual words from the Frankfurt
proceedings of 1964–5. The lines between the more or less factual (words
respecting what happened as it was directly experienced) and the more or less
imagined, narrativized, ideologically processing (words recasting, fictionalizing what is said to have happened) are in the Thomas and Weiss texts fairly
clear. And Young comes to no startling conclusions either, merely endorsing
old assumptions about the Novel's traditional blend of facticity and fictionality
in its devoted figuring of the Real which go back to the roots of English
fiction in the pages of Daniel Defoe.[4] Still, Young has realized that the
pronounced interest in history in historical novels, and these novels' manifest
work of blurring distinctions between so-called historical writing and fiction,
do make them of peculiar interest in any debate about fictionality and history,
and, for that matter, about the rhetoricity of historiography.

I prefer to take an older and less obvious example, Thomas Hardy's *The
Trumpet-Major* (1880). This seems as good a test case as any for the classic
historical novel, which is to say a test case for the strong profession of interest
in history, in being historical, by what is manifestly also a fiction. Even
before deconstruction came along *The Trumpet-Major* had had a bad press,
downgraded by a critical orthodoxy which has seen it as charming enough
pastoral stuff but not up to the powers of the Big Five, those far less pro-
nouncedly 'historical' of Hardy's fictions that box it in chronologically – *Far
from the Madding Crowd* (1874) and *Return of the Native* (1878) before it and
The Mayor of Casterbridge (1886), *Tess of the D'Urbervilles* (1891), and *Jude the
Obscure* (1896) after it. It's usually been taken as one of the obviously lesser
novels.[5]

And even those critics who have seen themselves as sticking up rather
more vigorously for *The Trumpet-Major* by actually praising its originality as
an historical novel have tended to hedge their enthusiasm by thinking of it
mainly as an early, feebler push at the epic matter of the Napoleonic era that
the long poetic text *The Dynasts* would later do more grandly. This is an
assessment incited by Hardy himself. He often encouraged slighting
judgements of his work in his Prefaces, and his Preface to *The Dynasts* talks
self-denigratingly of his having only dabbled in his novel – of 'having touched
the fringe of a vast international tragedy without being able, through limits

of plan, knowledge, and opportunity, to enter further into its events'. Would-be defenders of the importance of the historical material in *The Trumpet-Major* cannot even look to Hardy for encouragement. And now, of course, much poststructuralist theory would endorse the old denigration on large theoretical grounds.

But *The Trumpet-Major* is not so easily degradable, not even with the support of recent arguments suspicious of any kind of historical writing. *The Trumpet-Major* seems to me, rather, to grab attention for itself on several important counts: as a novel in serious contention with Hardy's Big Five, as an historical text that simply outdoes *The Dynasts* (which seems to me a much more awkwardly contrived, unflinchingly embarrassing, and generally dismaying version of the Napoleonic age), and as an historically based fiction that problematizes the relationship between textuality and history in dynamically provocative and exemplary ways.

Scrutineering

Textuality first. To a quite astonishing degree, *The Trumpet-Major* foregrounds – as they say – the business of perception, making sense, interpreting, reading.[6] What Hardy's people do most of is look at others and be looked at in turn. Everyone here is a scrutineer. Everyone gets scrutinized. They are all constantly engaged in acts of reading: literal reading of books and newspapers and letters and other publications, and metaphorical reading – that is, sense-making activities which in their interpretative busyness are emblems and analogies of reading. Hardy himself was, we know, a lifelong eavesdropper, a confirmed voyeur, a man who (as one early reviewer put it) 'sees more than others', who famously expressed the hope in his poem 'Afterwards' that he would be remembered after his death for what he prided himself in life as being noticeable for – the one who 'used to notice'. Hardy was forever wielding the family's old ship's telescope that his father for his own part had tirelessly deployed before him. Hardy stuffed his writings with the apparatuses and appurtenances of seeing and spying – eye-glasses, spy-glasses, spectacles, optical devices of all sorts. He was obsessed with the most recent instruments of visual reproduction such as cameras and magic lanterns. So it's not surprising that his characters should use their eyes so much. But the extent of visual activity in Hardy's texts still strikes one as extraordinary. There would be, simply, little left in *The Trumpet-Major* if every scene in which seeing goes on as the primary activity were removed.

Everywhere the characters stare and watch and survey and glance and peep and pry and peer and squint and catch (or decline to catch) one another's eyes. Human intercourse in these pages is primarily visual. 'Mrs Garland wanted to catch her daughter's eye . . . But Anne's eye was not to be caught'; 'The young women . . . glanced round towards the encampment from the corners of their blue and brown eyes' (ch. 2); 'the door opened about an inch, and a strip of decayed face, including the eye . . . appeared'; ' "Well, nephy . . . ?" said the farmer, looking dubiously at Festus from under one eyelid. "You see how I am" ' (ch. 6): that's how life is conducted in this novel. The eyes have it. All Hardy's attractive women attract attention to their eyes, even quiet Anne of the 'thoughtful' eyes. The reader is never allowed to lose interest in what the characters' eyes are turned upon. What the characters are being made to observe is what the reader is allowed to focus on. The beginnings of a modernist fiction that will be transmitted only through the perceptions of subjective and therefore unreliable narrators – the essence of Henry James's great fictional art – are astir here. Deliberately and self-consciously the Hardy text keeps surveying its scenes with and through the eyes of some actual or implied onlooker. 'Though nobody seemed to be looking on but the few at the window and in the village street, there were, as a matter of fact, many eyes converging upon that military arrival in its high and conspicuous position, not to mention the glances of birds and other wild creatures. Men in distant gardens, women in orchards and at the cottage doors, shepherds on remote hills, turnip-hoers in blue-green enclosures miles away, captains with spy-glasses out at sea, were regarding the picture.' That's a fine, but not extreme, example from the novel's opening chapter. Defining the angle and the mode of vision is simply normal in this novel. And the detail of what's seen is usually intense too.

Take the scene in chapter 4 at the miller's little fest for his son John and his military cronies. 'Those among the guests who first attracted the eye were the sergeants and sergeant-majors of Loveday's regiment.' The eye of the implied observer is, as usual, busily and self-consciously at work. It's also characteristic of Hardy's method that the means of vision should be so dwelt on. These particular men strike the implied gazer's eye because they sit 'facing the candles'. Hardy's favourite activity is to bring people and things into vision and focus just like this. His text keeps contriving sights, views, scenes, keeps making something or some person visible, just for a moment or for some longer time. As Virginia Woolf put it, enthusiastic about an activity in Hardy that would be the essence of her own fictional effort, 'His own word, "moments of vision", exactly describes those passages of astonishing beauty and force . . . a single scene breaks off from the rest . . . Vivid to the eye.' To be sure, Virginia Woolf went on to declare that the scenes she was most interested in were not vivid 'to the eye alone'; but she was undoubtedly right about the force of the moments of vision.[7] Hardy's great scenic splendours grow out of his regular, even banal, habit – almost a reflex or tic – of the set, sighted, picked-out, framed scene.

Framing the Seen

And as Hardy's most visionary moments do, these recurrent, habitual, bread-and-butter moments of seeing rely regularly on some stated device of lighting, such as those candles of chapter 4. It is always lighting-up time in this novel. The sources of light vary. Frequently they're natural ones, like the sunlight that illuminates the great royal military review in chapter 12 or the dawn that shows off John Loveday's splendid gear in chapter 11 ('the blue and the yellow and the gold of Loveday's uniform again became distinct; the sun bored its way upward, the fields, the trees, and the distant landscape kindled to flame, and the trumpet-major, backed by a lilac shadow as tall as a steeple, blazed in the rays like a very god of war') or the sunlight cruelly offering Matilda's ageing features for our cynical inspection (ch. 16) and tempting John's and Anne's variously controlled expressions into some sort of self-betrayal (ch. 38 and 39). But as if to emphasize that no lighting effect in a fiction is ever completely natural, Hardy also makes great use of artificial means of illumination like those candles of chapter 4. Thus Bob's battle scars are revealed when 'a candle is thrust against' his cheek (ch. 39). In the same chapter Bob pursues Ann with the candle that will be the means of his (and our) seeing her emotional turmoil. Budmouth (Weymouth) becomes strangely visible at night because of all the 'lanterns, lamps, and candles' that are lit there in expectation of the King's arrival (ch. 11). And the impression of contrivance is increased when these artificially lit scenes come framed – especially by window-frames.

Anne, for example, is watched by lovesick John (ch. 21) as he lurks about the mill for a glimpse of his beloved by night:

> he watched the lights in the different windows till one appeared in Anne's bedroom, and she herself came forward to shut the casement, with the candle in her hand. The light shone out upon the broad and deep mill-head, illuminating to a distinct individuality every moth and gnat that entered the quivering chain of radiance stretching across the water towards him, and every bubble or atom of froth that floated into its width. She stood there for some time looking out, little thinking what the darkness concealed on the other side of that wide stream; till at length she closed the casement, drew the curtains, and retreated into the room. Presently the light went out.

Again, on the night of 'The Alarm' (ch. 26), we are allowed to see old Derriman's face as he spies from an upstairs window on Festus, who is preparing to move off to do battle, because of 'the distant light of the beacon fire touching up his features to the complexion of an old brass clock-face'. Nothing could be more clearly rigged than these moments of visibility. And in fact, so many views through windows outwards from rooms, and through windows into rooms, not to mention views through doorways both inwards and outwards, have been laid on in this novel that it might be supposed that here was another clear example of that clumsiness of touch, that refusal to leave a good thing well alone (what T. S. Eliot complained of in *After Strange Gods* as Hardy's incapacity to resist giving 'one last turn of the screw himself' to his fiction's doings) that readers find so embarrassing in Hardy.[8] And there *is* something more than a mite heavy-handed in this zeal for obvious framing of scenes. Naturalistically speaking, all this coincidence of the right people at the right window with the right lighting arrangements and at times so convenient to the plot and the reader's need to know is highly improbable. It's simply hard to believe that any group of people with jobs to do and busy lives to lead would spend so much time looking out of, and being looked at through, windows, as do the people in this novel. But another explanation suggests itself. The accumulation of the device can be read less as the result of Hardy's heedlessness, carelessness in revision, or silly overdoing, and rather as a deliberate signalling to the reader of a much more than simply naturalistic interest in the processes of seeing and in what is happening in these epistemological transactions at the thresholds of vision. From the moment in this novel's development when chapter 1 lost its original neutral title in the manuscript – 'Account of One of the Principal Young Persons' – and got turned into 'What was seen from the Window overlooking the Down', we can be fairly certain that Hardy had become conscious that his numerous window scenes were carrying something more than straightforwardly realistic, plot-furthering significances. It certainly became easier after that for readers to suppose that he actually knew that at this repetitious series of moments he was compiling a sequence of locations where his favourite textual and, more than that, his favourite metatextual investigation into the business of perception, and in the end, of reading itself, could proceed.

And the window-framed, door-framed scenes are not the end of this kind of matter. In a novel which has an actress as a main character and draws for historical reasons on the theatrical life of Weymouth and the doings of a theatrically devoted Royal Family, the framed, illuminated scene is, on occasion, quite naturally, a literally staged one. In chapter 30, 'At the Theatre Royal', Anne and Bob watch a performance in which Matilda has a small part. But, characteristically of this novel, there are other performances to be watched as well. The Royal Family is also on show ('the King had appeared in his place, which was overhung by a canopy of crimson satin fringed with gold'). So too, unbeknown to himself, is John Loveday, watched by Bob and Anne to see if any change of expression will reveal which actress he's fond of: ' "we can see him", replied Anne, "and notice by his face which of them it is he is so charmed with. The light of that corner candle falls right upon his cheek." ' What's more, Bob and Anne and John (who didn't, as a matter of fact, know in advance that Matilda was to be in the show) are all being watched from the stage by the observed Matilda herself: 'The trumpet-major, though not prominently seated, had been seen by Matilda already, who had observed still more plainly her old betrothed and Anne in the other part of the house.' The whole scene is a highly theatrical, hepped-up version of the watcher–watched arrangement that Hardy is so extremely fond of in this text and elsewhere. And clearly, while most of the actors in this novel are not on a literal, metonymic stage, many of them are placed metaphorically on one. John, for instance, pretending not to love Anne, is called a 'counterfeiter', and as he walked he 'threw fictitiousness into his very gait' (ch. 28). Later on (ch. 37) he confesses to Anne that his claim to have loved Matilda 'was all make-up'; 'I had an idea you were acting,' she replies. But John is also being made to act a part even when he's unconscious of it, as in the Theatre Royal. So is Bob, in full naval rig in chapter 39 ('Bob Loveday struts up and down'), dramatically framed in the window of Anne's upstairs 'chamber': 'Well, he was a pretty spectacle, she admitted . . . and if she could care for him one bit, which she couldn't, his form would have been a delightful study, surpassing in interest even its splendour on the memorable day of their visit to the town theatre.'

Moreover, the theatrically framed scenes shade over into the painterly frame. Hardy is most keen to work into his story references to Anne's late father having been a landscape-painter (a result of Hardy's developing thought in this novel: his first idea was that old Garland should be a schoolmaster). Little John Loveday had wanted to learn painting from the old painter (ch. 3). John's preference for a uniform and a horse as against 'a dirty, rumbling flourmill' had been widely admired in the locality as evidence of this 'artistic taste' (ch. 13). Captain Hardy turns out to have one of old Garland's village scenes hanging on his wall (ch. 33). And though Bob's efforts in painting her summer-house are put down by the landscape-painter's knowing daughter ('But perhaps not quite so much art is demanded to paint a summer-house as to paint a picture?': ch. 22), the novel's ordinary lives do keep being presented as if in paintings. Bob himself, home from the sea, is 'of such a rich complexion by exposure to ripening suns that he might have been some connection of the foreigner who calls his likeness the Portrait of a Gentleman in galleries of the Old Masters' (ch. 15). The clothes of John Loveday's soldier-chums produce striking effects 'chromatically' (ch. 4). When Miller Loveday appears (ch. 3) to invite Anne and her mother to his son's home-coming festivity and mentions the late landscape-painter's 'lovely picters', he makes a not unpretty picture himself in 'his blue coat, yellow and red waistcoat with the three lower buttons unfastened, steel-buckled shoes and speckled stockings'.

Little Boxes

Nor is this sort of presentation the end of the novel's busy roster of analogies for textual presentation. Great play is made not just with things and people illuminated, framed, staged and painted, but also with things taken from boxes and drawers – models of the business of revelation and disclosure that readers have traditionally expected novels to indulge in. These repeated acts of disclosure – Anne unlocking her 'receptacle for emotional objects of small size' (ch. 14; it's 'a little drawer' in chapter 10) and taking out the lock of once treasured hair and burning it; the packages, the bird-cages wrapped in cloth, the seaman's chest and its 'queer little caskets' that are opened up to disgorge the exotic presents Bob brings home from abroad (ch. 15); the private apartments of Widow Garland and Anne that are broken into and knocked through when Mrs Garland marries the miller ('The door burst open, and Bob stood revealed on the other side, with the saw in his hand': ch. 22); the whole serio-comic drama involving Squire Derriman's deed-box and the sealed paper containing its secret location that was entrusted to Anne's short-lived safe keeping – all these should be taken as strong emblems of that revealing of hitherto secreted informations that all writing and read-ing have traditionally been thought anxious to effect.

And, of course, all these analogues of textual activity, these moments that are metaphoric of what reading and writing are about, are present in a text just stuffed – as Hardy's novels frequently are – with literal texts, and intertextual tradings with texts, of all sorts: epistles galore; newspapers; quotations openly taken from the Bible and the Book of Common Prayer and Shakespeare and Dickens and from Hardy's historical sources for the period (such as that extended notice about invasion pinned to a tree in chapter 23); textual stuff lifted less openly from other men's books, such as the material that caused Hardy to be accused of plagiarism in chapter 23;[9] words re-worked from earlier writing of Hardy's own; Bob's marriage licence (ch. 22); as well as that whole cache of secreted documents in the tin box that passes through the novel like some grotesque parody of Poe's 'The Purloined Letter'.

There's also the sealed note about the whereabouts of that tin box that Anne loses and Matilda finds, and old Derriman's distracted diagram of the location of the box drawn in the dust of the road ('Festus was curious enough to descend and look at the marks. They represented an oblong, with two semi-diagonals, and a little square in the middle. Upon the diagonals were the figures 20 and 17, and on each side of the parallelogram stood a letter signifying the point of the compass': ch. 28). And there's the set of calculations scrawled behind the mill door (ch. 2):

> Behind the mill door, and invisible to the mere wayfarer who did not visit the family, were chalked addition and substraction sums, many of them originally done wrong, and the figures half rubbed out and corrected, noughts being turned into nines, and ones into twos. These were the miller's private calculations. There were also chalked in the same place rows and rows of strokes like open palings, representing the calculations of the grinder, who in his youthful ciphering studies had not gone so far as Arabic figures.

Almost Nothing

The novel is certainly, one way or another, focusing continually upon the graphic matters of reading and writing. It is most devotedly about the textual and intellective processes that are central to the production and existence of any fiction. And it is equally noticeable that these heaped-up examples of the textual keep anticipating some sort of difficulty or failure in the business of writing and reading. Textuality in this novel is constantly under threat, and a matter of threat. What is enclosed in the framed scene frequently carries some hint of incipient anguish, or is the occasion of present anguish. Even – perhaps especially – the most splendid and memorable sights in *The Trumpet-Major*, the regal and soldierly panoramas of chapters 11 and 12, a great patriotic drama that's laid on for the affirmation of the people's loyal enthusiasms for King and Country (' "Thank God, I have seen my King!" said Mrs Garland'), are exposed as a set of views and reviews laid on to allure, but also to lull, the citizenry at home with their attempt at glossing the slaughters abroad that this spectacular ceremonial is in reality a preparation for.

Momentarily, the soldiery is granted a part in the abiding rural scene that frames its manoeuvres:

> It was a clear day with little wind stirring, and the view from the downs, one of the most extensive in the county, was unclouded. The eye of any observer who cared for such things swept over the wave-washed town, and the bay beyond, and the Isle, with its pebble bank, lying on the sea to the left of these,

like a great crouching animal tethered to the mainland. On the extreme east of the marine horizon, St Aldelm's Head closed the scene, the sea to the southward of that point glaring like a mirror under the sun. Inland could be seen Badbury Rings, where a beacon had been recently erected; and nearer, Rainbarrow, on Egdon Heath, where yet another stood: further to the left Bulbarrow, where there was yet another. Not far from this came Nettlecombe Tout; to the west, Dogberry Hill, and Black'on near to the foreground, the beacon thereon being built of furze faggots thatched with straw.

But already the familiar natural scene is seeded with the beacons which, when lit, will turn the landscape into a semiotic of alarms and distress. What's more, the gorgeous splendours enclosed in this proleptically distressing geography are themselves transitory: 'the King and his fifteen thousand armed men, the horses, the bands of music, the princesses, the cream-coloured teams – the gorgeous centre-piece, in short, to which the downs were but the mere mount or margin – how entirely they have all passed and gone! – lying scattered about the world as military and other dust.' It's Hardy's serious version of Humpty-Dumpty's fall – when all the King's horses and all the King's men couldn't put Humpty together again. And this great public and national vision of human loss implicit in what the dramatic and pictorial scene unfolds and what the illuminated moment reveals is backed by all the private occasions on which a similar vision is granted to the lowly characters whose small-time existences are caught up, in times like the novel's, in the national drama. The most moving of these is in chapter 34, where Anne climbs effortfully up Portland Bill in order to catch a last glimpse of Bob's ship, the famous flagship of Horatio Lord Nelson, the *Victory*, as it sails off to war (there's a lot of climbing up onto physical heights and promontories in this novel, as in other Hardy fictions, in order to secure some better look at a passing event).

This is most extraordinary scene on any reckoning. It is comparable with some of the greatest moments in early modernist novels by Conrad and James and Virginia Woolf (as discussed in my opening chapter, and later in chapter 5, section i: 'Lexical Fix'), when the difficulties of some observer seeking to make out things and people and meanings at some watery edge are made exemplary of the whole narrative, linguistic, textual problematic that modernist scepticism is anxious to bring to the reader's attention. Portland Bill is a blank text of a place – 'scarce a mark was visible to show that humanity had ever been near the spot'. The surrounding sea with its specks of boats is deterringly difficult to read: 'the tremulous expanse of water . . . seemed to utter a ceaseless unintelligible incantation.' Anne's vision is directed by a knowledgeable old sailor; she's thus enabled to position herself more

correctly so as to 'unclose to her view' the right bit of sea and then 'discover'
the ship she seeks. Even then her unaided sight is insufficient. The sailor has
a spy-glass. However, his 'sight is so gone off lately that things, one and all,
be but a November mist to me', and he can nowadays see 'Almost nothing'.
So Anne takes over his telescope, rests it upon the old man's arm, describes
to him the ship she is then able to discern, and the sailor confirms that it's
the *Victory*. Thus the near-blind leads the myopic by gradual, limping stages
to some sort of vision. But certainty and confidence in alleged fullness of
vision do not last long. Anne asks the sailor whether he is '*sure* it is the *Victory* ?'
In any case she cannot actually see her Bob, only picture 'him on the upper
deck, in his snow-white trousers and jacket of navy blue, looking perhaps
towards the very point of land where she then was'. The ship is hard to read
with certainty, partly because (like a painting and the river-bank scene in *The
Ambassadors* and the jungle in 'Heart of Darkness') it is 'silent'. It is said to
be ghostly, passing 'like a phantom'. As it crosses Anne's gaze and passes into
the distance, its shape alters disconcertingly – like the clouds whose variable
interpretability ('very like a whale') Hamlet mocks Polonius with: 'Sometimes
her aspect was that of a large white bat, sometimes that of a grey one . . . the
breadth of her sails diminished by foreshortening, till she assumed the form
of an egg on end.' There is still light of a kind to see it by: the sun 'twinkles'
on the cabin windows at the ship's stern. But the illumination and so the
perception must finally fade:

> The courses of the *Victory* were absorbed into the main, then her topsails went,
> and then her top-gallants. She was now no more than a dead fly's wing on a
> sheet of spider's web; and even this fragment diminished. Anne could hardly
> bear to see the end, and yet she resolved not to flinch. The admiral's flag sank
> behind the watery line, and in a minute the very truck of the last topmast stole
> away. The *Victory* was gone.

And as if to confirm the implicit textual bearing of this frustration of vision,
of reading, Anne, with her 'wet eyes' still fixed on the 'vacant' horizon,
unwittingly speaks out loud some words from the Bible – Psalm 107, a
passage prominent in the *Book of Common Prayer*'s 'Forms of Prayer to be Used
at Sea': ' "They that go down to the sea in ships, that do business in great
waters――." ' And to further seal in the reader's mind the textuality and
intertextuality of the moment, John Loveday, who has come up behind her
in improbable silence, caps her quotation: ' "These see the works of the Lord,
and His wonders in the deep." '

The moment is said to be a 'solemn' one. And it's solemn not least for
Hardy's persistent hermeneutical investigations. This strong and exemplary

emptying of certainty from Anne's vision, the filling up of the frame of the picture, the optical moment, with confusing epistemological blur and negativity, and then the final collapse into ultimate hermeneutical blankness, powerfully focus all the other, though related, difficulties clustering about this novel's moments of vision.

Seemings

The Trumpet-Major never lets us forget that Hardy was a writer who was very early on captivated by moments when sunlight got filtered and his vision was in consequence partially occluded.

> One event . . . stood out, he used to say, more distinctly than any. He was lying on his back in the sun, thinking how useless he was, and covered his face with his straw hat. The sun's rays streamed through the interstices of the straw, the lining having disappeared. Reflecting on his experiences of the world so far as he had got, he came to the conclusion that he did not wish to grow up . . . but to remain as he was, in the same spot.

And even though he did grow up, his autobiography, *The Life of Thomas Hardy 1840–1928* (1928–30) – he pretended his wife had written it – keeps on siting him in this childish position: it might be with the 'yellow sun shining in on the drab paint through the skylight, through which also came the faint notes of a brass band' as, one August time, he awaits his Baptist friends in the vestry of Dorchester Baptist chapel; or sitting one September under the trailing tendrils of the stable-wall vine just after *The Trumpet-Major* came out, correcting the text of his novel *A Laodicean*, with the sun trying 'to shine through the great leaves, making a green light on the paper'. No wonder Hardy becomes a connoisseur of weird lighting effects.

He was attracted by the strange lights and optical illusions commonly associated with battlefields.[10] He was (of course!) the employee deputed by Blomfield the architect to make sure during the building of the Midland Railway through London that the removal of coffins, being discreetly effected after dark in the Old St Pancras Churchyard, was done decently: he went every night to inspect this lurid transferring of dilapidated coffins and rotting corpses 'by the light of the flare-lamps'. Naturally, too, Hardy was just the man to volunteer to hold a candle while the coroner performed an autopsy in a lonely cottage one dark December evening in 1877. Hardy's practice and advocacy of 'impressions' and 'seemings' in his own writing was, equally naturally, backed by a keen admiration for Turner's 'maddest and greatest'

pictures, the ones producing 'strange mixtures' – 'pictorial drug(s)', Hardy
called them – out of their wrestle with 'the impossibility of really reproducing on canvas all that is in a landscape', the paintings that led Hardy to
conclude that 'Art is the secret of how to produce by a false thing the effect
of a true.' The precariousness of sight was one good reason, Hardy's friend
Moule once warned him, for going in for writing and not relying on architecture for a living – advice brought home to Hardy 'one morning shortly
after by his seeing, for the first time in his life, what seemed like floating
specks on the white drawing-paper before him'. And Hardy evidently warms
in his wry way to the old man he encountered in 1882 on The Cobb at Lyme,
much as Anne met the myopic old sailor on Portland Bill, who had had an
operation for cataract – 'like a red-hot needle', it was – but only on one of
his bad eyes: 'I've saved half-crowns and half-crowns out of number in only
wanting one glass to my spectacles. T'other eye would never have paid the
expenses of keeping en going.'

These deficiencies and spottinesses of perception that Hardy keeps celebrating in the *Life,* the result of working with the crazed-over and wonky
lens of a gothic, Turnerian impressionism, infect *The Trumpet-Major* no less
than they do all of Hardy's more esteemed writings. Those specks floating on
the architect's drawing-paper turn up as 'A Speck on the Sea' (to quote the
title of chapter 34) or as the travellers reduced to ant-like dimensions on the
road to Weymouth when viewed from the top of the Downs (ch. 12): 'like
an ant-walk – a constant succession of dark spots creeping along its surface'
(a 'microscopic spectacle' consisting of specks, 'rattling dots', figures 'about
the size of a pin's head', whose physical and social diminution is emphasized
by contrast with the grander 'portraits and histories' that Anne's fanciful
'painting' turns them into in the serial version of the novel).[11] What shed light
reveals is often something grim like the scars on Bob's face or John's steely
pose of indifference or Matilda's true age under her make-up. The theatre is
a place of painful realizations, and stage-fire, as it were, lights up mainly
pretence (which is, of course, how *hypocrisy* got its bad reputation in the first
place). As often as not, the very means of illumination taunts the observer
by the feebleness of the lights it casts. The moon, for instance, in chapter 2,
obscures as much of the camp as it lights up: from her window, Anne makes
out 'the white cones of the encampment . . . softly touched' by moonlight;
the 'quarter-guard and foremost tents showed themselves prominently; but
the body of the camp, the officers' tents, kitchens, canteen, and appurtenances
in the rear were blotted out'. John can see Anne and Bob, but only 'acquainted
by the weak moon and mist', in chapter 28. And, of course, the illumination
from candles, and beacons, moonlight, and sunlight is always and inevitably
very short-lived. What's more, optical aids are commonly unreliable. The

first soldiers Anne and the reader see in chapter 1 appear as if they're covered all over in little looking-glasses — aids to vision and reflection — because the 'burnished chains, buckles, and plates of their trappings shone' so much. But in chapter 32, Bob's very similar reflective accoutrements have got dimmed by night dampness; 'there was a foggy film upon the mirror-like buttons of his coat': that sort of illumination is soon polished off. Again, old Granny Seamore's spectacles (ch. 8) are as prone to betray her as the old seaman's telescope is useless to him on Portland Bill.

> Shaking her head at Anne till the glasses shone like two moons, she said, 'Ah, ah; I zeed ye! If I had only kept on my short ones that I use for reading the Collect and Gospel I shouldn't have zeed ye; but thinks I, I be going out o'doors, and I'll put on my long ones, little thinking what they'd show me. Ay, I can tell folk at any distance with these — 'tis a beautiful pair for out o'doors; though my short ones be best for close work, such as darning, and catching fleas, that's true.'

But she's still mistaken about the relationship between Anne and Festus that she's so proud of her long-distance glasses for having revealed to her.

Not dissimilarly, the protracted drama over Squire Derriman's strong-box proves that it's not always easy to extract things and meanings from boxes and envelopes (and books) just when you wish to. The enigmas of personal lives and pent-up secret histories like Anne's are not for cracking open as easily as Bob's knocking the wall of the apartment down. This novel submits in the end to the convention that its people and plot should be made clear, but not all the contents of its secreting drawers are to be emptied just by tugging at them. When Bob arrives home, the good citizens gathered at the mill welcome him 'by pulling out his arms like drawers'. But they also 'shut them again' and hold 'him at arm's length as if he were of too large a type to read close'. And whilst all the novel's visions across window-sills and doorsteps signal the possibility of meanings being transferred across the perilously difficult border zones between people and people, people and things, word and world, sign and referent, the precarious and frustrating nature of such transactions is also frequently stressed. Those calculations of the grinder and miller scrawled on the back of the mill door are full of errors, rubbings-out, would-be corrections, and other signs of scant skill in numbering. Access in chapter 6 to the inner fastnesses of Squire Derriman's rambling mildewed place, on her way to collect the one neighbourhood newspaper, is for Anne a sequence of most awkward threshold negotiations: the wooden hurdles across the arched gateway, another hurdle across a second and tauntingly open door (it possesses no knocker), a passage, then an inner door which opens only 'about an inch' — all the cumulative measures of the Squire's fears about thieves, the French, and Festus's trustworthiness. Mrs Garland misreads her daughter's relationship with John and Festus by mistaking the one for the other from her window (ch. 8). In chapter 27 Anne is pursued by Festus to a lonely cottage, threatened as she looks out of the window, and then mightily dismayed by Festus's attacks on the boundaries of her sanctuary. She has to watch, peeping over the window-sill as he, frustrated by the barred door, tries to prize apart the shutters' boards with his sword. (Hardy didn't have to wait for Freud to inform him that such thresholds were symptomatic of sexual boundaries. Festus is still sexually sore about his earlier tumble crossing the frail bridge over the brook when he was chasing after Anne (ch. 25). Hardy hesitated with prurience over which woman should kiss the sleeping Bob in the stream under the bridge when the Press Gang was after him. Streams carry a keen sexual charge in *Tess* and *Jude*.[12] Here Anne 'could see by the livid back of his neck' that Festus 'was brimful of suppressed passion'.)

Making Out the Penmanship

And the problematics of the border where meanings are negotiated between subject and object, observer and observed, reader and text, are made absolutely explicit when some piece of literal reading is under way. Festus is 'able to make nothing' of his uncle's diagram traced in the dust (just as in Woolf's *Jacob's Room*, where Jacob's diagram of the Parthenon traced in the dust of the Park is variously interpretable in numerous conflicting ways). The art of letters is an enigma to the semi-literate miller and his cronies. The scarcity of epistles in their lives increases the status of letters as puzzle. They're thought to be full of deterring 'hieroglyphs' that pose advanced problems in 'deciphering'. The right 'slanting' and 'snuffing' of the candle needs supplementing by Mrs Garland's assistance and the neighbours' opinions when the miller endeavours to cope with Bob's missive (ch. 14). Hardy enjoys himself mightily over the rustics' plodding ways with this rare piece of literature. The miller seems 'disposed to let off his feelings by examining thoroughly into the fibres of the letter-paper': ' "Well, since she's coming we must make her welcome. Did any of ye catch by my reading which day it is he means? What with making out the penmanship, my mind was drawn off from the sense here and there." ' But an extremely serious sense of problem attaching to the business of writings and readings is present even at such comically semiliterate moments.

Plights of various sorts pervade the novel's many moments of reading. Letters go wrong for people. That letter from Bob has arrived late: the sailor will arrive any moment; Uncle Benjy Derriman gets crushed in the miller's over-excitement; the news of Bob's fondness for Matilda Johnson contained in the letter is terribly distressing to Anne; and so on. Later on, in chapter 24, Anne realizes that her letter asking John's forgiveness is liable to be misunderstood; but it has already been sent off without her knowledge. Anne soon loses old Derriman's letter with the deed-box location inside it (lost letters are often crucial like this to Hardy's plots). Matilda picks it up, but is 'Unable to make anything of its meaning' (ch. 25). Loss is compounded by textual enigma. As it is when Bob is away on the *Victory* (ch. 35): Anne scours the available newspapers for any 'fragment' of shipping news, but in vain; news leaks out about General Mack's surrender (Anne is 'depressed'; 'old misgivings as to invasion' are 'revived'); the stage-coaches roll through, 'chalked with the words "Great Victory!", "Glorious Triumph!" and so on', but no particulars are granted; 'suspense' mounts at the mill as 'a rough list of the numbers' of casualties is issued; the 'final and revised list of killed and wounded' is 'a useless sheet' because only officers are on it; 'letters from survivors began to appear in the public prints', but not one from Bob; John 'watched the mails with unceasing vigilance', but 'there was never a letter from Bob'. When a letter from him at last arrives (after Anne has abandoned reading those uninformative newspapers), it's 'a meagre line' only. The flaws in epistles and newspapers as means of communication could not be more bitterly felt by the Lovedays and Anne.

Texts tend in this novel to waste their readers' time, to turn into waste matters – like Bob's marriage licence (ch. 22), a document 'nullified' when Matilda disappears from the scene: 'Beautiful language' – even though these beauties are not construable by the miller ('That's not the point, father! You never could see the real meaning') – emptied of sense: 'But why should I read on? It all means nothing now – nothing, and the splendid words are all wasted upon air.' Writings monger distress – like Anne's troubles with Festus which result from her newspaper-reading visits to Squire Derriman, or John (observed by Bob through the window in chapter 29) evincing in private his real, gloomy feelings as he 'took' Anne's 'letter from his breast-pocket, opened it, and, with a tender smile at his weakness, kissed the writing before restoring it to its place', or John's pain ('When he had read a few words he turned as pale as a sheet': ch. 37) as Bob's letter informs him that he will return to reclaim Anne. This letter later 'crackled warningly' in John's pocket (ch. 38) as if to caution him not to get too fresh with Anne. In the same chapter another letter arrives announcing Bob's recent promotion to lieutenant and so new eligibility for marriage. John throws it in some despair into Anne's lap. She, consternated in turn by the news, throws it away unlooked at. Masochistically, like the moral hero he is, John then gets hold of 'the nearest pen-and-ink' to warn Bob to come and claim Anne 'post-haste'. The speedier the mails, the more promptly will John's distresses accumulate. Truly the letter is a killer.

Textual Doom

In fact, that communal reading of Bob's letter at the mill in chapter 14 has the villagers 'as silent as relations at the reading of a will'. And most of the textual and intertextual moments of this novel spell gloom and death. The newspaper stories it reports – results of Hardy's trawling in the British Museum – are mainly about wars and rumours of war. The 'Address to All Ranks and Descriptions of Englishmen' reproduced in chapter 23 likewise threatens 'Ruin', 'Destruction', 'Pestilence', and 'Death, or worse than Death'. And just as Hardy was to draw textual authority from Greek drama about what the President of the Immortals intended for Tess, so in *The Trumpet-Major* he afforces his gloominess about letters and literacy with reference to adverse, doomy bits of other classic texts.

The unpromising nature of the mill garden as a scene for John Loveday's courtship is signalled from the start in chapter 10, 'The Match-making Virtues of a Double Garden', when this snug erotic retreat is said to be like 'the land of Lot' (living there cost Lot his wife).[13] Festus drags in the Old Testament story of the soldier-husband Uriah, disposed of in battle by King David (ch. 36). John thinks of St Paul's advice against marrying (ch. 38). Anne's favourite reading during Bob's absence (ch. 35) is 'the office for the Burial of the Dead at Sea, beginning "We therefore commit his body to the deep" '. The Christian classics speak awful tidings almost without exception throughout this novel. The novel also enjoys a curiously repetitive and equally gloomy intertextual commerce with *Hamlet*. One's not at all surprised, for example, that the progress of the unique local newspaper around the community – another, though less amusing, reminder of Poe's 'The Purloined Letter' – should be described in chapter 6 in terms that unite it with Hamlet's spry narrative of the rake's progress of the corpse of Alexander the Great, from living splendour to beer-barrel bung. When Mrs Garland, letter-writer, reader, and 'general translator from the printed tongue' to benighted villagers 'had done with the sheet' she

> passed it on to the miller, the miller to the grinder, and the grinder to the grinder's boy, in whose hands it became subdivided into half pages, quarter pages, and irregular triangles, and ended its career as a paper cap, a flagon bung, or a wrapper for his bread and cheese.

Beyond Textuality

Textuality here spells mortality. But, equally clearly, mortality is never merely textual. And neither is this novel. In that great scene on Portland Bill in chapter 34, the *Victory* and its Captain Hardy and 'the admiral who was not to return alive' are of course textualized, made part of a fiction's system of signification, of a text's encoded semiotic. They are even part of an arresting metatextual demonstration of perception's difficulties and of fiction's condition as a mere preamble to blankness. But, like Portland Bill itself, the ship and its famous sailors are more than this; they are all at once historical as well as fictional; they are part of a real, given, historical world, as well as incorporated into a made-up story; they belong to the world's domain, as well as to the region of words; the drama they enact occurs in an historical and quasi-historical narrative of events centred in and about the real Battle of Trafalgar, as well as being part of a fictional affair got up by Thomas Hardy. The text of history is woven inseparably into the fictional text. Neither text can exist separately from the other. No Nelson, *Victory* or Captain Hardy, no Bob or John Loveday. And there's an especially instructive illustration of this interdependence and interweaving in the Theatre Royal scene in chapter 30. There the play, the *Theaterspiel*, the metatextual text of fiction within our text of fiction, is twice interrupted by the intrusive texts of history – first by the arrival of despatches for the King, then by the summary of those despatches for the audience's benefit and the singing of 'Rule Britannia'. The audience switches its attention excitedly, but easily, from the drama on the theatre's stage to the drama in the Royal Box and in the ships off the Finisterre coast ('the eyes of the whole house' are 'anxiously fixed' on the King's face as he reads the papers a messenger brings him, 'for terrible events fell as unexpectedly as thunderbolts at this critical time of our history'). It's a deft switching, from fiction to history and back again, that the reader is invited continually to imitate in this novel. Indeed, it's never possible to say as firmly as this particular chapter of the novel does that the historical matter forms the merely 'parenthetic excitement' of the novel. For history and fiction are here continuously intertwined, and jointly animate Hardy's and the reader's interest.

Past Things Retold

The *we* of chapter 30 ('this critical time of our history') is by no means unusual in this text. The historical past of the novel is a time that Hardy feels himself to be stimulatingly in living touch with. For him Captain Hardy of the *Victory* was as much a local man as Bob Loveday, and vice versa. The *Life* records Hardy's personal acquaintance with the Old Royal Hotel at Weymouth, 'where George III and his daughters used to dance at the town assemblies, a red cord dividing the royal dancers from the townspeople. The sockets for the standards bearing the cord were still visible in the floor.' The historical excitements featured in the novel were ones still remembered in Hardy's childhood. They played important roles in the oral traditions of his family and neighbourhood. The *Life* tells how Hardy's grandfather was a volunteer throughout the Napoleonic scare, 'and lay in Weymouth with his company from time to time, waiting for Bonaparte who never came'. The false alarm that makes for *The Trumpet-Major*'s central tragi-comic event is the subject of Hardy's poem 'The Alarm', written 'In memory of one of the writer's family who was a volunteer during the war with Napoleon'. The *Life* also records the way the French Revolution stamped itself on the memories of his mother and grandmother:

> 'My mother says that my [paternal] grandmother told her she was ironing her best muslin gown (then worn by young women at any season) when news came that the Queen of France was beheaded. She put down her iron, and stood still, the event so greatly affecting her mind. She remembered the pattern of the gown so well that she would recognise it in a moment.' Hardy himself said that one hot and thundery summer in his childhood she remarked to him: 'It was like this in the French Revolution, I remember.'

It mattered intensely to Hardy that he had known those who knew, that he'd been pressed, as the poem 'One We Knew (M. H. 1772–1857)' describes it, into personal acquaintance with history at granny's knee:

> She would dwell on such dead themes, not as one who remembers,
> But rather as one who sees.

'Past things retold were to her as things existent.' It was important for Hardy to bolt his fiction securely into history as an experience lived by such people. He went, of course, to written documents, the newspapers of the time, the magazines, standard historical works like C. H. Gifford's *History of the Wars Occasioned by the French Revolution* (1817) and Southey's *Life of Nelson* (1813), the sort of material he carefully garnered in the library of the British Museum and set down in his Notebook. But his sense of history as consisting of the lives of real persons lived out in real time and real places led him always to supplement the public documents by the private recollections and stories of relations and other survivors. He didn't attend only to his granny.

He checked details of Captain Hardy's life in letters to the great man's daughter. He visited the Chelsea Hospital to glean the old military pensioners' memories ('extraordinary to talk and shake hands with a man' who had 'served under Sir John Moore in the Peninsula, through the Retreat, and was at Waterloo'). In short, *The Trumpet-Major* was, as Hardy's Preface has it, 'founded more largely on testimony – oral and written – than any other' of his novels.

The novel's historical matter evidently carried a variety of attractions for Hardy. He clearly revelled, for instance, in the lives of the great, the megastars of history, whom he wanted to finger in his novels as desperately as he wanted to mingle with them in his daily life. The *Life* has annoyed and embarrassed most readers by its dedicated eagerness to drop aristocratic and poetic names, despite the fact that the second Mrs Hardy pruned a lot of Hardy's keen gazetting of illustrious contacts and how many times he had bumped into Lady So-and-So. Hardy's visitors'-book pride in the company of *soi-disant* social notables was as unashamed and naïve as his relish for his supposed relatedness to Captain Hardy (and his diligent upgrading of his own humble origins in the *Life*). But this sort of social pride is also a key part of Hardy's sense of history and of the historical motivation of his novel. 'I saw L[or]d Palmerston lowered into the grave,' he notes on 27 October 1865. And Hardy isn't simply being infatuated with Peers of the Realm and Westminster Abbey obsequies. Palmerston was a personal link with the past, and political action in the past at the highest levels. Hardy would recall 'hearing Palmerston speak in the House of Commons a short time before his death, Palmerston having been War Secretary during the decisive hostilities with Napoleon embodied in' *The Dynasts*, 'a personal conjunction which brought its writer face to face not only with actual participants in the great struggle . . . but with one who had contributed to direct the affairs of that war'.

It came naturally to Hardy to wish to work into his novel the meeting of George III and Anne Garland (ch. 34) – one more revival of the old myth of The King Among His People. This was a heartfelt reflection of Hardy's patriotic version of Englishness and of the history of England, and a conjunction of the sort that he himself daily craved. Just as naturally, he sent a copy of *The Trumpet-Major* to Queen Victoria, and in 1911 offered the manuscript of the novel to the Royal Library at Windsor Castle, where it is now lodged ('Queen Victoria was interested in the book when it came out thirty years or more ago, owing to its being concerned with the times of George III at Weymouth and her Majesty thanked me for a copy which I sent her for that reason. This is why the question of presenting the ms. has arisen'). But this obsession with history's great ones was not Hardy's

over-riding concern. The *Life*'s mention of Palmerston equates Hardy's emotion at meeting the great man 'face to face' with the writer's feelings for 'his
numerous acquaintance of rank-and-file who had fought in the Peninsula and
at Waterloo'. And what suffuses *The Trumpet-Major* is Hardy's sense of his
historical novel as a democratic medium that will revive and keep alive the
memory of people like his grandfather, the men such as the 'ordinary seamen
and marines' of Bob Loveday's sort, who were of less interest to the naval
authorities of Nelson's – or anybody's – time than their officers (ch. 35). And
while these 'minor Englishmen', as they're labelled in chapter 26, fuel Hardy's
attempts at bucolic Shakespearean humour, so that his text always keeps
some distance between the reader's deepest interest and these characters of
the lower social classes, they are also afforded the very highest kind of moral
status as the human stuff on which the better-known and written-down
history of England relied for its accomplishment. One of the female camp-
followers of chapter 2, for example, 'seemed to have seen so much of the
world, and to have been in so many campaigns, that Anne would have liked
to take her into their own house, so as to acquire some of that practical
knowledge of the history of England which the lady possessed, and which
could not be got from books' (it's the kind of reflection that comes to Jude
as he opens the 'book of humanity' in the centre of unbookish, demotic
Christminster).

'Corporal Tullidge, who sported the crushed arm, and poor old Simon
Burden, the dazed veteran who had fought at Minden' (ch. 26) move Hardy
by their perennial stoicism, and move him enough to want to be himself
absorbed into this record of their representative quiet courage. The ranks of
brave but unsung English people stretch from the past, through the present,
and on into the future. And Hardy is confident about this because, looking
back on battles that had not yet happened in the time he was writing about,
he knows the kind of thing the future gets up to. These lowly endurers are
one with 'the stream', as chapter 13 puts it, of England's and humanity's
'recorded history'. They are caught up into the play of time and the runaway
progression of history that Hardy is careful to keep stressing as his narrative's
at once dizzily aweing and deeply affecting location. Time has, then, the
same hegemony over this narrative about these lives as it has over these lives
themselves:

> The present writer, to whom this party has been described times out of number
> by members of the Loveday family and other aged people now passed away,
> can never enter the old living-room of Overcombe Mill without beholding the
> genial scene through the mists of the seventy or eighty years that intervene
> between then and now. First and brightest to the eye are the dozen candles,

scattered about regardless of expense, and kept well snuffed by the miller, who walks round the room at intervals of five minutes, snuffers in hand, and nips each wick with great precision, and with something of an executioner's grim look upon his face as he closes the snuffers upon the neck of the candle. Next to the candle-light show the red and blue coats and white breeches of the soldiers – nearly twenty of them in all besides the ponderous Derriman – the head of the latter, and, indeed, the heads of all who are standing up, being in dangerous proximity to the black beams of the ceiling. There is not one among them who would attach any meaning to 'Vittoria', or gather from the syllables 'Waterloo' the remotest idea of his own glory or death. Next appears the correct and innocent Anne, little thinking what things Time has in store for her at no great distance off. (ch. 5)

History evidently matters in this text, and matters enough to impel this writer to intrude with such historical pointedness into his text. And any attempt to denigrate this novel's dealings with history, or to deny its blatant concern with things that are so extra-fictional, so extra-textual – whether from keenness on the 'death' of authors, or hostility to authorial intentions, or antagonism to texts engaging in anything but figurative trade with contextual matters, or from any other of the whole array of anti-historicist critical nostrums still current – is not only to be prevented from doing justice to *The Trumpet-Major* and to be satisfied with a partial, wrenching, lopsided reading of it; it is also to demonstrate the unsupported dogmatism and wilful narrowness of a critical prejudice. This must be said very loudly in support of Hardy's devotion to the historical subject and the historically engaged text. But, of course, this is no more the whole case than the sort of wholly textual reading that we looked at earlier in this chapter was all. It is important also, in this matter of history, to go on to notice that for Hardy the business of history and of the historical novel is inevitably a highly fraught and disconcertingly friable, fragile set of concerns. Hardy the devoted historicist is also, so to say, an anxious meta-historicist of an almost Hayden White stripe. History turns out to be scarcely more sure and certain than anything else in Hardy's world. The record of history, as Hardy apprehends it, is an eroded, defaced, dismantled one; and so the texts of history are particularly subject to all the problems of decipherment that Hardy proves texts in general to be victimized by.

The Worsted Work of History

For example, the Old Royal Hotel in which Hardy himself witnessed the traces, as it were, of the times of George III is now, at the time of writing the entry in the *Life*, 'pulled down'. The sockets Hardy once saw remained visible only 'while the building was standing'. Even as his granny was telling the past

> She seemed one left behind of a band gone distant
> So far that no tongue can hail.

And now granny is dead and gone; and though Hardy, the devoted haunter of graveyards and the designer and maker of memorializing gravestones, is busily setting down his memory of her memories, he is never unconscious of the common fate of such oral traditions. As he spelled it out in a letter to Rider Haggard in March 1902 (it's in the *Life*):

> village tradition — a vast mass of unwritten folk-lore, local chronicle, local topography, and nomenclature — is absolutely sinking, has nearly sunk, into eternal oblivion . . . [T]here being no continuity of environment in their lives, there is no continuity of information, the names, stories, and relics of one place being speedily forgotten under the incoming facts of the next. For example, if you ask one of the workfolk . . . the names of surrounding hills, streams; the character and circumstances of people buried in particular graves; at what spots parish personages lie interred; questions on local fairies, ghosts, herbs, etc., they can give no answer: yet I can recollect the time when the places of burial even of the poor and tombless were all remembered, and the history of the parish and squire's family for 150 years back known. Such and such ballads appertained to such and such a locality, ghost tales were attached to particular sites, and nooks wherein wild herbs grew for the cure of divers maladies were pointed out readily.

And, of course, this consciousness of the oral tradition's perpetual slide towards and into blanked-out emptiness has already embraced an acknowledgement of the parallel, and still more terrifying, effacement of written records: the identity of the dead lying in particular spots is lost not least because the writing on tombstones gets inevitably eroded. Sturdy memorials, stone buildings, written — even printed — records, are no certain bulwark against time's eroding activities. It's an overwhelming awareness of mutability that is the burden of the opening paragraph of the *Life* — as powerful a meditation on mutability as Hardy, or anyone else, ever wrote. Hardy writes that he was born into a scene of decay, mortality, and rot. It was a pronounced demonstration, going on all over the scene of his childhood, of the fading memorableness of the Napoleonic era — of the non-endurance of the most traumatic and dramatic set of events that the world, let alone the inhabitants of rural Dorset and Somerset, had ever known. Higher Bockhampton's inhabitants included 'retired military officers, one old navy lieutenant', and 'an old militiaman'. What happened to their houses was apt to the inhabitants' bodily decay. Dubbed 'Veterans' Valley', this set of abodes has gone: 'the quaint residences with their trees, clipped hedges, orchards, white gatepost-balls, the naval officer's masts and weather-cocks, have now perished every one.' And the old Hardy house is now a sharer in this fate: 'weather-worn and reduced . . . sand-and-gravel pits, afterwards exhausted and over-grown: also stabling and like buildings since removed; while the leaves and mould . . . have risen high against the back wall of the house, that was formerly covered with ivy. The wide, brilliantly white chimney-corner, in his child-time such a feature of the sitting-room, is also gone.'

These faded veterans get, as it were, into *The Trumpet-Major* as Simon Burden, 'the military relic' of chapter 1, digging about in his 'worm-eaten magazine of ideas' for some 'dim' recall of his soldiering days. 'Ay, I be an old man, and of no judgement now,' he says, and his bits of recollection of what the soldiers are up to as they pitch camp keep slipping from him: 'I can call to mind that there was – ah, 'tis gone from me again! However, all that's of little account now' (except of course to Anne, who dearly wants to know what's afoot, and to Hardy, and to us). And then there's decaying Corporal Tullidge with a hole in his head and 'no life' in the bones of his wounded arm, not to mention 'wizened' old Squire Derriman whose skull is visible about his eyes 'through the skin' (ch. 6), and Widow Garland with the 'ploughed-ground appearance near the corners of her once handsome eyes' (ch. 11). The novel is packed with the aged and the ageing and persons – like all the lovers in it – who are not, as people say, getting any younger. And those perishing buildings of Hardy's own life-story get into the novel as the ancient mill 'whose history is lost in the mists of antiquity' (ch. 2) and the Derriman place, Oxwell Hall – 'in a state of declension', 'rambling and neglected', 'mildewed' and worn away (ch. 6):

Mustard and cress could have been raised on the inner plaster of the dewy walls at any height not exceeding three feet from the floor; and mushrooms of the most refined and thin-stemmed kinds grew up through the chinks of the larder paving. As for the outside, Nature, in the ample time that had been given her, had so mingled her filings and effacements with the marks of human wear and tear upon the house, that it was often hard to say in which of the two or if in both, any particular obliteration had its origin. The keenness was gone from the mouldings of the doorways, but whether worn out by the rubbing past of innumerable people's shoulders, and the moving of their heavy furniture, or by Time in a grander and more abstract form, did not appear. The iron stanchions inside the window-panes were eaten away to the size of wires at the bottom where they entered the stone, the condensed breathings of generations having settled there in pools and rusted them. The panes themselves had either lost their shine altogether or become iridescent as a peacock's tail.

Everywhere the implied observer's eye travels in this novel there is the human trace and smudge – the 'worn-out millstones' set into the courtyard of the mill and the stains on the green hat of one of the military women (ch. 2), the eroded Tudor flagstones of the mill, 'worn into a gutter by the ebb and flow of feet' (ch. 3). Human beings have made their mark here. But it's a mark condemned to gradual erosion and ultimate erasure. In chapter 16 the mill is spruced up for Bob's bride-to-be, and many of the ancient traces are wiped out as heedlessly as the old houses in the *Life* were pulled down and the old churches modernized:

> By the widow's direction the old familiar incrustation of shining dirt, imprinted along the back of the settle by the heads of countless jolly sitters, was scrubbed and scraped away; the brown circle round the nail whereon the miller hung his hat, stained by the brim in wet weather, was whitened over; the tawny smudges of bygone shoulders in the passage were removed without regard to a certain genial and historical value which they had acquired.

And the friability and fragmentation of relics deride the memorializing function they are expected and intended to perform. Hardy's Preface makes light of the difficulties of the historian-novelist's salvage operations among the 'casual relics of the circumstances amid which the action moves':

> An outhouse door riddled with bullet-holes, which had been extemporized by a solitary man as a target for firelock practice when the landing was hourly expected, a heap of bricks and clods on a beacon-hill, which had formed the chimney and walls of the hut occupied by the beacon-keeper, worm-eaten shafts and iron heads of pikes for the use of those who had no better weapons, ridges on the down thrown up during the encampment, fragments of volunteer uniform, and other such lingering remains, brought to my imagination in early childhood the state of affairs at the date of the war more vividly than volumes of history could have done.

The Trumpet-Major's historical stuff had to be wrested from the closeted, boxed-up pastness of the past with all the difficulty that those worm-eaten remains imply. The novel and *The Dynasts* began, Hardy tells us in the *Life*, in some 'torn pages' that were long before his time secreted in a cupboard and got stumbled across only accidentally: 'A History of the Wars – a periodical dealing with the war with Napoleon, which his grandfather had subscribed to at the time, having been himself a volunteer', crumbled and fragmentary pages 'found in a closet'. No wonder one central drama of *The Trumpet-Major* concerns the fate of some papers stashed away in a tin box. Small wonder, either, that this hidden container is filled with textual and metatextual advertisements – is itself such an advertisement – for the unreadability of the worn-out, frayed historical record. History is clearly marked down as a semiotic of uncertainty.

Emblematic clues to this condition mount up in arresting profusion. Anne Garland, to take an early example, weaves a rug (ch. 1). Rugs, the text informs us, are artefacts – textures, tissues – that take time to complete, take so long in fact that they come to mimic the lengthy processes of history in which they are themselves produced. They keep being shut back into the closet unfinished, then taken out for a bit more work, then closeted away again. So their oldest parts are doomed to fade before the latest parts are completed: 'the wools of the beginning became faded and historical before the end was reached.' This is the 'inherent nature of worsted-work' (*worsted*, i.e. woollen, but also *worsted* in the sense that it is always losing out in the battle with time).

This is also, by implication, the inherent nature of history and of texts and of all textural artefacts in their inevitably historical condition. The power-fully emblematic fading rug is not unlike the weather-vane at the mill (ch. 2), 'in the form of a sailor with his arm stretched out. When the sun shone upon this figure' – in, of course, one more of Hardy's illuminated moments – 'it could be seen that the greater part of his countenance was gone, and the paint washed from his body so far as to reveal that he had been a soldier in red before he became a sailor in blue.' The unreliability of this male image – a reflection, in part, of the fickleness of Anne Garland's affections, now variously directed at sailor Bob, now at soldier John – is matched by the figure's unreliability as an indicator of wind direction: 'This revolving piece of statuary could not . . . be relied on as a vane, owing to the neighbouring hill, which formed variable currents in the wind.' And this faulty signification of wind direction at the mill is rather like the flawed telling of the time of day going on at Oxwell Hall (ch. 6), where the gnomon of the old sun dial 'swayed loosely about when the wind blew, and cast its shadow hither and thither, as much as to say, "Here's your fine model dial; here's any time for any man; I am an old dial; and shiftiness is the best policy" '. Decrepitudes developed simply in time upset any would-be confident relationship between onlookers/readers and old weather-vanes and sundials.

All markers become distorted and make puzzling markings, given time. This is presumably why in chapter 25 Hardy evokes the old portrait of Napoleon consisting of a 'hieroglyph' – that is, an encrypted puzzle, disturbing and difficult to decode:

> It was a hieroglyphic profile of Napoleon. The hat represented a maimed
> French eagle; the face was ingeniously made up of human carcases, knotted
> and writhing together in such directions as to form a physiognomy; a band,
> or stock, shaped to resemble the English Channel, encircled his throat, and
> seemed to choke him; his epaulette was a hand tearing a cobweb that repre-
> sented the treaty of peace with England; and his ear was a woman crouching
> over a dying child.

This is an emblem of history's disturbing – and horrific, nightmarish –
puzzlingness that Hardy takes great pains to draw to the reader's attention
right from the start, by dwelling in his Preface on its importance as a
surviving token of the past that is the novel's subject: it 'existed as a print
down to the present day in an old woman's cottage near "Overcombe" '. The
impressive difficulty of making out history's signs and texts must be brought
home. And the more historical evidence and experience are afforded importance, the more they are proved to be afflicted with the general hermeneutic
anxieties of the novel – indeed, the general *Angst* of the novel. If Bob's face,
domestic, homely, familiar from of old, is like a page of type too difficult to
be read from up close (ch. 15), how much more difficult to make out, and
make sense out of, the overawing, public, grandiose figure of the equestrian
King that is being laboriously carved out on a chalky hillside (ch. 38):

> When they reached the hill they found forty navvies at work removing the
> dark sod so as to lay bare the chalk beneath. The equestrian figure that their
> shovels were forming was scarcely intelligible to John and Anne now they
> were close, and after pacing from the horse's head down his breast to his hoof,
> back by way of the king's bridle-arm, past the bridge of his nose, and into his
> cocked hat, Anne said that she had had enough of it, and stepped out of the
> chalk clearing upon the grass. The trumpet-major had remained all the time
> in a melancholy attitude within the rowel of his Majesty's right spur.

The Farce of History

What's most noticeable here is that a serious problem of hermeneutics, a
tragic drama of point-of-view and readerly distance, is stuck about with
farcical overtones. The problematic historical text is a playful, jokey one.
Hardy is, of course, distressingly notorious for being never averse in his
writing to a kind of clumsy buffooning with the materials of his most urgent
anxieties. And this absurd miniaturization of the ordinary citizens, Ann and
John, within the historical grandeur and heroic magnitude of the traced–out
cultic, hieratic figure of the King is not the end hereabouts of the curious

edging over into farce of the serious. Anne is marked by the very stuff that marks the King's importance in the historical reckoning. Her shoes get caked with the regal chalk. She can't readily wipe it off. Commoners, the implica- tion is, also bear the mark, the stamp, the trace of history. Hardy's demo- cratic defence of his ordinary people's moral importance is afforded a moment's vivid endorsement. But there's more. Anne also wants John as a lover; she would love him to touch her. So, coyly, she insists that he steady her while she scrapes her shoes clean. And his resolve not to touch the woman he's decided his brother has prior claim on can hardly withstand the temptation the moment offers.

The lightness of touch and tone cannot help seeming ill-timed. It's rather typical, in fact, of that vexatious Hardy who never seems able to agree with the average reader that some coyness or joke is out of place, or to share readers' worries about his habit of steering his tones towards silliness, in- appositeness, and grotesquerie. Often, in such moments, the effort at jokiness fails because it's no joke, being just too dumpy and laboured to make anyone laugh – as with Festus's braggadocio posturings, or the drilling scene done as a rerun of Falstaff's recruiting among the peasantry in *2 Henry IV*, or the dubbing of German soldiers *Klaspenkissen* and the like (ch. 10). Sometimes Hardy seems to be being embarrassed into clumsy jest. Whenever men and women touch or come close to touching – as up on the white horse-and-king, or in the incident when Bob is lugged about the countryside prone on a rustic seat by the two females who are rivals for his body (ch. 32), or the scalded hands and nearly-scalded knee incident (ch. 37), or the gloved hands and the elderberry tree scene (ch. 39), or the phallic fireworks episode (also in chapter 39) – the text tends to break out into a sweat of sniggering coyness and behind-hand roguishness of almost gothic dimensions. But sometimes the buffooning is at the centre of a most urgent and serious moment, as on the chalk effigy, or in chapter 40, where – much in the manner of Marlowe's Dr Faustus being reduced to knockabout leg-pulling – the novel's extremely earnest trade in framed visions, illuminated perceptions, and the eliciting of meanings from out of the hermeneutic closet comes perilously close to travesty. First of all, old Derriman and Anne go into a comic parody of locking and unlocking. He entrusts the iron box to her; she locks it away in the 'boxed receptacle' beneath the window-seat; he gives her a 'little packet' which, opened, proves to be 'snugly packed' with 'twenty new guineas'. But then, immediately, he takes back his present, unlocks the window-seat, opens the box, puts the coins inside for safe keeping, shuts the box, locks the seat, and pockets the keys. After this charade, Anne goes upstairs, but watches events below through a knot-hole in the floor (absurdest of all the novel's framed visions), and sees the old man attempting to sneak

back and retrieve his strong-box while Festus is not looking but using the
candle to light his pipe, and then Festus trying to snatch the box away from
his uncle, and Matilda spying on the proceedings through the window, and
Bob trying to secure the box because Anne has shouted a warning through
the flooring to beware a 'plot'. Meanwhile the Squire and his box succeed in
vanishing from this daft scene altogether.

It's hard at this point not to feel, certainly at first blush, that Hardy's text
is demeaning itself here with inappropriate drollery. Further reflection suggests,
however, that we should perhaps rather think of this sort of farcicality as the
direct expression of that wryness with which Hardy, for all his proper ear-
nestness about such matters, views the difficulty of getting history, or anything
else, straight. It might even be that the distortion into farce and grotesquerie
is part of Hardy's constant bid to outwit the effacings and dimmings of
history. Critics are fond of piously quoting Hardy's line of thought on the
importance of the skewed vision, of the 'idiosyncratic mode of regard', of
'disproportioning', as techniques for 'making old incidents and things seem
as new' and for causing 'a tale or experience' to 'dwell in the memory and
induce repetition'. But the actual disproportioning going on in Hardy's texts
is a good deal harder to stomach. This novel's farcing is, though, what makes
it and its author the more challenging. It may be what grants Hardy's
hermeneutic investigations their ultimate distinction. It is certainly an intimate part of Hardy's most serious question, the one that interpenetrates all
his sceptical dealings with texts and history, the question of mortality.

Death closes all, in this novel as in everything Hardy penned. Word and
world are made to submit to the solemn hegemony of death, pain, disaster,
to the twin threats of dictatorship and political terror that are the text and
subtext of that Napoleonic hieroglyph. The recurring problem, as far as
Hardy is concerned, with text, history, history-as-text, and text-in-history, is
the challenge to survival and understanding, meaning and coherence that is
continually offered by mortality.

The novel ends with John Loveday disappearing from the 'waving light'
of his father's single candle into the darkness of the surrounding night, to
travel down the novel's lengthening vista of bloody battlefields until his
trumpet shall have been silenced forever. History, time, death, compose a
black, engulfing margin that extinguishes the human figure and his tootling,
footling art that have together been the illuminated, but also fragile, flickering
and short-lived centre of the writing's attention and the reader's gaze. It's an
altogether solemn moment; but also an ironic one. That death can so easily
extinguish this bravely self-sacrificial, musical, colourfully clothed man – as
pretty and creative a picture as the novel has been able to provide – is a
wretched fact for us to have to swallow. But it's impossible to separate it

from the farce of old Derriman's death consequent upon the undignified play with knot-hole, candle, window, and tin box (ch. 40):

> Just after dawn in the following morning a labouring man, who was going to his work, saw the old farmer and landowner leaning over a rail in a mead near his house, apparently engaged in contemplating the water of a brook before him. Drawing near, the man spoke, but Uncle Benjy did not reply. His head was hanging strangely, his body being supported in its erect position entirely by the rail that passed under each arm. On after-examination it was found that Uncle Benjy's poor withered heart had cracked and stopped its beating from damages inflicted on it by the excitements of his life, and of the previous night in particular. The unconscious carcass was little more than a light empty husk, dry and fleshless as that of a dead heron found on a moor in January.

And after this failure – the commonest human failure, at yet another set of Hardy borderlines, the rail and the brook – Anne then inherits the historical ruination of Oxwell Hall, 'with its muddy quadrangle, archways, mullioned windows, cracked battlements, and weed-grown garden'. Who, we wonder, needs that? But this is what inheriting the past is all about. It's also what writing, for Hardy, is all about. Anne couldn't rub the chalk of that grotesque picture of the King off her shoes: she was ineradicably marked by the marking stuff of a magnificent indecipherability. Now, of course, it is recollections of the 'mud on the carpet' of Anne's room and the 'footprints on the back staircase' (ch. 40) that explain, belatedly and in the end, how the dead man's tin box got into Anne's fireplace and the novel's 'mystery' is after all solved – and in just the way fictional conventions about mystery stories demand. But these are fading, faded traces that add up to sense only long after the event. And in any case they cannot restore that dead old man to life again. Like the lines around Widow Garland's eyes, or the scar on Bob's cheek ('a jagged streak like the geological remains of a lobster'), or the blood-stains on the deck of the *Victory* (ch. 35: ' "you may swab wi' hot water, and you may swab wi' cold, but there's the blood-stains, and there they'll bide" '), the traces that persist and survive do so only to give evidence of impersistence and lack of survival, of pain and death, of the passing away of people, the brevity of life, and the failure of trying to make meaning and sense by efforts at resisting time's erosions.

Hardy's writing, on this reckoning, enjoys only the most ironic and pyrrhic of successes, comprising, as it were, a helpful demonstration of human, historical, textual helplessness, a writing out of the near (but not quite) impossibility of writing, a making that makes most present – represents – to us mainly history's deterring and deferring work of emptying, of absenting, of depresentation. But, to emphasize once again: this demonstration concerns at once history and text, the history in the text, the text in history, history as text, and text as historical writing. No text – for textual work is most evidently time-bound work – should be expected to do less, whatever loud critical voices may urge to the contrary.

NOTES

1 Hayden White, variously in *Metahistory: The Historical Imagination in Nineteenth-Century Europe* (Johns Hopkins University Press, Baltimore and London, 1973); *Tropics of Discourse: Essays in Cultural Criticism* (Johns Hopkins University Press, Baltimore and London, 1978); *The Content of the Form: Narrative Discourse and Historical Representation* (Johns Hopkins University Press, Baltimore and London, 1987). See my earlier discussion of Auschwitz and American thinking about history in chapter 1.

2 Stephen Greenblatt, 'Shakespeare and the Exorcists', in *After Strange Texts: The Role of Theory in the Study of Literature*, ed. Gregory S. Jay and David I. Miller (University of Alabama Press, Alabama, 1985), 102.

3 A point made, more or less, by Gertrude Himmelfarb, 'Telling It As You Like It', *TLS*, 16 October 1992, 13.

4 James E. Young, *Writing and Rewriting the Holocaust: Narrative and Consequences of Interpretation* (Indiana University Press, Bloomington and Indianapolis, 1988), Introduction esp. 2; ch. 3, 51ff.: 'Holocaust Documentary Fiction'; ch. 4, 64ff.: 'Documentary Theater, Ideology, and the Rhetoric of Fact'.

5 As in Richard H. Taylor, *The Neglected Novels: Thomas Hardy's Lesser Novels* (Macmillan, London, 1982).

6 By far the best accounts of Hardy as exponent of perception issues are J. Hillis Miller, *Thomas Hardy: Distance and Desire* (Harvard University Press, Cambridge, Mass., 1970), and Tom Paulin, *Thomas Hardy: The Poetry of Perception* (Macmillan, London, 1975).

7 Virginia Woolf, 'The Novels of Thomas Hardy' (January 1928), in *Collected Essays*, vol. 1 (Hogarth Press, London, 1966), 256–66.

8 T. S. Eliot, *After Strange Gods: A Primer of Modern Heresy* (Faber, London, 1934), 56.

9 A repeated and vexing charge in the 1880s and 1890s and, indeed, through the rest of Hardy's life, was that Hardy had plagiarized the drilling scene in chapter 23 from a book called *Georgia Scenes* (1835), by one A. B. Longstreet. (Documentarizing novelists are, of course, likely to be thought plagiarists if they co-opt, as they tend to, the documents of others. Cf. the fuss over D. M. Thomas's *The White Hotel*.) In declaring that he used C. H. Gifford's *History of the Wars Occasioned by the French Revolution* (1817) and had forgotten that Gifford was quoting an American account, Hardy was answering the accusation of deliberate and conscious plagiarism. Gifford's source was, apparently, an anonymous American sketch from 1807 by one Oliver Hillhouse Prince as

reprinted in John Lambert's *Travels through Lower Canada, and the United States of North America in the Years 1806, 1807 and 1808* (1810). Some people have thought that Hardy might have come by Prince's account independently. Nobody now supposes Hardy guilty of deliberately seeking to pass off another writer's words as his own. See Carl J. Weber, *Hardy of Wessex: His Life and Literary Career* (revised edn., Columbia University Press, New York, and Routledge and Kegan Paul, London, 1965), 116–22.

10 See Emma Clifford, 'Thomas Hardy and the Historians', *Studies in Philology*, 56 (1959), 654–68.

11 In the serialized version of the novel in the magazine *Good Words*, January 1880 onwards, this bird's-eye view paragraph of chapter 12 (except its opening sentence) appeared at the end of the preceding chapter. Hardy cut out from the 'first' edition, October 1880, the following paragraph that had expanded on the arresting microscopic vision of people drawn towards Budmouth by the King's arrival and that had Anne (unconsciously) endorsing one of the sharpest instances of Hardy's uplifted visionary ironizings:

> Anne, who had all that romantic interest in court people and pageantry which was natural to an imaginative girl of her tastes, frequently bent her eyes on this microscopic spectacle from the field near the front of her house, and allowed her fancy to paint the portraits and histories of those who moved therein. That speck was a coach, perchance full of ladies of resplendent charms, leading fairy lives in some gorgeous palace, and accustomed to walk in gardens of bewildering beauty. Those rattling dots of horsemen were perhaps gallant nobles and knights who had the privilege of jesting with Kings; that figure on the horizon about the size of a pin's head, was perhaps composed throughout of royal blood. That, as a matter of fact, the several coaches contained the elderly countess of A——, of placid nature, plain features, and dowdy dress; the virtuous and homely lady B——; the strange-tempered Marchioness of C——, and so on: that the horsemen were puffy, red-faced, General D——, a couple of grey and bald-headed colonels, a diminutive diplomatist, and numbers of commonplace attendants on the court, made no difference whatever to the transcendency of her mental impressions.

12 Hardy's original intention was to have Anne kiss Bob under the bridge. Sexual encounters involving water-crossings curiously fascinate Hardy – compare the way Sue escapes her training-college in *Jude*, wading across a river and having to put on Jude's suit because her clothes are so wet; or Angel Clare in *Tess*, chapter 23, carrying the four dairy maids across a flooded lane. The sense of sexual *rite de passage* is frequently strong in such scenes, which are often the focus of some troubling sensation for text, author, and readers. In *Jude*, Jude and his author are evidently worried by Sue's mannishness once she's in his clothes. The *Tess* scene was so openly erotic that the editor of *The Graphic* made Hardy have Angel transport the girls through the water more antiseptically in a wheelbarrow!

13   This is just one of the many places in this novel where Hardy assumes in his
     readers his own intense familiarity with the text of the Authorized Version of
     the Bible. Genesis 13: 10: 'And Lot lifted up his eyes, and beheld all the plain
     of Jordan, that it was well-watered everywhere . . . even as the garden of the
     Lord.' The snag was (as Hardy well knew) that the plain of Jordan led Lot
     towards Sodom and Gomorrah and the eventual apocalyptic disasters that in-
     cluded the death of his wife. In such a garden John Loveday's courtship would
     already sound ominous to nineteenth-century Bible-readers.

4

Facts and Fancies

Dickens's *Hard Times* (1854) is a famous test for assumptions about reading texts, in this case novels – novels in general and nineteenth-century novels in particular. On the one hand, it has long been a *locus classicus* of Victorian realism. You could hardly invent a sharper instance of the so-called classic realist novel than this one. And it has indeed been an appropriately happy hunting-ground for moralists and historians and Marxists, for any ideologue, in fact, who believes that fiction, and above all nineteenth-century fiction, connects with the real world, mirrors it clearly, instantiates it by numerous particularities and by thickness of Jamesian detail in the pages of the book, gives us back the world we daily inhabit, the life we live and that our forebears lived. This set of realist insistences is the famous and repeated burden of F. R. Leavis and Raymond Williams and of successors of theirs such as David Craig and Terry Eagleton and, of course, of every undergraduate essay rightly enthused by such wisdoms. Such readings reinforce the view that the Victorian novel – and possibly all good novels, certainly the ones not wrongly contaminated by false modernist preferences – is, like this one, worldly, metonymic, imitative of social realities, a set of windows on to society, properly full of political and social purposes and other clearly centred meanings. The Condition of England Novel, on these assumptions, represents the right condition of the novel. In other words, this novel, like all serious novels, comprises good historical data, social signifieds, extra-textual signata. It's a kind of writing clearly demarcated from the fiction that preceded it – that is, playful, gaming, self-referential eighteenth-century texts, fictional modes climaxing in *Tristram Shandy* – or that succeeded it – anti-realist, modernist, and postmodernist writing that takes its cue from the likes of *Tristram Shandy*, textualized texts, increasingly gamey, highly metaphoric, artfully retreating from any suspicion of merely transcribing the real, zestfully imploding into a Barthesian well of mere scripting or scribing, of *écriture*, whose greatest and most logorrheic example is, of course, *Finnegans Wake*. Revealingly, F. R. Leavis was fond of supporting Dr Johnson to the effect that nothing odd will do long and that *Tristram Shandy* did not last. Leavis and his followers counted the Bloomsbury enthusiasm for *Tristram Shandy* as symptomatic of what was wrong with modernism in general and Virginia Woolf in particular – all 'irresponsible (and nasty) trifling, regarded as in some way extraordinarily significant and mature'.[1]

More recently, and in keeping with the fashion for post-Derridian notions that all the old referential assumptions about literature are misplaced, *Hard Times* has been subjected, along with many of the canonical classics, the standard items of the literary syllabus, to re-readings aimed at proving rather that it is essentially of the order of *Tristram Shandy* or *Finnegans Wake*, is really about the condition of text and textuality rather than the Condition of England, that it's an affair only or mainly of trope, figure, metaphor, plunging into abysms of self-reference, of its own writtenness, that it decentres or deconstructs itself, and runs the interpretative reader finally up against *béance*, *aporia*, absence. And, once again the tendency is for the reading in question, now a condition-of-text reading, to be offered as exemplary of the Condition of the Novel.[2] All novels, all texts, on evidence such as this, become *écriture*, granting only poststructuralist experiences to their readers. As J. Hillis Miller puts it after offering a sequence of altogether similar deconstructive readings of *Lord Jim, Wuthering Heights, Henry Esmond,* and *Tess of the d'Urbervilles*:

> all four are versions of the invitation, generated by the words of the novel, to believe that there is some single explanatory principle or cause [i.e. some 'external' meaning or meanings to which the novel may be thought of as pointing], outside the sequence of repetitive elements in the text [i.e. the accumulating, self-mirroring, self-enclosing textual stuff], accompanied in one way or another by a frustration of the search that belief motivates.[3]

Which is, of course, to endorse the polarity between the apparent fullness of repetitive elements in texts and the tantalizing actuality of aporia – that is, voids, frustrations of the quest for meaning – which Paul de Man offered as characteristic of all literature in his influential *Blindness and Insight*,[4] and also to settle the apparent warfare between these two poles in the direction of the empty, the void, non-reference, the ahistorical, and so on, in the now classic preferential manoeuvre I deplored in chapter 1.

But what *Hard Times* does dramatically is to challenge the either-or-ism of the critical postures that cluster about it. It very firmly undoes, it disallows, the absolute polarities that critics have erected between Victorian and Modernist, realist and rhetorical, Condition-of-England and Condition-of-Text, old-fashioned reading and progressive reading, reference and self-reference, metonymic and metaphoric, and that have sadly infected readings of this novel ever since Leavis's *The Great Tradition*. In particular, the difficulties this novel experiences in handling the apparent opposition it sets up between Fact and Fancy focuses with extraordinary (and, of course, I think exemplary) clarity the real impossibility of separating world issues from word ones, realism from irrealism, metonymic from metaphoric.

La Baguette du Sorcier

As soon as David Lodge popularized Roman Jakobson's opposed pair of terms *Metaphor*: *Metonym* in his book *The Modes of Modern Writing*, they became convenient labels for the alleged polarities keenly mongered in the hothouse of deconstructionist critique: realist versus irrealist writing, old-fashioned realist reading versus progressive decontructionist approach, and so on. For Jakobson, 'the metaphoric and metonymic poles' came to characterize all cultural phenomena. Lodge followed him in sorting all writing, dream, discourse, the whole sign-making business of culture, into two opposed and largely discontinuous sets: the metonymic (realism, prose, epic, film, close-up, the contextual) and the metaphoric (non-realism, poetry, lyric, drama, montage, the a-contextual). For a time, as Barbara Johnson nicely puts it, metaphor and metonymy were 'the salt and pepper, the Laurel and Hardy, the Yin and the Yang', as well as 'often the Scylla and Charybdis' of literary theory. Roland Barthes called this rhetorical *couple* a magic wand – *une baguette de sorcier* – really enabling the 'possibilité d'écriture'.[5]

Roman Jakobson did not, of course, invent these terms. They come out of the great repertoire of rhetorical terms that fill the enormous corpus of ancient writings on the conduct of discourse, the books of instruction in rhetoric, and so on. What Jakobson tapped into, though, was a framework of Western thought about how discourse engages with reality: on the one hand distantly, or metaphorically; on the other hand closely, or metonymically. The Greek *metaphora* (*translatio* in Latin; 'the Figure of transporte' in the English version of George Puttenham in his late sixteenth-century *Arte of English Poesie*, which translated the classical terms into English for the benefit of women who hadn't the ancient languages) described the substitution of one word by another, a transfer of meanings, of ideas, from like thing to like thing, a declaration of similarities, but also a transfer or translation that carried some distance from the original, and so involved a good deal of distinct distortion or *katachresis*, thereby opening up a gap between original and substitute. *Metonymia* (variously *transmutatio* or *transnominatio* or *denominatio* in Latin; Puttenham's 'the Misnamer'), described a less dramatic exchange of terms, a lesser degree of *katachresis*, a substitution of one name for another, in a process that maintained a rather close proximity between the original and its substitute. *Metonymia* was always thought of as closely related to the work of *synecdoche* – the figure by which a term for part of something was taken to represent the whole of that thing. Metonym is rhetorical work conducted close up to reality.[6]

It's easy to see how Jakobson might come to develop this apparent dichotomy in ancient language and rhetoric to represent, on the one side, the high fictionality of fiction, the poeticism of poetry, the distance and difference of 'literature' from 'life' (i.e. metaphor), a relationship of *similarities* but one that involves significant distance between world and word; and, on the other side, the more realistic, world-hugging, context-fond mode of the prosaic, the photograph, documentary (i.e. metonym), a relationship of *association* that involves significant contiguities between world and word.

But the polarity between metaphor and metonym can only be approximate, as most recent commentators insist. Roman Jakobson himself recognized that the polarity was not absolute.[7] For his part, David Lodge cannot even define the two without blending them into each other. Steven Connor appears to get them mightily confused.[8] In any case, both figures do seem to be subsumed in many ancient rhetoric books under the overarching (and Shandyan) concept and activity of *katachresis*.[9] But, at the same time, Lodge follows Jakobson, and is eagerly followed by troupes of others, in insisting that certain literary periods and certain modes of discourse do indeed foreground, or give preference to, now metonymy, now metaphor: 'In normal verbal behaviour both processes are continually operative, but careful observation will reveal that under the influence of a cultural pattern, personality and verbal style, preference is given to one of the processes over the other.'[10]

Allowing the possibility of such a preference does, of course, suit the polarizing tendency of linguistic and critical theory ever since Saussure. Much poststructuralist discussion has been built on the assumption that the Western tradition has always preferred to hierarchize metaphor over metonymy. Paul de Man alleges this. So does Barbara Johnson. But this is by no means absolutely true. Abraham Fraunce's *The Arcadian Rhetoricke* (1588), for instance, while declaring that 'There is no trope more flourishing than a *Metaphore*', nonetheless puts *Metonymia* first among the tropes.[11] But recent analysis hasn't been much moved by the old rhetoricians' hesitancies over relations between these two figures, and in our diligently polarizing and hierarchizing climate it's been easy for critics to move dubiously from conceding that either metaphor or metonym might indeed *predominate* in any particular discourse, or even in a particular field or period of discourses, to the notion that in any discourse or set of discourses either metaphor or metonym may rule absolutely to the utter exclusion of the other. But texts are peculiarly resistant to the critics' absolutes. Certainly *Hard Times* is.

Cutting and Drying

One of the major discernible overt functions of *Hard Times* is that it's written to undermine the literal, the factual, the metonymic, the purely worldly way of reading the world, and to urge in place of any such harsh vision or practice the counter-importance of the fanciful, the figurative, the metaphoric, the fictional mode of seeing. Chapter 2, the novel's genetic schoolroom scene, is prime and fundamental. In it Sissy Jupe, a child of the Circus, whose existence is full of horses (the very name of the Circus is 'Sleary's Horse Riding'), is found unable to define a horse to the satisfaction of her schoolmaster, Mr M'Choakumchild; her industrialist benefactor, the school's founder, Mr Thomas Gradgrind MP; and a schools inspector in government pay. This unholy trinity of most factual males agrees that Sissy is deplorably short of facts: 'Girl number twenty possessed of no facts, in reference to one of the commonest of animals.' Sissy can illustrate, can tell stories, but story-telling will not do: 'You mustn't tell us about that [her father's life as a clown] here'; 'You mustn't tell us about the ring here.' By great contrast, the boy Bitzer does satisfy the inquisitors in the matter of horse-flesh. He does so with an encyclopedic, metonymic list, a string of extremely factual synecdoches. A horse is 'Quadruped. Gramnivorous. Forty Teeth, namely twenty-four grinders, four eye-teeth, and twelve incisive. Sheds coat in the spring; in marshy countries, sheds hoofs, too. Hoofs hard, but requiring to be shod with iron. Age known by marks in mouth.' 'Now girl number twenty', declares Mr Gradgrind, 'You know what a horse is.'

Nor is this all. The government inspector, who is, like Bitzer, a 'mighty man at cutting and drying', starts up another classroom interrogation, this time on representation. 'Would you paper a room with representations of horses?' No, you would not, because pictures – that is, figures – of horses, are not real enough for the reality of walls. 'I'll explain to you . . . why you wouldn't paper a room with representations of horses. Do you ever see horses walking up and down the sides of rooms in reality – in fact? Do you? . . . Of course no. . . . Why, then, you are not to see anywhere, what you don't see in fact. What is called Taste, is only another name for Fact.' Thomas Gradgrind, we're told, 'nodded his approbation'. What he was approving was the abolition, at a stroke, of imaginative leaps, invention, metaphors, and, in the end, even metonyms. And the inspector, warming to his task of critical annihilation, adds another case. There must be no carpets with representations of flowers on them. No figures in carpets! The reader of Henry James is perhaps not the only one to feel a frisson of horror at this point. But the broom of abolition is busy and brusque: away go flowers on carpets and butterflies on crockery. Mathematical figures will do, but no pictures or figures stained by non-factual, imaginative association: 'You must use . . . for all these purposes, combinations and modifications (in primary colours) of mathematical figures which are susceptible of proof and demonstration.' But Sissy Jupe is as unredeemable in this matter as she was in the case of realistic knowledge of horses. She, in fact, would like to have pictures of flowers on her carpets. No harm would come to them, she says, from people's heavy boots or the legs of tables and chairs because 'They would be the pictures of what was very pretty and pleasant'. Like Philip Sidney outflanking the Puritans of the later sixteenth century with his deft assertion that the poet never lies because 'he nothing affirms' in the conventional sense of affirmation, so Sissy has the answer to the heavy literalist. Pictures of flowers simply can't 'crush and wither' like real flowers. But the distinction is not allowed. Nor is the attempt at the language of poeticity. '[A]nd I would fancy . . .', Sissy adds, but is stopped: 'Ay, ay, ay! But you mustn't fancy . . . That's it! You are never to fancy.' And, afforced by a chorus of Gradgrind repetitions, the government critic goes on to insist that 'You must discard the word Fancy altogether'.

Sissy is, of course, as a 'horse-rider', well-known to be a liar. Bitzer's certainty about this (I. 5) is Coketown's certainty. Horse-riders 'are famous for never minding what they say . . . It's as well known in the town as – please, sir, as the multiplication table isn't known to the horse-riders.' And lying is, clearly, thought to be part and parcel of the fancying, story-telling, picture-making business, just as it was in Philip Sidney's time. And the Circus is offered as indeed guilty of everything Gradgrind and his allies accuse it of. It stands for art and fiction and the whole tradition of story and metaphor. The Circus people are 'strollers'. They're in a long line of en-tertainers, clowns, wandering thespians. Sissy's father, the clown, goes in, we're told twice, for 'chaste Shakspearian quips and retorts' (I. 3, 6). Sissy used to amuse him with fictions – just those novels that are 'wrong books' according to Gradgrind. Novels kept her father off the drink, Sissy says. So novels are moral goods in the Circus world. And this moral force is exercised through a kind of endless fictionality, for Signor Jupe likes precisely the engulfing protractedness of *The Thousand-and-One Nights*, the story of Scheherazade: 'And often and often of a night, he used to forget all his troubles in wondering whether the Sultan would let the lady go on with the story, or would have her head cut off before it was finished' (I. 9). Circus life is a life of fictionality. Their public shows include nursery rhymes, fairy-stories, allegories, exotic and wondrous scenes – everything reprehensible in officially puritan Coketown. The 'Fairy bithnith and the Nurthery dodge' – 'That'h Jack the Giant Killer – piethe of comic infant bithnith': Sleary's Horse Riding proposes a world of imaginative *bithnith* to the hard men of business (III. 7).

In great contrast to the Circus ménage, domestic and mental life in the Gradgrind family is being attempted as an exclusion zone for metaphor, emblem, allegory, none of which Mr Gradgrind understands at all. When, in book 1, chapter 15, Gradgrind's daughter Louise intimates her coming marital misery and a possible moral and personal break-out from this emotional and poetic desert by resorting to a figure, her father finds it simply impossible to follow her meaning. She's staring out of the window at the Coketown chimneys. Her father wonders why.

> 'Are you consulting the chimneys of the Coketown works, Louisa?'
> 'There seems to be nothing there, but languid and monotonous smoke. Yet when the night comes, Fire bursts out, father!' she answered, turning quickly.
> 'Of course I know that, Louisa. I do not see the application of the remark.'
> To do him justice he did not, at all.

It's a tellingly accusing moment for Mr Gradgrind's imprisonment in a world wilfully cut off from the uses of allegory. But, powerful as the moment is in revealing such deficiency in the man, there's also something very odd about the episode. What's most arresting here is not that Gradgrind can't at all comprehend a little extended fiction or allegory (by this stage in the novel we're ready for that), but that Louisa, starved from birth of fictional and imaginative sustenance – indeed, programmed to be averse to any metaphoric function of language and thought – should be able to produce a deft little moral emblem, manipulate a little allegory, just like that.

But a moment's reflection indicates that this is the kind of metaphoric or figurative activity which the Coketowners seem, somewhat to our surprise, to go in for on a rather massive scale. It's connected with the mystery of who, in this so factual world, keeps the Circus going by attending its shows. The factual Coketowners are shown engaged, whether willy or nilly, in the worlds of myth, fiction, metaphor, that they are said consciously and conscientiously to reject. The text contrives to have fiction creep up on Coketown and surround it against its declared will, against its masters' doctrine and its educators' judgement. Metaphor, fancy, picture, quite engulf, in fact, these merchants of fact and documentation, overthrowing their public resistance to fancy, showing up their favoured metonymy as unable to escape its own figurative nature, its alliance with metaphor, its rhetoricity, and revealing the futility of seeking to contrive any matter-of-fact freeing of discourse, thought, life, from the activity of figure. What Mr Gradgrind wants, he says, is facts. What he gets, what he is, what his listeners in the opening schoolroom scene are, is metaphor. Metaphor saturates Dickens's account of the man of Fact. Language itself rises against Gradgrindery. Even Gradgrind's neckcloth undergoes a personification, by a process of prosopopoeia that is the very basis of the poetic function:

> 'Now, what I want is, Facts. Teach these boys and girls nothing but Facts. Facts alone are wanted in life. Plant nothing else, and root out everything else. You can only form the minds of reasoning animals upon Facts: nothing else will ever be of any service to them. This is the principle on which I bring up my own children, and this is the principle on which I bring up these children. Stick to Facts, sir!'
>
> The scene was a plain, bare, monotonous vault of a schoolroom, and the speaker's square forefinger emphasized his observations by underscoring every sentence with a line on the schoolmaster's sleeve. The emphasis was helped by the speaker's square wall of a forehead, which had his eyebrows for its base, while his eyes found commodious cellarage in two dark caves, overshadowed by the wall. The emphasis was helped by the speaker's mouth, which was wide, thin, and hard set. The emphasis was helped by the speaker's voice, which was inflexible, dry, and dictatorial. The emphasis was helped by the speaker's hair, which bristled on the skirts of his bald head, a plantation of firs to keep the wind from its shining surface, all covered with knobs, like the crust of a plum pie, as if the head had scarcely warehouse-room for the hard facts stored inside. The speaker's obstinate carriage, square coat, square legs, square shoulders – nay, his very neck-cloth, trained to take him by the throat with an unaccommodating grasp, like a stubborn fact, as it was – all helped the emphasis.
>
> 'In this life, we want nothing but Facts, sir; nothing but Facts!'
>
> The speaker, and the schoolmaster, and the third grown person present, all backed a little, and swept with their eyes the inclined plane of little vessels then and there arranged in order, ready to have imperial gallons of facts poured into them until they were full to the brim.

But then, as we read on, Gradgrind and his world turn out to be jam-packed with myth and mythic references. Fairy-tale and fiction are by no means the exclusive property of the transient players of the Circus. Mr M'Choakumchild, the schoolmaster, turns out to work in his school like 'Morgiana in the Forty Thieves' (I. 2). The Gradgrind children, subjected to lectures instead of to childish pleasures such as fairy-tales, have been ill-treated by an ogre, 'a monster in a lecturing castle' who drags children off 'into gloomy statistical dens by the hair' (I. 3). A pub in Coketown is called the Pegasus's Arms (I. 6). Who, in Coketown, is responsible for that? Horse-riding is Circus work, but here's the mythic winged horse celebrated on a Coketown sign-board. What's more, the sign-board has a poem – admittedly poor verse, but still verse – painted on it in a 'flowing scroll', celebrating the goodness of booze. Further still, inside the pub is an effigy of the fabulous beast 'with real gauze let in for his wings, golden stars stuck on all over him, and his ethereal harness made of red silk'. The reality of the gauze and the silk – real stuffs indeed – does not belie the nature of the textual reality, the fiction, they're serving. The effect is as garishly fictional – 'theatrical' the text calls it – as any painted Spanish Madonna. After which, it's no surprise at all to find that Gradgrind himself can be turned into myth. Sitting in his study, a room lined with Blue Books, those statistical government reports on the Condition of England, he becomes a kind of Bluebeard. This may emphasize his domestic monstrosity – Bluebeard notoriously killed his wives – but at least he's a story-book monster.

The Fictions of Coketown

And as its story unfolds, Coketown appears to be more and more full of story. Biggest local story-teller of all is Josiah Bounderby, Gradgrind's egregious ally and Louisa's unwished-for spouse. Bounderby is a terrific inventor. He's concocted a story about his childhood destitution and a myth of his own self-making that conveniently leaves out the contribution of his loving mother, an inconvenient sponsor reported as having ditched him as a child and now kept out of sight. 'You shall never force' him, he declares oroficially, 'to suppress the facts of his own life' (I. 4). But these 'facts' are fictions. And he and his kind have other fictions to monger as well – the 'fictions of Coketown' (II. 1): the fiction that poverty is the fault of the poor (they marry too early, live too luxuriously on turtle soup and venison and off gold spoons, and will not save); the fiction that anyone can save up his money and become wealthy if he chooses; the fiction that large wage increases will ruin the mill-owners; and so on, all stories that Victorian manufacturers repeatedly told themselves.[12] No wonder Bounderby is, like Gradgrind, a farrago of metaphors, a clutch of poeticist stuff that his admirers tend liberally to baste his reputation with (I. 7):

> It was one of the most exasperating attributes of Bounderby, that he not only sang his own praises but stimulated other men to sing them. There was a moral infection of clap-trap in him. Strangers, modest enough elsewhere, started up at dinners in Coketown, and boasted, in quite a rampant way, of Bounderby.

> They made him out to be the Royal arms, the Union-Jack, Magna Charta,
> John Bull, Habeas Corpus, the Bill of Rights, An Englishman's house is his
> castle, Church and State, and God save the Queen, all put together.

These eulogists tend to end up quoting from Goldsmith's *Deserted Village*
lines about princes and lords flourishing and fading. Which is quite a feat
for the town whose MP 'should as soon have expected' his children to have
been caught reading poetry as trying to sneak a look at the Circus (I. 4). But
then, the textual matter in this local admiration for Bounderby might almost
sanction the poetry. Made up of proverbs, songs, writings of all kinds, a
heraldic royal device, the multivalent signifier of the British flag, a quite
mythical personage called John Bull, Bounderby the lying fictionist is a
gargantuan mess of fictions.

Bounderby's fictionalizing extends to his lady housekeeper Mrs Sparsit. 'In
the measure that he would not allow his own youth to have been attended
by a single favourable circumstance, he brightened Mrs Sparsit's juvenile
career with every possible advantage, and showered wagon-loads of early
roses all over that lady's path.' Her apparent come-down in the world is the
sponsor, as likely as not, of the common reference to princes and lords fading.
And poetry is not too unapt in her case. Certainly her nose is Shakespearian
– 'Coriolanian', in fact. Mrs Sparsit is not, we're told, 'a poetical woman'.
That would have been too much in general, perhaps, for Bounderby to stand.
But she does become possessed of 'an allegorical fancy', namely 'a mighty
Staircase, with a dark pit of shame and ruin at the bottom; and down those
stairs, from day to day and hour to hour, she saw Louisa coming' (II. 10). The
moral judgementalism thus practised by Mrs Sparsit is certainly in keeping
with coketown's puritanism. But what about the deft way in which Widow
Sparsit has concocted and manipulates her great moral allegory? Isn't it odd,
you might think, that at the heart of the Bounderby regime, at the core of
Coketown, this extended allegory in the most fluent Dickens manner should
be shown flourishing as a mode of keen, but also normal, hermeneutical
analysis?

In a sense, of course, it *is* odd, as odd as Gradgrind being all metaphor and
the local pub being called the Pegasus's Arms and Bounderby being a
compound of fictions. At the very least, it spoils the point of Dickens's
plotting for the redemption of Gradgrindery. In the plot, *Hard Times* contrives the ultimate triumph of the metaphor world, the Circus world, over
the fact world. The well-instructed, factual Bitzer helps undo the Gradgrinds;
Sissy Jupe, once held to be the agent of Circus pollution, a wicked introducer
of fanciful notions into the minds of Louisa and Thomas, helps redeem
the manufacturer's off spring. The Gradgrinds go wrong, the novel suggests,

because of their father's awful factualized influence. Fallen, a crook and a thief, the boy Tom is rescued from the Law by the Circus people. He and his father are shown emblematically as savable by being turned into clowns – united in the Circus ring, the father seated on 'the Clown's performing chair', the son, disguised in 'comic livery' and black face. 'And one of his model children had come to this!' (III. 7). Coming to 'this' is the salvation of both of them. But if 'this', or something like it, namely the presence and power of the fictional, the metaphoric – Horse Riding stuff – is not something that has to be brought in to rescue Coketown from the stultifying imaginative and moral famine of factuality, but is there, in fact, from the beginning as part and parcel of the Coketown scene, then the elaborately plotted work of the narration must come to seem not a little redundant. Unless it be supposed that without the proleptic presence of the fanciful in and behind the factual, the final supremacy of the fancy world might seem too abrupt and forced. And that, or something close to that is, perhaps, how we should regard the strong presence of the fanciful, of metaphor and fiction, so vividly there in Coketown, or, rather, in the text of Coketown, from the start. And that's instructive, for what it announces is the inevitability of imaginative figures, of metaphor, the fact that there is no final separation of the metaphoric from the metonymic, no writing without the intrusion, the invasion, of the one into the other.

Fairy Palaces

It's writing in *Hard Times*, language itself, that sustains the triumph of the metaphor world over the world of factuality, of merely factually reporting, and that ensures the complete coverage of narrativity, the impossibility of maintaining hedges between the Circus and the factory. The writing of *Hard Times*, the text itself, cannot wait for Dickens to plot the downfall of Gradgrind's factual hegemonizing. From the start, metaphor pokes through the systems of factual thinking and educating that Gradgrindery has concocted, ensuring the complicated liaisons and submissions that the plot's dénouement will finally confirm. Take legs – especially the sexy legs of female performers that Dickens was apparently so keen on in daily life. The Circus is where legs are unpuritanically prominent. Signor Jupe's dog is actually called Merrylegs. The women of the Circus show off their legs more than is decent in the eyes of the puritan Coketowners. Bare legs are Circus properties. But legs strongly infiltrate Coketown, from the start, in Dickens's metaphors. M'Choakumchild, we're told (I. 2), has been turned out of his teacher-training school with others, all alike, 'like so many piano legs'. The steeple of Coketown's New

Church (I. 5) terminates 'in four short pinnacles like florid wooden legs'.
These legs are, of course, wooden ones, mechanical, factory products, and it
is, symbolically, the function of the education being offered by Dickens's
novel to turn the mechanistic factory consciousness of the place over to the
warmly human and organic ways and assumptions represented by the Circus
– much in the fashion of that Biblical pressure for turning hearts of stone
into hearts of flesh – but, still, there they are, bare legs, visible all over the
Coketown scene.

And this presence of Circus stuff within the mechanistic structures of
Coketown is nowhere more manifest than in the physical descriptions of the
streets and factories of the town. Metaphoricization is of course rife in Dickens's
descriptions of the locality – it always is – but it's metaphoricization of a
strikingly Circus kind. In book 1, chapter 5, the satirical Key-Note chapter,
the blackened red brick of the place is said to be 'like the painted face of a
savage'. The factory smoke streams out of the chimneys in 'interminable
serpents'. The pistons of a steam-engine work up and down monotonously
'like the head of an elephant in a state of melancholy madness'. Further on
in the novel (I. 10) the factories at night, all lit up in the darkness, are said
to strike passengers in trains going by, as 'Fairy palaces'. In those factories,
the atmosphere can get as hot as a desert, with the air 'like the breath of the
simoom' (II. 1). But what's the effect of this hot flush of metaphors? Painted
savages, elephants, exotic winds from the Arabian deserts, Fairy palaces: if
that's how Coketown is, then it is, despite the doctrines of the Gradgrind
gang, already a Circus place. For, after all, the 'fairy business' is the Circus's
business, and it's in the Circus that you find elephants with pagodas on their
backs in which sit performers dressed as the Sultan of the Indies (III. 7). And,
of course, Dickens has a democratic faith in the redeemability of the common
people, and a notion that the ordinary Coketowner was actually at odds with
the wishes and assumptions of the dominant Gradgrinders. Louisa Gradgrind
herself had had, as a child, to be rebuked for 'wondering', much as Sissy Jupe
had to be stopped from fancying (I. 8). And if Gradgrind's own children have
a yearning for Circus, how much more might those brought up without their
educational disadvantages develop such tendencies.

The Coke town library ministers to wonder in a way particularly irksome
to Gradgrind. 'It was a disheartening circumstance, but a melancholy fact,
that even these readers persisted in wondering':

> They wondered about human nature, human passions, human hopes and fears,
> the struggles, triumphs and defeats, the cares and joys and sorrows, the lives
> and deaths, of common men and women! They sometimes, after fifteen hours'
> work, sat down to read mere fables about men and women, more or less like

themselves, and about children, more or less like their own. They took De Foe to their bosoms, instead of Euclid, and seemed to be on the whole more comforted by Goldsmith than by Cocker. Mr Gradgrind was for ever working, in print and out of print, at this eccentric sum, and he never could make out how it yielded this unaccountable product. (I. 8)

'According to Cocker' meant 'utterly factually', a tribute to the legendary seventeenth-century arithmetician and his arithmetic book. Dickens thought of using the phrase as title for his novel. And the way Dickens confirms this popular and child-like proneness to wonder, this resistance to the mathematical mode of Cocker and the figuring ways of school maths books, this readiness for Circus modes of thinking and living, the human openness to fiction, is by his intense work of letting metaphoricizing, another kind of figuring, invade and simply take over the text. Stephen Blackpool famously declares that life in Coketown, its politics and economics, is all a muddle. He might just as truthfully have declared that it was all metaphor, or, as Joyce puts it in *Finnegans Wake, justafication.*

Justafication; all metaphor. But to arrive at this point is not to confirm any simplistic, quasi-deconstructionist notion that what this text is about is simply a demonstration of the figurative nature of the real, or something of that kind. *Hard Times* is exemplary in revealing to us that the business of metaphoricization, the argument for fiction and fictional ways of seeing the world, for Circus values in fact, is a textual business and a business of text, but one that impinges dramatically on the real world, the historical outside of text. Dickens's textualizing text is speaking into a real world where actual Gradgrinds indeed lived and made profits and sought to shape reality to their commercial will. Dickens is labouring hard to effect a transformation of the factual, even the metonymic, into the metaphor world of the Circus, and is succeeding, hands down, in his textual battle inside the textual domain. But the reality, out there, was more intransigent. The manufacturers and the manufacturing North of England, in particular Preston, the town whose locked-out weavers Dickens visited before composing his novel, were harder to convert than Gradgrind, harder to overthrow than Bounderby. In and around the fiction and this intensely fictioneering text of *Hard Times* are truly hard facts, hard presences.

Texts for Real

The textualizing is, in other words, for real. *Hard Times* appeared in Dickens's own paper *Household Words*, 1 April–12 August 1854, as part of an ongoing campaign against the atrocities of real, live, practising northern manufacturers. Mrs Gaskell's writing was part of the same campaign, and her *North and South* followed *Hard Times* in *Household Words*, 2 September 1854– 27 January 1855. The crusade ran on into 1856. Its concerns stretched back into the Condition of England literature of the 1840s. *Hard Times* is by no means analysable only as a demonstration of proliferating metaphoricity. Here is no text existing only as *écriture*, for all its insistence on the necessity and potency of the metaphoric. Here, for that matter, is no text supporting the idea of authorlessness; nor, while Roland Barthes's famous views of text are in question, is this a text that allows the Barthesian division of writings into texts (which are about texts) and works (which trade in worldly stuff). This text announces itself as coming from the hand of Charles Dickens. Indeed, every title-page of *Household Words*, every week, declared that it was *A Weekly Journal Conducted by Charles Dickens*. What's more, across the top of every pair of the magazine's pages ran the banner 'Conducted by Charles Dickens'. Clearly, the real northern manufacturing subject was being grasped by a real writer's real writing hand holding a real pen *avant la lettre*, a hand belonging to a real perceiving author with a real biography and history into which the text of *Hard Times*, this text so much about text and yet also so much about the world, has to be fitted.

Charles Dickens, a Southerner with serious social concerns, had discovered a real North as well as inventing a fictional one, and their amalgamation in *Hard Times* is instructively hard to disentangle. Discovery and invention, making out and making up, had gone hand in hand in this case, as they tend to. The marriage began in 1838 when Dickens travelled the 'Factory Road' for the first time, a horrifying initiation that he then put into novel after novel – *The Old Curiosity Shop*, *Dombey and Son*, as well as *Hard Times*. His visit to Preston early in 1854 to report on the notorious lock-out of weavers by their employers had resulted in his article 'On Strike' (*Household Words*, 11 February 1854). That was only seven weeks before *Hard Times* began to appear. So no reader of the magazine, even a reader unable to focus very sharply on features like the transformation of the Trades Union agitator named Gruffshaw in the *Household Words* article into the character Slackbridge in the novel, would have failed to make the connection between the two, the journalistic text and the fictional one, the fictional and the real world. He or she might not have appreciated all of the connections that now appear so potent between *Household Words*'s devoted hostility to factory practices of the time and *Hard Times*, but the general link would have been inescapable. Now, of course, the connection seems peculiarly potent, and not least in its instructiveness for criticism. A main issue in the novel is, of course, rhetoricity, the nature of metaphor and metonym, the question of how imagining and textualizing are conducted. And Dickens's rhetorics have a startling way of overlapping onto the extra-textual. It's an extra-textual tendency that his dealings with the manufacturing robber-barons of his day seem to have made him peculiarly aware of. Take the character Bitzer, who's commanded by a terrible chop logic. His harsh discourse glibly chops up horses into grotesque synecdochic bits under the aegis of his awful 'cutting and drying' mentors, the men from the ministry and the factory. But in the factories of England the chopping up was for real, and the victims weren't just horses – though they could be horses, as Anna Sewell's crusading novel *Black Beauty* would make clear in 1877. They were people.

The workers of Coketown are known as Hands. The rhetoric of industrialism has reduced the workers to metonymic bits of themselves. Coketown knows its workers by a rhetorically reductive bit of their whole body, their whole selfhood. Which is bad enough. Worse, though, is that this casual way with names reflected an equally casual way with the bit of the body in question. An article by Dickens entitled 'Ground in the Mill' appeared in the very same issue of *Household Words* as chapters 7 and 8 of *Hard Times* (22 April 1854). It reports the recent statistics of industrial chopping up (statistics issued by the northern manufacturers, astonishingly, as a demonstration that the dangers of factory life, unfenced machinery, and so on, had been greatly exaggerated): 106 lives lost, 142 arms or hands chopped off, 1,340 bones smashed, 1,287 fingers cut off. The sheer bodily, material bulk of these lost limbs arouses Dickens's indignant imagination: 'in bulk, how many bushels', he wants to know, do 1,287 fingers make? He can see them amassed, heaped up in sacks. In such a context – the context of national debate and of debate within the pages of *Household Words* itself – talk of Hands, and of horses dismembered into bits, can only appear savagely ironic, and is, of course, potently polemical. The Coketowns of the North had lots of Bitzers in them – careless breakers up of God's creatures into bits, producers of sacks-full of bits of (bits o'; i.e. bitzer) people. In such a context, the metonym–metaphor, the rhetoric, question inevitably breaks any textual bound, impinging terribly on the reality of those cruel factory-made synecdoches. The terrible statistics relayed by *Household Words*, and Dickens's humane indignation about them, are hard to keep out of one's mind when encountering Barthes's cheerily casual relish for the reduction of the author to a writing hand without a voice.

Figures of Wonderful No-Meaning

And this admirable moralizing of the rhetoric issue affects, of course, a feature of the textualizing work of *Hard Times* that has naturally attracted the attention of critics in our post-deconstructionist times. Readers like Melvyn Haberman[13] have noticed how the devoted metaphoricization of Coketown – the textual demonstration that Coketown is knowable particularly as figure, is thoroughly metaphoricized, that its disfiguration at the hands of industrialism and its filths, its mechanistics, and so on, is a process of figuration – leads not only to a serious blurring of its features, but also to a voiding, a kind of *mise en abyme* that seems just up, or down, the street of recent critical expectation. Industrial pollution, 'the smoke and ashes', have turned the red brickwork of the place savagely, unnaturally, and obscuringly black. The numerous religious persuasions have built chapels which all look alike and are all pious versions of the warehouses. And 'All the public inscriptions in the town were painted alike, in severe characters of black and white.' And (sharp, Foucault-anticipating point) 'The jail might have been the infirmary, the infirmary might have been the jail, the town-hall might have been either, or both, or anything else' (I. 5). And this resistance to difference leads to an even more arresting kind of meaning void, a sort of textual plunge with the ill-fated Stephen Blackpool in a black emptiness, a void, a textual version of the Old Hell Shaft that he falls into.

There is indeed a curiously busy amount of absenting, disappearing, going missing, pushing off, voiding, in *Hard Times*. Stephen Blackpool, Signor Jupe, Tom and Louisa Gradgrind, Bounderby's mother, all absent themselves at various stages. Cash disappears. Bitzer has no heart. Love is missing. And signs have a dramatic way of being erased. When Gradgrind and Bounderby arrive at the Pegasus's Arms (its sign-board another reminder of the abundance of local legs on show, Pegasus's being so prominent on it; and yet another gesture in the direction of the novel's bodily synecdoches), the realist duo take no offence from the mythicist sign-board nor from the gaudy equine effigy displayed inside the pub: 'As it had grown too dusky without, to see the sign, and as it had not grown light enough within to see the picture, Mr Gradgrind and Mr Bounderby received no offence from these idealities.' Signor Jupe, the man they seek, is not there either. So the evening and the plot and the text collaborate in a general voiding. It's a prevalence of *béance* that applies widely to the citizenry and to the locality.

Bitzer not only has no heart; he is, in physical appearance, a whited-out man. His neighbour in the opening classroom scene, the dark-eyed, dark-haired Sissy Jupe reinforces this blanking out of Bitzer:

> But, whereas the girl was so dark-eyed and dark-haired, that she seemed to receive a deeper and more lustrous colour from the sun when it shone upon her, the boy was so light-eyed and light-haired that the self-same rays appeared to draw out of him what little colour he ever possessed. His cold eyes

would hardly have been eyes, but for the short ends of lashes which, by bringing them into immediate contrast with something paler than themselves, expressed their form. His short-cropped hair might have been a mere continuation of the sandy freckles on his forehead and face. His skin was so unwholesomely deficient in the natural tinge, that he looked as though, if he were cut, he would bleed white. (I. 2)

For its part, Coketown is blacked out in a haze of pollution and smog when you look at it on a 'sunny midsummer day'.

Seen from a distance in such weather, Coketown lay shrouded in a haze of its own, which appeared impervious to the sun's rays. You only knew the town was there, because you knew there could have been no such sulky blotch upon the prospect without a town. A blur of soot and smoke, now confusedly tending this way, now that way, now aspiring to the vault of Heaven, now murkily creeping along the earth, as the wind rose and fell, or changed its quarter: a dense formless jumble, with sheets of cross light in it, that showed nothing but masses of darkness:- Coketown in the distance was suggestive of itself, though not a brick of it could be seen. (II. 1)

These pictures, of Bitzer and of Coketown, hint at the way that painting would go as it entered the modernist era. Coketown's sunlit haze suggests a late Turner. Bitzer's whited-out features suggest an even more thoroughly modernist canvas, a play of allied tones of white and off-white. And, of course, such passages are ripe for seizure by devoted Derridians in the name of modernist hermeneutical and semantic doubting, of a textual collapse or retreat into absence, and of an argument that would turn Dickens and, by implication, the nineteenth-century novel or even The Novel into an exemplary monger of (post)modernist *néants* and refusals. But for this text these voidings do not exist in an ahistorical, unideological, merely textual void. Far from it. Like the issue of rhetoric in its particular metaphorical and metonymic functions, what might be legitimately interpretable as an inspection of writing's self-absenting propensity must also be seen as part of a sharp social-moral criticism directed at the moral and political aspects of the voiding that the textual absenting also clamantly registers.

Whatever else is in question in the matter of Bitzer's awful whiteness, for instance, it clearly alludes to the Biblical Pharisees, accused by Jesus of being whited sepulchres – pleasant enough on the outside but full of dead men's bones inside; that is, hypocrites. When Mr Gradgrind appeals to Bitzer to have a heart (III. 8) and to be forgiving over Tom Gradgrind, Bitzer can only think of William Harvey and the circulation of the blood. James Harthouse, gentleman-seducer of other men's wives, has no heart either, only a 'cavity where his heart should have been – in that nest of addled eggs, where the birds of heaven would have lived if they had not been whistled away' (III. 2). When Louisa almost succumbs to the Harthouse temptation, she and the novel blame the hollowness of her father's philosophy and teaching: 'All I know is, your philosophy and your teaching will not save me' (II. 12). It's a failure in the Gradgrind–Bounderby world signalled by the failures of the Sparsit hermeneutic and calculations. The railway-carriage that she expects to contain Louisa does not contain her: it's an emblem of the hollowness that's unable to save, a hollowness rendered in a rush of negatives ('no coach . . . The door not being opened . . . saw nothing . . . found it empty'). And Mrs Sparsit had no recourse but to burst into tears of bitterness and say, 'I have lost her' (II. 11). The pursuit and the loss are a reprise of the pursuit and loss of Lady Dedlock in the Dickens novel before this one, *Bleak House* (just as the rhetoric of Slackbridge the agitator is Chadband's rhetoric revisited). But the difference is that Mrs Sparsit's failure as detective, and spy, and moral scrutineer who will not do, is, unlike in *Bleak House*, outdone by a species of moral detection that succeeds. For Sissy Jupe, steady moral influence, is there to help Louisa draw successfully back from the moral brink. The 'wisdom of the Heart', as Gradgrind puts it (III. 1), shows its superiority to the 'wisdom of the Head', or what passes for it in the Gradgrind circle. Harthouse is outdone by the representative of the Circus and its values – 'Only a poor girl – only a stroller' (III. 3). He adds: 'only James Harthouse made nothing of.' This late voiding of all moral force from the Gradgrind world reads like an enactment of what Louisa had craved early on when she tried to erase the dire kiss of Bounderby (I. 4):

> He went his way, but she stood on the same spot, rubbing the cheek he had kissed, with her handkerchief, until it was burning red. She was still doing this, five minutes afterwards.
>   'What are you about, Loo?' her brother sulkily remonstrated. 'You'll rub a hole in your face.'

Louisa's reply is savage: 'You may cut the piece out with your penknife if you like, Tom. I wouldn't cry!' But the actual wielder of the penknife that in the novel erases Bounderby's mark is Charles Dickens: it's his pen, his text, that contrive the cutting and the rubbing out.

The power of the Dickensian pen both for erasing the false marks and textualizings of the Gradgrind system and for installing fullnesses of meaning in the place of those voids is perhaps nowhere more powerfully suggested than in the episode of the dying Mrs Gradgrind (II. 9). Her voice fading as she fades, reminding her daughter that she 'long ago left off saying anything' at all, she says that she wishes never to hear of any of the Gradgrind Ologies 'of any description', even if there's one left 'that has not been worn to rags in this house'. But she's aware of the need for a 'something' that's been missing from her life, and for the name of that something to replace the empty Ologies, or O-logies, the O-logics, the empty words and empty ideas, that have bred unhappiness and spiritual and moral ruin in her family. She can't name this thing or write it down, however, and she dies struggling to write to her husband for the missing name, but only with an imaginary pen. 'Figures of wonderful no-meaning' are all she manages to 'trace' on her 'covers': her blankets that turn thus into an accusingly empty epistle, a non-text:

> 'But there is something – not an Ology at all – that your father has missed, or forgotten, Louisa. I don't know what it is. I have often sat with Sissy near me, and thought about it. I shall never get its name now. But your father may. It makes me restless. I want to write to him, to find out for God's sake, what it is. Give me a pen, give me a pen.'
>
> . . .
>
> She fancied . . . that her request had been complied with, and that the pen she could not have held was in her hand. It matters little what figures of wonderful no-meaning she began to trace upon her wrappers. The hand soon stopped in the midst of them.

A missing term, an absent word, is, of course, something the reader has encountered before, in the harsh exchange between Louisa and her father when the prospect of marriage to Bounderby is under discussion (I. 15). There she demands of Gradgrind whether he asks her to love Mr Bounderby and whether Bounderby expects her to love him. Gradgrind assures his daughter that Bounderby does neither of them the 'injustice, of pretending to anything fanciful, fantastic or (I am using synonymous terms) senti-mental. . . . Therefore, perhaps the expression itself – I merely suggest this to you, my dear – may be a little misplaced.' The expression in question is the word *love*. Louisa asks: 'What would you advise me to use in its stead, father?' Gradgrind then resorts to a long paragraph of facts about older men marrying younger brides, culled from around the world, so that the disparity in age between Bounderby and Louisa 'almost ceases to be disparity, and (virtually) all but disappears'. But still Gradgrind has not managed, in making the disparity all but disappear, to provide a substitute term for the word *love* that he has thus buried under a mound of facts. So Louisa presses on: 'What do you recommend, father . . . that I should substitute for the term I used just now? For the misplaced expression?' And Gradgrind has no answer except to urge sticking to facts and to focus on marriage rather than love. And the 'misplaced expression' remains displaced. Even Louisa cannot now bring herself to repeat the word *love*. And, of course, this gap, this *béance*, this disappearing signifier, is not just any contingently missing term, it's at the heart of the novel's whole accusatory case against Gradgrindery. There is no love in that world. The Gradgrind marriage is truly loveless; so is Stephen Blackpool's; so will Louisa's be. Family life in Coketown is a sham. Only in the huge messy extended family of the Circus ('two or three handsome young women . . . with their two or three husbands, and their two or three mothers, and their eight or nine little children, who did the fairy business when required' I. 6) is family life built on true love. Only Sissy from the Circus – and even she suffers from a missing father – can suggest hope to Mrs Gradgrind, and generate more humanizing ways of life for Louisa's younger sister.

So there are failures of text and word and hermeneutic in plenty in *Hard Times*, and the voidings, hollowings-out, and emptyings so attractive to certain deconstructionists are indeed a pervasive feature of this text. But they are, in the first place, foremost features of the moral and political charges that Dickens and his text are bringing against Victorian industrialism and its values. And, brusquely, Dickens has no doubt that the missing term in Coketown domestic life is easy to supply, and the hollowness of the Gradgrind O-logics easily to be remedied. Just as he is sceptical about 'the fictions of Coketown' and the tendency it has to wish disappearance upon itself. *We*, of course, are entitled to remind ourselves, with not unapt critical excitement, when reading of the 'haze' that shrouds the place, of the modernist resistance that Conrad's Marlow offers to the conventional yarns of seamen – the meaning of his narrative 'enveloping the tale which brought it out only as a glow brings out a haze' (this famous passage is dwelt on later in my discussion of *Heart of Darkness*, chapter 5, section iii). But, for his part, Dickens was more concerned to go in for irony at the expense of the manufacturers who declare themselves ruined whenever government interference makes them spend money on education or on fencing machinery or when they're pressed to clean up their processes:

> The wonder was, it [Coketown] was there at all. It had been ruined so often . . . the millers of Coketown . . . were ruined, when they were required to send labouring children to school; they were ruined, when inspectors were appointed to look into their works; they were ruined when such inspectors considered it doubtful whether they were quite justified in chopping people up with their machinery; they were utterly undone, when it was hinted that perhaps they need not always make quite so much smoke.

The fictions of Coketown are lies, ideologically generated stories. The linguistic failures of Coketown are socially remediable. The opposed rhetorics of the place, metonyms and metaphors, are part of a wider political argument and analysis. So that, all in all, *Hard Times* is deeply instructive for current discussions about the nature of textuality. It is about writing and reading, about figure, about kinds of figurativeness – roughly speaking, about the opposed claims of the metonymic and the metaphoric, the literal and the figural. It is at great pains to demonstrate how the factual and the fanciful, the world of the real and the world of the textual (including the deep, as it were abysmal, textuality of *Ur*-Derridian deferrals and faint tracings of meaning), both reflect and also create ideological positions, assumptions, manoeuvres, beliefs. Here is an exemplary interlocking of both the literal and the figural, of things present and things absent, of the world and the word, text and history. And it would be improper, however understandable the motive, whatever the applaudable wish to ginger up either deeply entrenched realists or seriously polarized deconstructionists, if analysis of this text were to play up either side at the expense of the other. This text is immersed in both the literal and the figural, the worldly and the textual. And in fact, whatever pole of that bipolarity is repressed or devalued, it has a tendency to return, to resurface, to insist on its co-presence in the texture of the whole. That irrepressibility is the subject of the next chapter of this book.

NOTES

1   F. R. Leavis, *The Great Tradition* (Chatto and Windus, London, 1948), Intro-
    duction, 2, n. 2, and ch. 5: '*Hard Times*: An Analytic Note', 227–48; Raymond
    Williams, *Culture and Society 1780–1950* (Chatto and Windus, London, 1958),
    ch. 5: 'The Industrial Novels'; David Craig, Introduction to Penguin English
    Library edn of *Hard Times* (Harmondsworth, 1969), 11–36, repr. in Craig, *The
    Real Foundations: Literature and Social Change* (Chatto and Windus, London, 1973),
    109–31; Terry Eagleton, Introduction to *Hard Times* (Methuen English Texts,
    London, 1987), 1–11. These readings variously depend on the pioneer researches
    of Humphry House, *The Dickens World* (Oxford University Press, 1941), Kathleen
    Tillotson, *Novels of the Eighteen Forties* (Oxford University Press, 1954), John
    Holloway, '*Hard Times*: A History and a Criticism', in *Dickens and the Twentieth
    Century*, ed. John Gross and Gabriel Pearson (Routledge and Kegan Paul, London,
    1962), 159–74.
2   See, variously, Melvyn Haberman, 'The Courtship of the Void: The World of
    Hard Times', in *The Worlds of Victorian Fiction*, ed. Jerome H. Buckley, Harvard
    English Studies, 6 (Harvard University Press, Cambridge, Mass., and London,
    1975), 37–55; David Lodge, 'How Successful is *Hard Times*?', in *Working with
    Structuralism* (Routledge and Kegan Paul, London, 1981), 37–45; Steven Connor,
    'Deconstructing Dickens: *Hard Times*', in *Charles Dickens* (Blackwell, Oxford,
    1985), 89–106.

3 J. Hillis Miller, *Fiction and Repetition: Seven English Novels* (Blackwell, Oxford, 1982), 142.

4 Paul de Man, *Blindness and Insight: Essays in the Rhetoric of Contemporary Criticism*, 2nd edn (Methuen, London, 1983).

5 Barbara Johnson, 'Metaphor, Metonymy and Voice in *Their Eyes Watching God*', in *A World of Difference* (Johns Hopkins University Press, Baltimore and London, 1987), 155–71. Roland Barthes, 'La Machine de l'écriture', in *Roland Barthes par Roland Barthes* (Seuil, Paris, 1975), 114.

6 See the extremely useful *A Handbook of Sixteenth-Century Rhetoric*, ed. Lee A. Sonnino (Routledge and Kegan Paul, London, 1968). For George Puttenham, *The Arte of English Poesie* (1589), see the useful edition of Gladys Doidge Willcock and Alice Walker (Cambridge University Press, 1936).

7 As Hillis Miller points out (praising Jakobson's 'self-subverting genius') in 'Stevens' Rock and Criticism as Cure, II', *Georgia Review*, 30, no. 2 (Summer 1976); repr. in *Theory Now and Then* (Harvester Wheatsheaf, Hemel Hempstead, 1991), 128–9.

8 David Lodge, *The Modes of Modern Writing: Metaphor, Metonymy, and the Typology of Modern Literature* (Arnold, London, 1977). See Maria Ruegg, 'Metaphor and Metonymy: The Logic of Structuralist Rhetoric', *Glyph*, 6 (1979); and Johnson, 'Metaphor, Metonymy'. Much discussion of these tropes has centred on Hayden White's subsuming historical writing under the structural-genetic determining power of the allegedly four main tropes, metaphor, metonymy, synecdoche, and irony, in his *Metahistory: The Historical Imagination in Nineteenth-Century Europe* (Johns Hopkins University Press, Baltimore and London, 1973). See e.g. Dominick LaCapra, 'A Poetics of Historiography: Hayden White's *Tropics of Discourse*', in *Rethinking Intellectual History: Texts, Contexts, Language* (Cornell University Press, Ithaca and London, 1983), 72–83. Connor, *Charles Dickens*, 96ff. 'This is not to say that these distinctions are maintained absolutely' (96); but metaphor and metonymy are so blurred in Connor's book that it would be most difficult for his 'distinctions' to be maintained *at all*.

9 See Valentine Cunningham, 'The Necessity of Literary History', in *Anglisten Tag 1986 Kiel: Vorträge*, ed. Rudolf Böhm and Henning Wode (Hoffmann Verlag, Giessen, 1987), 155–71.

10 Jakobson, quoted by Lodge, *Modes of Modern Writing*, 79.

11 Johnson, 'Metaphor, Metonymy', 157f.: 'these two tropes have always stood in hierarchical relation to each other.' Compare Abraham Fraunce, *The Arcadian Rhetoricke*, ed. Ethel Seaton (Hyperion Press, Westport, Conn., 1950), 4, 15. Fraunce alleges there are only two tropes: in the *first* place metonym and irony, in the *second* (even though 'There is no trope more flourishing than a Metaphore') metaphor and synecdoche. It's an arrangement which cuts across, not least, the common modern link between metonym and synecdoche. Barbara Johnson is not perturbed by de Man's 'summary' of 'the preference for metaphor over metonymy by aligning analogy with necessity and contiguity with chance' (metaphor = analogy = necessity; metonymy = contiguity = chance) as a prelude to his overturning the alleged historical precedence or supremacy of metaphor.

But, of course, the distinction is a straw man, set up because it's easy enough to counter. Metaphor must have some element of unnecessity in it (why would poets interest us if their metaphoric labours were all among the necessary and inevitable – i.e. the known already?), and metonymy must have elements of unchanciness or necessity (taking this part for that whole is commonly not a matter of mere chance connections; cf. de Man's example, 'Ford' for 'motor-car': initially the metonym could indeed have been 'Smith', but not after the great success of the Model T: like the arbitrariness of signifiers, this kind of chanciness doesn't last long: Paul de Man, *Allegories of Reading: Figural Language in Rousseau, Nietzsche, Rilke, and Proust* (Yale University Press, New Haven and London, 1979), 14).

12 See W. R. Greg, review of Mrs Gaskell's *Mary Barton, Edinburgh Review*, 89 (1849), 402–35, and discussion in Valentine Cunningham, *Everywhere Spoken Against: Dissent in the Victorian Novel* (Clarendon Press, Oxford, 1975), 133ff.

13 See Haberman, 'Courtship of the Void'.

5

The Return of the Repressed
i: Lexical Fix / Lexical Fics

Consulting a dictionary suffices only for mediocre candidates to the baccalaureate.

Desbois, *Le Droit de'lauteur en France* (1978),
quoted by Derrida, 'Des Tours de Babel'.

Gradgrinding Fact seeks to repress Circus Fancy, but without success. The worlds and modes of metaphor and metonym cannot deny their deep affinities. Whatever is repressed, or appears repressible, on either side of the textual binary line has a curious way of insisting, uncannily, on its right to return, even if only as a Banquo-like reminder and accusation at the table of its enemies. My next series of discussions looks at this linguistic/textual irrepressibility in three cases: the (post) modernist suspicion of philology, or the lexical fix (and fics); the widespread worry over the apparent dissolution of fullness into emptiness, the retreat of the full word into the empty one; and the alleged rejection or transcending of history by the fictions of classic (post)modernism. First, the dictionary fix, and fictions about dictionaries.

The dictionary, lexicography, lexical certainties, the claims of philology, all went dramatically out of fashion in the post-Saussurean period. The professor of Sanskrit wrote, as it were, a death-warrant for professors of Sanskrit. In the recent period of francophonic, Gallophiliac triumphalism in Anglo-Saxon criticism, undecidability came to reign.[1] Saussure shelved diachrony in an attempt to turn the clock back on a great era of philology, the nineteenth-century triumph of the lexicon, the hegemony in the nineteenth century of the historical mode of linguistic research and analysis. Derridian discourse – hostile to fixity, rootedness, centredness of meaning; friendly towards deferral of meaning, the escape of language from the traps of definition – has aided and abetted this suspicion of the lexicon as a place where meaning can be helpfully defined, bounded, contained. The whole Derridian effort at obscuring boundaries, edges, borders, frontiers of text or meaning, has had the effect of making the putting of bounds, limits, around words in the classic dictionary fashion of defining seem redundant, even when it's not just 'obviously' impossible.

Resistance to etymology is inevitable in a time of resistance to the diachronic axis of words, to philology, and to definiteness, centredness of meaning. What's labelled 'Cratylism' – the quest for etymological certainties, conducted with never so much misguided energy as by Plato in his *Cratylos* – has gone right out of fashion with literary critics. Etymology falls from grace along with authors, authorities, patriarchs, teleological reference points, acts of fathering, moments of genesis, stories of beginnings. For the *etymon*, as Roland Barthes put it, stands for origins and truth. It, and the lexicons that proclaim its power and importance, propose a pseudo-scientific or logocentric myth of truth in languages and texts which must be abandoned, or at least demythologized, in 'la défection des origines':

> His work is not anti-historical (at least, so he intends), but always, persistently, antigenetic, for Origin is a pernicious figure of Nature (of Physics): by an abusive interest, the *Doxa* 'crushes' Origin and Truth together, in order to make them into a single proof, each reinflating the other, according to a convenient swivel: are not the human sciences *etymological*, in pursuit of the *etymon* (origin and truth) of each phenomenon?[2]

The appearance of such sceptical sentiments in a work whose sections are arranged, dictionary fashion, in alphabetical order, so as to comprise a kind of lexicon of the self of Roland Barthes, is part of their provocation. Whatever history of selfhood, whatever brand of authorship, whatever story of genesis survive hereabouts, will do so only despite the destabilization of the dictionary or encyclopedia mode, convention, rhetoric. Of the numerous violences offered by modernism and postmodernism to the word, the logocentric tradition, to what D. H. Lawrence called 'the old stable ego of the character', it is the authority of dictionaries, the histories they register, the origins they allege, that will be resisted or even abandoned.

The historical shift into scepticism about lexicography can be nicely registered by the change of atmosphere that's clearly decipherable between the first appearance of Tennyson's poem *Maud* in 1855 and T. S. Eliot's *Notes Towards the Definition of Culture* almost a century later in 1948. When *Maud* came out in July 1855, the end of the poem celebrated the outbreak of the Crimean War as an end to the *canker* of peace: 'For the long, long canker of peace is over and done' (Part III; Section VI, stanza iv; line 50). But in the 1856 edition this line had been rewritten: 'For the peace, that I deemed no peace, is over and done?' Why so? It was because *canker* had been objected to by the reviewer in *Tait's Edinburgh Magazine*, September 1855, not just on moral grounds but on lexicographical ones:

> If any man comes forward to say or sing that the slaughter of 30,000 English-
> men in the Crimea tends to prevent women poisoning their babies, for the
> sake of the burial fees, in Birmingham, he is bound to show cause, and not
> bewilder our notions of morals and of lexicography by calling thirty years of
> intermitted [sic] war (absolute peace we have *not* had during the interval) a
> 'long, long *canker* of peace'.[3]

And Tennyson, ever sensitive to public criticism of his writing, was prompt to alter the line. The power of lexicography, the authority of the dictionary definition, could have no sharper illustration.

By contrast, the fate of Eliot's *Notes Towards the Definition of Culture* – a fate that serves as an emblem of the fate of T. S. Eliot's recent reputation – provides just as sharp an illustration of the loss of dictionary power in the meantime – that is, in our time. The *Notes'* claims to be able to define culture have gradually pulled less and less weight with readers. On his title-page Eliot inscribes a definition of *definition*:

> DEFINITION: 1. The setting of bounds; limitation (rare) – 1483. *Oxford English
> Dictionary*.

This definition accords with Eliot's Christian conservatism, his authoritari-anism and logocentrism, as well as with his customary choplogic habit of pursuing verbal strictness. Here, in little, is clearly stated his Arnoldian hostility to verbal and political anarchy. The date of the definition offered, 1483, of course, predates the arrival of Columbus in the Americas in 1492, and undoubtedly signals Eliot's acquired Anglicanism and his acquired suspicion of his own native Americanness. The definition of *definition* deftly defines Eliot's text and its theologico-socio-philosophical ambitions. But where Tennyson was ready to be prevailed upon by appeals to lexicography, Eliot's public was not, and Eliot's demise as a critical authority – an authority that was at its zenith in 1948 – has been spectacular. His critical power and the authority of the lexicography he promotes have sunk together.[4]

Postmodernist criticism has in principle thrown the authority of the lexicon out of the window as vigorously as Thackeray's Becky Sharp, refusing her pedagogic mentor's parting gift at the opening of *Vanity Fair*, chucked the presentation copy of Dr Johnson's *Dictionary* out of the window of the coach in which she quit Miss Pinkerton's Academy for Young Ladies. Lexicons, those collections of patriarchal ideology and authoritarian doxas, are vigorously flung back at the academy that would sign them with its own name of authority, as central to the custodianship of syllabuses, canons, meanings, interpretations.

T. S. Eliot was desperately worried about words slipping and sliding. He craved the grounded confidence of definiteness, the true truth of true etymology. 'I owe to a friend, the late Richard Jennings', he writes in the Preface to the 1962 edition of his *Notes*, 'the correction of a spelling which gives a false etymology (*autarchy* corrected to *autarky* on p. 116).' His wrestle with the definition of *culture* takes place against the vexing slackness of the draft constitution of UNESCO in its effort to define itself in relation to the 'Culture' of its title (United Nations Educational Scientific and Cultural Organization). UNESCO's draft Articles of 1945 provide 'only one of numerous instances which might be cited, of the use of a word which nobody bothers to examine'. Eliot's own first chapter would, by way of rebuking contrast, endeavour 'to distinguish and relate the three principal uses of the word: and to make the point, that when we use the term in one of these three ways we should do so in awareness of the others. I then try to expose the essential relation of culture to religion, and to make clear the limitations of the word *relation* as an expression of this ' "relation".' And a footnote quotes Labour Prime Minister Clement Atlee and his Minister of Education, Miss Ellen Wilkinson, at UNESCO's founding London conference, both of them derisively slack, in Eliot's view, about the definition of culture: 'when it comes to talking nonsense about culture, there is nothing to choose between politicians of one stripe or another. . . . The pursuit of politics is incompatible with a strict attention to exact meanings on all occasions.'[5]

By revealing and symptomatic contrast, in the 'Etymologies' entry of his *Barthes by Barthes*, Roland Barthes chides himself precisely for limiting words in his own discourse to their strict etymological definitions. This etymologocentrism is a shaming personal vice. Like Eliot, he delimits the word *definition* to mean 'a tracing of a limit'. But this customary practice, sanctioned by traditional lexicographical assumption, is to 'cut off' words, 'so to speak, at the root' – to pluck them up, stop them growing, deaden them, for: 'in etymology it is not the truth or the origin of the words which pleases him but rather the *effect of overdetermination* which it authorizes: the word is seen as a palimpsest: it then seems to me that I have ideas *on the level of language* – which is quite simply: to write'.[6] And this kind of self-confessed pleasure in the exuberance of signification, the expansiveness of *écriture*, this postmodernist relish for the slippage and sliding of the verbal palimpsest – an immensely expanded update of New Critical ambiguity – is readily endorsed by postmodernists as, in fact, the real reality of the lexicon: the essence of the true anti-authoritarianism that's really built into dictionaries for those that have ears to hear and eyes to see what is the true anti-*etymon* nature of etymology. The lexicon, on this view, does not lead, or should not be thought of as leading, you back to firm roots, to stable origins of meaning. On this model, dictionaries leak, or they lead you round by the nose in circles, their attempts at definition and limitation a set of *ignes fatui*, a system no less of deferred meanings. And in the same brisk atmosphere of overturning of older assumptions, this model of the lexicon becomes a handy model for texts.

And how should it be prevented from doing so, for texts are comprised of the stuff of dictionary that is now defined thus as a bearer of delusion? HencetHillis Miller's triumphalist dictionary analogy for what he perceives as the Conradian system of forever deferred meaning that *Lord Jim* is held to consist of – triumphalist because it's offered as representing a whole scheme of textuality. 'Each . . . passage . . . refers to the others by way of anticipation or recollection . . . but when the reader turns to the other passage it is no easier to understand and itself refers to other such passages. No one of them is the original ground, the basis on which the others may be interpreted.' It's a tendentious enough reading, and one obviously fired by the Saussure-inspired Derridian deferral system in which signifiers are endlessly in pursuit of signifieds which keep on turning out to be merely other signifiers in pursuit of yet other signifieds. David Lodge's professorial novel *Small World: An Academic Romance* (1984) illustrates this Sisyphean quest for ever elusive grails of meaning with great comic deftness in the character Perse McGarrigle's endless rummage through the literary conference scene in pursuit of the gorgeous Angelica Pabst, who, by the time he arrives at any particular scholarly *entretien*, has always just moved on to the next one. Or, as another of Lodge's jokily plotted exempla has it: you ask for some *Durex* across the counter, but end up with a box of *Farex*, a baby food, and narrowly escape having to make do with *Exlax*, a laxative.[7] The signifying chain, the endlessness of verbal difference, knows no mercy: the signifying carpet is always being pulled from under every solid-seeming signified. Hillis Miller, being no novelist, has to make do with the lexicon by way of illustration of this process. '*Lord Jim* is like a dictionary in which the entry under one word refers the reader back to another word which refers him to another and then back to the first word again, in an endless circling.'[8]

Navel Uniform

This is a view of how texts and dictionaries mirror each other in their frustration of the Eliotic quest for definiteness and limits of meaning that is granted tremendous and exemplary succinctness by Samuel Weber in his discussions of Freud's view of the dream-text – that kind of text-making which literary criticism has come more and more to believe is paradigmatic of all text-making. The dream-text frustrates interpretation: 'the very forces' – this is Weber glossing the master Freud – 'that make interpretation possible – by forming the dream in the first place – also render its results uncertain, incalculable, and impossible to verify (or to falsify) definitively. For there can be no such "definitive" instance precisely because there is no Archimedean or transcendental point from which such a definition or delineation could be established.' And Weber, like many another reader of Freud, is drawn to that most celebrated of passages in *The Interpretation of Dreams* where Freud seeks to describe this structural indefiniteness of the dream by means of a heap of metaphors piled around the arresting central metaphor of an inevitably *dark navel* that's located at the centre of every dream-text:

> Even in the best interpreted dreams, there is often a place (*eine Stelle*) that must be left in the dark, because in the process of interpreting one notices a tangle of dream-thoughts arising (*anhebt*) which resists unravelling but has also made no further contributions (*keine weiteren Beiträge*) to the dream-content. This, then, is the dream's navel, the place where it straddles the unknown (*dem Unerkannten aufsizt*). The dream-thoughts, to which interpretation leads one, are necessarily interminable (*ohne Abschluss*) and branch out on all sides into the netlike entanglement (*in die netzartige Verstrickung*) of our world of thought. Out of one of the denser places of this meshwork, the dream-wish rises (*erhebt sich*) like a mushroom out of its mycelium.[9]

Freud's metaphoric impetus is considerable. But just what, Weber invites us to ask, is being located by these metaphors; where is the place of origin of the dream? Weber waives, as so many commentators do, the question of translation, Freud's German, his own English, and reaches straight for the *Oxford English Dictionary*. But this gets him, literally, nowhere: the quest for definition proves a circular line of research, a hoop-snake chase into frustration. If the dream-wish arises out of the dream-navel like a mushroom out of its *mycelium*, one had better know what a *mycelium* is. The *Dictionary* tells. It's a term in botany for 'The vegetative part of the thallus of fungi, consisting of white filamentous tubes (hyphae); the spawn of mushrooms'. But the *Dictionary* is telling in too unenlightening a way. What, Weber wonders, is the *thallus*? This turns out to be another botanical term: 'A vegetable structure without vascular tissue, in which there is no differentiation into stem and leaves, and from which true roots are absent'. Which is, of course, extraordinarily unhelpful: how more indefinite can one get than a piece of vegetation defined entirely by negatives and absences – no vascular tissue, no differentiation, no true roots? What, then, might it mean for the dream to *straddle* this, or a similar, unknowable place? Alas, the *Dictionary* meanings of *straddle* prove, likewise, a map of absences, a decentred sprawl of spreading signification involving deepening lunges into equivocation ('*US colloq.* To occupy or take up an equivocal position in regard to') and not-quite-struck targets ('*Gunnery.* To find the range of (an object) by placing shots first to one side of it and then on the other'), an exercise in lexicographical bracketing-fire that ends up not in any certainty but only with the offered synonym for *straddle* – namely, yet another botanical term, *divaricate*. And what does this mean, Weber then enquires of his dictionary? And he learns that it indicates a kind of super-straddling, a spreading, stretching, diverging in different directions. Straddling equals straddling; the definition of *divarication* is a kind of super-prevarication. The *Dictionary* by no means clarifies Freud's text of the dream-text. The lexicon rather postpones defining. Its professed processes of illumination comprise all too visible darknesses.

What the *Dictionary*, then, offers its readers is a classic, definitive experience of the *mise en abyme*, an exemplary voyage into Lacanian *béance*. And into *béance* upon *béance*. For what emerges 'from this brief recourse to the dictionary' is that locating even the Lacanian 'hole, gap, lack, or abyss' is most difficult. Freud, and his text, and the dream-text are, between them, all conspiring to defeat the quest for meaning, and in so doing are comprising an essential model of all such frustrated meanings within the postmodernist conception of how texts operate:

> the meaning of the thallus begins to appear to be – or rather *to play* – a very bad joke on all attempts to articulate meaning. For the ramifications of Freud's description of the dream-navel suggest that interpretation originates and ends in a kind of calculated deception: in a posture necessarily, and structurally, an imposture, and perhaps an imposition.[10]

And lexicography, as represented by the *Oxford English Dictionary*, is presented as playing a key role in this very bad joke, this harshly unwitty *Witz*. Like the dream, and all texts, including this one of Freud's on the dream-text, the lexicon is offered as celebrating a taunting, teasing indefiniteness that it professes to deny, but in practice cannot. The *Dictionary*'s insights are all blinds, its apparently hard foundations for definition all places where meaning sops and drips and leaks away. And, of course, this view of how the word-hoard, the linguistic resource-book, the domestic site of the *langue* at its most plausibly domesticated, is just playing a foxy verbal game with us coincides with, and is supposed to be providing a clinching analogy or base for, all those classic places in modernist fiction where hermeneutics and certainties collapse, where positive meaning is edged out, blurred, obscured at some exemplary watery margin.

Leaky Edges

Such watery margins – founding and compounding the business of lexical leak – abound in early modernist fiction. My chapter 3 dwelt on Hardy's Anne Garland in chapter 34 ('A Speck on the Sea') of *The Trumpet-Major*, up on Portland Bill, trying with the aid of an old sailor's telescope to make out her lover on board his departing ship, the *Victory*, but unable to read the scene with any certainty and gradually losing sight of the ship – 'absorbed into the main', the 'ceaseless unintelligible incantation' of the sea. But Hardy wasn't the only 'man' whose fiction 'used to notice such things'. Another such noticer was his contemporary Joseph Conrad, who contrives another extraordinary example of the collapse of certitudes at a watery edge at the end of chapter 35 of *Lord Jim* (1900), where Marlow tells how he last saw Jim on the beach at Patusan. Marlow is about to be rowed out to his schooner. Jim, already at a distance from the departing Marlow, appears to be about to shout some message for someone at home. ' "Tell them . . ." he began.' But Jim does not say who is to be told. His eyes look 'dumbly', and he fails to complete the message: ' "No – nothing," he said.' And as Marlow's ship sails away, the silent figure that is being gradually engulfed by the encroaching darkness of the evening disappears gradually from view, a figure 'veiled' still for his narrator, and so for us ('Was it still veiled? I don't know': but he does know that, and so do we; it's just about the sum of our knowledge):

> For me that white figure in the stillness of coast and sea seemed to stand at the heart of a vast enigma. The twilight was ebbing fast from the sky above his head, the strip of sand had sunk already beneath his feet, he himself appeared no bigger than a child – then only a speck, a tiny white speck, that seemed to catch all the light left in a darkened world. . . . And, suddenly, I lost him. . . .

And there, naturally, Marlow's narrative has to end, in an incompleteness emblematized in this absorption of Jim into another of modernism's watery enigmas. And like Marlow, Marlow's audience has nothing to say: the possibility of discussion and comment collapses with the failure of narrative information.

In chapters 30 and 31 of Henry James's *The Ambassadors* (1903) it's *moral* blurring that occurs dramatically at the watery edge; but again, it's the threat to the possibility of narrative certitudes that gives the accidental meeting of Strether with Chad and Madame de Vionnet its peculiar force. When the shirt-sleeved young man and the lady with a pink parasol, drifting into view in their rowing-boat around a bend in the river, prove to be Chad and Madame de Vionnet, the shock to Strether's moral sense as he perceives 'the deep, deep truth of the intimacy' between them is considerable. And it's a shock, too, for narratology, for the possibility of maintaining fiction's old confidences, the assurances of the Maupassant story or the Lambinet landscape which Strether had just been fantasizing himself as part of. This transaction on the river bank is the kind of upset for textuality ('not a breath of the cooler evening that wasn't somehow a syllable of the text') that fuels all of the narrative hesitancies, doubts, and blurs of *The Ambassadors'* narrative procedure – the essence of the problematic style of the later James.[11] And the same goes, in the same dualistic way, for Virginia Woolf's whole narrative enterprise in the parallel upset of a slightly later date at yet another watery margin, the one we looked at earlier (in chapter 1), which takes place beside the sea on the opening page of *Jacob's Room*.

And what all such fictionalized leaky margins are, as it were, preparing us for is the explosive assault on the lexicon that takes place in Beckett's *Watt* (1953 in French, 1963 in English). Watt gets into terrible epistemological knots in the house of his incomprehensible master Mr Knott. Watt succeeds an eloquently unhappy servant called Arsene, and thus stands at the end of an interminable line of puzzled men, all failed detectives trying and failing to traverse the labyrinths of Knott's house and wishes. Arsene was no doubt so named by Beckett in wry tribute to the French novelist Maurice Leblanc's detective Arsène Lupin, hero of such stories as *Arsène Lupin contre Sherlock Holmes* (1908). The name is there to ensure, not least, that we perceive that Arsene and Watt and the rest are all going round in circles on a lexical loop – or loopy – line, looping (or Lupin) the loop in an epistemological quest forever doomed to end in blanks, or *blancs*. Watt wishes he had paid greater attention to Arsene's long parting lament; for he is in need of words apt to his strange situation. But all the words he tries on prove to be misfits, and terribly susceptible to lexical leakage:

> . . . he desired words to be applied to his situation, to Mr. Knott, to the house, to the grounds, to his duties, to the stairs, to his bedroom, to the kitchen, and in a general way to the conditions of being in which he found himself. For Watt now found himself in the midst of things which, if they consented to be named, did so as it were with reluctance. . . . Looking at a pot, for example, or thinking of a pot, at one of Mr. Knott's pots, of one of Mr. Knott's pots, it was in vain that Watt said, Pot, pot. Well, perhaps not quite in vain, but

very nearly. For it was not a pot, the more he looked, the more he reflected, the more he felt sure of that, that it was not a pot at all. It resembled a pot, it was almost a pot, but it was not a pot of which one could say, Pot, pot, and be comforted. . . .

Then, when he turned for reassurance to himself, who was not Mr Knott's, in the sense that the pot was, who had come from without and whom the without would take again, he made the distressing discovery that of himself too he could no longer affirm anything that did not seem as false as if he had affirmed it of a stone. Not that Watt was in the habit of affirming things of himself, for he was not, but he found it a help, from time to time, to be able to say, with some appearance of reason, Watt is a man, all the same, Watt is a man, or, Watt is in the street, with thousands of fellow-creatures within call. And Watt was greatly troubled by this tiny little thing, more troubled perhaps than he had ever been by anything, and Watt had been frequently and exceedingly troubled, in his time, by this imperceptible, no, hardly imperceptible, since he perceived it, by this indefinable thing that prevented him from saying, with conviction, and to his relief, of the object that was so like a pot, that it was a pot, and of the creature that still in spite of everything presented a large number of exclusively human characteristics, that it was a man. And Watt's need of semantic succour was at times so great that he would set to trying names on things, and on himself, almost as a woman hats. Thus of the pseudo-pot he would say, after reflexion, It is a shield, or, growing bolder, It is a raven, and so on. But the pot proved as little a shield, or a raven, or any other of the things that Watt called it, as a pot. As for himself, though he could no longer call it a man, as he had used to do, with the intuition that he was perhaps not talking nonsense, yet he could not imagine what else to call it, if not a man. But Watt's imagination had never been a lively one. So he continued to think of himself as a man, as his mother had taught him, when she said, There's a good little man, or, There's a bonny little man, or, There's a clever little man. But for all the relief that this afforded him, he might just as well have thought of himself as a box, or an urn.[12]

The 'old credentials' have disappeared because 'the old words' for those credentials have lost their meaning, and so have the old books that sustained a sense of a definable lexicon – novels and, above all, dictionaries. Watt's distraught play over the naming and writing of pots is there, I take it, to reverse a long tradition of confident naming of things and writing about them instated classically for the English novel by Daniel Defoe in *Robinson Crusoe* (1719–20), where Crusoe's positive hermeneutics, his bookish faith in the legibility of Scripture, his exemplary capacity to know and express himself through writing, through his journal, are rooted in a confident epistemology that runs in happy liaison with his ability to learn, know, handle, the world of things, and in particular his soon acquired skill in the making of pots. The more or less secure sense of self founded for our tradition and for the greater part of the history of our novels by Defoe's fiction is grounded in an epistemologically positive lexicon, one that's as relaxed in its dealings with Crusoe's pottery as the Old Testament Book of the Prophet Jeremiah was in treating of Jehovah the divine Potter. Naming the self, naming God, naming anything, is focused for Crusoe in the successful making and naming of pots, in what Hillis Miller called 'a now exploded Cratylism' (in his Modern Language Association Presidential Address), 'the . . . belief that the phenomenality of words somehow naturally corresponds to the essence of things'.[13] For Crusoe, lexical failure goes hand in hand with manufacturing failure: 'I could not make above two large earthen ugly things, I cannot call them jars, in about two months' labour'. And so, conversely, do manufacturing success and lexical success, success in saying: 'in the morning I had three very good, I will not say handsome pipkins, and two other earthen pots, as hard burnt as could be desired; and one of them perfectly glazed with the running of the sand. . . . After this experiment, I need not say that I wanted no sort of earthenware for my use; but I must needs say. . . .' And the Novel form, the profoundest literature of selfhood produced in modern times, comes out of this confident labour at the lexical kiln. It's not surprising, in the light of *Watt*'s reworking of Crusoe, that Watt's incapacity to know and name himself should founder in his difficulties over knowing and naming one of Mr Knott's pots. When your need of semantic succour is as great as Watt's, your existential confidence goes rapidly to pot.

But Whose Dictionary?

But, we have to ask, how valid is this wide modern quarrel with the lexicon – from Freud's *Witz* to Beckett's *Watt* and beyond – this shortest of Becky Sharp ways with the dictionary? It depends, I take it, on whose dictionary we take as read.

Roland Barthes's concept of the writer's inner dictionary, his personal lexical tissue, is strikingly close to Hillis Miller's or Samuel Weber's lexical loop-line. The writer's

> only power is to mix writings, to counter the ones with the others, in such a way as never to rest on any one of them. Did he wish to *express himself*, he ought at least to know that the inner 'thing' he thinks to 'translate' is itself only a ready-formed dictionary, its words only explainable through other words, and so on indefinitely; something experienced in exemplary fashion by the young

Thomas de Quincey, he who was so good at Greek that in order to translate absolutely modern ideas and images into that dead language, he had, so Baudelaire tells us (in *Paradis Artificiels*), 'created for himself an unfailing dictionary, vastly more extensive and complex than those resulting from the ordinary patience of purely literary themes'. Succeeding the Author, the scriptor no longer bears within him passions, humours, feelings, impressions, but rather this immense dictionary from which he draws a writing that can know no halt: life never does more than imitate the book, and the book itself is only a tissue of signs, an imitation that is lost, infinitely deferred.[14]

The expressive self here gets reduced to an inner, formalist lexicon whose words do not register anything but a self-explanatory system of words cut off from 'passions, humours, feelings, impressions', only 'a tissue of signs' whose worldly reference is 'lost, infinitely deferred'. The year when Barthes offered this was 1968, a time ripe for new French revolutions, revolutionary manifests, and manifestations, and the Bastille that Barthes seems hankering to storm, or at least negotiate with, is Lévi-Strauss's 1960 piece, 'Reflections on a Work by Vladimir Propp'.

What Lévi-Strauss had objected to in the *Ur*-structuralist work of the Russian Formalist Propp was that he analysed the *form* of folk-tales but had nothing to offer on their *function*. And this 'Formalism destroys its object' because its analyses stick at the syntagmatic level, operate only a morphological, grammatical, syntactical model of story. The vocabulary, or lexical level, is being crucially ignored. This is the formalistic error, 'the belief that the grammar can be tackled at once and the dictionary postponed. But what is true for some linguistic systems is even more true for myths and tales. This is so because in this case grammar and vocabulary are not only closely linked while operating at distinct levels; they virtually adhere to each other on all surfaces and cover each other completely.' And for Lévi-Strauss the contribution of 'the dictionary' is concreteness, particularity (the particularity of the individual folk-tale that Propp's systemic analysis has abstracted away), the reality of ethnography, 'the complementarity of signifier and signified', the rootedness of words and of tales, in history and ideology:

> By restricting itself exclusively to the rules which govern the grouping of propositions, [formalism erroneously] loses sight of the fact that no language exists in which the vocabulary can be deduced from the syntax. The study of any linguistic system requires the cooperation of the grammarian and the philologist. This means that in the matter of oral tradition the morphology is sterile unless direct or indirect ethnographic observation comes to render it fertile. Imagining that the two tasks can be dissociated, that the grammatical study can be undertaken first and the lexical study postponed until later, one

is condemned to produce nothing but an anemic grammar and a lexicon in which anecdotes replace definitions. In the end, neither would accomplish its purpose.

Lévi-Strauss accepts the Saussurean proposition that language is 'structural at the phonological stage'. He is 'gradually becoming convinced it is also structural at the level of grammar'. But vocabulary – dictionary stuff, philology's word-children – remains stubbornly historicized, individualist, resistant to the structuralist, differential analysis ('we have not yet discovered the angle under which vocabulary would give a handle to structural analysis'). In other words, language, folk-tales, the ethnographical stories that Lévi-Strauss analyses, and thus by implication all text, exist dualistically; and the lexicon side of the coin, the dictionary, philological stuff, represent what is rooted in history, the concrete, the real. Franco Moretti, in a discussion aiming to weld together both the structure and the sociology of writing, rightly calls Lévi-Strauss's article a 'splendid attack'.[15] It's splendid because it refuses to accept the anaemia of Formalism – neither an anaemic grammar nor an anaemic lexicon. And this lack of anaemia characterizes the idea of the dictionary in other powerful cases besides Lévi-Strauss's and Franco Moretti's.

You the Weak Definer

To be sure, there is little quarrel anywhere among postmodernist critics with the enclosed and, as it were, self-defeating *mise-en-abyme* formalism of the Hillis Miller/Roland Barthes/Samuel Weber dictionary as such. But the trouble is that this model, like Propp's morphology, simply doesn't go far enough. Dr Johnson himself, great fount of lexicographical wisdoms, recognized that dictionaries are always (to use the title of Elisabeth Murray's marvellous book about James Murray of the *Oxford Dictionary*) *Caught in the Web of Words*.[16] The rub in the dictionary's only available *modus operandi* is that it has, as Johnson's Preface to his *Dictionary* (1755) put it, to 'interpret a language by itself'. And 'To interpret a language by itself is very difficult.' Often an appropriate synonym for the word being defined doesn't exist. Paraphrase is frequently impossible – 'simple ideas cannot be described.' It's bad enough that some words are so heavily freighted with meaning, have such an 'exuberance of signification' that it is 'scarcely possible to collect all their senses'. It's worse that some words have a 'signification . . . so loose and general' that 'it is hard to trace them through the maze of variation, to catch them on the brink of utter inanity, to circumscribe them by any limitations, or interpret them by any words of distinct and settled meaning' (and Johnson includes *get*, *do*, *go*, *make*, and *take* in his daunting list). And it's worse still that the quest for definition can spiral downwards in a search for ever simpler words to describe more difficult ones by that in the end simply runs out of words that are simple enough: 'To explain, requires the use of terms less abstruse than that which is to be explained, and such terms cannot always be found.' The tone of despair about the deceptively knowable common words undoubtedly came more or less straight from the thinker about language whom Johnson so greatly admired, namely John Locke: 'men talk to one another, and dispute in words, whose meaning is not agreed between them, out of a mistake that the significations of common words are certainly established, and the precise ideas they stand for perfectly known.'[17] It is, Johnson writes, 'the fate of hapless lexicography' to be always endeavouring to define, on the one hand, the overflowing cornucopian word and, on the other hand, the word as bucket with a hole in it.

So Johnson's Preface to his *Dictionary* makes an arresting blend of lexicographer's pride and despair. The dream of the poet, that he might settle the orthography, regulate the structures and ascertain 'the signification of *English* words', has foundered in the cold dawn of the lexicographer waking to another day in which 'I saw that one enquiry only gave occasion to another, that book referred to book, that to search was not always to find, and to find was not always to be informed'. No wonder the key self-mirroring definitions of Johnson's *Dictionary*, the ones about defining and about dictionary stuff, conspire to deconstruct the flawed ambitions they announce. To *define*, 'to give the definition; to explain a thing by its qualities and circumstances', is illustrated from Locke: 'though *defining* be thought the proper way to make known the proper signification, yet there are some words that will not be *defined*.' To *define*, 'To determine; to decide; to decree', gets illustrated with a quotation from Francis Bacon about the unjust judge who '*defineth* amiss of lands and properties'. *Definer* is illuminated by a quotation from the poet Matthew Prior about vain tries at definitions of God: 'Let your imperfect definition show, / That nothing you, the weak *definer*, know.' Likewise, *definitive* comes with a sentence from Brown's *Vulgar Errors* about authors writing dubiously, 'even in matters wherein is expected a strict and definitive truth'. Not dissimilarly, *word* is illustrated by more of Locke's scepticism ('Amongst men who confound their ideas with *words*, there must be endless disputes, wrangling, and jargon'). And *dictionary* is explicated by a very curious quotation indeed from the *Vulgar Errors* about people who are 'afraid of letters and characters, notes and dashes, which, set together, do signify nothing; and not only in the *dictionary* of man, but in the subtler vocabulary of Satan'. Fear of writing, Satanic vocabulary, a writing that signifies nothing: it's a perturbing set of notions to pack a dictionary definition of *dictionary* with.

But like all these self-erasing, self-questioning moments, this is only one more instance of the collaboration between the darkness and light that, as Johnson puts it, are always present to impede and distress the lexicographer – who is for ever stuck between the interactive polarities of insight and blindness.[18]

A Random House

This is a view of the plight of the dictionary given most memorable expression not just by critics but, of course, by postmodernist novelists, and by the blind Argentinian librarian Jorge Luis Borges in particular. Borges's texts create mazes not only of meaning but of lexicons, dictionaries, encyclopedias, which entice their fictional and real-life readers into their pages and into libraries in search of definitions and informations which they keep refusing to provide. Characteristically, the story 'Tlön, Uqbar, Orbis Tertius' has a narrative self and one Bioy Casares pursuing elusive names, places, characters and languages through a hermetic, labyrinthine sequence of actual and imaginary encyclopedias that are variously defective, misleading, specious, and pirated. What Borges gives his readers is fictions of libraries, books, especially dictionaries and encyclopedias, as circular, labyrinthine, layered on – to themselves, full of definitions and information that lead only to more books and further words, all revealing lacks of information that require further dictionary and encyclopedia entries and yet further dictionaries and encyclopedias – which we don't have or can't find – for a desired final clarification that will always finally elude us. Borges has even provided his own, as it were, anti-lexicon or anti-encyclopedia, *The Book of Imaginary Beings*, a dictionary of real, unreal, mythic, fictional, historical, literary creatures. Borges professes admiration for the sort of dictionary that would finally abolish doubt about language, the artificial, self-explanatory lexicon of a John Wilkins; but what he really relishes is the arbitrary, queered, freakish aspects of the encyclopedia claim, the dictionary premise and promise, that of sorting, defining, ordering things through words, and, usually, alphabetically. Wilkins's 'ambiguities, redundancies, and deficiencies recall', Borges writes, 'those attributed by Dr Franz Kuhn to a certain Chinese encyclopedia entitled *Celestial Emporium of Benevolent Knowledge*. On those remote pages it is written that animals are divided into (a) those that belong to the Emperor, (b) embalmed ones, (c) those that are trained, (d) suckling pigs, (e) mermaids, (f) fabulous ones, (g) stray dogs, (h) those that are included in this classification, (i) those that tremble as if they were mad, (j) innumerable ones, (k) those drawn with a very fine camel's hair brush, (l) others, (m) those that have just broken a flower vase, (n) those that resemble flies from a distance.'[19]

This wonderful reduction of lexicon to the chaos of inventive arbitariness, this shoving of dictionary down into an abysm where the real and actual consort with the fabulous, with fantasy and myth, with words about myth and myths about words, books, lexicons – Borges has, of course, invented this spry Emporium – all this mightily excited Michel Foucault and inspired him to embark on his great work of historical epistemology *Les Mots et les choses*.[20] And it has all had an even profounder effect on fiction. The fabulous realism, or fabulation, of South American fiction – indeed, what we may call the South-Americanization of the postmodernist novel – clearly owes much to this throwing of spanners by Borges into the lexicon certainties. Umberto Eco's *The Name of the Rose*, most critically knowing of post-modernist fictions, whose contents comprise a veritable catalogue of the tropes and concerns of postmodern criticism and fiction as it enfolds the reader ever more completely in the labyrinthine arcana of its scriptures, scriptoria, libraries, and semantic quests, naturally starts with a bibliographical preface from its implied author, which is a receding catalogue of accidental, confusing, frustrating textual encounters and researches done in obvious parodic tribute to Borges's 'Tlön, Uqbar, Orbius Tertius'. Just as naturally, Eco's monkish and scriptorial characters include one Jorge of Burgos – recognizably a close cousin of Jorge Luis Borges.[21]

Characteristic, again, of Borges's proliferating fictional brood is the way G. Cabrera Infante Cubanizes Joyce and Sterne under the blinding aegis of the blind Argentinian master in his novel *Three Trapped Tigers*. Borges puts in an appearance in it as George Ludwig Borgid, heir to the 'elephantine' pedantry of J'aime Joys, Earza Pounk, and Teas Eliot. This is in the novel's 'Brainteaser' section, hero of which is Bustrófedon, who constructs his worlds 'at random (house) out of a dictionary' (a reference to the USA's *Random House Dictionary*), conducting his 'semantic safaris' through dictionaries, 'happy trip(s) around the words', keenly involved in the dictionary's provision of a *roman policier* or Hitchcock movie of word-guilt, word-murder, word-police, word-suspense. He dies a hero of word-play, a 'new Adam' who 'gave everything a name as though he really was inventing language'. He's had a whale of a time, bringing forth imagined worlds out of lexicons, in a text that pays constant tribute – as Borges's own fictions do, of course – to *Moby Dick*. And aptly enough; for everything in that great fishy text of Melville from 1851 starts in, and plunges the reader back into, an originating array of etymologies and lexicons.

'Call me Ishmale,' writes Infante's 'I', questing about Havana for women, his car driver Cué 'looking like Cuéptain Ahab hunting Morbid Dyke'. The declaration is quite in keeping with the novel's dense web of 'literatured' intertextuality. And it holds out to us the taunting possibility of finding this text's roots in that antecedent text's originating moment: 'Call me Ishmael'.[22] But though everyone remembers that *Moby Dick* begins with those words, in fact it does not. Utterly in line with the lexicon obsessions of the Borgesian fan-club's texts and of Borges's own fictions, *Moby Dick* begins much earlier than that moment of self-naming that everybody remembers, with an Etymology – supplied by an Usher to a Grammar School, a duster of 'old lexicons and grammars' – followed by Extracts, 'higgledy-piggledy' bits of earlier texts about whales, supplied in turn by a Sub-Sub-Librarian, 'a pains-taking burrower and grubworm of a poor devil of a Sub-Sub' who has ransacked 'the long Vaticans and street-stalls of the earth, picking up whatever random allusions to whales he could anyways find in any book whatsoever, sacred or profane'. What the Borgesians between them conspire to keep reminding us is that writing, like *Moby Dick*, is inside the dictionary whale: it begins in dictionary stuff, is clothed in it, enclosed in it, is about it, has it perpetually girt about it, and, furthermore, that dictionaries are like this. Texts on this plan lead to dictionary stuff, and that dictionary stuff to the dictionary stuff that comprises it too.

But this formalistic lexical loop-line that so distressed Dr Johnson, and that's had all the Borgesians zooming and skidding so energetically round it, is not, and impressively not, the whole story of lexicon – neither of Dr Johnson, nor, for that matter, of Barthes or Borges either. 'In the end', Alvin Kernan has suggested, Johnson 'inevitably comes to and describes the tau-tology that structuralists have identified as the principle by which language – being "non-referential" or not connected to some extra-linguistic, prior reality – makes meaning.' But recognizing 'the semantic circle' was not the end of the story for Johnson, only the half of it.[23]

The Solid Things in Tongues

A *lexicon* as defined by Johnson's *Dictionary* is 'A dictionary: a book teaching the signification of words': a book of words about words whose definition comes enhanced with the aid of more words – namely, a quotation from Milton. The fixing quotation, however, not only firms up the offered defi-nition, it also snaps open the lexical loop-line's particular hermeneutical circle:

> Though a linguist should pride himself to have all the tongues that Babel cleft the world into, yet if he had not studied the solid things in them as well as the words and *lexicons*, yet he were nothing so much to be esteemed a learned man as any yeoman competently wise in his mother dialect only.

'Though I speak with the tongues of men and of angels and have not charity I am become as a sounding brass, or a tinkling cymbal': thus St Paul in the First Epistle to the Corinthians 13: 1, in a declaration that Milton (and Johnson) are rehearsing and rehashing. For here in the *Dictionary*, charity, the master trope of the Christian faith that relieves Babel of all its clangorous linguistic boasting, is replaced by a knowledge of the 'solid things in' words that will supplement mere words and mere wordbooks. Charity precludes linguistic and glossolalic pride, according to the Pauline conception: 'charity vaunteth not itself, is not puffed up.' In the Milton/Johnson recension of the argument, a study of 'the solid things in' words will prevent mere *lipwisdom* ('Wisdom in talk without practice').

Even Borges is aware of the human imperatives that drive encyclopedia-making, and he endorses the lexicon's attempt to grasp the solid things in words – even if he regards the effort as utopian and a futile mimicking of an uncontingent, and in the end humanly unwritable, divine lexicography ('we must conjecture the words, the definitions, the etymologies, the synonymies of God's secret dictionary').[24] Roland Barthes's concessions are more down to earth. In practice, Barthes concedes, linguistic theory keeps bumping into the world of practice, not least medical practice. When, he suggests, the signified in the semiological system of the body is a disease, semiological standoffishness yields to the operational demands of medical practitioners. So it is, he allows, with dictionaries: daily realities prize open the linguistic hoop-snake:

> theoretically, systematically, a dictionary is an impossible object, it is a dizzy-ing object and in some sense a demoniac one. Yet dictionaries are useful and are workable, precisely because, at a certain moment, we halt the infinite critique by the intrusion of the operational, i.e., we simply stop at a definition and make use of it for tasks of a practical or operational type.[25]

This realism, as refreshing and harsh as the second thoughts induced by the death of Barthes's mother, is not unakin to Locke's own. Locke keeps declaring that a dictionary providing 'as it were, a natural history' of usage is too difficult to accomplish ('requires too many hands as well as too much time, cost, and pains to be hoped for in this age'); but he also believes that the 'true signification of many terms' could be easily rendered in a Vocabulary Book, or lexicon, that had illustrations:

> yet methinks it is not unreasonable to propose, that words standing for things which are known and distinguished by their outward shapes should be ex-pressed by little draughts and prints made of them. A vocabulary made after

this fashion would perhaps with more ease, and in less time, teach the true signification of many terms, especially in languages of remote countries or ages, and settle truer ideas in men's minds of several things, whereof we read the names in ancient authors, than all the large and laborious comments of learned critics. Naturalists, that treat of plants and animals, have found the benefit of this way: and he that has had occasion to consult them will have reason to confess that he has a clearer idea of *apium* or *ibex*, from a little print of that herb or beast, than he could have from a long definition of the names of either of them. And so no doubt he would have of *strigil* and *sistrum*, if, instead of *currycomb* and *cymbal*, (which are the English names dictionaries render them by,) he could see stamped in the margin small pictures of these instruments, as they were in use amongst the ancients. *Toga, tunica, pallium*, are words easily translated by *gown, coat*, and *cloak*; but we have thereby no more true ideas of the fashion of those habits amongst the Romans, than we have of the faces of the tailors who made them. Such things as these, which the eye distinguishes by their shapes, would be best let into the mind by draughts made of them, and more determine the signification of such words, than any other words set for them, or made use of to define them.[26]

This Lockean faith that words, or at least many words, stand for things in a direct relationship capable of being revealed by pictures of those things — a limited version of the Baconian faith in words as *imagines rerum* that was sustained by Bishop Thomas Sprat and the Royal Society — got roughly handled by novelists. The sages of Swift's Laputa, laden with great bundles of things on their backs in order to facilitate laborious conversations consisting entirely of holding objects up to the other person — 'since Words are only Names for Things' — offer a destructive parody of the Lockean connection, as well as of Wilkins's craving for a universal language that would transcend the usual verbal limitations of Babel.[27] *Tristram Shandy*, a text that has Locke constantly in mind, seeks to provoke its readers into adding Locke's *Essay* to the long list of learned tomes she or he might rush away and read seriously — 'Pray, Sir, in all the reading which you have ever read, did you ever read such a book as *Locke*'s Essay upon the Human Understanding? — Don't answer me rashly — because many, I know, quote the book, who have not read it — and many have read it who understand it not.'[28] And *Shandy* makes much fun by offering its characters repeated chances of showing that pictures, or maps, are ways of eluding 'the unsteady uses of words' and the indeterminacy of sense. 'What little knowledge is got by mere words.' Indeed; but, nonetheless, the novel goes on roguishly to demonstrate what little extra knowledge is gained by supplementing those words with maps and diagrams, and even with pointings at or touchings up of the very things apparently signified by the words. 'You shall lay your finger upon the place — said my uncle Toby.

—— I will not touch it, however, quoth Mrs Wadman to herself.' When Trim guides Bridget's hand to the place of Toby's wounding – '*here*' – we are still left in bawdy doubt as to what precise thing, or place, on the map of the Namur battle or on his own surrogate body Trim is assisting her to touch. And, of course, what's being substantively mocked here is the Catholic or 'French' doctrine of the 'real presence' of Christ in the sacrament:

> an error which the bulk of the world lie under —— but the *French* every one
> of 'em to a man, who believe in it, almost, as much as the REAL PRESENCE, '*That
> talking of love, is making it.*'
> —— I would as soon set about making a black-pudding by the same receipt.[29]

As every reader of Saussure's *Cours* who is familiar with Locke's *Essay* will recognize, Saussure's use of 'little draughts or prints' in his Locke-obsessed discourses is calculated precisely to unsettle Locke's idea that to provide a picture-equivalent of *arbor, tree, equos,* or *horse* is in fact a way of illustrating the 'thing' in the word. Saussure's interpolation of the 'signified' – the private mental concept or picture corresponding to *tree* or *horse* – is to be thought of as breaking the link between Locke's picture-lexicon and the world of things.[30] And, to be sure, Saussure's challenge is a serious theoretical riposte to Locke, as Swift's and Sterne's are seriously parodic ones. But the edgy survival of the connection between words and world – that is, of *reference* – in the lexicon concept of Locke (and Dr Johnson) is more tenacious than Swift or Sterne or even Saussure supposed. Certainly the fictional lexicons and encyclopedias of Borges and Cabrera Infante, and Melville's steeping of lexicons in the half-light of his fiction, cannot – any more than can Sterne's fictional play with dictionary and encyclopedia, or Beckett's or Barthes's or Hillis Miller's scepticism – utterly undo the sturdy survival of the real in the lexicon theory of Locke and the lexicon practice of Dr Johnson.

Dr Johnson's practice reveals again and again that lexicons straddle the place where word and world connect, that the world of the vocabulary book is exactly Virginia Woolf's wor(l)d: made of words, words upon words, but also made of words pointing to things, words steeped in the world of persons, affairs, ideas. Lexicons have a double-edgedness, in fact, that's repeatedly brought home in a very practical way by the stain, the impression made upon them by the history, the ideological assumptions and practices that they repeatedly confront and trace. Lexicons have never been able to evade the messy historicity of meaning-change, meaning-making, that they seek, with more or less objectivity, to chart. They are all held in history, in ideology. The lexical palimpsest that Roland Barthes rejoices in is inevitably an archaeology, or archive, of ideology.[31]

Archives of Ideology

Older historians of the English language have tended to ape each other in deploring Johnson's personal involvement in his definitions as a mark of the limitations from which professionalism would rescue succeeding lexicographers. The *Dictionary* is 'marred', claims A. C. Baugh characteristically, 'by prejudice and caprice'.[32] The repetitive implication and constant explicit assumption in such quarters is that dictionaries should be above such Johnsonian lapses as inconsistent spellings, 'ludicrous etymologies', grotesquely Latinate definitions (*network*: 'Any thing reticulated or decussated, at equal distances, with interstices between the intersections': but how *do* you describe a thing made of holes and gaps?), pretended or unnatural naturalizations (*ataraxy*, *deuteroscopy*, *indigate*, and so on), and misleading, mistaken, prejudiced, or ironically personal definitions (*excise*: 'A hateful tax levied upon commodities, and adjudged not by the common judges of property, but wretches hired by those to whom excise is paid', pointedly illustrated by Marvell: '*Excise*, / With hundred rows of teeth, the shark exceeds, / And on all trades like Cassawar she feeds'; *grubstreet*: 'Originally the name of a street in Moorfields in London, much inhabited by writers of small histories, dictionaries, and temporary poems; whence any mean production is called *grubstreet*'; *patron*: 'Commonly a wretch who supports with insolence, and is paid with flattery').[33] But such moments – and not least among them the wryly gloomy illustrations of the *defining* set of words – are valuable precisely because they reveal the *Dictionary*'s inevitable imbrication in the messy, worldly existence of words as they are actually quotidianly made and used. It was an ideologically stained existence that Johnson was keen to play up rather than down. As Allen Reddick has nicely shown, the good Doctor packed his revised fourth edition with quotations from the orthodox high-Anglican monarchist supporters of his own brand of Established Church Christianity, using the *Dictionary* as a weapon in contemporary politico-theological debate.[34] Which wasn't at all to flout or pervert lexicography, merely to utilize the way that the repositories and store-houses of the *langue* – lexicons, encyclopedias, grammars – prove utterly unable to escape the human and ideological frailties and flaws that tend to be associated, rather, with *parole*. Both language in use and language in store reflect, as it were, the un-utopian Babelic fallenness of *langage*.

James A. H. Murray, Dictionary Murray himself, famously decided that the magisterial scope of the *Oxford English Dictionary* would stop short of the uncouth, but plain, English bodily and sexual vocabulary, *piss*, *shit*, *fuck*, *cunt*. But then he would do that, would he not, this impressively godly and strait-laced Scottish puritan and teetotaller, deacon of the Congregationalist conventicle in George Street, Oxford, notorious to his neighbours as 'the Dic' to be observed regularly leading a procession of 'little Dics' kirk-wards down the Banbury Road of a Sabbath morning and evening. What's more, in the light of these pronounced Christian and Dissenting circumstances – one son went as a missionary to China – Murray was perhaps not likely either to spot anything wrong with the dabbling in ethnography of the *OED*'s *M* section (edited by Henry Bradley, 1904–8). A *medicine man*, we're Christianly, imperialistically, Eurocentrically informed, is 'a magician among the American Indians and other savages'. A note to the definition of *medicine*, sb. 4, explains: 'As savages usually regard the operation of medicines as due to what we should call magic, it is probable that their words for magical agencies would often be first heard by civilised men as applied to medicine.' The *OED* is regularly savage about savages. *Waugh*, for example, is defined as 'An exclamation indicating grief, indignation or the like. Now chiefly as attributed to N. American Indians and other savages.' But what of the even more explosive ideological charges packed into one of this eminently civilized lexicographer's own particular sections, the definition of *hysteria* (Letter *H*, part 1 of volume 5, *H–K*, published in 1901)? Murray notes of *hysteria*: 'Women being much more liable than men to this disorder, it was originally thought to be due to a disturbance of the uterus and its functions.' 'Women being much more liable to this disorder': it was an odd gloss from the absent-minded lexicographer who relied on his wife Ada to organize his life, run his household, help him make important decisions, and write certain letters, and from the father of an extraordinary band of five daughters, all of whom were roped in, like their brothers, to sort the *Dictionary*'s entry slips, recording illustrative quotations, at a few pence a hundred.

Some of these women became long-time *Dictionary* labourers. Hilda combined being an Oxford undergraduate with providing statistics for the Introductions to the published parts of the great work. Elsie gave twenty-one adult years of her life to the Murray endeavour, Rosfrith thirty-one. Murray wrote tributes to these females into Letter *A* of the *Dictionary* at their births: 'As fine a child as you will see' (added to the proofs of page 2, column 1, on the birth of Elsie, 1 May 1882, to illustrate *as* as adjective); 'the new arrival is a little daughter' (illuminating the noun *arrival* and celebrating the arrival of Rosfrith, 5 February 1885) – thus inaugurating his daughters into life and lexicon in the appropriate beginning slot of the alphabet.[35] But by the time of the *hysteria* note, the unhysterical reality of these lexicographical females had evidently got itself forgotten, drowned by the preconceptions of Victorian ideology – prejudices at odds not just with these home truths but, more curiously still, at odds with the illustrating quotations garnered for *hysteria*, *hysteric*, *hysterics*, *hystericize*, *hysterical*. For alongside all the hysteric women,

'misses', shepherdesses, wives, Marias, screaming sisterhoods, and girls in
these quotations is a noticeable gang of hysterical men: 'hysteria in his whole
demeanour', 'The men [of the Brazils] . . . are a . . . hysterical . . . tribe'; 'This
of Pisek was but one of the many unwise hysterical things poor Broglio did';
'Professor Ruskin curses . . . with the . . . hysteric passion of his later days.'
One hopes that the unscreaming Murray sisterhood insisted that these particular illustrative slips be included as counterweights to their father's ideological slip. At any rate, they slipped in, and the *Dictionary* makes the reader
feel a sharp sisterly rebuke, even if editor Murray never felt it, in the quotation
from a medical textbook under *hysteric*: 'Swediaour . . . affirms that men may
labour under the hysteric passion as well as women.'

The mere history of the word *hysteria* as set out in the *OED* is a record of
varied assumptions about the temperament of women. And, whether consciously or not, the *Dictionary* lifts a veil on a particular Victorian family's
role in the history of that particular nexus of ideas. Any dictionary compiled
on historical principles would necessarily plunge one into the debate that is
packed into the stormy passage of the word *hysteria* through the history of
the English-speaking peoples. The Murray *Dictionary* is not prevented by its
being the greatest dictionary in the world from rendering that voyage of
ideological lexis. Indeed, its greatness consisting greatly in its passionate
and diligent historicity, it is the more likely to end up, as its *hysteria* words
did, imbrued in the ideological conflicts they register. With an indecipherable
mixture of knowingness and unconsciousness, Murray here taps inexorably
into the ideological logics and complexities of the lexicon. And so, most
arrestingly, do Murray's successors. R. W. Burchfield, editor of the *OED
Supplements*, claimed to be 'mindful' of the 'Victorian ideology of the editors
of the *OED*', especially their mealy-mouthedness about sex words and their
feelings about 'savages'. And the Second Edition of the *OED*, prepared by J.
A. Simpson and E. S. C. Weiner, duly goes in for slang and four-letter words,
prunes *medecine man* and *waugh* of their earlier associations with savages,
mightily rinses the entries on *jew*, noun and verb, of any trace of anti-Semitism,
whitewashes the old sturdily offensive Protestant entry on *Jesuit*, makes *Mormons*
less simply deluded as religionists, and improves the racist physiognomy of
negro ('black skin, black woolly hair, flat nose and thick protruding lips' give
way to 'black skin, black tightly-curled hair, and a nose flatter and lips
thicker and more protruding than is common among white Europeans').
Nobody, though, on the contemporary *Oxford Dictionary* staff has thought ill
enough of the old *heathen* definition ('in modern usage, for the most part,
restricted to those holding polytheistic beliefs, esp. when uncivilized or
uncultured'), or of the *hysteria* note ('Women being much more liable . . .')
to get them excised or amended. Did the male editors not notice that note,
or perhaps not listen, once again, to the large band of *Dictionary* females

(Burchfield goes out of his way to specify them as being on his staff)? And, for that matter, isn't the amended definition of *negro* still gratuitously Eurocentric? *Plus ça change. . . .*[36]

The insistent and clearly continuing ideological presence in even the best dictionaries is something that astute ideologists like Dr Johnson have turned to their particular polemical advantage, using dictionaries and encyclopedias to subvert social systems and governments – who, of course, commonly seek to control meanings and command the lexicon for their own purposes. Persons who want to change history have realized, and properly so, that the vocabulary book, inevitably steeped, like the vocabulary, in history, a great axis of ideology, has tremendous potential as a focus for subversion and an agent of change. The revolutionary *encyclopédistes* in France acted vigorously on this perception. Voltaire's *Dictionnaire philosophique* (1764), aimed mainly at Biblical and theological concepts, got itself onto the Catholic Church's Index of forbidden books. Voltaire's steadfast opponent, the Benedictine monk Dom Louis Mayeul Chaudon, replied, naturally, in lexicographical kind with the *Dictionnaire antiphilosophique* (1767–9). The Church and the police kept Diderot – France's Dr Johnson – on the run for years, from 1759 to 1772, as he clandestinely slaved to keep the volumes of his anticlerical, anti-despotic, heretical *Encyclopédie* coming out. Living as an outlaw was the heavy political and personal price he paid for not just docilely translating into French Ephraim Chambers's *Cyclopedia, or Universal Dictionary of Arts and Sciences* – as he and two others had earlier done with Robert James's *Medicinal Dictionary* (1746– 8) – but turning this rather anodyne project into what was attacked as 'chaos, nothingness, the Tower of Babel, a work of disorder and destruction, the gospel of Satan'. The French intellectual tradition had certainly caught on to the idea of subversion by lexicon. It was small wonder that the young Flaubert should have been excited by the idea of a *Dictionnaire des idées reçues*, a private, jesting lexicographical grouse against bourgeois thinking (*'Ecrit, Bien Ecrit*: Mot de portiers pour designer les romans–feuilletons qui les amusent'). But this francophone Johnsonianism didn't survive only in France. Horne Tooke notoriously used etymology as a radically subversive political weapon in *The Diversions of Purley* (1786). A right knowledge of etymology would, he thought, help establish people's democratic rights.[37] Ambrose Bierce's *Devil's Dictionary* (first published, incomplete, in 1911), sceptical, sardonic, cynical, wry, very funny, brought the satiric ambitions of the *encyclopédistes* up to date and home to contemporary America (*liberty*: 'One of Imagination's most precious possessions'; *reliquary*: 'A receptacle for such sacred objects as pieces of the true cross, short-ribs of saints, the ears of Balaam's ass, the lung of the cock that called Peter to repentance and so forth'; *diplomacy*: 'The patriotic art of lying for one's country').[38]

Voltaire and Bierce bad-mouth the cant and beliefs of institutions, pastors and masters, Church and State, the Crown, the Law. Other subversive lexicographers function by bad-mouthing both the ordinary, demotic bad-mouthers – Eric Partridge's *Dictionary of Clichés* (first published in 1940) has all slack talkers in its sights – and also the practitioners of respectable lexicography such as Dr Murray, who seek to keep naughty words, sex words and the like, and so naughty notions, from public view. Eric Partridge's great *Dictionary of Slang and Unconventional English* (first edition 1934) runs gleefully along in the mire and ephemera of the verbal gutters that Dr Murray chose not to step in between his weekly Sabbath walks to chapel. Partridge's *Shakespeare's Bawdy* (1947) – 'The apparently provocative title is merely a convenient abridgement of "Sexuality, Homosexuality, and Bawdiness in the Works of William Shakespeare" ' – effected a permanent change in the way the Bard was perceived. After Partridge, anyone wishing to use Shakespeare as a prop for respectable Englishness or Anglicanism or niceness in general had Partridge's lexicon of foul thoughts and uncouth words to contend with. Faced, say, with what the Revd M. R. Ridley, one-time chaplain of Balliol, does in his Arden edition of *Othello* with Iago's 'If ever mortal eyes did see them bolster / More than their own' (III. iii. 405–6) – 'I suppose just "share the same pillow" [a thought inspired, one supposes, by the *OED*'s separate entry devoted to this line: '?intr. To lie on the same bolster'], but is there a hint of the picture of "the beast with two backs"?' – it's a great joy to encounter Partridge's blunt 'to coit illicitly': 'The verb *bolster* appositely applies only to the man: cf. the synonym (and semantic parallel), "to **stuff**". Etymologically, a *bolster* probably = "the puffy, swelled, thing" (Wyld).' After such lexical knowledge, what forgiveness for Murray, the schoolmasters, the reverend dons, and all other bowdlerizers?

There'd be no forgiveness either for other kinds of thought-controllers after George Orwell's prophetic dips into the Eleventh Edition of the *Newspeak Dictionary* in 'The Principles of Newspeak' section that he appended to his novel *Nineteen Eighty-Four*. In this futuristic lexicon Orwell was tapping with uncanny power into the long history of politically radical counter-lexicography. So too is a book like the Orwell tributary *Nukespeak: The Media and the Bomb*, with its appended 'ABC of Nukespeak Jargon' (*Limited Nuclear War*: 'Much of Europe annihilated'; *Multiple Independently Targeted Re-entry Vehicle (MIRV)*: 'Nuclear version of a shotgun: hits lots of targets at the same time'). Orwell's Newspeak clearly set a standard that remains (cf. Jonathon Green's *Newspeak: A Dictionary of Jargon*, which came out in 1984 – a good year for Orwelliana, of course).[39] And from the start, modern feminism has seen that its work must be with lexicon and grammar, given that, as feminists go on powerfully arguing, those authorities have been main vehicles of male – hysterically male, you could even say – ideology.

Naturally enough, it's been easy, especially for unregenerate men, to poke fun at earnestly revised feminist spellings such as *womon* and *wimmin* and etymologically daft critiques of words like *human*; all too easy to jest at feminist worries over whether to do something about *manoeuvre* or *manage*, *mention* or *manhole*, and the like. And *The Official Politically Correct Dictionary and Handbook* by Henry Beard and Christopher Cerf (1992) makes glorious fun of neologisms such as *shero*, *femagefent*, *abdofem*, *vulvic symbol*, and other sexcessively strenuous readjustments of the old 'male' lexicon. The Beard–Cerf illustrations are particularly delighting spoofs ('After carefully considering a proposal to change the title of Louisa May Alcott's *Little Women* to *Vertically Constrained Wimmin*, the Committee for an Inclusive Curriculum finally decided to ban it altogether'). It comes as no surprise that this work should bear an epigraph from *Nineteen Eighty-Four* about Newspeak driving out Oldspeak and thus making 'a heretical thought . . . literally unthinkable'. But for all the sensible caution about neo-feminist lexicography along these lines, it is the case that *Ms* looks set for a long career in the English language, and so too does *chairperson* (or even, however awkward it might sound to old ears, *chair*). And though *they* as a singular pronoun (= *she/he*) and *she* as an inclusive singular pronoun (for old *he*) are struggling for survival, at least every thoughtful male has been made to pause before using *man* and *men* or the third-person pronouns *he*, *him*, *his*, when women are among the subjects in question.[40] And these changes in consciousness and practice have come about not least because feminist lexicographers have not been tardy either in criticizing the male hegemony in and over the dictionary or in stepping into the Johnson–Voltaire–Orwell shoes. In terms of potent feminist lexicography, *A Feminist Dictionary* by Cheris Kramarae and Paula A. Treichler clearly leads the field. But it's already in a large crowd of wordbooks by women that are utterly open about their ideological designs. Some of them are flamboyantly over the top (topmost among these excessive ones is Bina Goldfield's *Efemcipated English Handbook*, 1983), but most do battle with what seems unarguable lexical good sense, keen not only to unsettle old gender assumptions to which the dictionary has been prone (*hysterical*: 'An alternative role option for middle-class Victorian women': *A Feminist Dictionary*) but also, latterly, increasingly anxious to correct some of the loonier suggestions of sisterly lexicography ('*Manhattan*: non-sexist; it comes from an Indian word meaning "island" ': Rosalie Maggio's *Nonsexist Word Finder*).[41]

When he reviewed *A Feminist Dictionary* in the *Observer* (27 October 1985) Anthony Burgess invoked Saussure with a view to sweeping away all such political assumptions from lexical work – 'Language is arbitrary and inert, as Saussure taught us' (yet one more sign of the unthinking uses to which 'l'arbitraire du signe' has been put). But despite the likes of such self-appointed guardians of the apolitical case for lexicography, feminism has proved an astonishingly successful battle of the lexical and grammar books. And no one at all mindful of this ongoing history of such lexicon interference in history would deny that the political and ideological stakes are high. Least of all Dostoevsky.

Many novelists have developed their work out of a feel for the outward-facing ideological posture of the lexicon. Voltaire, Diderot, George Orwell, Jane Austen (of whom more later), make an impressive bunch to set against the Borgesian party of the internalized abysmal lexicon. But none of these ideologues risked more for the politicized dictionary than Dostoevsky, youthful member of the Petrashevsky circle – arrested, held for eight months, tried, actually lined up before the firing-squad before his 'reprieve' arrived, sent into Siberia for four years' penal servitude followed by enforced military service, in a truly grim sequence of traumatic events all going back to Petrashevsky's publication in 1846 of two volumes of a subversive *Dictionary of Foreign Words Incorporated into the Russian Language*. Like Voltaire's *Dictionnaire*, Petrashevsky's lexicon aimed at Christian nationalism, this time of Holy Russia (*optimism*: 'unsuccesful attempt to defend theism against the crushing attacks of practical atheism which is inspired by the facts of life itself'). The Tsarist censor, sustained by conventional notions of the social and political harmlessness of lexicons, passed the two volumes unread. They circulated unhampered for months. When authority eventually caught up with them, the unread copies were seized, the casual censor was himself censored, and the official memory was stung enough to store up a revenge that would consign Dostoevsky to years of lost liberty in the freezing cold of Siberia, the veritable house of the dead. What is surprising is not the Russian state's violent reaction to the Petrashevitski, but E. H. Carr's to their *Dictionary*: 'The work possessed in a high degree two qualities generally eschewed by makers of dictionaries; it was tendencious and it was readable.' Little in the history of lexicon-making supports this lenient vision of untendentiousness.[42]

When Raymond Williams argued in his book *Keywords: A Vocabulary of Culture and Society* (1976) – a kind of lexical supplement to his earlier *Culture and Society* – that the great Oxford *Dictionary* was inevitably marked by the ideology of its compilers – 'the air of massive impersonality which the Oxford *Dictionary* communicates is not so impersonal, so purely scholarly, or so free of active social and political values as might be supposed from its occasional use. Indeed, to work closely in it is at times to get a fascinating insight into what can be called the ideology of its editors' – the then editor of the *Supplements*, R. W. Burchfield, was rattled enough to reply with a curious blur of hurt acceptance and angered rebuttal. He accepted, as we've seen, the

'Victorian ideology' of the original editors in matters of sex and savages. He would leave others to judge whether his own passion for, say, rugger was biasing the *Supplements* and thus constituting 'a retreat from impartiality'. As for working-class usage, which Williams claimed was given short shrift in the *OED*, well, Burchfield jolly well knew as much about that as Raymond Williams. What irked Burchfield particularly was Williams's cool notion that Johnsonian bias, the presence of the lexicographer's personal preferences and assumptions, was 'inevitable'.[43]

But the more Burchfield protested, the more he revealed of his own living presence as a human being who happened to be a lexicographer, and the sheer refusal of the lexicographer to follow the Barthesian/Foucauldian Author in dying or disappearing. In a curious way Burchfield's fleering allusions to his working-class New Zealand background, his inherited religious Nonconformity, his liking of Anglo-Saxon and philology, his enjoyment of gardening and preference for soldiers over sailors and airmen, line him up with Williams rather than otherwise.[44] Williams's impressive introduction to *Keywords* carefully places his own interest in the vocabulary of culture and class in just such a mesh of personal particulars – the return from the War, specifically from the Kiel Canal, in 1945, to resume studies at Cambridge; the move out into Adult Education; the reading of the *OED* in the basement of the Public Library in Seaford, Sussex; the gift of 'three cardboard boxes full' of the original part-published paperback fascicles of the *OED* by Mr W. G. Heyman, a member of one of Williams's adult classes in 1950. Doing what Williams later defined as 'modulating' terms such as *culture* 'through history', resisting the 'rabid idealism' even of so-called leftist materialists and the arguments in which 'the epistemological wholly absorbs the ontological' and 'the very possibility of an "external referent" got doubted' – doing this required the autobiographical, gossipy placing of his dictionary work in particular times and places.[45] Those paperback fascicles are intended to act like the information about the cheap blue volumes of Dickens obtained by the Williams family with give-away newspaper coupons in the thirties and that Williams claimed in discussions of Dickens to have stuck by ever since. They're offered as authenticating, empirical, personal, historical, lived-out roots for the realist criticism or epistemology that ensues – as apt, instructive, and even as necessary as Humphry House's locating the Preface to the second edition of his realist *Dickens World*, 'In the Field, April 1942', or Erich Auerbach's *Mimesis: The Representation of Reality in Western Literature* appearing with the information that it was written during the author's exile from Nazi Germany 'in Istanbul between May 1942 and April 1945'.[46]

Above all, the detailed clutter of the military veteran's Cambridge in 1945 and the extra-mural teacher's Seaford Public Library is there to rebuke T. S.

Eliot, and beyond him Matthew Arnold, for not realizing that, logically speaking, all the local data and detail that comprise *Notes Towards the Definition of Culture* and *Culture and Anarchy* undercut those authors' blind bid for impersonality and for universalizing fixity of definition. Naturally enough, it's dissatisfaction with Eliot's *Notes* that figures large in the *Keywords* Introduction, as it was dissatisfaction with the *Notes* and with Arnold's *Culture and Anarchy* that prompted the investigations that became Williams's *Culture and Society*. 'My year in Cambridge passed. I went off to a job in adult education. Within two years T. S. Eliot published his *Notes Towards the Definition of Culture* (1948) – a book I grasped but could not accept – and all the elusive strangeness of those first weeks back in Cambridge returned with force. I began exploring the word in my adult classes.'[47] Culture, the tricky reality and the tricksy vocabulary for it, converge in a classic interaction between personal experience and book-knowledge, of political debate and reading matters: the paradoxical alliance of words in the world and words in the dictionary. The overlapping palimpsest they form in Williams's relishing account of the 'historical dictionary' is far more magnetically rich than Barthes's palimpsest:

> . . . when we go . . . to the historical dictionaries, and to essays in historical and contemporary semantics, we are quite beyond the range of the 'proper meaning'. We find a history and complexity of meanings; conscious changes, or consciously different uses; innovation, obsolescence, specialization, extension, overlap, transfer; or changes which are masked by a nominal continuity so that words which seem to have been there for centuries, with continuous general meanings, have come in fact to express radically different or radically variable, yet sometimes hardly noticed, meanings and implications of meaning. *Industry, family, nature* may jump at us from such sources; *class, rational, subjective* may after years of reading remain doubtful. It is in all these cases, in a given area of interest which began in the way I have described, that the problems of meaning have preoccupied me and have led to the sharpest realization of the difficulties of any kind of definition.[48]

In his own way, Williams is assuming the great Johnsonian task of definition, and recognizing, equally Johnsonianly, that the task is not the simple one that the title-page of Eliot's *Notes* professes to define. Lexicography, the lexicon, the historical task of philology, the necessity of defining, are at once affirmed, but also, if not actually undone, at least seriously problematized. It is a Johnsonian borderline position and one amply suited to the temperament of Williams in his role as the novelist of border country.[49] And it is, I'm arguing, an inescapable position: the lexical fix. And, inevitably perhaps in this lexicon context, a fix in several of the many senses of *fix*: *fix* as mere condition, or state, or working order, the situation as is, the modus of dictionary living that writing and writers can't avoid; *fix* as direction-finding, the determination of bearings; *fix* as drug, as narcotic dose, the lexicons that writing and writers are hooked on and cannot live without, a habit that can be kicked only by suffering very painful withdrawal symptoms; *fix*, even, as dubious transaction, illicit arrangement between the proper forces of law and the improper transgressors of it, cops and crooks; and, certainly, *fix* as trouble, problematic, dilemma, predicament, what we're stuck with, where we're stuck, where we get stuck and come unstuck, 'a position', as the Oxford *Dictionary* has it, 'from which it is difficult to escape'.

The dictionary imperative, the necessity of defining, are urgencies that writing, especially the new writing of the novel, took readily to, especially in the wake of Johnson's *Dictionary*. Pride, prejudice, sense, sensibility: the earnest novel of Jane Austen, spiritual daughter of Dictionary Johnson, turns itself into a moral lexicon in which the importance of seeking to define such terms of the moral and social life is accepted as a main task. At the same time, the difficulties in the way of such moral lexicography also emerge very clearly. Who is the more proud or the more prejudiced in *Pride and Prejudice*? What indeed is signified by these nouns? My later discussion of the ambivalences of the word *candid* in *Emma* (chapter 6: 'Games Texts Play') will amply illustrate Jane Austen's ambivalent lexical posture.

Gallygaskinish

It's an ambivalence that *Tristram Shandy*'s astonishing activity as an anti-encyclopedia and a self-undoing lexicon only endorses on a busier scale. This novel continually celebrates the undecidability of form and the ambivalence of vocabulary. At one typical place where the narration meditates yet once more on the potential bawdiness of an otherwise clean-looking word ('here are two senses . . . two roads . . . a dirty and a clean one') and contemplates this ambivalence yet again in the case of words with an exemplary hole or holes in them – noses and crevices – the narrator declares that 'to define – is to distrust' (Bk. III, ch. 31). At the centre of the novel's sequence of mishaps is the maidservant Susannah, a leaky lexical sieve. She's quite the opposite, at least hermeneutically and semantically, of the Vestal Virgin Tuccia, who proved her virtue by carrying water safely in a sieve. She's entrusted with carrying Mr Shandy's desired name for his new-born son to the birth-room, despite his paternalistic doubts – '*Trismegistus*, said my father —— But stay – thou art a leaky vessel, *Susannah*, added my father; canst thou carry *Trismegistus* in thy head, the length of the gallery, without

scattering?' Alas, she cannot, and bits of *Trismegistus* spill *en route*, and only
'Tris-something' arrives, to be gallantly, but erroneously interpreted as Tristram by the curate (IV. 14).[50] 'Well might *Locke* write a chapter upon the
imperfection of words', declares the narrative of Susannah's sloppy way with
names (V. 7). In its characteristic eighteenth-century role as lexicon or encyclopedia, this novel's particular entries will keep daunting and letting
down the reader, just as Susannah let down Mr Shandy.

   Tristram Shandy finds a lot of dictionary work a glorious source of embarrassment. *Zounds*, for instance, is 'a word of all others in the dictionary the
last in that place to be expected – a word I am ashamed to write – yet must
be written —— must be read – illegal – uncanonical . . .' (IV. 26). Furthermore, the novel is dense with eloquent signs, facial expressions, gestures,
blank and black and marbled pages, silences, exclamations, that cannot be
contained in lexicons, that are beyond the scope and authority of dictionaries,
even a dictionary armed with Locke's 'little draughts and prints'. For some
verbal traces make 'prints' or 'etchings' in the face or heart, rather than on
a lexicon's page. 'There are some trains of certain ideas which leave prints of
themselves about our eyes and eye-brows; and there is a consciousness of it,
somewhere about the heart, which serves but to make these etchings the
stronger – we see, spell, and put them together without a dictionary.' And
this statement is followed in the text by a chorus of sub-words – *Ha, ha! he,
hee! Ho, ho! Whist! st, st, hush*, and *poo, poo* – and then by a list of words that
might follow the word *whiskers* into oblivion, driven out of the lexicon by
potentially indecent associations: *beds, bolsters, nightcaps, chamber-pots, trouse,
placket-holes, pump-handles, spigots, faucets* (V. 1). When a hot chestnut falls
painfully into the gap in the galligaskins of symposiast Phutatorius, the
aperture in question can't be named because polite words for it don't exist
in Johnson's *Dictionary* – they've fallen, as it were, through – they've even
made – a gap in the lexicon ('it fell perpendicularly into that particular
aperture of *Phutatorius*'s breeches for which, to the shame and indelicacy of
our language be it spoke, there is no chaste word throughout all *Johnson*'s
Dictionary') (IV. 27).

   At the same time, though, there is a word in dictionaries, not least in Dr
Johnson's, for gaps of the sort that afflict Phutatorius. At least, when in pain
he cries aloud the word that the narrative-I declares himself ashamed to set
down, the cut-off cry of agony as the heat of the hot chestnut penetrates to
a vital genital organ, the word Z——*ds*!, the narrator is able knowledgeably
to label the utterance an *aposiopesis* ('that interjection of surprise so much
descanted upon, with the aposiopestic break after it, marked thus, Z——ds').
Aposiopesis, the rhetorical term for naming by not naming, occurs several
times in *Tristram Shandy* (as we shall see in the next section of this chapter,

'Give Me An Aposiopestic Break'). Its occurrence is typical of the way this novel comes peppered with learned vocabulary, scientific terms, difficult words whose meaning is crucial and that rebuke the ignorance of Uncle Toby and Mrs Shandy, and that the reader is invited, by contrast with Mrs Shandy's complacent and incurious bad example, to look up in a dictionary, and with some expectation of enlightenment:

> . . . she had a way . . . that was, never to refuse her assent and consent to any proposition my father laid before her, merely because she did not understand it, or had no ideas of the principal word or term of art, upon which the proposition or tenet rolled. She contented herself with doing all that her godfathers and godmothers promised for her – but no more; and so she would go on using a hard word twenty years together – and replying to it too, if it was a verb, in all its moods and tenses, without giving herself any trouble to enquire about it.
>
> This was an eternal source of misery to my father, and broke the neck, at the first setting out, of more good dialogues between them, than could have done the most petulant contradiction —— the few which survived were the better for the *cuvetts* ——
> – 'They are foolish things'; said my mother.
> —— Particularly the *cuvetts*; replied my father.
> 'Tis enough – he tasted the sweet of triumph – and went on. (IX. 11)

It's bad luck for these characters, the novel's progress reveals, if they try to get on without knowing the meaning of the abundant 'terms of art', *curtain, phimosis, hypallage,* and the like, that fill these pages; and it's even worse hermeneutic practice, the reader soon learns, if we try to go on reading without finding out what *aposiopesis, catachresis, farcy, cataplasm,* and all that, mean, and what this text exploits the lexicon to have them stand for.

It's Johnson, Always Johnson

And this paradox of the lexical fix – the recurrent inadequacy of lexicography coupled with the insistent need for it – is an edgy plight that has increased, rather than diminished, in the modern and postmodern period. The more our literature has insisted on linguistic uncertainty, indeterminacy, difference, untranslatability – in other words, on the helplessness of *lexis* – the more it seems that authors, texts, and readers have come to need and to rely on assistance from dictionaries. Twentieth-century fiction and writing and culture in general comprise nothing if not an era of translation. By necessity, in the case of exiles from their native tongues, and by choice in the case of 'world' literature, we possess our fiction by courtesy of the dictionary. The vocabulary of a Conrad, a Nabokov, is peculiarly rich. It stretches the common resources of the native speaker of English. We have to read a Conrad's or a Nabokov's novels dictionary at hand. Which is because these writers acquired their English and wrote their novels dictionary in hand. The writings of Samuel Beckett have rightly become the usual examples of texts steeped in dictionary stuff: they are a particularly sharp instance of the modern case. And what they sharply prove is, once more, the duality and duplicity of the dictionary as well as its utter necessity.

Beckett's texts go in for cross-Channel ferry work. They effect busy Channel crossings, between their French and English versions. They have an extraordinarily versatile series of lexical tricks up their sleeve – or *Manche*. They prove the subtlety and aptness and, in the case of monolingual readers, the sheer necessity of dictionary ploys and plays. But they also end up instructively in a kind of interlinguistic limbo, a place of linguistic betweenness. For example, Estragon declares in *En attendant Godot* that he has never been 'dans la Vaucluse': 'J'ai coulé toute ma chaude-pisse d'existence ici, je te dis! Ici! Dans la Merdecluse!' In *Waiting for Godot*, however, he was never 'in the Macon country. I've puked my puke of a life away here, I tell you! Here! In the Cackon country!'[51] And in one sense, translation, the dictionary, work triumphantly; without them, the English-only or the French-only speaker is indeed in a fix; with them, Beckett's sourly invective jests can be enjoyed in two languages: Cackon, Merdecluse – a piece of linguistic genius, a wonder of translation. But in another sense, the dictionary only partially works, and translation is having to fall back defeated: warm piss is not puke; the Vaucluse is not the Mâcon.

Not dissimilarly, one might observe that the place in which the French reader finds Murphy at the beginning of his story, 'dans l'impasse de l'Enfant-Jésus, West Brompton, Londres', is, and at the same time is not, a version of the 'mew in West Brompton' in which the English reader finds him. Translation includes transposition; this kind of replacing of one word, one text, by another, is also displacing; these friendly linguistic transactions confirm, as well as seek to dispel, linguistic alienation. Cooper, we're told in the English version of *Murphy*, 'had a curious hunted walk, like that of a destitute diabetic in a strange city'. The metaphor imagines the plight of a sick Londoner in some unhelpful foreign place. The French version declares of Cooper: 'On aurait dit un homme traqué faisant de son mieux pour ne pas le paraître, ou un diabétique continental sans ressources dans une grande ville des Iles Britanniques'. The narrative point of view has shifted, in keeping with the translation, dramatically across the Channel, and Cooper has become, for the metaphorical moment, a sick European destitute in a British city.

Once more the dictionary has helped, but it has also been transcended or subverted. And it's almost as if in signal token of this combined triumph and failure (but what a failure!) that in the same paragraphs Cooper is also described thus: 'He was a low-sized, clean-shaven, grey-faced, one-eyed man, triorchous and a non-smoker'; 'C'était un homme de petite taille, sans barbe ni moustache, au teint plombé, borgne, triorchite et non-fumeur'.[52] *Triorchous?* *Triorchite* translates it alright; but neither word is, as such, in any dictionary, not even in the second edition of the *OED*. Etymology comes, as often, to our aid. *Tri*: three; *orchous*: from Greek *orchis*, a testicle; so *triorchous*: 'having three testicles'. Cooper is a genital freak, one-eyed, but three-testicled, a man with an embarrassingly lapsed or displaced ball, and clearly a character compounded of physical improbability over whom Beckett is having a linguistic ball. *Triorchous* is a piece of linguistic undermining, a covert sapping operation, lurking there in an innocent-seeming paragraph to spring a joyously explosive verbal surprise on us, luring us into a triumphant little demonstration that reading (like writing) involves us inevitably in dictionary work, but also leads us subversively beyond straight lexical activity into zones of linguistic play beyond the mere referential frame of the dictionary work. It's no surprise in the light of all this to learn that Dr Johnson obsessed Beckett: 'it's Johnson, always Johnson, who is with me. And if I follow any tradition it is his.'[53]

According to Littré

In the case of Jacques Derrida: for Dr Johnson, read Littré. It's French dictionaries and this French dictionary in particular that are always, apparently, with him. Derrida is, of course, the great guru of lexical leak, the biggest current charmer into the open of lexical hoop-snakes. Hillis Miller and Samuel Weber are only two of the critical eminences who get their lexicon and their view of lexicons from him. Under Derrida's guiding hand, that view has become a deconstructionist cliché. The translator of *De la grammatologie*, Gayatri Chakravorty Spivack, turns naturally to the lexicon to illustrate the alleged perpetual absence of full meaning: 'As even such empirical events as answering a child's question or consulting the dictionary proclaim, one sign leads to another and so on indefinitely.'[54] Lexicons are what Derrida's writings profess to deconstruct – invoking them in order to supplant their certainties. Or so the theory goes. Take this typically ingenious anti-logocentric flurry, which rejects Saussurean binaries and crypto-theological trinaries in the anti-prefatorial preface to *Dissemination*:

Dissemination *displaces* the three of ontotheology along the angle of a certain re-folding [*reploiement*]. A Crisis of *versus*: these marks can no longer be summed up or 'decided' according to the two of binary oppositions nor sublated into the three of speculative dialectics (for example 'differance' [sic], 'gramme,' 'trace,' 'broach/breach' [*entamer*], 'de-limitation,' 'pharmakon,' 'supplement,' 'hymen,' 'mark-march-margin,' and others; the movement of these marks pervades the whole of the space of writing in which they occur, hence they can never be enclosed within any finite taxonomy, not to speak of any lexicon as such); they *destroy* the trinitarian horizon. They destroy it *textually*: they are the marks of dissemination (and not of polysemy) in that they cannot be pinned down at any one *point* by the concept or the tenor of a signified.

Thus Barbara Johnson's translation. And she provides a footnote on Derrida's own lexicon-which-seeks-not-to-be-one, in order further to scorn 'lexicons as such':

Because Derrida's discourse operates a displacement of traditional binary logic, it tends to amass and foreground a series of terms like those listed here which contain within themselves skewed contradictions and which render undecidable any proposition in which they occur. It is therefore tempting for translators and other prefacers to try to facilitate the reader's entrance into Derrida's writing by constructing a 'lexicon' of such terms. Derrida is here both inviting and warning against such a procedure, which, while it points up Derrida's neologistic innovations, reinscribes the effects of those innovations within a finite, pointillistic topology.[55]

But, of course, the footnote's worried tone signals precisely what is happening here: lexicons 'as such' are refusing to have themselves totally deconstructed, finally rubbed out. Lexicon work is in fact predominant here. Barbara Johnson's access to Derrida's thinking is, like ours, strongly dependent upon lexicons 'as such': hence the bilingualism of Ms Johnson's text at certain difficult key moments – 'refolding [*reploiement*]', 'broach/breach [*entamer*]' (a misprint, incidentally, for the French, Derrida's *entame*). This is manifestly a translated text, and one translated only by dint of lexicons 'as such'. It's also at certain moments a scarcely translatable text. Either way, though, it's locked into lexicons 'as such' – *en tant que tel* – for even the untranslatability is revealed to us by means of cross-Channel lexicography, dictionary reminders and remainders. But then, this paradoxical duality is true of all Derrida's efforts at what is offered as a new lexicography: the writing that seeks to go beyond, to sap lexicon as such, is also stuck in and with the lexicon as such. And everywhere in Derrida's texts, whether in French or in English, such dictionary activities and implications enfold us. Nowhere in these texts may the reader manage to avoid getting wrapped up tightly in dictionary textures. Ironically, the English-speaking reader has access to attacks on the dictionary only by means of an English–French dictionary. And all readers of these pages are promptly inducted into this French writer's total reliance on the French dictionary, and at the very places in his text where the lexicon is being denigrated for misleading logocentrism:

> *La brisure.*
> Vous avez, je suppose, rêvé de trouver un seul mot pour désigner la différence et l'articulation. Au hasard du *'Robert'*, je l'ai peut-être trouvé, à la condition de jouer sur le mot, ou plutôt d'en indiquer le double sens. Ce mot est *brisure*: '– Partie brisée, cassée. Cf. brèche, cassure, fracture, faille, fente, fragment. – Articulation par charnière de deux parties d'un ouvrage de menuiserie, de serrurerie. La brisure d'un volet. Cf. joint.'
> Roger Laporte (*lettre*).
>
> The Hinge [La Brisure]
> *You have, I suppose, dreamt of finding a single word for designating difference and articulation. I have perhaps located it by chance in Robert {'s Dictionary} if I play on the word, or rather indicate its double meaning. This word is brisure { joint, break}* ' – broken, cracked part. Cf. breach, crack, fracture, fault, split, fragment [brèche, cassure, fracture, faille, fente, fragment]. – Hinged articulation of two parts of wood- or metal-work. The hinge, the brisure [folding-joint] of a shutter. Cf. joint.'
> – *Roger Laporte* (letter)[56]

Deftness in dictionary work couldn't be more necessary for the reader who would follow this lexicon-wielder. The extraordinary multilingualism of Derrida's texts, like that of Freud's, leads the reader into an extraordinarily dense labyrinth of verbal tradings – Channel-crossings, cross-border ferryings – involving intense delvings into English and French and German and Latin and Greek dictionaries, all of which in practice affirm just as strongly as they professedly deny dictionary certainties, logocentrism, etymology, and all the rest. It amounts to an extraordinary expansion and cosmopolitanizing of Heidegger's fiercely, even monomaniacally, narrow delvings for truth into the German–Greek lexicon:

> The hymen enters into the antre. *Entre* can just as easily be written with an *a* . . . . Indeed, are these two (*e*) (*a*)*ntres* not really the same? Littré: 'ANTRE, s.m. 1. Cave, natural grotto, deep dark cavern. "These antres, these braziers that offer us oracles," *Voltaire, Oedipe* II, 5. 2. Fig. The antres of the police, of the Inquisition. 3. *Anatomy*: name given to certain bone cavities. – *Syn: Antre, cave, grotto. Cave*, an empty, hollow, concave space in the form of a vault, is the generic term; *antre* is a deep, dark, black cave; *grotto* is a picturesque cave created by nature or by man. *Etym.* Antrum, 'ἄντρον; Sanscrit, *antara*, cleft, cave. *Antara* properly signifies "interval" and is thus related to the Latin preposition *inter* (see *entre*). Provenc. *antre*; Span. and Ital. *antro*.' And the entry for ENTRER ['to enter'] ends with the same etymological reference. The *interval* of the *entre*, the in-between of the hymen: one might be tempted to visualize

these as the hollow or bed of a valley (*vallis*) without which there would be no mountains, like the sacred vale between the two flanks of the Parnassus, the dwelling-place of the Muses and the site of Poetry; but *intervallum* is composed of *inter* (between) and *vallus* (pole), which gives us not the pole in between, but the space between two palisades. According to Littré.

We are thus moving from the logic of the palisade, which is always, in a sense, 'full,' to the logic of the hymen. The hymen, the consummation of differends, the continuity and confusion of the coitus, merges with what it seems to be derived from: the hymen as protective screen, the jewel box of virginity, the vaginal partition, the fine, invisible veil which, in front of the hystera, stands *between* the inside and the outside of a woman, and consequently between desire and fulfillment. It is neither desire nor pleasure but in between the two. Neither future nor present, but between the two . . . .

There exist treatises on membranes or *hymenologies*; descriptions of membranes or *hymenographies*. Rightly or wrongly, the etymology of 'hymen' is often traced to a root *u* that can be found in the Latin *suo, suere* (to sew) and in *huphos* (tissue). *Hymen* might then mean a little stitch (*syuman*) (*syuntah,* sewn, *siula,* needle; *schuh,* sew; *suo*). The same hypothesis, while sometimes contested, is put forth for *hymn,* which would thus not be a merely accidental anagram of *hymen* [*hymne/hymen*] (see figure V). Both words would have a relation with *uphainō* (to weave, spin – the spider web – machinate), with *huphos* (textile, spider web, net, the text of a work – Longinus), and with *humnos* (a weave, later the weave of a song, by extension a wedding song or song of mourning). Littré: . . . 'according to Curtius, 'ὕμνος has the same root as 'ὑφάω, to weave, 'ὑφή, 'ὕφος, textile; in that long ago era when writing was unknown, most of the words used to designate a poetic composition were borrowed from the art of the weaver, the builder, etc.'

The hymen is thus a sort of textile. Its threads should be interwoven with all the veils, gauzes, canvases, fabrics, moires, wings, feathers, all the curtains and fans that hold within their folds all – almost – of the Mallarméan corpus. We could spend a night doing that.[57]

You could indeed spend a night doing that. This night-work, the task of penetrating this hymen and its meanings, are offered by Derrida as, and have become for the critical world, metaphor and metonym of decentred betweenness, the elusiveness, the unlocatability of meanings. And *hymen*, the word, as presented here, exists in-between lexicons. But we only get close to defining its indefiniteness, its dislocatedness, and that of its associated verbal cluster, in and through dictionaries. It's been argued by Derek Attridge in loyal deconstructionist fashion that when Derrida thus relates *hymen* to *hymn* with the help of Littré, it's like other etymological ventures popular in current criticism, such as Freud's investigation of *heimlich* in Grimm's *Dictionary*, or Heidegger's argument for a common source of *bauen* and *bin*, or

Barthes's relating of *text* to *textus* (the woven); in other words, it is 'turning the etymological dictionary against itself by using the power of etymology to undermine the easy mastery of language implied in much of our literary and philosophical tradition, and to shake our assurance in fixed and immediately knowable meanings'.[58] But this gloss fails to go far enough into the business.

The reality of the case is deeply ironic. To be sure, Attridge acknowledges some irony surrounding the lexical fix that Derrida has got himself into. Irony plays freely through Derrida's writing, Attridge observes, and to illustrate he quotes a footnote from the English text of *Dissemination* in which Derrida dips once again liberally and literally into Littré in connection with *penne* (*penna*) and *pénil* (*pubis*) while at the same time prefacing his lexical foray with a disclaimer: 'We turn to Littré, from whom we have never, of course, been asking for the *truth*.' *Truth* is a bit strong as a version of Derrida's French *savoir* – knowledge, learning, know-how – but even so, one is only incredulous at the waiving of *savoir* claims, for Derrida acts always and consistently as if Littré were precisely the place to get savvy about meanings. When, for example, the ear is 'at issue', so is 'the sheltered portico of the tympanum' and 'the vestibular canal'. And what's that? Littré knows what a *vestibule* is:

> 'Anatomical term. Irregular cavity that is part of the inner ear. Genital vestibule, the vulva and all its parts up to the membrane of the hymen exclusively. Also the name of the triangular space limited in front and laterally by the ailerons of the nymphs [small lips of the vulva], and in back by the orifice of the urethra; one enters through this space in practicing a vestibular incision. E. *Lat. vestibulum*, from the augmentative particle *ve*, and *stabulum*, place in which things are held (see *stable*), according to certain Latin etymologists. Ovid, on the contrary, more reasonably, it appears, takes it from *Vesta* because the *vestibule* held a fire lit in the honor of Vesta [goddess of the proper, of familiarity, of the domestic hearth, etc.]. Among the moderns, Mommsen says that *vestibulum* comes from *vestis*, being an entryway in which the Romans left the toga (*vestis*).' Littré.[59]

And here lies the most massive irony in Derrida's use of lexicons. He's the world's most notorious anti-logocentrist, yet he's always so hot for etymologies, for dictionary certainties; so logocentrist in other words. In fact he keeps sounding oddly close to the English tradition's hyper-logocentrist, the Jesuit priest and poet Gerard Manley Hopkins, when he's on one of his etymological binges – those passionate forays into lexicons by the devoutest of Christian Cratylists, God's etymologist no less, intent on proving to himself that language comprises a vast divine order or poem, that the words in his tradition chime with each other in sound and meaning by divine design, that linguistic rhyming-clusters mirror the ordered rhyming sets of the things that they signify, and that it's God's eternal purpose that's daily revealed in onomatopoiea, etymology, reference. God's *telos* was revealed, Hopkins believed, in the *etymon*, in onomatopoiea. The lexicon declared the glory of God. Glory be to God for dappled things – which God had organized – and also for all the words for dappled things which He had also arranged: that was Hopkins's line of thought. And therefore the task of the observant Christian poet would be to re-enact God's creative and lexical order. Hopkins's co-ordinating in verse his great rashes of rhyming (usually alliterative) words was a mode of access to God's poetic arrangement of rhyming things in the world which was rooted, in other words, in reflections like the characteristic philological notes in Hopkins's undergraduate journal (September 1863):

Horn.
    The various lights under which a horn may be looked at have given rise to a vast number of words in language. It may be regarded as a projection, a climax, a badge of strength, power or vigour, a tapering body, a spiral, a wavy object, a bow, a vessel to hold withal or to drink from, a smooth hard material not brittle, stony, metallic or wooden, something sprouting up, something to thrust or push with, a sign of honour or pride, an instrument of music, etc. From the shape, *kernel* and *granum, grain, corn.* From the curve of a horn, κορωνίς, *corona, crown.* From the spiral *crinis*, meaning ringlets, locks. From its being the highest point comes our crown perhaps, in the sense of the top of the head, and the Greek κέρας, horn, and κάρα, head, were evidently identical; then for its sprouting up and growing compare *kere-, cornu,* κέρας, horn with grow, *cresco, grandis,* grass, great, *groot.* For its curving *curvus* is probably from the root *horn* in one of its forms. κορωνη in Greek and *corvus, conix* in Latin and *crow* (perhaps also *raven*, which may have been *craven* originally) in English bear a striking resemblance to *cornu, curvus.* So also γέρανος, *crane, heron, herne.* Why these birds should derive their names from *horn* I cannot presume to say. The tree *cornel*, Latin *cornus* is said to derive its name from the hard horn-like nature of its wood, and the *corns* of the foot perhaps for the same reason. *Corner* is so called from its shape, indeed the Latin is *cornu.* Possibly (though this is rather ingenious than likely, I think) *grin* may mean to curve up the ends of the mouth like horns. Mountains are called *horn* in Switzerland; now we know from Servius that *herna* meant *saxum* whence the Hernici, *Rock-men*, derive their name; *herna* is a horn-like crag. ἔρνος, a shoot, is so called from its horn-like growth. Curiously enough the expression κεράων ἔρνος occurs in Oppian, and another word, ἔρνοξ, in the *Poetics* of Aristotle. Or it is possible that ἔρνος, may be so called from its shooting up as, not in the shape of, a horn.
    Expressions. He hath raised up a horn of salvation for us.

See *horn* above. On the other hand the derivation of *granum, grain* may be referred to the head.

Grind, gride, gird, grit, groat, grate, greet, κρούειν, *crush, crash*, κροτεῖν, etc. Original meaning to *strike, rub*, particularly *together*. That which is produced by such means is the *grit*, the *groats* or crumbs, like *fragmentum* from *frangere*, *bit* from *bite. Crumb, crumble* perhaps akin. To *greet*, to strike the hands together (?). *Greet*, grief, wearing, *tribulation. Grief* possibly connected. *Gruff*, with a sound as of two things rubbing together. I believe these words to be onomatopoetic. *Gr* common to them all representing a particular sound. In fact I think the onomatopoetic theory has not had a fair chance. Cf. *Crack, creak, croak, crake, graculus, crackle*. These must be onomatopoetic.[60]

Hopkins's etymological delvings and speculation affirm divine origins, meaning, intention. And this is clearly the kind of affirmation whose traditional shadow Derrida's wrestle with the lexicon finds it hard altogether to evade. In seeking to prove that meaning eludes the old fixing claims of the dictionary, Derrida is perpetually fixed in a quite traditional lexicographical position – the work of fixing, establishing meanings, past and present; showing how meanings grow and shift; trading in etymologies. But the contradictoriness is, I'm suggesting, utterly germane to the nature of what lexicons do. Derrida can't be blamed for inventing inconsistency: the inconsistency, the paradox of his practice, pertains to the two-facedness of meaning and of the word-hoards that chart it. It's a two-facedness that is illustrated with unrivalled vividness in one of the most striking of lexicon-minded modern novels, William Golding's *Rites of Passage* (1980).[61]

Dictionary of the Marine

Rites of Passage is unique in Golding's oeuvre, and very different from the two novels that succeeded it in a so-called trilogy. It's difficult to believe that Golding intended to produce a trilogy of fictions when he set out on the voyage that *Rites of Passage* initiates; difficult not to guess that the formidable commercial and critical success of *Rites* induced him to pick up the threads of the mere sea-story that *Rites of Passage* contains but is by no means reducible to (a critical guess confirmed in Golding's Foreword to the one-volume version of this 'Sea Trilogy', *To The Ends of the Earth* (1991): 'But the truth is I did not foresee volumes two and three when I sat down to write volume one').

Rites of Passage is evidently the response of a strong old-fashioned moralist fiction-maker to that postmodernist theory which has sought to outlaw realism, parable, fictions about knowable or 'real' persons, novels with moral or theological ambitions, stories keen to make truth-claims about the world and human behaviour – Golding's kind of novel, in other words – in favour, instead, of novels about text, writing, narrativity, whose mode is metatextual and intertextual. *Rites of Passage* is, I suggest, Golding's act of old man's defiance. Anything the postmodernist Young Turks can do, he can do better. The novel comes from a man who was no doubt exceedingly fed up over being sniped at for years on end as too traditionalist (changes mindlessly repeated upon his death in June 1993). It's a sharp demonstration that he can easily outsmart the postmodernist whipper-snappers, can knock off a self-reflexive, metatextual, textualizing novel, but one that will, however, also function, as his novels have always done, right from the start with *Lord of the Flies* (1954), in the traditional zones of the moral, onto-theological, old-fashioned human subject-matter.

With great critical knowingness, Golding chooses a setting at the end of the eighteenth century for his demonstration. He parodies the tone and exploits some classic forms of eighteenth-century fiction (in his book a journal encloses a letter). His diary-keeping narrator Edmund Talbot is a devoted quoter of eighteenth-century novels. And all this is canny, for this is the period aptest to any effort at producing a novel that's self-conscious about fiction, narrative, text, and also concerned with selfhood and morality. This is the time when the English novel combined continuous questioning self-consciousness about its formal procedures – in an intensity of internal enquiry that sustains the various attempts by Richardson, Fielding, and Sterne to start up each novel afresh, each time on cleverer or more moral or more sustainable critical grounds than every predecessor – combined self-reflexivity with devoted attention to the selfhood and meaning of the persons who peopled its pages. *Rites of Passage* sets out to be as dualist as the eighteenth-century texts that it gently pastiches; and at the heart of that dualism is a dictionary, *An Universal Dictionary of the Marine: or, A Copious Explanation of the Technical Terms and Phrases Employed in the Construction, Equipment, Furniture, Machinery, Movements and Military Operations of a ship*, by the Scottish poet William Falconer, first published by T. Cadell of London in 1769, the year Falconer was lost at sea, and reprinted many times there after.[62]

The story of how the naïve youthful voyager Talbot received his moral education through an encounter with the terrible shipboard downfall of the Reverend Mr Colley is done in terms of a foregrounded literariness that is at once recognizably Shandyesque and postmodernist. This is writing about writing. Writing is manifestly this writing's object. 'With these words I begin the journal I engaged myself to keep'; 'let this sentence be inserted'; 'The book is filled . . . I shall lock it, wrap it & sew it unhandily in sailcloth & thrust it away in the locked drawer'; 'But now I am sufficiently recovered from my nausea to be able to hold a pen, I cannot refrain from harking back to . . . .' And so on. Talbot reads, refers to, echoes likely novels and other current texts. Seduction is not the least of his actions framed, sustained, ironized by bookish precedent and allusion. 'She retired in disorder . . . I attacked once more . . . The bookshelf tilted. *Moll Flanders* lay open on the deck, *Gill Blas* fell on her . . . Hervey's *Meditations among the Tombs (MDCCLX) II vols London* covered them both. I struck them all aside and Zenobia's tops'ls too.' The premature ejaculation that follows – Zenobia clutches Talbot frantically, thinking an explosion on deck portends French attackers – is straight out of *Tristram Shandy*: 'Was there ever anything more mistimed and ridiculous? . . . *confound* the woman.' And this is immediately followed by a paragraph correcting Coleridge in the matter of sailors not shooting seabirds.[63] Moreover, this steady peppering of the writing within the writing – the journal – with bookish allusions all occurs within the larger framework of considerable intertextual dealings between Golding's text and the anthropological classic by Arnold van Gennep, *Les Rites de passage* (1909) from which Golding has derived his title, and Melville's nouvelle *Billy Budd* (first published posthumously, in 1924), whose plot Golding recasts in designing the fate of the Revd Mr Colley at the hands of the awful seaman Billy Rogers.

Everything, in fact, in this novel has a postmodernist habit of turning out to be textualized, literatured (to use *Finnegans Wake*'s word), substantially a matter of writtenness, of linguisticity. For instance, Talbot's shipboard servant, old Wheeler, helpfully calms his master's neophyte stomach with *paregoric*, a soothing medicinal potion made of tincture of opium. It's a drug that Talbot refuses the next time it's offered. And it's a drug that is, characteristically of this novel, connected with writing. 'I believe there is a gentleman ashore as has wrote a book on it,' says Wheeler (p. 44). And Talbot suggests that his own writing is a kind of drug in effect rather like the paregoric: 'Can it be that I have evaded the demon opium only to fall victim to the *furor scribendi*?' (p. 45). And, of course, as recourse to a dictionary reveals, *paregoric* in the sense of something soothing or encouraging derives from Greek words for speaking and the public place of speaking, the public assembly of the vocal electorate. *Paregoric* implies, at root, sweet talking, smooth talk. So, in a single word, Golding sums up his textual purposes, encapsulates the overlap he's demonstrating between the inside and the outside reference of words and text: *paregoric*, a word for talk, for words, for what comes out of the mouth; but also a word for the non-verbal, a medicine that comes from the outside, invading the mouth, the domain of words that it will not allow to be occupied only by words. It's a mouth business, an intimate play between the verbal and the non-verbal, that stands with terrible proleptic irony, as the

reader finally discovers, for what brings about Colley's downfall. His particular oral action, his fellatio with Rogers, is what the sailor slangily called
'getting a chew off a parson' (p. 273). The clergyman comes to die of shame
essentially because that phrase did not stay just a phrase, a noise in the
mouth, but got itself tragically translated into action, in another kind of
mouth activity. And in encapsulating all this in a single word, Golding has
taken a spectacular leaf out Derrida's books. This is the deconstructionist
practice turned against deconstructionists. And there's even more salt being
rubbed in the wound, in that *paregoric* is one of that huge lexicon of words
beginning in *para* that Derrida (and J. Hillis Miller) have used to such good
effect on their side of the argument. (Of *para*, much more later, in my
chapter 7: 'The Logics of Para', and 8: 'The Rabbins Take It Up one After
Another'.)

Wheeler is, of course, a great smooth-talker, a kindly-ish but increasingly
irksome buffer between Talbot and the more awful truths about life aboard
ship that will finally overtake Talbot. What's more, Wheeler's sweet-talking
is, in great part, lexicon work. This handy explicator of nautical terminology
is called by Talbot 'that walking Falconer' (p. 14). Talbot relies heavily on
this 'living *Falconer*' (p. 62), and also on the copy of Falconer that he keeps
'by my pillow': 'for I am determined to speak the tarry language as perfectly
as any of these rolling fellows!' (p. 8). And Talbot is right to rely on Falconer.
Subsequent readers of his *Marine Dictionary* have all done so, not least other
lexicographers (Falconer is included in the 'List of Books Quoted in the
Oxford English Dictionary', which is appended to the *OED*). Falconer refers, in
the classical fashion of lexicography, with utter confidence to the marine
world that its vocabulary embraces. This dictionary comes usefully illustrated
with Lockean 'draughts' – a 'Variety of Original Designs of Shipping, in
different situations; Together with separate Views of their Masts, Sails, Yards,
and Rigging'. It boasts its superior copiousness and accuracy of reference. Of
rival marine lexicons, its Preface declares: 'Far from exhibiting an enlarged
and comprehensive view of naval affairs, these productions are extremely
imperfect, according to the very circumscribed plan which their authors have
adopted.' 'Of the machinery of a ship; the disposition of the rigging on her
masts and yards; and the comparative force of her different mechanical powers, their accounts are *vague, perplexed*, and *unintelligible*.' And with the help
of Falconer's definitions, Talbot repeatedly banishes his vagueness about sailors'
jargon, undoes his perplexities, and makes his voyage, and so his writing,
more intelligible. 'I was on all fours, the door having been caught neatly
against the transverse or thwartships bulkhead (as Falconer would have it) by
a metal springhook . . .' (p. 20). 'So we stood for a few more moments, one
leg stiff, one leg flexing like reeds in the wind while the shadow of the *driver*
(thank you, Falconer!) moved back and forth across us' (p. 32).

With Falconer's aid, Talbot, and we, get clued up about the maritime meanings of words, and not least the meaning of *clewed up*. Colley's body is about to be committed to the deep: 'Almost all our sails were *clewed up* and we were what the *Marine Dictionary* calls, technically speaking – and when does it not? – *hove to* . . .' (p. 260). But at what looks like just another of the novel's many moments of lexical cluing-up, the dictionary definition and the actuality of the ship come adrift: '*hove to*, which', Talbot adds, 'ought to mean we were stationary in the water'. But they weren't. The *pintles* fixing the rudder to the *stern-post* are getting loose. And so too is Falconer's lexical grip on events. And this moment of dictionary failure – when 'the spirit of farce' is rightly invoked – is not unique.

The Revd Mr Colley doesn't own a Falconer, and so his definitions and etymologies are rather chancy ones. 'The seamen call the material "tarpaulin" if I am not mistaken; so the phrase "Honest Tar" here finds its original' (p. 231). Access to Falconer would have confirmed the point about sailing *tars*, but would have given him *tar-pawling* or *tarpauling* for his guessed-at *tarpaulin*. But even with his Falconer, Talbot is left on occasion all at sea, lexically speaking. The 'privehouse, the loo – I beg its pardon, I do not know what it should be called since in strict sea-language the *heads* are at the forward end of the vessel, the young gentlemen should have a *roundhouse*, and the lieutenants should have – I do not know what the lieutenants should have' (p. 11). But *heads* is not one of Falconer's words. *Roundhouse* is, but it doesn't have reference in his pages to any privy purposes. *Loo* is a quite modern word for lavatory and one for which no dictionary feels confident about offering derivations. Talbot's seasick confusion, his desperate need for the loo, is here registered very nicely in lexical chaos. 'Oh Falconer, Falconer!' he exclaims two pages later in a tone of apparent despair, referring to the great number of ropes humming over his head which he cannot name and to the *ratlines* – an attempt at technicality only approximate to Falconer's *ratlings*. So it's scarcely surprising that three pages after that he suggests that true comprehension of ships will take him well beyond the mere scope of Falconer's definitions:

I began, as Wheeler had put it, to *ride a ship*. Her masts leaned a little. The shrouds to windward were taut, those to leeward slack, or very near it. The huge cable of her *mainbrace* swung out to leeward between the masts; and now here is a point which I would wish to make. Comprehension of this vast engine is not to be come at gradually nor by poring over diagrams in Marine Dictionaries! It comes, when it comes, at a bound. In that semi-darkness between one wave and the next I found the ship and the sea comprehensible not merely in terms of her mechanical ingenuity but as a – a what? As a steed, a conveyance, a means working to an end. This was a pleasure that I had not anticipated. It was, I thought with perhaps a touch of complacency, quite an addition to my understanding! A single sheet, a rope attached to the lower and leeward corner of a sail, was vibrating some yards above my head, wildly indeed, but understandably! As if to reinforce the comprehension, at the moment when I was examining the rope and its function there came a huge thud from forward, an explosion of water and spray, and the rope's vibration changed – was halved at the mid-point so that for a while its length traced out two narrow ellipses laid end to end – illustrated, in fact, the *first harmonic*, like that point on a violin string which if touched accurately enough will give the player the note an octave above the open one. (pp. 16–17)

Mainbrace, as a matter of fact, does not occur in Falconer, though *brace* does. But Talbot's new capacity to read the ship is not hindered by this omission from the dictionary. This particular dictionary has its failings, but his previous knowledge of harmonics and chords comes to the rescue, and comprehension is able to proceed despite the limited assistance of the lexicon.

So, exemplarily, the usefulness of Falconer fades in and out. Now it clues Talbot up, now it does not. Now the real meshes with the lexicon, and dictionary-reference triumphs. Now the real exceeds or falls short of the lexicon. One clamantly large failure concerns the ship's conniving, morally derelict captain. According to Falconer, a captain 'is enjoined to show a laudable example of honour and virtue to the officers and men, and to discountenance all dissolute, immoral, and disorderly practices, and such as are contrary to the rules of discipline and subordination, as well as to correct those who are guilty of such offences, as are punishable according to the usage of the sea.' But vice and corruption reign under this ship's senior officer. Falconer's failure to encompass this case parallels the crucial blur over *chew*. Some cruces of naval discourse and practice will elude the dictionary's best efforts to encompass them.

Colley's funeral, writes Talbot, was conducted in 'Tarpaulin language. You know how I delight in that! You will already have noted some particularly impenetrable specimens as, for instance, mention of a *badger bag* – does not Servius (I believe its was he) declare there are half a dozen cruxes in the *Aeneid* which will never be solved, either by emendation or inspiration or any method attempted by scholarship? Well then, I shall entertain you with a few more *naval cruxes*' (p. 259). And *Rites of Passage* stands as a large and telling testimony to the power of the lexicon all at once to solve and also to fail to solve the verbal crux. The troubles of Talbot, and of Colley, are a parable of the lexical fix, as it interacts with the moral dilemma.

The irresoluble lexical crux, like all lexical leaks, blank walls, black holes, and hoop-snakes, remains a striking problematic of dictionaries. The role of this crux in Golding's novel is as exemplary as anything of the sort in poststructuralist criticism or fiction. Equally, though, the use and demonstrable usefulness of Falconer are never finally impugned in this novel by such lapses. Falconer remains the focus and the locus of being all at sea and yet also managing not quite to be so, of getting profoundly lost on the ocean and yet also making a kind of progress there. The dualism becomes in Golding's hands intensely powerful and moving. His manipulation of it is why *Rites of Passage* is a fiction of such extraordinary importance for our lexically sceptical times.

NOTES

1 For useful discussion of indeterminacy, see Gerald Graff, 'Determinacy/Indeterminacy', in *Critical Terms for Literary Study*, ed. Frank Lentricchia and Thomas McLaughlin (University of Chicago Press, 1990), 163–76.
2 *Roland Barthes by Roland Barthes* (1975) (Macmillan, London, 1977), 139. See also p. 67.
3 *The Poems of Tennyson*, ed. Christopher Ricks, 2nd edn, 3 vols (Longman, London, 1987), vol. 2, p. 584, n. iii. 50.
4 Robert Burchfield, *OED* reviser, adds to the demotion by noting that 'someone' had consulted the *Shorter Oxford English Dictionary* for that sense 1 of *definition*, and not the *Oxford English Dictionary*: Robert Burchfield, *Unlocking the English Language* (Faber, London, 1989), 61.
5 T. S. Eliot, *Notes Towards the Definition of Culture* (1948) (Faber, London, 1962), 7; 14–15 and n. 1.
6 *Roland Barthes by Roland Barthes*, 85.
7 David Lodge, *Small World: An Academic Romance* (Secker and Warburg, London, 1984), e.g. 47 and 53.
8 J. Hillis Miller, *Fiction and Repetition: Seven English Novels* (Blackwell, Oxford, 1982) 39.
9 Samuel Weber, 'The Meaning of the Thallus', in *The Legend of Freud* (University of Minnesota Press, Minneapolis, 1982), 75. Weber's discussion reworks his original article, 'The Divaricator: Remarks on Freud's *Witz*', *Glyph*, 1 (1977), 1–27.
10 *Legend of Freud*, 76–82. Cf. Hillis Miller, 'Constructions in Criticism', in *Theory Now and Then* (Harvester Wheatsheaf, Hemel Hempstead, 1991), 259–61.
11 The 'excessive' framing of this episode is discussed by Mary Ann Caws, *Reading Frames in Modern Fiction* (Princeton University Press, 1985), in her ch. 5: 'High Modernist Framing', 154ff. It's hard to agree with her about the lack of surprise in 'all this frame'. Rather, the 'excess' is part of the powerful moral accusation Strether takes on the chin: 'framing' in the police court/criminal sense endorsed by Browning's Duke ('That's my last duchess painted on the wall'), fingering, as the criminal argot has it, his allegedly adulterous wife.
12 Samuel Beckett, *Watt* (Calder Jupiter Book, London, 1963), pp. 78–80.

13   J. Hillis Miller, 'Presidential Address 1986', *PMLA*, 102, no. 3 (May 1987), 282.

14   Roland Barthes, 'The Death of the Author', in *Image–Music–Text*, ed. and trans. Stephen Heath (Fontana, London, 1977), 146–7.

15   Claude Lévi-Strauss, 'Structure and Form: Reflections on a Work by Vladimir Propp', in *Structural Anthropology*, vol. 2, trans. Monique Layton (Peregrine, Harmondsworth, 1978), 115–45; Franco Moretti, 'Clues', in *Signs Taken for Wonders: Essays in the Sociology of Literary Forms*, trans. S. Fisher, D. Forgacs, and D. Miller (Verso, London, 1983), 132.

16   K. M. Elisabeth Murray, *Caught in the Web of Words: James A. H. Murray and the Oxford English Dictionary* (Oxford University Press, paperback edn, 1979).

17   John Locke, 'of the Remedies of the Foregoing Imperfections and Abuses of Words', in *An Essay Concerning Human Understanding* (1690), bk 3, ch. 11, ed. Alexander Campbell Fraser (Dover edn, New York, 1959), vol. 2, 162.

18   Samuel Johnson, Preface (1755) to *A Dictionary of the English Language*, in e.g. *Rasselas, Poems, and Selected Prose*, ed. Bertrand H. Bronson (Holt, Rinehart and Winston, New York, 1958), 222–31. Definitions from first edition, 2 vols 1755.

19   'Tlön, Uqbar, Orbis Tertius', in Borges, *Fictions* (translation of *Ficciones*, 1962), ed. Anthony Kerrigan (Calder Jupiter Book, London, 1965); Borges and Margarita Guerrero, *The Book of Imaginary Beings*, rev., ed. and trans. Norman Thomas di Giovanni in collaboration with the author (Penguin, Harmondsworth, 1974); *idem*, 'The Analytical Language of John Wilkins', in Borges, *Other Inquisitions 1937–1952*, trans. Ruth L. C. Simms (Souvenir Press, London, 1973), 101–5.

20   See Michel Foucault, *The Order of Things: An Archaeology of the Human Sciences* (Tavistock, London, 1974), esp. Foucault's Preface, discussing Borges's Chinese encyclopedia, where not the least interesting aspect is the translation's difference from the Spanish of Borges. Cf. Dogberry, *Much Ado About Nothing*, V. i. 204ff.

21   Umberto Eco, *Il nome della rosa* (1980), trans. William Weaver as *The Name of the Rose* (Secker and Warburg, London, 1983).

22   G. Cabrera Infante, *Three Trapped Tigers*, trans. Donald Gardner and Suzanne Jill Levine in collaboration with the author (Picador, London, 1980), 213–33, 395.

23   Alvin Kernan, *Samuel Johnson and the Impact of Print* (Princeton University Press, 1989), 189.

24   Borges, 'Analytical Language of John Wilkins', 104.

25   Barthes, 'Semiology and Medicine', in *The Semiotic Challenge*, trans. Richard Howard (Blackwell, Oxford, 1988), 210–11.

26   Locke, *Essay*, bk 3, ch. 11, Dover edn, vol. 2, 163–4. Cf. 'The picture theory of signs' in Stephen K. Land, *From Signs to Propositions: The concept of form in eighteenth-century semantic theory* (Longman, London, 1974), 21ff.

27   Jonathan Swift, *Gulliver's Travels* (1726), ed. Paul Turner (Oxford University Press, 1971), 184–5, and Notes, pp. 350–1.

28   Laurence Sterne, *The Life and Opinions of Tristram Shandy, Gent.* (1759–1767), bk 2, ch. 2 (Everyman, London, 1912), 62.

29   Ibid., bk 9, ch. 20, 'The Eighteenth Chapter', chs. 26–28 (Everyman edn), 460–61, 468, 471–2.

30 It's a challenge, too, to John Wilkins's notion that the 'mental Image'
    is equivalent to the 'natural thing'. Saussure's examples, *horse* and *tree*, indicate
    a keen desire to undo Wilkins's idea of steadfast universal referents which
    could be reflected in a utopian universal language:

> That conceit which men have in their minds concerning a Horse or Tree,
> is the Notion or mental Image of that Beast, or natural thing, of such a
> nature, shape and use. The Names given to these in several Languages,
> are such arbitrary sounds or words, as Nations of men have agreed upon,
> either casually or designedly, to express their Mental notions of them.
> The Written word is the figure or picture of that Sound.
>
>   So that if men should generally consent upon the same way or manner
> of Expression, as they do agree in the same Notion, we should then be
> freed from that Curse in the Confusion of Tongues, with all the unhappy
> consequences of it. (John Wilkins, *An Essay towards a Real Character and
> a Philosophical Language* (1668), quoted in Susie I. Tucker, *English Ex-
> amined: Two Centuries of Comment on the Mother Tongue* (Cambridge Uni-
> versity Press, 1961, 50)

31 For much spry information about linguistics and ideology, and not least about
    the conservative ideology of Johnson's *Dictionary*, see Olivia Smith, *The Politics
    of Language 1791–1819* (Clarendon Press, Oxford, 1984).
32 Albert C. Baugh and Thomas Cable, *A History of the English Language* (Routledge
    and Kegan Paul, London, 1981 reprint), 270.
33 Ibid. 270, n. 3, quoting Noah Webster; Margaret Schlauch, *The English Lan-
    guage: In Modern Times (Since 1400)* (PWN, Warsaw; Oxford University Press,
    London, 1959), 138–9; Barbara M. H. Strang, *A History of English* (Methuen,
    London, 1970), 107–8, quoting Simeon Potter.
34 Allen Reddick, *The Making of Johnson's Dictionary 1746–1773* (Cambridge
    University Press, 1990), 141–69: ' "Factions in a Factious Age": Theology and
    Politics in the Fourth Edition'. Cf. Robert DeMaria Jr, 'The Politics of Johnson's
    Dictionary', *Publications of the Modern Language Association of America*, 104 (1989),
    no. 1, 64–74; Alvin Kernan, 'The Battle for the Words: Dictionaries, Deconstruc-
    tors, and Language Engineers', in *The Death of Literature* (Yale University Press,
    New Haven and London, 1990), 152–88.
35 Murray, *Caught in the Web of Words*, 179–80, 200–1.
36 See R. W. Burchfield, 'A Case of Mistaken Identity', *Encounter* (June 1976), 57–
    64; *OED*, 2nd edn prepared by J. A. Simpson and E. S. C. Weiner (Clarendon
    Press, Oxford, 1989); R. W. Burchfield, 'The Treatment of Controversial Voca-
    bulary in *The Oxford English Dictionary*', *Transactions of the Philological Society*, [72]
    (1973), 1–28.
37 See 'Horne Tooke on Etymological Metaphysics', ch. 11 in Roy Harris and
    Talbot T. Taylor, *Landmarks in Linguistic Thought: The Western Tradition from
    Socrates to Saussure* (Routledge, London, 1989), 136ff.
38 See *The Enlarged Devil's Dictionary*, ed. E. J. Hopkins (Gollancz, London, 1967).

39 Crispin Aubrey (ed.), *Nukespeak: The Media and the Bomb* (Comedia Publishing Group, London, 1982). Jonathon Green, *Newspeak: A Dictionary of Jargon* (Routledge and Kegan Paul, London, 1984).

40 Henry Beard and Christopher Cerf, *The Official Politically Correct Dictionary and Handbook* (Grafton, London, 1992). Robin Lakoff, *Language and Woman's Place* (Harper and Row, New York, 1975). Alette Olin Hill, *Mother Tongue, Father Time: A Decade of Linguistic Revolt* (Indiana University Press, Bloomington and Indianapolis, 1986). Dennis Baron, *Grammar and Gender* (Yale University Press, New Haven and London, 1986).

41 Francine Wattman Frank and Paula A. Treichler, *Language, Gender, and Professional Writing: Theoretical Approaches and Guidelines for Nonsexist Usage* (Commission on the Status of Women in the Professions: Modern Language Association of America, New York, 1989), *passim*, but esp. Treichler, 'From Discourse to Dictionary: How Sexist Meanings Are Authorized', 51–79. Cheris Kramarae and Paula A. Treichler, *A Feminist Dictionary* (Pandora, London, 1985). Ruth Todasco, *The Feminist English Dictionary: An Intelligent Women's Guide to Dirty Words* (Loop Center YWCA, Chicago, 1973). Casey Miller and Kate Swift, *The Hand-book of Nonsexist Writing* (Lippincott and Crowell, New York, 1980). Bobbye D. Sorrels, *The Nonsexist Communicator: Solving the Problems of Gender and Awkwardness in Modern English* (Prentice-Hall, Englewood Cliffs, N.J., 1985). Florence Hervé, Elly Steinmann, and Renate Wurms, *Kleines Weiberlexicon* (Weltkreis Verlags, Dortmund, 1985) – actually a very sizeable lexicon. Rosalie Maggio, *The Nonsexist Word Finder: A Dictionary of Gender-Free Usage* (Oryx Press, Phoenix, Ariz., and New York, 1987). Rosalie Maggio, *The Dictionary of Bias-Free Usage: A Guide to Nondiscriminatory Language* (Oryx Press, Phoenix, Ariz., 1991). Bina Goldfield, *The Efemcipated English Handbook* (Westover Press, New York, 1983).

42 E. H. Carr, *Dostoevsky 1821–1881* (1931; Unwin, London, 1962), 38ff.

43 There's a parallel common assumption about the neutrality of Grammars, and a parallel actuality of the highly ideological organization and content of Grammars, not least ones published in the colonial context, e.g. *Cooly Tamil as Understood by Labourers on Tea and Rubber Estates, Specially Arranged for Planters and Planting Students*, by W. G. B. Wells, 4th edn (The Ceylon Observer, Colombo, 1927), or the *Guide To Military Urdu and the Elementary Examination*, by Major W. Turner (Educational Publishing Co., Karachi, 1942(?)), or the *Introduction to Chinyanja*, by Dr Meredith Sanderson of the East African Medical Service and W. B. Bithrey of the Nyasaland Police (Government Printing Office, Zomba, Nyasaland, 1925), found by Richard Boston, like my copies of the Tamil and Urdu guides, in a junk-stall (see 'Tongue with the Cheek', *Guardian*, 27 April 1987, 21), all of which initiate the white man into the syntax, vocabulary, tone of boss, master, superior, waited-upon one, and fix the native Singalese, Indian, and African as a bossable and bossed, recalcitrantly subordinate, servant class. There's also a parallel knowing subversion of this ideological actuality and political potential, especially in William Cobbett's *Grammar of the English Language, In a Series of Letters. Intended for the Use of Schools*

and of Young Persons in General; But More Especially for the Use of Soldiers, Sailors, Apprentices, & Plough-Boys (1817), full of subversive examples ('Sometimes the hyphen is used to connect many words together: 'The never-to-be-forgotten cruelty of the Borough tyrants'). Cobbett manifestly owes much to the subversive example of Horne Tooke. Again, there's also a parallel feeling by writers for the fictional potential of grammar and Grammars, from Eugene Ionesco's beginning as a dramatist when *The Bald Prima Donna* grew out of the grammatical examples of his Assimil English textbook *Anglais sans peine*, to Monique Wittig's novel *Le Corps lesbien* (Minuit, Paris, 1973) which experiments with French pronouns to indicate divided female selfhood (*j/e* and *m/a* for *je* and *ma*; thus creating problems for translators: *m/y* works in English; *j/e* became merely *I* in the English version). See also Baron, *Grammar and Gender*, for extended discussions of gender, especially in relation to nouns and pronouns (for a book professing to be about grammar, Baron is concerned to an astonishing extent with *lexis*; though, by the same token, the authors writing about *lexis* and compiling feminist lexicons (see n. 41) are also frequently engaged with grammatical questions). For varied discussions of politics and language, see e.g. Ali A. Mazrui, *The Political Sociology of the English Language: An African Perspective* (Mouton, The Hague and Paris, 1975), and Tony Crowley, *The Politics of Discourse: The Standard Language Question in British Cultural Debates* (Macmillan, London, 1989), published in the USA as *Standard English and the Politics of Language* (University of Illinois Press, Urbana and Chicago, 1989).

43   Burchfield, 'Case of Mistaken Identity'.

44   Later on, Burchfield seems to have absorbed and internalized the Williams point, as his review of some Johnsonian material shows, with its ringing declaration, nicely illustrated, that the lexicographer's personal bias is inevitable – his own, H. W. Fowler's, Murray's, as well as Johnson's: 'The Great Index', *Times Higher Educational Supplement*, 5 October 1990, 16.

45   Raymond Williams, *Keywords: A Vocabulary of Culture and Society* (Fontana/Croom Helm, London, 1976), Introduction, 9–24; *idem, Politics and Letters: Interviews with New Left Review* (Verso, London, 1979), 109, 167.

46   Erich Auerbach, *Mimesis* (1946), trans. Willard Trask (Princeton, University Press, 1953), information on obverse of title-page.

47   Williams, *Keywords*, 11.

48   Ibid., 15.

49   Cf. Raymond Williams, *Border Country* (Chatto and Windus, London, 1960), originally conceived as *Border Village*. It's disappointing, after all her indictments of the *OED* for (male) ideologism, that Paula Treichler should call Williams's *Keywords* (and Flaubert's *Dictionnaire des idées reçues*, and Bierce's *Devil's Dictionary*) 'eccentric' ('From Discourse to Dictionary', in Frank and Treichler, *Language, Gender, and Professional Writing*, 58.

50   For Tuccia, see 'The Sieve of Tuccia', ch. 11 of Marina Warner, *Monuments and Maidens: The Allegory of the Female Form* (Picador, London, 1987), 241–66.

51   Samuel Beckett, *En attendant Godot* (Éditions de Minuit, Paris, 1952), 86; *Waiting for Godot* (Faber, London, 1956; 2nd edn 1965), 62.

52   Beckett, *Murphy* (1938; John Calder, London, 1963), 41; *Murphy* (Éditions de Minuit, Paris, 1965), 44.
53   Deirdre Bair, *Samuel Beckett: A Biography* (Cape, London, 1978), 257.
54   Gayatri Chakravorty Spivack, Translator's Preface to *Of Grammatology* (Johns Hopkins University Press, Baltimore and London, 1976), xvii.
55   Jacques Derrida, *La Dissémination* (Éditions de Seuil, Paris, 1972), 32; *Dissemination*, trans. Barbara Johnson (University of Chicago Press, 1981), 25 and note.
56   Derrida, *De la grammatologie* (Éditions de Minuit, Paris, 1967), 96; *Of Grammatology*, 65.
57   Derrida, *Dissemination*, 212–13.
58   D. Attridge, 'Language as History/History as Language: Saussure and the Romance of Etymology', in D. Attridge, G. Bennington, and R. Young (eds), *Post-Structuralism and the Question of History* (Cambridge University Press, 1987), 202–3.
59   Derrida, *Marges de la philosophie* (Éditions de Minuit, Paris, 1972); *Margins of Philosophy*, trans. Alan Bass (Harvester, Brighton, 1982), xvii, n. 9.
60   *The Journals and Papers of Gerard Manley Hopkins*, ed. Humphry House and Graham Story (Oxford University Press, London, 1959), 4–5. See also entries under *slip*, *Earwig*, *Flick*, *fly-flow*, *Shear*, *Steel*, *Twig*, etc. (ibid., 9–19, 47).
61   For other recent lexicon fictions, see Monique Wittig and Sande Zeig, *Lesbian Peoples: Notes for a Dictionary* (Avon, New York, 1979; Virago, London, 1980), trans. of *Brouillon pour un dictionnaire des amantes,* 1976); Milorad Pavić, *Dictionary of the Khazars: A Lexicon Novel*, trans. Christina Pribićević-Zorić (Hamish Hamilton, London, 1988); Lawrence Norfolk, *Lemprière's Dictionary* (Sinclair-Stevenson, London, 1991); Sebastian Faulks, *A Fool's Alphabet* (Hutchinson, London, 1992). In some senses Roland Barthes's *Roland Barthes par Roland Barthes* and his *A Lover's Discourse: Fragments*, trans. Richard Howard (Cape, London, 1979), and Derrida's 'Limited Inc abc . . .' are also lexical fictions. Angela Carter enthuses wisely about Pavić in her *Expletives Deleted: Selected Writings* (Chatto and Windus, London, 1992), 9–16.
62   The new and corrected edition of Falconer (1780) was reprinted by David and Charles in 1970: it's my guess that it was this republication that led Golding to Falconer.
63   William Golding, *Rites of Passage* (Faber, London, 1980), 86–7.

ii: Give me an Aposiopestic Break

'Reading maketh a full man,' declared Francis Bacon in his little essay 'On Studies'. It was the traditional notion. Books filled you up, they satisfied. Books were the meat and drink of the mind and spirit. 'Some books are to be tasted, others to be swallowed, and some few to be chewed and digested.'[1] Such was the commonest medieval and Renaissance assumption. It animates the poetry of George Herbert as it does the sermons and allegories of John Bunyan. Words are commonly regarded as comestible stuff in Bunyan's texts, because Christ the Word and God's Word, the Bible, are. The logocentric sacramental assumptions in the Bible about the Word overflowed onto other books, onto other words. Reading of every kind was thought to give readers access to plenty, presence, satisfaction, fulfilment, *copia, pleroma*.

The sense of the plenitudes of books was rooted in a sense of the plenitudes of God's Book. The felt capacity of words to make things, people, ideas, present was founded in the notion of the Word becoming flesh. Once it was accepted that Christ could be made present through the Word, it was a short step to thinking that any person or thing could be manifested in language. The episcopal preacher and Biblical translator Lancelot Andrewes – he whose sermons provided T. S. Eliot's poetry with so many of its best lines – expounds the position with classic vigour in his Christmas Day sermon of 1611. This discourse is an exultant restatement of the power of the Word, preached before the patron of the Authorized or King James Version of the Bible, King James himself, in the year of its publication by one of that version's own translators. His text is from St John 1. 14: 'And the Word was made flesh, and dwelt among us (and we saw the glory thereof, as the glory of the only-begotten Son of the Father), full of grace and truth.' And fullness is as much on Andrewes' mind as it is the substance of his text – the fullness of God, the fullness of Christ the Word, the fullness of Scripture: '. . . that as He came not obscurely but was seen, so He came not empty but "full of grace and truth". This fullness was not for Himself, but for us; *et de plenitudine Ejus omnes accepimus.*' The Word was made flesh; Christ, the transcendent Logos, assumed immanent human form, became present in history; the Scriptural words about the Word have the capacity to keep on entering the human, historical world, ever full of the presence of Christ. The Incarnation is *factum* not *fictum*, a fact indeed, not a light invention. The Word and the word are incarnational fact, not incarnational joke, deception, fiction. To believe otherwise is to join the heretic Manicheans. '"Made" it was; against Manicheus holding that He had no true body: as if *factum* had been *fictum*, or making mere mocking.' And the real presence of the Word in the word is a surety of all the other real presences in words. What's *fictum* – formed, fashioned, made, mentally conceived, represented, sketched out, imagined (all meanings of the Latin verb *fingere*) – is in this logocentric case by no means the merely *fictus* (the adjective derived from *fingere*) – that is, feigned, false, deceiving, fictitious.[2]

The essence of Christian fact within Christian fiction, the *factum* in the *fictum*, the incarnational ground of the Christian faith in linguistic presence and fullness, was of course sited emphatically, as another Andrewes sermon expounds it, in the very birth of Christ. When T. S. Eliot started in his un-Christian phase, in his poem *Gerontion*, to manifest his sense of the importance of Andrewes' Christmas Day sermon of 1618 ('Signs are taken for wonders'), he was responding to this fundamental Christian proposition that meaning in language, in any sign-system, depends on, and is in effect guaranteed by, the central logocentric moment when the Word became flesh and was manifest in the manger. For at that moment, according to Andrewes, the meaning of the word *signatus* (= signed, signified) was realized in its enactment of the *natus* (= born) that it already had packed into it, as it were, plenipotentially. 'So we come from *Christus natus* to *Christus signatus*. *Natus* "born", to be found; *Signatus*, "signed or marked", that He may be found.' Christ *signatus*, the word, the sign, the occasion of signs and sign-systems, is also Christ *natus*, the baby, the manifested one; and there is no signifying without the birth. This Word becomes flesh; this sign is incarnated; and so all signs may – indeed, must – ultimately realize their significance in such manifestations, such engagements with the historical, timely world, the zone of presence, the present, the presented. On this model, the *signatum* in general, the person or thing that signs refer to and make present in words, acquires its entire legitimacy from this divine *Signatum*. 'Some kind of proportion there would be between *signum* and *signatum*.' And a chief feature of this proportionality between the Christ-sign and Christ-*signatum* is eloquence. It's eloquence that transcends the astonishing temporary dumbness of the infant word – the 'Verbum infans' that so attracted Eliot, 'the Word without a word; the eternal Word not able to speak a word'. Even when for the moment infantilely dumb in the manger, this sign speaks out. 'For *loquitur signis*, "signs have their speech", and this is no dumb sign.'[3] And the eloquence of the Word's becoming audible, in the now, not least in the era of the Authorized Version, speaking out of the silence of the divine transcendence and from the quiet writtenness of the text, the pages of Scripture, is the essence of its current fullness, its contemporary accomplishment, its power for *pleroma*.

What is continuously present in all explications such as Andrewes' is some recollection of the paramount Christological moment in the Gospel of St Luke chapter 4 in which Jesus enters the synagogue of Nazareth on the Sabbath and, exercising his privilege as a male Jew, stands up to read from the Scripture, unrolling the scroll of Isaiah until he comes to the place where it is written: 'The Spirit of the Lord is upon me, because he hath anointed me to preach the gospel to the poor.' And when he has finished reading, he folds up the scroll, sits down, and says: 'This day is this scripture fulfilled in your ears.' This giving of voice to the written text, the utterance of these words by this person, the bringing of the old words out of the past into the present, by a person full of a sense of mission ('And Jesus being full of the Holy Ghost . . .'): here, daringly claimed, is the realization, the fulfilment, of the silent potential of the word. The French version has particular force for literary criticism: 'Aujourd'hui cette parole de l'Écriture, que vous venez d'entendre, est accomplie.' 'Cette parole de l'Écriture': this *écriture*, this scripture, this writing, will not stay locked up *in potentia*, in writing, or in mere Saussurean *langue*; it has a capacity for utterance, for *parole*, and that capacity has been eloquently achieved in and by a person, by this singular presence in this moment of presentedness. 'Hodie impleta est haec scriptura in auribus vestris': so the Vulgate version's Latin. The *scriptura impleta*, in your ears: the scripture that has been voiced, by this reader, and so been filled up, swollen with meaning for readers, as if the very text were satisfied by eating, satiated with food, like a belly swollen, fattened, pregnant even, and so a scripture brought into prominence, having achieved due emphasis. (Quintilian uses the verb related to *impleta* as a technical term of rhetoric: this fulfilling is what rhetoric is desired to do.) This is a writing that has discharged its destiny, come into its own, achieved its appointed end or function. It has done what writings should do.

All of which, of course, has been repudiated by the counter-arguments of our post-Saussurean times. Instead of providing satisfaction, plenitude, fullness, and presence, texts are alleged to provide, rather, experiences of emptiness and absence. In place of the old logocentric rhetoric of plenitudinousness, there comes to reign instead a usurping alternative Babelic lexicon of preferred counter-terms: *aporia* (Greek for being at a loss, in an impasse or doubtful position), gap, *béance* (French for a yawning hole), *manque* (French for what's missing, a lack), *kenosis* (Greek for emptying).

Kenotic Energy

The language of lacks, gaps, cut-offs, and cut-outs – unkind cuts, but allegedly necessary ones – seeds the texts of Derrida and Lacan and of their disciples. The Freudian metaphor of the significant navel is taken as a fundamental clue to, and sign of, the nature of selfhood and writing. This anatomical place of emptiness, a *béance* or abyss where a scar, a graphic trace of the necessary childhood cut, marks the absence – the cut-off point – of the navel cord and the mother, is offered as the essence of the knowledge got by writing. It declares the ultimate mystery of the graphing process, the deterring *dernier terme* of being and of text, the very heart of Lacan's vision of the unconscious's being 'structured like a language'.[4] So when Samuel Weber probes and pokes at Freud's dark navel-place in order to chart the lexical difficulties that defining it proposes, and discovers a vast hinterland of yet further gaps, a regressive scene of *béance* upon *béance*, he's only pursuing a well-defined Lacanian logic. All utterance, on this view, all text, all lexicons, all critical enquiry, get you deeper into *béance*, the *manque d'un manque*, the deeps of emptiness.

> Whatever else may be unclear in Lacan's discourse, there seems little doubt that, 'in the final analysis' – *au dernier terme* – its terms lead us to the 'center of the unknown' and to *derniers termes* such as *béance*. Lacan here repeats the gesture that we have retraced in Freud: the gesture of the final analysis itself, of a certain termination and determination: that of the dernier terme designed to put an end to the indetermination of an interminable proliferation. The final term, here *béance* (there *manque*), designates the place where one can stop and get off the train, having finally arrived at the desired destination.[5]

The dream-wish, the desire that drives text-making, is a ticket into emptiness.

This particular desire is one that came more and more to characterize modernist literature, a fictional glorying – as Henry James put it in his 1914 review of Conrad's novel *Chance*, in a discussion of Conrad's reluctant, lapsing, even refusing narrator – 'in a gap'. The bridge, wrote James, between narrative authority and the subject of the narration keeps breaking down, and Conrad comes 'once more and yet once more to "glory in a gap" '. As so often, in his readerly embrace of an amenable text, James is here sympathetically selecting for approval narrative features that reflect his own practice. The lapsing, unreliable narrator had become increasingly a feature of James's own fictions. Conrad's Marlow and James's Strether are twin brothers. There is some danger, James thinks, in such intense deployment of faint and fading impressions – in Conrad's case a great clutter of rebarbative narrative stuff, lapsing narrative voices afforced by the broken bits of textual evidence, fragments of letters, scraps and shreds of writing, the heaps of difficult or contradictory witness that become normal in, say, Beckett or B. S. Johnson (or, in their different but connected ways, in Kafka's diaries or T. S. Eliot's *Waste Land* manuscripts and typescripts or Saussure's lectures or, for that matter, the postmodernist version of *King Lear* recently broken into two by the Oxford Shakespeare editors). The danger James scents in this sort of Conradian practice – that of 'steeping his matter in perfect eventual obscuration' – is one that Conrad seems to be consenting to with a 'grace' unequalled by any other artist that James knows. But already James was himself coming to accept the slippage that his discussion was arranging from a state of danger into one of grace. 'This grace', his next sentence begins, 'presently comes over us as the sign of the whole business.'[6] And after 1914, the obscuration that occurs in the vicinity of the Conradian gap would come to be accepted as the great grace of a whole modern literature of silence, exiled meanings, refusal, Beckettian *néant*.

Characteristically, Frank Kermode glories in that Conradian and Jamesian glorying in a gap. Fictions that clam up rather than disclose, that guard their secrets rather than utter them, that go in for narrative breaks and hermeneutic gaps, are germane to Kermode's master-argument that great texts are about emptiness rather than fullness, absence rather than presence, *kenosis* rather than *pleroma*. And, importantly, although much of Kermode's major evidence comes from twentieth-century texts – for example, Conrad, James, Ford Madox Ford, Joyce, Henry Green – and his major critical stimulus is to be found in the critical pushes of the nineteen-sixties and seventies, nonetheless his argument is offered as generally applicable. What all texts are about, it's alleged, is the genesis of secrecy. The ambition of Kermode's immensely important book *The Genesis of Secrecy* is to describe how all texts work. In making the New Testament's Gospel of St Mark his central case, he's trying to grant the argument power to embrace our whole tradition of narrative, as well as seeking to challenge at its Biblical source the old idea that texts are actually about *pleroma*, fulfilment, satisfaction, presence. 'We are in love with the idea of fulfilment, and our interpretations show it.' 'We are all fulfilment men, *pleromatists*.' What we should all rather be, by contrast, is alerted to the pervasiveness of the *vide* in literature, 'the unarticulated sentence, the aposiopesis'.[7] We'd be wiser to recognize the centrality of *kenosis* in Scripture, as in texts generally.

Kenosis, the New Testament word used to describe Christ's emptying himself of Godhead in order to be incarnated as a human being, is the third of the 'revisionary ratios', or rhetorical strategies, that Harold Bloom proposes in *The Anxiety of Influence: A Theory of Poetry* (1975) as governing the relationship between poets and poems and their influential predecessors. And it's not just *kenosis* that has a long textual history behind it. Gaps, voids, mysteries, secrets, are, of course, easily discoverable in ancient as well as modern texts. The hoariness of terms like *aporia* and *aposiopesis* bears loud witness to the negative rhetorical possibilities on offer to text-makers from of old. *Aporia* has always been an option. Puttenham in his *Art of English Poesie* (1589) Englished the ancient figure of *aporia* as *the Doubtfull*. The *OED* nicely cites John Smith's *The Mysterie of Rhetorique Unvail'd* (1657): 'Aporia is a figure whereby the Speaker sheweth that he doubteth, either where to begin for the multitude of matters, or what to do or say in some strange or ambiguous thing.' This recognition of the possibility of self-doubting, self-stymying, self-deconstructive utterance, is as old, then, as rhetorical reflection and instruction. What's new is the generalization of aporia in our time – the allegation that all texts are aporetic – and the reductiveness of this allegation: the notion that aporia is what all texts mainly, or only, consist of.

The generalization and the reductiveness are at the heart of the deconstructionist, or postmodernist, case. The generalization is dubious; the reductiveness is demonstrably an exaggeration, even a complete falsehood. At the core of this matter lies a variant of the Cretan Liar paradox. 'All Cretans are liars, said the Cretan': and you're expected to accept as truth a Cretan's statement that all Cretan statements are lies. Not dissimilarly (and the point really is, as it were, a Princeton First Year one), the argument that things made of words, all texts, are empty, comes with the counter-claim built implicitly into it that the emptiness doesn't apply to this sentence about emptiness. And, of course, some such persistent positivity is indeed the wry essence of the logic of all such claims about linguistic negativity. For words about negativity are inevitably themselves positive terms – positive about negatives. Language and texts do not empty simply by virtue of proposing emptiness. And in fact, emptiness, blankness, silence, are not states of language. As long as language is in play, in existence, in however exiguous a form, it is not a nothing, not silence. Speakers and texts can, and do, fall silent. But silence is not a version of language, not a possible state of language; it is the absence of it. If you are in the presence of a complete blank page, if you cannot hear any words, you are not in the presence of language as such. Words, written texts, pieces of music, can exploit silence, talk about it, countenance it, have it as a theme, build moments of it into their structure, frame it. But once they have been utterly overtaken by it, they have ceased to exist as textual structures and entities. The ludicrously elementary error in much recent criticism is to suppose that texts which mark absences, which discuss and are about emptiness, gaps, incompleteness, voids, do by virtue of such subject-matter themselves comprise emptiness. But the marks, vocabulary, rhetorics, of absence are, in their way, full signs, just as eloquent in their fashion as any mark of presence or fullness.

Empties Not Empty

So that, naturally, the whole postmodernist lexicon of emptiness words is actually full of meaning. This vocabulary would not, of course, have ever been brought into action if that were not the case. Which is a discomfiting, even deconstructing, truth that is acknowledged, where it's acknowledged at all, only with embarrassment. Samuel Weber, for example, is driven with some reluctance to own up to the case that the Lacanian *béance* offers a very positive, 'curiously full, oversaturated', centre to the Freudian dream-text. Freud's vague heart of darkness, his, so to say, wayside station that doesn't seem to be in the railway timetable, has got itself turned into a mainline terminus well-known to Baedeker. Labelled *Béance*, the nearly-nowhere place of the Freudian dream has become in Lacan's analysis 'the final station, the Terminus or Terminal, where every voyage begins and ends; very different from the obscure, out-of-the-way Haltestelle, where, according to Freud, one must be prepared to wait patiently for a connection (Anschluss)'.[8] But, of course, the same applies to all of the labels that Freud sticks on or about this place: navel, mycelium, and so on. There could not be a more telling illustration of the fact that, once uttered, all words enjoy a provocative fullness, a challenging presence, even words about absence, the very vocabulary for emptiness.

Take *béance*. It's a word full of meaning, much like the act of yawning that it denotes. Yawns occur in faces. They're not simple absences, but complex facial actions constrained by facial musculature, lips, teeth, tongue, and glottis. Mouths are not bottomless pits. *Le Bâilleur*, 'The Yawner', Peter Brueghel the Elder's portrait of a yawning man in the Musée des Beaux Arts in Brussels, brings home very sharply indeed the complicated facial manoeuvres required by a yawn, as also the complex significations that might be implied by one. The fact that *bâillon* is a term for a gag or muzzle, as well as for a device to keep mouths open during surgery, is further neat indication of how meanings continually rush in to fill the vacancies that yawns might be felt to propose and impose.

As if to bring home the great richness of the yawning situation, there is a vivid concatenation of overlapping and historically confused verbs hereabouts in French: *bâiller*, to yawn, gape, or (of doors and windows) to fit badly, to be ajar; (the older verb) *bayer*, to stand gaping with mouth open, to gawp; (the even older) *béer*, to open, yawn, desire, aspire; *bâilloner*, to gag, muzzle, silence. The central cluster of meanings, to open wide the mouth, to gape, to aspire after, focuses in *bâiller* and its variants: the noun *bâillement*, yawn, yawning, gaping, fissure, crack, gap (in curtains); the adjective *bâillant*, gaping (as shirt or bodice), yawning (as chasm), ajar (as door). Out of the *mélange* of all such terms came *abeance* and *abeyance*, legal terms in Old and Anglo–French for the condition of an heir or some other person hopeful of coming into a title or property, which gave us our English legal term *abeyance* for the condition of property (*in abeyance*) whose ownership is thus claimed or liable to be claimed by someone. And, to stress the point, this condition of abeyance is clearly not a nothing, nowhere condition. As the focus of desire and aspiration, it's a state of some potency and potential (capable, for example, of sustaining the hundreds of pages of a novel about people caught up in legal expectancy, such as *Bleak House*). How the verbs basic to this cluster of French words arose exactly is a matter of speculation, but they are commonly traced to the noise that infant lips make at the breast or when sucking in air: *bayer à la mammelle* in older French was to crave the breast. Again, a something, not a nothing, is going on here.

And so it is with other terms accepted as keys to the deconstructionist allegation. *Difference* itself is an ancient term proposing real differentiation in mathematics and logic and heraldry. 'What's the difference?' asks Paul de Man in his *Allegories of Reading*, quoting the awful US TV-soaps racist Archie Bunker, as a way of wryly debunking the power of words and grammar to offer authoritative statements, ask positive questions. The passage is taken up approvingly by Barbara Johnson as the epigraph for her book *The Critical Difference* (1980). But if you're a member of a family whose coat-of-arms is distinguished from that of another branch of the family by a variant known as a *difference*, 'What's the difference?' is no empty question. As it wasn't for onlookers at mad Ophelia, sadly different from what she'd been, handing out tokens of that difference with a queered knowingness about heraldic differentiation: 'You must wear your rue with a difference' (*Hamlet*, IV. v). 'What's the difference?' asks one of the boys in Christopher Hope's novel satirizing racist separation laws in South Africa, *A Separate Development* (1981), during a discussion about the alleged difference of Blacks from Whites. The views of the boy van Dam and his White kind matter immensely, as one of the chums discovers when he's reclassified as Black. One way or another, with or without Archie Bunker, Ophelia, or van Dam, *difference* refuses to have itself negated, emptied out, drained of content, de-differentiated.

In other words, language continually reaches out for fullness and presence just as the infant mouth reaches out for the breast. Language aspires towards fullness. It is precisely in a state of *abeance*, of *aspiration*. Which is the condition, in fact, of its tiniest and most fragile units of meaning, such as aspirates. Or, for that matter, commas and apostrophes. *Aspirates* are breathing sounds in speech. In writing, they're signs such as the letter *h* in English or the mark in Greek looking like a comma or apostrophe which denote a breath or breathing place. Like commas and apostrophes, aspirates mark an absence or gap or pause in speech, which, however, is by no means negative or empty but full, in the first place, of the very essence of speech – namely, breath, air.

The curiously emphatic commas that punctuate the Biblical warnings painted on walls and fences in Hardy's *Tess of the d'Urbervilles* (chapter 12) rightly attract Hillis Miller: 'THY, DAMNATION, SLUMBERETH, NOT'; 'THOU, SHALT, NOT, COMMIT.' The itinerant evangelist, says Miller, places 'a comma after each word, as if to give pause while that word was driven home to the reader's heart'. Miller, though, wants little to do with that significant, thoughtful pausing. He prefers to dwell on the 'gap . . . designated by the comma'. He adds that 'The comma is a mark of punctuation which signifies nothing in itself but punctuation, a pause.'[9] Which is manifestly not true. At least, one must take Shakespeare and *Hamlet* into account before deciding that commas are marks 'signifying nothing' in themselves. When Hamlet forges the letter to the King of England that does mortally for Rozencrantz and Guldenstern, he prefaces the epistle's nitty-gritty with some of the usual approach-shots of ambassadorial, courtly rhetoric:

> As England was his faithful tributary,
> As love between them like the palm might flourish,
> As peace should still her wheaten garland wear
> And stand a comma 'tween their amities,
> And many such-like 'as'es of great charge,
> That . . .
>
> (V. ii. 39–44)

And whatever meaning we attach to the vexed crux *comma* – even if, like Harold Jenkins's Longer Note in the new Arden edition (1982), we grant it very little as 'the least of the marks of punctuation, and therefore a type of something small and insignificant' – the equation between *love* and *comma* as buffers or links, the fact that it's *peace* that is to stand like a comma, do suggest a certain degree of fullness of meaning in this central mark of an absence, enough at least to give any paid-up deconstructionist some pause.

Something similar is the case with the apostrophe ('), the full superscript mark denoting an absent letter or letters (as in Hamlet's *'tween* for *between*). Apostrophe is also the label in rhetoric for addresses to some person or thing not present with the speaker and otherwise missing or even dead, at any rate not present on-stage or at the moment. As with commas, it's the absentings of apostrophe that have attracted most recent notice. Jonathan Culler's compact little essay 'Apostrophe' complains that critics have ignored apostrophe, acting as if it weren't so dominant a presence, particularly in lyric poetry. But his own thoughts on apostrophizing tend towards confirming that critical absenting rather than correcting it. For a start, Culler has nothing to say about apostrophe as written sign (though he does make a feeble pun about Baudelaire's *Cygne* as *signe*). And the baneful presence of Paul de Man dominates the discussion. Culler agrees with, and quotes lengthily from, de Man's oddly lopsided reading of Rilke's apostrophic lyric in *The Book of Hours*, 'Ich liebe dich, du sanftestes Gesetz'. The joint Culler–de Man line is that the *Gesetz* (law) apostrophized so repeatedly in the poem is addressed by such a plethora of names, is granted so many metaphoric designations, that its identity gets lost; and anyway since these many titles (law, homesickness, forest, song, net) all imply reactions inspired by the addressee in the addresser, the real interest of the poem lies in the speaker, so that the poem refers rather to 'an activity of the speaking subject.' Culler makes this instantiation of the speaker a key function of apostrophic verse. Which is as may be; but to argue that the implication of a drama going on between addresser and addressee means the effective wiping out of the addressee is absurd; as is the notion that the more metaphoric attributes the addressed *Gesetz* earns, the less specificity it enjoys. That way every title added, say, in the Old Testament to the name Jehovah would be a diminution of the Deity's selfhood. And nobody's ever had the gall to suggest that. Clearly, what's afoot here is a rather desperate effort to resist the traditional instantiating power of the rhetoric of apostrophe.[10]

Traditionally, and I think rightly, apostrophe has been felt to own the curious power of making the absent present, of raising the dead, giving present existence to persons and things that otherwise appear to lack it (as discussed in my final chapter). In an apostrophe such as 'O death, where is thy sting? O grave, where is thy victory?' (i Corinthians 15: 55), the grave and death are called into being, granted identity and selfhood. Clearly, apostrophe is the essence of the 'pathetic fallacy', a key agent in the rhetorical work of *prosopopoeia*, the granting of humanity to non-human entities. And, far from surprisingly, Paul de Man is suspicious of the work of prosopopoeia too.[11] Furthermore, in ancient rhetoric, as explained by Quintilian, it was clearly accepted that apostrophe could just as easily address persons present as persons absent (as in St Paul's 'Whereupon, O King Agrippa, I was not disobedient to the heavenly vision': Acts 26: 19). And self-evidently, this is a power that apostrophe still retains. It really is hard to divorce apostrophic work from the actuality of presence in some form or another.

Famously, Jacques Lacan polarized the *empty* word (the constipated utterance of obsessives) and the *full* word (the verbal diarrhoea of hysterics).[12] One of the preoccupations of postmodernist criticism has been to spot apparently full words imploding to become 'actually' empty ones. What I am suggesting is that apparently empty words – and not least, the key postmodernist terms for emptiness – keep returning as actually full ones. It is not, generally speaking, a mistake to perceive the possibilities of textual emptiness, the textual dalliance with it; but it is an error to think it ever exclusive. The unabated persistence of emptiness in some form, coupled with the insistent return of the fullness with which it is at odds, provides dramatic occasions of contradiction, but also challenging paradox and complementarity. What's really going on in key metaphors like *béance*, what's really being marked by aspirates, commas, and apostrophes, is, I think, the true drama of marginality, a continuing struggle between emptiness and fullness, a persistent convergence of, and clash between, absence and presence.

Hachette Jobs

Is *abeance*, aspiration, a drawing in of air or a releasing of it? Hard to decide, for is it not both or either? Aspiration is inspiration and also expiration. Just so, the 'uneasiness' of the waves on Mrs Flanders's sea-shore in *Jacob's Room*, the place and emblem of her writing-problematic, might be the mark of a rising or a receding tide. Again, a *béance* in curtains is difficult to specify instantly as the result of faulty opening or closing. The verb to *draw*, used of curtains, registers the ambivalence precisely. What does the instruction to *draw the curtains* order? To draw them back, to open them; or to draw them to, to close them? It can mean either. (One's not surprised to find the yellow curtains in *Mrs Dalloway* blowing in as well as out; as emblems of consciousness and meaning, they register the entrancing marginality of curtains with great flair.) Derrida's *brisure*, the articulating hinge action or place of a shutter, also means a breach, a gap, a kind of disarticulation. Doors both open and close about hinges: that movement of articulation is also a motion of disarticulation. One's not surprised, again, that squeaky hinges are so prominent in *Tristram Shandy* and *Mrs Dalloway*; attention needs calling to the difficulties of articulation. As she goes in and comes out, manoeuvring her way through her front door as across a dangerous strand, thinking of Rumpelmayer's men arriving to remove the inside doors, and thus complexly involved in an extraordinary beginning emblem of the difficulties of beginning a text, of negotiating the borders of text and being, it's small wonder that Mrs Dalloway should remember a squeaking hinge. Likewise, aspirates have a disconcerting way of arbitrarily coming and going that proper folks believe to be improper, but which defeats all efforts at regulation. As the *OED* puts it with disconcerting frankness about *aspirate*: '*Esp*. applied to the initial *h* – so often "dropped", or improperly inserted, by the uneducated in England.' Which is another example of old social prejudice retained in the *OED*'s Second Edition, for doubtfulness over initial *h* straddles class borders as it transgresses national ones. The gentry still go 'untin', shootin' and fishin' in England. In England the posh as well as the cockney stay in 'otels. Think, too, of the jumpy *h* in *herb*. The politest of chefs in the USA pronounce it '*erb*. No doubt they're thinking of the French *herbe* as their model, which has no initially sounded aspirate. Indeed, the French never aspirate their *h*'s. There's much losing or gaining of *h*'s depending upon which way you cross *la Manche*. (Absent thee from your *h* awhile 'Oratio, as one might say.)

This business of a now-you-hear-it-now-you-don't initial *h* is, in fact, a rather potent apostrophic drama of presence and absence, and one hinted at briefly in a nicely jesting moment in Derrida's *Signéponge* where the *h* in *franchise*, inscribed on a leaf (of a tree) in a Francis Ponge text, is made expungeable (along with the ultimate *e*) to yield (shades of Saussure's anagrams) Ponge's forename *Francis* – a detachable insignificant aspirate that can in the right hands chop a whole tree down (the letter *h* in French – *hache* – is also the French word for an axe – the big version of a hatchet – *hachette*).[13] It's a drama of hatcheting out and hatching in that's focused quite sensationally in the pedantic sniffing out of an apparently missing apostrophe by schoolmaster Holofernes in *Love's Labours Lost* (IV. ii). Nathaniel reads out a sonnet. Holofernes, his nose as keen as Ovidius Naso's for 'smelling out the odoriferous flowers of fancy, the jerks of invention', detects a missing 'apostrophus' in the reading of the poem's last line. But what is actually present or absent in the sonnet has never proved positively identifiable, however, by any subsequent scholarship or pedantry. Many commentators have thought that Holofernes should have said *diaeresis* rather than *apostrophus*. In any case, the Arden edition's preferred word *apostrophus* is a reading dithering between the extant textual variants *apostraphas, apostrophas, apostrophes*. *Apostrophus* is what Furness called an *emendatio certissima*. It came, interestingly enough, from Dictionary Murray himself in a parenthesis in the *OED*'s quotation from this very passage of Shakespeare under the entry *apostrophe*.

So Murray puts in an *apostrophus* where one was missing from every extant text of Shakespeare, in imitation of Holofernes, who puts in *apostrophas/ apostrophes* where he should probably not have. And Holofernes talks of *apostrophes*, makes one present, only to note that an apostrophe has not been discovered, has been left out of the reading ('You find not the apostrophus, and so miss the accent'), a dual sin, of commission and omission, a little textual drama of finding and losing, of both looking overhard and overlooking, that is in turn very neatly reflected in Arden editor Richard David's footnote on the matter:

> Ben Jonson gives a careful definition (overlooked in the *New Eng. Dict.*) in *The Second Book of the English Grammar* (*ante* 1637): '*Apostrophus* is the rejecting of a vowel from the beginning or end of a word. The note whereof, though it many times through the negligence of writers and printers, is quite omitted, yet by right . . . hath his mark, which is such a semi-circle (') placed in the top.' It is this negligence the pedant complains of as misleading Nathaniel.[14]

The complex logic of *apostrophe* appears all the more as the rather desperate editors increase their interpretative squeeze. Which is the case also with Hamlet's *comma*. Harold Jenkins's wonderfully useful Longer Note on *comma* in the new Arden edition, crucially reveals the persisting dialectic between presence and absence in the metaphor, which is of course the dialectic in the mark of the comma itself. 'And stand a comma 'tween their amities': the context suggests a bond; the practice of commas in marking gaps, denoting pauses, implies a break. The sense of bond has led many editors variously to amend *comma* to read *commere, cement, co-mate, cov'nant, compact*. On the other side, John Dover Wilson preferred the sense of 'briefest possible pause', following the *OED*'s sense 2c, 'Break of continuity, interval, pause', the citations for which lead off with this passage. But the truth of the matter is that the two complementary senses bond/break will not simply resolve their opposition into a domination of either sense by the other. So that even when Jenkins suggests that *comma* may be a guess by the compositor of the Second Quarto, he calls it, with perhaps unconscious aptness, a stopgap. For here gap and stopgap are interacting with arresting, if puzzling, vivacity.[15] And I would argue that this particular moment of Hamletian pause over the meaning of *comma* is exemplary in the widest fashion. And exemplary in a similarly arresting bifocal way, though of course on a far larger textual scale, is Laurence Sterne's keen rewriting of *Hamlet* – that is, the novel *Tristram Shandy*.

Phimotic Devices

The Russian Formalist Viktor Shklovsky took *Tristram Shandy* as the arch-example of what the Formalists thought made texts important, namely (in Russian) *obnaženie priëma*, the exposure of textual mechanism, the engine or works of the text, within the proceedings of the text itself. *Tristram Shandy* 'lays bare' its 'device', goes in for what Tzvetan Todorov translates as 'la dénudation du procédé', and it does so on nearly the hugest scale of any of the great fictions. And this self-exposure of fictional workings, this metatextual preoccupation, made this novel for Shklovsky the world's essential novel: 'One often hears an assertion that *Tristram Shandy* is not a novel. . . . Actually, the reverse of this is true. *Tristram Shandy* is the most typical novel in world literature.'[16] And the particular aspect of the exposed guts of *Tristram Shandy* that I wish to stress — and to offer as typical of how novels, and language, work — is the way that procedures making for emptiness, that undo, subvert, frustrate, the process of the novel, are coexistent with their opposite — those tactics making for fullness, satisfaction, completion. Exemplarily, I think, the apparent emptiness or self-annihilation of *Tristram Shandy* (what *Finnegans Wake* glosses as *lexinction*, 83: 25, or the *abnihilisation of the etym*, 353: 22) keeps returning as a kind of satisfactoriness, a fullness — but always a skewed, flawed fullness, perpetually interfered with by, and as it were conscious of, failure, textual distress, silence.

Tristram Shandy keeps offering itself as a mess. It is one long confession of assorted failures. It can't, in the words of the Gershwin song, work up any confidence about 'getting started'. It can't manage straightforward progress. Its apparent progressions are digressions. It makes headway with the circling, stuttering motions of Watt's walk in Beckett's novel — a 'headlong tardigrade'. It anticipates Joyce in being what *Finnegans Wake* calls an 'exprogressive process' (614: 31). It stumbles dramatically at its own threshold, is confused about how to begin, about where to begin, about whether it has begun. Things keep being got back to front. Characteristically the text provides the rhetorical term for this: *hypallage*. 'What's that? cried my uncle Toby. The cart before the horse, replied my father.' And this is in a chapter (VIII. 13) that provides a cock-eyed handy-dandyish alphabet of love's progress in which *S* precedes *R*. The novel's Preface comes very late indeed in the text.

Emblematic of this formal hesitation, Tristram's christening — which follows a mock-learned discussion in French about the papist possibility of baptizing a child before it's born (I. 20) — is a sloppy, hasty farce of awful misnaming. Tristram's circumcision (or what might be his circumcision, when the sash-window crashes down onto his little penis) occurs very belatedly, and only by accident, when he's five years old. But then Tristram's begetting is a farce, and so is his parturition, and so too is his Uncle Toby's laying siege to Widow Wadman's charming body and attractive front door. The *obstetrical* is said to inform the *scriptical* (III. 8), and both are disaster areas. This is not just a text of what Beckett's *Murphy* called 'maieutic saws', but of sore maieutics. Here midwifery of every kind, whether the bringing of a child or a text into the world, keeps going wrong. 'Unhappy *Tristram*: child of wrath! child of decrepitude! interruption! mistake! and discontent! What one misfortune or disaster in the book of embryotic evils, that could unmechanize thy frame, or entangle thy filaments! which has not fallen upon thy head, or ever thou camest into the world — what evils in thy passage into it! — what evils since!' The lamentation of Tristram's father for his unhappy son (IV. 19), in a novel as full of unhappy sons as *Hamlet*, is a lamentation too for *Tristram Shandy* the text.

And much in the text supports, both metaphorically and metonymically, the central failures that have to do with procreation and birth, of getting into, and getting along in, life. Tristram's damaged penis is of a piece with Uncle Toby's wounded groin and his father's difficulties in fathering – the particular act of coitus interruptus with which the novel opens ('Did ever woman, since the creation of the world, interrupt a man with such a silly question?'). And the damaged penis has a vast roster of analogues, bawdy, sad, comic – Mr Shandy's snapped-off tobacco pipe, the bridge of Tristram's nose crushed and broken at birth by Dr Slop's heavy-handed forceps, the damaged drawbridge in Toby's dinky-model fortifications on the bowling green, the pair of hereditary riding-boots Trim saws up to make model gun barrels, the broken names (Tristram for Tristram-gistus, bastardized version of the desired Trismegistus), broken sentences, paragraphs with gaps in them, the collapse of discourse into asterisks, dashes, silence, gap – including a torn-out chapter (IV. 24; 'a chasm of ten pages made in the book by it' as the chapter after that describes its missing neighbour) – a black page, a marbled one, lots of blank whitenesses, all swapped for the print that you'd normally expect, and that normally you get.

This text is full of holes. And holes, orifices, gaps, gulfs, spell trouble here. Calamity builds around and at them. Centrally, of course, there are the disruptions of normal bodily orificial activity – at the ends of penises (Mr Shandy's, Uncle Toby's, Tristram's) and in the birth passage, the vagina of Mrs Shandy (and, potentially, of Bridget and Widow Wadman). And these main disastrous holes are surrounded by numerous others in an exuberant profusion of distress: the opening of Dr Slop's bag of obstetric instruments crucially tied up in knots, holes in trousers or breeches in breeches, slits in petticoats, buttonholes, nostrils, muzzles of guns, windows, doors, crevices, cracks, openings of all sorts. And disasters in, and at, holes overlay each other most alarmingly. Tristram is born disastrously, and misnamed, and has his nose crushed, all while his father is struggling to don his breeches and rushing along the gallery with only one button only half into his buttonhole so that it slips out on the way (IV. 14). What comes before this (III. 21, 22) is a set of reflections on the parlour door whose hinges have lacked oil and so squeaked for ten years (as well as much matter about noses). What follows, includes the tearing out of the chapter, promises of a chapter on buttonholes (IV. 15), and the mock symposium of talkative friends who, it's hoped, will resolve the question of whether Tristram can be rechristened, renamed – at which discussion poor Phutatorius gets terribly burned in the penis because a hot chestnut rolls out of its bag (or damask napkin) into an 'aperture' of his breeches or galligaskins (IV. 27). Shortly to follow is the crashing down of the sash-window on the hapless Tristram because Corporal Trim has plundered the window fittings to make model artillery for Toby: the pulleys for the wheels of gun-carriages, the lead counterweights for the barrels of the siege-cannons themselves. In one sequence or another, and in a paragraph with a distinct Beckettian ring to it (compare *Murphy*'s paired opposites and the perverse sequences of series in *Watt*), all the windows in Toby's house have become potential weapons and places of destruction and fatality:

> He had dismantled every sash-window in my uncle *Toby*'s house long before, in the very same way, – though not always in the same order; for sometimes the pullies have been wanted, and not the lead, – so then he began with the pullies, – and the pullies being picked out, then the lead became useless, – and so the lead went to pot too. (V. 19)

People and text, then, are continually stuck, and coming unstuck, at thresholds, the threshold of life, of fatherhood, of writing. Promises are made, and commonly not fulfilled. The text reaches forward, towards fullness, completion, promising chapters on this or that, on noses, buttonholes, pishes, digressions, on chapters even. The continual note is promissory, hopeful, proleptic: 'my father (availing himself of the *Prolepsis*) . . .' (IX. 33). But the perpetual result is frustration. The narrator's lengthening narration keeps lagging behind the actions that it is seeking to narrate. Mr Shandy's Tristrapaedia, encyclopedic record of his son's existence, is likewise lagging furiously. Phrasis diverts continually into periphrasis (IX. 33). No wonder this text has so many muzzles in it. No wonder it offers constipation as a model for itself. The alphabet of *Tristram Shandy* takes, as it were, the alphabet of love (VIII. 13) and makes it stand for what the novel turns out to be – *Confounded, Futilitous, Gallygaskinish, Misgiving, Ridiculous*, and, of course, *Obstipating* – that is, constipating. In other words, the novel's promise, like its promises, keeps ending in the phimotic, as Dr Slop declares Tristram's damaged penis might. 'Twill end in a *phimosis*, replied Dr Slop' of the nearly castrated boy. After all the panic, he has not actually been castrated ('Nothing is left, cried *Susannah*, – nothing is left – for me, but to run my country': V. 17). Nor has he even been circumcised (despite Mr Shandy's readiness, as ever, with a learned Latin tome or two on that subject: V. 27). But he has been struck in such a way that Slop thinks the foreskin will grow over the head of the penis, so occluding it and making its natural functions difficult, painful, and, even, without surgery, impossible. '*Phimosis*: from Greek φιμωβις, muzzling: contraction of the orifice of the prepuce, so that it cannot be retracted' (*OED*). And it's inviting indeed to take this phimotic orifice for all the novel's damaged, occluded, rusty orifices. Phimosis, as stigma, burden, fate, and future, threatens and marks this text as it threatens its wounded hero.

And yet phimotic, or potentially phimotic, though things are in *Tristram Shandy*, the story of emptiness, the fiction, the forms, the rhetorics of emptiness, are all continually backed by their opposite. This novel turns out also to be a very full text indeed, and one that rejoices in abundance of materials. Tristram does, after all, get engendered; does come into the world, survive, get christened, acquire a name; does manage not to be castrated (for all Trim's dramatic sawing away at his finger). He's not even circumcised. The knots on Slop's bag do eventually get undone. The broken bridge of Tristram's nose is mended, albeit farcically 'with a piece of cotton and a thin piece of whalebone out of *Susannah*'s stays' (III. 27). At the same birthing time, or thereabouts, 'The Author's Preface' actually appears (III. 20). Just so, the door with the squeaky hinge has its uses in a kind of queered communication that's factilitated as much as it's hindered by the badness of the hinge:

> . . . whenever an extraordinary message, or letter, was delivered in the parlour – or a discourse suspended till a servant went out – or the lines of discontent were observed to hang upon the brows of my father or mother – or, in short, when anything was supposed to be upon the tapis worth knowing or listening to, 'twas the rule to leave the door, not absolutely shut, but somewhat a-jar – as it stands just now – which, under covert of the bad hinge (and that possibly might be one of the many reasons why it was never mended), it was not difficult to manage. (V. 6)

The awkward hinge is not, after all, a completely bad thing in terms of domestic arrangement.

In similar vein, direction, as Hamlet found out before Tristram, can sometimes be by indirection found out. Some progress is to be made, even by way of intense digression. Some textual promises are in fact kept. 'Have not I promised the world a chapter of knots? two chapters upon the right and wrong end of a woman? a chapter upon whiskers? a chapter upon wishes? — — a chapter of noses? – No, I have done that –' (IV. 9). A digression is promised for chapter 15 of book IX. Should it go into chapter 14? No, 'I have this chapter to put to whatever use I think proper ———— . . . I could write my chapter of Button-holes in it ——— Or my chapter of *Pishes*, which should follow them ——— Or my chapter of *Knots*' (IX. 14). But they remain deferred. Then chapter 15 comes, 'at last' – 'and brings nothing with it but a sad signature . . . For in talking of my digression —— I declare before heaven I have made it!' The chapter with 'nothing' in it has proved an ironic, self-spiting, contradictory success: the digression has been made despite every appearance of its being continually evaded. And this is a model of the novel: it's steadily getting made in and through all the deferring metatextual talk about it. Text is accumulating, beneath and through the mountain of denying metatext. The motions of apparent failure are the motions also of evident success. Textual pieces fall off and out of this text. Their emblem is the paper that falls unexpectedly out of the volume of Stevinus that Trim has carried redundantly from Toby's house. Trim fails to find a sailing chariot in the book, but finds a sermon instead. So the loss is also a gain, the absence also a presence, the falling out also a falling in. The sermon, one of Sterne's own, Shandyanly provides textual material for a long chapter (II. 17).

Farce Feeding

The unexpected arrival of the sermon, the stuffing-in of something rather serious into the rather light surrounding text, is the technique of farce. *Farce* is what is stuffed in: forced meat, stuffing, male sexual organs, light bits of text (Latin in Greek liturgies, French in Latin liturgies, gags and knockabout in religious dramas). The sermon arrives like farce, as an unexpected inter-polation. Its content, though, is very unfarcical. And this contradiction be-tween form and tone in the discourse is also exemplary of the novel. *Tristram Shandy* works by playing farcical methods against tragic tones. And the trick of textual provision by such farcical means is, again, exemplary. In times of textual need, there's always something Sterne can stuff in. His text, continu-ally lamenting and demonstrating its anorexia, is also at the same time busily padding itself out, stuffing itself full of textual stuffing. 'Had this volume been a farce . . .' (V. 15): and this particular chapter, an interval of mere noises and verbal nonsense, certainly is; and so is this particular volume, beginning with talk of *farcy* and 'a good farcical house'; and so is the novel as a whole.

Shandy comes stuffed full, like the Roman *satura lanx*, the full plate that's one of the alleged origins of the word *satire*, and like sausages, those co-mestibles consisting of forced-meat that are classically phallic emblems of the Rabelaisian carnivalesque which informs talk of even the most threatened phalluses in this fiction. One aspect of that sort of stuffing is a kind of excess, the doing that's also overdoing, a laying on thickly. The verb *to farce* also means to overlay thickly, to overdo. Like *cataplasm*. Cataplasm is Dr Slop's proposed cure for Tristram's wounded penis – a plastered-on poultice (VI. 3). And the novel goes in strongly for textual cataplasm – laying on thick the farcical devices, the textual stuffing. It might even be thought that it does so too thickly, or with a too mechanical exuberance. The thought is one the novel anticipates. While Slop is away looking to the cataplasm, Mr Shandy puts in some work on the Tristrapaedia (V. 41), talking, writing, reading ('half reading and half discoursing': V. 42). His subject is textual stuffing, the expansion of knowledge, stories, books – what Erasmus, in his famous treatise *De Copia* on how to keep your texts going, thought of as copiousness. Mr Shandy's home recipe for copiousness is auxiliary verbs. By use of modal auxiliaries, even an unlikely story about a white bear can be kept going indefinitely. 'Have I ever seen one? Might I ever have seen one? Am I ever to see one? Ought I ever to have seen one? . . . If I should see a white bear, what would I say?' (V. 43). And so on. Auxiliaries comprise a textual engine for bringing countless textual offspring to birth: 'Now the use of the *Auxiliaries* is, at once to set the soul a-going by herself upon the materials as they are brought her; and by the versability of this great engine, round which they are twisted, to open new tracts of inquiry, and make every idea engender millions' (V. 42).

The word *auxiliaries* sets Trim thinking, in the usual punning style of verbal association in this novel, of military auxiliaries. The Danes 'who were on the left' at one of the sieges that preoccupy him and Toby, the siege of Limerick, 'were all auxiliaries'. Toby, misunderstanding as ever, assures Trim that he conceives Mr Shandy to be talking about 'different things'. Mr Shandy is not so sure of the difference ('You do? said my father, rising up'). And nor should we be sure. The left-handedness of the Limerick auxiliaries recalls the '*bend-sinister*', 'the vile mark of illegitimacy' that a blundering or left-handed coach-painter accidentally added to the Shandy coat-of-arms, a sign of 'the sinister turn which every thing relating to our family was apt to take', a distorting Shandyan heraldic difference no less, emblem of all the difficulties of life and text that accumulate around Tristram: 'like the affair of the hinge, it was one of the many things which the *Destinies* had set down in their books ever to be grumbled at . . . but never to be mended' (IV. 25). It's why Mr Shandy won't go in his coach any more – not least in the journey to talk with Phutatorius and company that would have occupied the torn-out chapter.

Blunder, illegitimacy, sinister turns, faulty hinge, distorting heraldic difference, missing chapter, prelude to gallygaskinish horrors: the negative associations could scarcely be more intense. Yet out of the left-handedness of auxiliaries arises Mr Shandy's recipe for coping copiously with narratives. And his auxiliary enthusiasm is such that several pages of the Tristrapaedia are encompassed, and he goes on to announce a related grammatical mechanism

for transcending all difficulties with words and for effecting mental copiousness in the small human subject of his writing, the boy Tristram:

> When my father had danced his white bear backwards and forwards through
> half a dozen pages, he closed the book for good and an' all, – and in a kind
> of triumph redelivered it into *Trim's* hand, with a nod to lay it upon the
> 'scrutoire, where he found it. —— *Tristram*, said he, shall be made to conju-
> gate every word in the dictionary, backwards and forwards the same way; —
> every word, *Yorick*, by this means, you see is converted into a thesis or an
> hypothesis; – every thesis and hypothesis have an offspring of propositions; –
> and each proposition has its own consequences and conclusions; every one of
> which leads the mind on again, into fresh tracks of enquiries and doubtings.
> —— The force of this engine, added my father, is incredible in opening a
> child's head. (VI. 2)

Copiousness outfaces, as it were, the muzzles of failure. Recipes for textual
bulk build copiously in spite of all opposition:

> I am this month one whole year older than I was this time twelve-month; and
> having got, as you perceive, almost into the middle of my fourth volume – and
> no farther than to my first day's life – 'tis demonstrative that I have three
> hundred and sixty-four days more life to write just now, than when I first set
> out; so that instead of advancing, as a common writer, in my work with what
> I have been doing at it – on the contrary, I am just thrown so many volumes
> back – was every day of my life to be as busy a day as this – And why not?
> —— and the transactions and opinions of it to take up as much description
> – And for what reason should they be cut short? as at this rate I should just
> live 364 times faster than I should write – It must follow, an' please your
> worships, that the more I write, the more I shall have to write – and conse-
> quently, the more your worships read, the more your worships will have to
> read. (IV. 13)

There's no reason why the narrator's life and the narration shouldn't last a
very large number of volumes, nor why the narrator shouldn't 'in other
words . . . lead a couple of fine lives together'.

Snags, however, remain. A cavilling voice is added at the end of the long
paragraph just quoted: 'Will this be good for your worships' eyes?' Just so,
when Mr Shandy proposed his great conjugation machine, Toby cried
dyspeptically that it was 'enough . . . to burst' the child's head 'into a thousand
splinters' (VI. 2). The 'bend-sinister' may be mitigated in the left-handed
textual power of auxiliaries, but it has still not been 'brush'd out' of the
Shandy arms painted on the family coach. This blot on the Shandy escutcheon
remains. As does the squeaky hinge that goes on squeaking, declaring the
continuing awkwardness of thresholds, the perpetual *béance* or empty gape of
the door perpetually ajar. Not unlike the cataplasm, the cure for future

phimosis, that never actually gets applied. Susannah and Slop quarrel; mutual abuse over nostrils and noses is exchanged; Slop throws the cataplasm in Susannah's face; she returns 'the compliment with what was left in the pan'; Tristram, the cataplasm having 'failed', has to make do with a supplementary 'fomentation' instead (VI. 4). These instances of, and metaphors, recipes for copiousness, for amendment of failure, for the outfacing of emptiness, are never entirely to succeed. The novel, though, as ever, has just the rhetorical formula for this puzzled final mixture – *aposiopesis*.

Aposiopesis

While Mrs Shandy is in difficult labour with Tristram, her husband and brother discuss her reluctance to have the man-midwife Slop attend her. Toby cannot bring himself to name the genital region that Mrs Shandy is reluctant to display to a man. His incomplete sentence is abetted by the coincidental snapping of Mr Shandy's pipe. The narration dwells on the incompleteness and on alternatives to silence:

> —— 'My sister, mayhap,' quoth my uncle *Toby*, 'does not choose to let a man come so near her ****.' Make this dash, — 'tis an Aposiopesis. - Take the dash away, and write *Backside*, — 'tis Bawdy. - Scratch Backside out, and put *Cover'd way* in, 'tis a Metaphor; – and, I dare say, as fortification ran so much in my uncle *Toby's* head, that if he been left to have added one word to the sentence, —— that word was it. (II. 6)

It's characteristic of the text to offer overt verbal strategies, variously bawdy and metaphoric, for outmanoeuvring, and filling up with explicit content, the gap left by the missing word. The 'world stands indebted', we're told, 'to the sudden snapping of my father's tobacco-pipe for one of the neatest examples of that ornamental figure in oratory, which Rhetoricians stile the *Aposiopesis*'. *Backside* and *covered way* only gloss what is implied by the **** or the dash, and what the reader had already guessed. (Rough-tongued contemporary satirists were quick to suggest that Mr Shandy's real 'hobby' was Mrs Shandy's **** or *arse*.) *Aposiopesis*, from Greek words for keeping silent and being taciturn, is the theoretical activity of communicating by silence, stating something by not stating it, implying some content by banishing or deferring it. Johnson co-opted John Smith's *Mysterie of Rhetorique Unvail'd* (1657) for his definition of *aposiopesis*:

> A Form of speech, by which the Speaker, through some affectation, as sorrow, fear, anger, or vehemency, breaks off his speech before it be all ended. A figure, when, speaking of a thing, we yet seem to conceal it, though indeed we

aggravate it; or when the course of the sentence begun is so stayed, as thereby some part of the sentence, not being uttered, may be understood.

The moment of rhetorical self-consciousness around Mrs Shandy's **** is indeed aposiopestic, and in the conflicting dualism of its play between absence and presence, unstatedness and statedness, it focuses all the novel's indulgent investment in the gappiness-that-isn't-quite. As does the novel's gaudier and bawdier aposiopestic moment, the one when the hot chestnut rolls into Phutatorius's breeches.

The narration arrives at the symposium looking for canonical answers to the question whether Tristram can be rechristened, renamed, only to hear Phutatorius's cry of anguish over what's occurring in the porches of his galligaskins, in the very threshold of his person: the 'desperate monosyllable Z——ds' (IV. 27). In pain from the hot chestnut, panicky that some 'detested reptile, had crept up, and was fastening his teeth ——', Phutatorius 'leapt incontinently up, uttering as he rose that interjection of surprise so much descanted upon, with the aposiopestic break after it, marked thus, Z——ds – which, though not strictly canonical, was still as little as any a man could have said upon the occasion'.

The moment is a drama of apertures, trouserly and verbal; a scene of layered linguistic absences (there's no chaste word in Johnson's *Dictionary* for the aperture in the breeches, we're told; the utterance is uncanonical; and the exclamation is incomplete, printed with a blank decently imposed on it). But emptiness and absence are by no means complete. Phutatorius's mouth is not a gape, a *béance* of pain – his lips are Stoically pursed ('with the help of some wry faces and compursions of the mouth'). He's saying little – 'as little as any man could have said upon the occasion' – but it is not nothing. And, as usual, this is a little that the narration is able to 'descant upon' at great length. A verbal break there is – as there is a fatal gap in the galligaskins – but it's an 'aposiopestic break'. And one could say that all of *Tristram Shandy*'s breaks are such. A chapter of noses (IV. 9)? 'No, I have done that'. Not *Yes*, I have done that; but *No*, I have done it. But still, 'I have done that.' *Aposiopesis* by no means banishes the breaks that comprise it. It does, however, display the power of a rhetoric that will not absolutely succumb to the silencing forces that will always be part of its essence. And this, I suggest, is the resistant power of rhetoric itself. It is what texts do all the time.

NOTES

1   *The Essayes or Counsels Civill and Morall of Francis Bacon Lord Verulam* (1597–1625), Everyman edn (London, 1906), 150.

2 Sermon VI, 'Of the Nativity', Christmas Day 1611: in Lancelot Andrewes, *Seventeen Sermons on the Nativity*, The Ancient and Modern Library of Theological Literature, 6 (Griffith, Farran, Okeden, and Welsh (new edn, n.d.), 85, 89.

3 Andrewes, *Sermons on the Nativity*, 193–211: XII, Christmas Day 1618, Luke 2: 12–14, 'And this shall be a sign unto you . . .' (Et hoc erit vobis signum . . .).

4 See 'The Freudian Unconscious and Ours', in Jacques Lacan, *The Four Fundamental Concepts of Psychoanalysis*, trans. Alan Sheridan (Penguin, Harmondsworth, 1979), 20–3.

5 Samuel Weber, *The Legend of Freud*, (University of Minnesota Press, Minneapolis, 1982), 78–9.

6 Henry James, 'The New Novel', *TLS*, March–April 1914; *Notes on Novelists* (1914), in *Selected Literary Criticism* of Henry James, ed. Morris Shapira (Peregrine, Harmondsworth, 1968), 381–2.

7 Frank Kermode, *The Genesis of Secrecy: On the Interpretation of Narrative* (Harvard University Press, Cambridge, Mass., and London, 1979), 65–72. For other glorying in gaps, secrecies, *vides*, see Kermode's *Essays on Fiction 1971–82* (Routledge and Kegan Paul, London, 1983), 95, 68, and *passim*. The essay focusing on Conrad's *Under Western Eyes*, 'Secrets and Narrative Sequence', 133–53, is particularly strong.

8 Weber, *Legend of Freud*, 79.

9 J. Hillis Miller, *Fiction and Repetition; Seven English Novels* (Blackwell, Oxford, 1982), 141.

10 Jonathan Culler, 'Apostrophe', in *The Pursuit of Signs: Semiotics, Literature, Deconstruction*, 135–54; Paul de Man, *Allegories of Reading* (Yale University Press, New Haven and London, 1979), 29–30.

11 Culler, 'Apostrophe', 153, refers warmly to de Man on 'the latent threat that inhabits prosopopoeia'.

12 Jacques Lacan, 'The Empty Word and the Full Word', ch. 1 of 'The Function of Language in Psychoanalysis' section, in *The Language of the Self: The Function of Language in Psychoanalysis*, trans. and ed. Anthony Wilden (Johns Hopkins University Press, Baltimore and London, 1968), 9ff.

13 For the *hache* – hatchet job see 'Signsponge', in *Jacques Derrida: Acts of Literature*, ed. D. Attridge (Routledge, New York and London, 1992), 365–6. Hachette is, of course, also the famous Paris publishing house. The volatility of *h* resonates curiously, too, with Roland Barthes's difficulties over the letter *H* in his lexicon of selfhood *Roland Barthes par Roland Barthes* – because it stands for the *homosexualité* he had difficulty in confessing publicly. There's no entry for *Homosexualité* at the appropriate alphabetical position; instead, there's an entry at an unexpected place under *D, La Déesse H.*, all about the Goddess Homosexuality and Hashish, and, later in the book (reproduced), one of Barthes's handwritten slips of paper with the heading *la déesse Homo*, and, fainter, the word *Homosexualité*, but with the final *é* half cut off: a whole sequence, then, of disappearances, reappearances, and partial disappearances again – the case of apostrophes and *h* with a vengeance!

14 *Love's Labour's Lost*, ed. Richard David, Arden edn (Methuen, London, 1951), 88.
15 *Hamlet*, ed. Harold Jenkins, Arden edn (Methuen, London, 1982), 557–8. For Hamlet and writing, see Jonathan Goldberg, 'Hamlet's Hand', *Shakespeare Quarterly*, 29, no, 2 (Summer 1988), 307–27, and also, more generally, Goldberg, *Writing Matter: From the Hands of the English Renaissance* (Stanford University Press, Stanford, Calif., 1990). See also Valentine Cunningham, 'A comma 'tween their amities? Hermetic versus Pleromatic Readings', *Revue Belge de Philologie et d'Histoire/Belgisch Tijdschrift voor Filologie en Geschiedenis*, 62 (1984), 3, 449–62.
16 See Victor Ehrlich, *Russian Formalism: History-Doctrine* (1955), 3rd edn (Yale University Press, New Haven and London, 1981), 190–1; Tzvetan Todorov, *Théorie de la littérature: textes des formalistes Russes* (Seuil, Paris, 1965), 300–1. A translation of a large part Shklovsky's writing on *Shandy* appears as 'A Parodying Novel: Sterne's *Tristram Shandy*', trans. W. George Isaak, in *Laurence Sterne: A Collection of Critical Essays* (Twentieth-Century Views series), ed. John Traugott (Prentice-Hall, Englewood Cliffs, N.J., 1968), 66–89.

iii: Reading Biscuits, Reading Gaol

Joseph Conrad's *Heart of Darkness* (1899) is that student's friend, the multi-illustrative text. It's an exemplary modernist text, an exemplary modern metafictional fiction, an exemplum too of the modernist text of epistemological doubt turning itself into the postmodernist text of ontological doubting. This blur between epistemology and ontology is particularly exemplary. Try as he might, Brian McHale fails again and again in his influential discussion *Postmodernist Fiction* to keep apart the epistemological subject which he takes as the essence of modernist fiction and the ontological one which he offers as the essence of the postmodern.[1] Incidentally, and less attractively, *Heart of Darkness* is also exemplary in being one of those classic texts about which interpreters feel licensed, in Kermode's words, to say absolutely anything they like.[2] Crazily, the shrinking calibres of the gun barrels of the French ships firing incomprehensibly into Africa – ten-inch in the manuscript version, eight-inch in the typescript and in the *Blackwood's Magazine* serial version, six-inch as they finally appeared in the volume *Youth* – become for John Batchelor exciting emblems of the white man's shrinking of sexual potency in Africa (whoever heard of phalluses six inches in diameter – let alone ten-inch-wide ones?!).[3] Talk of 'chains and purchases' in the Towson/Tower book on seamanship that Marlow finds on the river bank on his way up to Kurtz has one Marxist critic babbling of the fiction's reference to economics, as if *purchases* weren't to do with leverages and the laws of mechanics but were things you bought in shops. No doubt he also thinks *chains* are fetters to be thrown off in revolutions rather than old imperial and cricketing measures of length.[4]

Still, as far as the expectations of sceptical (post)modernist criticism go, it would be hard to find a more succinct set of occasions than *Heart of Darkness* provides by way of illustration. This *nouvelle* grants *bonnes nouvelles* for the deconstructionist. It's the busiest of refusing, sceptical, self-emptying texts. It steadily inducts the reader into negativity, blankness, crypticity, the hermetic. It's full of narrative failure – the failure of narrators, of narrating, and so, it's possible to argue, of narrativity itself. The text's busy array of gaps, puzzles, lacks, *béances*, faint traces of meaning, sense, and certainty, all bring vividly home the modern collapse of language into ambivalence, puzzle, and silence, and so illustrate the twentieth-century novel's widespread sense of the difficulty of keeping up story-telling, old-fashioned subjects, character and reference, the old assurances about the selfhood of persons and narratives. Here, if anywhere, is the traditional novel as box, a container of goodies for readers – content, presence, even good ideas about goodness – being emptied before one's eyes, made to elude one's acquisitive, inquisitive, desirous grasp. Here the promise of the full fictional container opens onto a disappointingly bare cupboard, an emptied casket. If this container contains anything, it's only a boxful of verbal tricks; or a prison-house full of empty signs; or a den of thieves presided over by Hermes, the god of tricksters, thieves, and tricky interpreters, and patron of the hermetic; or an echo chamber of impossible meanings, an *antre*, a Cave of Marabar, as in Forster's *A Passage to India*, where orderly syntax, grammar, alphabet, get reduced to mere noise, nonsense, glossolalia, *ou-boum*, chaos.

Heuristic, Nein!

Heart of Darkness undermines the heuristic confidence that the nineteenth-century novelists taught us to accept as normal. 'This is heuristic, ja?': a young German woman at the party that comprises the core of Malcolm Bradbury's *The History Man* (1975) voices an assumption normal in the pages of traditional British fiction. Novels are, on this traditional reckoning, heuristic systems, that is, places of learning, of self-education, offering positive results to their studious participants. The protagonists in most traditional novels, as in most traditional narratives, are breezy with confidence that something positive is to be gained by their time in the narration. They're on a kind of voyage of discovery simply by dint of being in the fiction. It's a voyage that has many convergent aspects and analogues – the epic journey of adventure and heroism, the colonizing journey of capture and discovery, the Dantesque moral journey of personal discovery and salvation, the journey that sorts out puzzles for oneself or for others. The traveller on such a journey may be variously pilgrim, soldier, picaro, agent of imperialist expansion, detective – Ulysses, Quixote, Crusoe, Theseus, Sherlock Holmes, Everyman. But whatever particular label on the luggage, everyone involved in the ancient business of story is on a learning road. Authors and narrators – the text-producers; characters – the subjects of texts; and readers – the consumers of texts: all of them traditionally travel the same path, in turn, from greater to lesser ignorance, from less to more knowledge. The traditional story business comprises a generally triumphant heuristic triad. The traditional participants in story – teller, character, reader – make a hopeful, and commonly successful, learning trio.

> His servants he with new acquist
> Of true experience from this great event
> With peace and consolation hath dismissed,
> And calm of mind all passion spent.

That's how Milton's *Samson Agonistes* ends. It is more or less how all tragedy, all serious traditional fiction, hopes to end. The traditional plot is a sequence of cognitions, anagnorises, recognitions, opened eyes, an affair of knowledge, knowing, acknowledging, and being acknowledged.[5] At the end of such a plot sequence the voyaging trio are united in 'new acquist of true experience'.

Henry James's method gave publicity to a common enough process. First of all, James would give himself up to a private, often lengthy, heuristic engagement, giving an extensive interpretative squeeze to the *germs* of stories as they presented themselves, letting them germinate in his mind, listening hard for the *notes* sounded by the stories or phrases that he was always so keen to pick up, until the potential fictional shape the material might assume became clear at last. Then he would write out his story – and commonly as a story of that heuristic process, one in which the characters are presented with problems to which they must apply their own interpretative squeeze, treading in James's own footsteps ('There is the story of one's hero', as he put it in the Preface to *The Ambassadors*, 'and then, thanks to the intimate connexion of things, the story of one's story itself'). After which the writing is handed over to the reader, to engage for herself in the business of readerly heuristicism, tracking the character's heuristic efforts, which in their turn had aped their author's own. (And, intriguingly, of course, as his notorious Prefaces show, James himself would often, some time after publication, join the public in reading and (re)interpreting his own writings.)

All this represented a serious faith in what heuristicism could or might do that the modernist novel made it its business to doubt, frustrate, and invert. What's intriguing, again, about James is that this modernist doubting is already settling in, bedding down, in his own practice. Strether in *The Ambassadors* is characteristic of the later Jamesian character in being both a successful voyager and also a failing one; he gets to know, and also to have his knowledge, his certainties, unsettled, all at once. By the time of, say, Bradbury's *The History Man*, the doubting has become a pretty easy kind of

trope to go in for. For a Bradbury the walls of the old fictional Jericho are
a pushover. It's simply no problem at all for such a latecomer to overturn a
whole sequence of traditional heuristic systems: parties, and universities, and
the novel that he himself is writing, about a party at a university. The
slickness of Bradbury's heuristic setbacks has been enabled by a lengthy and
difficult history of earlier sceptical struggles. Others – the likes of James and
Conrad – did the huffing and the puffing that have already blown the Bradbury
house of fiction down. And at the very heart of that late-Victorian, early
twentieth-century revisionist effort stands *Heart of Darkness*.

Amazing

In *Heart of Darkness* several traditionally successful sorts of fictional journeys
get invoked, but only as a prelude to some pronounced failure in, or hesitancy about, the successes customarily claimed by the tradition. Here, a
colonial journey is shown going wrong. The trek that Marlow's on raises
awkward questions about the white man's exercise of power over Blacks, his
moral and legal right to take African territory and grab African spoils. Also,
a kind of pilgrimage is proving to be in effect a Divine Anti-Comedy, a
journey bogged down in an Inferno, or at best a Purgatorio, with no suggestion of a saving Paradiso at the end – 'like a weary pilgrimage amongst hints
for nightmares'. 'I had stepped', declares Marlow, 'into the gloomy circle of
some Inferno.' And he never really escapes from it – not unlike Samuel
Beckett's favourite anti-hero Belacqua, named for the man whom Dante
encountered, slumped, his head between his knees, on the mount of Purgatory,
in despair, going nowhere, having given up the struggle to climb out of
Purgatory. What's more, this is a detective story that's failing to come up
with the moral confidences and clarifications that readers of Poe and Dickens
and Conan Doyle had been schooled to expect.

Detective stories are updates of the Theseus story. In that archetypal detective fiction an insoluble moral problematic is sited in a labyrinth. Young
Athenian men and women are being sacrificed to the labyrinth's inhabitant,
the transgressive offspring of an animalized god and a woman, the beast-man
named the Minotaur. Our hero Theseus enters the maze, kills the beast-man,
and re-emerges physically and morally triumphant from the heart of darkness. How? By following the ball of thread helpfully provided by Ariadne
which he unravelled as he entered the maze and which helped him find his
way back. The word for such a ball of archetypally woman's stuff, this
particular sort of yarn, the very stuff of weaving and text? Why, it's a *clew*.

And that's just an older spelling of the modern *clue*. Success in mazes comes from following the given clue or clues. It's the success detectives enjoy in that form of fiction invented at the zenith of the novel's epistemological confidences in the nineteenth century. The heroes of that fiction, the detectives Dupin, Inspector Bucket, Sherlock Holmes, and their successors, are models of confident authors, characters, and readers in the process of getting wised – or clued – up. The mode they triumph in assumes that they'll rapidly shed their initial puzzledness – their amazement, no less – over whatever problems life and story can throw at them. Your traditional detective is never stuck long in the dark, in the labyrinth. But when, with the onset of modernism, confidence starts to lapse within a widespread Western failure of old assurances of all sorts – about God and morality and economics and truth and text – then the detective model starts to waver, and though detective certainties continue as an axiom of the popular detective fiction genre, they start to come unstuck or to get eschewed in more high-minded novels. These fictions begin to offer heroes and heroines who aren't getting out of the maze and who are actually being vanquished by the problems, moral, theological, characterological, textual, that were once assumed to be soluble by their kind of person.

So Stephen Dedalus, a youth much preoccupied by mazes, actually becomes the Minotaur, a bestial man, as he goes through the Dublin streets at the end of chapter 2 of Joyce's *A Portrait of the Artist as a Young Man*, 'like some baffled prowling beast', happy to lose his virginity and his Catholic orthodoxy in the city's brothel quarter which is an actual labyrinth, 'a maze of narrow and dirty streets'. Young Dedalus, arrestingly named for King Minos's original labyrinth-builder, is compelled to accept amazement – moral damnation in the urban maze. As a wilful blasphemer Stephen even seems happy with his labyrinthine predicament. T. S. Eliot's Prufrock is much less content with his particular urban maze. Unhappy or not, however, saving clues about ways out are not on offer for Prufrock. They would only come later, from Eliot's new-found old Christian orthodoxy. For his part, Henry James nudgingly names his youthful heroine Maisie in a ghastly pun on the labyrinthine cluelessness that to the end undermines her repeated confident epistemological claims to 'know' what's going on in the adulterous adult world – as well as undercutting whatever confident expectations about novels banishing amazement the reader might otherwise entertain. Even at the end of *What Maisie Knew* (1897), we and Mrs Wix 'still' have 'room for wonder at what Maisie knew'. And labyrinthine fictions have been making modernism's antidetective point ever since. But what would triumph in Robbe-Grillet's *Dans le labyrinthe* (1959) – translated by Christine Brooke-Rose as *In the Labyrinth* (1967) – or

in the labyrinthine libraries of Borges or Umberto Eco, or up Borges's forking garden path, gets an explicit generative kick from the insistence in *Heart
of Darkness* that Marlow's layered journeys – the African voyage, the journey
recalled, the experience narrated – are voyages into the labyrinth, the amazing, which in great measure fail to end with the maze cleared up, straight-
ened out, commanded, explained.

Marlow's experience, we're told, thoroughly amazes him. And his narrative
has little to offer us by way of clarifying or abolishing his amazing experiences. Amazement remains right to its end the condition of Marlow's story,
of this fiction. Marlow fails to become what he seems set up to resemble:
namely, a type of the detective narrator, the sleuthing hero, the one who
sports ample keys to mazes. *Amazing* is – unamazingly, then – one of the key
words woven with studied care into Conrad's text. The trading company's
chief accountant, or book-keeper, whom Marlow encounters in the jungle,
the one who first names Kurtz in his hearing, is an extraordinarily spruce
white man, got up in emblematic white shirt and trousers, wielding a ready
pen as he keeps his account books in 'apple-pie order' and toting a green-
lined parasol. He's everything that experience of Africa makes impossible and
absurd for Marlow. The moral whiteness of the Whites is precisely what
Marlow learns has been put at issue. That's why Marlow's own book is, so
to say, not in apple-pie moral, political, and narratological order. As for
parasols, Marlow has nothing with which to keep the stark sun of Africa off
him. The white man's cover, his *parasol* or *parapluie*, his European moral
umbrella, no less, his cover-up, his cover-story – and one of the two knitters
of black wool in Brussels wore a dress 'as plain as an umbrella-cover' – is off,
or, at least, in process of being taken off, or blown. By the end of his story,
Marlow's concept of *para*-items will have become rather more like Jacques
Derrida's than this other book-keeper's: he'll not know the ins of his para-
concepts from their outs. No green linings, or restfully green thoughts at all,
for Marlow, as is clear only a couple of pages later, where, expressing vexation
at the mollycoddling of a fat white man who's always having to be carried,
he declares how annoying it was 'to hold your own coat like a parasol over
a man's head while he is coming to'. (For more paragraphs and paraphrasing,
not to say paradoxes, in the matter of para-, see the discussion in my final
two chapters.) And thus the Kurtz-namer, the owner of a proper parasol, the
one who finds 'everything here . . . very satisfactory', is a *miracle, amazing*. So
also is the land itself – 'its mystery, its greatness, the amazing reality of its
concealed life'. So is the narrative of Kurtz's Russian sidekick and apologist,
whose 'amazing tale' was 'not so much told as suggested to me in desolate
exclamations, completed by shrugs, interrupted phrases, in hints ending in
deep sighs'. And so, of course, is Kurtz's primeval horde: its earth-plastered

chiefs shouting 'periodically together strings of amazing words that resembled no sounds of human language; and the deep murmurs of the crowd, interrupted suddenly, were like the responses of some satanic litany'.

The Africa Marlow narrates, then, is, and crucially remains, an enigma. 'Watching a coast as it slips by the ship is like thinking about an enigma.' This enigma whispers, 'Come and find out.' Clues are in short supply, both in Africa and in Marlow's narration. At one point, as Marlow pauses in his story, lost for words in the dark, the frame-narrator who is our first narrative access to Marlow, tells us that he listened 'for the sentence, the word, that would give me the clue to the faint uneasiness inspired by this narrative'. And the clue evades him just as it evaded and is still evading Marlow. The two females who guard the Belgian company's offices, knitting black wool, are no pair of Ariadnes preparing helpful clues for Congo traders and Congo narrators, but are rather like the Fates, knitters of doom, preparers of winding sheets – 'knitting black wool as for a warm pall'. Not surprisingly, in the offices whose entrance they guard, Marlow signs a document covenanting 'not to disclose any trade secrets'. 'Well,' Marlow adds, 'I am not going to.' Later on, he repeats the claim: 'I am not disclosing any trade secrets.' And he assures the Russian that 'Mr Kurtz's reputation is safe with me'. Crucially, at the end, Marlow keeps his mouth shut about Kurtz. And how, in a sense, could he do otherwise? For Africa is a place of deep reserve, confronting its interpreter with problems of visibility and audibility that provide near-impossible conditions for the one seeking to make sense of it. How to invent anything – to tell your story – when it's so hard to invent – to make out, discern, decide, discover – what's around you? The jungle is silent, a place of intense solitude, a great primeval deaf mute. 'We penetrated deeper and deeper into the heart of darkness. It was very quiet there.' 'Dumb immobility sat on the banks'. This is the essence of the labyrinthine. 'You looked on amazed, and began to suspect yourself of being deaf – then the night came suddenly, and struck you blind as well.'

> I wondered whether the stillness on the face of the immensity looking at us two were meant as an appeal or as a menace. What were we who had strayed in here? Could we handle that dumb thing, or would it handle us? I felt how big, how confoundedly big, was that thing that couldn't talk, and perhaps was deaf as well. What was in there? I could see a little ivory coming out from there, and I had heard Mr Kurtz was in there. I had heard enough about it, too – God knows! Yet somehow it didn't bring any image with it . . . .

In the moonlight, as Marlow waits for rivets, obscurity of sight and sound interlock: 'a rioting invasion of soundless life'. No wonder the story is another 'one of Marlow's inconclusive experiences': 'Not very clear . . . No, not very clear', throwing only 'a kind of light'.

Of Our Time Distincly

The atmosphere of the African enterprise and of the narrative that enables such access to it as we have, is hazy, a flicker. 'We live in the flicker.' *Flicker* was the word unerringly picked up by the Conrad-obsessed T. S. Eliot to endorse and expand *Heart of Darkness*'s gloomy reading of the modern situation. 'I have seen the moment of my greatness flicker,' bewails Prufrock. And in the tube-train section of 'Burnt Norton' the flickering Conradian half-light merges into the twilight of the cinema – the flickers, or flicks – to compound a sombre critique of England's mindless emptiness: 'Only a flicker / Over the strained time-ridden faces.' And haziness is said to be the characteristic of Marlow's yarns, the narratives he weaves, according to his listening friend, in that famous passage that has become so beloved of deconstructionists such as Hillis Miller:

> The yarns of seamen have a direct simplicity, the whole meaning of which lies within the shell of a cracked nut. But Marlow was not typical (if his propensity to spin yarns be excepted), and to him the meaning of an episode was not inside like a kernel but outside, enveloping the tale which brought it out only as a glow brings out a haze, in the likeness of one of those misty halos that sometimes are made visible by the spectral illumination of moonshine.

'The subject', Conrad wrote to William Blackwood, proposing to offer him *Heart of Darkness* as his contribution to the thousandth number of *Blackwood's Magazine*, 'The subject is of our time distinctly.' Except that he didn't write *distinctly*, but – shaky as ever with his English – *distincly*. Distinctness faltered in the very writing of the word for it, even as Conrad sought to claim distinctness for his proceedings.[6] The lapse was symptomatic of the failure of the text of Africa precisely in the matter of distinctness.

The map itself, prime text of Africa, the one Marlow starts his journey by being confronted with, the would-be accurate mirror held up to Africa's geographical nature, was blank, and is now dead, dark, yellow. The boyhood glamour once held out to Marlow by the atlas's blank spaces, in South America, Africa, Australia, has gone. 'The glamour's off.' The Congo is not the blank space it once was: 'by this time it was not blank space any more. It had got filled since my boyhood with rivers and lakes and names. It had ceased to be a blank space of delightful mystery – a white patch for a boy to dream gloomily over. It had become a place of darkness.' And so, in a way,

it's still enigmatically blank, with the tail of the great Congo river 'lost in
the depths of the land', an emblem of what remains 'the biggest' empty place
on the map, 'the most blank, so to speak'. More, in other words, is known
about Africa than before, and Marlow's narrative will add to that knowledge;
but still the text, the narrative, the mirror of Africa, is a blank, a mirror of
enigmas.

Hence the devoted rhetoric of negative capability that has so offended so
many readers, notably F. R. Leavis, who blamed Conrad for a kind of self-
indulgent negative whimsy. It was the same argument that Leavis and others
used against the later style of Henry James. Why did these texts not get on
with it, come right out and say what they meant plainly?

> Hadn't he, we find ourselves asking, overworked 'inscrutable', 'inconceivable',
> 'unspeakable' and that kind of word already? – yet still they recur . . . The
> same vocabulary, the same adjectival insistence upon inexpressible and incom-
> prehensible mystery, is applied to the evocation of human profundities and
> spiritual horrors; to magnifying a thrilled sense of the unspeakable potential-
> ities of the human soul. The actual effect is not to magnify but rather to
> muffle.[7]

But this is to miss the point. When what's experienced is inscrutable, it is
also unspeakable. Marlow's negative rhetoric composes itself into two large,
and necessarily connected, groups – a set of words to do with the failure of
conception, epistemology, hermeneutics, which inevitably generate a vocabulary of defeated narration. Africa is *incomprehensible, incredible, inscrutable,
impenetrable, unfathomable, inconceivable, insoluble*; and so it is *indefinable, in-
explicable, innumerable, unspeakable*. Given all of which, it's also *improbable* and
intolerable. It's no surprise at all that there's so much talk here of nightmare,
madness, absurdity. Africa is truly dementing for narrators, whose business
is, precisely, with the speakable: 'Nowhere did we stop long enough to get
a particularised impression . . . general sense of vague and oppressive wonder
. . . like a weary pilgrimage among hints for nightmares.' Marlow has got
himself stuck in a narrative theatre of the absurd. A sense of absurdity
abounds. The cumulative absurdities of Africa – 'absurd long staves', 'cruel
and absurd mysteries', 'bits of absurd sentences' – generate a sense of absurdity
in Marlow's audience: 'Why do you sigh in this beastly way, somebody?
Absurd? Well absurd. Good Lord!'

> Absurd! . . . This is the worst of trying to tell. . . . Here you all are, each
> moored with two good addresses, like a hulk with two anchors, a butcher
> round one corner, a policeman round another, excellent appetites, a tempera-
> ture normal – you hear – normal from year's end to year's end. And you say,

Absurd! Absurd be – exploded! Absurd! My dear boys, what can you expect
from a man who out of sheer nervousness had just flung overboard a pair of
new shoes! Now I think of it, it is amazing I did not shed tears.

Narration has, then, run up against serious labyrinthine impossibilities:
lack of clarity, inconclusiveness, enigma, secrecy, absurdity. And they infect
the narration in all its dimensions. In a world where language flagrantly fails
as the instrument of truth, where it can be distorted to say what Swift's
Houhynhyms deplore as 'the thing that is not' – and so centrally in the case
of Kurtz's name ('Kurtz – Kurtz – that means short in German – don't it?
Well, the name was as true as everything else in his life – and death. He
looked at least seven feet long') – in this world, the would-be truth-teller
Marlow succumbs to lies. Marlow hates lies; they're tainted, he thinks, with
death. Lying 'is exactly what I hate and detest in the world. . . . It makes me
miserable and sick, like biting something rotten would do.' But Marlow
'went for him [Kurtz] near enough to a lie'. In fact, when he told Kurtz's
fiancée back in Brussels that the last word Kurtz had uttered had been her
name, he got so near a lie as to make no difference. The lie always there in
the name of Kurtz – 'He was just a word for me' – has so filled Marlow's
mouth that it's turned all words, all names in that mouth, especially the
innocent fiancée's name, for the moment at least, into a lie. Just so, it could
be said that the Babel of Africa – the incoherent babble that precedes speech
or marks the apocalyptic dissolution of it: the 'amazing words', the 'bits of
absurd sentences', the jabberings that occur when the jungle's menacing
silence is dispelled; 'and the momory of that time lingers around me,
impalpable, like a dying vibration of one immense jabber, silly, atrocious,
sordid, savage, or simply mean, without any kind of sense. Voices, voices . . .'
– that this Babelic turmoil is an influenza epidemic the sign of whose affliction
is exactly that pervasive rhetoric of negative capability that Leavis could not
stand.

And as if these problems of orality, the verbal difficulties for story-telling
Marlow, weren't enough, the infection is shown spreading through and beyond
Marlow's business, which is the voicing of words, to Conrad's (and the novel's)
task, which is writing them down. For Conrad, the novelist building his
fiction around the yarning Marlow, the oral and the written cannot be
disentangled. And in this dark place, at this dark nadir, writing proves to be
in as parlous a state as speaking. There's a lot of 'rot' about progress 'let loose
in print and talk', Marlow is made to reflect, before his aunt (Charlie Marlow's
Aunt!) prattles about enlightening the ignorant millions. But Africa makes
him less sure that any talk or any print is immune from rotting.

The terrifying realization of the possibility of rottenness in talk and print runs, of course, through Marlow's whole engagement with the Kurtz affair. For Kurtz is a writer. Writing is a central part of the huge corrupted talent of this poet, musician, painter, journalist. And just as Marlow can't bring himself to repeat to the Intended Kurtz's actual last words, 'The Horror! The Horror!', so he also tears off the revealingly awful footnote 'Exterminate all the brutes!' appended to Kurtz's pamphlet written for the International Society for the Suppression of Savage Customs. This particular text makes Marlow 'tingle with enthusiasm. This was the unbounded power of eloquence – of words – of burning noble words.' But 'the magic current of phrases' ended in that terrifying command. This discourse wasn't only unspeakable, it was unprintable.

The shakiness of print is focused with perhaps even more power in the curious figure of Kurtz's sidekick, the fantastic Russian seaman who looks like someone wandered in from a Dostoevsky novel, as eerie as mad Mrs Marmeladov in *Crime and Punishment* who turned her fatherless family into a zany troupe of street performers. His clothing is an extraordinary patch-work – 'patches all over, with bright patches, blue, red, and yellow, – patches on the back, patches on the front, patches on elbows, on knees' – so that he looks like a harlequin in his bizarre version of motley: 'as though he had absconded from a troupe of street mimes, enthusiastic, fabulous'. He is, of course, a living emblem of Africa's dividedness, a walking, talking version of the map that Marlow encountered in Brussels: the 'large shining map, marked with all the colours of a rainbow. There was a vast amount of red . . . a deuce of a lot of blue, a little green, smears of orange, and, on the East Coast, a purple patch, to show where the jolly pioneers of progress drink the jolly lager-beer . . . I was going into the orange.' And this mobile sculpture of Africanness is, naturally, a key focus of all Marlow's rhetoric of defeated conception and harassed narration: 'His very existence was improbable, in-explicable, and altogether bewildering. He was an insoluble problem. It was inconceivable how he had existed.' He brings home with peculiar vividness the truth Marlow is gradually unfolding, that the failure of the African glamour – 'The glamour's off' – is intimately connected with the threat to grammar. Glamour; grammar: at root they are the same word. The Russian is especially glamorous: 'Glamour urged him on, glamour kept him unscathed.' Marlow envies him his youthful adventurousness. But his devotion to Kurtz means that his particular glamour will wear off as the glamour of the blank map did. His personal charm will prove, in fact, as deceiving as his grammar, his writing, his book.

On his way up river, Marlow had found, at a deserted hut, some wood, a message, and a book, all, it eventuated, left by the Russian. The enigma of this scene encapsulates the whole African enigma. The signs and texts in it are either illegible, or, if readable, incomprehensible. There is a leaning flagpole, but the tatters of a flag it bears are unrecognizable. A faded and cryptic message which someone has left is puzzling, gappy, useless:

> a flat piece of board with some faded pencil-writing on it. When deciphered it said: 'Wood for you. Hurry up. Approach cautiously.' There was a signature, but it was illegible – not Kurtz – a much longer word. Hurry up. Where? Up the river? 'Approach cautiously.' We had not done so. But the warning could not have been meant for the place where it could be only found after approach. Something was wrong above. But what – and how much? That was the question. We commented adversely upon the imbecility of that telegraphic style. The bush around said nothing, and would not let us look very far, either.

Some Such Name

As usual, Africa has imperilled speech – 'the bush around said nothing' – and the general absurdity has encroached onto this abandoned piece of writing. It's faded, illegible, tauntingly telegraphic. And the old book that Marlow finds in 'a heap of rubbish' in 'a dark corner' is little use either, at least in giving clues to the Congo situation. It's a confusing mixture of decrepitude and care. *An Inquiry into Some Points of Seamanship*, it's called. Its pages are blackened with use. It's been recently stitched together with white cotton. But its covers have gone. It's been annotated, but Marlow can't read the annotations. They must, he guesses, be in cipher. All the labyrinthine puzzlement of Africa is here: 'this amazing autiquity', this 'wonderful' find, these 'astounding' notes: 'I couldn't believe my eyes! They were in cipher! Yes, it looked like cipher. Fancy a man lugging with him a book of that description into this nowhere and studying it – and making notes – in cipher at that! It was an extravagant mystery.' And the mystery attaches still, even as he relates all this, to the author of the book. Marlow professes uncertainty as to his name: 'Tower, Towson – some such name'; 'Towson or Towser'.

The illegible, faded, pointless writing, the hesitation over the name of the book's author: all this impresses Marlow and us as the true nature of writing in Africa. The apple-pie order of the parasol-toting accountant's 'books' is the anomaly. The litter of 'torn envelopes and open letters' scattered on Kurtz's bed, among which his 'hand roamed feebly', comes to seem typical of the condition of Marlovian textuality. It's very easy for us to read the problematic writings and inconclusive written matters of Kurtz and his Russian devotee as centre-pieces in Conrad's stern and massive repertoire of despairing emblems and figures of a collapse of narrative coherence, the demise of textual certainty. And of course *Heart of Darkness* is jammed with enough such figures to gladden the heart of any deconstructive analysis. The tattered flag and the 'torn curtain of red twill' that hung in the doorway of the Russian's abandoned hut and 'flapped sadly in our faces' join all the other bits of cloth, yarn in disarray, *tissus* torn and gone wrong, that could be said to function as vivid metaphors of narrative collapse, textual raggedness, the disintegration of story: those 'black rags' that the chinking chain-gang have 'wound round their loins'; the 'bit of white worsted' round the neck of the inert and dying black man; the harlequin's rags and patches, his 'miserable rags'; the traders' 'rubbishy cottons' exchanged for ivory; the curtain behind which the dying Kurtz is laid; the metaphorical 'veil' that, in curious recall of the Crucifixion, is said to have been 'rent' as, with his dying breath, Kurtz pronounces 'The horror! The horror!'

Conrad came to *Heart of Darkness* as a man proud of his expertise in *voile*, or sail. His experience of naval command, he told his aunt, Marguerite Poradowska, had been *principalement à voile*.[8] And in this fiction he commands the *voiles* – in French, the veils, fogs, mists, screens, palls, covertnesses – of meaning like an advanced Derridian *avant la lettre*. For Marlow's narrative is an attempt to squeeze meaning out of an extraordinarily deterrent and Derridian-style lexicon of borders, edges, doors, windows, blinds, shutters, fences, gaps, cracks, holes, scars, and faint traces of footpaths.

Marlow's narrative ends in the drawing-room of Kurtz's Intended, a room that has three huge and paradoxical windows, at once 'luminous and bedraped'. The semi-concealment, half-revelation, that they betoken aptly climax what had begun in the same city's silent shadowed streets of houses that had 'innumerable windows with venetian blinds' – *jalousies*, jealous guardians of half-lighting – and 'immense double doors standing ponderously ajar', 'cracks' through which Marlow 'slipped' into a Chinese-box interior of bureaucratic doors and, after that, into further encounters with yet further enigmatic doorways – the bookkeeper's ('in going out I stopped at the door'), the Russian's (guarded by that torn twill), the curtained threshold of Kurtz's final cabin.

Sailing into this place is a nightmare of edginess: a rebarbatively edged jungle, 'the gloomy border of the forest', grim river banks. These enigmatic borders make rotten fences. The Central Station is a backwater 'surrounded by scrub and forest, with a pretty border of smelly mud on one side, and on the three others enclosed by a crazy fence of rushes'. What might this mean? 'I asked myself sometimes what it all meant. They wandered here and there with their absurd long staves in their hands, like a lot of faithless pilgrims bewitched inside a rotten fence.' Meaning collapses at, or with, these fragile, crumbling walls and fencings. 'There's something pathetically childish in the ruins of grass walls.' What's learned at the gaps in these crazy or ruined

fences is never consoling. 'A neglected gap was all the gate it had, and the
first glance at the place was enough to let you see the flabby devil was
running that show.' The river bank's 'wall of matted vegetation' stands 'higher
than the wall of a temple'; in the moonlight Marlow can see 'through a
sombre gap' the river 'glittering' as it flows by – but it flows mute. The gap
offers only half-lit, partial, unhelpfully dumb access to understanding. The
amazing accountant, for his part, works permanently behind something like
the Brussels *jalousies*. His office is constructed, in fact, so as to become
one huge shutter, which makes the actual shutters redundant: 'It was built
of horizontal planks and so badly put together that, as he bent over his
high desk, he was barred from neck to heels with narrow strips of sunlight.
There was no need to open the big shutters to see.' And on the river a
complex metaphorical shutter presides tantalizingly over the day's passing
enlightenments:

> When the sun rose there was a white fog, very warm and clammy, and more
> blinding than the night . . . At eight or nine, perhaps, it lifted as a shutter
> lifts. We had a glimpse of the towering multitude of trees, of the immense
> matted jungle, with the blazing little ball of the, sun hanging over it – all
> perfectly still – and then the white shutter came down again, smoothly, as if
> sliding in greased grooves.

Small wander, than, that Kurtz lies dying in a shuttered pilot-house.
'Close the shutter', he says suddenly one day, 'I can't bear to look'. Africa
affords only barred and shuttered glimpses. They sort well with all the holes
and the leaks. Marlow comes across a hole in the ground, and it's a meaningless
hole: 'a vast artificial hole somebody had been digging on the slope, the
purpose of which I found impossible to divine. It wasn't a quarry or a
sandpit, anyhow. It was just a hole.' When there's a fire at the Central
Station in the grass shed that houses the trashy cloth and beads the pilgrims
trade in, 'the stout man with moustaches came tearing down to the river, a
tin pail in his hand, assured me that everybody was "behaving splendidly,
splendidly", dipped about a quart of water and tore back again. I noticed
there was hole in the bottom of his pail.'
    Meaning leaks away, or is simply not present enough, at all of these
repellently absurd, sometimes exuberantly daft, but almost invariably allegorical thresholds, gaps, fences, holes. The African scene is simply packed
with such emblematic zones, places where meaning cries out for recognition,
where readings are on the verge of becoming available, where signs appear
to be becoming apparent. The scars of potential readings are everywhere,
marks of the white man's presence; but, like the ravine that Marlow comes

across full of broken drainpipes – 'almost no more than a scar in the hillside' – the 'smash up' of intelligibility, of hermeneutic possibility, is 'wanton'. Africa, and the Marlow/Conrad text of Africa, comprise, in short, the sort of text that's welcomed by modernist and postmodernist criticism, one that's blurred, eroded, effaced – and in, and through, the very places (and figures, metaphors, of places) where meaning is looked for and might, under certain circumstances, have been anticipated: 'Paths, paths, everywhere; a stamped-in network of paths spreading over the empty land, through long grass, through burnt-grass, through thickets, down and up chilly ravines, up and down stony hills ablaze with heat; and a solitude, a solitude, nobody, not a hut.' The paths – and one's reminded of Derrida's notorious (and rather startling) allegation that such paths are a kind of *Ur*-writing, a primitive original textuality, whose ubiquitous and pre-alphabetic existence 'proves' the original nature of writing that his grammatology alleges, the founding precedence of text over speech – the paths go nowhere. They connect no existent people, and join up only 'abandoned villages'. They are a devastated, emptied network of graphic traces. Trying to make sense of them is, in fact, insane, farcical; for here narrative, the textual trade, the naming business, have been reduced to farce. Amidst so much imprecision you would expect the certainty of established place-names to have been welcomed as stepping-stones across otherwise marshy vastnesses. Far from it. The place-names Marlow meets are 'farcical' ones – 'names like Gran' Bessam, Little Pope: names that seemed to belong to some sordid farce'. And where is this farce enacted? Why, 'in front of a sinister back-cloth'. This farce proclaims its affinity with woven stuff, cloth, and, what's more, painted cloth, cloth with images on it, theatrical, rhetorical, textual stuff. And once again there's something wrong with this tissue: it's a *sinister* piece of figured cloth.

Mais Après?

Is all this, however, all that *Heart of Darkness* has to bring home to the reader? Is this *nouvelle* at all in danger of affirming the post-modernist 'fear' that Patricia Waugh detects haunting it (the possibility that 'Experience becomes [only] text. History is [only] narrative', with 'No way out of text')? Of course not. This so textualizing text isn't bounded only by textuality. This text whose material presses so insistently towards the establishment of heuristic vagueness, this hard-working set of self-emptying epistemological and hermeneutic scenarios, this group of narratives that so impressively inducts the reader into what Tzvetan Todorov has labelled the 'connaissance du vide' – knowledge of the void – is by no means just a matter of an exemplary self-reflexive textual self-doubting.[9] When Conrad writes that 'the subject is of our time distincly', the intention to announce a temporal pertinence can, and must, be allowed him. And his subject is manifestly political, arising out of the particularities of his Congo experiences, as he emphasized in his letter to his radical friend Cunninghame Graham:

> You must remember that I don't start with an abstract notion. I start with definite images and as their rendering is true some little effect is produced. So far the note struck chimes in with your convictions – mais après? There is an après. But I think that if you look a little into the episodes you will find in them the right intention though I fear nothing that is practically effective.[10]

Politically practical, or no, the fiction's episodes are historically and politically particular enough. The absurdity, the farce, are theatres of cruelty in which black lives are wasted. The frustration at the narrative and narratological levels is matched by anger at the political and moral levels. The pilgrims are on an exemplary literary journey, an intertextual engagement with Dante, one that inverts the Dantesque tradition of happy endings and heavenly comic conclusions. They are also trigger-happy nigger-killers. Those emblematic textual holes are also bullet holes. The network of erasures, the figures of meaning's traces, are also demolished homes, communities, lives. And Marlow carefully unites the bullet holes and the erased roadways in a single sarcastic instance. He comes across a drunken, uniformed white man guarded by armed Zanzibaris: 'Was looking after the upkeep of the road, he declared. Can't say I saw any road or any upkeep, unless the body of a middle-aged negro, with a bullet-hole in the forehead, upon which I absolutely stumbled three miles farther on, may be considered as a permanent improvement.'

The *vides* of this text are full of political and moral accusation. The hollowness at the heart of *Heart of Darkness* is by no means limited to a process of narrative self-emptying. The metatextual writing subject is also a colonial one. The astonishing bookkeeper is the agent of a colonialist system that makes money the supreme value, whose fetish is successful accountancy, spruce book-keeping. Kurtz's writing is done at the behest of a colonial agency. At the centre of the labyrinth of the Belgian head offices squats 'a heavy writing-desk'. Colonizing means writing, and writing – whatever else it might mean – spells colonizing. The ink-stains on the Belgian clerk's jacket sleeves come to look like proleptic emblems of the whole enterprise's moral stains that Marlow would soon encounter out in the field. And much of the consternation buzzing about Marlow's encounter with Towson-Tower's *Inquiry* clearly has to do with its being an emphatically British piece of writing. One comes to feel that it stands at the centre of a piece of guilty

self-accusation, a moral despair on the part of the narrator intimately connected with his criticism of imperialist enterprises, including British ones.

Marlow can scarcely stop himself reading the *Inquiry*. 'I assure you to leave
off reading was like tearing myself away from the shelter of an old and solid
friendship.' Approving adjectives, especially high moral terms, stud Marlow's
account of this arresting text – it's dull, but also sound and good:

> Not a very enthralling book; but at the first glance you could see there was
> a singleness of intention, an honest concern for the right way of going to work,
> which made these humble pages, thought out so many years ago, luminous
> with another than a professional light. The simple old sailor, with his talk of
> chains and purchases, made me forget the jungle and the pilgrims in a deli-
> cious sensation of having come upon something unmistakeably real.

What Marlow is evidently feeling is what the text's opening narrator calls
'the bond of the sea', and it's clearly a powerful moral affinity.

The values centred for Conrad in the British Merchant Marine – a shining
professional work ethic that made 'Polish Joe' so keen to acquire his British
merchant officer certificates, a moral touchstone of all his writing as the so-
called Prose Laureate of the British Merchant Navy – could not be much
clearer: *singleness, honest, right, work, luminous, real*. The tone of this readerly
response to the *Inquiry* chimes in with Marlow's reflections in Brussels on the
'vast amount of red' on the map, the overseas possessions of Britain: 'good to
see at any time, because one knows that some real work is done in there'.
Towson-Towser was a 'Master in His Majesty's Navy'. Marlow is also a
British master mariner. So, since November 1886, had Conrad been. 'Possède
certificat anglais de Cap^ne marin': it was one of the 'avantages' that this 'Polish
nobleman, cased in British tar' boasted of.[11]

And the trouble is that the *Inquiry* turns out to belong to Kurtz's Russian
devotee. The annotations prove not to be in cipher after all, but in Russian.
And hatred of Russians was in Polish Conrad's blood. In fact, the terror at
the heart of this fiction's darkness is like an archetypal Polish nightmare,
concocted by a man with a German name and a Russian friend, harsh reminders of the two enemies traditionally given to squeezing Poland in their
unfriendly pincer embrace. 'Il y aura des Russes. Impossible!,' Conrad replied
to Cunninghame Graham's invitation to sit on an international peace-meeting
platform. He felt no fraternity with Russians.[12] The Russian reader of the
Inquiry is one with the likes of Vladimir, the nasty stirrer-up of trouble from
the Russian Embassy in *The Secret Agent*, or the whole crew of Russians,
especially Russian exiles, in *Under Western Eyes*. Particularly offensive to Conrad
about Russians was their proneness to happiness abroad. His Russians tend
to be people with internationalist politics, like Laspara in *Under Western Eyes*,

the Russian Jewish anarchist exiled to Geneva, where he edits a subversive journal ironically titled *The Living Word*. 'We'll have it translated,' he assures Razumov of the article he wants him to write. In great contrast, Conrad was an unhappy exile whose foreign accent was reported to have worsened the longer he stayed in England. His fictions sank ever deeper into gloom about the livingness of the word, the possibility of translation, the nature of exile. Laspara's cheerfully *deraciné* politics and linguistics must have been designed to smell offensively rank. And Kurtz is another such internationalist. 'All Europe contributed to the making of Kurtz.' And from the look of his patched rig-out, you'd think the whole map of the world had contributed to the making of Kurtz's Russian admirer. If anything, this man's rootless internationalism is even more pronounced than Kurtz's. And yet, staggeringly, this vagabond owns, reads, and admires Towson-Towser. Kurtz tells Marlow that 'his sympathies were in the right place' – namely, with the English, and with the England where he went to school. This claim is clearly treated by Marlow with a pinch of salt. There's no getting away, however, from the shock of learning who actually owns the *Inquiry*. The book's power to *amaze* climaxes in what is for Marlow a terrible piece of knowledge.

Now That's Brotherly

What price, after this information, the bruited rightness of the British naval way of working if it may so enthral Kurtz's man? The luminosity of that moral professionalism abruptly darkens. It had already dimmed a lot when the Russian rubbed in other affinities with Marlow. He laid claim to a brotherhood of the sea that Marlow was not only helpless to rebuff but sealed with a gift of tobacco: 'Brother sailor . . . honour . . . pleasure . . . delight . . . introduce myself . . . Russian . . . son of an arch-priest . . . Government of Tambov . . . What? Tobacco? English tobacco; the excellent English tobacco! Now that's brotherly. Smoke? Where's a sailor that does not smoke?' When they part, he helps himself to another handful of Marlow's tobacco – 'Between sailors – you know – good English tobacco' – and cadges a pair of Marlow's old shoes. He also begs a few cartridges for his Martini–Henry rifle. And he goes off with his copy of Towson in one pocket (dark blue), and another pocket bulging with cartridges. The pocket with the ammunition in it is bright red. So much for 'the real work done in there'. The complicity of Marlow and the British Empire he represents and admires with the savage imperialism that comes from the barrel of an internationalist gun (the Martini–Henry combined the Swiss-made breech action invented by the Hungarian-born Frederick Martini with the American barrel developed by Tyler

Henry), the complicity with Kurtz, with his sidekick, with what's going on in this heart of darkness, could not have been made clearer. And central to this complicity is a book.

The gift of the shoes is as arresting as the shared interest in the *Inquiry*. The Russian will henceforth walk in Marlow's shoes. In a measure, Marlow has already been shown to stand in the Russian's shoes. The gift of shoes seals their connection in the same way as the loan of pyjamas seals the bond between the neophyte ship's captain and the alleged murderer in Conrad's story 'The Secret Sharer'. By such exchanges do you recognize your Double, your *Doppelgänger*, your mirror-self, in Conrad's fiction. This writing is commonly built on the widespread nineteenth-century trope of the *Doppelgänger*. *Lord Jim*, for example, is composed of several sets of Double relationships: the Patna: Patusan; Marlow: Jim; Jim: the French Lieutenant; Jim: Gentleman Brown. And central to such Double fictions, in which Conrad is such a specialist, is a kind of cross-over effect or *chiasmus*, an exchange of relative moral identity and status. In such fictions the overground, respectable man – Dr Jekyll, it might be – discovers his shocking identity with the unrespectable, underground, dark, repressed, evil Other – with the terrifyingly bestial Mr Hyde, or the unconscious, or the libido, or the Id (Freud's several ingenious variants on the *Doppelgänger* myth are inventively supple). And what occurs in this exchange is not only moral chastening for the ostensibly good person, but also rather general moral confusion. Learning he's also Mr Hyde reduces Dr Jekyll's grounds for moral self-priding. Equally, though, as Dr Jekyll's moral self-esteem collapses, some of our initial revulsion from Mr Hyde also dilutes. The *Doppelgänger* fiction is a great moral leveller. And so it is in this passage between Marlow and the Russian. Marlow's central position as moral arbiter, proud Englishman, incorruptible British merchant mariner, is deeply shaken. And Marlow's decrease is the Russian's increase. It's rebuking enough to Marlow to have his instinctive assumption that Towson belonged to an Englishman ('He must be English') overturned. It's even more sobering when this non-Englishman cheerfully assumes the right to teach Marlow a thing or two about keeping a tight ship ('My faith, your pilot-house wants a clean-up!') and when Marlow, inextricably locked into this new and estranging fraternalism, expresses envy and admiration for the person who is on the face of it an obnoxious wanderer: 'seduced into something like admiration – or envy'.

And this extravagant 'phenomenon' of a man is only the prelude or threshold to the even more momentous individual, Kurtz himself. The Russian isn't moved only by Towson, but by Kurtz. Whenever the Russian pockets, as it were, Towson, the approval is accompanied by an endorsement of Kurtz. At the end of chapter 2, when Marlow returns the book and is nearly kissed in gratitude, the Russian, the *Inquiry*'s devoted annotator, instantly declares that 'this man' – Kurtz – 'enlarged my mind'. When he leaves Marlow, Towson and the bullets carefully pocketed, he enthuses about Kurtz's poetry: 'You ought to have heard him recite poetry – his own, too, it was, he told me. Poetry!' And again: 'Oh, he enlarged my mind.' These are his last words.

Marlow's own last words, at least to Kurtz's Intended, were his lie about Kurtz's last word, a lie about naming: 'The last word he pronounced was – your name.' Our narrator has thus got himself locked into a *Doppelgänger* relationship even more morally rebuking and upsetting than the one with the Russian. 'It is strange how I accepted this unforeseen partnership.' This particular moral chiasmus is particularly stunning. Kurtz, the hollow man, the person intimately associated with the unspeakability of Africa, with the unspeakable rituals conducted there by both Blacks and Whites, the man whose very name is a lie, is nonetheless a voice, a word-monger whose word not only persists but has a degree of affirmation that Marlow seeks and signally fails to achieve. Marlow has to be content with knowing life only as a 'riddle'. 'I was within a hair's breadth of the last opportunity for pronouncement, and I found with humiliation that probably I would have nothing to say. This is the reason why I affirm that Kurtz was a remarkable man. He had something to say. He said it.' Kurtz's ghastly revelation is a summation, a 'sort of belief'. It has 'candour' and 'conviction': 'it had the appalling face of a glimpsed truth.' What Marlow has to say is, by contrast, inconclusive, 'futile', tepidly sceptical, 'a vision of greyness'. Kurtz has the positive assurance of the believing damned, Marlow the lukewarm Laodiceanism of the troubled agnostic. Not surprisingly, his story peters out in hesitations, a lie, and the allowing of lies, in the scene with the Intended that might be a pastiche of scenes in the later Henry James – *What Maisie Knew*, say, or *The Golden Bowl* – a farcical dance of dubious and finally quite false claims to knowledge, a grim comedy in which the fiancée supplies the desirable but self-deluding words that Marlow cannot. ' "It was impossible not to ——." "Love him," she finished eagerly, silencing me into an appalled dumbness. "How true! How true!" ' And as Marlow concludes his miserable confession, the darkness that he thought to avert by endorsing untruths ('I could not tell her. It would have been too dark altogether') descends anyway as the frame-narrator's thoughts lead away, under an overcast sky, to 'the uttermost ends of the earth', 'into the heart of an immense darkness'.

Everything has collapsed for Marlow through meeting Kurtz and the Russian who acts as preface or *hors-texte* to Kurtz. Most notably damaged is Marlow's rhetorical confidence; and that's momentous because it was that confidence which sustained the ancient self-righteous tradition of seafaring Britain. This awful collapse eventuates in the texture of narrative hesitancy that comprises our prime experience here as readers. It's the thing we immediately encounter and learn most forcibly, perhaps, from this fiction. It's an experience of the failure of language and language stuff – the spoken, the written, narrative, rhetoric, story – that arises within a striking series of language encounters, a clash of voices, a war of rhetorics, a business of discourses, words, writings, books, bookishness. But this textual affair could and would not exist were it not for the historical, moral, and political; in short, the ideological experience that engenders it, first for Conrad, then for Marlow. It's Africa, the colonial scene, the imperialist endurance test, the nineteenth-century business of foreign trade, that are, in the end, responsible for generating this famous display of narrative and rhetorical powerlessness, this decline in story-teller's confidence.

As with all of modernism's exemplary engagements with despair – its devoted revulsion from narrative, detective-style success – the rhetorical, hermeneutic, narrative issues never arise *in vacuo*. There is always, whether for Browning or James, for Joyce or Conrad, some experience or sense of moral, theological, political, social loss that is also significantly, and I would argue fundamentally, in play. No Kurtz, no Russian, no Towson, no African horrors: and no Marlow, no *Heart of Darkness*. And if the rhetorical collapse so prominent in this fiction cannot be considered separately from the experience it registers and reflects of a collapsed confidence in the values of white imperialism, especially the rightness and righteousness embodied in Towson's *Inquiry*, in Marlow's own moralizing seafaring craft, then neither does the reader have a choice in deciding which aspect of this so modernist text to emphasize. The historical and the rhetorical, the contextual and the textual, are no more separable than Kurtz the ivory-trader is separable from Kurtz the poet, or the Russian as adventurer from the Russian as reader.

What *Heart of Darkness* is doing is unpicking a tradition of the English novel in which writing and colonizing have gone intimately together. Robinson Crusoe, founding father of the English Novel, was a man with a pen in one hand and a gun in the other. The Russian with cartridges in one pocket and a book in the other, Kurtz the ivory-trading poet, are Crusoe's updated analogues. They are also a focus of the modernist cavilling at the tradition of Defoe, the undoing of Crusoe's certainties. And the cavilling is aimed not just at the tradition's textual features, the writing confidences, the faith in reading and writing that got into the tradition from Defoe's puritan background, but also at that tradition's sustaining moral and political assumptions, its belief in the God-given right to plunder and enslave. Targeting both is merely logical. These things hung together in their eighteenth-century ascendancy, and now they were inseparable in their late nineteenth-century downfall.

The notorious problem of yarns and yarning in *Heart of Darkness* is also a problem with yarn. The text's famous difficulties with textual stuff are inextricable from the questions it's asking about literal stuff, *Stoff*, cloth. Textual problems converge upon, are intricately woven into, problems with textiles – especially the trade in textiles between Europe and Africa. And where do they come from, the 'confounded spotted cotton handkerchiefs', the 'ghastly glazed cotton' trade goods, the torn twill curtain, the bit of white worsted around the neck of the dying Negro, the stuff the tattered flag is made of? Why, assuredly, from England. Lancashire was where the world's cotton goods were processed. Yorkshire was where the world's worsted woollen things were produced. Of course, the story's Martini–Henry rifles call the whole violent culture of Western white man into question. The railway boiler 'wallowing in the grass', the upturned railway truck, the stack of rusty rails, doubtless came, like the energetically farcical railway engineers, pointlessly blasting away at a cliff, from Belgium. But the colonialist cloth, the yarns so carefully woven into the *tissu* of this Conradian yarn, are English.

And thus the *Doppelgänger* relationship arranged between Marlow and Kurtz and the Russian is extended, subversively, even secretively, to a Double relationship between nations, Belgium and England. Conrad's satiric anger over the imperialist despoliation of Africa is intense. The 'vilest scramble for loot that ever disfigured the history of human conscience and geographical exploration', he called it, famously, in his late essay 'Geography and Some Explorers'.[13] And imperial Britain, Towson's home, Conrad's and Marlow's ground of assurance and of righteous feelings, turns out also to be on trial in this satire. We are compelled in the end by Marlow's progress to recognize the allegedly benign British Empire as the fraternal double of the obviously terrible Belgian enterprise of King Leopold. ' "And this also", said Marlow suddenly, "has been one of the dark places of the earth." ' Marlow's slow realization, and ours, is that it is still dark even at the end of the civilized nineteenth century, and that the 'dreams of men, the seed of commonwealths, the germs of empires', do not enjoy a simple 'greatness' just because it's our Commonwealth, our Empire that's in question.

An Empty Huntley & Palmers Biscuit Tin

And if all the yarn in this story is critically exemplary for this story of empires, both global empires and narrative empires, forcing us to read this material, this *Stoff*, as emblematic of what's going amiss with yarns of the narrative sort and also as representative of what's up with Britain's huge colonial export trade not least in cloth; even more exemplary, I'd say, in both of these directions, is the sudden arrival on the Congo river and in our text of a Huntley & Palmers biscuit-tin. The tin arrives with a consoling clatter of English reassurance amidst the annoying absence of rivets, the dumbness of the jungle, and after the jabber of the hook-nosed agent, the 'papier-mâché Mephistopheles' of the Central Station, the man who makes bricks without straw:

> It was a great comfort to turn from that chap to my influential friend, the battered, twisted, ruined, tin-pot steamboat. I clambered on board. She rang under my feet like an empty Huntley & Palmer [sic] biscuit-tin kicked along a gutter; she was nothing so solid in make, and rather less pretty in shape, but I had expended enough hard work on her to make me love her. No influential friend would have served me better.

Why a biscuit-tin? Why this particular brand of biscuit-tin? To be sure, biscuits and biscuit-tins make a curiously pervasive presence in the literature of classic modernism. James Joyce, for example, is oddly obsessed by the products of Dublin's Jacob's biscuit factory. Stephen Dedalus seems to hang about at its gates. He's hailed by one of its female employees, 'a girl he had glanced at, attracted by her small ripe mouth, as she passed out of Jacob's biscuit factory'. We're not told precisely what 'musty biscuits' the lads buy in the story 'An Encounter' in *Dubliners*, but the biscuit-tin that the irate citizen picks up off the bar and throws at Bloom in the Cyclops episode of *Ulysses* is specified, and it is of the Jacob's variety. There's some satisfying ironic aptness in the anti-Semitic citizen aiming a Jacob's tin at one of Jacob's latter-day sons. Jacob's biscuits are part of the Dublin life that Joyce is eager to register, a newly distinctive feature of the city's topography (William Jacob, an Irish Quaker, not in fact a Jew, had started making the first cream crackers in Dublin in 1885). Huntley & Palmers biscuits, though, appear to have more obviously textual resonance when they appear in *Finnegans Wake*. 'Huntler and Pumar's animal alphabites, the first in the world from aab to zoo': this mock advertisement appears in footnote 1 on page 263 of the *Wake*, offering in characteristic Wakean fashion a metatextual, self-referential tag advertising the counter–logos-centric assumptions of Joyce's great modernist text. The tag deftly manipulates different sorts of nursery biscuits made by Huntley & Palmers – ones shaped like animals (and so naturally produced by a firm called Huntler and Pumar) and ones in the form of letters of the alphabet. The prime quality of these biscuits ('first in the world') suggests primacy, firstness, origins, genesis, in a world whose animal existence is, then, a kind of A to Z, a whole alphabet (aab to zoo). Or, to unpack this densely folded talk of nursery foodstuffs more bluntly: the world begins in, and consists of, text; its *telos* is language; it's an alphabet-game or procedure, whose alpha and omega, its ontology (shouldering aside the Christian *telos* and ontology resident in Christ the Logos, the Alpha and the Omega of Biblical tradition) are merely alphabet-stuff, *a* to *z*, aab to zoo. What's more, it's being suggested, *Finnegans Wake* is the A–Z guide – the lexicon and the street map – to this A to Z condition, a text that here, and elsewhere, proposes itself as merely alphabeticist, consisting of just such an exemplary alphabeticism, bits (or bites, or even bytes) of mere alphabet, alphabites, just like this bitable alphabetical bit. Should the reader look to feed on fiction as filling stuff (the founding stuff of Western metaphysics, grounded in Greek and Christian logocentrism, as deconstructionists have insisted), she/he gets instead the *Wake*'s alternative sacrament, modernism's post-Christian alphabet-biscuits – the tokens of, and miniature texts for, an alternative genesis story, another kind of nursery rhyme than the Judaeo-Christian story of beginnings, the orthodox Father's story that *A Portrait* begins in. This one approximates rather to what's offered in the 'Oxen of the Sun' section in *Ulysses*, where the Garden of Eden is a beginning in and with alphabet, *aleph*, *alpha*. On such a reading, Huntley & Palmers biscuits are made into modernist emblems of the world as text, of text as a layered farrago of text upon text, of text as the origin and the be-all and end-all of things. In short, the Huntley & Palmers condition thus neatly touched in by Joyce is a textual condition, the condition of reading matter. And, after all, these biscuits were (and still are) made in Reading, the place known to the Victorian world as Biscuit City.

It's as if Joyce were aware of the once current pun – current in Oxford and Cambridge, at least (and Shem the Penman's lair in *Finnegans Wake* has 'once current puns' papered on to its walls (183: 22)) – the jest that referred to these Reading biscuits as 'reading biscuits'. From the start of their manufacture, the Reading biscuit-tins had exploited the reading connection by being made in the form of little collections of books, shaped like novels by Scott, Dickens, assorted Victorians, and so on. The so-called 'Library' tin of 1900, a simulated group of eight books bound by a simulated leather strap, brought the Reading biscuit's bookish self-reference to a certain peak: the titles of the 'books' include *Modern Reading*, *History of Reading*, *Biscuits*, and *Cakes*.

The gingerbread biscuits in *Jude the Obscure* scarcely match the Huntley & Palmers biscuits of *Finnegans Wake* for textual and metatextual force. But then, how could they, for it's Joyce's design to have everything in *Finnegans Wake* more-metatextual-than-thou, to out-textualize the whole world. But Hardy's biscuits, the ones offered for sale by Sue and Jude at country fairs – 'reminiscences of the Christminster Colleges. Traceried windows, and cloisters, you see' – are manifestly made a part of *Jude*'s devoted reduction

of things to miniaturized, shrunken, cut-down, dinky-toy, and otherwise
lacking and disappointing bits of text, metatext or emblems of text: signa-
tures, photographs, newspaper cuttings, carved or sign-written portions of
Scripture, Sue's private cut-up version of the Bible, Christian and pagan
effigies, a travelling model of Jerusalem ('I fancy we have had enough of
Jerusalem,' says Sue: II. v), and the 'Model of Cardinal College, Christminster:
by J. Fawley and S. F. M. Bridehead', shown at the Great Wessex Agricultural
Show (V. v). All hopes, all beliefs, all Old and New Jerusalems, all Promised
Lands, shrink and collapse in *Jude*. Christ and Christminster alike are just
more spoiled sacramental stuff, just bits of gingerbread.

Murphy's lunch of tea and biscuits in Samuel Beckett's *Murphy* represents
more biscuity material deftly absorbed into a modernist novel's play with
symbolic systems. The novel *Murphy* (as ambitiously solipsistic as its
eponymous hero) is schemed around closed systems of diads, paired opposites.
Murphy's lunch (ch. 5) is ' "A cup of tea and a packet of assorted biscuits".
Twopence the tea, twopence the biscuits, a perfectly balanced meal'. Exploiting twonesses as deftly as any mean Christian absorbed by Biblical
pairings (such as the story of the Two Thieves on the Cross, one saved, the
other damned, that so obsessed Beckett), Murphy cons a second cup of
tea out of waitress Vera. ' "I ask for China and you give me Indian," ' Murphy
declares, 'in an egg and scorpion voice.' Egg and scorpion: it's another of the
New Testament's Manichean binaries that Beckett is much drawn to: 'If a
son shall ask bread of any of you that is a father, will he give him a
stone? . . . Or if he shall ask an egg, will he offer him a scorpion?' (Luke 11:
11–12). The biscuits, however, Murphy saves for later, to eat in Hyde Park
– always supposing he's able to cope with their difficult difference: 'Murphy
fell forward on his face on the grass, beside those biscuits of which it could
be said as truly as of the stars, that one differed from another, but of which
he could not partake in their fullness until he had learnt not to prefer any
one to any other.' Alas, the bitch (dog or bitch: of course Murphy likes to
ask which) belonging to the panpygoptotic passer-by, Miss Dew, the medium
who suffers from Duck's Disease, eats up all the biscuits except for the ginger
one, which she/he does, however, masticate keenly. Murphy refuses to eat
doggy rejects: ' "The depravity of her appetite," said Murphy, "you may be
glad to hear, does not extend to ginger, nor the extremity of mine to a
rutting cur's rejectamenta." ' Murphy's friend Wylie, we're told, 'might have
consoled himself' in this situation 'with the thought that the Park was a
closed system in which there could be no loss of appetite'. But, again and
again, these apparent closed systems split dangerously open. As Vladimir and
Estragon remind each other in *Godot*, only one of the Four Evangelists actually records that one of the two thieves was saved. So much, then, for the

apparent evens-balance between the odds on salvation and damnation. Damnation looks the more promising. Murphy's carefully contrived enclosing refuge at the Magdalen Mental Mercyseat proves incapable finally of shutting out death and dissolution. In these blackly Irish closed systems there's often some provocative or irking residue, some grit in the oyster. On this occasion, the ginger biscuit slobbered at and finally spurned by Miss Dew's Dachshund is that telling *disjectum* or *rejectamentum*. Its role as metaphorical, symbolic, textual actor is clear. It must not be thought of as a simply realistic biscuit. It's much more in the Christminster gingerbread, Huntler and Pumar line of allegorical comestible.

Empire Biscuits

The connection between Joyce's Huntler and Pumar's biscuits and the Huntley & Palmers biscuit-tin of *Heart of Darkness* is, naturally, an inviting one. It is, of course, eminently possible to read this metaphorical transformation of Marlow's river-steamer into an empty Huntley & Palmers biscuit-tin as if it were drawing out a subterranean proleptic Joycean pun on Huntley & Palmers biscuits as textual items originating in a place called Reading-reading and so endorsing the Conradian text's pervasive stress on narrative and verbal hollowed-out-ness. This tin is empty. It exists for us as metaphor, the essence of rhetoricism. Furthermore, it is a metaphor of emptiness. But attractive, and even highly plausible, though this reading might be, the precision in the naming of the biscuit-tin seems to require some further interpretative response. This is not just any old biscuit-tin, but one supplied by Huntley & Palmers. Thus named, it has a quite specific identity and origin. And the specificity of this thing takes it way beyond the very suggestively British material stuff, the cottons and worsted wool, that so clamantly indict themselves as part and parcel of European colonial enterprise.

For what Huntley & Palmers stood for was one of the most extraordinary and far-flung triumphs of colonialist marketing and propaganda that Victorian Britain knew. Huntley & Palmers biscuits, well-preserved in their tins, went simply everywhere. They were with Scott on his 1910–12 journey to the South Pole: British foodstuffs that encapsulated the spirit of the Empire and the British class system all at once. In Scott's hut at Cape Evans, a wall of Huntley & Palmers biscuit-tins made the boundary between officers and men: the ward-room of Scott and his fellow officers and the scientists on one side of the metal hedge, the mess-deck for ordinary seamen on the other. (Thomas Kenneally, the Australian novelist of *inter alia* colonial adventurism, has a fossilized piece of Huntley & Palmers biscuit from Scott's last expedition hanging on his study wall.) Henry – 'Dr Livingstone I presume' – Stanley once pacified a war-like tribe in Suna (now Central Tanzania) with Huntley & Palmers biscuit-tins. Ugandan Christians kept Bibles and Prayer Books in theirs – good for warding off ants and such. When a Royal Navy landing party went ashore on the Pacific island of Juan Fernandez off the coast of Chile – one of the candidates for Robinson Crusoe's island – they found only a few goats and an empty Huntley & Palmers biscuit-tin. These biscuits were sold 'By Appointment to the King of the Belgians'. Their various names revealed the company's colonialist ambition and success – Traveller, Camp, Cabin, African, Cape, Colonial, Empire, Prince, Queen, and so on. Their highly ornamental tins (extremely 'pretty in shape', as Marlow puts it) also proclaimed the imperialist association. There, were, for example, tins labelled Indian, Arctic, Orient, Ivory, Arabian (brought out in 1891, this one had boat scenes on it from around the world, including the Congo). When in 1896 Prince Henry of Battenberg, husband of Victoria's youngest daughter, caught a fever fighting the Ashanti in West Africa and died on the boat journey home, his body was preserved in rum in a casket hammered together from Huntley & Palmers biscuit-tins. The municipal museum at Reading owns two swords taken as trophies from the battlefield of Omdurman where, in 1898, the year before *Heart of Darkness* was published, General Kitchener defeated the Sudanese Mahdi and finally avenged the death of General Gordon. Their scabbards are bound together with bits of tin. The name *Huntley & Palmers* is clearly legible, stamped into these metal straps. Once again the Reading biscuit-tin had proved its versatility in the colonial effort. The Reading museum also holds a photograph taken by a Reverend R. D. Darby of a Conrad-style Belgian trading steamer on the Upper Congo river. A large Huntley & Palmers tin is clearly visible on the roof of the vessel. The photo is captioned 'Huntley & Palmers Biscuits foremost again'.[14]

When Conrad put such a biscuit-container into a metaphor on the Congo river in his intensely anti-colonial fiction, he knew the inference that his British readers would draw. Once again, British trade is being implicated, clearly and by name, in the Belgian horrors.[15] What's more, we are invited to contemplate an empty biscuit-tin. Someone, in the metaphor, has eaten the sweet contents. Huntley & Palmers's African and Empire biscuits were advertised at the time of Conrad's tale as 'slightly sweetened'. The suggestion of sweetness, even of slight sweetness, is, in the context of Conrad's tale, most ironic.

It will take more than the sweet exports of Biscuit City to sweeten the horrors Marlow has discovered, just as it will need more than the Swedish ship's biscuit that Marlow felt compelled to give the dying Black with the bit of white worsted round his neck to halt his death by malnutrition – 'The fingers closed slowly on it and held – there was no other movement and no other glance.' As an opium of the people, biscuits are of little avail. They represent a failure of nutrition, though, that the metaphor-as-meaning does not share. The biscuit-tin in question is empty of biscuits but not of point. In fact, the metaphor fills up very busily with bleakly unconsoling meanings: political, ideological messages from Reading to supplement whatever self-referential message of bookish, textual emptiness, the abysmality of reading, which this trope might also be construed as conveying.

Prison Breakfasts

Arrestingly, this insistent intrusion of Reading into our reading of *Heart of Darkness*, especially as that reading is relevant to critical concern with relations between text and history, has another most arresting supplementary twist to it. In the later 1890s, all writers in England, including, no doubt, even the quite recently settled Polish immigrant Joseph Conrad (who only really set up house in England in September 1896), had had a major connection between reading matter and Reading matters brought vividly home to them. This was the two-year prison sentence passed on Oscar Wilde, most of it spent in Reading Gaol. And the release of Wilde from custody (he left Reading 18 May 1897 and was discharged from Pentonville the next morning 19 May) brought strange publicity to the close connection between Reading's prison and its biscuits. In his last months in prison Wilde had been befriended by a Belfast-born warder called Thomas Martin, who smuggled in for him each morning the *Daily Chronicle* and apparently also supplied him secretly with occasional ginger biscuits. And biscuits were to be the well publicized cause of Martin's downfall. Shortly before his release, Wilde had been upset to observe three children, in the prison because they'd stolen some rabbits and had been unable to pay their fine. The smallest of the three had been quite unable to eat the prison food, and was found by warder Martin crying with hunger. Taking pity on the lad, Martin had given him some sweet biscuits to eat instead. For this act of kindness Martin was dismissed from his post. The newspapers reported the dismissal, and Wilde, just then released, wrote a long letter protesting about his friend's sacking, about the treatment meted out to children in Britain's gaols and related cruelties, and giving an inside story of Martin and the biscuits. His letter was published in the *Morning Chronicle*, 28 May 1897, just ten days after his liberation. It was the first publication of Wilde's new freedom.[16]

In the case of the little child to whom Warder Martin gave the biscuits, the
child was crying with hunger on Tuesday morning, and utterly unable to eat
the bread and water served to it for its breakfast. Martin went out after the
breakfasts had been served, and bought the few sweet biscuits for the child
rather than see it starving. It was a beautiful action on his part, and was so
recognised by the child, who, utterly unconscious of the regulation of the
Prison Board, told one of the senior warders how kind this junior warder had
been to him. The result was, of course, a report and a dismissal.[17]

He 'went out after the breakfasts . . . and bought the few sweet biscuits.'
Where did he go? Where else could he go? Why – and this is something no
biographer of Wilde seems to have noticed – straight across the street to the
Huntley & Palmers biscuit factory, the huge sprawling red-brick production
centre of Reading's and the world's biscuits which was the prison's gargantuan
neighbour.

The prison and the biscuits are still neighbours, though the factory has in
recent years been greatly demolished; knowledgeable travellers by rail through
Reading can still just about observe the neighbourliness. But no Victorian
rail traveller could fail to miss the proximity of the giant biscuit complex to
the gaol. Huntley & Palmers were keen to make rail travellers notice their
works. As a publicity stunt they used to hand first-class passengers a packet
of their biscuits at Paddington station with instructions on the packet to
look out for the factory when the train reached Reading. They were inviting
their customers to look, in the same glance, willy-nilly, at Reading Gaol.
When Oscar Wilde landed up there, this was a proximity that severely
embarrassed the Palmer family. In his days of glory Wilde had visited the
Reading factory as a guest of honour, courted by Jean Palmer, arty wife of
George Palmer's son Walter. Wilde had signed the Visitors' Book as 'Poet'.
His name was on the roll of distinguished visitors. When he turned up as
an unwanted neighbour, somebody added dissenting exclamation marks in
the Visitors' Book alongside his entry, and his name was pasted over on the
Roll of distinction. But the connection, Prison: Wilde: Huntley & Palmers
biscuits, was less readily erasable. And it's there too, for us, shadowily but
still forcefully, in *Heart of Darkness*.

What Wilde's connection with our text vividly underlines is Conrad's
anti-colonialist point, that the dire circumstances of oppression are not to be
alleviated by mere biscuits. For all their sweetness, the products of Huntley
& Palmers satisfy or sweeten as little in Africa's colonial confinements as in
Reading Gaol. What the Wilde link further endorses is the revelation singing
through *Heart of Darkness* of the limitations of merely textualizing assumptions and readings. It brings home joltingly that what matters in reading
has this uncanny way of impinging, so to say, on what goes on in Reading,

and vice versa. As Edward Said has nicely argued, Oscar Wilde was in prison, according to his own account in *De Profundis*, because he had mistakenly supposed that writing was just writing, that the art of letters could exist for its own sake, that texts were just texts, reading just reading, and the meaning of a writing something safely locked up within a textual or reading gaol.[18]

Wilde's misplaced faith in the textual insulation of a letter landed him in Reading Prison. 'Look at the history of that letter . . . I go to prison for it at last'. A grim experience of harsh Foucauldian truths about inhumanity, oppression, the organized power of the state apparatus, as evidenced in the institution of Reading prison, was the terrible reward for too lax – even too arrogant – a faith in the safety of the reading prison. In other words, Wilde's encounter with the mixed blessings of Reading brought vividly home to this notable contemporary of Conrad's and of *Heart of Darkness* the embarrassingly mixed nature of writing and reading that is so major a thrust of Conrad's narrative. We con only speculate about the extent of Conrad's acquaintance with this particular sweet and sour story from Reading. But our knowledge of it surely offers us a piquant allegory about the impossibility of any faith in the absoluteness of reading prisons, and one that grants the parallel message sounding from Conrad's emptied biscuit-tin even more resonance than it enjoyed by itself. And that was already a lot. For tough resistance to the prison-house view of language, text, and fiction, *Heart of Darkness* really does take the biscuit.

NOTES

1   See Brian McHale, *Postmodernist Fiction* (Methuen, New York and London, 1987), *passim*. Patricia Waugh's discussion accepts the challenge of this text's straddling of any simple modernist–postmodernist divide: *Practising Postmodernism/Reading Modernism* (Arnold, London, 1992), 85, 89–98. The centrality of Conrad's and *Heart of Darkness*'s modernism is widely recognized. 'Modernist fiction is pioneered in England by James and Conrad': thus David Lodge, *The Modes of Modern Writing: Metaphor, Metonymy, and the Typology of Modern Literature* (Arnold, London, 1977), 45. The recognition is commonly a bit pawky and thin, as in McHale, *Postmodernist Fiction*, 9; John Batchelor, *The Edwardian Novelists* (Duckworth, London, 1982), 37; and Douglas Tallack (ed.), *Literary Theory at Work: Three Texts* (Batsford, London, 1987), ch. 1: 'Narratology'; ch. 6: 'Dialogics'. But Conrad's modernist and postmodernist centrality is a *donnée* of Ian Watt's 'Impressionism and Symbolism in *Heart of Darkness*', *Southern Review*, 13, no. 1 (January 1977), 96–113 (repr. in *Joseph Conrad: Modern Critical Views*, ed. with an introduction by Harold Bloom (Chelsea House, New York, 1986), 83–99); J. Hillis Miller's *Fiction and Repetition: Seven English Novels* (Blackwell, Oxford, 1982); Peter Brooks, 'An Unreadable Report: Conrad's *Heart of Darkness*', in

Reading for the Plot: Design and Intention in Narrative (Clarendon Press, Oxford, 1984); Cedric Watts, *The Deceptive Text: An Introduction to Covert Plots* (Harvester, Brighton, 1984). Frank Kermode's *The Genesis of Secrecy* made the greatest difference to the postmodernist reading of Conrad – as is clear from Allon White's chapter 'Conrad and the Rhetoric of Enigma' in his *The Uses of Obscurity: The Fiction of Early Modernism* (Routledge and Kegan Paul, London, 1981), from Jakob Lothe's *Conrad's Narrative Method* (Clarendon Press, Oxford, 1989), and most notably, of course, from Kermode's own rereading of *Under Western Eyes*, 'Secrets and Narrative Sequence', in Kermode, *Essays on Fiction, 1971–82* (Routledge and Kegan Paul, London, 1983). The difference is measurable in the shifts between Cedric Watts' 1984 book and his earlier prolifically suggestive, but ragged, *Conrad's Heart of Darkness: A Critical and Contextual Discussion* (Mursia, Milan, 1977). Conrad's rebarbative textuality, the glorying in gaps which Henry James celebrated in his *TLS* discussion of *Chance* ('The New Novel', in James, *Notes on Novelists* (1914), and in, e.g., *Henry James: Selected Literary Criticism*, ed. Morris Shapira (Penguin, Harmondsworth, 1963), 358–391) and which Leavis so influentially castigated in his 1948 discussion of *Heart of Darkness* in *The Great Tradition* (buttressed there by his attacks on the style of the later James), is now cheerfully accepted, regarded as all cut and dried, and all on the convenient docket of the (post)modern.

2 See Frank Kermode, 'Can We Say Absolutely Anything We Like?', in *Essays on Fiction*, 156ff.

3 Batchelor, *Edwardian Novelists*, 44 and n. 24.

4 Tallack, *Literary Theory at Work*, 190.

5 See Terence Cave, *Recognitions: A Study in Poetics* (Clarendon Press, Oxford, 1988).

6 Letter to Blackwood, 31 December 1898, in *Collected Letters of Joseph Conrad*, ed. Frederick R. Karl and Laurence Davies, vol. 2; *1989–1902* (Cambridge University Press, 1986), 140.

7 F. R. Leavis, *The Great Tradition* (Chatto and Windus, London, 1948), 177–9. It's interesting, albeit astonishing, to see this accusation adapted in the simple-minded anti-racist polemic of Frances B. Singh: 'he uses words like . . . *implacable, inscrutable* . . . so constantly . . . that the people of Africa begin to be tinged by the qualities that these words connote': 'The Colonialistic Bias of *Heart of Darkness*', *Conradiana* 10 (1978), quoted in the excellent Norton edition of *Heart of Darkness*, 3rd edn, ed. Robert Kimbrough (W. W. Norton and Co., New York and London, 1988), 271.

8 Letter of 1? February 1891, in *Collected Letters of Joseph Conrad*, ed. Frederick R. Karl and Laurence Davies, vol. 1; *1861–1897* (Cambridge University Press, 1983), 67.

9 Waugh, *Practising Postmodernism/Reading Modernism*, 90. Tzvetan Todorov, 'Connaissance du vide: coeur des ténèbres', in *Les Genres du discours* (Seuil, Paris, 1978), 161–73.

10 Letter of 8 February 1899, in *Letters*, vol. 2, 157–8.

11 Letter to Marguerite Poradowska, February 1891, and to Karol Zagorski, 22 May 1890, in *Letters*, vol. 1, 67 and 52.

12   Letter of 8 February, 1899, in *Letters*, vol. 2, 158.

13   Quoted, e.g., by Gérard Jean-Aubry, 'In the Heart of Darkness', in *Conrad's Heart of Darkness and the Critics*, ed. Bruce Harkness (Wadsworth, Belmont, Calif., 1960), 96.

14   Information about Reading biscuits and tins from T. A. B. Corley, *Quaker Enterprise in Biscuits: Huntley & Palmers of Reading 1822–1972* (Hutchinson, London, 1972); M. J. Franklin, *British Biscuit Tins 1868–1939: An Aspect of Decorative Packaging* (New Cavendish Books, London, 1979); Ian Bradley, *Enlightened Entrepreneurs* (Weidenfeld and Nicolson, London, 1987), chapter on 'George Palmer (1818–1897)'; Paul Brown, 'Scott's Last Outpost, Frozen History', *Guardian*, 15 February 1989, 24; Tim Toni, 'My Style: Tom Kenneally', *Sydney Morning Herald*, 26 September 1985.

15   In other words, the direct involvement of Britain in the *nouvelle*'s critique of imperialism is far wider than Hunt Hawkins allows in 'Conrad's Critique of Imperialism in *Heart of Darkness*', *Publications of the Modern Language Association of North America*, 94, no. 1 (1979), 286–99. And, of course, at no point does Conrad's text sustain the colonialist racism Chinua Achebe professes to detect in his curious misreading of it in the notorious 'An Image of Africa: Racism in Conrad's *Heart of Darkness*', repr. in the Norton edn, 251–62. For a more temperate discussion of the racism charge, see 'Epilogue: Kurtz's "Darkness" and Conrad's *Heart of Darkness*', in Patrick Brantlinger, *Rule of Darkness: British Literature and Imperialism, 1830–1914* (Cornell University Press, Ithaca and London, 1988), 255–74.

16   Richard Ellmann, *Oscar Wilde* (Hamish Hamilton, London, 1987), 485; H. Montgomery Hyde, *Oscar Wilde: The Aftermath* (Methuen, London, 1963), 107.

17   Oscar Wilde, 'The Case of Warder Martin: Some Cruelties of Prison Life', *Daily Chronicle*, 28 May 1897, in *The Annotated Oscar Wilde: Poems, Plays, Lectures, Essays, and Letters*, ed. H. Montgomery Hyde (Clarkson N. Potter Inc., New York, 1982), 466–71. *Selected Letters of Oscar Wilde*, ed. Rupert Hart-Davis (Oxford University Press, 1979), 269–275.

18   Edward Said, 'The World, the Text, and the Critic', in *The World, the Text, and the Critic* (Faber, London, 1984), 42–3.

6

Games Texts Play

Lesen, so konnte man in einer Formulierung Batesons sagen, 'ist wie das Leben – ein Spiel, dessen Zweck darin besteht, die Regeln herauszufinden, wobei sich die Regeln andauernd verändern und immer unentdeckbar bleiben'.

(Reading, it could be said in a formulation of Gregory Bateson's, 'is, like life itself, a game whose purpose is to discover the rules, but in a process by which the rules perpetually change and always remain undiscoverable'.)

Wolfgang Iser, Das Fiktive und das Imaginäre (1991)

The Joker has become a definitive hero of our time. It's a symptom of high critical and textual significance that Tim Burton's 1989 reworking of the Batman epic in the movie *Batman* should have followed Brian Bolland and Alan Moore's *The Killing Joke* (DC Comics, 1988) in shrinking the erstwhile hero's part, robbing him of his ephebic assistant Robin, normalizing his magic and his technics, in order to clear centre-stage for the magnetically manic Joker, as played by Jack Nicholson. For the centre-stage Joker is a quintessence of our strongest fictions. He is, as it were, the messiah that our (post)structuralist textual practices and critical preferences have been awaiting – indeed, loudly acting as John the Baptist for. Nicholson's Joker is the emblem and apotheosis of all the recent years of critics and writers supposing art to be *Just Gaming*, mere game, play, *ludus*, carnival, *Spiel*, a 'freeplay' of significance, *un jeu des signifiants*.[1]

The joking text is indeed a currently pervasive one at this end of the twentieth century. Even the deeply suspected concept of the author has been allowed to reappear in the shape of Yahweh, the great originator and ultimate author as impish ironist, a kind of cosmic comedian created by the so-called J-texts of the Pentateuch. Harold Bloom, uncanny cabbalist, agonistic rabbi, powerfully reads off the J-texts of the Old Testament as presenting sublime instances of divine low cunning, trickery, caprice, uncanniness, and bad etymology in the person of the Jehovah who breaks his own command-ments by making a clay effigy that he punningly calls Adam, who picnics with Israel's elders, tries to bump off Moses, arranges to out-trick the trick-ster Jacob in a night of wrestling, and later finds a servant to really suit his jokey moods in grumpy Jonah, the pissed-off prophet who's had a bellyfull of preaching doom and gets his come-uppance in the belly of a great fish. Jehovah regains critic-credibility thus as a joker. *Deus Ludens*. J-text stands for joking text. It's the new, readable, Carnivalized Version of the Bible.[2]

Tristram Shandy, dismissed by the sober-sides critical tradition that reigned bossily from Dr Johnson to Dr Leavis as too freakishly jokey for a permanent residence permit in the House of Fiction, is now taken as the quintessential novel of the English tradition precisely because it exists as *Spiel* – a game of fiction-making, fiction as game, a self-conscious, self-representing *Theaterspiel* whose subject is itself, its own fictionality. Wolfgang Iser has very persua-sively applied the standard game-theory tropes of Roger Caillois's influential book *Man, Play, and Games* – *agon* (contest games), *alea* (games of chance), *mimicry* (pretend reality), *ilinx* (subversive, entropic, self-cancelling games) – to *Shandy*. The war-games of Uncle Toby and Corporal Trim that fill out the novel act, Iser argues, as a subversively metatextual, self-referential *ilinx* as they 'play *agon* by means of *mimicry* according to aleatory rules'. The result is a 'triumph of gaming'.[3] It's a triumph that anticipates the thorough penetration of fiction in the twentieth century by games and gamesters, and the modernist assumption of gaming as the self-reflexive essence of fiction. Virginia Woolf turned quite naturally to *Tristram Shandy* as a model – where-as the fad for Sterne in Bloomsbury only pepped up Leavis's distaste. The Shandyan gaming inheritance is writ large across the modernist fictional scene from James to *Finnegans Wake*. The more self-conscious and metafictional modern fiction became, the more it used games as allegories, analogues, models of fictional proceeding. The numerous games and metaphors from games that fill, say, *What Maisie Knew* – chess, shuttlecocks, billiards, forfeits – or *The Golden Bowl* (in which billiards are central), the chess-playing that preoccupies Beckett's *Murphy* or Nabokov's *The Defence* (1964) or, for that matter, Saussure's *Cours*, are all alerting signposts to, and exempla of, the pervasive play with the form of the novel that's the essence of metafiction.[4]

A Reel of Funnish Ficts

Finnegans Wake is a new piece of grown-up child's play in which old juvenile games and rhymes get absorbed and rewritten. Jack and the Beanstalk and

Little Red Riding Hood reappear as 'Jests and the Beanstalk with a little rude riding rod' (307, fn. 1). The House that Jack Built is an old J-text particularly appealing to James Joyce and his own latest J-text. This particular fictional house that Jim builds is advertised as 'the hoose that Joax pilled', or the one that Jokes pulled (369: 14, in reference to the celebratory volume by Joyce's disciples *Our Exagmination*). It's 'the hoax that joke bilked' (511: 34) – a reminder that Shem the Penman's lair is papered or literatured with, among other things, 'cans of Swiss condensed bilk'. This writing will not play the game of fiction straight, will not meet conventional expectations (to *bilk* is to evade payment of a debt, and early on meant a spoiling action in the card-game of cribbage). This text will be no conventional monument of fiction, nor even a proper monument to, say, the Duke of Wellington – unlike the Wellington Monument that it's preoccupied with. From first to last, from 'the first joke of Willingdone' (9: 14) to 'the last joke of Willingdone' (10: 12), the *Wake* is a monumental game and a monument to the subversiveness of game, jest, pastiche, parody, satiric catachresis. The list of credits given for this particular cinema reel or spiel includes 'Jests, jokes, jigs and jorums for the Wake lent down from the properties of the late cemented Mr T. M. Finnegan' (221: 26). Games involving the 'rude riding rod' naturally abound in a text that delights scurrilously in all kinds of sexual activity commonly accounted perverse. Sex-games and language-games keep converging in a way that's certainly not cricket — especially when they're both jointly elaborated in an extended set of naughty cricket metaphors:

Quick, pay up!
Kickakick. She had to kick a laugh. At her old stick-in-the-block. The way he was slogging his paunch about, elbiduubled, meet oft mate on, like hale King Willow, the robberer. Cainmaker's mace and waxened capapee. But the tarrant's brand on his hottoweyt brow. At half past quick in the morning. And her lamp was all askew and a trumbly wick-in-her, ringeysingey. She had to spofforth, she had to kicker, too thick of the wick of her pixy's loomph, wide lickering jessup the smooky shiminey. And her duffed coverpoint of a wickedy batter, whenever she druv behind her stumps for a tyddlesly wink through his tunnilclefft bagslops after the rising bounder's yorkers, as he studd and stoddard and trutted and trumpered, to see had lordherry's blackham's red bobby abbels, it tickled her innings to consort pitch at kicksolock in the morm. Tipatonguing him on in her pigeony linguish, with a flick at the bails for lubrication, to scorch her faster, faster. Ye hek, ye hok, ye hucky hiremonger! Magrath he's my pegger, he is, for bricking up all my old kent road. He'll win your toss, flog your old tom's bowling and I darr ye, barrackybuller, to break his duck! He's posh. I lob him. We're parring all Oogster till the empsyseas run googlie. Declare to ashes and teste his metch! Three for two will do for me and he for

thee and she for you. Goeasyosey, for the grace of the fields, or hooley pooley, cuppy, we'll both be bye and by caught in the slips for fear he'd tyre and burst his dunlops and waken her bornybarnies making his boobybabies. The game old merrimynn, square to leg, with his lolleywide towelhat and his hobbsy socks and his wisden's bosse and his norsery pinafore and his gentleman's grip and his playaboy's plunge and his flannelly feelyfooling, treading her hump and hambledown like a maiden wellheld, ovalled over, with her crease where the pads of her punishments ought to be by womanish rights when, keek, the hen in the doran's shantyqueer began in a kikkery key to laugh it off, yeigh, yeigh, neigh, neigh, the way she was wuck to doodledoo by her gallows bird (how's that? Noball, he carries his bat!) nine hundred and dirty too not out, at all times long past conquering cock of the morgans. (583: 25–584: 25)

Even if *Finnegans Wake* avers a certain relish for oral games, not least Joyce's particular version of 'pigeony linguish', or speaking sexually with tongues, the kind of glossolalia it utters is not of course primarily an oral but a written matter. And what Shem the Penman – or Punman – gets up to is the most extended game of all – namely, massive word-play, endless textual, metatextual, and intertextual gaming, 'patpun for all' (301: 13). The great epic list of games on page 301 informs us that this particular writing game (there's a sequence of verbs describing how 'he' would 'scripple', 'pen', and 'pine' for his lady and 'patpun fun' for everyone) is 'A nastilow disigraible game'. It's only thought of as being disagreeable, though, to the orthodox reader, the one who would object to the heretical, blaspheming take-over of orthodox fiction and texts, orthodox beliefs and practices, in a text that's turned Devil's advocate, siding with the great Satanic adversary in the match 'Christ's Church varses Bellial!' (301: 9). Earlier, on page 175, just before the text's long listing of games, when 'All Saints beat Belial' by 'Mickil Goals to Nihil', this result is declared 'Notpossible!' And what the *Wake* applauds loudest is the kind of game, or *Spiel*, in which orthodox textuality, not least the Word of God and words referring to God, are routed and displaced by its own anti-theologocentric, modernist, self-referential *ilinx* play. Which is what's arranged, more or less, on page 257. There a ranting run of invented terms appears to link diaspora, *deus*, and deity with de-inspiration, desperation, despair, disappearance, and expiration: 'in deesperation of deispiration at the diasporation of his diesparation'. This is immediately followed by the *Wake*'s most extraordinary *coup de théâtre*, its greatest vocable, all ninety-nine letters of it. Applause for this feat breaks out: 'Upploud!' And then God Himself is turned into a game and His day into a play, as Ellerton's famous evening hymn ('The day Thou gavest, Lord, is ended, The darkness falls at thy behest') is subverted into 'The play thou schouwburgst, Game, here endeth. The curtain drops by deep request'. And the applause is even louder – 'Uplouderamain!' – for a play which is simply 'play' (the proleptic echo of Beckett's play *Play* is of course most suggestive) written by 'Game'. This is the apparent evidence that plays nowadays are all only play, texts mere games, and all authored by one 'Game'. The text's next words are 'Gonn the gawds'. Gods – and rejoicing in them: *gauds* – are gone. The old texts, the old authors, especially the divine ones that sustained the secular ones, are disappeared.

More will be said in my final chapter about the theological nature of the exemplary game that this most exemplary of modernist texts is playing. Here we must consider the more formal aspects of what gives *Finnegans Wake* all this self-congratulatory pleasure and what is being imagined as prompting its readers to applaud as they stand on the touchline at the Christ's Church versus Bellial match or sit watching the curtain rising and falling on the *Theaterspiel*, or Play, by 'Game'.

What gave most pleasure in the non-Shandyesque, pre-modernist text was, as we've outlined earlier, the business of following the spool or clew into the labyrinth and out again. When, as it were, the real, or mimesis, world becomes what Joyce celebrated as the *reel world* – 'the reel world, the reel world, the reel world!' (64: 24): 'a reel of funnish ficts' (288: 8–9) – and Theseus's determined and terminal spool work gets transformed into the indeterminate, interminable enjoyment of the labyrinth for its own sake as a place of endless spiel, it's clear that we've gone beyond any ordinary principle of textual-reading pleasure into the place where Ariadne's clew has turned into the cotton-reel or bobbin that Freud's grandson famously toyed with, to the intense fascination of his grandfather and so many others, including Jacques Lacan and Jacques Derrida.

Curious Principles of Pleasure

The hero of Freud's 1920 text *Beyond the Pleasure Principle* is a tiny boy on the threshold of articulateness, throwing small objects about and hunting for them. Freud and the boy's mother believe the lad to be trying to say the German word *fort* (away, off, gone) as he throws his toys away and shouts 'o-o-o-o'. He's thought to be articulating, or nearly articulating, a disappearance game. 'I eventually realized that it was a game and that the only use he made of any of his toys was to play "gone" with them.' The nature of the repeated game is confirmed by what the boy does with his bobbin on a string.

The child had a wooden reel with a piece of string tied round it. It never occurred to him to pull it along the floor behind him, for instance, and play at its being a carriage. What he did was to hold the reel by the string and very skilfully throw it over the edge of his curtained cot, so that it disappeared into it, at the same time uttering his expressive 'o-o-o-o'. He then pulled the reel out of the cot again by the string and hailed its reappearance with a joyful 'da' ['there']. This, then, was the complete game – disappearance and return.

The curious economy of the game is what magnetizes the interpretative grandfather and mother. It's a drama in two acts – Act One, the arranged disappearance of the bobbin; Act Two, the bobbin's recovery – a drama, as it were, of entering the labyrinth, unreeling the clew, and then reappearing from the labyrinth and rolling up the clew again. And it's endlessly repeated: 'repeated untiringly as a game in itself'. The interpreting observer is confident that 'the greater pleasure was attached to the second act', but 'As a rule one only witnessed' the 'first act'. So disappearance, loss, absence, appear to be more important than return, gain, presence. At any rate, absence, the labyrinthine loss, is compulsively engaged with again and again. This is a game, a play, a source of pleasure, then, that seems arrestingly paradoxical, built as it is out of miming pain – the pain of loss, absence, disappearance.
Freud cast about for concrete analogues and explanations. The boy is variously suggested to be staging the disappearance of his mother from the room or the house, or his own disappearance (he makes the *fort* noise as he dodges his own image in a mirror), and, later, the disappearance of his father into the trenches of the First World War. Freud is frankly perplexed at a pleasure economy, a game, in which pain and not pleasure seems to predominate. Why repeat it if it's so hurtful? 'The child cannot possibly have felt his mother's departure as something agreeable or even indifferent. How then does his repetition of this distressing experience as a game fit in with the pleasure principle?' And Freud repeats the fact 'that the first act, that of departure, was staged as a game in itself and far more frequently than the episode in its entirety'. What's in it, runs the underlying question, for the boy? Why play painful games? What kind of play pushes you beyond the pleasure principle into repeated experiences of absence, losing your thread, clewlessness? And as the boy emerges as a magnificently potent version of that peculiar modernist hero, the failed detective, his grandfather's text turns into a dramatic example of the amazed early-modernist text – holding on to hopes of meaning ('His mother and [I] were agreed in thinking . . .'; 'One day I made an observation which confirmed my view'; 'The interpretation of the game then became obvious'), but lapsing into tentativeness, inconclusiveness, puzzle. Meaning is stuck in a maze of possibilities: 'It may perhaps be

said'; 'No certain decision can be reached'; 'still another interpretation may be attempted'; 'We are therefore left in doubt'; 'Nor shall we be helped in our hesitation'. And, astonishingly, the case, elaborated so lengthily, and one in which so much seems to be personally at stake for Freud and his family, is allowed to peter out in an offhand reference to adult 'artistic play', especially tragedies in which pleasure seems to be derived from the enactment of painful experiences.

> The consideration of these cases and situations . . . should be undertaken by some system of aesthetics with an economic approach to its subject matter. They are of no use for *our* purposes, since they presuppose the existence and dominance of the pleasure principle; they give no evidence of the operation of tendencies *beyond* the pleasure principle, that is, of tendencies more primitive than it and independent of it.[5]

The lack of usefulness in the announced but rejected connection between the *fort-da* boy and the texts of adult artistic play has not been felt by other influential proponents of modernist theory. The enigmatic endlessness and possible pointlessness or lack of purposiveness beyond itself of the play that so gripped Freud is exactly what defines play for Hans-Georg Gadamer when he proposes play as the clue to the ontology of the work of art. Play in Gadamer's sense, as in Freud's, is

> the to-and-fro movement which is not tied to any goal which would bring it to an end. This accords with the original meaning of the word spiel as 'dance', which is still found in many word forms (e.g. in Spielmann, jongleur). The movement which is play has no goal which brings it to an end; rather it renews itself in constant repetition. The movement backwards and forwards is obviously so central for the definition of a game that it is not important who or what performs this movement. The movement of play as such has, as it were, no substrate. It is the game that is played – it is irrelevant whether or not there is a subject who plays. The play is the performance of the movement as such.

Language, according to Gadamer, is play on this model. 'As far as language is concerned, the actual subject of play is obviously not the subjectivity of an individual who among other activities also plays, but instead the play itself.' Language is, in other words, about itself, for play is always self-representative. 'Play is really limited to representing itself. Thus its mode of being is self-representation . . . to ask what its life-function is and its biological purpose is is an inadequate approach. It is, pre-eminently, self-representation.'[6]

The connection between this particular playful view of language's self-

representing function and modernist or Shandyesque textuality is obvious,
and Wolfgang Iser's discussion of *Tristram Shandy* makes it clear in a crucial
passage where he calls that novel's narrator on his hobby-horse – at once
actor and director – a fool, a specially playful kind of player (though one, we
might add, whose speciality is to go beyond the pleasure principle as the
essence of tragedy's peculiar combination of jest and pain), and links him in
that dual role with the post-Saussurean notion of difference as the essence of
textuality.

> He hangs [an unfortunately literal translation of German *hängt*, I suspect; better,
> 'is suspended' or 'is poised'] between his self and his other self, and at best one
> could say that he 'is' the being between the two selves, but this, of course, is
> the being that defies definition. His intermediate position, however, is what
> enables him always to be other than what he is at any given moment. This
> makes him into the fool that he is forever calling himself, because the fool
> embodies 'difference' between the roles to be acted out. Difference, however,
> is not a place to linger in, but one which triggers a constant back-and-forth
> movement, which indeed is *the* basic play movement and features the fool, who
> keeps forever moving to and fro, as the player *par excellence*. (p. 93)

When D. H. Lawrence presented the rhetoric of his fiction as a verbal
back-and-forth movement, a repetitions 'pulsing, frictional to-and-fro', he
had in mind the kind of pleasurable bodily friction that eventuates in the
closure, however temporary, of sexual climax.[7] That was the essence of what
was still a pre-modernist game. By contrast, Iser (following Gadamer, whom
he doesn't, by the way, mention except in his bibliography) sees the repetitive
self-representative textual play of Shandyism as constituting its indeterminable and modernist, Joycean, Derridian openness. In playing like this, 'The
novel no longer imitates a world, but becomes an imaginary set where the
indefinable is acted out. However, as the indefinable eludes definition, freeplay
takes over and constantly undoes what appears to be a tangible result, thus
conveying the indeterminable as an experience.'[8]

For his part, when confronted with the play of *fort-da*, Jacques Lacan craves
the interpretative closure that eluded his master. He claims to have penetrated
'the true secret of the ludic'. Once again, the possible interpretations are so
numerous as to crowd out definiteness (the cotton-reel stands for the subject;
the subject as signifier; the subject in its earliest childish self-manifestation
'as an insistence that the story should always be the same, that its recounted
realization should be ritualized, that is to say, textually'; the subject in its
enigmatic otherness as the '*petit a*'; it stands too for the possibility that bits
of the male self can be cut away – that is, for the fear of castration). Above
all, though, Lacan ends up repeating his master's insistence on this game as

a play of absence, a ritual of denial, that's manifest even in the cry of *da* – that is, the claim of *Dasein* (presence, existence), the apparent phenomenology of presence. However one looks at it, there's going to be more *fort* than *da*, and this is offered as central to any view of the game or dance of representation. 'It is the repetition of the mother's departure as cause of a *Spaltung* [split, division, cleavage] in the subject – overcome by the alternating game, *fort-da*, which is a *here or there*, and whose aim, in its alternation, is simply that of being the *fort* of a *da*, and the *da* of a *fort*. It is aimed at what, essentially, is not there, *qua* represented – for it is the game itself that is the *Repräsentanz* [the representation dance] of the *Vorstellung* [performance, idea, representation].' What's being complexly elaborated here, in other words, is the Lacanian point that the situation of traumatic lack, or absence, is the very essence of selfhood and of textuality. 'What will become', he goes on to ask, 'of the *Vorstellung* when, once again, this *Repräsentanz* of the mother – in her outline made up of the brush-strokes and gouaches of desire – will be lacking?'[9] And this is a cry of radical despair that's even clearer later on in the pages of *The Four Fundamental Concepts of Psycho-Analysis* when Lacan returns to the *fort-da* game in order to stress its 'inaugural force' for the subject and to present it once again not as a drama in which a problematic of the self is mastered, but one in which a split or alienated self is ritualistically re-enacted.

> There can be no *fort* without *da* and, one might say, without *Dasein*. But, contrary to the whole tendency of the phenomenology of *Daseinanalyse*, there is no *Dasein* with the *fort*. . . . If the young subject can practise this game of *fort-da*, it is precisely because he does not practise it at all, for no subject can grasp this radical articulation. He practises it with the help of a small bobbin, that is to say, with the *objet a*. The function of the exercise with this object refers to an alienation, and not to some supposed mastery, which is difficult to imagine being increased in an endless repetition, whereas the endless repetition that is in question reveals the radical vacillation of the subject.[10]

It is, as ever, difficult to be confident that you've grasped precisely what Lacan is driving at, but the drift of his reading of Freud's *fort-da* story is clear enough. And in essence it runs in the same direction as Derrida's far more powerful and greatly extended reading of it in *La Carte postale*. In this immense and complex text 'the radical vacillation' that Lacan writes of, the uncertain and alienated to-ing and fro-ing around a *fort* that essentially denies a *da* or *Dasein*, is put with extraordinary vividness as expressing the nature of text and, in fact, the nature of the whole effort at communication by writing that has developed the modern postal system and of which the post, and in this case especially the humble postcard, are potent emblems. Not least impressive about *La Carte postale* is the way in which in its multivalent function as a powerful polemic for modernist textuality and a strong exemplum of that textuality, it not only sums up a huge repertoire of Derrida's own texts and tropes, but also draws out the meanings of so many other great modernist texts – *Beyond the Pleasure Principle*, of course, but also such central and subversive Post Office fictions as Poe's 'The Purloined Letter', James's *In the Cage*, *Finnegans Wake*, *Jacob's Room*, or even Thomas Pynchon's *The Crying of Lot 49* (1972).

Bobbin Along

La Carte postale de Socrate à Freud et au-delà (1980) is an extraordinary set of meditations on writing and selfhood set in a Western tradition of thought about these matters determined by the legacies of Plato and Judaeo-Christianity and, latterly, dominated by Freud and the Holocaust and, yes, Jacques Derrida himself. It was prompted by a postcard found on sale in Oxford's Bodleian Library (where copies are still on sale), a reproduction of Matthew Paris of St Albans's title-page for a thirteenth-century fortune-telling text, *The Prognostics of Socrates the King*. A man sits writing in a high-backed chair wearing a hat that looks somewhat like an unrolled, or used, condom. Behind him, apparently instructing or even admonishing, stands another man. They are Plato and Socrates. But their expected roles are reversed. Some scribal hand, who knows whether cannily or mistakenly, has labelled the writer 'Socrates' and the instructor 'plato' [sic]. It's this reversal that arrested Derrida, for here was deconstruction *avant la lettre*, seemingly ancient proof of his repeated case. An image from out of the lineage of the Western logocentric tradition, on sale in the foyer of one of the greatest monuments to that tradition, appearing out of the blue as a welcome supplement to a Balliol (cf. Joyce's Bellial) seminar on *la différance* (painful reminder of the embarrassment with which the Oxford Philosophy Sub-Faculty, Ryle, Ayer, Strawson, in the old home of J. L. Austin, had once greeted Derrida), the postcard could be read as a *latearly* endorsement of the Derridian problematic of writing at a reversible, troubled margin.

The logical, historical order and hierarchy Socrates–Plato is, on the postcard in question, troublingly but excitingly reversed. The inversion is to be taken, Derrida suggests, as standing for the inversions inscribed in all postcards and so, the argument goes on, in all postal communication, all writing. 'You don't know what's before or what's behind, what's here or there, near or far, who's Plato who Socrates, what's recto what verso. Nor which is more important, the image or the text, and (in the text) whether the message or the address or the description of the illustration matters most.' The chance encounter with the Bodley postcard that brought this home amounted to 'my post-card apocalypse'.[11]

Once launched on his analysis, of course, Derrida is typically and rhapsodically unstoppable. The first, *Envois* section of his book, a sequence of messages to a distant beloved allegedly written on a great pile of these same Bodley postcards during his pedagogical absences from home, is 273 pages long. That's some heap of postcards! The subsequent material, some of it reprinted from earlier appearances, mainly speculations on the legacy of Freud and refutation of Lacan's reading of Poe's 'The Purloined Letter', adds another 276 pages. What's of greatest importance here is the amount of attention devoted to *Beyond the Pleasure Principle* – a beyondness adverted to, of course, in the *au-delà* of the book's title. The chair-back (the *dossier*) standing between Plato and Socrates is assimilated to the curtain of the cot across which Freud's grandson threw his bobbin, a margin denoted by Derrida's great roster of tissues or textual stuffs that characterize what he calls the law of writing. He'll let his reader open that cot-curtain to reveal all the other curtains, 'mots et choses (rideaux, toiles, voiles, écrans, hymens, parapluies, etc.)', with which he has long been associated.[12] The *fort-da* boy is a transgressor of the limen, the hymen. The undecidable Derridian hymen is the border between the boy's *fort* and *da*, the presence and the absence that his reel of thread at once connects and disconnects, and so calls vividly into question.[13] The to-and-fro of the bobbin stands for the to-and-fro of the mails, of postcards, even of telephone calls (the unreeled thread is a telephone line – akin to the Joycean umbilical cords that telephonically link *Ulysses'* Dedalus to Edenville). But in the case of these postal or telephonic movements, chronology and hierarchy and the logical order of addressers and addressees are all back to front, like the relation of Plato to Socrates on the postcard. In this text Socrates can write to Plato, can pick up the phone and say 'Hold on, I'll give you Freud or Heidegger'. It's a scene of communication that's offered as the latest version, disruptive and transgressive, of the *Symposium*.[14]

What's being called into question, of course, is the classic Jakobsonian speech-act model of communication in which a particular addresser sends an encoded but decipherable message to a particular addressee. The letter, the postcard, the postal system, are the clearest expressions of practical faith in this classic model. They are the emblems, as Gregory Ulmer points out in the sharpest reading of *La Carte postale* I've come across, of logocentrism's faith in communication, in the knowability of texts and in the identity, the selfhood, of writers. 'The feature that makes the letter exemplary of the logocentric era (a synonym for "postal era") is that it is addressed and signed, directed or destined ("destinaire" = addressee). We take for granted the postal institution . . . The entire history of the postal *tekchné* rivets "destination" (and

destiny, *Geschick*) to identity. "To arrive ["arriver" – to succeed, to happen]
is for a subject to attain ["arriver"] my self".' 'Identity', Ulmer goes on,
following Derrida most closely, 'in all its aspects (truth and being) is the
ideology of the postal principle.'[15] As P. D. Juhl rather plaintively points
out, what's precisely at issue in the deconstructionist game-theory of text is
the classic speech-act model: 'Now if this theory of the text is even roughly
correct, it is clear that anything like a speech act model of literary interpretation
cannot be right. Conversely, if there is such a thing as understanding a text
and if that is essentially like understanding a person's speech act and hence
necessarily involves reference to the speaker's intentions, then not much
remains' of the deconstructionist game-plan.[16] And the speech-act model
sustains not only the practice of letter-writing, but also the kind of fiction
that regarded the epistolary mode as a fundamental model of narrative. The
traditional novel, not least the epistolary novel – and it's no accident hereabouts
that Trollope invented the street letter-box – gets vividly called into question
in and around Derrida's unravelling of the postcard business.

Starting with his Plato–Socrates card, Derrida insists that postcards are
marginal sites of doubtful readability. They look open to all comers, but in
practice they are other, cryptic, labyrinthine. As bobbins – and he's thinking
of the *fort-da* boy, but also of all texts that appear to offer clues and act as
clews, everything that passes along telephone lines and that's on film (French
bobine is also a reel of film) – postcards are locked into the differential system
which is for him the essence of a 'postal code', a Postal Principle, that
hinders, slows down, impedes, the arrival of messages, preferring to keep
them tauntingly in circulation.[17] So that epistles, like postcards, are seen as
poised between sender and receiver, marooned at a margin of (un)readability:
'ni lisibles ni illisibles, ouvertes et radicalement inintelligibles'.[18]

It's the fate of epistolary missives to be poised between *fort* and *da*, with
the emphasis, as ever, on *fort*. In fact the dead-letter office, the knacker's yard
of the epistolary, is destined to be, as likely or not, their destination. For
Derrida it's no accident that in the Bodleian postcard Socrates is crowned by
what looks to him like a condom and that the letter *a* in the name inscribed
over his head (*le a*: a nudge and a wink towards Lacan's *petit a*) 'mimes' this
condom shape. For he detects a strongly prophylactic *préservatif* (French word
for condom) situation in all postcards – a case brought home by the immediate conjunction of words rhyming in *p*: Plato, *prophylactique, préservatif* (*le
petit p* of Plato's name on the card is far more relevant here than any *petit a*).[19]
But this is the fate of all missives headed for the Post Office's dead-letter
morgues, or destroyed in holocausts and apocalypses such as Hitler's or the
private one Derrida describes himself as arranging. This is a textual occlusion
or withholding, a going into the dark, that's offered as endemic to all texts

– all essentially condomized, locked up, encrypted, preserved. Much play is made of the etymological link between prophylactics and phylacteries, the parchment rolls or little boxes containing portions of Scripture that orthodox Jews were – and are – compelled ceremonially to tie about their wrists and foreheads and attach to the hems of their garments and their door-posts. 'You will understand why I immediately jumped when I read this definition in my dictionary: "*phulaktèrion . . .* lieu pour garder, *poste*, corps de garde . . . *préservatif . . .* talisman, amulette . . . chez les Juifs, *pancarte* qu'on portait suspendue au cou et où étaient inscrits des versets de la loi mosaïque . . ."'[20]

The writing situation is, as Derrida says, disconcertingly, contradictorily, legalistic. 'La loi et la police ne sont pas loin.' Meaning is confined, imprisoned, guarded, put under surveillance by laws – the Law of Moses, the laws of states and institutions, or (even) of textuality, whose laws, the law of genre for example, Derrida diligently expounds.[21] Dictators, and philosophers, order books and letters to be burned. They can and do arrange textual holocausts. *Une bobine* happens to be a slang word for face, a mug. Police photographers take mug-shots of criminals. The mug-shot incriminates. The Bodley postcard is a sort of mug-shot of Plato and Socrates – and somebody in the cop-shop of textual transmitters seems to have mixed up their names.[22] Police stations, cop-shops, are in French 'postes de police'.[23] Police posts and post offices are thus worrying linguistic neighbours. In Derrida's explication, the bobbin of Freud's grandson becomes a firing-squad (to pull, *tirer*, on a thread is in French, as in English, the same word as to pull, *tirer*, on a trigger): 'Et la bobine du petit, c'est un peloton d'éxécution. Quand quelqu'un donne l'ordre de tirer, et donner l'ordre c'est déjà tirer, on y passe tous'.[24]

La Carte postale includes a very serious reading of *Beyond the Pleasure Principle* as being about the play of Freud's personal and institutional authority within the psychoanalytic movement. Traditional *bobinarité*, as Derrida calls it, is dictator stuff, an authoritarian, patriarchal, institutional, legalistic (and psychoanalytical) business of policing.[25] *La littérature epistolaire* is also *la littérature policière*.[26] And, after all, the genre that developed so dramatically into epistolary form very quickly came to know itself, and most potently, as the *roman policier*. And it is the old assumption – the detective-story Theseus–Ariadne policeman-reader faith – that clews are readable, and that the post-card, the letter, the text-as-letter, are translucent arrangements for clued-up triumphings over the labyrinth, which Derrida's play with the postcard as bobbin, and his offering of the postcard = bobbin model of textual play, are out to challenge. The old kind of *bobinarité* won't do because it's oppressive: 'donner à la police juste de quoi la semer, et avec elle tous et toutes les postes, les institutions, les ordinateurs, les pouvoirs, les dupin [the fictional

detectives, the Dupins] et toute leur bobinarité (*fort/da*), les Etats, voilà ce
que je suppute, ou compute, ce que je trie pour défier tous les tris [that's
what I reckon on, what I pull from the bag in order to defy everything that
goes on in sorting-offices]'.[27]

And so, on this view, Freud, anxious to maintain his authority in the
movement he founded, and Lacan, anxious to police readings of Freudian
texts and of Poe's 'Purloined Letter', are playing an interpretative game
flawed by the old policing urges. 'Une lettre arrive toujours à destination,'
concludes Lacan's Poe seminar. The logic of the postcard is rather, Derrida
ripostes, that 'une lettre peut toujours ne pas arriver à destination' (and he
points out that Lacan's confidence is achieved in a repeated distortion of the
word *dessein* in Poe's text to *destin*).[28] Derrida steadfastly proposes an alternative to what he argues is the persistent old-fashioned *bobinarité* even of Freud
and Lacan – or rather, the infection of their sceptical, negative reading of the
fort-da boy by old-fashioned models of communication. (Once again, Derrida
is trying to out-modernize his modernist forebears, just as he did with
Saussure.) And this alternative, one that *La Carte postale* declares Derrida to
have been offering to the world all along, is the ultra-modernist, Shandyan,
Joycean, classic Freudian version of the bobbin play. It is the *Theaterspiel* in
which texts are truly enigmatic word-games, elusive world-puzzles that keep
the possibility of solution always in play but nonetheless hold it persistently
at bay. In other words (to take key tropes from *La Carte postale*, which are
also key tropes in the whole modernist or, if you prefer, postmodernist enterprise), the textual business here becomes a game in which the clew, reel,
bobbin, is a *ficelle*. Which is to say, a set of *ruses*, a tricky, deceitful, deceptive
affair of the text as *rebus*.

Les Ficelles du Metier

The word *ficelle* comes inscribed in Derrida's French translation of Freud's
Beyond the Pleasure Principle, which Derrida both carefully annotates *en courant*,
in order to make sure we spot the connections between his own lexicon and
Freud's, and which he also encodes, once again, within the so-called 'postal
code' that he is seeking to elaborate:

> L'enfant pour l'envoyer [i.e. to send the bobine or epistolary missive] ne
> manquait pas d'*adresse*.
>   C'est la suite. [And here follows Derrida's translation of a key Freudian
> passage.] 'Un jour je fis alors l'observation qui confirma mon interprétation.
> L'enfant avait une bobine en bois (*Holzspule*) qui avait une ficelle (*Bindfaden*)

enroulée autour d'elle. L'idée ne lui était jamais venue de traîner par exemple cette bobine sur le sol derrière lui, donc de jouer avec elle à la voiture, mais il jetait la bobine tenue au fil avec une grande adresse (*Geschick*) par-dessus le bord de son petit lit entouré d'un rideau (ou d'un voile, *verhängten Bettchens*), de telle sorte qu'elle y disparaissait, ce sur quoi il prononçait son o-o-o-o significatif (*Bedeutungsvolles*) et retirait alors la bobine tenue au fil hors du lit, mais saluait son apparition cette fois d'un joyeux "*Da*". Tel était donc le jeu complet (*komplette Spiel*), disparition et réapparition (*Verschwinden und Wiederkommen*).'

The affair was, of course, by no means *complet*, Derrida is at pains to point out, neither as game nor as a piece of observation or interpreting. 'Si la complétude était évidente at assurée, Freud y insisterait-il, la ferait-il remarquer comme s'il fallait vite fermer, clore, encadrer? On soupçonne d'autant plus l'incomplétude (dans l'objet ou dans sa description).' In the first place, the game went on and on: 'La scène est celle d'une supplémentation interminable répétée.' In the second, 'Il y a comme un axiome d'incomplétude dans la structure de la scène d'écriture.' It's another in Derrida's magisterial sequence of 'il y a' pronouncements: 'There is a sort of axiom of incompleteness, or lack of fullness or fulfilment, in the very structure of the scene of writing.'[29] Derrida's lengthy account of the postal system is there to prove it; and the word *ficelle* shows that analysis to be already embedded (like other key Derridian concepts, such as *voile*), as it were genetically, in the Freudian text.

Une ficelle is a thread, a cord, a piece of string, what's rolled up in clews. But it is also a trick, especially a trick performed onstage. As well, it's trickster, a cheat, and the tricky or trickish. The French lexicon elaborates the potential of *ficelle* as a term of art, performance, and crime: *tenir la ficelle*, literally 'to hold on to the string' like Freud's grandson, is 'to manage puppets'; *montrer la ficelle*, to betray the secret; *on voit la ficelle*, you can spot the game, the trick; *il connaît toutes les ficelles*, he's up to every dodge; *il connaît toutes les ficelles du métier*, he knows all the tricks of the trade.

The referee, then, in this game its presiding deity and tutelary genius, is the con-artist Hermes, winged god of interpreters, but also the ancient patron of tricksters, rogues, thieves (*voleur*: flyer and thief), and so the acclaimed modern guardian of the hermetic, difficult text. The text as postcard, an affair of ruse and counterfeit,[30] drags or limps along, even as it appears to speed towards its destined addressee and meaning: 'tout y est merveilleusement *hermétique*, c'est à dire postal et *traînant* – souterrainement ferroviaire, mais aussi boiteux, traînant la patte: il ne nous dit RIEN, ne fait pas un pas qu'il ne retire au pas suivant' (everything about it is marvellously hermetic, that is to say postal, on the ball, and at the same time dragging, reluctant – making its way subversively, in a kind of undercover operation, at once speeding along by rail but also wobbling on its pins, dragging its feet: not that it says NOTHING to us, rather it never takes one step forwards without immediately taking a step backwards – or, utters a negative, a *pas*, that it doesn't instantly withdraw). Even as he flies, Derrida's Hermes limps. In fact he's Hermes as Wrestling Jacob (of whom more later), or Hermes locked into the paralysis of Joyce's Dublin, the Daedalian stasis of the hero of *A Portrait of the Artist as a Young Man* (*stasis*, the condition of to-and-fro argument or fighting, an animated deadlock pronounced by the commonest Greek word for the irresoluble clash of argument in the assemblies of argumentative citizens). 'Tu diras qu'Hermès ne boitait pas, il avait des ailes au pied, oui, oui, mais ce n'est pas contradictoire, boiter ne l'empêche pas de courir et de voler, le vieux. Rien ne marche, mais tout va très vite, absolument vite, dans cette paralyse' (You will say that Hermes did not limp, he had wings on his feet, yes, yes, but this is not contradictory, because his limping does not prevent the old boy from running and flying. Nothing makes progress here (nothing works) but everything travels very fast, absolutely fast, in this state of paralysis).[31]

And this limping aspect of the postal revision of the *fort-da* game, or vision of the writing business as the essence of the *fort-da* frustration, is also prompted by the Freudian text. Derrida is very taken by the fact that *Beyond the Pleasure Principle* ends with two lines from the German version by Rückert of one of the *Maqâmât* of the Arab writer al-Hariri (lines that Freud himself was obviously much drawn to: he also quoted them in a letter to Fliess, 20 October 1895):

> Was man nicht erfliegen kann, müss man erhinken
>
> . . .
>
> Die Schrift sagt, es ist keine Sunden zu hinken.

What you can't attain by flying, you must reach by limping. . . The Scripture says it is no sin to limp.

Bilderrätsel

But which Scripture says that? In the reading of Freud and Derrida, all Scripture, all script, apparently. The poet's message from Islamic Scripture (like the word for the Koranic Scripture), when translated into German uses the common word *Schrift*, writing, which is also the Jewish and Christian word for Scripture. So a word from the Islamic world comes disguised as a Judaeo-Christian Biblical message, which is also a message about writing in general. And Derrida's text inevitably mimics the process: German *Schrift* becomes *Écriture*, the standard French word for Scripture, the Biblical Writings, that French criticism also uses to stand for all writing. So here text is solemnly piled upon text, sacred text, poetic text, text from three great bookish traditions, Islamic, Judaic, Christian, to endorse the retarded, hermetic limp that Derrida alleges characterizes all postal stuff. And the text of Freud's *Beyond the Pleasure Principle* is the pivot. It's his book that 'se ferme en boitant par une référence poétique au boitement. Citation de l'Ecriture citée par l'écriture d'un poète ("Ce qu'on ne peut gagner [ou atteindre] en volant, il faut le gagner en boitant . . . L'Ecriture dit que boiter n'est pas un péché").'[32]

But then the Freudian text, and the Freudian view of text, in particular of the fundamental dream-text, are continually pivotal hereabouts. When Derrida presents himself as a man who produces rebuses (on a bathroom mirror in lipstick, for instance), who presides over text and the history of philosophy as the master reader of their rebus condition, who presents the Bodley postcard as a rebus (which he, and, as a matter of fact, he alone, can and will interpret), he is self-consciously mindful that it is as rebus that Freud offered the deterring dream-text, and so, in effect, all texts.[33] Derrida's postcard story bolts firmly, then, onto Freud's story of the dream-text as a *Bilderrätsel*, or picture-puzzle, which must be treated as a rebus, a pictorial device of images and letters of the alphabet or words, whose meaning isn't going to be a simple matter of transcribing a sequence of picture-signs into their seemingly obvious equivalent in a sequence of word-signs. A commonsensically obvious reading of such a puzzling text would be, says Freud, a syntactical nonsense. Sorting out the true grammar of the dream-as-rebus depends on unobvious connections, on accepting that dreams present riddles for really deft analytical cracksmen to penetrate:

> The dream-content is presented as it were in picture-writing whose signs have to be translated one by one into the language of the dream-thoughts. You would clearly be led into error if you wanted to read these signs according to their mere pictorial value instead of according to their signifying relationship. I have a kind of picture-riddle [*Bilderrätsel*] (a rebus) in front of me: a house, on whose roof a boat is visible, then a single letter of the alphabet, then a figure running, whose head has been apostrophized away. I could now descend to criticism and declare that this combination and the parts that comprise it were crazy nonsense. A boat does not belong to the roof of a house, and a person without a head cannot run; what's more, the person is bigger than the house, and if the whole thing is supposed to represent a landscape, then the individual letters of the alphabet don't fit in because you don't come across them out in the fields. Clearly the correct critical judgement only yields itself if I raise no such objections against the whole ensemble and its individual

components, but rather take the trouble to replace each image by a syllable or a word that may be represented by that image according to some referential aspect or another. The words which find themselves brought together in this manner are no longer senseless but could even yield the most beautiful and significant of poetic statements. Now the dream is just such a picture-riddle, and our predecessors in the province of the interpretation of dreams have committed the error of criticizing the rebus as if it were a straightforward pictorial composition. As such it seemed to them meaningless and of no value.[34]

Clearly – even though Freud talks about incorrect critical judgements and arriving at beautiful and significant poetic statements – he wishes to play up the riddling, enigmatic features of the dream-work. It's not surprising that he should also have talked about dark navel-places in the dream-text-as-rebus that resist even the critical analysis he approves of as correct. And as we've seen, interpretation and explanation are plunged into a kind of interpretative endlessness when they try to figure out and provide figures for the dream-work in and about the abysm of the dark navel. There, playing with the rebus proves an endless game, in effect the postmodernist game of the apparently endless play of signifiers. On this plan, the dream, the text in effect, turns into a stage for the Joker. At least for the Joker as explicated by Michel Serres.

The Cow is a Joker

Serres's Joker erupts into his extraordinary book *The Parasite* (1982 in English; 1980 in French) as the essence of Serres's reading of a great Biblical story of the interpretation of a dream, namely Joseph's reading in Genesis of Pharoah's dream of the fat and lean cows and the thin and the full ears of corn, which followed his success in reading the dreams of the king's chief baker and butler in prison – a sequence of events which itself curiously follows the oddly interpolated story of the rape of Tamar in Genesis 38. Serres theorizes the Joker as a character or other element in a story that upsets a seemly narrative or textual procession, disrupts an otherwise serenely flowing series of elements, causing bifurcations and thus sparking multiple meanings or interpretative confusions in what started out as an apparently simple sequence. This Joker is an identity- or meaning-shifter, insisting that *a* is not after all *a* but is really *b* or *c* or *d*. In certain card-games the joker in the pack has this power of becoming any other card. When the text, whether of the dream or of the interpretation of a dream, admits a joker, or admits itself as Joker, it starts going crazy ('wild, as they say in English'), becomes Saturnalian, turns the text into *bricolage*; in other words, goes

Freudian, becomes differentialist, celebrates its condition as rebus. The joker, Serres argues, 'has no value so as to have every value. It has no identity, but its identity, its unique character, its difference, as they say, is to be indifferently, this or that unit of a given set. The joker is king or jack, ace or seven or deuce. Joseph is a joker; Tamar, queen, just, despised, whore, is also a joker. *A* is *b*, *c*, *d*, etc. Fuzzy.' The key to the anti-method, *bricolage*-method, of the dream-text, whether interpreted by Freud or by Joseph, is the joker: 'The only describable difference between a method and *bricolage* is the joker. The principle of *bricolage* is to make something by means of something else, a mast with a matchstick, a chicken wing with tissue meant for the thigh, and so forth. Just as the most general model of method is game, the good model for what is deceptively called *bricolage* is the joker.' And the joker, once let loose, tends to multiply, and this proliferation can become insolubly labyrinthine. The Joker text is in some danger of becoming too labyrinthine, too polyvalent, for interpretation. Start stacking up jokers, and their potential meanings will go everywhere and stop nowhere. Thus the Freudian dream-text can become a hermetic and hermeneutic nightmare of saturation where 'polysemy overtakes the space with multivalence and equivocity' and meaning is driven to the dream-limit, 'completely filled with polyvalence'.

> This is something else. I dreamt of a sheaf of wheat, of the sun, and of eleven stars. This sheaf is not a sheaf, yet it remains a sheaf, and you are the sheaf. The moon is your mother; the stars are your brothers. The wheat bends like a moon; the sun places its forehead on the earth, in the wheat field. This is something else. I am a star and a sheaf of wheat; you are a sheaf and the sun; in the beginning is hatred.
> This is again something else. You dreamt of a vinestock with three branches, and of three baskets of cakes on your head. And I say to the bailiff and to the butler: the baskets are days, the cakes are your flesh and body, the branches are days; the days are branches and they are baskets. Here is the meaning: this is something else. In the middle, servitude, life, and death.
> This is yet something else. Pharaoh dreamt of cows and wheat; the thin cows ate the fat cows; the thin and wind-burnt wheat covered wheat that was ripe and in abundance. I shall tell him the meaning; this is yet something else. The cows are years; the wheat sheaves are years; time is a cow; it is divided into clusters of grain, just as it was divided into branches or baskets. If the sheaf were a sheaf, if the star were a star and the cow a cow, there would have been no meaning, no key, no explanation, no interpreter. No rhyme or reason. This has to be something else. Finally a logic of light; we will finally eat to stop our hunger. We shall send caravans of grain and fruit toward the Promised Land.
> All these chains of words abound with jokers. Given some series whose links are well identified, where there is a law, an explicit one. The same is diffused

the length of the differences, constituting the axis, be it rigid or supple. Suddenly, a joker. Can I read it? Certainly. It is enough to recognize the upstream law and the downstream laws. The joker, in the position of bifurcation, makes it possible by the confluence of values that it insures. It is both what has been said and what will be said. It is bi-, tri-, or poly-valent, according to the complexity of the connection. The ramification of the network depends on the number of jokers. But I suspect that there is a limit for this number. When there are too many, we are lost as if in a labyrinth. What would a series be like where there were only jokers? What could be said of it?

Dream logic seems to me to be of this nature. Multivalent because of jokers. Connections *ad libitum*. Time is the cow; time is the sheaf; time is the branch and the basket. The cow is a sheaf; this is something else. The cow is a joker; the basket, the sheaf, other jokers. Beyond a certain density, or a certain number of multivalent elements, the series cannot be known.[35]

The dream-place where meaning reaches its impossible limits – it also represents, of course, a dream of, or wish for, text at the limit – is clearly no joke. Reminders of the Saturnalian, carnivalesque aspect of the rebus text keep being offered to us by its exponents. And indeed there is ground for thinking that the rebus is at root carnivalesque. It's been suggested that the use of the word *rebus* for puzzle arises in medieval Carnival tracts put about by Rabelaisian priests.[36] But, it must be asked, is being locked in the semic labyrinth really fun? Are the relentless polysemic punning ploys of an early Shakespeare comedy, for instance, or, for that matter of *Finnegans Wake*, actually 'patpun fun for all?' For the author maybe, showing off his ingenuity; but what about the reader? Doesn't the experience of being pushed up to and even beyond the limit in *Finnegans Wake* often feel indeed like 'A nastilow disigraible game'? (301: 13 and n. 4). Was the *fort-da* game not rather obsessive and dismaying, a very curious kind of pleasure-seeking, as grandfather Freud kept noticing? Is not all that curious pleasure indeed at some kind of limit? Shouldn't we allow Derrida's talk of police surveillance and firing-squads to colour our appreciation of the endlessly recursive circulation game of the postcards? Aren't we to tremble with this scrutineer of the curtained Torah, this Jewish custodian of the writings, one in a long line of wearers of the phylactery, as he offers himself, as not just another little boy playing the *fort-da* game but also as one who arranges and is the victim of holocausts?[37] (And isn't it hard hereabouts not to be reminded again of the posthumously revealed link between Paul de Man's oppressive resistance to closure of meaning and the guilty wartime secrets hermetically embedded in his own career as Fascist collaborator in wartime Belgium?) Mustn't we keep reminding ourselves of the awfulness of what passed between Joseph and his brothers, of the terrible nature of Tamar's forced sexual experiences, of the direct connection between Pharaoh's dream, famine in Egypt, and, as Serres argues, the whole business of money circulation, even if Joseph and Tamar and their stories and their stories' dream-texts are all examples of the Joker at work? What's being enacted in *Tristram Shandy* is indeed Wolfgang Iser's endless play, a great Ring Cycle of textual self-representation; but it's also a painful affair of damaged penises, groin wounds too awful to be speakable, hurt lives, all on a small stage on which a mimic sequence of sensationally bloody battle scenes is being repeated. Carnivalesque on these models is no carnival. But then, neither was Carnival. Having dog shit poured on you by drunken clerics or yobboes dressed as clergymen during some mock Easter ritual was doubtless as little amusing as the Rabelaisian wheeze, so celebrated by Mikhail Bakhtin as the fullness of the carnivalesque, for Pantagruel to revenge himself on the Woman of Paris by spraying her clothes with the essence of dismembered pudenda of bitches in heat so that the dogs of Paris will pursue her home, pissing on her as she goes, and turning her house into an island lapped by a great lake of urine.[38]

The gamey postmodernist story of the text as word-puzzle is not a new one. What's new about it is its intense specialization – the allegation that this is all a text is – and a specialization supported by an intense lack of proportion, precisely a shortage of moral and political perspective, which includes blindness as to the game's mixed blessing when considered as a bundle of fun. Older texts are well aware – as *Tristram Shandy* and the Book of Genesis both are – of the mixed nature of this blessing, and make a business precisely of dramatizing that mixture.

The Reader's Friend

Henry James makes much of the 'fun' involved in deploying his so-called *ficelles*, that is, the women characters – Maria Gostrey of *The Ambassadors* in particular, but also Henrietta Stackpole of *Portrait of A Lady* – whom he provides as modern versions of Ariadne, people offering 'threads' to guide other characters and the reader through the interpretative maze, at least as far as they're ever going to be guided in James's dawningly modernistic texts. Again and again, in his New York edition's Preface to *The Ambassadors* and in the long Project of *The Ambassadors* that he wrote for Harper his publisher, James returns to Maria Gostrey in her function as *ficelle*, as thread and provider of threads. And he keeps striking the note of amusement: his own, his characters', the reader's, and the critic's. Strether is on 'holiday', is going in for ' "amusement" ' (James's own inverted commas), is trying to 'lounge'. It's time he went in for some 'free play' [*sic*] after a lifetime of puritanism and work.[39] Having devised the part of Maria Gostrey as *ficelle* or hermeneutical helper for Strether and for us, James is evidently very chuffed at his own method ('quite incalculable but none the less clear sources of enjoyment for the infatuated artist') and pleased to be granting us the joy of working with the *ficelle* ('how many copious springs of our never-to-be-slighted "fun" for the reader and critic susceptible of contagion').[40]

But the amusement for James consists in the practice of the sort of masterful deceptions that the label *ficelle* always announces. And these are doubly dubious delights, because *ficelle*-tricksters delight not only in deception but also in being able to hide the deceptiveness. 'Half the dramatist's art, as we well know . . . is in the use of *ficelles*; by which I mean in a deep dissimulation of his dependence on them.' 'The *"ficelle"* character of the subordinate party is as artfully dissimulated, throughout, as may be. . . .' There's ecstasy in the trickery: 'delightful dissimulation . . . ecstasies of method'.[41]

Miss Gostrey is offered as 'the reader's friend . . . in consequence of dispositions that make him so eminently require one; and she acts in that capacity, and *really* in that capacity alone, with exemplary devotion, from beginning to end of the book. She is an enrolled, a direct, aid to lucidity; she is in fine, to tear off her mask, the most unmitigated and abandoned of *ficelles*.'[42] The reader's friend, the *ficelle* or thread or clew that James places in the readerly hand, will, with apparent devotion, guide him or her to the destination of ultimate lucidity and elucidation. What's more, James's description professes the same elucidatory zeal: just as Miss Gostrey will (as the description in the Project has it) provide fullness of information, act as 'a little palpable gold thread that plays through all the pattern', help to trace the figures in this novel's particularly complicated carpet, 'meet a want', elicit 'for us luminously the conditions in which Strether is involved', so James's accounts of her will be a 'tearing off' of her 'mask'. Her function is elucidated for us in James's arrestingly to-ing and fro-ing critical commentary – proleptic in the Project, retrospective in the belated Preface. But to tear the mask off a *ficelle* is to announce that a mask is still in place; for the art of the *ficelle*, as James prides himself, is the art of trick, ruse, dissimulation. And so his paragraphs describing Miss Gostrey turn out to offer a dauntingly tricky mixture of lucidity and darkness, revelation and concealment, copiousness and emptiness, overtness and covertness, definiteness and indefiniteness. In this they are, of course, models of *The Ambassadors*, representative of all the great later James texts, and so also typical of modernism's larger rusing. With supreme aptness, the workings of the *ficelle* character are analysed in paradoxical, self-undoing terms that embody in miniature the larger workings of the text as *ficelle*, of which Miss Gostrey – character as *ficelle* – is just one rusing element:

availing myself of the opportunity given me by this edition for some prefatory remarks on [*The Ambassadors*], I had mainly to make on its behalf the point of its scenic consistency. It disguises that virtue, in the oddest way in the world, by just *looking*, as we turn its pages, as little scenic as possible; but it sharply divides itself, just as the composition before us does, into the parts that prepare, that tend in fact to over-prepare, for scenes, and the parts, or other-wise into the scenes, that justify and crown the preparation. It may definitely be said, I think, that everything in it that is not scene (not, I of course mean, complete and functional scene, treating *all* the submitted matter, as by logical start, logical turn, and logical finish) is discriminated preparation, is the fusion and synthesis of picture. These alternations propose themselves all recogniseably [sic], I think, from an early stage, as the very form and figure of 'The Ambassadors'; so that, to repeat, such an agent as Miss Gostrey, pre-engaged at a high salary, but waits in the draughty wing with her shawl and her smelling-salts. Her function speaks at once for itself, and by the time she has dined with Strether in London and gone to a play with him her interven-tion as a *ficelle* is, I hold, expertly justified. Thanks to it we have treated scenically, and scenically alone, the whole lumpish question of Strether's 'past,' which has seen us more happily on the way than anything else could have done; we have strained to a high lucidity and vivacity (or at least we hope we have) certain indispensable facts; we have seen our two or three immediate friends all conveniently and profitably in 'action'; to say nothing of our begin-ning to descry others, of a remoter intensity, getting into motion, even if a bit vaguely as yet, for our further enrichment. Let my first point be here that the scene in question, that in which the whole situation at Woollett and the complex forces that have propelled my hero to where this lively extractor of his value and distiller of his essence awaits him, is normal and entire, is really an excellent *standard* scene; copious, comprehensive, and accordingly never short, but with its office as definite as that of the hammer on the gong of the clock, the office of expressing *all that is in* the hour.[43]

It's typical of this small and very dynamic critical text ('the composition before us') that it should stress lucidity, copiousness, and fullness of expression in relation to a scene which nowhere, neither in the Project, nor the novel, nor the Preface, actually yields up 'the whole situation at Woollett'. For all the Project's declaration that the 'distinctly vulgar article of domestic use' manufactured at Woollett, the source of all the Newsome–Strether cash, would be 'duly specified', it never was.[44] That thread, like so many others, led nowhere specific. But that's the essence of *ficelles* – they're false trails, misleading impressions, takings-hold of threads that turn out to be mistakings.
Small wonder, then, that mistaking is a keynote in *The Ambassadors'* Preface, and that the probability of mistaking always frames the business of taking, possessing, having – of experience, impressions, guiding threads,

conclusions – that Strether and most other Jamesian characters and their
readers are embarked on. The 'whole case' of the novel, James informs us,
is in Strether's 'irrepressible outbreak' to Little Bilham in a moment of
'candour':

> 'Live all you can; it's mistake not to. It doesn't so much matter what you do
> in particular so long as you have your life. If you haven't had that what *have*
> you had? I'm too old – too old at any rate for what I see. What one loses one
> loses; make no mistake about that. Still, we have the illusion of freedom;
> therefore don't, like me to-day, be without the memory of that illusion. I was
> either, at the right time, too stupid or too intelligent to have it, and now I'm
> a case of reaction against the mistake. Do what you like as long as you don't
> make it. For it *was* a mistake. Live, live!' Such is the gist of Strether's appeal
> to the impressed youth, whom he likes . . . the word 'mistake' occurs several
> times, it will be seen, in the course of his remarks – which gives the measure
> of the signal warning he feels attached to his case. He has accordingly missed
> too much.[45]

James urged one of his readers, Millicent Duchess of Sutherland, to 'Take
. . . the *Ambassadors* very easily and gently', five pages a day, but above all to
hang on to *'the thread'*: *'don't break the thread.* The thread is really stretched
quite scientifically tight. Keep along with it step by step – and then the full
charm will come out.'[46] But the trouble is that when the thread is a *ficelle*,
fullness of knowledge is what might not come out. Readers are commonly
placed in the position of the governess in *The Turn of the Screw*, just one more
of James's stories where all kinds of skewed possession – in this case epistemological, personal, demoniac – are in play. 'I seized his . . . supposition. . . .
I was so determined to have all my proof . . . "What does he matter now, my
own? . . . *I* have you . . . but he has lost you forever!"' But a terrible mistaking accompanies all this claimed seizing and possessing. The *ficelle* has led
to terrible loss in the alleged gain:

> With the stroke of the loss I was so proud of he uttered the cry of a creature
> hurled over an abyss, and the grasp with which I recovered him might have
> been that of catching him in his fall. I caught him, yes, I held him – it may
> be imagined with what a passion; but at the end of a minute I began to feel
> what it truly was that I held. We were alone with the quiet day, and his little
> heart, dispossessed, had stopped.

And the charm of this farrago of taking and mistaking for the novelist is
precisely the trickster's pleasure in the wielding of his *ficelle*-text, his having
led his characters on, as the saying goes, and in their having in turn led us
on: 'Exquisite . . . the mere interest and amusement of such at once "creative"

and critical questions as how and where and why to make Miss Gostrey's false connection carry itself, under a due high polish, as a real one.'[47]

The magician is, of course, likely to feel pleasure if he believes himself in control of his tricks. And James's delight in his concoction and manipulation of *ficelle*-characters and of the fiction as *ficelle* is no doubt akin to Freud's or Derrida's delight in rebuses whose interpretations they think of themselves as mastering ('je te dépêche encore . . . plato et Socrates', writes Derrida to his correspondent female in *La Carte postale*, 'avec un rébus pour toi au-dessus du doigt levé. Comme je suis sûr que tu ne trouveras pas, je ne te l'expliquerai, à mon retour, qu'à une condition'; 'là, tu ne comprends pas, faute d'avoir lu le rébus'; and so on[48]). For Strether, stuck with a slow interpretative quest through all the tempting Parisian otherness on his way to the startling realization about his friend Chad's adulterous relationship with Madame de Vionnet and to questions about puritanical American values, fun doesn't seem much in the question. As for the reader applying a patient interpretative squeeze as she trudges along in Strether's footsteps, in the labyrinthine ways of this text, just trying to keep up with Strether is hard work, sweat-of-the-brow, post-lapsarian labour. With threads like these, who needs enemies? In fact, James's repeated suggestion in the Preface to *The Ambassadors* that for Strether, and for us, playing ball or *ficelle* in this Jamesian text of a Parisian encounter is more like a life sentence than a bundle of fun, does seem closer to the mark. Strether has, the Preface reports, a 'lifelong trick of intense reflexion'. He is 'encaged and provided for as "The Ambassadors" encages and provides'. His, and our, threading 'through winding passages, through alternations of darkness and light very much *in* Paris', is indeed to be 'in the cage'.[49]

In the Cage

'In the cage': as it were in Derrida's *antre* or Forster's Marabar, where confusing linguistic noise reigns, or in Hermes' den of interpretative thieves. It's where all of classic modernism's interpretative heroes and heroines are – James's, Eliot's, Conrad's, Woolf's, Joyce's – all locked into the dual modernistic problematic, all at once commanded by the imperative of interpreting and condemned to the impossibility of making sense of such fragmented discourses and texts as are presented for interpretation. This is where the girl telegraph clerk is in James's *nouvelle* entitled 'In the Cage' (the story was published in the same volume of the New York edition as *What Maisie Knew*), her days spent behind the wire grille or cage in the post office in the posh London district where she works. Every working day is for her a close encounter with the aristocratic telegrams – that is, encoded, cryptogrammic discourses, puzzling bits of mysterious text, sentences syntactically abrupt, maimed and limping – that are pushed across her counter, inciting her curiosity into decipherment but still keeping their privacy, retaining much of their essential hermetic discretion. Here is, then, a 'world of whiffs and glimpses', of 'clues', a continual 'tangle' of meanings that invite her to 'fill out some of the gaps, supply . . . the missing answers'. These messages excite her confidence in her own reading powers. They taunt her with the possibility of right interpretation, and so delude her into thinking she has grasped and fully translated their possible senses. The outcome, result of getting hold of both the right and the wrong end of the stick, taking and mistaking all at once, is ghastly embarrassment and the breaking up of her whole private life.

'And what game is that?', the telegraph girl is asked when she's let slip that she's an attentive reader and recaller of aristocratic telegrams. It's an echo of the cockney or proletarian question, the policeman's interrogative – 'What's your game?' – when something hurtful, nasty, or wrong is in the air. And T. S. Eliot recognized this whiff of the hurtful, the criminal even, about the modernistic interpretative plight when he sought for a framing title for the powerful opening sections of *The Waste Land* (1922). What might best encapsulate his awesomely difficult *mélange* of texts and voices, this jigsaw-puzzle array of scattered discourses, this bitty sequence of readings and rereadings of so many plundered texts, the amassed booty of so many traditions in disarray, this new Shakespeare in rags? 'O O O O that Shakespeherian Rag', cried the new century's ragtime hit song, and modernism's most agonistic text repeats the cry in an odd echo of its contemporary of 1920, Freud's grandson's 'o-o-o-o'. So many reminders of a literary tradition in, as it were, criminal disorder made Eliot mindful of James's encaged interpreter. He also remembered an arrestingly odd episode of *Our Mutual Friend*.

In Book I, Chapter 16, of Dickens's novel, entitled 'Minders and Re-minders', John Rokesmith and Mrs Boffin visit child-minder Betty Higden in search of a baby for Mrs Boffin to adopt. What they encounter is an extraordinary reading situation. The scarcely literate Mrs Higden loves news-papers, and is assisted in her taste by a retarded youth called Sloppy. 'You mightn't think it, but Sloppy is a beautiful reader of a newspaper.' He came to Mrs Higden as one of her 'Minders' – she fosters orphans for the Parish authorities – and he has stayed on, a minder like her (in the sense of minding or feeling for the sufferings of others), one who minds about 'the worn-out people', 'the decent poor' trying to avoid the workhouse, whom she is reminded of as she and Sloppy read the newspapers. For these two, reading is a theatrical process of minding and reminding, of powerfully performative re-enactment. Sloppy dramatizes what he reads, plays the parts of people in the newspaper stories (he's a version, in fact, of Dickens himself, reanimating his fictions on his reading tours). Mrs Higden and Sloppy (and Dickens) go in for performance, an obvious kind of performative reading. When they are thus re-enacted, voices speak again, minds and selves are resurrected, feelings are revived, those who minded once are made, as it were, to do their minding all over again. On this plan, reading is recovery, a kind of *pleroma*, successful repetition, reminding. As with the textual and other visions of Eliot's *Prufrock*: the prospect of revision is held out.

But it's also clear that *Prufrock* is a poem mindful that attempted revisions are always fraught with the danger of corrupting revision. It's hard to get originals to recur in any simple unrevised way. And so with Mrs Higden's and Sloppy's remindings. Sloppy's dramatic skill in reading the newspaper is praiseworthy. But he's also a mangler: literally a mangler, hard at work turning the enormous washing mangle that fills Mrs Higden's room; and perhaps also, in a nice pun, a mangler of text. Reminding – we're thus emblematically reminded – can also be mangling. No wonder, then, that the threshold which Rokesmith and Mrs Boffin negotiate in order to enter this homely reading-room is so *Ur*-Derridianly awkward. 'The board across the doorway' – put there to keep the little Minders safely in – 'acting as trap equally for the feet of Mrs Higden coming out, and the feet of Mrs Boffin and John Rokesmith going in, greatly increased the difficulty of the situation.' And, of course, what Mrs Higden particularly praises the reminding mangler for re-enacting in this reading-enclosure is police reports. 'He do the Police in different voices.' If rereading is a kind of mangling, it includes mangling in the sense of wrongdoing. These are criminal proceedings, done behind barriers, behind threshold bars.

Eliot's *The Waste Land* offers the modernist text – comprising in great part a rag-bag of remembered and half-remembered reminders of precedent texts, a deprecatory celebration of the damage the modern world is doing to the half-forgotten texts of the past – in true modernist fashion as a game. Part II of *The Waste Land* is entitled 'A Game of Chess'. But this claim upon game has never shrugged off – and now the published *Waste Land Manuscript* volume is there perpetually to remind us of it – the lack of jokiness encapsulated in all such modernist play. The great opening sections of the poem were originally headed 'He Do the Police in Different Voices'. Part II, now 'The Game of Chess', was 'He Do the Police in Different Voices, Part II'; its subtitle: 'In the Cage'.

Alphabetical Crushes

And the way that textual games can land the free-wheeling interpreter in a very unfunny cage is at the heart of one of the most discomfiting fictions from the Shakespearean canon, the treatment of Malvolio in *Twelfth Night*. This egregiously confident hermeneute is deceived by a letter he thinks himself capable of reading for his own pleasing advantage. Up to one kind of game, his play of fast and loose with an epistle, he falls victim to another, the ruse of Maria – a 'devil of wit', an Ariadne who has turned into a fearsome Penthesilea or Amazon Queen of textual gaming. Maria's epistolary deception of Malvolio, situated very near the centre of *Twelfth Night* – a play which seems to have been occasionally performed under the title *Malvolio*[50] – is a 'fiction' within the fiction (III. iv. 129), a play staged within the play (III. iv. 128), a comic 'interlude' within the comedy (V. i. 371), a 'sport' within the general sportiveness (IV. ii. 73), a game with a 'whirligig' or spinning-top (V. i. 375). Within the general provocation of pleasure that *Twelfth Night* is set up to provide, the gulling of Malvolio will, says Maria, have her allies Toby Belch and company 'laugh' themselves 'into stitches'.

And Malvolio is trickable, is predisposed to become the victim of this sport, because he accepts it as normal that texts should play games, that they regularly come as riddles, that they're alphabetical puzzles, hieroglyphs, cryptograms, obscure communications requiring ingenious 'contemplation' in order to generate an acceptable 'construction' (cf. 'obscure epistles of love': II. iii. 155; 'observe his construction': II. iii. 175; 'this letter will make a contemplative idiot of him': II. v. 19–20; 'Contemplation makes a rare turkeycock of him': II. v. 30–1). 'Let me see, let me see, let me see,' says Malvolio, wrestling in Act II, scene v, with the 'fustian riddle' beginning 'I may command where I adore' and ending with the puzzling 'M.O.A.I. doth sway my life':

> 'I may command where I adore'. Why, she may command me: I serve her, she is my lady. Why, this is evident to any formal capacity. There is no obstruction in this. And the end: what should that alphabetical position portend? If I could make that resemble something in me! Softly! 'M.O.A.I.'

And, of course, given time, thoughtfully repeating these bits of alphabetical stuff long enough, he might make them resemble anything at all, for he's the model of an ingenious riddling word-player: ' "M.O.A.I." This simulation is not as the former: and yet, to crush this a little, it would bow to me, for every one of these letters are in my name.' And Shakespeare has his own alphabetical fun to layer onto Maria's and Malvolio's, in a little hermeneutical game played with the audience, as it were, over Malvolio's shoulder. 'By my life, this is my lady's hand: these be her very C's, her U's, and her T's, and thus she makes her great P's. It is in contempt of question her hand.' And in order to put one meaning of this particular turn in the alphabet-game beyond question, Shakespeare has silly Sir Andrew Aguecheek echo Malvolio: 'Her C's, her U's, and her T's: why that?' Why, because C. U. T. reminds you of *cunt* and because it spells *cut*, a waterway, along which great pees or copious pissings might flow. Not dissimilarly, as Malvolio wrestles with M.O.A.I. and spots that *M* is his own initial, but is prevented from reading all of his name there because ' "A" should follow, but "O" does' and ' "I" comes behind' *O* rather than before it, Fabian puts in the hope that ' "O" shall end' to remind the audience – if they needed it – not just that *A* and *O* refer us to the first and last letters of the Greek alphabet, familiar to church-goers as a Biblical title for Christ – the Alpha and Omega – but also that the *O*, or vagina, is where Malvolio and every would-be hero of comedy (and many a tragic hero too, not least Hamlet himself) desire to end up.

Games can certainly be played with texts, and Shakespeare plays with us this game of codes and nicknames for private bodily parts and intimate bodily functions as a neat mimicking of comedy's larger expression of the human desire to participate in such body sports (comedies commonly end in marriages). But *Twelfth Night* is also making play with the evidence that not everything a player takes from playing the textual game or deduces from textual riddles is going to avoid mis-taking. Some interpretative uses will in fact be abuses. And Malvolio is abused – and *abuse* becomes a key token in this drama's rhetoric – in order to disabuse him of his too ready assumptions about the way letters, letters of the alphabet and epistles, might be construed. And the punishment of Malvolio fits the crime. He's taken from the solipsistic cage of over-zealous interpretation to be locked up in a 'prison' (IV. ii. 19) or 'dark room' (III. iv. 136), a place where ignorance and puzzle reign, as during the plague of darkness or 'fog' that Moses afflicted the Egyptians with. 'Sir Topas' informs Malvolio (IV. ii. 43–5) that his darkness is really light, but, like the meanings he squeezed from Maria's letter, this illumination is para-doxical, illusory, a series of sick jokes: 'Why, it hath bay-windows trans-parent as barricadoes, and the clerestories toward the south-north are as lustrous as ebony: and yet complainest thou of obstruction?' (IV. ii. 37–40).

A different order of letter-writing and reading finally sets Malvolio free. Release from his imprisonment within the foggy world of the 'fustian riddle' comes when he writes a sensible letter, one that proves thus his sanity. Light and clarity are the essence of this releasing writing. They can – indeed must – be the companions of writing stuff, the text implies, as Malvolio calls three times for writing materials: 'a candle, and pen, ink, and paper'; 'some light and some paper'; 'some ink, paper, and light' (IV. ii. 84, 109, 113–14).

Malvolio's reading game, and the tricks played upon him as a reader, distinctly sour *Twelfth Night*. Few members of any audience leave the theatre feeling that Malvolio has not been, as Olivia puts it, 'notoriously abused' (V.

i. 378). Malvolio refuses to take his treatment as a joke, as a piece of 'sportful
malice' that should provoke 'laughter' rather than 'revenge' (V. i. 364–5). His
angry exit, shouting 'I'll be reveng'd on the whole pack of you' (V. i. 377),
damages the play's conventional attempt at comic conclusions in peace,
marriage, and song. Why, then, since the textual sport with Malvolio is so
upsetting to comedy's generic disposition to pleasure, leave it in? One possible
answer is that the intended fun misfired and that Shakespeare was too short
of time or will to sort things out, to get the fun back on the rails again, and
so let his play go ahead just as it was anyway. This seems implausible.
There's plenty of evidence (*Othello* and *King Lear*, for instance) that Shakespeare was ready to rewrite plays wholesale, though intrinsic implausibility
hasn't stopped such an argument being applied to *Measure for Measure* and its
notorious formal wobbles. It's more pertinent, I think, to recall the other so-
called comedies whose comic endings are aborted or thwarted, *Love's Labours
Lost* and *As You Like It*. In both of these cases, too, games with texts, textual
riddling, absurd writing, and ridiculous reader expectations are predominant.
So it does look as if Shakespeare would take strong risks with comedies, even
to the extent of having them run quite aground, in order to prove that textual
gaming, playing with textuality to the extent of supposing it entirely
swallowed up in riddle and having it overwhelmed by the cryptic, was not
only silly but dangerous. In all three of these cases, it's the contemporary
mannerisms of lovers' discourse, the conventional codes of love-poems and
love-letters, that are under satiric fire. But that's not all. In the case of
Twelfth Night, the spiteful energy with which Malvolio is abused seems to be
directed at him as a type of theological reader.

Whether Shakespeare was, as is sometimes suggested, a secret Roman
Catholic or not, it's clear that he's very down on Protestants and their hermeneutic habits. Hamlet, anguished reader, is a graduate of Wittenberg, the
university of Martin Luther. Macbeth, convinced he's a predestined killer,
seems to be offered as a demonized type of Scottish Calvinist, reading his life
as filled with transcendent direction. And Malvolio is 'a kind of Puritan' whose
reading of Maria's letter is attended with a curious density of theological suggestions. Toby and his gang pretend he's inspired by the Devil
and must be exorcised by the Clown as Parson. His way with epistles, says
the Clown, is anathema to Gospel truths: 'a madman's epistles are no gospels'
(V. i. 285f.). Like Bible readers from the beginning of Bible reading, Jewish
and Christian, Malvolio plays quite arbitrarily with the overt meanings of
Maria's text. He's a metaphoricist or allegorist where it suits, ready patiently
to 'crush' out some very recessive meanings, but a literalist where that is
more convenient: 'Daylight and champaign discovers not more! This is open.
I will be proud, I will read politic authors, I will baffle Sir Toby . . . I will

be strange, stout, in yellow stockings, and cross-gartered' (II. v. 140ff.).
Maria's uncanny acquaintance with the expectations of amorous but, more
particularly, theological readers means that she can play him on her textual
hook every which way she pleases, now allegorical, now literal. And the
result is Malvolio's plunge into 'vain bibble babble' – Babelic nonsense
which, it's hinted, is even Bible babble, the kind of cabbalistic textuality
that *Finnegans Wake* would reduce all textuality to.

Mad Fun-House

Once again, Shakespeare looks as if he's been reading his Joyce. He's certainly
been minding the reading ways of lovers and preachers. In the case of Joyce's
countryman, Jonathan Swift, it was politicians and preachers whom he watched
reducing text to a very convenient complex of arbitrarily manipulable liter-
als, figurals, allegories, hermeticisms. And for Swift, these self-servingly
arbitrary and supple readers such as Jack the Protestant Dissenter aren't
going to be cured by a quick spell in Malvolio's dark room. They deserve a
life sentence to Bedlam.

> JACK had not only calculated the first Revolutions of his Brain so prudently,
> as to give Rise to that Epidemick Sect of *Æolists*, but succeeding also into a
> new and strange Variety of Conceptions, the Fruitfulness of his Imagination
> led him into certain Notions, which, altho' in Appearance very unaccountable,
> were not without their Mysteries and their Meanings, nor wanted Followers to
> countenance and improve them. I shall therefore be extreamly careful and
> exact in recounting such material Passages of this Nature, as I have been able
> to collect, either from undoubted Tradition, or indefatigable Reading; and
> shall describe them as graphically as it is possible, and as far as Notions of that
> Height and Latitude can be brought within the Compass of a Pen. Nor do I
> at all question, but they will furnish Plenty of noble Matter for such, whose
> converting Imaginations dispose them to reduce all Things into *Types*; who can
> make *Shadows*, no thanks to the Sun; and then mold them into Substances, no
> thanks to Philosophy; whose peculiar Talent lies in fixing Tropes and Allegories
> to the *Letter*, and refining what is Literal into Figure and Mystery.
>   JACK had provided a fair Copy of his Father's *Will*, engrossed in Form upon
> a large Skin of Parchment; and resolving to act the Part of a most dutiful Son,
> he became the fondest Creature of it imaginable. For, altho', as I have often
> told the Reader, it consisted wholly in certain plain, easy Directions about the
> management and wearing of their Coats, with Legacies and Penalties, in case
> of Obedience or Neglect; yet he began to entertain a Fancy, that the Matter
> was *deeper* and *darker*, and therefore must needs have a great deal more of Mystery
> at the Bottom. *Gentlemen*, said he, *I will prove this very Skin of Parchment to be*

Meat, Drink, and Cloth, to be the Philosopher's Stone, and the Universal Medicine.
In consequence of which Raptures, he resolved to make use of it in the most
necessary, as well as the most paltry Occasions of Life. He had a Way of
working it into any Shape he pleased; so that it served him for a Night-cap
when he went to Bed, and for an Umbrello in rainy Weather. He would lap
a Piece of it about a sore Toe, or when he had Fits, burn two Inches under his
Nose; or if any Thing lay heavy on his Stomach, scrape off, and swallow as
much of the Powder as would lie on a silver Penny, they were all infallible
Remedies.[51]

'He had a Way of working it into any Shape he pleased': it's the madness
of the textual, hermeneutical fun-house. For its part, the Bedlam of Laputa
in *Gulliver's Travels* is characterized by truly systematized craziness, a meth-
odical madness that supposes itself scientific, experimental truth. Ingenious
interpretative gaming is now set up as *Wissenschaft*, a sport for professors. But
it's a game to be played by police-state rules for the benefit of repressive
regimes. The hermeneutic professoriate has some useful tips, a handy project,
for politicians.

Another Professor shewed me a large Paper of Instructions for discovering
Plots and Conspiracies against the Government. He advised great Statesmen
to examine into the Dyet of all suspected Persons; their Times of eating; upon
which Side they lay in Bed; with which Hand they wiped their Posteriors; to
take a strict View of their Excrements, and from the Colour, the Odour, the
Taste, the Consistence, the Crudeness, or Maturity of Digestion, form a Judgment of their Thoughts and Designs: Because Men are never so serious,
thoughtful, and intent, as when they are at Stool; which he found by frequent
Experiment: For in such Conjunctions, when he used merely as a Trial to
consider which was the best Way of murdering the King, his Ordure would
have a Tincture of Green; but quite different when he thought only of raising
an Insurrection, or burning the Metropolis.

But Gulliver can do even better than simply project such hermeneutic
bedlam, for he comes from Langdon (or London) where anagrammatism is
already well established as a practice among those who wish to discover plots
where none exist, in order to promote their own or their Party's advantage.
First they select their victims:

Then, effectual Care is taken to secure all their Letters and other Papers, and
put the Owners in Chains. These Papers are delivered to a Set of Artists
very dextrous in finding out the mysterious Meanings of Words, Syllables
and Letters. For Instance, they can decypher a Close-stool to signify a Privy-
Council; a Flock of Geese, a Senate; a lame Dog, an Invader; the Plague, a
standing Army; a Buzard, a Minister; the Gout, a High Priest; a Gibbet, a

Secretary of State; a Chamber pot, a Committee of Grandees; a Sieve, a Court Lady; a Broom, a Revolution; a Mouse-trap, an Employment; a bottomless Pit, the Treasury; a Sink, a C———t; a Cap and Bells, a Favourite; a broken Reed, a Court of Justice; an empty Tun, a General; a running Sore, the Administration.

And if this ingenious, but simple, hieroglyphical method fails to produce the desired readings, 'they have two others more effectual; which the Learned among them call Acrosticks, and Anagrams':

First, they can decypher all initial Letters into political Meanings: Thus, *N*, shall signify a Plot; *B*, a Regiment of Horse; *L*, a Fleet at Sea. Or, *secondly*, by transposing the Letters of the Alphabet, in a very suspected Paper, they can lay open the deepest Designs of a discontented Party. So for Example, if I should say in a Letter to a Friend, *Our Brother* Tom *has just got the Piles*; a Man of Skill in this Art would discover how the same Letters which compose that Sentence, may be analysed into the following words; *Resist,* ———*a Plot is brought home*———*The Tour*. And this is the Anagrammatick Method.[52]

Apple-Pie Histories

Word-games are also presented as the tricky essence of institutionalized power in the writings of a more modern satirist, Charles Dickens. As presented in *Bleak House* (1852–3), the Law and Parliament, the corrupt but magisterial ruling systems of England, conspire together to blight the lives of their citizens, the characters of Dickens's novel, the inhabitants of Dickens's London, by playing the Joker. As Hillis Miller has nicely observed in his Introduction to the Penguin edition of *Bleak House* (1971), everybody in this novel is caught up in writerly business, reading, writing, trying to make sense of texts and of systems of all kinds cast in textual form. And much of this work is to malign effect.

Dickens tends to produce all his major scenes as scenes of interpretation, to play all his texts for their metatextual meanings, to present existence as a business of naming, writing, reading, as a general hermeneutics. And of none of his novels is this truer than of *Bleak House*. Here solipsistic textual games, riddling exercises of catch-the-meaning, dominate private and public life. Politics is a self-consuming alphabetical artifact operated by Sir Leicester Dedlock's parliamentary cronies: Lords Boodle and Coodle, Sir Thomas Doodle, the Duke of Foodle, and Messrs Hoodle, Joodle, Koodle, Loodle, Moodle, Noodle, Poodle, Quoodle (ch. 12), and 'all the fine gentlemen in office, down to Zoodle' (ch. 16). And if not by that gang, then by Buffy, Cuffy, Duffy, Fuffy, Guffy, Huffy, Juffy, Kuffy, Luffy, Muffy, Puffy, and their lot (ch. 12). As political teams these form a perfect chain of elusive signifiers, a bunch of endlessly proliferating Jokers, the meaningless heart of a heartless but self-perpetuating political world. And Parliament is in this respect exactly like the Court of Chancery, where the passage of legal paper from lawyer to lawyer comprises another endless and nonsensical alphabet-game, a huge batch of signifiers endlessly circulating in search of some end-point, some satisfying rest for meaning. As Mr Jarndyce explains (ch. 8): 'cartloads of papers' perform

> an infernal country-dance of costs and fees and nonsense and corruption, as was never dreamed of in the wildest visions of a Witch's Sabbath. Equity sends questions to Law, Law sends questions back to Equity; Law finds it can't do this, Equity finds it can't do that; neither can so much as say it can't do anything, without this solicitor instructing and this counsel appearing for A, and that solicitor instructing and that counsel appearing for B; and so on through the whole alphabet, like the history of the Apple Pie.

What Jarndyce is referring to is the apple-pie alphabet rhyme, one of the earliest recorded children's alphabets:

> A was an apple-pie;
> B bit it,
> C cut it,
> D dealt it,
> E eat it,
> F fought for it,
> G got it,
> H had it,
> I inspected it,
> J jumped for it,
> K kept it,
> L longed for it,
> M mourned for it,
> N nodded at it,
> O opened it,
> P peeped in it,
> Q quartered it,
> R ran for it,
> S stole it,
> T took it,
> U upset it,
> V viewed it,
> W wanted it,
> X, Y, Z, and ampersand
> All wished for a piece in hand.[53]

This alphabetic mnemonic offers a ludic but also crazy, nonsensical economy of signifier and signified. It has signifiers endlessly in circulation, just as in Serres' reading of Joseph's dream-texts: *a* becomes *b* becomes *c*, and so on. An apple pie is also in circulation, the object of perpetual desire and point of constant reference. But though the pie appears from time to time to be graspable and eatable (B bit it, G got it, H had it, T took it), in the end no one has it, and everyone is left still wishing 'for a piece in hand'. What remains endlessly, circularly present, circulated, consumed, and consumable is letters of the alphabet. And hungry children, though they obviously enjoy having words in their mouth, especially in word-games and chants like this one, would also like, would undoubtedly prefer, to chew some apple pie from time to time.

And the point of *Bleak House* is not that it's simply advertising an un-satisfactory economy of signifier and signified, the failure of alphabet systems to achieve their desire for reference. The novel may indeed be doing that, and alerting us to the way in which texts proceed Derridianly as self-enclosed alphabet-games. But in the first place it's complaining about political and legal systems which frustrate the desires of children, and adults, for satisfactions of a material kind. Children have grown old waiting for the complacently weary windbag of a Court of Chancery to deliver their apple pie. The youth Richard, his inheritance tied up in the Chancery case of Jarndyce v. Jarndyce, is only the latest in line for life-smashing frustration. Lower in the social scale, Jo the crossing-sweeper, inhabitant of the slum called Tom-all-Alone's, a street of houses in dilapidation because their ownership is also in question in the long-running Jarndyce saga, is such another. Except that Jo can't read, so his plight is doubled, for he thus misses the satisfactions of alphabets as well as of apple pies. He's a creature of thresholds and crossings, an ironic little Hermes no less, squatting for breakfast 'on the door-step of the Society for the Propagation of the Gospel in Foreign Parts', brushing it clean in pathetic gratitude, spending his days sweeping a path through the horse dung to let delicate feet cross the road cleanly, but unaware of the meanings that Derridians might perceive clustering about him and his labour.

The Great Teetotum

At one arresting point, Jo's London is described as 'the great teetotum' that spins and whirls every day. A teetotum was a spinning-top with letters of the alphabet on it, an alphabet-game or puzzle, a textual toy.[54] London, so ob-viously a place of text and signs and signifying systems, is thus presented as a textual game. But this child Jo can't play this game. He is a child without a childhood, excluded from all kiddy games. At an age when the bourgeoisie thinks he should be playing, he's working. In any case, play with a teetotum makes no sense at all to the unlettered. 'The town awakes; the great tee-totum is set up for its daily spin and whirl; all that unaccountable reading and writing, which has been suspended for a few hours, recommences. Jo, and the other lower animals, get on in the unintelligible mess as they can.' And Jo's plight inspires at this point (ch. 16) one of Dickens's most passionate outbursts, an attack on the nation that produces illiterate children:

> It must be a strange state to be like Jo! To shuffle through the streets, un-familiar with the shapes and in utter darkness as to the meaning, of those mysterious symbols, so abundant over the shops, and the corner of streets, and on the doors, and in the windows! To see people read, and to see people write, and to see the postman deliver letters, and not to have the least idea of all that language – to be, to every scrap of it, stone blind and dumb! It must be very puzzling to see the good company going to the churches on Sundays, with their books in their hands and to think (for perhaps Jo *does* think, at odd times) what does it all mean, and if it means anything to anybody, how comes it that it means nothing to me? To be hustled, and jostled, and moved on; and really to feel that it would appear to be perfectly true that I have no business here, or there, or anywhere; and yet to be perplexed by the consideration that I *am* here somehow, too, and everybody overlooked me until I became the creature that I am! It must be a strange state, not merely to be told that I am scarcely human (as in the case of my offering myself for a witness), but to feel it of my own knowledge all my life! To see the horses, dogs, and cattle, go by me, and to know that in ignorance I belong to them, and not the superior beings in my shape, whose delicacy I offend! Jo's ideas of a Criminal Trial, or a Judge, or a Bishop, or a Government, or that inestimable jewel to him (if he only knew it) the Constitution, should be strange! His whole material and imma-terial life is wonderfully strange; his death, the strangest thing of all.

Jo is the victim of a system that will play word-games without him, content to destroy children and childishness in a riddling chaos of signs. Of course, Dickens manages to make us laugh at aspects of this chaos. Dickens's text can get up to some very funny fun and games in and through the revelations about the awful word-games the grown-ups are playing to the detriment of Britain's children. There is joke in the Coodle–Boodle satire. And there's Mr Chadband's abundant rhetorical excess, his wrenching of Biblical signifiers away from every sensible reference in crazed and wilful misapplication to Jo. A huge feeder, Mr Chadband gets lots of apple pie. For his part, Jo gets empty Biblical metaphors. 'We have here . . . a Gentile and a Heathen, a dweller in the tents of Tom-all-Alone's. . . .' And so on. The preacher's questions ('. . . why do I say he is devoid of these possessions?

Why? Why is he?') are put 'as if he were propounding an entirely new riddle, of much ingenuity and merit, to Mr Snagsby, and entreating him not to give it up'. The effect on the audience at this religious house-meeting – groans passing from one person to the next – is 'like a game of forfeits' (ch. 25). Chadband's rhetoric is a riddle and a game that excludes Jo, and hilariously so. Again, there's the chaotic Jellyby household (ch. 4), a kind of domestic syntax gone wrong through Mrs Jellyby's being massively distracted by her incessant correspondence about charitable schemes in Africa. In this house metonymic displacement reigns, with potatoes in the coal-scuttle, a kettle on the dressing-table, envelopes in the gravy, a pie dish on the wash-hand stand, curtains held up by a dinner fork, and a commemorative mug from Tunbridge Wells doing duty as a candle-holder. We laugh. And Esther and Ada laugh off the dampness of their bedroom at the Jellyby house.

Others laugh too. Jarndyce and Jarndyce 'has passed into a joke' (ch. 1). The court case ends, at long last, in general amusement, with the clerks and court officials, everyone, all laughing, 'more like people coming out from a Farce or a Juggler than from a Court of Justice' (ch. 65). But the laughter is hollow. Just so, dining with the Jellybies is not fun for Esther and her friends. Nor is there pleasure for Jo as the small victim of Chadband's riddling words, helplessly lost in the labyrinth of adult linguistics. Even when Babel is pint-sized – and Guppy and Jobling encounter (ch. 20) 'a model of the tower of Babel' in a cafe: 'a pile of plates and flat tin covers' – Babel is still Babel. The tiny tots of the Jellyby family are all potential Tristram Shandies, set up to be victims of thresholds, their 'noses and fingers' in constant 'situations of danger between the hinges of the doors' (ch. 4). Caddy Jellyby, her mother's exploited amanuensis, sobs on her wedding-eve at the thought of leaving her father in his wife's 'nest of waste-paper', the awful litter of literary rubbish, detritus of a life turned over to writing, in a house whose jam-packed closets greatly resemble the evilly ponging literatured cell of Shem the Penman in *Finnegans Wake*: 'bits of mouldy pie, sour bottles, Mrs Jellyby's caps, letters, tea, forks, odd boots and shoes of children, firewood, wafers, saucepan-lids, damp sugar in odds and ends of paper bags, footstools, blacklead brushes, bread, Mrs Jellyby's bonnets, books with butter sticking to the binding, guttered candle-ends put out by being turned upside down in broken candle sticks, nutshells, heads and tails of shrimps, dinner-mats, gloves, coffee-grounds, umbrellas' (ch. 30).

Amidst such rubbish, litters of letters, litter provoked by literature, rubbish as the current condition of the world as text, writing, and alphabet-game, human lives are being rubbished – Lady Dedlock, Nemo, all the actors and branches of the Jarndyce case, Richard, the Man from Shropshire, Miss Flite (her reticule of legal 'documents' a litter of junk), Jo, and Krook – he whose shop is a garbage tip of old law documents, ink-bottles, waste paper, rags for recycling into yet more paper, a scrap-heap that he truffles and rummages endlessly in (ch. 5). The novel's wastes of paper are the scene where lives also get wasted, all consumed by a principle of inherent deadliness, so that Krook's gothic death by 'spontaneous combustion' has an inevitable emblematic aptness about it.

It's perfectly proper and critically pertinent to read *Bleak House* deconstructively. Its packets of mysterious papers, the documentation, epistle, and vital signature of Nemo/Hawdon, travelling entrancingly across a criminal scene as the object of intense commercial, legal, and police-detective attention – this is English literature's first major detective story – should remind us of Poe's 'The Purloined Letter' and of its extreme attraction for deconstructionists. The central role of a writer-copyist called Nemo in the house of an illiterate called Krook sticks out like a provocatively poststructuralist sore thumb. The text's self-consuming alphabet-games vividly illustrate and enact the post-Saussurean allegation that language is a system of differences with no positive terms. The novel's presentation of writing as waste, writing as limping, writing as erasure – as in Krook's arresting technique of writing letters back to front, bottom to top, and then rubbing them out even as he builds words from them – all look like enticing deconstructionist plums. But where readings focusing on such matters would go wrong would be in limiting the text to such word-gaming aspects. And this is where Hillis Miller's Penguin Introduction does indeed go wrong. Dickens's characters, he alleges 'exist only in language', they're 'only figurative', 'just a figure of speech'.

Bleak House, Miller argues, is allegory, that is, 'a temporal system of cross references among signs rather than a spatial pattern of correspondence between signs and referents'. The novel's purpose is to demonstrate the fragility of reference, the death of Cratylism, and so on.[55] But to stick at this level of analysis is precisely to play along with the system that Dickens is challenging – and that Shakespeare and Swift were, *mutatis mutandis*, challenging. This is to side with the treacherous word-gamers and riddlers, with Parliament and Chancery, with Chadband and Mrs Jellyby and the rest, and to refuse to call their bluff and expose the dangerous kind of world-game that they're about. It is simply to miss Dickens's political and social point, to evade the full force of his double-jointed attack on demystifying systems of thought and practice (and incidentally, to be quite stammeringly self-contradictory, for after all Hillis Miller can't live with the force of his limiting *onlies*, and has, for very shame, to mention Parliament, Disraeli, crises of 'the early fifties', Dickens's Christian humanitarianism, and the doctrine of original sin, because such things inevitably figure hugely in Dickens's text). In other words, no reading of *Bleak House* as a text devoted to rebuses and to the functions of text as rebus can ignore the world of things that are inevitably signified by the word *rebus* itself.[56]

A Sort of Practical Rebus

If the carnivalesque explanation of the origin of *rebus* as word-puzzle has any truth in it, then rebuses inevitably embrace or straddle the word–world, word–game/world–game dualism that is so major a theme of *Bleak House* and that forms the major interest of my discussions in this book.

> Menage says the name is derived from certain tracts issued annually by the priests of Picardy, about Carnival time, for the purpose of exposing misdemeanours which had been committed in their neighbourhood. These pamphlets were entitled, *De Rebus quae geruntur* ('about things which are going on'), and the breakings and joinings of the words were filled in with pictures.[57]

De rebus: rebuses, word-games, but also *res*, things, actualities, abuses, out there in the world beyond the text. And this dramatically two-faced aspect of rebuses at their point of alleged origin – carnivalesque word-games with serious moral intentions, rebuses directed at the world of *res*, affairs, things – is clearly a condition that rebuses have found it hard to shed. As George Eliot's *Middlemarch* brings startlingly home. In chapter 60 of this vast panorama of English provincial life (1871–2), there occurs an auction of one Edwin Larcher's goods. The atmosphere is said to be carnivalesque. A sale in Middlemarch is always 'a kind of festival', 'as good as a fair'. Bidding for the sale-goods is a kind of play, like 'betting at the races'. The auctioneer, Mr Trumbull, a man 'keenly alive to his own jokes', gets rid of a dubious steel fender, with a crack about using its sharp edge as a knife for cutting down suicides: ' "It was worth six shillings to have a fender you could always tell that joke on," said Mr Clintup, laughing low.' And then Trumbull offers a 'very recherchy lot', a tray of 'bijoux', 'a collection of trifles'. In case we should overlook these objects as mere trifles, or this scene as merely bucolic trifling, just a sentimental padding out of the novel's rural scenario, Trumbull is made to add that 'trifles make the sum of human things – nothing more important than trifles'. And central to this little gatherum of importantly trifling stuff is a rebus:

> 'This I have in my hand is an ingenious contrivance – a sort of practical rebus I may call it: here, you see, it looks like an elegant heart-shaped box, portable – for the pocket; there, again, it becomes like a splendid double flower – an ornament for the table; and now' – Mr Trumbull allowed the flower to fall

alarmingly into strings of heart-shaped leaves – 'a book of riddles! No less than five hundred printed in a beautiful red. Gentlemen, if I had less of a conscience, I should not wish you to bid high for this lot – I have a longing for it myself. What can promote innocent mirth, and I may say virtue, more than a good riddle? – it hinders profane language, and attaches a man to the society of refined females. This ingenious article itself, without the elegant domino-box, card-basket, &c., ought alone to give a high price to the lot. Carried in the pocket it might make an individual welcome in any society. Four shillings, sir? – four shillings for this remarkable collection of riddles with the et caeteras. Here is a sample: "How must you spell honey to make it catch lady-birds? Answer – money." You hear? – lady-birds – honey – money. This is an amusement to sharpen the intellect; it has a sting – it has what we call satire, and wit without indecency. Four-and-sixpence – five shillings.'

The moment of the auction is, of course, central to the plot of *Middlemarch*. It happens that Will Ladislaw has been sent along by Bulstrode as a man the banker knows fatally little about but who has a reputation for knowing about pictures, to see whether a painting of Christ's supper at Emmaus catalogued as by Guido is worth the purchase. Banker Bulstrode is a man who has all his life combined shrewd calculation about financial advantage in religion and commerce. How momentously so, the reader, and the town of Middlemarch, will soon learn, and not least because an old associate of Bulstrode's, the man Raffles, happens to turn up at the sale, recognizes Will's family likeness, and starts making connections that will lead to Bulstrode and to startling moral revelations and crises for Bulstrode and also for Will, Dr Lydgate, and Dorothea. Numerous questions are about to be answered, riddles resolved, rebuses sorted out. The progress of *Middlemarch* as an earnest detective story, a fiction about a group of serious people seeking to cope with life as private detectives desperate for solutions, thus takes a great leap forward at this innocuous-seeming juncture. No hinge moment, no fortuitous encounter, not even Ladislaw's chance meeting with Dorothea in Rome, is more serious than this one.

Trumbull's jests are misleading. Raffles may sign himself John Raffles W. A. G. (ch. 41), but nothing he'll provoke is waggish. Solving the rebuses of Middlemarch isn't a comic affair. The sacramentalism with which George Eliot commonly loads her characters' life-choices is particularly present in this moment. If only Trumbull knew it, he is himself in a deeply solemn 'book of riddles', a text that wants to be taken as sacredly as the picture of Christ's meal at Emmaus. At that sacramental supper Christ was 'made known' to his previously unknowing disciples 'in the breaking of the bread': the real divine presence, transcendence within the common experience, great and ultimate meanings at a deceptively ordinary-looking moment. That

Emmaus meal stood for the kind of hidden, encrypted meaningfulness that George Eliot is continually trying, in the manner of Ludwig Feuerbach, to alert us to as the condition of ordinary life. Its revelation of the Christ was the kind of decrypting, unriddling, enigma-solving moment that her fiction is always seeking to contrive. This auction is by no means one of the great humanistic moments of Eliotic vision. In its hard-edged plotting way, though, it is a moment of truth that's like an echo of the great sacral rendings of veils that George Eliot continually works for. And it's done, characteristically of *Middlemarch*, through that 'sort of' rebus, a book of riddles, and a painting by 'the celebrated *Guydo*' – an 'Old Master', so called, as Trumbull puts it, 'because they were up to a thing or two beyond most of us – in possession of secrets now lost to the bulk of mankind'. The textual and metatextual nature of the proceedings could scarcely be more self-advertised.

And this is typical in huge respects of *Middlemarch*. So much of this fiction appears as text, as a serious play with texts, its significations repeatedly refracted through texts. Middlemarch is extraordinarily, abundantly, even (sometimes) gratuitously bookish. It's the kind of novel in which even a man like Trumbull, wanting to impress a Mary Garth, will (ch. 32) pick up a book – any book would do, but it happens to be Walter Scott's *Anne of Geierstein* – will read aloud its opening paragraph, and a moment later venture on a little heavy-footed literary criticism. 'You have an interesting work there, I see, Miss Garth . . . It is by the author of *Waverley*; that is Sir Walter Scott. I have bought one of his works myself – a very nice thing, a very superior publication, entitled *Ivanhoe*. You will not get any writer to beat him in a hurry, I think – he will not, in my opinion, be speedily surpassed. I have just been reading a portion at the commencement of *Anne of Jeerstein*. It commences well.' The jeer in the auctioneer's mispronunciation of *Geierstein* is perhaps not accidental. George Eliot is mocking a cumbersome piece of flirtation. But the fact that chatting up Mary Garth, the rural beauty, has to be done by means of books, indicates just how far literariness goes in George Eliot's fictional world.

This novelist, of course, prepared for her fictions very bookishly. She did research in libraries, kept extensive notes, and reproduced those notes, that scholarship, in the course of her fictions – sometimes with an overburdening excess, as in *Felix Holt* and *Romola*. She wasn't England's leading woman-scholar, the country's most eminent translator, one of its most telling critics, for nothing. She lived by books and writing, and the bookishness of her life inevitably shades all her writing with the colours of her learning. *Middlemarch*, studded with references to books, full of quotations, is well to the fore as characteristically Eliotic bookworm stuff, matter for librarians culled from libraries. In its super-literary self-fashioning it's a distinct precursive echo of bookish things to come from Joyce, Borges, Eco, and their kind. (One of W. J. Harvey's most useful notes in the Penguin edition brings the point vividly home. Sleepless old Casaubon wants Dorothea to read him some 'pages of Lowth' (ch. 37). 'There are', Harvey points out, 'three possible candidates – William Lowth (1660–1732), Simon Lowth (1630–1720), and Robert Lowth (1710–87); all prolific writers on theological subjects. The reader has a free choice; Professor Haight favours the first while I incline to the last, since he engaged in controversy with Bishop Warburton, mentioned elsewhere in connection with Casaubon. But only an editorial Casaubon would wish to pursue the matter further.' Readers who dislike this kind of intertextual density steer clear of *Middlemarch* – it's lousy, or Lowthy, with it.[58])

What's more, the novel's plot relies vividly on the power of writing that the text keeps registering. A signature, *Nicholas Bulstrode*, on a scrap of a letter to Joshua Rigg (now Featherstone), casually thrown into the fireplace ('within the fender' – this novel keeps reminding us to mind such commonplace objects), picked up with equal insouciance by Raffles to wedge his loose hip-flask with, will lead Raffles to Bulstrode, and both of them to catastrophe. It's George Eliot's writing practice to make us pause reflectively over matters of form and content that she feels important. Naturally enough, the prelude to Raffles's acquisition of that bit of vital epistolary trash (ch. 41) is a typically portentous (and not a little typically ponderous) but still important paragraph on 'the effect of writing':

> Who shall tell what may be the effect of writing? If it happens to have been cut in stone, though it lie face downmost for ages on a forsaken beach, or 'rest quietly under the drums and tramplings of many conquests', it may end by letting us into the secret of usurpations and other scandals gossiped about long empires ago: – this world being apparently a huge whispering-gallery. Such conditions are often minutely represented in our petty lifetime. As the stone which has been kicked by generations of clowns may come by curious little links of effect under the eyes of a scholar, through whose labours it may at last fix the date of invasions and unlock religions, so a bit of ink and paper which has long been an innocent wrapping or stop-gap may at last be laid open under the one pair of eyes which have knowledge enough to turn it into the opening of a catastrophe.

Book 5 of the novel is entitled 'The Dead Hand', but the hands that keep reaching out from the past on signed pieces of paper – Bulstrode's on his epistle to Rigg, old Featherstone's on wills and codicils, Casaubon's on research documents for Dorothea and on his cruel will disinheriting her should she marry Ladislaw – have tenacious powers to disturb and alter the lives of the living, the present.

The writing hands that offer these momentous unlockable secrets to future readers are not always catastrophic, or not simply so. The lesson of renunciation that Maggie Tulliver learned in *The Mill on the Floss* (1860) from reading the passages marked by an unknown annotator in her copy of Thomas à Kempis's *Imitation of Christ* affects her whole life painfully, perhaps even helps on her death; but George Eliot believes it's for her good. Maggie won't give in and marry Stephen Guest, not least because of this long-dead writing hand whose words, endorsed by a second, equally dead reading–writing hand, are accepted as coming from the hand of God, or from the humanized version of the divine imperative now enshrined in a vague but still overwhelmingly authoritative textuality: 'The words that were marked by the quiet hand in the little old book that she had long ago learned by heart rushed even to her lips and found a vent for themselves in a low murmur . . . "I have received the Cross, I have received it from Thy hand; I will bear it, and bear it till death, as Thou hast laid it upon me" ' (VII. 5).

A Fine Quotation

There's nothing in *Middlemarch* that quite equals the intensity of that life commanded by a single book even unto death. But most of the characters who matter most in the later novel are under some sort of bookish shadow for much of their career in the fiction. Casaubon, of course, works himself to a bookish death, wrestling in libraries with antiquities and out-of-date theology. Dorothea is a great reader of old-fashioned texts, on easy terms with the Bible, Milton, Hooker, John Locke. 'She knew many passages of Pascal's *Pensées* and of Jeremy Taylor by heart' (ch. 1). Her marriage to Casaubon is fired by her desire to be his research assistant. Lydgate would return home of an evening, before his marriage at least, and read medical textbooks 'far into the smallest hour' (ch. 16). Will Ladislaw is a painter and art critic who turns radical journalist. Even feather-brained and ill-educated Rosamond reads something. She's devoted to the silver-fork school of fictions and other low-brow, high-life literature for women (ch. 27). Still more surprising, even old Featherstone has a few tomes around the house: Josephus on Jewish antiquities, Culpepper (not on herbs but on usury), Klopstock's *Messiah*, the *Gentleman's Magazine*. We learn this on the occasion of a conversation with Fred Vincy in which he deprecates Mary Garth's insatiable zest for reading (ch. 12). And she does indeed seem to have an encyclopedic acquaintance with fictions of all kinds. She can reel off Shakespeare and allusions to Scott, Goldsmith, and Madame de Staël with no bother at all (ch. 14). Fred brings her books (*Anne of Geierstein* was one of his gifts). 'She is very

fond of reading' is his explanation to Featherstone. Mr Brooke is also fond
of reading, or has been so, and he has an apparent passing acquaintance with
a vast host of literature. His recall of bits of Smollett novels is typically vague
but enthusiastic: 'I remember they made me laugh uncommonly – there's a
droll bit about a postilion's breeches. We have no such humour now. I have
gone through all these things . . .' (ch. 30). For his part, Caleb Garth's feel
is for Biblical echoes of a more or less apt, but also more or less vague sort:
' "The soul of man . . . when it gets fairly rotten, will bear you all sorts of
poisonous toad-stools, and no eye can see whence came the seed thereof." '
Clearly, 'It was one of Caleb's quaintnesses, that in his difficulty of finding
speech for his thought, he caught, as it were, snatches of diction which he
associated with various points of view or states of mind; and whenever he had
a feeling of awe, he was haunted by a sense of Biblical phraseology, though
he could hardly have given a strict quotation' (ch. 40).

Reading shapes people's lives to such an extent, in fact, in *Middle-march*
that they're actually presented as texts or as bits of grammatical function.
The wonderfully acerbic Mrs Cadwallader, claiming that Casaubon 'dreams
footnotes', agrees with Sir James Chettam that the scholar has 'got no good
red blood in his body': 'No. Somebody put a drop under a magnifying-glass
and it was all semicolons and parentheses' (ch. 8). Dorothea is described as
a quotation on the novel's opening page – a piece of text within our text by
analogy with a piece of text within another text: she dressed plainly, 'which
by the side of provincial fashion gave her the impressiveness of a fine quotation from the Bible, – or from one of our elder poets, – in a paragraph of
to-day's newspaper'. And one kind of textualized being leads to another.
These characters become paintings. Ladislaw's friend Naumann flatters
Casaubon by painting him as Saint Thomas Aquinas disputing with the
doctors of the Church. He tries to fix Dorothea in the role of Santa Clara,
though the result fails to please him (ch. 22). Dorothea's plain sleeves are like
'those in which the Blessed Virgin appeared to Italian painters' (ch. 1). She
supposes that Casaubon's hair and eyes resemble 'the portrait of Locke' (ch.
2). Mary Garth is said to be plain, but 'Rembrandt would have painted her
with pleasure, and would have made her broad features look out of the canvas
with intelligent honesty' (ch. 12). (Being the potential subject of a Dutch
painting means that you've successfully passed George Eliot's moral-aesthetic
test, at least as that high standard is spelled out in chapter 17 of *Adam Bede*.)

And when the people of Middlemarch are not being turned into painted
versions of themselves in the action or in some direct painting analogy,
they're being posed, framed, reflected, and reflected upon, in some position
analogous to the freezing or fixing work of painting and sculpture. One way
or another this text will present its people to our gaze as if they were works

of plastic art. Rosamond and Mary Garth are poised in front of, and variously reflected in, the mirror of a toilette-table placed near a window (it's the context for the observation about Rembrandt in chapter 12). Casaubon is shown reflected in the distorting and diminishing views of his neighbours – so many 'small mirrors' – as if Milton's face or 'portrait' were to be reflected in a spoon (ch. 10). Repeatedly, characters go static, caught in some tellingly contrived tableau – Dorothea, posed like a statue among the marble figures in the Vatican gallery, prompting Naumann to envision her painted ('I would dress her as a nun in my picture': ch. 19); Mr and Mrs Bulstrode, side by side, united in mute shame (ch. 74); Rosamond and Will, immobilized on the threshold of a guilty liaison that short-sighted Dorothea blunders upon, only gradually focusing on this upsetting relation's 'terrible illumination': 'Will, starting up . . . seemed changing to marble' (ch. 77).

Getting to know the world demands a sequence of interpreting, reading engagements not at all helped by poor eyesight. Dorothea's bad eyes, like Casaubon's, become telling emblems of a pervasive hermeneutic difficulty. And these eye problems are exacerbated by the challengingly cryptic silences of the novel's recurrent moments of text-as-paintedness. Dorothea is a silent figure in the Vatican; Bulstrode is unable to utter a confession of guilt; his wife's 'promise of faithfulness' was silent too; Will was speaking to Rosamond 'with low-toned fervour', low enough to give the myopic observer distinct pause. And the power of such textualized moments lies precisely in their quietness, the quietness of paint on canvas and of words on the page. It's a muteness that shocks and arrests because it offers only tantalizing glimpses and whiffs of important depths that might or might not yield to the insistently interpretative gaze. And *Middlemarch* continually demands such a gaze from its readers. Like statuary or paintings, it never shouts. When Celia tries to draw out her sister Dorothea on the subject of Roman honeymoons, the reply is off-putting and 'quietly' voiced: 'No one would ever know what she thought of a wedding journey to Rome' (ch. 28). No wonder Henry James liked George Eliot above all her contemporaries, for all of her great texts closely approached the Jamesian condition of self-reflectingly cryptic, riddling fictions, a set of puzzles to readers, about puzzled characters compelled constantly to behave as readers presented with a world, other people, life, as a rebarbative set of shockingly difficult textualities.

Stupendous Fragmentariness

Dorothea's Roman experience (ch. 20) is central to the novel's presentation of the combination of necessity and difficulty in life-as-reading. Rome has a 'stupendous fragmentariness'. It presents an 'oppressive masquerade' of the ages, 'in which her own life too seemed to become a masque with enigmatical costumes'.

> To those who have looked at Rome with the quickening power of a knowledge which breathes a growing soul into all historic shapes, and traces out the suppressed transitions which unite all contrasts, Rome may still be the spiritual centre and interpreter of the world. But let them conceive one more historical contrast: the gigantic broken relevations of that Imperial and Papal city thrust abruptly on the notions of a girl who had been brought up in English and Swiss Puritanism, fed on meagre Protestant histories and on art chiefly of the hand-screen sort; a girl whose ardent nature turned all her small allowance of knowledge into principles, fusing her actions into their mould, and whose quick emotions gave the most abstract things the quality of a pleasure or a pain; a girl who had lately become a wife, and from the enthusiastic acceptance of untried duty found herself plunged in tumultuous preoccupation with her personal lot. The weight of unintelligible Rome might lie easily on bright nymphs to whom it formed a background for the brilliant picnic of Anglo-foreign society; but Dorothea had no such defence against deep impressions. Ruins and basilicas, palaces and colossi, set in the midst of a sordid present, where all that was living and warm-blooded seemed sunk in the deep degeneracy of a superstition divorced from reverence; the dimmer but yet eager Titanic life gazing and struggling on walls and ceilings; the long vistas of white forms whose marble eyes seemed to hold the monotonous light of an alien world: all this vast wreck of ambitious ideals, sensuous and spiritual, mixed confusedly with the signs of breathing forgetfulness and degradation, at first jarred her as with an electric shock, and then urged themselves on her with that ache belonging to a glut of confused ideas which check the flow of emotion. Forms both pale and glowing took possession of her young sense, and fixed themselves in her memory even when she was not thinking of them, preparing strange associations which remained through her after-years. Our moods are apt to bring with them images which succeed each other like the magic-lantern pictures of a doze; and in certain states of dull forlornness Dorothea all her life continued to see the vastness of St Peter's, the huge bronze canopy, the excited intention in the attitudes and garments of the prophets and evangelists in the mosaics above, and the red drapery which was being hung for Christmas spreading itself everywhere like a disease of the retina.

This Rome is an eye disease. Gazing at it causes the eye un-ease. Like all texts-as-rebus, this one gives too few or too many clues. No textual encounter has prepared the previously well-read Dorothea for being caught up in such a hermeneutic 'wreck' of unintelligibility, ruin, confusion – this 'glut of confused ideas'. The experience, this 'inward amazement of Dorothea's' that's intimately, though only implicitly, connected with loss of virginity, learning grisly truths about Casaubon, and getting on the steep slide downwards into domestic and intellectual unhappiness, is dementing enough. But it could be worse. The chapter goes on, in a famous passage, to declare that having the ability to penetrate all of nature's silences would kill us: 'If we had a keen vision and feeling of all ordinary human life, it would be like hearing the grass grow and the squirrel's heart beat, and we should die of that roar which lies on the other side of silence. As it is, the quickest of us walk about well wadded with stupidity.'

The thought here, then, is that stupidity, the blunting of our senses, saves our life. Which is just as well, for otherwise we might not be greatly consoled in being stuck with the awkward necessity of enigma. The connoisseur seeks the sureties of connaissance, knowledge. He would like to be, in the nice malapropism of auctioneer Trumbull when addressing Ladislaw in the matter of 'Guydo', 'a connoiss*ure*' (ch. 60). But, like the unsafe attribution of that painting to 'Guydo', no 'connoissure' in this novel is sure. Who or what, for example, is Dorothea in the Vatican gallery when she's considered as a sculpture by the novel's pair of well-travelled connoisseurs, Ladislaw and Naumann (ch. 19)? Is she a 'perfect young Madonna'? Or rather 'a sort of Christian Antigone – sensuous force controlled by spiritual passion'? She's poised next to 'the marble voluptuousness' of 'the reclining Ariadne'. Her form, we're told, is 'not shamed by the Ariadne'. But if anything of Ariadne is, so to say, rubbing off on Dorothea, this woman, even considered as Ariadne, is offering precious few certain clues as to her identity. Indeed, in a curious act of corrective authorial informing, the narrative tells us that the Vatican's Ariadne was not actually so described at the time of this incident. It was 'then called Cleopatra': just one more tangle in the devious weave of potential names and possible identities which leaves the gazing connoisseurs as incapable of conclusion about the character of Dorothea as she is herself. (Is she the Midlands St Teresa of the novel's prelude? Or an Old Testament Sara, or New Testament Dorcas, as in chapter 3? And so on.) As readable art-object, Dorothea's 'significance' remains as undecided as the obscurity that Will alleges to be the characteristic of Naumann's paintings.

A Difficult Kind of Shorthand

Will is a joker about symbolic meanings. When, in chapter 22, Mr and Mrs Casaubon visit Naumann's studio, Will not only lets on that he twits Naumann about his 'excess of meaning', but he teases Casaubon about the 'breadth of intention' in his own sketch of Marlowe's Tamburlaine Driving the Conquered Kings in his Chariot ('I take Tamburlaine in his chariot for the tremendous course of the world's physical history lashing on the harnessed dynasties . . . a good mythical interpretation'). He also teases Dorothea about the language of pictures. And she is ripe for teasing. She had earlier (ch. 9) told Mr Brooke and Casaubon, in relation to a sketch of Will's, that the 'language' of pictures was all Greek to her. Pictures 'are a language' that others understand, but not she – just as Casaubon sees 'what a Greek sentence stands for which means nothing to me'. And now Will lays the daft meanings on thick. His Tamburlaine stands for 'earthquakes and volcanoes', as well as 'migrations of races and clearings of forests – and America and the steam-engine. Everything you can imagine!' And the narrative clearly endorses the tease as Naumann explicates his own work: George Eliot's text is also teasing Dorothea. 'Dorothea felt that she was getting quite new notions as to the significance of Madonnas seated under inexplicable canopied thrones with the simple country as a background, and of saints with architectural models in their hands, or knives accidentally wedged in their skulls.' But already that sentence's progression is shedding its banteringly distant tone: those skulls have become perceptibly serious. And the next sentence seems thoroughly to endorse the idea of pictorial enigma, allegory, covertly puzzling meanings. 'Some things which had seemed monstrous to her were gathering intelligibility and even a natural meaning.' Dorothea is still unhappy with enigma. 'What a difficult kind of shorthand!' all this is, she declares: 'I think I would rather feel that painting is beautiful than have to read it as an enigma.' But though the jokily endless significances of Will's Tamburlaine ('yours with the very wide meaning') are unacceptable, she feels she's learning how to read Naumann's painted text ('I should learn to understand these pictures').

But if Will's pictures can be offered, even in jest, as packed with infinitely 'wide meaning' – 'Everything you can imagine!' – Naumann for his part, now that it's his turn for satire, professes to believe that Will's preferred medium of writing is possessed of even wider potential. 'Oh, he does not mean it seriously with painting. His walk must be *belles-lettres*. That is wi-ide.' Casaubon admires the satirical 'stretch' of the word (ch. 22). But Naumann's gibe is not at all wide of Will's earlier defence of language's capaciousness (ch. 19). Paint cannot do justice to women, he'd said. 'Language is a finer medium.' Painting is too superficial. 'Language gives a fuller image . . . . true seeing is within. . . . You must wait for movement and tone. . . . This woman whom you have just seen, for example: how would you paint her voice, pray?' And why is language a finer medium? Because it's vaguer: 'all the better for being vague'.

Questionable Riddle-Guessing

Writing is, of course, the medium of Casaubon's investigations. He refuses
to be drawn into the discussion (ch. 22) about the reading of painting, even
when Dorothea, taking seriously Will's jest about Tamburlaine representing
America, earnestly points the allegation in the direction of Casaubon's own
hermeneutics: ' "What a difficult kind of shorthand!" said Dorothea, smiling
towards her husband. "It would require all your knowledge to be able to read
it." ' He's silent and 'uneasy', perhaps because Will's 'off-hand treatment of
symbolism' is too warmly close to the nub of his own critical practice. Later
on, Dorothea is appalled to realize just how close. She comes (ch. 48) to fear
a lifetime devoted to sorting out the results of Casaubon's long years of
'questionable riddle-guessing', the dubious jigsaw-puzzle pictures he's cobbled together, 'shattered mummies, and fragments of a tradition which was
itself a mosaic wrought from crushed ruins'. His key to all mythologies is
conveniently supple in the face of the mythic riddle. It's almost as flexible
an interpretative practice, in fact, as Freud's readings of dream-texts as rebuses,
based in a belief in dreams as a word-master's *bricolage* of etymological
punning. 'Mr Casaubon's theory of the elements which made the seed of all
tradition . . . floated among flexible conjectures no more solid than those
etymologies which seemed strong because of likeness in sound, until it was
shown that likeness in sound made them impossible.'

To be this flexible in riddle-guessing, to play the game of utterly labyrinthine meanings, is to endorse the labyrinth as a meaning-prison. Casaubon's
hermeneutic 'shorelessness' (ch. 29), his interpretative bottomlessness, his too
'wide' a conceptual 'embrace' (ch. 3), are unfortunate conditions that Dorothea
only remains enthusiastic about while she's still naïve, untutored, and not
actually married to the old brute hermeneute. 'Dorothea . . . looked deep into
the ungauged reservoir of Mr Casaubon's mind, seeing reflected there in
vague labyrinthine extent every quality she herself brought . . . and . . .
understood from him the scope of his great work, also of attractively labyrinthine extent' (ch. 3). As he unfolds the story of his encounters with the
rebus of myth, offers his personal key to 'the vast field of mythical constructions', so that they 'became intelligible, nay, luminous with the reflected
light of correspondences', Dorothea thinks of Milton's 'affable archangel'
copiously instructing Adam and Eve in heavenly truths. We, rather, are supposed to think of Milton's fallen angels, lost in labyrinths of speculation as
they debate the abstruse points of Calvinist theology in the hellish labyrinth
of their constricted city of Pandaemonium, and find 'no end, in wand'ring
mazes lost'. And as in interpretation Casaubon is lost, so also in writing is
he perpetually deflected from any straight path. The great Ergon of the Key

to All Mythologies waits as he publishes his interim position papers, 'pamphlets – or "Parerga" as he called them'. It's Casaubon's fate to hesitate for ever on the disconcertingly indecisive threshold between *ergon* and *parergon*, work and side-work, word and by-word, path and by-path. The projected unified Ergon splits and bifurcates all too easily into many little Parerga. It has this daunting potential, seemingly, of proliferating endlessly into a distraught, distracted, for ever delaying and deferring network of forking paths.

Entangled in Metaphors

But then, this condition of Casaubon's reading and writing – or something very like it – is one curiously familiar to George Eliot herself, as witnessed by many moments of textual and metatextual reflection on the supple powers of metaphor or figurativeness. For George Eliot, metaphor comprises the labyrinth we're all fatally and necessarily enclosed in: 'we all of us, grave or light, get our thoughts entangled in metaphors, and act fatally on the strength of them' (this of Casaubon, ch. 10). Whether or not that is true for 'all of us', metaphorical entanglement is the condition that George Eliot's writings keep recognizing themselves as inhabiting. Take this passage about Mrs Cadwallader as an observer of the Middlemarch social scene (ch. 6):

> Now, why on earth should Mrs Cadwallader have been at all busy about Miss Brooke's marriage; and why, when one match that she liked to think she had a hand in was frustrated, should she have straightway contrived the preliminaries of another? Was there any ingenious plot, any hide-and-seek course of action, which might be detected by a careful telescopic watch? Not at all: a telescope might have swept the parishes of Tipton and Freshitt, the whole area visited by Mrs Cadwallader in her phaeton, without witnessing any interview that could excite suspicion, or any scene from which she did not return with the same unperturbed keenness of eye and the same high natural colour. In fact, if that convenient vehicle had existed in the days of the Seven Sages, one of them would doubtless have remarked, that you can know little of women by following them about in their pony phaetons. Even with a microscope directed on a water-drop we find ourselves making interpretations which turn out to be rather coarse; for whereas under a weak lens you may seem to see a creature exhibiting an active voracity into which other smaller creatures actively play as if they were so many animated tax-pennies, a stronger lens reveals to you certain tiniest hairlets which make vortices for these victims while the swallower waits passively at his receipt of custom. In this way, metaphorically speaking, a strong lens applied to Mrs Cadwallader's matchmaking will show a play of minute causes producing what may be called thought and speech vortices to bring her the sort of food she needed.

Kinds of metaphor, uses of metaphor, reflections upon metaphor, accumulate
here in an arrestingly self-conscious layering. Mrs Cadwallader is a great
observer, reader, and interpreter of the Middlemarch locality. Her interpreting,
though, depends upon what metaphorical lens she chooses to apply to the
social text of the town. Change the lens — and the metaphor — and what's
to be read changes, the interpretation alters. And, what's more, our reading
of Mrs Cadwallader equally depends on what metaphorical lens is applied to
her, on how she's disposed of, or offered to us, metaphorically speaking.

Many kinds of web famously preoccupy <i>Middlemarch</i>, both as formal method
of fictional organization and also as analogue of social and moral community.
But the basic webbing is a web of metaphor, of figure. And the dense webs
of Eliot's metaphoricity make her text's meaning continually slippery, elusive,
fragile, always prone to shifts or transferences; they make it precisely rebus-
like. And when the condition of text is so thoroughly metaphorical, fullness
and emptiness of meaning are all at once continuously present — kissing, overlapping, eliding, turning the one into the other. Play, puzzle, ruse, are never,
in such a text, not in question. It is a dauntingly energized condition of
textual unpinnability based in the prevailing metaphoricity's propensity for
surprise, perpetual motion, continual rusing acts of interlocked self-emptyings
and refillings, repeated difference and alterity, that's vividly brought home
by a now notorious passage in <i>The Mill on the Floss</i>.

In <i>The Mill</i>, schoolmaster Stelling thinks of brains as cultivatable fields,
and his pupil Tom Tulliver's brain as in particular need of ruthless ploughing
and harrowing. But the pedagogue's consequent reading of Tom's educability,
of his selfhood altogether, is at the mercy of such metaphors that define and
constrain it (II. 1):

> It is astonishing what a different result one gets by changing the metaphor!
> Once call the brain an intellectual stomach and one's ingenious conception of
> the classics and geometry as ploughs and harrows seems to settle nothing. But
> then it is open to someone else to follow great authorities and call the mind
> a sheet of white paper or a mirror, in which case one's knowledge of the
> digestive process becomes quite irrelevant. It was doubtless an ingenious idea
> to call the camel the ship of the desert, but it would hardly lead one far in
> training that useful beast. Oh, Aristotle, if you had had the advantage of being
> 'the freshest modern' instead of the greatest ancient, would you not have
> mingled your praise of metaphorical speech as a sign of high intelligence with
> a lamentation that intelligence so rarely shows itself in speech without meta-
> phor that we can so seldom declare what a thing is except by saying it is
> something else?

And this scepticism is manifestly self-directed at George Eliot's own writing
procedures. Tom Tulliver's lack of 'abundance' in speech means that he has

no metaphors for lessons in Latin ('he never called it an instrument of torture'). But George Eliot has no such lack. Her medium is metaphor and more
metaphor. Her texts are utterly abundant in metaphor. *The Mill* even has one
immediately on hand for describing, and countering, Tom's blankness about
metaphor: 'At present, in relation to this demand that he should learn Latin
declensions and conjugations, Tom was in a state of as blank unimaginativeness
concerning the cause and tendency of his sufferings, as if he had been an
innocent shrew-mouse imprisoned in the split trunk of an ash-tree to cure
lameness in cattle.' Imagining unimaginativeness; metaphor for the absence
of metaphor; metaphoric copiousness for blankness about metaphor: what
neater demonstration could there be of metaphoricity's slipperiness, its off-
hand sleights of hand, or of George Eliot's rightful watchfulness about her
own fluency in metaphor and the need continually to suspect metaphor's
plausibility, to watch out for its epistemological lures and traps?[59]

Not More Than Figuratively Ungenteel

Clearly we should take seriously *Middlemarch*'s warnings about the metaphoric or figurative medium that is its own habitat. And the more jokey they
are – like Will's thoughts on pictorial allegories – the more seriously, perhaps,
we should take them. As in that curious passage about writing upon low
subjects at the end of chapter 35, in which Featherstone's will is read out.
Treat low subjects as parables, as mere rhetorical figures of ungentility, and
that way, we're told, they acquire elevation, if only in terms of stylistic description, because they're then being considered in rather a high-flown way
as figures of style. So the meanings of parable, of figure, are thought of here
as being as flexible as any of Casaubon's mythography:

> And here I am naturally led to reflect on the means of elevating a low subject.
> Historical parallels are remarkably efficient in this way. The chief objection to
> them is, that the diligent narrator may lack space, or (what is often the same
> thing) may not be able to think of them with any degree of particularity,
> though he may have a philosophical confidence that if known they would be
> illustrative. It seems an easier and shorter way to dignity, to observe that –
> since there never was a true story which could not be told in parables where
> you might put a monkey for a margrave, and *vice versa* – whatever has been
> or is to be narrated by me about low people, may be ennobled by being
> considered a parable; so that if any bad habits and ugly consequences are
> brought into view, the reader may have the relief of regarding them as not
> more than figuratively ungenteel, and may feel himself virtually in company
> with persons of some style. Thus while I tell the truth about loobies, my
> reader's imagination need not be entirely excluded from an occupation with

lords; and the petty sums which any bankrupt of high standing would be sorry to retire upon, may be lifted to the level of high commercial transactions by the inexpensive addition of proportional ciphers.

Margrave was a German title for a ruler of border territory. And parable, in this version, is a textual border zone, or rebus condition, where monkeys can become margraves, and vice versa, according to the writer's or reader's wish. But what's not least noticeable about this astonishing passage is that its 'off-hand treatment' (to borrow George Eliot's phrase about Ladislaw's artcritical talk) of the slidings of interpretation, figure, rhetoric, should end up referring to cash. The example of how loobies can become lords, socially mean figures become figures of and for gentility, by being treated as only figuratively ungenteel, is the numerical elevation of the figures for small sums of money into figures for larger sums by the mere addition of noughts. The implication of paper delusions, a mere trick with figures, of fraud and deceit, and easy ('inexpensive') fraud at that (just add a few noughts), all undergirded by the suggestion that this figurative power is indeed a kind of emptiness, a game of ciphers, a juggling with noughts: this is arresting, even appalling. On this reckoning, the rhetorical medium is indeed a trickster's zone. Crooks and cheats, the whole tribe of Hermes, would be at home here. Here you play with rebuses with intent to deceive. Nothing on this view, whether apparently full or empty, low or elevated, is ever what it seems. The real is a game of perpetual verbal illusion. Everything is metaphorical, and everything metaphorical is a manipulation. And it's all a kind of naughting – a game with noughts, a sort of textual, even moral, bankruptcy.

And if this were in fact all, the rebus condition as presented by *Middlemarch* would indeed spell a terrible kind of *Ur*-deconstructive bankruptcy for meaning. It is not, though, all. *Middlemarch*'s medium is not just simple rebus work in this rather limited sense. To be sure, this text repeatedly welcomes its troubling condition as metaphor, parable, allegory, figure – that is, as rebus. In this text we are indeed in the midst of rebuses. But we are also *in mediis rebus*, in the midst of *res*, things, thinginess, and what's more, amongst middle, or middling, things. This medium of the textual rebus is also the medium of Middlemarch, the English Midlands, provincial mediocrity, mean ordinariness. The medium of fluid metaphoricity is also a medium of rather solid – even dully, banally, solid – moral, social, religious, political mediumness (and, it seems to me, a medium that George Eliot is happier with than Franco Moretti's use of the phrase *punctum dolens* suggests: the Midlands scene is narrow, but also beautiful and joyful for 'midland-bred souls'[60]). The text that is so much about figures of speech, the stuff of books, is also about figures in bank-books, and – perhaps the most momentous point to observe in the passage just quoted – simultaneously so. For George Eliot's text, and in her view of text, the one set of figures blurs into the other sort. As we read about Fred Vincy, Mr and Mrs Casaubon, Mr and Mrs Bulstrode, old Featherstone, Mr and Mrs Caleb Garth, Dr and Mrs Lydgate, we are indeed continually reminded of their condition as variously writable, readable, textual figures. They are, of course, figures in and of text. But we're also shown how much of their existence consists of, and is determined by, what figures, what numbers, what ciphers, figure in their bank balances, and how they acquired those numerical figures, how they spend those sums, and to whom they will eventually bequeath them.

The jokey Trumbull, jestful introducer of that eloquent rebus at the auction, a gleeful player with language ('an amateur of superior phrases'), plays on just this Eliotic duality of figures. After Trumbull has been allowed upstairs to see his dying second cousin, old Featherstone, much to the consternation of closer relatives excluded from the rich man's miserly presence and desperately greedy for his cash, Solomon Featherstone asks him whether anybody might ask what Featherstone has said:

> 'Oh yes, anybody might ask', said Mr Trumbull, with loud and good-humoured though cutting sarcasm. 'Anybody may interrogate. Any one may give their remarks an interrogative turn', he continued, his sonorousness rising with his style. 'This is constantly done by good speakers, even when they anticipate no answer. It is what we call a figure of speech – speech at a high figure, as one may say.' The eloquent auctioneer smiled at his own ingenuity. (ch. 32)

Figures of speech, on this model, are empty ornaments of style, high-flown but hollow. Trumbull affects to believe that Solomon's enquiry is what is known popularly as a 'rhetorical question'. Such questions expect, and normally get, no direct reply. They have some stylistic pretension, though, which makes them 'high' figures: a stylistic elevation, at least as Trumbull reckons it, that's enough to provoke his sick joke about a 'high figure' – alluding to the big sums of money the Featherstone cousinhood craves and will fail to receive. Their hopes of obtaining such high financial figures, characteristic of a general *Middlemarch* aspiration for financial fortunes, will prove as vain, as unanswered, as Solomon Featherstone's unwitting 'figure of speech' has been.

Old Maid's Rubbish

Figures and figures. Quite clearly *Middlemarch* is directing us to the possible moral and social dimensions of rhetoricity, its worldly connections. Allegory, parable, figure, metaphor – all names for, and rhetorical dimensions of, the text as rebus – are steeped here in something other than just rhetoric. Rhetoric is not, to use Hillis Miller's metaphor (see this chapter's note 59), the only bottom the text touches, so to speak. Trumbull's rebus, that emblem of Middlemarch's textuality, is also a 'practical' object, a piece of 'old maid's rubbish', banal as all of the town's provincial practicalities. Money is of its essence. The sample riddle that Trumbull reads out from the rebus rhymes *honey* with *money*. This rebus is about honey traps for women. And it comes at a price. It's finally knocked down for a guinea. As with all the other dodgy stuff on sale, cash is the be-all and end-all of Trumbull's witty talk. Figurative, and figurative of figurativeness, the rebus may be, but its fate is to be reckoned nonetheless at a certain money figure. Its purchaser, Mr Spilkins, a youth 'reckless with his pocket-money', pays over the odds for it. Banker Bulstrode, never reckless with *his* pocket-money or any other kind of cash, will soon get his 'Guydo' and a certain religio-aesthetic consolation for a more appropriate ten guineas. It would be 'an insult to religion', Trumbull assures his audience, 'that a subject like this should go at such a low figure' as a mere six guineas.

Pricing the picture properly, says Trumbull, 'touches us all as Christians'. And what's going on here, as Bulstrode's religiosity is measured out in petty cash and Raffles moves into a position to recognize and expose key facets of the social text of Middlemarch and Bulstrode's life, touches us all as socially engaged readers. There's moral accountancy being done – and to be done – here. This auction, a blunt convergence of opposite kinds of accounting materials, narrative stuff and money stuff, in a keenly revelatory engagement between figures of rhetoric and cash figures, brings home the extent to which the rebus of textuality can't shake off the perpetual drag of the worldly *res* – 'this petty medium of Middlemarch' (ch. 18) which Lydgate and Dorothea find it so hard to come to terms with, this world of 'low people by whose interference, however little we may like it, the course of the world is very much determined' (ch. 41). However high the rhetorical claim – and there are some astronomically high critical claims made for rhetoricity these days – *Middlemarch* insists on down-to-earth calculations about the imbruing of rhetoric, the textual rebus, in the strong undertow of middling or lowering considerations, in quotidian realities such as economics, morals, politics, history. Whatever figure rhetoric cuts in it, George Eliot's book is always going to be spotty with the 'commonness' of the *realium* that brings Lydgate's great ambitions down (ch. 15).

Out of the Library

Res, in fact, continually tests, hedges, frames *rebus* in Middlemarch. Just as Dorothea is disconcerted by her husband's flexible way with myth and etymologies, so one major strand of the novel is directed precisely at the freedoms which Bulstrode – and by implication also whole schools of Evangelical and Calvinist theology – take with metaphor. The young Bulstrode found it easy to accommodate making money at a crooked pawnbroker's with his higher religious claims to Evangelical probity, his life's devotion to saving souls and working for God's sake, because 'Metaphors . . . were not wanting'. Over the years he spun out these handy religious metaphors into 'intricate thickness, like masses of spider-web, padding the moral sensibility' (ch. 61). Lydgate is not the only person to be irritated by the banker's habit of 'broken metaphor and bad logic' (the phrase is used twice in ch. 67). *Middlemarch* is devoted to exposing the deceptive, canting logic of a metaphoricity that works so much to Bulstrode's cash benefit, to others' financial detriment, and, in the case of Raffles, to loss of life. The game of metaphoricity – it's Dickens's point, too, not least in relation to Chadband – is an intensely serious moral business.

In fact, textual games of all sorts, both reading and painting, those twinned artistic activities whose importance George Eliot so devotedly registers, tend to exist under a moral cloud in this novel. Studios and libraries and what goes on in them all attract, at times at any rate, the same Eliotic frown that's directed at gambling dens. 'Work is worship': George Eliot never repudiated the formula for the moral life that she first brought to the notice of English readers as the translator of Ludwig Feuerbach's *The Essence of Christianity* (1854). The opposite of such secular sacramentalism is play, exemplified for her in its most horrifyingly demonized version as gambling – playing the tables for money, rather than working for it. Fred Vincy bets and loses catastrophically. Lydgate tastes the same opiate, snuffing the vain possibility that gambling might get him off the financial hook that the extravagances of marriage to Rosamond have pinned him on. The scene of Fred's downfall and Lydgate's temptation is the billiard-room at The Green Dragon, haunt of the sporty and horsey. Nobody finds Caleb or Mary Garth there, playing billiards or laying bets. Nor do you find them pinning their financial hopes on big windfalls from old Featherstone's will – unlike Fred or the ugly tribe of Featherstones. Nor, for that matter, do you find the Garths locked into the total bookishness of the Casaubonian library enterprise, or the allegorical excitements of the studio world of Ladislaw and Naumann, that so attract Dorothea. Mary may remind you of a Rembrandt, but her 'brown', 'rough', 'stubborn', 'low' 'plainness' remains unpainted. If Rembrandt had indeed done her portrait, he 'would have made her broad features look out of the canvas with intelligent honesty'. Rembrandt's kind of Dutch art always looks honestly out of the canvas, which is why it remained an aesthetic touchstone for George Eliot. By contrast, Will's kind of allegorizing looks primarily inwards, as it were, into the canvas, absorbed by the paintedness of paint, and there is about his critiques more than a touch of playful dishonesty.

And, of course, Will eventually quits painting and the circle of his arty German chums, as well as his habit of 'taking all life as a holiday'. Morally wised-up, he goes over to the world of Caleb Garth and manual labour, all at once in marked antithesis to Fred's gambling, to Bulstrode's elastic Biblicism, and to what the German art community in Rome stands for. 'I should not like to get into their way of looking at the world entirely from the studio point of view,' he tells Dorothea in their important Roman conversation (ch. 21), the one in which she admitted to finding much of the art lifeless in a city that had revealed to her that 'there were so many things which are more wanted in the world than pictures', and he deplored the artifice of 'a great many' of the 'styles' of the 'old language' of art – where 'sometimes the chief pleasure one gets out of knowing them is the mere sense of knowing'. And it's no accidental part of George Eliot's approach to these matters that Dorothea and Will should then progress to the question of whether Casaubon's 'persevering devoted labour' is worthy work. Will is stung by sexual jealousy into gibing at Casaubon's distaste for German scholarship and his inability to read German. For the first time Dorothea senses that Casaubon's kind of textuality might be as vain as Roman artworks. She 'felt a pang at the thought that the labour of her husband's life might be void'. Growing up for Dorothea will include – in a major sense, will consist of – realizing that books and bookishness are not enough.

Increasingly, bookishness comes to seem to Dorothea like a prison. Even her own books. 'There was a little heap of them on the table in the bow-window – of various sorts, from Herodotus, which she was learning to read with Mr Casaubon, to her old companion Pascal, and Keble's *Christian Year*. But to-day she opened one after another, and could read none of them. Everything seemed dreary: the portents before the birth of Cyrus – Jewish antiquities – oh dear! – devout epigrams – the sacred chime of favourite hymns – all alike were flat as tunes beaten on wood. . . . Books were of no use.' After dinner, though, in a chapter (ch. 48) most of whose action consists of her work of wifely reading, she has to read to Casaubon as usual in the library. Then there's more reading out of his notebooks during the night. It's this night-time reading and Casaubon's uneasy attempt at extracting from her a promise of obedience to him after his death that provoke Dorothea's profound crisis of confidence in his dubious 'riddle-guessing'. After this awful night with books, Dorothea is sickened – indeed, quite ill with fatigue and despair. But despite her maid Tantripp's exhortation not 'to go into that close library', she does so, prepared for yet one more day of pointless bookwork. She knows she'll 'submit completely' to her husband's request for a life of post-mortem literary imprisonment, 'her own doom'. And she weeps again, as in Rome, fearful of the library as what Tantripp, who'd seen the Roman catacombs, calls a 'caticom'.

Happily, however, Dorothea is saved, for Casaubon is already lying dead out in the summer-house. Soon she'll be able to resist the 'dead hand' of his will and marry her own Will. Meanwhile, she refuses to carry on Casaubon's library work, turning her back on 'the rows of note-books' as the sun shines into the library, illuminating 'the weary waste planted with huge stones, the mute memorial of a forgotten faith'. Still wifely, still loyal to her husband's memory, she tidies the library materials, and arranges the notebooks 'in orderly sequence'; but she also gets out (ch. 54). The moment of liberation is a reprise of the earlier, proleptic occasion (ch. 34) when Mrs Cadwallader winkled her out of the library to look at Featherstone's funeral procession. On that occasion Casaubon slipped back into the library 'to chew a cud of erudite mistake about Cush and Mizraim'. But Dorothea, like a 'monk on his holiday tour', drank in the everyday scene of unbookish 'prosaic' Middlemarch life (and death) going on outside. It was a turning-point, a recognition scene that would be as memorable in later years 'as the vision of St Peter's at Rome'. 'I am fond of knowing something about the people I live among,' she said. This is the direction her life would eventually take – absorption into the mediocrity of worthy Midlands communality. 'I am quite obliged to Mrs Cadwallader for coming and calling me out of the library.'

Wanting Spiritual Tobacco

And so the dodgy middle where slippery rebuses preside, the flexible medium of Casaubon's conveniently versatile metaphoricity and Will's infinitely deft allegorizing, gives way to the unbookish, moral, worldly medium of the surrounding *res*. Bulstrode, that other self-serving metaphoricist, will be disgraced. Ladislaw the critical dilettante will side with Garth, will have great moral stature thrust upon him in repudiating Bulstrode's tricksy deals, will be brought back from the brink of sinning with Rosamond, and will marry his rescuer. So it's QED, then, for *res*? Well, not quite. For, once again, there's no simple either/or, no absolute opposition between word and world. Just as the author who warned of the versatile power of metaphorical descriptions to change utterly the nature of a pedagogy nevertheless ploughed metaphorically on in *The Mill on the Floss*, so in *Middlemarch* the power of bookishness, so criticized, resisted, subverted even, still asserts itself.

The Reverend Mr Farebrother mocks with considerable satirical zest any microscopic philological and scientific learning and writing on the plan of

Casaubon's kind of Biblicism: 'bad emendations of old texts, or small items about a variety of *Aphis brassicae*, with the well-known signature of Philomicron, for the *Twaddler's Magazine*; or a learned treatise on the entomology of the Pentateuch, including all the insects not mentioned, but probably met with by the Israelites in their passage through the desert; with a monograph on the Ant, as treated by Solomon, showing the harmony of the Book of Proverbs with the results of modern research' (ch. 17). This is wasteful 'spiritual tobacco'; at worst, words going up in smoke; at best, mere armchair consolation and pastime. But Farebrother still needs to put it, or something like it, in his pipe and smoke it. As the raconteur of the ways of dumb animals, he's said to be 'like another White of Selborne' (ch. 80).

Writing is the natural corollary of natural history as practised by Gilbert White and Farebrother. So too with George Eliot. The natural history she advocates as The Natural Historian of Our Social Classes (to adapt a phrase from her formative essay of July 1856 on the German social historian Wilhelm Heinrich von Riehl) is literary history, infused with, caught up in, textuality and intertextuality.[61] The opening of chapter 15 of *Middlemarch* is nicely revealing. It begins with Fielding. He's designated 'a great historian'. George Eliot cannot match his practice. Time, Victorian life and reading, no longer allow leisurely critical discussions on the model of Fielding's *Tom Jones* (as also in *Joseph Andrews*) – those 'copious remarks and digressions . . . especially in those initial chapters to the successive books of his history, where he seems to bring his own arm-chair to the proscenium and chat with us in all the lusty ease of his fine English'. The new kind of historian, the natural historian, must get on rather with grappling, in the manner of Lydgate's up-to-date pathology that preoccupies chapter 15, with the great 'web' of structural connections in the organic body of Middlemarch society and of the novel's plot, 'unravelling certain human lots, and seeing how they were woven and interwoven'.

Belated Histories

'We belated historians': that's George Eliot's label for herself on this occasion. But, clearly, her belatedness involves no simple rebuttal of Fielding. Her new practice finds it necessary to define itself in relation to the old. Natural history is still a kind of history; it still involves story, and the telling of Fieldingesque critical stories about story. This new and allegedly scientific mode of writing is still writing. And, of course, so far from having no time to indulge in a prefatory Fielding-like critical chat, this opening paragraph of chapter 15, in the very process of rejecting prefaces in the Fielding fashion, in fact comprises one. George Eliot cannot bring herself actually to name either Fielding or *Tom Jones*; but though she is able to erase their names, she can't blank out the power of their example. Her text of self-declared worldly, communal, natural-historical engagement is still a writing, a fiction, in a tradition of writing. For that matter, natural history remains a metaphor, just one of the several, as it were, Cadwallader lenses through which the novelist might have chosen to filter her practice and her concept of her practice. George Eliot's real world, the Riehl world no less, is by that very token a bookish world.

The inspiration for this kind of realism came, as so often (witness, clamantly, Feuerbach and all the rest), from a book. This author was belated in relation to a very great deal of precedent textualizing. Even before she'd written a word of fiction, the real had been decisively imprinted by the Riehl, had been recognized as writable, had been acknowledged by this potential novelist as a writable potential, a *res* to-be-written, to be turned into textual rebus. In a sense, too, George Eliot knew that whatever she might write was already written, that all writing was a kind of rewriting. Riehl, Fielding: they'd all got in first. So that the observation in the novel's Finale on Middlemarch town's belief that Mary must have written Fred's book on Crops and Feeding and that Fred wrote Mary's little book for boys, *Stories of Great Men* – 'there was no need to praise anybody for writing a book, since it was always done by somebody else' – seems to be not just an ironic recollection of George Eliot's own early experience with readers and family frantically speculating about the identity of the author of *Adam Bede*, but to reflect wryly on the perpetual belatedness of text.

After this novel's careful rejection of bookwork for work, of disturbingly enigmatic textualities for the moral glories of quiet lives, it comes as no little shock to be informed that Fred and Mary, quintessence of the opting for a married and Middlemarch ordinariness, should have written anything at all. But bookishness in *Middlemarch* sticks like glue. Chapter 83 finds Dorothea in the library again, still wrestling with books. This time, though, they're on 'political economy and kindred matters'. She will redistribute her fortune by the book. But once again she's failing to concentrate on bookwork. Again, bookishness, even of this worldly sort, irks. She still needs rescuing from the bind of bookish belatedness. And, on fairy-prince-like cue, Will Ladislaw arrives. The two are united in the library. They will marry. The stormy world outside the library's window-panes is to be theirs. They'll not enjoy the high figures of Casaubon's cash. Dorothea will be short of the wherewithal now to act out the advice of the political economy texts. Her craving for bookish elevation, so greatly diminished in her time with Casaubon, must come down an even lower peg or two. But still there remains a future with writing.

As a political journalist, Will faces the prospect of selling himself 'as a mere pen and a mouthpiece' (ch. 83). He enters the word-arena of Parliament. As for the text that contains him and Dorothea, its conclusions simply revel in the belatedness of intertextuality. Chapter 85 opens with a long quotation from Bunyan, 'immortal Bunyan', as a frame for concluding Bulstrode's fate. Chapter 86 has an epigraph from Victor Hugo about the conserving power of love. This epigraph is also about the conserving power of texts and the transmissions from one text to another, one set of storied lovers to another. 'C'est de Daphnis et Chloë que sont faits Philémon et Baucis' – and, by implication, Fred and Mary. The next, Finale chapter has Mary writing her book *Stories of Great Men*. They are *Taken from Plutarch*. After all of which it's easy to recall that when Dorothea waived Casaubon's plans for her to continue his life's work of riddle-guessing, she sealed his 'Synoptical Tabulation for the Use of Mrs Casaubon' in an envelope along with a rejection of his rebus practice and his synoptic gospel of that misguided bookish devotion: 'I could not use it.' But the rejection of the textual life was a writing, a note written and signed by herself – against a life of writing but in writing, against a testament but in a testament, against text but a text itself. Which is as pointful a complexity to recall as the case of Mr Spilkins, the rash purchaser of the 'practical rebus'. Spilkins is described as 'a young Slender of the neighbourhood'. He buys the rebus-riddle collection because 'he felt his want of memory for riddles'. Not unlike Slender, the idiotically hapless lover of Shakespeare's *The Merry Wives of Windsor*, who needs his books about him to help out in small talk and wooing – his 'book of Songs and Sonnets', it might be, or his 'Book of Riddles' (*Merry Wives*, I. i. 179–86). And the bookish connections are, like these, everywhere in George Eliot's text. *Res* and *rebus* are here indissolubly intertwined. There is never any absolute escape from the medium of the one into the medium of the other.

And riddling texts, texts as riddle, do have this way of turning out, like *Middlemarch*, to be emphatically dualistic, suffused in the paradox of rebus. *Finnegans Wake*, for example, the big riddler, several times invokes rebuses as clues to its identity. It proceeds *rebustly* (368: 17). It's a text that founds its textual city of Dublin as a punning antithesis to Rome, the city of Romulus and Remus, in a 'robulous rebus' (12: 34). It tells us it 'needs a rebus' to explain itself by. The *Wake* is the text as puzzle on the most massive scale known to modernist or postmodernist literature. But even *Finnegans Wake* sites itself squarely within the true dualistic ambivalence of rebus. It is *Rebus de Hibernicis* (104: 14). It's an Irish rebus – the most extreme and impossible kind, perhaps, along the lines of Irish jokes, or even Irish virgins as celebrated in Beckett's *Murphy*. But it's also a writing mightily preoccupied with the stuff, the geography, history, politics, of Ireland – *de rebus Hibernicis*. In short, as it says, it is a rebus, an extraordinary word-game, a text about words and texts and their slippery ways, which is also *de Hibernicis*, about Ireland and the Irish.

Let Us Consider Letters

And what could be more candid than that, you might wonder, as an under-lining of the bilingualism of rebus? But, of course, candour is precisely what is in question in the text-as-riddle, as is indicated by another of the great canonical texts of English literature, and one that seems at first just about as far removed from *Finnegans Wake* as you could get, namely Jane Austen's *Emma* (1816).

Emma is one of those texts whose self-reflexive inspections of the nature and consequences of writing is built about that epistemological equation – basic to the novel in general as it is basic to Derrida's *La Carte postale* in particular – the equation between the function of letters, epistles, and the function of literature itself. *Epistolae* and *litterae*; letters and Letters: their communicative ambitions, assumptions, functions, have run continuously in parallel in the whole Western tradition, so that they have rightly served as natural and comprehensive analogues of each other. 'La lettre, l'epître, qui n'est pas un genre mais tous les genres, la littérature même.' Thus Derrida in *La Carte postale*, providing the rationale for his notion that if the epistle, the art of letters, the business of the mails, the postal era, get subverted, are undone, so also is the whole art of Letters, *Litterae Humaniores*, and especially the postal era's greatest and most humanely humanist mode, the novel. It's this assumption of interdependence between epistles and Letters that drives and sustains Virginia Woolf's novel *Jacob's Room*. 'Let us consider letters,' Mrs Woolf invites us, as she squares up to one more inspection of the postal services which so preoccupy her in that novel, and the whole business of writing goes once more under the hammer. And, in its own quiet fashion, the same is true of *Emma*.[62]

Jane Austen inherited classic assumptions about the sufficiency of com-munication by epistle that sustained – and sustains – Derrida's post-age and the age of the classic realist novel. Her fiction grew up within the Richardsonian faith, the belief that letters can tell all, can be relied upon as modes of access to knowledge, avenues of self-revelation, means of truth-telling, instruments of personal, sexual, family power. Epistemology in what Foucault (not least in *Les Mots et les choses / The Order of Things*) called the Classical Age is commonly epistolary. There's even a suggestion in Samuel Richardson's practice of fiction that effective communication is of necessity epistolary: letter-writing is an imperative that Pamela and Clarissa and Lovelace and the rest eagerly subscribe to. And Jane Austen's own early attempts at fiction are naturally not behind in yielding to the going epistolary creed. *Love and Freindship, Lesley Castle, A Collection of Letters, The Three Sisters*, are of their era – the post-age – epistolary. But already in these Austinian beginnings there are signs of heretical, revisionary thoughts (they're there, arguably, in *Pamela* and *Clarissa* too, and they're certainly there in Fielding's send-up of *Pamela* in his *Shamela*). The young Jane Austen is already subverting the conventions she's exploiting – mocking female letter-writers' gush, exposing by over-exposure their exuberant fullness, their excess of stylistic self-confidence in their communicative procedures: 'There is a pattern for a Love-letter Matilda! Did you ever read such a masterpiece of Writing? Such Sense, Such Sentiment, Such purity of Thought, Such flow of Language & such unfeigned Love in one Sheet? No. . . .' And already in *A Collection of Letters* a pattern is being established – and it's the Richardsonian pattern too – of calling attention to what goes on in letters, not simply for the fun of it, but with sceptical, undermining intent. These youthful epistolary fictions are, in a complex ambivalent-mindedness, not wholly happy with the condition of letters which is their own condition. It's a wary self-scrutiny that *Emma*, not itself an epistolary novel but a novel built visibly upon the bones of one, manifestly continues (as also, though to a lesser extent, do *Pride and Prejudice* and *Persuasion*).

Epistles matter terribly in *Emma*. They enjoy a kind of absolute centrality in the world of its Highbury gentlefolks. Even Mr Knightley, jokily prone to dismiss the 'charm' of letters as a youthful aberration of Jane Fairfax's, can't profess complete 'indifference' to epistles. As for Jane Fairfax, there's no question of indifference: letter-writing is the only way that she is likely to escape the awful fate looming over all of Jane Austen's respectable poor girls – that is, having to 'sell' herself in the 'governess-trade' (ch. 35). Caught in the act of going to the post office despite the rain – intercepting the mail at the post office is the only way she will keep her transgressive correspondence with Frank Churchill secret – she sticks up boldly for letters as the seal of friendship, against Knightley's patronizing male gibes: 'till I have outlived all my affections, a post-office, I think, must always have power to draw me out, in worse weather than to-day' (ch. 34). Socially, Jane Fairfax is a 'nothing' who'll only become a something, a Mrs Frank Churchill, by dint of flouting the convention that respectable young women do not write privately to unmarried young men. And the Highbury women understand the desperation that motors her unconventionality. ' "And how much may be said in her situation for even that error!" ', declares Mrs Weston. ' "Much, indeed!" cried Emma, feelingly. "If a woman can ever be excused for thinking only of herself, it is in a situation like Jane Fairfax's" ' (ch. 46).

Jane Austen, of course, enjoys her joke at Jane's expense in chapter 34 as Mr Woodhouse, Mrs Elton, and Mrs Weston all join in chiding her for risking her health in the rain, and Mrs Elton makes Jane very nervous by suggesting that her letters be collected by one of her servants. The nervousness sponsors an excessively bright burst of chat from Jane about the wonders of the post office ('a wonderful establishment! . . . The regularity and dispatch of it!'), and especially the skill of its employees in deciphering handwriting. And once again the bright bubble of the young woman's talk is pricked by heavy Knightley, who dryly observes that the clerks are expert at reading because they're paid to be so. But now that the talk has got round to questions of deciphering, Knightley himself becomes utterly serious. For reading letters and interpreting epistolary hands are central to the morally discriminating life he leads. Emma professes to admire Frank Churchill's handwriting. Knightley can't endorse the enthusiasm – 'I do not admire it . . . It is too small – wants strength. It is like a woman's writing.' Knightley has already (ch. 18) found wanting the content of Churchill's epistle which made excuses for not visiting the Westons. 'He can sit down and write a fine flourishing letter, full of professions and falsehoods, and persuade himself that he has hit upon the very best method in the world of preserving peace at home and preventing his father's having any right to complain. His letters disgust me.' And Knightley goes on to locate the task of epistolary hermeneutics at the heart of the lexicography that preoccupies Jane Austen's texts. Reading letters is for him like reading Austen's novels is for us, a matter of engaging with the definition of moral terms. 'No, Emma, your amiable young man can be amiable only in French, not in English. He may be very "aimable", have very good manners, and be very agreeable; but he can have no English delicacy towards the feelings of other people: nothing really amiable about him' (ch. 18).

But for all Knightley's bluff certainty, there is already nothing simple about the writing and reading of letters. Letters, which circulate so freely in Highbury, and are read aloud in the family circle, and whose meanings are so openly debated, are also, apparently, circulating clandestinely. So the overtness of epistles and the post-age comes backed also by the possibilities they arrange for covertness. It's too easily overlooked – and I was only prompted to notice the fact by Marilyn Butler's arresting remark that the farmer Robert Martin never says anything in the novel – that we never see or hear directly from Martin's letter to Harriet, nor, for that matter, from her reply to it.[63] And silences cluster busily like this around all the postal activity of *Emma*. In chapter 34 Emma does not counter Knightley's accusations by submitting Churchill's hand to any public test: a note from him remains locked up in her writing-desk next door. What's more, she keeps quiet about 'the expense of the Irish mails; – it was at her tongue's end – but she abstained'. Further, we suspect Knightley of reading Churchill's letter with a jealous eye on Emma's obvious keenness for the young man. Emma, too, wonders at the degree of Knightley's vexation. She's happy to profess her 'prejudice' in Churchill's favour, but shocked to discern an 'unjust' reading in Knightley (ch. 18).

'Prejudiced! I am not prejudiced', was Knightley's indignant response to Emma's objection to his reading. But it does seem likely. Letters in *Emma*, in other words, provide tests for readers even more complex than the ones they offer writers. Emma's prejudice as a reader is only one aspect of her sloppiness with all writing and reading materials. Her early efforts (ch. 7) over Robert Martin's letter to Harriet – biased, grudging, foolishly snobbish, wilfully myopic – set the reading pace. She'll misread deliberately, read against the clear moral and social grain. Martin's letter is so obviously good – *plain, strong, unaffected,* 'good sense, warm attachment, liberality, propriety, even delicacy of feeling' – that 'one of his sisters must have helped him'. It just won't do. It may be better than expected, but Martin himself is still 'illiterate' and 'vulgar', and his letter, after all, only 'tolerable'. And this tricksy reader of a letter becomes, as it were, just as tricksy a writer of one. With constant waivings of any intention to interfere, Emma steers Harriet into a letter of refusal. It was 'particularly necessary to brace her up with a few decisive expressions'. Even if Martin can manage to 'write a good letter', his 'clownish manner' would probably offend Harriet 'every hour of the day'. And Harriet agrees: 'Nobody cares for a letter.' Emma lets the observation pass. But it's simply not true. Harriet cares, and so do Emma and all her friends. Emma's bossy deviousness has painted her into a discomfiting corner. But clearly, once you start playing fast and loose with epistles, you can't stop. Soon Emma is luxuriating in a delicious misreading of Frank Churchill's letter to Mrs Weston (ch. 31).

Wilfully self-deluded, Emma inhabits at this stage of her career an atmosphere of high epistolary imaginativeness, constantly 'forming a thousand amusing schemes for the progress and close of their attachment, fancying interesting dialogues, and inventing elegant letters'. The invention of letters goes hand in hand with the invention of meaning in letters. Churchill's letter proves gratifyingly 'stimulative' – but stimulative of silliness. Emma decodes every reference in it to 'Miss Woodhouse' as a confirmation that he loves her – a love that, of course, she spurns. She's prejudiced alright, and her epistolary errors and mismanagements are central to the comic exposure of 'one who sets up as I do for Understanding' (ch. 49) as an egregious misreader of self and world. Mr Knightley, though, is set up as a true centre of moral intelligence and rational understanding, of reading capacities grounded always in appropriate conscience. That his reading of a letter might be thrown out of true because of jealousy is truly disconcerting.

But Knightley's prejudice – and his mistaken jealous belief that Emma is really in love with Churchill will increase until it climaxes in that angry solicitude over her supposed upset at the news of Frank and Jane's wedding: 'The feelings of the warmest friendship – Indignation – Abominable scoundrel!' – Knightley's prejudice is important in generalizing the idea that reading is difficult. It isn't just the young or girls who make heavy weather of the business. Of course, even for the merely nosey girl or the older female gossip in Jane Austen's world, people are, like their texts, delicious puzzles which do often yield to the keen decoder. Why, for instance is Jane Fairfax hanging on for months in Highbury when she might be with her guardians the Campbells in Ireland where they've gone to join Jane's old friend the former Miss Campbell and her new husband Mr Dixon? Jane is 'a riddle, quite a riddle', says Emma. 'Here is quite a . . . puzzle' (ch. 33). And Emma will puzzle out an answer (Jane is peeved: she wanted Dixon herself). But reading people, reading letters, is also, and for everybody concerned, an engagement with riddle, puzzle, conundrum – a self of hard reading encounters – in which mistaking is also eminently on the cards. Guessing the truth of the Dixon business helps keep Emma in the dark about Jane's clandestine affair with Churchill.

More Equal to the Covert Meaning?

The three occasions on which actual riddles or word-puzzles occur in *Emma* sharply extend the *litterae–epistolae* equation: for both of these turn out also to equal riddle. Emma is as devoted a misreader of riddles as she is of letters, and in just the same areas of Harriet's future and the intimations of suitors. Riddles (ch. 9) are, we're told, Harriet's only kind of literature (she never got far in books, no 'more than a few first chapters, and the intention of going on tomorrow'). She aims for a collection of riddles 'on a very grand scale'. 'Emma assisted with her invention, memory and taste.' And Mr Elton is invited to 'contribute any really good enigmas, charades, or conundrums that he might recollect'. He contributes 'their two or three politest puzzles', then recalls an old chestnut they already have. They press him to 'write one yourself'. The result is intended for Emma. He tries to privatize it, keep it covert, telling Emma it's for her, not for the collection. But Emma briskly makes it public, as it were, in consigning it wholly to Harriet: 'it is for you. Take your own.' Harriet, all fluttery with girlish anxiety, is puzzled. 'What can it be, Miss Woodhouse? – what can it be? I have not an idea – I cannot guess it in the least. What can it possibly be? . . . do help me. I never saw anything so hard . . . It must be very clever, or he would not have brought it. Oh! Miss Woodhouse, do you think we shall ever find out?' Emma, though, knows – 'Give me the paper and listen' – and returns a clamantly wrong solution: 'There is so pointed, and particular a meaning in this compliment that I cannot have a moment's doubt as to Mr Elton's intentions. *You* are his object.' Clearly, reading a riddle is no push-over. And Emma, the reading subject or agent, turns out to be just as much the concentrated focus of mistaking when she becomes the reading patient, the subject herself of a riddle and the object of someone else's misplaced reading confidences.

On the lamentable outing at Box Hill (ch. 43) Emma proposes a guessing game. What are people thinking of? Every key participant, indeed every reader, would like to know that; but propriety forbids such truth games. So the game is changed, hurriedly. Can people instead say one clever thing, or two immoderately clever things, or three dull ones? Emma, of course, cannot resist saying just what she thinks about boring Miss Bates when the old dear asks the picnickers whether or not they think her capable of saying 'three dull things'. Emma puts her foot heavily in it: 'Ah! ma'am, but there may be a difficulty. Pardon me – but you will be limited as to number – only three at once.' It's a truly terrible moment that's not at all alleviated by Mr Weston coming instantly in with his attempt at something clever, a conundrum. 'What two letters of the alphabet are there, that express perfection?' Like Francis Bacon's Pilate enquiring about truth, he won't stay for an answer, and rushes on with his own solution. 'Ah! you will never guess. You, (to Emma), I am certain, will never guess. – I will tell you. – M. and A. – Em-ma. – Do you understand.' Nothing could be for the moment more inappropriate. To be sure, some of the players are too stupid even to grasp this kind of puzzle and this sort of social mistaking. Mrs Elton, who 'had an acrostic once sent to me upon my own name, which I was not at all pleased with', takes herself and her husband off for some less stationary 'exploring'. But the pained Miss Bates and the morally censorious Knightley are right to suppose that such easy solutions are misleading ones. '*Perfection*', says Knightley, 'should not have come quite so soon.' Being 'clever' on this plan will not do. And one more attempt at joke has failed. 'Better pass it off as a joke,' Churchill had said to Emma about the guessing proposal. But conundrums and their particular brand of hermeneutic wit, at least Weston's sort, aren't funny either. Only Emma, Frank, and Harriet 'found a great deal to laugh at and enjoy' in Weston's cleverness.

The joke is on Emma. And the reader is in a position to share the text's sense of satirizing superiority. It's part of a sense of knowing where we are in our reading of Emma through the riddling going on through and around

her. When we come, though, to Frank Churchill's alphabet game the sense
of word-games as no joke continues, but now it's the reader's own hermeneutic
footing that becomes unsure. In chapter 41 *Emma* plays riddling games with
the reader as well as with the characters.

    Churchill has just accidentally let slip some local gossip, knowledge of which
can only have come from Jane Fairfax. So his clandestine correspondence
with her is in danger of being exposed, with terrible possibilities for social
opprobrium. He needs to communicate his mistake to Jane, to warn her he's
made a blunder. Quick on the up-take, he gets Emma to produce her nephew's
'alphabets – their box of letters'; they provided so much amusement the
previous winter; 'I want to puzzle you again'. 'It was', as Knightley soon
guesses, 'a child's play, chosen to conceal a deeper game on Frank Churchill's
part.' The clandestine covertness of the private correspondence, the letters
that have passed between Frank and Jane, runs in parallel with the attempt
to communicate covertly with Jane through the private messages of this
alphabet-puzzle. Mr Woodhouse likes the 'quietness of the game'. And quiet
communication has been the appeal of the private correspondence for Churchill
and Jane Fairfax. Moreover, just as it has been hard for the Highgate community to get at the truth of the Churchill–Fairfax correspondence, so it's now
difficult for onlookers to perceive the truth of the alphabet-puzzle which
mimics and repeats it. The hermeneutical difficulties of reading, of epistles
and texts in general, are emblematized in the puzzle of these particular
letters of the alphabet and the words Churchill forms from them. He makes
two or three alphabetical clusters: *blunder*, *Dixon*, and possibly also a third
word which remains, however, unspecified. What does all this signify? What,
especially is that last word? What *is* Churchill's game?

    Harriet Smith is, once again, the crudest reader. She 'exultantly proclaimed'
the word *blunder*, thus shouting out the truth of the Churchill–Fairfax
correspondence that Miss Bates had nearly stumbled upon with her rambling
reflections on how Churchill might have got to hear of the plan Mr Perry had
of getting a carriage, and that Knightley had guessed almost immediately
(his 'eyes had preceded Miss Bates's in a glance at Jane'). For her part, Emma
sets up, once more, as the confident reader, but again gets things wrong or
not really right enough. ('My dear Emma', Knightley presses her, 'do you
perfectly understand the degree of acquaintance between the gentleman and
lady we have been speaking of?' 'Oh! yes, perfectly. – Why do you make a
doubt of it?') And Knightley is, of course, the most superior reader around.
He's the best-placed observer of all these alphabetical manoeuvrings: 'so
placed as to see all' the players; 'it was his object to see as much as he could'.
He picks up the meaning of *blunder* straightaway, noting the 'blush on Jane's
cheek which gave it a meaning not otherwise ostensible'. So that in the same

movement of hermeneutical discovery he's onto the meaning of the letters of the alphabet and of the letters that have apparently travelled through the mails between the covert lovers. Still, though, and arrestingly, even Knightley fails to understand quite what *Dixon* means. This remains a private joke between Churchill and Emma (she 'found it highly entertaining') at the expense of Jane. But the joke is once again also on Emma, who is in this apparent moment of complicity also being put off the scent of Churchill's real affection. Naturally enough, Jane understands about Dixon much better than Knightley. He notices 'the poignant sting' of the word, but that's all. Her 'comprehension was certainly more equal to the covert meaning . . . of those five letters so arranged' than Knightley's was. What's more, Emma refuses to explain later: 'it all meant nothing, a mere joke among ourselves.' But even more arresting is the truly stubborn enigma of the third word.

'Mr Knightley thought he saw another collection of letters anxiously pushed towards her, and resolutely swept away by her unexamined.' In the general confusion of guests leaving, he cannot be certain whether any word has actually passed. Nor is he clear about the mood of the suspicious pair: 'how they parted, Mr Knightley could not tell.' That the novel's most acute observer and moral censor is so confused is to be felt by the reader as particularly telling. And the confusion is one endorsed by the text. The Austen family liked to continue the puzzling out of this particular word-game: family tradition had it that this third word was *pardon* – Churchill apologizing for the *Dixon* jest that so hurt Jane's feelings. But our text remains silent. In other words, the novel's insistence upon the enigmatic difficulties of reading is absorbingly strengthened at this point. There is, clearly, clarification to be had by means of letters, but their deterring enigmas will remain also in play. The generally recognized puzzling quietness of words, letters, whether letters of the alphabet or epistles in the post, converges dramatically onto the unuttered and, in fact, the unutterable silences of the word and of meanings which are actually withheld. Small wonder, you feel, hereabouts, that Virginia Woolf should have thought that Jane Austen could have been, had her work continued, 'the forerunner of Henry James and of Proust'.[64]

It is, as George Eliot's texts keep reminding us, the quietness of certain texts that conspires to assist their enigma. And it's the quietness of the silent word, the covert epistle – and, for that matter, of painting (one thinks of the portrait of Darcy in *Pride and Prejudice* before which Elizabeth Bennet says not a word), or a garden or landscape (not least in *Emma*, chapter 42, where the 'nothing' of Robert Martin's Abbey-Mill Farm is read by Emma's party, by the text, and by us, as so 'English') – it's the quietness that endorses the enigma, and also provokes the necessity of coming seriously to grips with the possibility of comprehension. Jane Austen's importance lies *inter alia* in her insistence that there is a moral imperative in this provocation that goes beyond the mere hermeneutic pleasures to be got from textual games. The moral seriousness of interpretation is, in her reading, beyond a joke. Not least important for her is that better reading can be learned and that this betterment has moral aspects. There is a moral betterment that can accompany, afforce, and be afforced by, hermeneutical improvement: a self-improvement by hermeneutical diligence. Emma learns her failures as a hasty interpreter who is prone to be too much of an imaginist. She has to learn to control her impetuosity in reading, by sense and seriousness. And she does learn. Contrast, for example, her reaction to Robert Martin in the early letter to Harriet and her agreement with the text's late reading of the English verdure, culture, and comfort of his farm-scape just referred to. And Knightley is the novel's best reader precisely because he is so morally earnest. At the end of the novel Churchill is still finding the whole affair of the correspondence a joke. Emma appreciates the 'high entertainment' he got from outwitting, 'tricking', them all. He jokes about Jane's embarrassment on the day when he made his blunder. And Emma laughs with him, or at least smiles 'completely'. But this is only 'for a moment'. She cannot now understand how Churchill can keep on laughing and wanting to laugh (how he can *'court'* such recollections). She sees now with Knightley's eyes, the vision of the morally serious writer and reader. She 'felt, that pleased as she had been to see Frank Churchill, and really regarding him as she did with friendship, she had never been more sensible of Mr Knightley's high superiority of character' (ch. 54).

And the morally serious kind of reading proposed by *Emma* is reading that notices and respects the deterring enigmatics of letters, but at the same time refuses to give up the quest for right meanings – which is also at the heart of the Austinian quest for the meaning of righteousness. Struck, for example, by what he perceives as the reserve of Jane Fairfax, Knightley is determined to probe what is suggestive of some morally deplorable covering up: 'I love an open temper.' He refuses to accept either the world or the word as void of meaning, empty of moral concerns and of the possibility of a moral lexicon.

> Mr Knightley began to suspect [Churchill] of some inclination to trifle with Jane Fairfax. He could not understand it; but there were symptoms of intelligence between them – he thought so at least – symptoms of admiration on his side, which, having once observed, he could not persuade himself to think entirely void of meaning, however he might wish to escape any of Emma's errors of imagination. (ch. 41)

Knightley does not want to be an Emma – filling up the spaces of meaning with the richly fanciful. But he will avoid the opposite error of supposing no meanings present at all, a 'void of meaning', an absence behind the manifest symptoms of presence. He believes – and the text proves him right – that there is a something centred within the awfully quiet enigma of puzzles, word-games, alphabets, letters. 'He could not understand it.' Not yet, at any rate. But he will go on trying. And in the process he becomes, not least, the model of a model reader of Jane Austen's own texts – texts whose power is, notoriously, implicitness and quietness – whether of action or meaning or of social and moral criticism.

Candid Camera

What we are confronted with in *Emma*, what *Emma* confronts, is, in other words, the problematic frankness or candour of letters. Frankness is obviously in question in *Emma*. When a key protagonist in a fictional episode of covert letter-writing, the transgressive circulation of undercover meanings, is named Frank, you should certainly prick up your ears and look for trouble.[65] To be frank is to be open and outspoken; which Frank Churchill is not, at least, not when it comes to his affair with Jane Fairfax. At the time of *Emma*, to frank a letter was to put your signature on its outside and so own up before the world to being its sender; which is not the nature of Frank Churchill's correspondence with Jane. Clearly the nature of frankness – what it means to be frank and Frank – is under frank inspection. What perturbs this novel is precisely the lack of openness in *Emma*'s world, and it's a lack provocatively embodied, it turns out, in the bearer of a name that's utterly central to the vocabulary of sincerity: one Frank. So Jane Austen's usual moral lexicography has focused – unusually for her: no Dickens she – in a proper noun, a personal name. More usually in her fictions the sharp-tongued moral lexicographer sticks to probing the semantics of the common nouns and adjectives of moral praise and blame, the traditional novelist's verbal tools of description and discrimination – good, better, best, kind, wrong, amiable, and the like. When Knightley criticizes Churchill for a lack of English amiability ('He may be very "aimable" . . .' (ch. 18)) he's only doing Jane Austen's customary hatchet-job of moral lexicography. Which is momentous enough. But when this novel, with the so unfrank doings of the unfrank franker of unfrank letters Frank Churchill at its core, focuses its moral-lexical doubting through the then currently uncertain meanings of the words *candid* and *candour*, something rather special, and even rather momentously exemplary, does seem to be going on, even for Jane Austen.

At the period when Jane Austen was writing, the meanings of the words *candour* and *candid* were undergoing a complete turn-about, as William Empson noted in 1951 in *The Structure of Complex Words* and as Donald Davie has been

more recently keen to repeat (as part of his running battle with the insinceri-
ties of the eighteenth-century Unitarians who, as he sees it, pretended to be
Christians when they were not, because they could not hold with the Holy
Trinity). Commenting on a discussion of the 'affectation of candour' in *Pride
and Prejudice*, Empson noted that novel's scepticism about 'just what kind of
truth-telling is involved' in being *candid* at the end of the eighteenth century. The word, he points out, implied no simple or normal semantic equation.
'In other words' – this is Davie glossing Empson – 'in the 1790s, if one were
in any way scrupulous and alert and honest as a speaker or writer of English,
one had to recognize that "candour" and "candid" were suspect words, very
problematical.'[66] And by 1816, in *Emma* and the manifestly unfrank world
of Frank Churchill, the problematic is even more acute (and a far cry, by the
way, from Marilyn Butler's feeling about *Emma* as being full of 'directness'
and 'openness', 'the greatest novel of the period because it puts to fullest use
the period's interest in articulate, sophisticated characters, whose every
movement of thought finds its verbal equivalent in a nuance of speech'[67]). What
was happening to *candid* and *candour* – for reasons upon which Empson and
Davie disagree sharply – was a semantic shift from the original Latinate
meanings, to do with kindly, benign frankness, a tolerant whitewashing or
covering up of people's faults, a dwelling only on their better aspects and
best motives, to the modern senses where to be candid is to be brutally frank
about people's faults. Jane Austen stands at the cusp of the shift, so that her
texts can make great play with the revaluation of the virtue of being candid
in the old sense, the generous liberality of judgement that Dr Johnson thought
so highly of (Johnson's *Dictionary*: 'Freedom from malice, favourable disposition, kindliness; "sweetness of temper, kindness" '), a revaluation that was
going on in contemporary England and English.

Candour is naturally in question in relation to Frank Churchill and to
Emma on Box Hill. 'In general', Churchill 'was judged, throughout the
parishes of Donwell and Highbury, with great candour; liberal allowances
were made for the little excesses of such a handsome young man – one who
smiled so often and bowed so well; but there was one spirit among them not
to be softened, from its power of censure, by bows and smiles – Mr Knightley'
(ch. 25). Knightley is not prepared to be candid (old sense), and in so
refusing he becomes utterly candid in our sense – extremely frank and open
about Churchill's character, as opposed to the general Highbury (and female)
tendency towards moral cover-up, tolerance, and forgiveness. He speaks out,
and his is a speaking out that the novel appears to endorse. But speaking out
is clearly not something always admired. Emma is candid (in our sense) and
uncandid (in the old sense) about Miss Bates's stupidity and dullness, and
that perturbs the novel as it perturbs Knightley and the others. Miss Bates

'felt your full meaning', says Knightley (ch. 43). 'She has talked of it since. I wish you could have heard how she talked of it – with what candour and generosity.' The implication is that Emma could have done with some of Miss Bates's old-fashioned candour and repressed her more up-to-date urge for a candidly expressed (in our sense) fullness of meaning.

So the moral dilemma remains. Should one speak out frankly on all occasions? Is fullness of meaning always the aspiration of moral people? And these moral issues are, obviously, also writing issues, ones focused in the business of epistles. Most of the novel's letters are common property, to be read openly and passed about among relations and friends for free and public comment and interpretation – just as they were in Jane Austen's own family. In other words, epistles are normally candid (in our sense) affairs; which is what Knightley prefers in a correspondence. To be candid (old sense) about epistles is to incur the wrath of a Knightley. Covert, that is candid (old sense), writings smack of the immoral. Nonetheless, however, old-fashioned candid Highbury will still, in the end, condone Jane Fairfax and Frank Churchill almost to the hilt for their joint crime of epistolary uncandidness (our sense), their concealed writing relationship. And, of course, Jane Fairfax is saved by this epistolary uncandidness (our sense) from going off to be a governess, saved from a heavy misery that no gentlewoman in Highbury would wish upon her and that every lady felt to merit the desperate strata-gem of the unfrank epistle. And she's rescued in particular when, as Churchill confesses in his long letter of explanation to Mrs Weston, he discovers that he has accidentally locked up his letter of reconciliation with Jane 'in his writing-desk' and gets it out to send to her. So the uncandid one (our sense) is finally rescued by a piece of epistolary discovery, a gesture of anti-covert-ness, of candidness in our sense, frankly owned up to in a for once frank epistle from Frank. Clearly, candour and uncandour are in a confused state, and the opposite merits of candid and uncandid words, open and closed letters, letters locked up in the privacy of writing-desks and letters released from that privacy, are to remain ambivalent right (or, indeed, write) to the end.

And this moral ambivalence is also an ambivalence about possibilities of meaning. As *Emma* cannot resolve the debate about the morality of candid speech and candid writing, so it doesn't finally resolve the issue between the powers of candour and those of uncandour, the tendencies to covertness and overtness, in letters, epistles, novels, as telling issues of its epistemology and hermeneutics. Famously, Jane Austen's own writing style is a concealing one – candid (in our sense: prickly, waspish, the vehicle of the notorious 'regulated hatred') within an appearance of candour in the old sense (kind concealment, gentle ironies). And in place after place, but especially in the extraordinarily

canny courtship scene between Knightley and Emma (ch. 49), *Emma* tends
to become all at once exemplarily candid (in our sense) about the tendency
of texts towards uncandidness (our sense), reaching a sort of exemplary equilibrium where the candour of texts survives despite the continuing obstacles
of linguistic uncandidness (both in our sense). The practical textual result can
be a quite Conradian or Jamesian jostle of frankness and unfrankness, as
crucial words are, just as in the alphabet-game, simply withheld. 'What did
she say? – Just what she ought, of course. A lady always does.' As the text
gives us Emma's (non)reply to Knightley's offer of love, it becomes appallingly
unfrank, uncandid (our sense). Doubtless there was some liaison here for our
author between choice and necessity. What does a lady say? Did Jane Austen
actually know? Certainly, we'll never know. But, too, and crucially, 'She said
enough to show there need not be despair – and to invite him to say more
himself.' And, after all, Knightley, inveighing against Emma's silence and
pleading to hear her voice, disclaiming the capacity to make speeches himself,
does manage to speak out most candidly, or at least candidly enough (in our
sense), just as he had spoken out morally before. ' "You hear nothing but
truth from me. – I have blamed you, and lectured you, and you have borne
it as no other woman in England would have borne it. – Bear with the truths
I would tell you now, dearest Emma, as well as you have borne with them . . .
you understand me . . ." ' 'While he spoke, Emma's mind was most busy,
and, with all the wonderful velocity of thought, had been able – and yet
without losing a word – to catch and comprehend the exact truth of the
whole.' There's clearly a time when a person wants to catch an exact truth,
just as there was a time when feeling a full meaning (as Knightley put it of
Miss Bates) was something to be avoided, if possible. And the clear implication of *Emma* is that there are times when you might want to do either,
and neither is quite within your power to control.

Full meanings and not-so-full ones; concealed meanings and open ones;
words locked up in the writing-desk and words let out from it; letters
franked and unfranked; a text candid and not so candid (both in our sense)
about textual candour (in either the old or the modern sense), and also a text
candid and not altogether candid (both in our sense) about the morality of
persons: in these contradictions *Emma* demonstrates, then, the inevitable and
troubling mixture of openness and concealment in human affairs and also the
concomitant mixture, just as necessary and just as troubling, of possibilities
both for revelation and for enigma in human texts, writings, the arts of letters
in every mode. And in this, as in other great Joker texts built about the puzzle
of words and word-puzzles, no one side of the binary array of the frank and
unfrank ever has the last laugh all to itself. As the para-logics of my next
chapter would have it, both are indistinguishably parasitic upon each other.

NOTES

1   Jean-François Lyotard and Jean-Loup Thébaud, *Just Gaming*, trans. Wlad Godzich, Theory and History of Literature, 20 (Manchester University Press, 1985). See, for an interesting summary and hostile critique, P. D. Juhl, 'Playing with Texts: Can Deconstruction Account for Critical Practice?', in *Criticism and Critical Theory*, ed. Jeremy Hawthorn (Arnold, London, 1984), 59–72.

2   Harold Bloom, *Ruin the Sacred Truths: Poetry and Belief from the Bible to the Present* (Harvard University Press, Cambridge, Mass., and London, 1989), ch. 1: 'The Hebrew Bible', 3–24.

3   Roger Caillois, *Les jeux et les hommes* (Gallimard, Paris, 1958); *Man, Play, and Games*, trans. Meyer Barash (Thames and Hudson, London, 1962). Wolfgang Iser, *Sterne, Tristram Shandy*, Landmarks of World Literature series, trans. David Henry Wilson (Cambridge University Press, 1988), ch. 3: 'The Play of the Text', 91ff. For wider applications of game-theory by Iser, see 'The Play of the Text', in *Prospecting: From Reader Response to Literary Anthropology* (Johns Hopkins University Press, Baltimore and London, 1989), 249–61.

4   For discussion and other examples see Patricia Waugh, *Metafiction* (Methuen, London, 1984), 'Play, Games and Metafiction', 34ff.

5   Sigmund Freud, *Jenseits des Lustprinzips* (1920); *Beyond the Pleasure Principle* (1922), trans. James Strachey (1950, 1955), in Pelican Freud Library, vol. II: *On Metapsychology: The Theory of Psychoanalysis*, ed. Angela Richards (Penguin, Harmondsworth, 1984), 283–7.

6   Hans-Georg Gadamer, *Truth and Method* (*Wahrheit und Methode*, 2nd edn (J. C. B. Mohr (Paul Siebeck), Tübingen, 1965), trans. W. Glen-Doepel, ed. John Cumming and Garrett Barden (2nd English edn, Sheed and Ward, 1979), Part 1, ch. 2: 'The Ontology of the Work of Art and its Hermeneutical Significance. 1. Play as the Clue to the Ontological Explanation. (A) The Concept of Play', 93, 97.

7   D. H. Lawrence, 'Foreword to *Women in Love*', in *Phoenix II: Uncollected, Unpublished and Other Prose Works*, ed. Warren Roberts and Harry T. Moore (Heinemann, London, 1968), 275–6.

8   Iser, *Sterne, Tristram Shandy*, 93.

9   Jacques Lacan, *The Four Fundamental Concepts of Psycho-Analysis*, (Paris, 1973), trans. Alan Sheridan (1977) (Peregrine Books, Harmondsworth, 1986), 61–4.

10 Ibid., 239. The *objet petit a* is the always elusive end of writing and discourse (forever in *a*lterity).

11 Jacques Derrida, *La Carte postale de Socrate à Freud et au-delà* (Flammarion, Paris, 1980), 17, 19 (my translation). 'Latearly! Latearly! Latearly! Latearly!': *Finnegans Wake*, 502: 16.

12 *La Carte postale*, 330.

13 Ibid., 337.

14 Ibid., 36.

15 Gregory L. Ulmer, 'The Post-Age', *diacritics*, 11 (1981), 41. The piece appears, supplemented, in Ulmer's *Applied Grammatology: Post(e)-Pedagogy from Jacques*

Derrida to Joseph Beuys (John Hopkins University Press, Baltimore and London, 1985), ch. 5, 125–53.

16 P. D. Juhl, 'Playing with Texts', 60.

17 Derrida, *La Carte postale*, 61.

18 Ibid., 88.

19 Ibid., 27. Matthew Paris was clearly fond, it has to be said, of kitting out his ancient philosophers in used-condom headgear, as can be seen from another Bodley postcard, reproducing Paris's drawing of Pythagoras at his writing-lectern, from the *Prenostica Pitoragice*. Both drawings come from a collection of 'scientific' texts copied out in the thirteenth century, Bodley MS Ashmole 304. For ascription of these drawings to Paris see Francis Wormald, 'More Matthew Paris Drawings', *The Walpole Society*, 31 (1942–3), 109–12.

21 Derrida, 'La Loi du genre/The Law of Genre', *Glyph* 7 (1980), 176–237.

22 Derrida, 'Regarde bien leur bobine', in *La Carte postale*, 27: 'Look closely at their mugs.'

23 Ibid., 199–200.

24 Ibid., 266.

25 Ibid., 199–200.

26 Ibid., 194.

27 Ibid., 208.

28 Ibid., 472, 482, 524.

29 Ibid., 334.

30 Ibid., e.g. 58.

31 Ibid., 153.

32 Ibid., 414 (cf. 152, where Derrida, who seems to be suffering from a broken leg as he writes, is naturally reminded of this Scriptural consolation for limpers).

33 The bathroom rebus: ibid., 131. The Bodley postcard as rebus: ibid., 43. The history of philosophy as rebus: ibid., 44.

34 Sigmund Freud, *Die Traumdeutung* (1900; Fischer Taschenbuch Verlag, Frankfurt am Main, 1981 imprint), ch. 6: 'Die Traumarbeit', 234–5 (my translation).

35 Michel Serres, *The Parasite*, trans. Lawrence Schehr (Johns Hopkins University Press, Baltimore and London, 1982), 160–3.

36 See the chapter on *The Rebus* in Tony Augarde's wonderfully useful *Oxford Guide to Word Games* (Oxford University Press, 1984), esp. 85.

37 Derrida, *La Carte postale*, e.g. 58ff., 262, 270–1.

38 See Wayne C. Booth, 'Rabelais and the Challenge of Feminist Criticism', in *The Company We Keep: An Ethics of Fiction* (University of Press, California Berkeley, 1988), 382–418.

39 Henry James, Project of *The Ambassadors* (1 September 1900), in *The Complete Notebooks of Henry James*, ed. Leon Edel and Lyall H. Powers (Oxford University Press, New York and Oxford, 1987), 544–5.

40 James, Preface to *The Ambassadors,* in *The Art of Criticism: Henry James on the Theory and the Practice of Fiction*, ed. William Veeder and Susan M. Griffin (University of Chicago Press, Chicago and London, 1986), 373.

41 Ibid., 372, 373, 374.
42 Ibid., 372.
43 Ibid., 372–3.
44 Project, *Complete Notebooks*, 547.
45 Preface to *The Ambassadors*, 361–2.
46 Letter of 23 December 1903, in Henry James, *Letters*, ed. Leon Edel, vol. 4: *1895–1916* (Belknap Press, Harvard University Press, Cambridge, Mass., and London, 1984), 302.
47 Preface to *The Ambassadors*, 373.
48 Derrida, *La Carte postale*, 43, 44.
49 Preface to *The Ambassadors*, 368, 371.
50 Introduction to the Arden edition of *Twelfth Night*, ed. J. M. Lothian and T. W. Craik (Methuen, London, 1975), lxxix. All my quotations are from this edition of the play.
51 Jonathan Swift, *A Tale of a Tub &c*, ed. A. C. Guthkelch and D. Nichol Smith, 2nd edn (Clarendon Press, Oxford, 1958), sect. XI, 189–90.
52 Jonathan Swift, *Gulliver's Travels* (1726), pt III, ch. 6, ed. Paul Turner (Oxford University Press, 1971), 190–2. Paul Turner's notes connect Swift's jeering list with several actual political events of the early eighteenth century. Turner also calls attention to the similarly sarcastic poem of Swift (1722), 'Upon the horrid Plot discovered by Harlequin the B[ishop] of R[ochester]'s French Dog'. Exiled to France, Bolingbroke had himself known as M. La Tour – i.e. *The Tour* of Swift's text. Ibid., 352–3.
53 Augarde, *Oxford Guide to Word Games*, 127.
54 Teetotums occur again in *Our Mutual Friend* (IV. 1): Eugene Wrayburn 'rowed past a line of wooden objects by the weir, which showed like huge teetotums standing at rest in the water'.
55 J. Hillis Miller, Introduction to *Bleak House* (Penguin, Harmondsworth, 1971), 23, 25, 29–30.
56 Cf. D. A. Miller, 'Discipline in Different Voices: Bureaucracy, Police, Family, and *Bleak House*', *Representations*, 1 (February 1983), 59–88. (Hillis) 'Miller's account keeps characteristic silence about what even *Bleak House* . . . is quite willing to publicize; that the hermeneutic problematic itself is an instrument in the legal establishment's will to power' (88, n. 21). For once, a claim by Paul de Man seems apt: 'What we call ideology is precisely the confusion of linguistic with natural reality': *The Resistance to Theory* (Manchester University Press, 1986), 11.
57 'A Cantab.', *Charades, Enigmas, and Riddles* (1862), quoted by Augarde, *Oxford Guide to Word Games*, 85.
58 *Middlemarch*, ed. W. J. Harvey (Penguin, Harmondsworth, 1965), 905, n. 4 (ch. 37). See Michael Wheeler, 'The Spectacles of Books: *Middlemarch*', in *The Art of Allusion in Victorian Fiction* (Macmillan, London, 1979), 78–99.
59 J. Hillis Miller has reflected on this passage several times in print with some force. See e.g. 'The Two Rhetorics: George Eliot's Bestiary', in *Writing and Reading Differently: Deconstruction and the Teaching of Composition and Literature*, ed. G.

Douglas Atkins and Michael L. Johnson (Kansas University Press, Lawrence, 1985), 101–14. Miller analyses it to underline 'The claim of "deconstruction" ' that 'language is figurative through and through, all the way down to the bottom, so to speak' (p. 113). He's very fond of the figure: 'Deconstruction . . . has patiently shown . . . that . . . language . . . is figurative through and through, all the way down to the bottom, so to speak' ('The Ethics of Reading', *Style*, 21, no. 2 (Summer 1987); repr. in *Theory Now and Then* (Harvester Wheatsheaf, Hemel Hempslead, 1991), 335. Cf. 'the irreducibly figurative nature of language,' ('The Function of Rhetorical Study At the Present Time' (1979; 1988), in *Theory Now and Then*, 206. *Irreducibly* has a way of sliding into *exclusively*. (For Miller again on the George Eliot passage, see 'Composition and Decomposition: Deconstruction and the teaching of writing,' originally in *Composition and Literature*, ed. Winifred B. Horner (University of Chicago Press, 1983); repr. in *Theory Now and Then*, esp. 233ff.

60 *Middlemarch* ch. 12. Franco Moretti, *The Way of the World: The Bildungsroman in European Culture* (Verso, London, 1987), 220.

61 'If any man . . . would devote himself to studying the natural history of our social classes . . .': 'The Natural History of German Life', *Westminster Review*, July 1856; repr. in George Eliot, *Selected Essays, Poems and Other Writings*, ed. A. S. Byatt and Nicholas Warren (Penguin, Harmondsworth, 1990), 112.

62 The quotation from Derrida in this paragraph is one of the epigraphs to the Prologue of Linda S. Kauffman, *Discourses of Desire: Gender, Genre, and Epistolary Fictions* (Cornell University Press, Ithaca and London, 1986), which is much preoccupied with the doubling of 'The letter as literature, literature as a letter' (p. 17), but not as this is manifest in Jane Austen or Virginia Woolf.

63 Marilyn Butler, *Jane Austen and the War of Ideas* (Clarendon Press, Oxford; paperback reissue with new introduction, 1987), 273.

64 Virginia Woolf, 'Jane Austen', in *Collected Essays*, vol. i (Hogarth Press, London, 1968), 153.

65 See U. C. Knoepflmacher, 'The Importance of Being Frank: Character and Letter–Writing in *Emma*', *Studies in English Literature*, 7 (1967), 639–58.

66 William Empson, *The Structure of Complex Words* (Hogarth Press, London, 1951), ch. 15. Donald Davie, 'An Episode in the History of Candor', in *Dissentient Voice* (University of Notre Dame Press, Notre Dame, Ind. and London, 1982), 83–93.

67 Butler, *Jane Austen and the War of Ideas*, ch. 11: '*Emma*', edn *cit.*, 250–74.

7

The Logics of Para

Deconstructionists are the para-troops of criticism. A para-troupe. The paras. Deconstructive paragraphs about words beginning in *para* or related to *para* have dominated much criticism in the seventies and eighties. The ones, of course, not actually by Derrida, a man devoted to the exemplary significance of *parasites, parerga, parages, parures, parafes, parapluies* and so on, have been parasitical upon Derrida, in a great act of what John Llewellyn has labelled *paracitation*.[1]

A rhetoric, and activity, of the parasite flow naturally from the centrality of parasitism in Derrida's thought. The order of writing, he insisted in *Of Grammatology*, thinking of the 'Saussurian formulas', is the order 'of the "parasitic" ' – a statement that is itself exemplarily parasitic in being a quote from Jakobson and Halle.[2] Derrida's lexicon of exemplary tropes for un-decidable doubleness, the convergence of insides and outsides, open and shut meanings (naturally, he likes *parapluies*), comprises a repertoire of terms precisely for the repeated logocentric parasitic feeding of one set of meanings off another. The *pharmakon* (poison/medicine) works, Derrida wrote in 1972 in *Dissemination*, like 'a *literal parasite*', the one meaning preying interferingly upon the other, like an outsider upon an insider (and Barbara Johnson, translating, added, 'like static, = *"bruit parasite"* ').[3] In 1977 Derrida went on to declare that the symptom of parasitism had long interested him: 'The parasitic structure is what I have tried to analyze everywhere, under the names of writing, mark, step [*marche*], margin, *différance*, graft, undecidable, supplement, *pharmakon*, hymen, *parergon*, etc.' (and he quoted John Searle quoting *Of Grammatology* quoting Jakobson and Halle – the passage I've just referred to: parasitism layered upon parasitism).[4]

In an influential paragraph of 'Limited Inc abc . . .', Derrida dwells on the nature of the parasite, the allegedly unwelcome guest:

It should also be remembered that the parasite is by definition never simply *external*, never simply something that can be excluded from or kept outside of the body 'proper,' shut out from the 'familial' table or house. Parasitism takes place when the parasite (called thus by the owner, jealously defending his own, his *oikos*) comes to live *off the life* of the body in which it resides – and when, reciprocally, the host incorporates the parasite to an extent, willy nilly offering it hospitality: providing it with a place. The parasite then 'takes place.' And at bottom, whatever violently 'takes place' or occupies a site is always *something* of a parasite. *Never quite* taking place is thus part of its performance, of its success as an event, of its taking-place.[5]

And so when in 1977 deconstruction was described by its conservative opponents as producing strange readings that were nonetheless 'parasitical' upon 'obvious or univocal' readings, Hillis Miller could, I guess, scarcely believe his luck. The reactionaries were leading with their chin. And Miller's response, 'The Critic as Host'– it appeared in the course of a very sharp critical fracas in the pages of *Critical Inquiry* – was, simply, his finest hour, a knockdown finessing of the opposition (and, naturally enough in the circumstances, utterly parasitical upon Derrida on parasites). 'There is no parasite without a host,' Miller declares, and 'the strange logic of the parasite' means in fact that it's hard to distinguish anywhere, in literary criticism as in biology, who precisely is the parasite, who the host. The evidence was in the lexicon, where English (and French) words built on the Greek preposition *para* (= alongside, beside, along, by, near, with) comprise a labyrinthine set of tricksy border conditions, multiplex versions of the Derridian *hymen*:

'Para' is an 'uncanny' double antithetical prefix signifying at once proximity and distance, similarity and difference, interiority and exteriority, something at once inside a domestic economy and outside it, something simultaneously this side of the boundary line, threshold, or margin, and at the same time beyond it, equivalent in status and at the same time secondary or subsidiary, submissive, as of guest to host, slave to master. A thing in 'para' is, moreover, not only simultaneously on both sides of the boundary line between inside and outside. It is also the boundary itself, the screen which is at once a permeable membrane connecting inside and outside, confusing them with one another, allowing the outside in, making the inside out, dividing them but also forming an ambiguous transition between one and the other. Though any given word in 'para' may seem to choose unequivocally or univocally one of these possibilities, the other meanings are always there as a shimmering or wavering in the word which makes it refuse to stay still in a sentence, like a slightly alien guest within the syntactical enclosure where all the words are family friends together.[6]

Miller went on to provide a long list of para-words (pruned in the *Deconstruction and Criticism* version of the piece): parachute, paradigm, parasol, *paravent, parapluie,* paradox, parataxis, parapraxis, parabasis, paraphrase, paraph, paragraph, paralysis, parallel, parallax, paramnesia, paregoric, parergon, paramorph, Paraclete, paramedical, paralegal, parasite – and so on. A parasite feeds off a host. But in line with the paradoxical logics and placings of these para-words, the word *host* itself turns out to be paradoxical as well; in fact, it's perplexingly cognate with both *guest* and *enemy.* So the conventional parasite–host antithesis turns out to comprise a self-subverting lexical support system where apparent opposites converge and overlap in uncannily Derridian fashion: 'Each word in itself becomes divided by the strange logic of the "para", membrane which divides inside from outside and yet joins them in a hymeneal bond, or which allows an osmotic mixing, making the stranger friend, the distant near, the *Unheimlich heimlich*, the homely homey, without, for all its closeness and similarity, ceasing to be strange, distant, and dissimilar.'[7]

So what, on this view and evidence, the arguments of Wayne Booth and M. H. Abrams and the *Critical Inquiry* forum on deconstruction, and indeed the whole business of writing and criticism, are locked into is, Miller asserts, a given linguistic frame, the 'strange' linguistic, textual, conceptual 'logic of the parasite' which insists on making 'the univocal equivocal in spite of itself, according to the law that language is not an instrument or tool in man's hands, a submissive means of thinking. Language rather thinks man and his "world", including poems, if he will allow it to do so.'[8]

And so, yet once more, as the US academy roped in Derrida and Barthes ('Language writes the man . . .') for support, the textual, linguistic labyrinth turned out to be where meanings were headed, there to be inescapably engulfed. Once again, acute linguistic internalization, triumphalist abysmality, dominated the argument about language, poeticity, and reference.

But there is so much more here than Hillis Miller is letting on. Striking about the para-list that Miller culled with such diligence from *The American Heritage Dictionary of the English Language* is the presence in it of words that form intense nexuses of meaning in major texts – parasol (*Heart of Darkness*), paralysis (*Dubliners*), parallax (*Ulysses*), paregoric (*Rites of Passage*), parergon (*Middlemarch*), Paraclete (St John's Gospel ch. 14–16: *parakletos* – Comforter – Holy Spirit). And, inescapably, these words do not only announce specifically linguistic problematics of the kind Derridians can endorse in the fashion Hillis Miller so powerfully approves. They also manifest a blatant set of extra-linguistic logics of the para. These para-words are also manifestly folded into the extra-linguistic debates which their texts engage with – the politics of the European presence in *Heart of Darkness*, the condition of being and experience in Joyce's turn-of-the-century Dublin,[9] moral knowledge in *Rites of Passage*, questions of the direction of religious and theological history and

belief that focus in Casaubon's researches in *Middlemarch*, the nature of God
and Christ and the Holy Trinity in *St John's Gospel*. When Artur Schopenhauer
modestly titled his *Kleine Philosophische Schriften* of 1851 his *Parerga and
Paralipomena*, he wasn't simply making a canny reflection about supplementation, nor was he simply offering a fluent reflection on the difficulty of
separating one's *erga* from one's *parerga*; he was seeking to make a placing
claim about the secondary status of the contents of his two volumes. Of
course the late-Latin word *paralipomena*, from the Greek verb to leave on one
side or omit, carries all of Hillis Miller's linguistic logic of para and Derrida's
logic of supplement: it means things all at once omitted in the main body
of a work and yet also not (quite) omitted because they're appended as an
extra, a supplement. But there's more to *paralipomena* than just a Shandyan
game about what's in or out of a text, or where the reader is in a writing –
a playing of homage to Sterne's 'great saint *Paraleipomenon*' (*Shandy*, III, 36).
Paralipomenon is the title given in the Septuagint and the Vulgate versions
of the Old Testament to the Books of the Chronicles – so-called because
these Chronicles contain things omitted in the Books of the Kings that
precede them. And no traditional or normal reader of the Old Testament
would suppose the Books of the Chronicles, the *Paralipomenon*, to be comprising only a sort of seminar example of the textuality of supplementation.
The issue of supplement and textual parasitism is clearly in question in the
relation between the narratives of Kings and Chronicles. But the *Paralipomenon*
also lays claims on historicity; it offers itself as an historical narrative in its
own right. The question of the status of this paralipomenon has to do with
history as well as with text. And, of course, the historical issues cannot be
separated from the textual ones – or vice versa – here, as everywhere else, in
the putatively historical parts of the Old Testament. There's parasitism here
precisely of a sort that the American deconstructionist is not at all keen on.
History, the extra-textual, and the textual are indeed parasitical upon one
another, here, as throughout Hillis Miller's list of para-words, making it as
hard as ever to distinguish between them. As the man says, who indeed is
the parasite and who the host?

    This uncanny *historical* feature of the linguistic case which Miller unfolds
indeed emerges – as how could it not? – from his own analysis. His display
of the para-effect is a kind of 'J'accuse' directed at the conservative bastions
of criticism represented particularly by M. H. Abrams. It's offered 'as an
"example" of the deconstructive strategy of interpretation'. But no context is,
it seems in the end, excludable from the analytical sweep. Chasing para- and
host-words through the dictionary – being so cheerfully parasitical, as his
critics were prompt to charge him, upon the dictionary – led Miller very
far and wide. He professed to think it a search specialized irrefragably to

language and the language of criticism – 'To get so far or so much out of a little piece of language . . . is an argument for the value of recognising the equivocal richness of apparently obvious or univocal language, even of the language of criticism' – but in fact he was only able to get so far by means of extra-linguistic proofs and propositions. As he himself put it, but blinded, as so often, to the implications of his insight, his case rested in 'context after context widening out from these few phrases to include as their necessary milieux all the family of Indo-European languages, all the literature and conceptual thought within those languages, and all the permutations of our social structures of household economy, gift-giving and gift-receiving'. You can't, to put it bluntly, discuss the emblematic force, the deep linguistic logics of parasites and hosts, without also pondering some of the actual social, historical, biological relations of those real parasites and hosts who share each others' tables, salt, bodies, life. The para-logics of language, text, hermeneutics, are inseparable from the para-logics of dependency and ownership, slavery and mastery, colonies and colonized, subordination and authority. Which is, to take a great literary example, what *Jane Eyre* (1847) succinctly demonstrates.

Lost in a Book

The girl-woman Jane Eyre is clamantly bookish. So is *Jane Eyre*. Heroine and text conspire together to comprise a packed, devoted, textual, and intertextual scene. The reader of *Jane Eyre*, inescapably confronted with her or his own readerly condition ('Reader . . .'), finds it impossible, right from the start, to evade contact with the readerly condition of Jane Eyre and her fictional compatriots. The mere act of introducing oneself into the pages of this book is an act of discovering a fictional reading self who has already introduced herself into the pages of a book within our book. We first encounter Jane meditating on 'certain introductory pages' of Thomas Bewick's *History of British Birds*. Little Jane cannot pass over those 'introductory pages', she tells us, 'quite as a blank': no mere *hors-texte* these. Haunted by 'the haunts of sea-fowl', these initiating pages impress her by their pointful desolateness. And as we read on in our book, those introductory pages have their proleptic intelligence massively endorsed for us too.

Books are not blanks, not even in their introductory pages. And what they are not least full of is the telling force of books. In this book, books prove to be prophetic of life and development. Books here are necessary mirrors and generators of selfhood. The pages of books here predict, sponsor, create, their readers' existences. Jane's character, her selfhood, are continually being

generated out of her reading. We know her by her relationship to her reading
materials. Her life, and the life of the bourgeois reading classes who people
this text, are predicated upon books, defined by reading, are inextricably
bound up with the powers of letters and the letter.

By their books and their readings and their response to others' reading do
we know them: Jane's readings of Bewick, of Goldsmith's *History of Rome*,
Gulliver's Travels, some Arabian Tales, the hell-fire *Child's Guide* ('this book
about the Liar') that the Revd Mr Brocklehurst doles out, and of St John
Rivers's missionary letters; Helen Burns's devotion to *Rasselas*; Brocklehurst's
and St John Rivers's Calvinistic use of the Bible; Eliza Reed's Anglo-Catholic
preference for 'the Rubric' of the Prayer Book (ch. 21). Rochester is said to
be a Byronic Corsair-type (ch. 17). Georgiana Reed's frustrated story of brilliant
London seasons and titled conquests is an 'improvised' 'volume of a novel of
fashionable life' (ch. 21). And so on. The selfhood of Jane and the others,
which has so much to do with matters of reading, is, in other words, clearly
parasitical upon reading matters. And this textual parasitism of the people
in *Jane Eyre* is part and parcel of the extreme parasitism of *Jane Eyre* as text,
this novel that's cobbled together inspirationally from its author's own
kaleidoscopically various reading stew of Biblical, Gothic, and Romantic
texts, and which diligently rewrites so many of the texts it encounters – the
clergymen's Systematic Calvinist theology (the Brontës were brought up in
Wesley-inspired Arminianism, and Jane Eyre pushes that generous theology
on towards Helen Burns's Universalism – 'My maker and yours . . . will
never destroy what He created' (ch. 9)); the tract account 'of the awfully
sudden death of Martha G——, a naughty child addicted to falsehood and
deceit' (Jane Eyre does not die awfully or suddenly, but rather survives into
a prosperous long life); the sexual adventurism of Byronic heroes; even the
missionary letters of St John Rivers.

Battles of the Books

But to reach this point in observing what's going on in *Jane Eyre* is already
to have pressed beyond the limits of the purely textual. Books are fundamental to the existence of this fiction and its people, but so also are battles of the
books. And the novel's bookish battlefield is a scene where ideologies clash
in and through the conflict of readings. *Jane Eyre* keeps asking who owns the
books, who owns the meanings of books. Such questions of readerly authority
are, of course, rooted in the problematics of authorship that made the Brontës
squirm so when they offered their writing to the world. If Currer Bell was
only the editor of *Jane Eyre* ('Edited by Currer Bell', the early title-pages

announced), who then was 'The Author' who 'respectfully inscribed' the novel's second edition to William Thackeray? What was at issue here was the traditionally male authority of authors that the gender-unspecificity of 'Currer Bell' was seeking to side-step and that the second edition's prefatory pretence of maleness ('The world may . . . hate him who dares to scrutinize and expose . . .') was pretending to claim. And male authority, the male hegemony over books and writers and their interpretation, is what's continually at stake in this book's narrative of battles over books.

Books, in the world in which Jane Eyre grows up, are men's stuff. The repeatedly heard male suggestion is that women readers are parasites upon a male host, dubious guests at a male table. In the Reed household, the reading may be done by little Jane, but the books are in the ownership of John Reed, heir apparent of house and tomes: 'I'll teach you to rummage my bookshelves: for they *are* mine.' The Reed ménage is full of women – a mother, two sisters, a girl cousin, the servant Bessie, the ladies-maid Miss Abbot – but one fat little boy lays claim to own all the books. Just so, the Revd Mr Brocklehurst and the Revd Mr St John Rivers lay claim to unique understanding of the great Biblical doctrines of grace and nature. Both of them construe St Paul's (and William Cowper's) fear of becoming a 'castaway' from grace with reference to Jane (ch. 7 and 35). Brocklehurst has the *Child's Guide* up his sleeve. The sources of heavy book-learning are male too. Jane does of course become a teacher, and she was herself taught by women at Lowood School. And Diane Rivers teaches Jane German (ch. 30). But the proprietor of Lowood is Brocklehurst; the Latin that Helen Burns knows was taught her by her father (ch. 8); and it's St John Rivers who teaches Jane Hindustani. The male missionary-to-be makes Jane 'give up' the sisterly pursuit of German for the altogether more male domain of Hindustani, the learning that Rivers commands, male knowledge, 'the crabbed characters and flourishing tropes of an Indian scribe' – the 'mystic lore of his own' (ch. 34).

But for all their attempts to patrol the male domain of books, to preserve their old hegemony of interpretation, these interpretative, pedagogic males can't prevent the women from reading subversively, against the male grain. The blinded Rochester's final dependence on Jane as scribe and reader is symptomatic of the rebellion of female textualists that this text contrives. The pen ends up in Jane's hand – she writes Rochester's letters for him – and so does the book: 'Never did I weary of reading to him.' Rochester may regain some vision, but 'he cannot read or write much'. From now on, Jane will do that for him. It's an emblematic or token victory that climaxes the novel's steady work of undermining the male hold on reading and writing matters.

The main female hermeneutic challenge that's offered repeatedly and from the start is to male claims over the Biggest Book of all in the Western tradition, the Bible.[10] Little Jane informs big Brocklehurst that she doesn't like the Psalms ('not interesting'). She cavils inwardly over how God might, in Brocklehurst's borrowed Biblical phrases, 'take away your heart of stone and give you a heart of flesh' (ch. 4). She and her novel share an outraged wonderment at Brocklehurst's confusion between her being sent away to school ('the inestimable privilege of her election' to Lowood) and St Paul's doctrines of grace (ch. 4), at the connection he makes between burnt porridge and suffering hunger and thirst for Christ's sake, at his absurd hostility to natural curls ('we are not to conform to nature. I wish these girls to be the children of Grace'), and his refusal to connect Biblical hostility to 'braided hair and costly apparel' with the fashionable get-up of his own wife and daughter in their 'velvet, silk, and furs' (ch. 7). Naïve though she be, when she confronts the Inscription written up over Lowood's extension (ch. 5), Jane spots the clash between male and female interpretations of the Bible implicit in the place from its foundation. She also senses a larger problematic in any attempt to marry female actions and female texts with the great text of Judaeo-Christian patriarchy:

> 'Lowood Institution. – This portion was rebuilt A. D. ——, by Naomi Brocklehurst, of Brocklehurst Hall, in this county.' 'Let your light so shine before men that they may see your good works, and glorify your Father which is in Heaven.' – St Matt. v. 16.

> I read these words over and over again. I felt that an explanation belonged to them, and was unable fully to penetrate their import. I was still pondering the significance of 'Institution', and endeavouring to make out a connexion between the first words and the verse of Scripture, when the sound of a cough close behind me made me turn my head.

The cougher is Helen Burns, 'bent over a book', intently reading *Rasselas*. Helen, the strong little reader, can answer some questions ('Can you tell me what the writing on that stone over the door means? What is Lowood Institution?') for her fellow-reader ('I, too, liked reading'). And the interpretative collaboration between these two female readers already feels momentous. It is as yet only cagily critical. Is Naomi Brocklehurst's son 'a good man', Jane asks? The reply is studiedly vague: 'He is a clergyman, and is said to do a great deal of good.' But the difficult question of male goodness has been broached: not a little like the question carefully left open about the link between the text declaring Naomi Brocklehurst's good works and that text's own appropriation of the Biblical words about letting your light shine before *men* and glorifying your heavenly *Father*. Unanswered question or not, though, we are given pause over this arresting public textual submission by 'Naomi Brocklehurst' to the text of 'St Matt'. Who, we are made to wonder, has the right of the matter, of these reading, textual matters? Who here, in fact, is parasitical upon whom?

Such wondering about readings of male books, especially the Bible, and the awe-full suggestion that the problem might lie for Christian women readers with the great male text itself as much as with its male interpreters, with St Matthew and the 'heavenly Father' as much as with the Revd Mr Brocklehurst, are all the kind of worry that steers the schoolgirls Jane and Helen into continual sparring with authority figures. Jane's troubled career would be marked throughout by such textual troubles. And serious trouble, for the place where the female worm, or parasite, chooses to turn, the place where a line is drawn between old male and new female rights of access to books and interpretation proves a perpetually fraught, even dangerously bloody one. In this respect the opening chapter of *Jane Eyre* is proleptic and exemplary in the astonishing violence of its proceedings.

Bleeding Edge

Here, at the extraordinary and momentous beginning place of the novel, John Reed winkles his cousin out from her curtained retreat, intrudes roughly into her happy reading of Bewick, claims that book as his, snatches it from her, and then hurls it at her. The male book becomes a male weapon against the female who has had the temerity to appropriate it and its meanings for herself. And what an arresting array of dangerous edges or thresholds there is here! Jane bleeds at the edge where the reader is, the opening of our book, because the complexly edged retreat she contrived for herself in the window-seat, between the curtain and the window-panes, and in the introductory pages of her book, proves too edgy for comfort, and is no safe haven at all. She bleeds on the threshold where Reed carefully disposes her – 'Go and stand by the door, out of the way of the mirror and the windows' – trying in vain to dodge the hurled book and striking her head 'against the door and cutting it. The cut bled, the pain was sharp.' A woman of these many margins, she bleeds at the edge of her own body, from her vulnerable female skin. She's then physically banished to the red room, out of the way, upstairs.

It is a most arresting, overwhelmingly powerful, complex moment. A marginalized female, the alien in the family, the unwanted orphan, the one who is kept 'at a distance' ('Me, she had dispensed from joining the group': ch. 1), whose habitat is the physical margin, off-stage, in the breakfast room off the drawing-room, behind the curtain, in the window-seat, upstairs, out of the way, in the unlived-in red room, is made to bleed in a doorway: 'I felt a drop or two of blood from my head trickle down my neck, and was sensible of somewhat pungent suffering.' And though the immediate prime cause and physical agent of her bleeding is a book, this moment is far far more than merely bookish. It is obviously about male physical tyranny. 'He ran headlong at me: I felt him grasp my hair and my shoulder. . . . I really saw in him a tyrant: a murderer.' And the sub-text insistently poking through the motifs of rape and murder feels even more widely valent. What seem to be in question are those powerful demarcations and mythic discriminations that marginalize women, pronounce them taboo, precisely because they bleed at an edge, their bodily edge, the porches of their body. That is, because they menstruate.

From this astonishing start to her story, Jane Eyre is marked out as of the margin and bleeding, a tabooed person. Like all the ritual liminars so powerfully analysed by Arnold van Gennep in his classic *Les Rites de Passage* (1908) – brides, adolescents, initiands, novices, neophytes of all sorts – Jane will finally come through her long ordeal by separation, deprivation, marginalization, her repeated experiences of being on edge, behind curtains, on the run, in the discomfited position of outsider, exile, beggar, prodigal, governess.[11] But the stain of her initial curse – indeed, of The Curse, the menstrual blight dwelt on so movingly by Mary Douglas in *Purity and Danger* and Julia Kristeva in *Pouvoirs de l'horreur* – is not so easy to erase.[12] It marks Jane as one of the permanently scarred ones of Victorian literature, the great throng of those exiled from Matthew Arnold's 'centre' for various causes, political, social, geographical, religious, genderized.

As provincial people, northerners, dwellers in the County of Yorkshire so far from London, as women, as spinsters, as daughters of the vicar, as daughters of a poor and cranky vicar from Ulster with pronounced Wesleyan sympathies, the Brontës had numerous marginalizing factors heaped about them. 'A little, plain, provincial . . . old maid': George Henry Lewes fingered the provincial and the female factors of Charlotte Brontë's marginality with deft precision. She shared as victim in that massive act of Victorian religio-socio-geographical scorning that isolated Dissenters from Anglicans, kept Nonconformists out of Oxbridge, divided northerners from southerners, working class from bourgeoisie, London suburbs from London centre, that calculatedly defined the industrial poor as subhuman trash or 'Human Soot', that shoved out Robert Browning the Dissenting poet from Camberwell into exile in Italy. There were, naturally, grades and shadings in all of these marginalizing manoeuvres. Charlotte Brontë was not a Nonconformist but an Anglican, as was Charles Kingsley, whose 'Human Soot' sermon and novel *The Water Babies* stuck up so potently for those defined as trash by the Victorian centre.[13] For all his Methodist sympathies, Patrick Brontë was an Anglican vicar. So was Charlotte's eventual husband, the Reverend Arthur Nicholls – and he seems to have discouraged personal contacts between his wife and Mrs Gaskell, wife of a Unitarian pastor and thus considered to be far beyond the pale of Trinitarian orthodoxy.[14] But *Jane Eyre* stands, as Kingsley's *The Water Babies* does, with Mrs Gaskell's *Mary Barton*, that eloquent defence of the humanity of people condemned to live in the unhealthy foulness of Manchester's cellars, among the oozing and flooding excrements, the penetrating shit and piss, that Engels dramatically drew attention to.[15] These Christians – Charlotte Brontë, Kingsley, Mrs Gaskell – were of course rebuking Christian England for its consignment of certain citizens to live in filth and excrement, its definition of some people as offal, trash, waste, *Abfall*, and so taboo. And they were administering this rebuke in the name of the Christ who became taboo, who mingled with publicans, sinners, Samaritans, and other outcasts, and who died in the Jerusalem garbage dump, Golgotha, outside the city wall. And for a woman like Charlotte Brontë, who defines Jane Eyre's unwanted, outlawed difference by the shedding of blood in a doorway, there seems little doubt that a powerful subterranean connection exists between this tabooed bleeding female creature and the Christ who did not shun the Samaritan woman or the woman taken in adultery or lepers, who let himself be touched by the woman with 'an issue of blood', and who died to redeem those whose 'righteousnesses' were, in the words of the updated Authorised Version of Isaiah 64 : 6, 'as filthy rags'. Or, as earlier versions of the same King James text of Isaiah had it: 'as menstruous rags'.

Unposh Nosh

The taboo place of trash and of the trashed ones is, of course, the place where waste-matters are cast beyond socially pleasing bounds, the dubious excremental end of the human feeding cycle. And the kind of alleged parasites *Jane Eyre* focuses on – whether orphans, schoolgirls, governesses, homeless refugees, or Victorian wives – naturally enough raise questions of good and bad eating and concentrate on issues of appropriate provisions of foodstuffs, for parasitism always has to do with feeding. The story of Lowood School is a sorry chronicle of short and horrid commons – burnt porridge, stew that stinks of 'rancid fat', inadequate supplies of brown bread and oatcake (ch. 5). Brocklehurst's readings of Scripture support his policy of bad feeding – 'Oh, madam, when you put bread and cheese, instead of burnt porridge, into these children's mouths, you may indeed feed their vile bodies, but you little think how you starve their immortal souls!' (ch. 7). At Rochester's house, Thornfield, food is more plentiful. Jane is served 'a little hot negus' and 'a sandwich or two' the moment she arrives (ch. 11), and the servants' dinner consists one memorable night of meat and cheese and sago pudding (ch. 16). But still, while Rochester's posh guests dine splendidly – 'The dessert was not carried out till after nine' – Jane has to forage for 'cold chicken, a roll of bread, some tarts, a plate or two, and a knife and fork'. Governesses did not dine with guests, and while the guests drink their coffee, Jane, curtained once again in a window-seat and coffee-less, is subjected to their overheard abusive remarks about the 'anathematized race' of the governess (ch. 17). Escaped from Rochester, she becomes a famished wanderer begging bread and, at the nadir of her fortunes, turns into a version of the destitute Prodigal Son of New Testament parable who 'would fain have filled his belly with the husks that the swine did eat' when she's driven to consume some cold porridge destined for a pig trough ('T' pig doesn't want it': ch. 28). And when in her hunger she's taken in by the compassionate Riverses, she's only risen once more to the level of impoverished guest at someone else's table, an alien eater, dependent, parasitical.

But the parasitism is, as usual, not a one-way process. Jane is a giver as well as a mere receiver. She becomes a teacher at Lowood School. At Rochester's she works for her keep. Refusing to be a mere dependent of the Riverses ('I will be a dressmaker; I will be a plain-workwoman; I will be a servant, a nurse-girl, if I can no better': ch. 29), she opens a village school for St John Rivers. When she comes into her inheritance, she divides it out between herself and her new-found cousins. When she finally becomes Rochester's wife, having refused first time around to be his doll, a mere dressmaker's dummy loaded with the silk frocks of his generous providing ('I never can bear being dressed like a doll by Mr Rochester, or sitting like a second Danae with the golden shower falling daily round me' (ch. 24)), she is not only bringing him her newly acquired wealth ('What, Janet! Are you an independent woman? A rich woman?: ch. 37), she becomes the blinded cripple's devoted reader, amanuensis, and guide: 'He loved me so truly that he knew no reluctance in profiting by my attendance' (ch. 38). And who is the parasite, who the host, in such a relationship as that? It would be difficult to decide.

Foul Vampire

As ever, Bertha Mason, Jane's predecessor as Mrs Rochester, is Jane's cracked mirror image, this time as a spectacularly Gothicized version of the dependency paradigm of Victorian wifehood. And she provides a particularly lurid, but also very telling, version of the parasite's ambivalent status when she assumes the character of the vampire. In chapter 20 Jane is admitted to the house's third storey and 'one of its mystic cells' in order to tend the wounded stranger called Mason. Animal noises – 'like a dog quarrelling', 'snarling, canine noise' – with supernatural overtones – a 'goblin ha! ha!'; 'movements of the wild beast or fiend' – are heard off. Locked in with the bloody Mason, wiping the 'trickling gore' from his bleeding arm and shoulder, Jane feels she's been locked into a 'web of horror'. Daylight and the doctor – one more of the novel's many curtains having been drawn back – reveal that Mason has been ferociously bitten, and by some sort of female bloodsucker. 'The flesh on the shoulder is torn as well as cut. This wound was not done with a knife: there have been teeth here!' 'She bit me.'

'I must look to this other wound in the arm: she has had her teeth here too, I think.' 'She sucked the blood: she said she'd drain my heart.' Jane assumes this female vampiric attacker to be the enigmatic Grace Poole, though how this assumption is thought to tally with Rochester's immediate confession to Jane about standing 'on a crater–crust' as a consequence of wild youthful actions in 'a remote foreign land' is left unstated. When Jane actually sets eyes on the so-called vampire (ch. 25), it's none of the women she knows, 'not even that strange woman, Grace Poole'.

The materials of the vampire encounter are once again the edgy woven stuffs that perpetually shroud the parasitic females of the text. This terrifying female Other appears in a white garment, 'but whether gown, sheet, or shroud, I cannot tell'; she 'drew aside the window-curtain'; she rends Rochester's gift, Jane's wedding veil, in two, 'from top to bottom'. This is another of the text's great complex moments, a little parable about the pains of marriage for Victorian women, an emblem perhaps of violent sexual deflowering and harsh penetration, that's built on a conscious echo of the Biblical tearing of the veil of the Temple, 'rent in twain from top to bottom' at the crucifixion of Jesus, that was read by the Biblical writer to the Hebrews as an emblem of the redemptive tearing of the 'flesh' of Christ (Hebrews 10: 20), and is one more of the novel's associations between females and the wounded Christ. But the violent ripper and tearer is a woman vengeful against the men who buy and arrange the veils that females wear and who control the moments of veil-removal, hymen-tearing, and so forth. She reminds Jane 'Of the foul German spectre – the vampire'. And vampires are parasites as vengeful eaters – they're biters who've been bitten and who bite back.

Rochester would later claim Bertha Mason as his 'Indian Messalina' (ch. 27) – an updated version of the violent, profligate, adulterous wife of the Roman emperor Claudius, who capriciously ensnared lovers and had numerous enemies killed, and whose downfall came when she bigamously married a beautiful young lover Caius Silius, whom she'd forced to divorce his wife. One of the first things Jane tells her readers in chapter 1 is that she'd 'read Goldsmith's *History of Rome*, and had formed my opinion of Nero, Caligula, &c'. In that book Goldsmith is righteously eloquent about Messalina and the unbounded enormities, impurities, vices, and cruelties of this lustful, 'abandoned and infamous woman', as well as about the 'lascivious' and 'indecent' bacchanalia with which she and Silius celebrated their adulterous and bigamous marriage. Her name, Goldsmith informed his readers, 'is almost become a common appellation to women of abandoned character'.[16] And Messalina's life-story has strong parallels with Rochester's. The 'heartless, sensual pleasure' that he confesses to Jane (ch. 20) is reminiscent of Messalina's. She achieved the sort of bigamous marriage that Rochester at first craved for himself and Jane. At the same time, Rochester does try to distance his 'dissipation' from Bertha's Messalina-like 'debauchery': 'That was my Indian Messalina's attribute: rooted disgust at it and her restrained me much, even in pleasure' (ch. 27). But still, like the weak-willed Claudius, he married her and is chained to her even as he seeks to keep her imprisoned. One clear implication is that if men are 'like the Roman emperors', as John Reed is said to be (ch. 1), then they deserve the Messalinas, or Bertha Masons, that they get. The male 'slave-driver' of women who is also enslaved by women: it's a powerful variant on the parasite–host paradox. But this is not by any means the whole story. Touching Victorian England far more closely than debauched Roman emperors and their gaudily corrupt womenfolk, this particular vampire is also a Creole from the West Indies.

Creole Love Call

It is by now an established notion of literary history that 'the Gothic' provides 'a very intense, if displaced, engagement with political and social problems'.[17] And the later nineteenth-century vampires, Dracula in particular, have been described with some power as representing the anxieties, the personal terrors, and cultural guilts of colonial Britain through stories in which the colonized, the exploited, the victims of empire, keep returning as dark, primitive re-vengers.[18] In the shape of the vampire, the colonial Other, bitten, consumed, eaten up – and, commonly, eaten up in the world-wide imperial enterprise of providing means of life, raw materials, foodstuffs for consumption in the colonial home-base – returns to do some consuming, some blood-sucking on its own account. So when the West Indian Creole Bertha Mason turns vampire, she's acting out these anxieties for the 1840s, and widening the political question of who the parasites in the family are to embrace the then increasingly vexed question of Victorian England's self-enrichment at colonial expense.

This female vampire has negroid features. Her face is said to be *savage, discoloured, blackened, purple*. Her lips are 'swelled and dark' (ch. 25). When, next day, and the wedding abandoned (ch. 26), Rochester owns up to being married to this creature and exposes her in her padded, curtained room ('He lifted the hangings from the wall'), Jane 'recognized well that purple face – those bloated features'. Yet this bestial maniacal negroid Jamaican woman is also the source of English Rochester's great wealth. The huge sum of £30,000 came to him through marriage to 'tall, dark, and majestic' Miss Mason, 'the boast of Spanish Town' (ch. 27). Jane too is enriched, to the tune of £20,000, from the same geographical source. Her money has been safely invested in 'the English funds', and so given the outward appearance of white righteousness. But like Rochester's great English house and his life of flirtation with respectable white women with white names like Blanche Ingram, it's the product of far-off, edged-out black toilers in the colonial margins. It's loot, the satisfying cash pay-off of repressed economic truths and realities consigned to the unspeakable edges, cellars, attics, of consciousness. Jane's uncle, John Eyre, made his money in Madeira, but his business is intimately linked with the Mason plantations in Jamaica: he's the Funchal town correspondent of Mason's business house. So Madeira and Jamaica, a Portuguese and a British possession, are here married together as joint colonial sources of European wealth. And not just any old European wealth: this cash comes from foodstuffs. Madeira produced sugar and wine, Jamaica sugar. Madeira pioneered sugar plantations, Jamaica carried them on. These colonies richly sweetened the European table. When news of her Eyre money reached her, Jane felt instantly like a guiltily gargantuan feeder, 'like an individual of but average gastronomical powers sitting down to feast alone at a table spread with provisions for a hundred'. The discomfiting truth about England's prosperity at colonial expense was coming home to her. Who was the female vampire, who the parasite, who the destructive biter, who the bad eater now?

And the ambivalence of parasites holds up strongly in this tale of the returned colonial repressed. A 'feeder' is a consumer of food, but also a provider of it. The apparent victims of this circulation of eating matters – Creoles, women, wives – turn out not only to be this economy's beneficiaries, but also its benefactors. The Masons make money; Jane is in a position to give money away to the Riverses. (Just so, Messalina was wife as victim, but also wife as imperious wielder of sexual, domestic, and political power.) It all makes for a most messy set of ambivalences, worthy, after all, of the conceptual and biological ambivalence of the Creole.

Creolization is a mixing process, a blending of European and non-European elements in race, music, food, language. But just what proportion of Europe, what amount of American Negro or Pacific islander, there is in jazz or New Orleans cuisine or creole (or pidgin) speech is impossible to determine with accuracy. And what kind of Creole Bertha Mason is remains as indeterminate as the term Creole itself. Was Bertha Mason's mother, 'the Creole', white or black? The term was used to cover everybody born and raised in the West Indies or South America whose ancestors came originally from elsewhere. But these could be Spanish or French or African Negro. So *Creole* could signify more or less white (the offspring of European settlers) and more or less black people (the offspring of some settled black family, as distinct, in the *OED*'s blunt terms, 'from one freshly imported from Africa'). By calling Bertha's mother 'Creole' the text could signify West Indian Spanish or French descent, or West Indian black descent. The Masons' residence in Spanish Town appears to signify the one, Bertha's negroid features the other. Either way, the 'pure' white Englishman Rochester was a good catch ('Her family wished to secure me, because I was of a good race': ch. 27). And the concealment of the bride's mother ('I understood she was dead . . . she was only mad, and shut up in a lunatic asylum') begins to acquire racial overtones along with its other features when Bertha's own madness makes her appear less 'dark, and majestic' than bestial and black. But whatever might have been revealed racially by a sight of the creole mother, our guesswork about it must necessarily be stained with irresolution about the precise nature of the creolization.[19]

One aspect of the irresolution has to do with questions of subordination, subjection, the subaltern. Bertha Mason's identity as West Indian, a Creole or daughter of a Creole, seems to mark her as racially inferior, even as the stuff of slavery, certainly someone about whose identity and origins the whole truth must be concealed, an apt candidate for, and model of, the inferiorities, servitudes, and occlusions of English marriage. But this woman's standing in relation to slavery remains, like so much else in her story, rather murkily contradictory. Dating in this novel is kept deliberately vague. If, as has been suggested, there is good reason for a dating in the twenties and thirties before the abolition of slavery and the collapse of the Jamaican plantation system in 1838, then this would strongly argue that the Mason–Rochester money is a proceed of slavery.[20] What could be apter than that the white male husband, enriched by slavery, should be the possessor of an actual creolized wife from the slave plantations? The Eyre Madeira money, though, is not the product of slavery. Slavery was abolished in Madeira in 1775, and the wine and sugar industries had long recovered from the slump in trade that followed. But just as Bertha Mason is the Creole whose family were planters in their own right and so not enslaved, however creolized they were, so it's hard, conversely, to rinse the taint of servitude from the still ongoing colonial enterprise that has generated Jane's cash. So, White: Black; colonizer: colonized; centre: margin; Britain: Empire; free: slave – the apparent oppositions interact, feeding, in fact, parasitically off each other. And, of course, such ambivalence runs very fiercely in regard to the novel's central dealings with Jane's marriage, and the intricate parasite–host questions of dependency and choice, bondage and freedom, that marriage raises so starkly for her, as for other Victorian women.

The ambivalent interactions of England and the Indies, West and East, are crucial hereabouts. Bertha Mason, the 'Indian Messalina', is a woman of the West Indies. For her part, Jane will not leave England for the East Indies. Bertha is a free West Indian who enters on a life of dramatic servitude and incarceration in England. Jane resists St John Rivers's pressured invitation to service as a missionary-wife in India, preferring a marriage freely entered into in England, which turns out, however, to be laden with uncanny Eastern associations.

Eastern Allusions

At the end of the novel Jane refuses to go East. But for all of her life, and for the whole life of her novel, she has in fact been in an Eastern condition. It is perhaps no accident that the second edition of Jane Eyre should have been dedicated to Thackeray, who was born in India and remained obsessed by it. As girl, young woman, wife-to-be, and ultimately as wife, Jane's situation is pointedly presented by the text as an Eastern one. The opening chapter of the novel has her sitting reading Bewick in the window-seat, 'cross-legged, like a Turk'. She reads 'Arabian tales' and 'usually' finds them 'fascinating' (ch. 4). And as a developing woman Jane finds herself increasingly inside a story that's dominated by enslaving Eastern males. 'You are like a slave-driver,' she tells John Reed. And even males who appear in kindlier guise, as Rochester does in the immediate run-up to the aborted marriage ceremony, cannot shed their part as Eastern tyrants. Marriage in Britain is demonstrated to be enslaving along Eastern lines. The arresting charades enacted by Rochester and Blanche Ingram (ch. 18) have the pair 'attired in oriental fashion'. She is got up like 'some Israelitish princess of the patriarchal days'. He, turbanned, swarthy, with 'Paynim features', 'looked the very model of an Eastern emir'. The scarcely cryptic solution to the pantomime they put on turns out be 'Bridewell' – the generic name of a notorious prison for women in London that became the name of prisons for women all over the country. And this notion of English marriage as an Eastern transaction involving the locking up of women in the power of bridegrooms who resemble Eastern potentates pervades the text. When Rivers fantasizes himself as a husband of Rosamond Oliver (ch. 32), he imagines himself 'stretched on an ottoman in the drawing-room'. And Jane's resistance to such oriental wifely subservience has necessarily to be cast in Eastern terms.

On the eve of the aborted marriage attempt (ch. 24) Rochester 'obliges' Jane to go to a 'silk warehouse' with him, where he 'orders' her to choose material for half-a-dozen dresses. Hostile to extravagance, she beats the number down to two. She will not be 'dressed like a doll by Mr Rochester'. He is not to be her 'idol' – Christianity forbids idol worship – and she will not be his idol either. He smiles possessively: 'and I thought his smile was such as a sultan might, in a blissful and fond moment, bestow on a slave his gold and gems had enriched.' Jane expostulates ('You need not look in that way'), and there follows an exchange about harems which is peculiar only if it's read apart from the novel's carefully contrived set of 'Eastern allusions':

> He chuckled; he rubbed his hands, 'Oh, it is rich to see and hear her!' he exclaimed. 'Is she original? Is she piquant? I would not exchange this one little English girl for the Grand Turk's whole seraglio – gazelle-eyes, houri forms, and all!'
>
> The Eastern allusion bit me again. 'I'll not stand you an inch in the stead of a seraglio,' I said; 'so don't consider me an equivalent for one. If you have a fancy for anything in that line, away with you, sir, to the bazaars of Stamboul, without delay, and lay out in extensive slave-purchases some of that spare cash you seem at a loss to spend satisfactorily here.'
>
> 'And what will you do, Janet, while I am bargaining for so many tons of flesh and such an assortment of black eyes?'
>
> 'I'll be preparing myself to go out as a missionary to preach liberty to them that are enslaved – your harem inmates amongst the rest. I'll get admitted there, and I'll stir up mutiny; and you, three-tailed bashaw as you are, sir, shall in a trice find yourself fettered amongst our hands: nor will I, for one, consent to cut your bonds till you have signed a charter, the most liberal that despot ever yet conferred.'

'I'll be preparing myself to go out as a missionary to preach liberty to them that are enslaved.' But the idolatrous and possessive sultans and pashas, the purchasers and owners of female flesh, are at home too. They're called husbands. Jane Eyre does not need literally to go out East to aid the cause of women's emancipation from despotic oriental husbands. That particular missionary work is, metaphorically speaking, required to be done also at home in England. And Jane and the novel she's in will co-operate in the insistence that this particular missionary enterprise, laudable and necessary though it might also be overseas, must start at home.

English marriage is presented as a form of West Indian slavery and Eastern servitude, a species of colonialism that its female victims should resist. And yet, after all, Jane finally submits to it, giving up her emancipating (if morally tainted) Madeira money, allowing herself to be taken in marriage by a man self-confessedly enriched by slavery and an imprisoner of his former spouse. Admittedly, Rochester is physically broken by this time, and Christianly repentant ('I began to experience remorse, repentance, the wish for reconcilement to my Maker': ch. 37). He's now greatly dependent on Jane, and relieved to become 'one flesh' with her ('We must become one flesh without any delay, Jane': it's a candidate, this, for the most explicitly physical marriage proposal anywhere in Victorian literature). And Jane avows herself (ch. 38) 'supremely blest beyond what language can express; because I am my husband's life as fully as he is mine. No woman was ever nearer to her mate than I am: ever more absolutely bone of his bone and flesh of his flesh.' But though this Biblical rhetoric from the Book of Genesis is suggestive of mutuality – and notoriously too much so for many Victorian readers – Adam remains in it still Adam and occupant of the prime place, while Eve is still Eve, in the traditional secondary position, with her highest expectation as a lover only the absorption into *his* bone and *his* flesh. The potential missionary liberator of the harems of Istanbul, the female version of the great English Evangelical opponents of the slave-trade, succumbs here to English wifehood. Radical critique has seemingly given place, spectacularly – and not unakin to what happens at the end of *Emma* or *The Mill on the Floss* – to convention.

What hovers over the marriage in this most Christologically-minded of fictions is, of course, something like the old Christian paradox about free submission to Christ, 'whose service is perfect freedom'. But old formulae do not make such paradoxes any less dramatic or contentious. As appears with supreme force on the very last page of the novel. Jane has rejected Christian wifehood in India – missionary service as St John Rivers's wife was too little like perfect freedom, however Christian the terms on which it was offered – but still St John is allowed the novel's last word, indeed a whole spate of last words.

Missionary Letters

Suddenly, at the novel's ultimate margin, its frame – as it were, its parergon, its ultimate para-site – quite out of the blue (for we thought we'd heard the last of him, a discredited male like Brocklehurst), out of distant India, from the far-away colonial margin, comes word of, and the words of, St John Rivers. And they're extraordinarily approving ones. The missionary is said to be *resolute, indefatigable,* a *pioneer*. 'Firm, faithful, and devoted, full of energy and zeal, and truth, he labours for his race; he clears their painful way to improvement; he hews down like a giant the prejudices of creed and caste that encumber it.' His *sternness* is that of Bunyan's warrior Greatheart. His *exaction* is that 'of the apostle, who speaks but for Christ, when he says, "Whosoever will come after Me, let him deny himself, and take up his cross and follow Me." ' His ambition is to stand with the triumphant saints of the Book of Revelation 'who share the last mighty victories of the Lamb, who are called, and chosen, and faithful'. And his 'last letter' is quoted. It's a medley of Biblical quotations. In it Rivers 'anticipated his sure reward, his incorruptible crown'. 'His own words' are not, to be precise, his own; they're the words of his namesake, St John the Divine, the named author of the last book of the Bible: 'Amen; even so come, Lord Jesus!' And these are the very last words of the last book of the Bible, which is, perhaps, an unbeatable degree of ultimateness. So the ultimate affirmation for St John comes in a densely layered feat of intertextualizing that appears to reverse some of the novel's most sharply critical thrusts. Jane Eyre brushes, as it were, her own text aside to give place to what had apparently been discredited: the unadulterated male word, the male missionary text, the male appropriation of texts, especially of the Biblical text, and of writing matters in general.

Earlier (ch. 35) Jane had resisted St John's ultimate push for her body in marriage when he read at family prayers from the twenty-first chapter of Revelation, that book's penultimate chapter, with its 'last glorious verses' about having your name 'written in the Lamb's Book of Life', but also containing threats of fire and brimstone to unbelievers. The Book of Revelation was St John's ultimate weapon against Jane. He appropriated its pages, much as John Reed (so many Johns . . .) used Bewick's *Birds*, as a weapon to assault Jane with, to force her submission to him. And Jane nearly succumbed to the male exegete, the pointedly male reader, 'as he sat there, bending over the great old Bible', using Biblical words to warn Jane of damnation exactly in Brocklehurst's vein. But just then she hears Rochester's call. 'It was *my* time to assume ascendancy. *My* powers were in play and in force.' So another kind of Christianity than Rivers's, another kind of prayer, another kind of relationship with Christ than Rivers proposed – 'my soul rushed out in gratitude at His feet' – proved, after all, to be available, and redemptive. Rivers's attempt to colonize the Bible, the Book of Revelation, as his own book, all his canny repetitions of St John's words for his own purposes, had failed in their purpose. So, giving the Book of Revelation back to Rivers at the end of the novel, after all this, does come as a shock.

Just so, the affirmation of a male as missionary is disconcerting. In the 1840s the word *missionary* was of a uniquely male gender. There was at the time of *Jane Eyre* no scope on mission-fields for unmarried women, and scarcely any for women whose missionary husbands had left them widowed while out in the field. Women went out to Africa and India and elsewhere as missionary wives or not at all. St John Rivers is right about that, and that's what makes Jane's readiness to go to India as a single woman so challengingly unorthodox. 'God and nature intended you for a missionary's wife', Rivers declares, and that was all a contemporary woman was allowed to be on a mission-field. Jane counters by saying that she would go as a 'fellow-missionary'. But by then-current definition – a definition that irradiates Charlotte Brontë's poem 'The Missionary', about an itinerant male hero of the faith – the 'fellow-missionary' who was female did not really exist. But Jane is adamant: she could go to India unwed, 'quite as well as if I were either your real sister, or a man and a clergyman like yourself' (ch. 34). But Jane's 'as if' won't do: she's not his sister, and though she has 'a man's vigorous brain', she's still no man. And not being a man, she can as little be a 'missionary' as she can become a clergyman of the Church of England. What Jane proposes would upset the entire male order of missionary work, usurping the established male place and male function on mission-fields. She'd like to be like a man, in effect. No wonder Rivers labels her words as 'violent, unfeminine' (ch. 35). He can scent the challenge of the new kind of missionary Jane would be – not the male of the poem 'The Missionary', who sheds his 'missionary blood' in foreign climes, sweating 'such blood-drops' as fell from Christ in 'old Gethsemane', but the female harem-liberator who shed her blood in this novel's opening pages of a battle of the male books, a missionary in her own right. So, again, it comes as a shock that the missionary as male, and this particular, recently discredited, male missionary to India, should right at the end of the novel get such apparently vigorous recuperation as heroic, should seemingly be so utterly sanctioned, and at the highest possible divine level.

A Stranger's Hand

At this ultimate border of the novel a theologocentric letter from India seems, then, brusquely to have overturned much of what the novel has carefully achieved. Oddly, though, this final border-event recalls an earlier disconcerting paper margin that was written on in 'Indian ink': the 'ravished margin of the portrait cover' on which Jane Eyre had 'traced in Indian ink, in my own handwriting, the words "JANE EYRE"', which St John Rivers pulled from his pocket-book, and which was the physical link between the girl he knew as Jane Elliott and Mr Rochester's Jane Eyre, the legatee of the Madeira fortune. Indian ink was – and is – indelible ink. Is, we then wonder, Jane's selfhood, her name, Jane Eyre, her paper-work, her text, to be forever indelibly, as it were, in St John Rivers's possession, in his pocket-book, in his pocket? Is Jane's kind of Indian ink – her rewriting of the role of women, of missionaries, and Eastern missionary work – to prove in the end inerasably subservient to Rivers's Indian ink, to his epistolary endeavours, his textuality, his personality, coming home to her and to us in the colonial, the Indian mails? To an extent the answer must be yes. But only to an extent. For St John Rivers's inked paper from India is not in fact the very last ink from India that *Jane Eyre* contemplates. Satisfyingly apocalyptic and ultimate in tonality though the melding of the last words of this book into the last words of the Big Book might be (to some), there is, it appears, a word, a letter, an Indian letter, yet to come: 'I know that a stranger's hand will write to me next.' Admittedly, it's anticipated that this text of the stranger from India will also carry on in the same vein as Rivers's own last letter and say, using the words of the Master in Christ's parable (Matthew 25: 21) 'that the good and faithful servant has been called at length into the joy of his Lord'. But still, St John Rivers is to be denied, after all, the last word. At last there will come a time when he is dead and silenced and a stranger's hand will take up the pen he held so firmly, and a stranger will speak, add more, have more to say. The Indian ink that the novel appeared to have found so ultimate and indelible is, after all, not his alone.

The thematic of the stranger, the alien, the Other, abounds, of course, in *Jane Eyre*. Bertha Mason and Jane Eyre, its polarized pair of wives, the one from the West Indies, the other an honorary East Indian, compress into their variegated selfhoods an abundance of Other–wise characteristics. They are variously the foreigner, the Black, the colonized, the poor, the mad, the prisoner, the menstruating, the mannish woman, the theologically sceptical. Their alterity, their difference, their role as critics of the male worlds of empire, home, theology, textuality, represent many of the alterities the Stranger might stand for, and does stand for, in *Jane Eyre*. In being made submissive to Rochester as wife and to St John Rivers as reader or textualist, Jane Eyre's force as alternative voice is, of course, softened if it's not altogether suppressed. But in allowing that the 'stranger' might have more to say after St John Rivers has claimed and been granted the 'final' word, room for more radical possibilities, the telling survival of the voice of the 'stranger', is suddenly opened out. Of course, this space is filled proleptically with yet more endorsements of the male missionary. There's to be no clear victory here for the repressed woman, the extinguished female, in a piece of writing that will simply take over where the male text leaves off, such as Richardson contrived for Clarissa in having her write her own coffin inscription or Tennyson granted to the Lady of Shalott in having her write her own name 'round the prow' of the boat she dies in.[21] But the power of the letter, at the end of a novel in which so much – Jane's broken wedding ceremony, her coming into the Madeira money – depended crucially on epistles sent and received, is once again affirmed, and affirmed as the posthumous prerogative of the 'stranger'. And who knows what might happen if the likes of the strangers we've encountered in this novel were to carry on writing? And in a sense they do. St John Rivers has written his last words, but the recording pen has not, by implication, fallen from Jane Eyre's hand, and it is still, at the end, in Charlotte Brontë's fist. And she was just one of the huge throng of menstruating, pen-wielding strangers already moving strongly in to shake up the old hegemonic male scene of reading and writing once dominated by Brocklehurst, St John Rivers, and all the other reverend gentlemen. And the 'female hand', as Johnathan Goldberg nicely puts it in a discussion of Renaissance women being taught to write by male writing masters, 'the female hand makes the rift in the ideology' – of writing as a male domain – 'more apparent'.[22]

For all this, however, Jane Eyre, the erstwhile social parasite and focus of the novel's angry defence of the parasitized female, continues as such, for Victorian wives were indeed such. And the novel that she's in remains in every sense parasitically attached to the male things it's worried by, defining itself in relation to them, feeding in a basic way off the old male stories, male modes of mission, male readings and writings – especially Biblical and theological ones. It's more or less content to endorse marriage and colony, and to have its heroine live off the proceeds of empire. But then, this is the logic and essence of the para-condition: the parasite and host are locked inextricably together in a closed cycle of economic dependence, a closed circle of sustenance. Vampires are always sustained only by those they would bleed to death.

And once again, a fiction proves instructive for criticism in the matter of text and history. The case of *Jane Eyre* comes to rest, as it began and continued, in affairs of text – battles of books, opposed readings, struggles for hermeneutical mastery and for ownership of meaning, jostlings for the last word, for command of the quotation, for possession of the pen, the epistle, the mails. And ineluctably, inerasably so: for the Eastern question, these affairs of the Indies, are (and it didn't depend on literary gents like Macaulay or the epistolary father and son, James and John Stuart Mill, masters of the Indian correspondence, to bring this home to us) inevitably matters of (Indian) ink. And the ink spilled in these matters is *Indian* ink: indelible (one might even say in-Delhi-ble) marking ink. And some of that indelibility marks the degree to which the textual and textualized issues of *Jane Eyre* are also matters of history, politics, theology, and so on. Once again, text and ideology cannot escape from the way they are indelibly involved, the one in the other, each at once parasitical upon, and host to, the other.

NOTES

1 *Parerga*: e.g. Jacques Derrida, *La Verité en peinture* (Flammarion, Paris, 1978); *The Truth in Painting*, trans. G. Bennington and Ian McLeod (Chicago University Press, 1987). See below, chapter 8: 'The Rabbins Take It Up One After Another'. *Parages*: see *Derrida, Parages* (Galilée, Paris, 1986). *Parures* and *parapluies*: in Derrida, *Éperons: les styles de Nietzsche* (Flammarion, Paris, 1978), 49ff., 103ff.; *Spurs: Nietzsche's Styles/Éperons: Les de Styles Nietzsche*, Preface by Stefano Agosti, trans. Barbara Harlow (University of Chicago Press, Chicago and London, 1979), 62–3, 122–3. *Parafes*: in Derrida, *Signéponge/Signsponge* (1984), and Derrida, *Acts of Literature*, ed. D. Attridge (Routledge, New York and London, 1992), 346 and 346, n. 1. See also Derrida, 'Some Statements and Truisms about Neologisms, Newisms, Postisms, Parasitisms, and other Small Seisms', in *The States of 'Theory'*, ed. David Carroll (Columbia University Press, New York, 1990), 63–94. For other paramongers see e.g. Cynthia Chase, 'Paragon, Parergon: Baudelaire Translates Rousseau', in *Decomposing Figures: Rhetorical Readings in the Romantic Tradition* (Johns Hopkins University Press, Baltimore and London, 1986), 196–208; Gerard Genette on textual titles as paratexts: 'Structure and Functions of the Title in Literature', *Critical Inquiry*, 14 (Summer 1988), 692ff (from *Seuils* (Seuil, Paris, 1987): which appeared in German as *Paratexte* (Campus Verlag, Frankfurt and New York/Éditions de la Maison des Sciences de l'Homme, Paris, 1989)); Sylvère Lotringer, on paramorph, paramime (paronymic renewal/avoidance): 'The Game of the Name', *diacritics*, 3 (Summer 1973), 5. See also Shuli Barzilai, 'Lemmata/Lemmala: Frames for Derrida's *Parerga*', *diacritics*, 20, no. 1 (Spring 1990), 2–15. For John Llewellyn on *paracitation*, see his *Derrida on the Threshold of Sense* (Macmillan, London, 1986), 60.
2 Jacques Derrida, *Of Grammatology*, trans. Gayatri Chakravorty Spivack (Johns Hopkins University Press, Baltimore and London, 1976), 54.
3 Jacques Derrida *Dissemination*, trans. and ed. Barbara Johnson (University of Chicago Press, 1981), 128.
4 Jacques Derrida, 'Limited Inc abc . . .', *Glyph*, 2 (1977), 247.
5 Ibid., 232.
6 J. Hillis Miller, 'The Critic as Host', *Critical Inquiry*, 3, no. 3 (Spring 1977), 439–47 (adapted in *Deconstruction and Criticism*, introduced by Geoffrey Hartman (Routledge and Kegan Paul London, 1979), 217–53; and in *Criticism Now and Then* (Harvester Wheatsheaf, Hemel Hempstead, 1991), 143–70): *Critical Inquiry* version. The piece has a central place in Jürgen Schlaeger's important

anthology *Kritik in der Krise*: *Theorie der Amerikanischen Literaturkritik* (Wilhelm Fink Verlag, Munich, 1986), 'Der Kritiker als Gastgeber', 166–75.

7   Amended *Deconstruction and Criticism* version, p. 221: oddly parasitical, of course, upon its *Critical Inquiry* predecessor.

8   Ibid., 224.

9   See Hugh Kenner, *Ulysses* (George Allen and Unwin, 1980), ch, 8: 'The Aesthetic of Delay', 72ff.

10 Labelling the Bible as the 'Big Book' seems to derive from Frank Kermode: 'Deciphering the Big Book', *New York Review of Books*, 29 June 1978; repr. in Kermode, *The Uses of Error* (Collins, London, 1990), 17–28.

11 See e.g. Victor Turner, *Dramas, Fields, and Metaphors: Symbolic Action in Human Society* (Cornell University Press, Ithaca and London, 1974), esp. ch. 6: 'Passages, Margins, and Poverty: Religious Symbols of Communities'. Turner draws heavily on his own earlier book *The Ritual Process: Structure and Anti-Structure* (Routledge and Kegan Paul, London, 1969).

12 Mary Douglas, *Purity and Danger: An Analysis of the Concepts of Pollution and Taboo* (Routledge and Kegan Paul, London, 1966); Julia Kristeva, *Powers of Horror: An Essay on Abjection*, trans. Léon S. Roudiez (Columbia University Press, New York, 1982).

13 See Valentine Cunningham, 'Soiled Fairy: *The Water Babies* in its Time', *Essays in Criticism*, 35, no. 2 (April 1985), 121–48.

14 This seems to lie behind Mrs Gaskell's failure to visit her friend once she married: Winifred Gérin, *Charlotte Brontë: The Evolution of Genius* (Oxford University Press, 1967), 559.

15 Friedrich Engels, *The Condition of the Working-Class in England in 1844*, trans. F. K. Wischnewetsky (1892); graphically commented on by Steven Marcus in his *Engels, Manchester, and the Working Class* (Weidenfeld and Nicolson, London, 1974).

16 Oliver Goldsmith, *The Roman History, from the Foundation of the City of Rome to the Destruction of the Western Empire*, 2 vols (London, 1769), vol. 2, 197ff.

17 David Punter, *Literature of Terror: A History of Gothic Fictions from 1765 to the Present Day* (Longmans, London, 1980), 62.

18 Stephen D. Arata, ' The Occidental Tourist: Dracula and the Anxiety of Reverse Colonization', *Victorian Studies*, 33, no. 4 (Summer 1990), 620 – 45.

19 The desire to resolve the irresolution infects many current readings. Bertha becomes utterly White or Black, especially (why?) in feminist readings. She's 'a white Jamaican Creole' (Gayatri Spivack); she's 'fixed as white by her status as daughter of settler planters' (Penny Boumelha). The critically much sharper Susan Meyer is rightly sceptical about Spivack's glib and confused reading of *Jane Eyre*, but even she insists – this time on Bertha's outright blackness: 'an actual Jamaican black woman'. See Gayatri Chakravorty Spivack, 'Three Women's Texts and a Critique of Imperialism', *Critical Inquiry*, 12 (1985), 243–61; Penny Boumelha, *Charlotte Brontë* (Harvester Wheatsheaf, Hemel Hempstead, 1990), 61; Susan L. Meyer, 'Colonialism and the Figurative Strategy of *Jane Eyre*', *Victorian Studies*, 33, no. 2 (Winter 1990), 247–68.

20 Susan Meyer discusses implied datings, 'Colonialism', 254–5.
21 *Clarissa* (1747 – 8), letter 451, Penguin Classics edn, ed. Angus Ross (Penguin, Harmondsworth, 1985), 1305 – 6. In the 1832 version of *The Lady of Shalott* Tennyson had his heroine write her name 'Below the stern', but the jeers of critics made him raise the writing more clearly above the water-line in the 1842 version: *Poems*, ed. Christopher Ricks, 2nd edn, 3 vols (Longman, London, 1987), vol. 1, 395, n. 161.
22 Jonathan Goldberg, *Writing Matter: From the Hands of the English Renaissance* (Stanford University Press, Stanford, Calif., 1990), 145. (ch. 3: 'Copies: Institutions of the Hand', is particularly pertinent to the Brontë usurpation of male pen/letter/ink.), I am grateful to Alan Sinfield's *Faultliness* (Clarendon Press, Oxford, 1992) for calling this discussion to my attention.

8

The Rabbins Take It Up
One After Another

I wondered whether a professor at large . . . wasn't rather like the person
who in the old days was called *un ubiquiste*, a 'ubiquitist', if you will,
in the University of Paris. A ubiquitist was a doctor of theology not
attached to any particular college.
Jacques Derrida, 'The Principle of Reason: The University in the Eyes of its Pupils',
diacritics, 13 (Fall 1983), 6.

The intricately bifocal logics of para which invade and command *Jane Eyre*
inevitably lead that text, one of the great modern texts of parasitism, into
that tense and difficult dialectic between word and world, rhetoric and history,
formalism and reference, that has featured at each stage of this book's engagement with great Western fictions. This is not surprising; in fact, it's the
least surprising of all the rhetorical manoeuvres I've been dealing with. For
if, as I've been constantly arguing, no rhetoric, no rhetorical system, can exist
without its worldly connection, without being, in itself, parasitic upon the
worldly host – or without having the worldly host parasitic upon it – then
it's hardly likely that a text built overtly upon the ways of parasitism is
going to be the unique candidate for escaping from the linguistic-historical
double-bind.

But what is even more arrestingly suggestive about *Jane Eyre* is that its
parasite issues are conducted so much in terms of theology. However, a
moment's thought suggests that this too is utterly normal, for when the
word–world relationship is at issue, then the question comes down, sooner
or later, to theology, because in the Western tradition, the Graeco-Judaeo-
Christian tradition, all thinking about the word is inevitably done in the
shadow of logos and the Logos. Our linguistics, our critical theory, our
writing, are all performed under the shadow of our traditional Graeco-Christian
metaphysics, a logocentrism – indeed, theologocentrism – or onto-theology,

especially as these are manifested in and through the scripturality of Judaeo-Christianity. From their opposed positions, Jacques Derrida and George Steiner are both right about that.[1]

In other words, if we are to seek to historicize modernism and post-modernism, to provide or recognize historical and ideological frames for the state of our writing and our thinking about writing, for our textuality and our theory – and we are constrained to do so because there is no rhetoric, no system of rhetoric such as a body of fictions or theory, without a history and an ideology – then we must certainly look at, indeed we will not be able to miss, the relationship – belated, punning, parodic, parasitic – with the meta-physical, the theological, the Scriptural. I would even go so far as to allege that this particular connection is not simply one among many possible his-torical relationships such as are called for by Linda Hutcheon,[2] but that it is the big one, the master trope or master relationship, and that in all our con-temporary engagements between word and world, in all our words about words, and especially in all our words about words-and-the-world, our practice and our theory are commanded above all by a relationship with – are in fact parasitical upon – traditional thought and traditional words about the Word that have been of the essence of the preceding so-called Christian centuries. No history; then no rhetoric. But also, no history of Logos, Scripture, Theologocentrism, then no modernist–postmodernist textuality or critical rhetoric – indeed, no textuality at all.

Modernism knows itself, of course, as beginning in theology. *Modernism, modernist, modernistic*, were terms of theological application, pertaining in particular to an early twentieth-century anti-tradition movement within the Roman Catholic Church, as well as more widely to early twentieth-century modes of thinking theology and reading the Bible, before they got themselves applied to movements in painting, architecture, and writing. These shifts of meaning are particular twentieth-century phenomena. They happened too late for registration in the original *OED*, for example. And these modern semantic shifts within the *modernism* set of words are undoubtedly important as indicators that theology sits in this particular cultural driving seat. But evidence for the theological and the Biblical as being the scarcely concealed agenda of the (post)modernist – the awkwardly persistent subtext of what our critical theory is about, the *ergon* upon which it is *parergonic*, the set of namings or *onomatoi* upon which it is *paronomastic* or punning, the earlier textuality upon which it is *paralipomenic*, the host on which it is parasitic: the evidence for all this is, like God, omnipresent.

In a striking passage in his Life of Roland Barthes, Louis-Jean Calvet meditates on the posthumous revelation that Barthes preferred to read Pascal or Saint-Simon or Chateaubriand rather than 'les Modernes'. He was an apparent convert to his age, 'au modernisme', but he 'conservait en secret son goût' for *Les Pensées* of Pascal: like a 'marrano', one of the Spanish Jews who were forcibly converted to Christianity but secretly followed Judaism.

> Il était, déclare Jean-Paul Enthoven, comme ces juifs qui, forcés par Isabelle la Catholique à abjurer leur foi ou à s'exiler, s'étaient convertis au catholicisme, faisaient montre d'une grande piété, ces juifs que les Espagnols avaient baptisés d'un terme pejoratif, *marranos* (en espagnol 'porcs', d'un mot arabe signifiant 'chose interdite par la religion'), mais qui conservaient leur religion en secret, de génération en génération.[3]

And the passage is revealing both for the fact of Barthes's secret fascination with Pascal and also for the analogy from religious history that comes so readily to hand. The question of loyalty or otherwise to 'les Modernes' is tellingly seen as analogous to questions of loyalty to religious beliefs and rivalries between faiths. And, even more arrestingly, it's an issue between modern texts and the thoughts of Pascal, the writer who made famous the wager on God's existence and the validity of the Christian faith.

At such a moment, Barthes's life and the Barthesian enterprise are focused in their insistent relation to issues of belief in general and of Pascal in particular. They appear parasitic upon matters of Judaeo-Christian history, not least in the sense of the French noun *parasite* that's invoked by Michel Serres in the reflections upon parasitism referred to earlier in chapter 6. In French *parasite* is also, as we noted Barbara Johnson observing in the previous chapter, radio interference, static. Barthes wrote (and lived) within the crackle, the static, of the Judaeo-Christian past – though (and again paralogic comes vigorously into operation) just who was jamming whose frequency remains a question.[4]

The Parerga of Religion

The insistent intrusion of the religious question at this point is not dissimilar to, though it is much simpler than, that extraordinarily and wonderfully layered moment in Derrida's *The Truth in Painting* where a characteristically deconstructionist discussion of the para-based ambivalences of *parerga* (German *Zierathen*: frames to pictures, drapery on statues, colonnades in palaces), as Derrida reads them in Kant's *Critique of Judgement*, turns to Kant's other uses of *parergon* and *parerga*, which happen to crop up in his *Religion Within the Border of Reason Alone* (*Die Religion innerhalb der Grenzen der blossen Vernunft*, 1793). The location of these uses of *parergon* and *parerga* in *Die Religion* in what, for Derrida, constitutes a little Kantian thesis on the supplementary marginality of the parergon is mightily attractive to the margins-obsessed deconstructionist, for Kant's discussion there is itself extremely, self-referentially even, parergonic. The place is a long Note added to the second edition of *Religion* (1794) at the end of the first of the four General Remarks on religious matters (on the effects of grace, miracles, mysteries, and the means of grace) which were appended to each section of Kant's text. These Remarks are described by Kant in his Note as being 'as it were *parerga* of religion within the borders of pure reason'. So this particular Kantian Note is a *parergon* upon *parerga*, and since these *parerga* are religious ones, the Note nicely enacts the way in which, according to Kant, religion arrives – indeed, is required – as a set of frames, or *parerga*, to the operations of reason: it supplements the moral lacks of reason. And of course in Derrida's *The Truth in Painting* the discussion of the *parerga* of religion stands parergonically to the discussion of aesthetic *parerga*. Or, put another way, the question of religion comes in as parergonic, a necessary framing, to the deconstructive critical position or argument.

Derrida glosses Kant's parergonic note on the *parergon* about grace: reason 'needs the supplementary work' of religion. So also, it would seem, does deconstruction. At least, Derrida's discussion of Kant brings home to us the persistent presence of the religious as the constant frame, and frame of reference, of the deconstructionist case. Of course, the theme of the lack – the lack of meaning, truth, reference, presence, consolation – and the craving we have for some supplementary provision of what's lacking are well-established parts of the Derridian critique of what's illusory in traditional philosophy, text, and reading. The search for supplements to lacks of meaning is seen as a human, but doomed effort. And neither Kant nor Derrida is happy about the apparent necessity for the religious. It carries with it a threateningly high price, 'the theory of which is elaborated'. Each of Kant's four *parerga* of religion threatens a corresponding danger (fanaticism, illuminism, superstition, thaumaturgy). But still, the religious *parergon* of reason, the concern with 'transcendent questions', cannot be excluded or banished, because it fulfils a persistent lack within reason that Reason on its own can't ever satisfy: 'Le *parergon* inscrit quelque chose qui vient en plus, *extérieur* au champ propre (ici de la raison pure et de *La religion dans les limites de la simple raison*) mais dont l'extériorité transcendente ne vient jouer, jouxter, frôler, frotter, presser la limite elle-même et intervenir dans le dedans que dans la mesure où le dedans manque.' So religion and reason are joined parergonically – parasitically – of necessity and with complete intimacy. The *manque*, or lack, in reason demands that play of religion – that abutting of religion, brushing, rubbing, and pressing against reason's limits, that intervening on the interior of the zone of reason – by the very nature of reason. And so again, observably, does deconstruction. 'Le *parergon* inscrit.' The *parergonic* Note of Kant itself inscribes the necessary role of religion as the 'transcendent exteriority'. And, by the same token, the parergon – parergon work, the theory of the parergon and of the para in deconstruction – all inscribe the persistent and necessary presence of the religious, the transcendent. Religion is the perpetual frame, or *parergon*, of the deconstructive argument. And Derrida's tone hereabouts is characteristically tinged with a sense of Nietzschean tragedy about the lack of God. But it is also arrestingly accepting of the necessity of making that lack good. We are of course reminded that Kant's acknowledgement of the religious necessity – which is also deconstruction's acknowledgement – is a matter of dangerous distractions and seductions for reason; but, nonetheless, what is allowed to be clearly in view in it is 'un certain plaire, le plaire-à-Dieu (*gottgefälliger Absicht*)' – a certain act of pleasing, a pleasingness-to-God (a God-pleasing aim or intention). To have Derrida arrive at this point is as magnetic and, as it were, as scandalous as to find Lacan declaring that the Pascalian wager is still open.[5]

Circonfessional

Now something of what is going on here can, naturally enough, be ascribed to simple Western nostalgia for former religious consolations now occluded in (post)modernistic secularism. George Eliot wept as she translated David Friedrich Strauss's demythologizing book *Das Leben Jesu*, but this didn't make her a Christian again. Nor is Derrida made a Christian by being able to write that 'les schémes de la philosophie chrétienne restent efficaces' (characteristically the observation comes prefaced by a reference to 'la foi disparue').[6] He's not really a rabbi just because he can sign off an elliptical pseudo-rabbinical meditation on The Book as 'Reb Derissa'.[7] Nostalgia for lost childhoods is normal. Which is not to say that though people reshape their origins, repudiate their upbringing, deny or utterly transform the religion of their fathers, they may not still be crucially marked by where (as we say) they're coming from. Biographical criticism may induce its follies and fallacies, and the explanatory power of origins has no doubt been rightly cast under a cloud by criticism (though both scepticisms have, I take it, been mightily shaken in recent times by the Paul de Man scandal: once publicized, the youthful Fascist allegiances and their cover-up proved very insight-provoking clues to, and cast immense shafts of light upon, his critical writings and their particular emphases). Nonetheless, it seems important to trace Derrida's persistent fascination with Jewish textuality and his self-presentation as a master of Jewish hermeneutic, a rabbi no less, Reb Rida, Reb Derissa, back to his being born the son of Algerian Jews, circumcised on the eighth day, and named Elijah ('mon nom secret, Elie'), and one who haunted the synagogue, watching eagerly as the Torah was carried out from within its veils, from behind its curtains, *derrière les rideaux*, and so was marked for life, not only by the circumcizer's knife but also by the punning proximity of that Scriptural veiling and unveiling to his own patronymic: Derrida – De Rideau – a *fort-da* boy for whom meaning would be forever bound up with what's behind *that* curtain, *derrière-da*.[8] Likewise, it's important to track Harold Bloom's obsession with the J-texts of Genesis back to the fact that 'I have read the Hebrew Bible since my childhood',[9] and ascribe Roland Barthes's promptness in interpreting the Bible to his childhood in the Protestant Temple,[10] just as it is revealing to see Joyce's aesthetics of epiphany as contingent upon his boyhood Catholicism and Jesuit schooling, and to think of Beckett's textual spareness as an outgrowth of his Irish protestantism or D. H. Lawrence's obsession with the Biblical Sons of God who desired and copulated with the Daughters of Men before the Flood as consequent upon his chapel childhood.

But even more is going on in (post)modernism's literary and theoretical parergonic relationship to Judaeo-Christianity than simply an aggregate of biographical accidents or nostalgic childish traces such as are likely to be endemic to Western culture at a particular phase of its meandering dance with the wolves of secularism. The biographical facts and traces, the nostalgias and memories, exist and are extremely important. 'Circoncision, je n'ai jamais parlé que de ça', Derrida confesses in 'Circonfession': all his edges, margins, cuts, limits, closures, pharmakons, and so on, were really about circumcision (*Jacques Derrida par Geoffrey Bennington et Jacques Derrida*, 70ff). And such admissions are important because they're part of a massive textual and theoretical structure in which is inscribed again and again the question of the 'extériorité transcendente' and what Judaeo-Christianity has built upon the wager on the existence of the Divine Other – 'the big Other', as Jean-François Lyotard has put it,[11] that greatest case of Otherness which Michel de Certeau, Lacanian disciple and Christian, has argued as definitively provoking the whole Lacanian discourse. The house of (post)modernism is 'haunted by monotheism':

> But what is, after all, this Other whose irreducible brilliance streaks through the entire work? 'The Other is there precisely as it is recognized, but as it is not known.' 'This Other [is] that I call here *the dark God*.' Such formulations, and a thousand others similar to them, like the analyst's apparatus, gradually bring the strange impression that the house is haunted by monotheism. This monotheism resides in the concepts scattered throughout the discourse, concepts whose theoretical (and/or mythical) promotion is most often marked by

a capital letter: *the* Word [*Parole*] is articulated on *the* Other by *the* Name of the father, *the* Desire, *the* Truth and so on. Repeated throughout is the mono-theistic form of the capital letter singular, an index of something which, under the signifier of the Other, always amounts to the same.

All this is not something which Lacan would render hidden and mysterious. On the contrary, he reiterates that 'there is a One' which is always the Other. On condition that one 'never have recourse to any substance' nor to 'any being,' 'speaking [*dire*] brings God' and 'as long as something will speak, the hypothesis God will be there.' Such a hypothesis, such a 'song' (an expression of the mystics) does not come from a void. In Lacanian discourse, it has its history, its narratives, and its theoretical loci: it is Christian. Trailing its apparitions, one is impressed by the corpus which is there quoted and com-mented upon: Biblical and evangelical texts; theological texts (St. Paul, St. Augustine, Pascal, of course, and also authors of a theological inclination like Nygren and Rousselot); and especially mystical texts (Hadewijch of Antwerp, Master Eckhart, the *Imitation of Christ* or *Internal Consolation*, Luther, Theresa of Avila, Angelus Silesius, etc.). They punctuate the Lacanian space where they figure as *exordia* (where does it begin?) or as exits (where to end?). To this fundamental grillwork is added the central figure of the speaking analyst, 'Master of truth,' even 'director of conscience,' a 'saint' who 'wastes away,' one whose speaking, devoted to the price which the body must pay for having access to the symbolic, is a speech structured like that of the person praying.[12]

And de Certeau can be even more specific than this. Noting the 'strange' dedication of Lacan's thesis (1932) 'To the Reverend Father Marc-François Lacan, Benedictine of the Congregation of France, my brother in religion', he suggests that Lacan was claiming a brotherhood not just of flesh and blood but in the Benedictine Order, and so was laying the foundation of a career as a kind of Benedictine master or monk. The detail of this relationship is arguable, but that doesn't matter so much as the twin features of de Certeau's point: the unarguable observation that the issues, the rhetoric, the critical vocabulary of (post)modernistic debate, keep running up against the theological and Scriptural, and the powerful inference that Judaeo-Christian logocentrism is the continual provocation of the whole business, the great origin that the various deconstructionisms would subvert but cannot avoid, the ultimate impasse or *aporia* they're stuck in or with.[13] It's a situation curiously adumbrated in the *OED* definition of *aporia* itself: 'Aporia . . . 1657 J. SMITH *Myst. Rhet.* 150 Aporia is a figure whereby the speaker sheweth that he doubteth, either where to begin for the multitude of matters, or what to do or say in some strange or ambiguous thing. 1751 in CHAMBERS; and in mod. DICTS. [E.g. *Luke* xvi. 3.].'

In any French church, of course, the punning overlap between critical and theological discourse emerges with the power of a startling reminder. There the ordinary talk is of *la Texte*, *l'Écriture*, *les Écritures* – the Text, Scripture, the Scriptures. So much so that during French expositions of Scripture you have to blink hard sometimes to remind yourself that you're not in some literary-critical seminar where the very same vocabulary with equal naturalness prevails. In such circumstances it's easy to sense that reading books is an activity that's framed inevitably by readings of the Big Book, with all the intricate challenges that entails. Indeed, it has been pointed out, that the idea of the 'interpretive community' of readers who, in Stanley Fish's influential view, make the poem and its meanings, started life in an account of the Christian community of interpretation making the Christian story under the authority of the figure of Jesus.[14] Both the paronomastic vocabulary and the challenges hereabouts are well recognized by Protestant-born Barthes, not least in his analysis of the Biblical Book of Acts 10–11, the story of St Peter and the Gentile Cornelius. '[T]he very notion of Scripture, the fact that the Bible is called Scripture, Writing, would orient us toward a more ambiguous comprehension of the problems, as if effectively, and theologically too, the base, the *princeps*, were still a Writing, and always a Writing.' Just so; but the historical claim of the Acts of the Apostles ('There was in Caesarea a man called Cornelius'), the question of reference in this text, which makes it a model of the logocentric, has also to be confronted, for the Biblical text, the essence of onto-theological textuality, stands out starkly as the ultimate test for the anti-logocentric claim that texts are only self-reflexively written structures, are only textual and intertextual.

Barthes does his best to grip the Biblical story of Cornelius tight in a mesh of written, literary codes – topographic, onomastic, semic, rhetorical, symbolic, and so on. This text, like all others (for such is 'the very nature of meaning'), is pronounced meta-linguistic: it's a piece of text about other pieces of textual stuff. But still the question remains: is this all there is? For the 'ideological problem' still goes on being provoked by such a text: 'the problem of the final signified: does a text possess in some way a final signified? And by scouring a text clean of its structures do we arrive, at a certain moment, at a final signified which, in the case of the realistic novel, would be "reality"?' Naturally, Derrida is invoked. 'Jacques Derrida's philosophical investigation has taken up in a revolutionary fashion this problem of the final signified, postulating that there is never ultimately, in the world, anything but the writing of a writing: a writing always refers to another writing, and the prospect of the signs is in a sense infinite. Consequently to describe systems of meaning by postulating a final signified is to side against the very nature of meaning.' But still the awkward counter-claim of Scripture remains: 'the realm which brings us together here, to wit Scripture, is a privileged domain for this problem, because . . . theologically, it is certain that a final signified is postulated: the metaphysical definition or the semantic definition of theology is to postulate the Last Signified.'[15] Intransigently Barthes's analysis runs up against the Scripture's obdurate alterity.

Roland Barthes is not alone. Embarrassingly and definitively logocentric, Scripture simply will not be written off. It will keep returning as a daunting logocentric reminder, persistently forcing itself upon the modern reader and theorist as the awkward site of the repeated postmodernist *agon*. The great swathe of recent books about the Bible from secular literature departments in universities in the West, the appearance of the Bible on the syllabus of so many English faculties, the coming out of so many neo-rabbinical critics from the diaspora closet of Jewish, especially US-Jewish, assimilation, the general re-establishment of the Bible as a test case for textuality, are only late symptoms of the way modern writing, modern theory, have been fleshed out on the bones of Scripture. We are all Biblicists, all rabbis nowadays, taking up the Scriptural thematic, as Lancelot Andrewes so memorably put it, 'one after another'. But then modernism has never really been minded otherwise.

J-Texts

Indeed, the postmodernist scene comprises a kind of vast post-Biblical J-text, or set of J-texts, written (of course!) by writers with names like James Joyce son of John Joyce, Jacques Derrida, Jacques Lacan, Edmond Jabès (and, for that matter, Dan Jacobson and Gabriel Josipovici), about (Joker) characters called Joyce, Jabès, Jehovah, Joseph, Job, Jeremiah, Jonah, and haunted not least by the J-text(s) and the so-called J-author of the Old Testament.[16] And especially haunting is the J-text story of Jacob, Wrestling Jacob. This ancient Biblical story (Genesis 32) about a foundational struggle for life, selfhood, mastery, naming, and an authenticating blessing has provoked numerous critical wrestling matches. Modern critics have returned again and again with uncanny celerity to this particular text, quite hypnotized by its rich suggestiveness. Struggling with its meanings has become almost *de rigueur* for recent readers and theorists. The struggle this text describes between Jacob and his mysteriously transcendent opponent has evidently become a potent emblem of (post)modernism's larger struggle with the divine Other and the notion of ultimate signification. Through struggling with the ancient story of Jacob struggling, in mimicking and repeating that old story by rereading it, the critic locks closely in a necessary wrestling match with the ultimate divine antagonist, puts him or herself fearfully, but optimistically, in the arena with Jacob, the man who toughed it out with God.[17]

So Roland Barthes offers a reading of Genesis 32 on a structuralist model – 'a very classical, almost canonical structural analysis' he calls it – that resists 'reducing the text to a signification, whatever it may be (historical, economic, folkloric, or kerygmatic)'. This reading 'no longer reveals *where* the Text comes from (historical-critical analysis), nor even *how* it is made (structural analysis), but *how* it is unravelled, exposed, and disseminated, and which coded stages *go into it*'. At one point the analysis turns God into a *logothète* and Jacob is described as a morpheme of 'a new *langue* of which the election of Israel is the message'. Be that as it may, what's also clearly going on here is that in such manoeuvres Roland Barthes is himself acting as *logothète*, commander of the structuralist critical *langue*, and that the Biblical text has become a most exemplary set of graphemes in the structuralist discourse.

For his part, Harold Bloom, devoted and persistent reader of the Biblical J-texts, which he offers as main contender for a unique Western aesthetic originality ('If there is an aesthetic originality in our Western tradition beyond interpretive assimilation, then it inheres in J's texts'), reads the Jacob story as the very type of the critical agon that he has made particularly famous, the model of literary history as a story of the Anxiety of Influence, a sequence of struggles for mastery between belated poetic ephebes and strong poetic predecessors. More, and even more tellingly than this, he reads Freud – master story-teller and master critic of the modern tradition – as Wrestling Jacob's great modern successor. Freud becomes Wrestling Sigmund, the modern author who is 'the only possible modern rival of the Yahwist'. Browning wrestles exemplarily with Shelley, Wordsworth with Milton, but these are only local struggles in the great power-game defined by the Biblical J's text of Jacob's struggle and by Freud's texts of neo-Jacobean struggle, in and through which our whole tradition wrestles with Big J, Jehovah himself.[18]

We all, then, wrestle with Jacob – both alongside him, and against him? It's a notion shared completely by Geoffrey Hartman, yet one more Jewish (post)modernist who finds explanations and roots in Jacob's struggle. In the volume that Hartman edited with Sanford Budick, promoting rabbinical Midrash as an exemplary critical technique, he not only comes forward as himself the model of a modern Midrashi, engaged in a model rereading of a Biblical text; he also offers the story of Jacob's struggle – and his own struggle with it – as *the* quintessential model and fount of all reading. 'The universality of Jacob's combat with the angel lies, finally, in the struggle for a text.' As such, critical faith must be kept with this text: 'The accreted, pro-missory narrative we call Scripture is composed of tokens that demand the con-tinuous and precarious intervention of successive generations of interpreters, who must keep the words as well as the faith.'[19] It's an imperious demand, which Jacques Derrida has, of course, massively met, and a textual-religious imperative that Derrida finds obeyed exemplarily in the most exemplary of modern fictions in the whole Western tradition, namely *Finnegans Wake*.

The *Wake* is by no means alone among great modernist texts in its Jacob preoccupations. Jacob Epstein's hugely squat marble figure of Jacob locked in combat with a great overshadowing, engulfing winged creature (now in the London Tate Gallery) is one of the most haunting and provocative of modernist icons and of Epstein's Biblical subjects. The tip of what looks uncannily like Jacob's massively erect phallus sticks out from behind the Angel: this patriarch is seeking a rebarbatively sexual subjugation of his opponent. The poems of I. A. Richards, inventor of Practical Criticism, the man who declared foundational modernist texts such as *Lord Jim* and *The Waste Land* to have been built precisely upon the absence of Christian belief, are also mightily haunted by Jacob's struggle. In Richards's poem about Wittgenstein, 'The Strayed Poet', a poem mindful perhaps of T. S. Eliot's 'intolerable wrestle With words and meanings', Wittgenstein is cast as Jacob the Wrestler.[20] But James Joyce's interest in Jacob-matters is most strikingly recurrent. Reference was made earlier, in chapter 5, section iii, to the encounter between Stephen Dedalus and the girl from Dublin's Jacob's biscuit factory and to the *Ulysses* episode in which the irate Citizen throws a Jacob's biscuit-tin at Bloom. The growing pains of Stephen, his struggle with Catholic priests and teachers, the exile sorrows of Bloom, and the colonial grief of Dublin and Ireland – for it's possible to read the mock-heroic smash-up of central Dublin caused by the thrown biscuit-tin as a representation of what the British shelling did during the Easter Rising[21] – are thus made to seem like modern traces of Jacob's ancient pains. In the *Wake* Jacob's biscuits are basic foodstuffs, 'Jacob's lettercrackers' (26: 30), 'Jacob's arroroots' (138: 14), indicative of the kind of Biblical text this great mock-Bible is parasitic upon, its 'Primanouriture and Ultimo-geniture' ('with a sweet me ah err eye ear marie to reat from the jacob's': 300: 11–12 and margin), but they're also signals of the pain such Biblical and theological struggles entail.

James the son of John has made aesthetic beauty out of J-texts and J-stories, but the beauty of Biblical sons is geared into the sorrows of Biblical parentage: 'Joh Joseph's beauty is Jacq Jacob's grief' (366: 35–6). And this wearying struggle is so pervasive in *Finnegans Wake* that Jacques Derrida can sum up Joyce's text *tout court* by an encrypted allusion to it. Egged on to brevity by the lateness of the hour at which he was called on to speak at the Pompidou Centre in 1982 ('It is very late'), but driven by the same un-timeliness to thoughts of belatedness – the critic's belatedness mimicking the writer's ('it is always too late with Joyce') – Derrida compressed his awed reading of the *Wake* and of Joyce into a comment on two words ('I shall say only two words'), two words he offers as summarizing Joyce's enterprise, which is to be taken as the central (post)modernist one. The words come from a very exclamatory Bible-imitating passage of the *Wake*: 'he war' (258: 12). Characteristically, Derrida bends the words about, licensed by the allusions to Babel in Joyce's text at that point, reading them as 'he wages war', and he *war*, as in German – that is, he was, he who was. And who is 'he who is or who am' if not Yahwe? And *he war* even rhymes, albeit babelically, grotesquely, with Yahwe. (*Nicht wah?*) And behind this little reflection about the Jehovah who 'declared war in language and on language and by language, which gave languages . . . the truth of Babel', and so enabled rival Babels such as *Finnegans Wake*, is the story of Jacob who struggled for a name in a kind of war with Yahwe. And in a bustle of Js – 'James (the two, the three), Jacques, Giacomo Joyce' – Jacques (or Elijah) Derrida brings in quotations from and comments on his own *La Carte postale*, thus underlining the way in which that text is haunted by the *Wake*, and especially by this very *he war* passage with its babelic Jehovah, and by the necessity of struggle with that original bookish deity. And as Jacob would not let the Angel go, so this phrase won't let go of Derrida, nor will he let go of it. On one of his later tours to and around the Tower – or *Tour* – of Babel, meditating on the fallenness and untranslatability of language, originating in the God of Babel who declared linguistic warfare upon language by deconstructing the Tower's ambitions, its building materials, and the tongues of its builders, and whose linguistic warfare upon language began in the very unpronounceability of his name, the tetragrammaton YHWH, Derrida is again drawn to consider the *Wake*: 'And he war.'[22] And in all of these protracted struggles with the Lord God, with his Book and his linguisticity, Derrida sides with Joyce. Both of them (and what they both stand for as twin peaks of postmodernist writing and reading) have taken Jacob's biscuit.

The process is, of course, blasphemous, usurping, transgressive, heretical, and commonly most violently so.[23] Punning is always what Barthes called 'une rhetorique noire', as Walter Redfern, doyen of punmanship, points out. Redfern notes too that *paronomesis*, a close relative of *paronomasia* (pun), means illegality.[24] Homage to Jacob is not only homage to the punning wit of the Judaeo-Christian Scripture – Jacob's name is derived from the Hebrew for *heel* because he was born clutching his twin brother Esau by the heel – but also homage to the low-down treachery of Jacob the Heel, the Supplanter, or tripper-up, who usurped his brother's birthright.[25] Puns are supplanters, displacers of meaning. *Finnegans Wake*, this giant of (post)modernism, key work of one of modernism's blackest rhetoricians, a giant act of anti-Christian usurpation, is naturally built on the pun. Shem the Penman, its figure of the writer, is Shem the Punman. The pun is this text's commonest mode of local operation at the level of word and sentence. And the pun is also its large-scale formal *modus*, for the *Wake* is calqued at large on Biblical books and liturgical texts. And Jacob the Supplanter, the Bible's equivalent of Hermes the trickster, is the *Wake*'s tough trickster hero. 'Shem is as short for Shemus as Jem is joky for Jacob' (169: 1). Jem Joyce as Joky Jacob turns earnest Biblical stories of trickery with a 'mess of pottage' and night-time wrestling with angels into Dublin jokes about Jacob's biscuits, but the steely intent to supplant and usurp is clear. 'I gave bax of biscums to the jacobeaters and pottage bakes to the esausted' (542: 29–30). Esau, elder brother, predecessor, emblem of the orthodox tradition, had better beware. He who sups with this Jacob will be supping with the proverbially devilish long spoon. The floor and walls of Shem's writing lair are (183) 'literatured' with the literary ingredients of the written past that the *Wake* is comprehensively parasitic upon. Naturally they include 'fallen lucifers', 'broken wafers, unloosed shoe latchets, crooked strait waistcoats', 'lees of whine', 'glass eyes for an eye, gloss teeth for a tooth, war moans' (i.e. reduced echoes of the Salvation Army's journal the *War Cry*), and other 'blasphematory spits' from the Judaeo-Christian past. Naturally, too, the numerous stolen and distorted bits of neo-sacramental eating stuff – the broken wafers, lees of w(h)ine, but also 'Swiss condensed bilk' and 'once current puns, quashed quotatoes' – include 'messes of mottage'.

Sacrificial Offerings

Jacob is a violent wrester of names, blessings, heritages. And so is Joky Jacob Joyce. So, to take another exemplary modernist example, is D. H. Lawrence. The writer who would undo the old stabilities of the ego, shake the solidities of selfhood as he found them in the classic nineteenth-century realists, Turgenev and Tolstoy and their like, would do so in the name of the Italian Futurists, those *Ur*-Fascist aestheticians of doctrinaire violence.[26] And, of course – for this is modernism's commonest usurping move – the assault is built on Lawrence's early violent grapplings with the Bible. 'Let's make a sacrifice of Arabella,' says little Paul Morel at one of the most extraordinary and uncanny moments of his early career in *Sons and Lovers* (ch. 4); 'Let's burn her.' And he arranges a mock Old Testament altar on which apocalyptically to dispose of his sister's doll:

> He made an altar of bricks, pulled some of the shavings out of Arabella's body, put the waxen fragments into the hollow face, poured on a little paraffin, and

set the whole thing alight. He watched with wicked satisfaction the drops of
wax melt off the broken forehead of Arabella, and drop like sweat into the
flame. So long as the stupid big doll burned, he rejoiced in silence. At the end,
he poked among the embers with a stick, fished out the arms and legs, all
blackened, and smashed them under stones.

'That's the sacrifice of Missis Arabella', he said. 'An' I'm glad there's nothing left of her'.

In one arrestingly strange manoeuvre, then, Lawrence violently assaults and
usurps the tradition on several fronts, Biblical and Hardyesque. Arabella is
named for the fearsome wife of Jude Fawley in *Jude the Obscure*. To destroy
a proxy Arabella is to attack the navel string uniting Lawrence with his great
fictional predecessor. But beyond that, the target is Hardy's own Biblical
target. *Jude* is the novel in which Sue Bridehead, Arabella's female rival for
Jude's affections, cuts up the Bible with a pair of scissors, rearranging its
parts to suit her Higher Critical tastes. This Lawrentian sacrificial altar,
replicating the Old Testament altars on which the 'cuisine of sacrifice' was
prepared and from which the fat of the burnt-offering animals dropped down
and the smell rose as a 'sweet savour' into the nostrils of Jehovah, is a blaspheming, punning mime which signifies Lawrence's intention to displace
what it parodies. What comes later is Paul Morel's destructive assault on
Miriam's chapel beliefs and values, an attack that is cast in terms of explicit
violence to the text of the Bible.

Paul Morel turns into a pseudo-Biblical character, a harvester, a thresher
of wheat and treader of grapes, a persona laden with Biblical and Christological
associations (Christ the reaper, the thresher of the harvest, and treader of the
wine-press), engaged in work that may be pleasantly garbed in the familiar
agrarian metaphors from the Bible but that's done adversely, violently, against
the grain of Scripture and orthodoxy (and, incidentally, once more against a
female object): 'They were at the Renan *Vie de Jésus* stage. Miriam was the
threshing floor on which he threshed out all his beliefs. While he trampled
his ideas upon her soul, the truth came out for him. She alone was his
threshing floor.' And in the very next episode of chapter 9 ('Defeat of Miriam':
successor to 'Strife in Love'), Paul has become another Sue Bridehead, the
private Biblical editor. He reads aloud a chapter of St John's Gospel to
Miriam, but gratuitously cuts out a discomfiting verse about woman's sorrow
in the travail of parturition. Paul Morel is thus, as it were, well on the way
to joining the later Lawrentian heroes Birkin and Skrebensky, who are both
cast in terms of Lawrence's obsessively favourite progenitor figures, those
mysterious Sons of God who in Genesis 6 'saw the daughters of men that
they were fair; and they took them wives of all which they chose', and so bred
a race of giants who seem to have provoked the Noahic Flood because of their

wickedness. These fathers are absorbed into Lawrence's fantastic cult of stallion virility – 'The sons of God who came down and knew the daughters of men and begot the great Titans, they had "the members of horses", says Enoch.'[27] Either way, as transcendent beings copulating with earthly women or as stallion-men, those Sons of God were engaged in violently transgressive sex that provoked divine wrath and apocalyptic revenge. And it's transgression that Lawrence celebrates by offering Birkin and Skrebensky as applaudable modern updates of the ancient sexual sinners, and replicates, for his own part, in his usurping of this Biblical story for his own apocalyptical and modernist ends.

For Lawrence, violently transgressive acts are what free the self and the fiction, and in his writing such allegedly liberating dealings are commonly cast in Biblical terms and directed at theological orthodoxy, Christian belief, at God and his Book. Vronsky's 'sin' in Tolstoy's *Anna Karenina* was, Lawrence thought, 'the greatness of the novel itself',[28] and he kept on seeking to achieve this sort of trespasser's greatness for his own texts and characters. Lawrence and his people never asked forgiveness for their sexual trespasses; trespasses were the very heart of their desires.

Violent dealings with tradition are of course *de rigueur* all across the pages of literary history. But modernistic aesthetics are particularly violent. The characteristic heroes of modernism are Oedipus and his clones – father-killers and mother-fuckers. Lawrence's texts are full of them. The era of the First World War, with its battlefield hells of shelling, high explosive and machine-gun fire, and its international framework of revolutions, now seems the aptest location, and analogue, of modernistic writing. After 1916, imagining literary arguments as warfare and revolution came all too naturally. The Revolution of the Word pronounced by Eugene Jolas around Joyce's *Work in Progress* (i.e. *Finnegans Wake*) is Great War destructiveness applied to textuality.[29] And postmodernist discourse frequently continues this rhetoric of destruction. The well-known postmodernists are past masters (and mistresses) of violent tropes and figures, their key metaphoric a body-threatening *mélange* of cutting, gashing, dismembering, mutilating, decapitating.[30] Literary theory and commentary in the postmodern era comprise an extensive and obsessive metalanguage of mutilation and allied physical damages. The body returns in New Historicism, abetted and aided by a Feminism that's rightly preoccupied with rape and other violences against females, as the troubled analytic locale of torture, sadism, physical distress. The new access of somatic materiality in criticism is, of course, welcome, but the specialization is noteworthy: the new materialism is the materialism of pain. *Clarissa* displaces *Robinson Crusoe* as the generic English novel. It's the mutilations in *Tristram Shandy* that make it typical. And so on.[31] But even more noteworthy about (post)modernist violence than its mere prevalence is its Biblicism. Insofar as his discourse of violence is provoked and shaped Biblically and theologically D. H. Lawrence is utterly representative of his, and our, time.

A Law of Sacrifice pervades (post)modernist discourse. René Girard is only one modern hermeneutic prophet to find *Le Bouc émissaire*, the Old Testament scapegoat, a potent emblem of our age and its meanings. Paul Morel's sacrifice of Arabella is replicated, oddly but arrestingly, in a childhood recollection Derrida offers in *La Carte postale* of burning his sister's celluloid doll. It's a sacrifice that's in some way the disturbing genetic centre-piece of all the burnt offerings, of postcards, and of Jews, that haunt this text: 'Ce fut sans doute le premier holocauste désiré (comme on dit un enfant désiré, une fille désirée).'[32] Biblically shaped violent struggles with the metaphysical, against God and the Judaeo-Christian tradition, are for Derrida the essence of modern philosophy. They are the quotidian basis of what he and his literary and philosophical masters – whether Nietzsche or Heidegger or Levinas or Joyce – are all engaged in.[33] The essay in *Writing and Difference* that's selected to precede 'Violence and Metaphysics', Derrida's piece on the Jewish thinker Emmanuel Levinas, is the essay on another great Jewish writer, Edmond Jabès, in which Derrida again assumes his characteristic role as rabbinical commentator, Reb Rida, masterfully Midrashic upon Midrashics. And in this piece Derrida strikingly traces the beginnings of deconstruction to the moment when Moses angrily smashed the Tables of the Law, thus instigating the necessity of interpretation in a colossal moment of Jahwe-displeasing violence.[34] And even more striking, perhaps, as Derrida continues his great quest for the Biblical origins of deconstruction and decides on the still earlier transgressive moment at the Tower of Babel as yet another beginning or telos, is his siting of the tragic moment not just in that divinely prompted confusion of tongues, but in a self-division within the very divine name itself, the 'I Am that I Am'. The textual wars of the tradition have followed, Derrida suggests, the war 'that first raged within his name: divided, bifid, ambivalent, polysemic: God deconstructing'.[35]

What, of course, is going on, *inter alia*, in (post)modernism's blasphematory wrestle with the Biblical is a massive sequence of attempted repressions – in texts and metatexts, in repressive collaborations between writers, commentators, translators. It is a struggle to silence, nullify, annihilate, the prime father and his textual fathering. These repressions are occasionally admitted to. Often they're hotly denied – are repressed, in fact. But even when they're displayed prominently, they're often not spotted – just like a series of teasing purloined letters.

Jacques Lacan, a perpetually Biblically-minded analyst, but one whose Biblicism is often in the purloined letter-rack, highly visible but ignored, tellingly presents Freud as presiding over a kind of collective Western repression of God. In Lacan's reading, Freud becomes a Pontius Pilate washing his hands of discomfiting questions about divinity. The centre of the unconscious, the dark navel of the dream, is reread as a place of would-be oblivion, of the non-, or un-, a lack or gap, the navel scar marking the repressed presence of nothing less than God. This repression, Lacan suggests, is not just individual, but is characteristic of our culture as embodied in the influential psychoanalytic enterprise. And Lacan seizes on a particular Freudian example of forgetting in the aftermath of a cathedral visit, 'his inability to remember the word *Signorelli* after his visit to the paintings at Orvieto'. What's crucial for Lacan here is 'the term *Signor, Herr*' – that is, Lord – 'that passes underneath' the word *Signorelli* that Freud can't bring himself to recall. Masters, fathers, fear of castration, are thought, naturally enough, to be in question. But under all these, Lacan senses, is the troubling repressed presence of God the Father. And Lacan brings in Nietzsche: 'who declares, in his own myth, that God is dead. And it is perhaps against the background of the same reasons. For the myth of the *God is dead* – which, personally, I feel much less sure about, as a myth of course, than most contemporary intellectuals, which is in no sense a declaration of theism, nor of faith in the resurrection – perhaps this myth is simply a shelter against the threat of castration.'[36] The sweep (and the Biblicism) of the argument are by no means untypical of Lacan's readings of Freud. But with its picture of Freud's life and work and of the Freudian enterprise and of the whole notion of the work of the unconscious as being built upon systematic repressions of the Signor, the Herr, the Lord God, in Western selfhood and textuality, the argument is simply breathtaking in its challenge. And, of course, such Freudian repressions – aided and abetted by parergonic activities such as translation and commentary – can be found notoriously, and I'd say with Lacan, representatively, seeded across the Freudian texts and metatexts.

Deflowering Dreams

Take a well-known dream from *The Interpretation of Dreams*. A prudish young woman has a dream around the year 1912 of expensive flowers, ones you pay a high price for – 'lilies of the valley, violets and pinks or carnations'. Her analyst, Alfred Robitsek, is speedy to associate the flowers with fear of sex, especially sex with a flower-giving fiancé. *Valley* is thought to stand for the female genitals and so for loss of virginity. Violets associate with French *viol* (and English *violate*), and *carnations* with the *carnal*. The 'language of flowers', to use Robitsek's phrase, is thus perceived as loaded with sexual fears. The rhetoric of these flowers – the 'flowers' of (dream) 'rhetoric', to use the ancient metaphor used by Derrida in allusion to this very analysis – is thoroughly carnal; it's about deflowering. The woman says she associates the carnations, her fiancé's recurrent gift, with *colour* : 'determined', writes Robitsek, 'by the meaning of *"carnation"* (flesh colour)'. The woman's flowery list had linked *pinks* with carnations. Trouble, though, rapidly arises for this silky analytical smoothing out of the dream's 'lack of straightforwardness'. 'Suddenly', at the end of her comments, the woman 'confessed of her own accord that she had not told the truth: what had occurred to her had not been *"colour"* but *"incarnation"* '. She had tried to repress the real association of carnations with *incarnation*. And, interestingly, so does Robitsek; and so in effect does Freud, who quotes this piece of analysis at great length and at face value in his *The Interpretation of Dreams*; and so also, by its clumsy fiddlings with the German text of Freud's book, does the standard English translation of the episode.

What's clear from the German text, though not from the English translation, is that the analysand is English. Her words are all reproduced in English in the German text, with German glosses. In English the punning association between carnations and incarnation – which is, of course, the centre-piece of Christian theology and the master-trope of all logocentric thinking about real presences in the word, the aptly named 'incarnationist' linguistics – is obvious, and so, when the woman gets around to confessing it, not at all surprising.

But it was an association that Robitsek rejected at first. To his way of thinking, carnations meant *flesh*, and so it must be for his patient: 'Bei *"pinks"*, die sie dann *"carnations"* nennt, fällt mir die Beziehung dieses Wortes zum "Fleischlichen" auf ': 'It strikes me that the association of this word "pinks", which she then calls "carnations", is with "the fleshly" – not with English *incarnation*, you notice, nor even with the standard German word for in-carnation, namely *Incarnation*, but with *Fleischlich*, the fleshly. His analysis is determined to have and hold its pound of flesh. And when the woman does reveal the absolutely natural English association with *incarnation*, her analyst still, in great measure, will not have it: 'es sei ihr nicht *"colour"*, sondern *"incarnation"* (Fleischwerdung) eingefallen, welches wort ich erwartet hatte' – 'it wasn't "colour" but "incarnation" (becoming flesh) that had occurred to her'. And he adds: 'whch word I had expected'. Well, he may have expected the word 'becoming flesh'; what he had actually been given was the English word *incarnation*. *Fleischwerdung* is cognate with *Fleischlich*, but that was his association, not hers. What he got was something a bit different from what he wanted: it was *incarnation*, the word which he won't bring himself to repeat in its German form, *Incarnation*.

What's more, none of this artful dodging really appears in the standard James Strachey text whose translation of *Fleischlich* as *carnal* ('I thought of the connection between that word [carnations] and "carnal"') completely obscures this devoted resistance on the part of a collective of analysts – Robitsek, silently endorsed by Freud – their refusal to name the Incarnation. Further, by getting rid of Robitsek's *Fleischwerdung* parenthesis, Strachey savagely obscures the foot-shuffling going on in that gloss of the English *incarnation* by the rather unusual *Fleischwerdung*: 'what had occurred to her had not been "colour" but "incarnation" – the word I had expected.' In the English version, Robitsek (and Freud) thus appear to find the incarnation association logical, when in fact that was precisely what they were resisting. By repressing the fact of their repression, this resistance to naming the intensely theological term, the English text compounds the repression. So that there's an extraordinary fourfold erasure going on: by the woman first, by Robitsek's original paper, by Freud's incorporation – even incarnation – of it in the *Interpretation*, then by Strachey's standard English text. And after all that there's Derrida, coming in as a supportive fifth member of the silencing band. His renowned 'Flowers of Rhetoric' discussion is headed by a *mélange* of quotations from the *Interpretation*, centred precisely on this dream. The flowers of deconstructive rhetoric are gleaned not least from such Freudian encounters, and in this particular case they're founded on this densely layered Freudian repression. 'There is a gap, a little space in the flowers': Derrida eagerly seizes on some of the woman's words. But the larger gap opening out in these particular floral arrangements is the one left by the collectively desperate attempts to embargo the Incarnation word. The whiting-out mythography of deconstruction, exfoliating from this massed convergence of (post)modernist texts, once again proves itself very theological indeed.[37]

Tours of Babel

Translation is, of course, notoriously a problem. But the *incarnation–Fleischwerdung* troubles, like the misleading *jeu–freeplay* messiness referred to earlier (in chapter 1), are only the tip of a large repressive iceberg. Mistranslation conveniently aids and abets the anti-logocentric wish all over the shop. Take the wittily deconstructive piece about the US adulation of Derrida that mightily vexed some US deconstructionists, in which Jeffrey Mehlman made play with the 'mouvement de baguette' passage from Rousseau's *On the Origin of Language*. The passage was, as Mehlman put it, rather unhappily translated by Gayatri Spivack in the American-English version of Derrida's *Grammatologie*. 'The origin of language . . . appears to have been lost in the translation,' and

Derrida's arguments have been 'botched'. What Mehlman failed to spot (and
I only noticed by accident) is that the mistranslation in question did not
originate with Spivack, but goes back to a standard US student paperback
translation of Rousseau's essay which Spivack seems to have reached for
whenever she came across passages from Rousseau in Derrida's text. This
particular translator's laziness is thus reminiscent of that nineteenth-century
translator of Milton's *De Doctrina Christiana* who didn't bother to translate
Milton's carefully manipulated Latin version of Scriptural passages, saved
himself effort by simply using the Authorized Version at every point, and so
obscured Milton's studied theological pointings. In his comments on
Rousseau's *baguette* passage, Derrida was at pains to refute its suggestion of
an originating gesture of linguistic inscription – God's arm, God's finger
– as being too logocentric or theologocentric. The student paperback
mistranslation had weakened the Rousseauesque logocentricity, blunting its
point, emptying its fullness, and so, when it appeared in the English
Grammatology, contributed unfairly to Derrida's hostile effort. It was an argu-
mentatively convenient act of translation-repression in which Spivack's
slackness as translator and her ideological preferences gladly collaborated.[38]

That Spivack's casualness got itself taken very seriously by Mehlman ('the
translation seems to convey its own myth') is unfortunately symptomatic of
our theologically repressive, and generally rather slap-dash times. On another
occasion, a pair of Germanic-sounding interviewers, Harold Schweizer and
Martin Heusser, rightly picked up an example of Hillis Miller's casual way
with Kant's German in Miller's book *The Ethics of Reading*, but they were too
respectfully inclined to the great man simply to jeer at his translation howlers.
Miller must have 'deliberately' translated *als so* as if it meant *as if*, 'and we
were wondering how functional the questionability of that translation is? Is
it a deliberative narrative or fiction on your part to exemplify an unavailable
literal language?' Well, no, it's just an elementary howler, as a footnote has
the grace to admit (and it's by no means unrelated to problems with Hillis
Miller's use of German elsewhere in his writings). But this didn't stop Miller
from huffing and puffing in his next long paragraph with an apparently
learned example of how a standard student translation perverts an anti-
logocentric-sounding passage of Kleist about causality – which, it eventually
turns out, Miller anyway got at second hand from Andrzej Warminski. Too
discipular by half, and mistranslation being so useful a tool of repressive
misreading, the interviewers took all this solemnly in. But then they had also
been genially unpressing when Miller earlier wriggled under their question
about 'the religious dimension of writing'. His talk of the other and otherness,
should not, he declared, be confused with 'god or some onto-theological
"one"'. To be sure, his Protestantism had placed him in a heritage where the

private judgement of the reader before the book was highy valued, but 'that's only a kind of analogy with what I've been saying about the "other" in reading', and thus, quick as a flash, Miller had executed a big, anxiously evasive side-step away from the obviously rather insistent, and Lacanian, link between otherness in general and (divine) Otherness in particular. Relieved, he was happy to go on with quite unconnected talk of revolution in reading. But the repressive (mis)translator had shown himself utterly one with the repressor of the religious connection. It's the usual twin violence.[39]

It should come as no surprise, then, to find that recent discussions of the (manifold and manifest) problems of translation keep coming back to questions of Scripture, and that theological repressions, or tactics approaching such repression, are so busily under way in the (post)modern scene of translation theory. Walter Benjamin's essay 'Die Aufgabe des Übersetzers' is rightly granted pride of place in such wrestlings. It ends, famously, with an arresting allegation, very characteristic of this most rabbinically minded of Jewish hermeneutes: 'Denn in irgendeinem Grade enthalten alle grossen Schriften, im höchsten aber die heiligen, zwischen den Zeilen ihre virtuelle Übersetzung. Die Interlinearversion des heiligen Textes ist das Urbild oder Ideal aller Übersetzung.'[40] Derrida, whose piece 'Des tours de Babel' is also a tour around the problematics of translation as tackled by Benjamin, ends by quoting these last words of Benjamin's essay. In the English translation of Derrida's essay they are: 'For, to some degree, all the great writings, but to the highest point sacred Scripture, contain between the lines their virtual translation. The interlinear version of the sacred text is the model or ideal of all translation.'[41]

Aptly enough, the English is spectacularly ropey (it conceals the very close link that Benjamin's German makes between the great texts and sacred texts: 'all great texts [or Scriptures], but above all the sacred ones'), but at least Benjamin's main point is clear: interlinear versions of the Bible, those useful tools for Bible students which keep the original intact as well as attempting a clarifying transference to another tongue, mixed texts which thus honour the givenness of God's Word but also recognize the necessity and possibility of spreading it beyond the linguistic-geographical bounds of its first audiences, are the model, even the ideal, of all translation. The task, then, of the translator includes a respect for this feature of Scripturality, which is a feature of all great texts' Scripturality.

And, naturally, Derrida carefully misreads. He takes Benjamin's interlinearly translatable Scripture as at the limit of translation; that is, as a model, in effect, of untranslatability. The text, he argues, offers itself up for a translation that it then refuses to allow. We're present here, then, at a version of what we might call the Two Versions of Translating, or, indeed, Two Versions of the Sacred. In one version we have a commonly, and theologically, envisaged set of possibilities; in the other, a possibility at the very limit, its meaning escaping between the lines of the effort to translate it, a (sacred) text, and texts, whose untranslatability reflects the unpronounceability of the very name of its presiding babelic deity, YHWH. *Finnegans Wake* thus, so to say, returns, lending its Scriptural inspirer the Babelism it borrowed from it – or him – in the first place:

> That is what is named from here on Babel: the law imposed by the name of God who in one stroke commands and forbids you to translate by showing *and* hiding from you the limit. But it is not only the Babelian situation, not only a scene or a structure. It is also the status and the event of the Babelian text, of the text of Genesis (a unique text in this regard) as sacred text. It comes under the law that it recounts and translates in an exemplary way. It lays down the law it speaks about, and from abyss to abyss it deconstructs the tower, and every turn, twists and turns of every sort, in a rhythm.
>
> What comes to pass in a sacred text is the occurrence of a *pas de sens*. And this event is also the one starting from which it is possible to think the poetic or literary text which tries to redeem the lost sacred and there translates itself as in its model. *Pas de sens* – that does not signify poverty of meaning but no meaning that would be itself, meaning, beyond any "literality." And right there is the sacred. The sacred surrenders itself to translation, which devotes itself to the sacred. The sacred would be nothing without translation, and translation would not take place without the sacred; the one and the other are inseparable. In the sacred text "the meaning has ceased to be the divide for the flow of language and for the flow of revelation." It is the absolute text because in its event it communicates nothing, it says nothing that would make sense beyond the event itself. That event melds completely with the act of language, for example with prophecy. It is literally the literality of its tongue, "pure language." And since no meaning bears detaching, transferring, transporting, or translating into another tongue as such (as meaning), it commands right away the translation that it seems to refuse. It is transferable and untranslatable. There is only letter, and it is the truth of pure language, the truth as pure language.[42]

Pas de sens. Inevitably that recalls the 'il n'y a aucun sens à se passer des concepts de la métaphysique' of the original Two Interpretations of Interpreting lecture. There's no *sens*, no way, of avoiding metaphysics, but no *sens*, no route, by which to meet the sacred either. The *sens* has come full circle: we can't avoid the encounter with meaning and text; they must be translated; but, like God, whose name can't be pronounced and who can't get his Word translated, translation won't work. The classic deconstructionist double-bind snaps closed once again. But at least it's clear from Derrida's discussion what it's snapping closed on. Whereas, to move to another neck of the deconstructionist wood, Paul de Man, for his part, did his very best to conceal where his theory was coming from.

De Man's 'Conclusions: Walter Benjamin's "The Task of the Translator"' is keener even than Derrida on the impossibility of the translator's task. *Die Aufgabe*, the task, depends greatly for its meaning, he insists, on its base verb in German, *aufgeben*, to give up: so this is a task the language itself gives up on before it's even begun. But this is not a feeling any native German speaker ever has about 'Die Aufgabe' (let alone any schoolchild: no teacher would accept incompletion of the day's *Aufgaben*, the homework tasks, on the grounds that students had been implicitly asked to 'give them up' before they'd even begun them; such an argument would be too much even for a Just William, or Richtiger Wilhelm, to dare to concoct!). The point, though, is typical of de Man's magisterial dust-throwing play with the languages of his European authors – which monolingual American in his audience would dare challenge the so obviously European master on his linguistic home turf? Typical, too, is de Man's diversionary tactic, his turning smartly from the *Aufgabe* at hand to Benjamin's 'Theologico-Political Fragment'. And so is his hermeneutic way with that Fragment, his worming the *Geist* out of Benjamin's (and Hegel's) *Geisteswissenschaft* (taking it away, too, from Gadamer and Hartman), and his barring both God and history from the linguistic and the literary domains in one neat and dubiously *ficelle*-like conjuring trick.

Benjamin had argued that messianism put an end to history and that theocracy had no connection with politics; but because, de Man says, 'the political and historical is due to purely linguistic reasons', you can therefore substitute the poetical for the political in Benjamin's formula; so Benjamin is 'really' alleging that questions of theocracy, sacredness, and so on, are actually distinct and separate from language, criticism, aesthetics. Which is a truly astonishing place to have Benjamin come out! But then, as de Man's editor reveals, this sneaky result was based in no less tricksy a dealing with a translation of the very Scripture that Benjamin was offering as a model of translation – a tricksiness in Biblical translation that all this so characteristic, and would-be deconstructive, finagling seems designed to obscure.

De Man's surviving prompt-notes for this talk on Benjamin apparently included a sheet that read simply: 'Im Anfang war das Wort und das Wort war bei Gott/Dasselbe war bei Gott/ohne Dasselbe' – the last two words underlined. These are, the editor tells us, 'the beginning of Luther's translation of the Gospel according to John'. But, of course, they both are, and are not, the first three verses of Luther's translation. They omit *im Anfang* from verse 2 ('Dasselbe war *im Anfang* bei Gott': 'the same was in the beginning with God') and most of verse 3: 'Alle Dinge sind durch dasselbe

gemacht and ohne dasselbe ist nichts gemacht, was gemacht ist': 'All things
are made by him himself and without him himself is nothing made that is
made.' De Man's cut-down version of Luther's translation thus attempts at
a stroke what his reading of Benjamin's essay on translation tries to achieve;
namely, it modifies the originating power of the divine Word and represses
the connection between words and things (i.e. the link between God's rhetoric
and history), in order to bring out the nicely juxtaposed, but wholly unjustified
self-deconstructing pair, *Dasselbe war bei Gott: ohne Dasselbe* – 'the self-same
was with God: without the self-same'. Distortive hermeneutical practices and
wrenching manoeuvres with translation such as these can help you prove
almost anything you fancy. The craving to repress the logocentric God reveals
its strength in the sheer desperateness of the textual measures it incites.[43]

Scriptural Penalties

In the case of Kafka the violence of translation into English elides into, as
it tends to obscure, what precisely is going on in his textuality's appallingly
violent tradings with the Jewish Scriptures. The man being punished in the
extraordinarily sadistic writing-machine of Kafka's *Novelle* 'In der Strafkolonie'
– generally known in English as 'In the Penal Settlement' – is presented in
usual Kafkan terms as a distorted update of the Old Testament sacrificial
victim, an ineffectual *bouc émissaire*, a scapegoat gone wrong. Suggestions early
in the narrative of some redemption to be wrought through his sufferings
prove vain – 'no sign was visible of the promised redemption.' The victim
connives in his own death, letting himself be strapped into the killing writing-
device, much as Joseph K at the end of *The Trial* appears to welcome the
killer's knife. Sacrifice on this model turns too easily into suicide. But what
the English versions of 'In der Strafkolonie' obscure is the thoroughly Biblical
nature of the victim's sufferings. In English the sufferer is sentenced to have
a writing incised into his flesh by a mechanical needle that's a cruel parody
of a pen. This writing is a deadly 'script' with 'lots of flourishes'. And in
English this sounds merely like a very extreme version of that modern anxiety
over the word and the morality of writing and of the writer, the worried idea
of the poem and the poet *maudit*, that links Kafka with Conrad and Dickens
and Baudelaire and the rest. But in Kafka's German, the Scriptural and, even,
rabbinical aspects of the case are unmistakable. *Schrift* is indeed writing, mere
script, but it is also Scripture. The machine writes a punitive Scriptural text
directed by the cogs in the machine's 'Designer' device (*Zeichner*), and these
cogs are set to the design (*Zeichnung*) of the lawcourt's judgement on the
victim. The present commandant of the punishment colony follows the plans

(*Zeichnungen*) of the original commandant. The run of German rhymes, *Zeichner, Zeichnung, Zeichnungen*, makes clear connections which the English obscures. The machine's script or Scripture follows the originally given script or Scripture, which is also the sentence of the court. The commandant carefully exposes the first page of the original designs (the *Zeichnungen*) to the researching traveller. He can't read this generic text because its lines are so densely packed together. It's very artistic (*kunstvoll*), he says, but also so labyrinthine (*labyrinthartig*) that he can't decipher it ('ich kann es nicht entziffern'). And this original text, so quintessentially modernist in being so genetically labyrinthine, is, in Kafka's German, arrestingly packed with Biblical features. It is no mere 'Schönschrift für Schulkinder', that is, no *hupogrammos*, the exemplary line of writing that ancient Greek pedagogues would write out for children to learn writing from: it's a *Schönschrift* for grown-ups. To understand it, you have to read long in it ('Man müss lange darin lesen'). It is, of course, and necessarily, no simple script or Scripture: 'Es darf natürlich keine einfache Schrift sein.' Which is precisely the rabbinical view of God and his writing endorsed by Jabès and Derrida: '"*there is no writing without a lie and writing is the way of God*"'; 'there can be no *simplicity* of God.'[44]

Because this writing is designed to kill its victims slowly, it has to be complicated, and it's complicated even further by many *Zieraten*. 'Es müssen also viel, viel Zieraten die eigentliche Schrift umgeben': *Zieraten*, Kant's and Derrida's *parerga*, the essence of the aesthetic and of the deconstructive, now emphatically seen as Scriptural postils, commentaries, the flourishes around the text that are absorbed inseparably into it. And this Scripture, with these *Zieraten/parerga*, is a performative utterance, 'die wirkliche Schrift'. This letter killeth; its working is (to borrow the old Puritan term) effectual, but effectually damaging. Kafka's man dies, his body finally torn to shreds by Scripture and by the accumulations of Scriptural commentary. He's an extreme version of maimed, lamed Jacob.[45]

Most of this is obscured by English translations of Kafka, though occasionally even the English version is compelled to 'incline its ear' (good Biblical phrase) to Kafka's Biblicism – not least when the traveller 'inclines his ear' to his machine-minder ('hatte das Ohr zum Offizier geneigt': rendered, for once, quite literally). But Derrida, who knows his Kafka not least because he inhabits a similar post-Biblical Jewish terrain, knows precisely what's going on: 'Kafka said: "We are nihilist thoughts in the brain of God" . . . there can be no *simplicity* of God'; 'the situation of the Jew becomes exemplary of the situation of the poet, the man of speech and of writing'.[46] Like Freud, Kafka accepts the violent hurtfulness of the Biblical heritage, grants it its central place in the struggles of modernist transgressivity, and professes to live with it. 'It's no sin to limp' – the defiant assertion of *Beyond the Pleasure Principle* and *La Carte postale* is an attempt to recuperate the maiming as a blessing, to join limping 'Jacob' in turning into the renamed 'Israel', Prince of God. Geoffrey Hartman called the assertion about limping sinlessness 'Freud's genial self-defense', which Hartman himself, in the course of dwelling on Jacob as exemplary interpreter, 'can only repeat'.[47] But geniality seems in the main far removed from modern writing's participation in the Scriptural heritage. Here is indeed a scene – the tragic modernist scene – of hurt, maiming, anguish, difficulty.

The Scriptural inflects the modernistic at its most agonizing. The Bloomian Agon is indeed agonistic, agonizing. Jacob remains a heel. His struggles and those of his modernist successors are, as many of them believed, Satanic, and the Satanic hubris of the 'old trickster' – whether Stephen Dedalus's or Wittgenstein's as elaborated in I. A. Richards's poetic celebration of the philosopher – always invites a wrestling fall. 'Il est vrai que je boîte, mais je suis en compagnie distinguée,' Conrad wrote to his aunt in 1891: 'It's true that I limp, but I'm in distinguished company.' And he referred to Tamburlaine, the lame conqueror (confusing him, incidentally, with Timoleon, the Greek statesman). He'd also heard, though, of the Devil who limps, specifically in Lesage's novel *Le Diable boiteux* (1707). It is also Satanic to limp.[48]

In *The Breaking of the Vessels* Harold Bloom corrects Lacan's famous adage that the unconscious is structured like a language: no, it is 'structured like *Freud*'s language, and the ego and superego, in their conscious aspects, are structured like Freud's own texts, for the very good reason that they *are* Freud's texts. We have become Freud's texts, and the *Imitatio Freudi* is the necessary pattern for the spiritual life in our time.' 'Alas', Bloom adds; for this is a horrific, catastrophic condition, far beyond anything you'd think of as a pleasure principle. 'It is not, I think, hyperbolic to observe that, for the later Freud, human existence is quite as catastrophic a condition as it was for Pascal and for Kierkegaard, for Dostoevsky and for Schopenhauer.' Being haunted by God is to limp indeed. 'There is a crack in everything that God has made, is one of Emerson's dangerously cheerful apothegms.' We are all, Bloom suggests, caught up in the remorseless wrestle between superego and ego – 'shockingly like the Gnostic vision of the relation of Yahweh to human beings'. And so on. To be inside this J-text is to be struggling with the Jehovah who actually tried to kill Moses.[49]

An Absolute Text

'[D]as haben wir behandelt wie einen heiligen Text': 'we treated it – the dream-text – like a sacred text.' Freud's ringing assertion in *The Interpretation of Dreams* is a declaration of faith in the Scriptural importance of every jot and tittle of the exemplary dream-text, a hermeneutic credo that turns every dream into a kind of Holy Writ, every analyst into a rabbi, and, by implication, every reading encounter into a Biblical engagement. And the text in which nothing is insignificant and everything is endlessly weighable and interpretable – every 'nuance of the verbal expression', even the *Mängel*, the gaps and deficiencies, the apparent insufficiencies of meaning in the *Wortlaut*, the wording – has not only become a piece of pseudo-Holy Writ, but is a text full of endless obligations for interpreters that are (forgivable pun in the circumstances) nightmarish to contemplate. No wonder that it was in this very section of the *Interpretation* that Freud went on to talk about the finally deterring dark navel-place of the dream: the interpreter's black hole, or the cabbalist's graveyard.[50]

Borges has some inkling of the dementing nature of the cabbalist's vision of the text – and the world – as endlessly significant:

> Bloy (I repeat) did no more than apply to the whole of Creation the method which the Jewish Cabalists applied to the Scriptures. They thought that a work dictated by the Holy Spirit was an absolute text: in other words, a text in which the collaboration of chance was calculable as zero. This portentous premise of a book impenetrable to contingency, of a book which is a mechanism of infinite purposes, moved them to permute the scriptural words, add up the numerical value of the letters, consider their form, observe the small letters and capitals, seek acrostics and anagrams and perform other exegetical rigours which it is not difficult to ridicule. Their excuse is that nothing can be contingent in the work of an infinite mind. Léon Bloy postulates this hieroglyphical character – this character of a divine writing, of an angelic cryptography – at all moments and in all beings on earth.[51]

Borges well appreciates, of course, that the secular literary Classic, however subject to repeated interpretation, usually fails to rise to the provoking hermeneutical density of the Bible. Homer can be said to have nodded at times; the Holy Spirit, by definition, never nods. So the Spirit-breathed text lacks the contingency, the blank or slack passages, the dead water, that are to be found even in the Classic. To think otherwise, even of Classics, would be extremist. Anyone reading *Don Quixote* or *Macbeth* or the *Chanson de Roland* as the Bible has been read would be reckoned, Borges properly believes, quite mad.[52] But this is precisely what has happened and is happening. Umberto Eco is right to observe that critical history is crowded with secular texts that are in fact treated as sacred for their culture, and this is especially true in the field of postmodernist critique. *Finnegans Wake* is the big symptom and example of this. This particular acme of the (post)modernist text was set up precisely out of a desire to rival the Judaeo-Christian Scriptures in luring in the interpreter forever. Its wishes have been massively respected *per se* and *per exemplum*.

The assumption that some such Scripture-rivalling absoluteness of text is central to textuality has come massively to dominate hermeneutical theory in our time. It commands the Freudian notion of the dream-text as Holy Writ in particular, and, opening out from that, the idea of the more-or-less Surrealist text in general as a cabbalistic play of signifiers. It infects the Revolution of the Word as pronounced in exemplary style in the Joyce circle by the likes of Eugene Jolas.[53] It is profoundly present in the concept of the word as revolutionarily proposed by Saussure's generic lectures. It is no accident that Saussure was so much attracted by the idea of glossolalia. What his linguistics was based in historically, and what it in principle led back to, was a faith in the tongues of men being akin to the tongues of angels. (Post)modernist literary theory and practice endorse the parallel. Engaging now with the Enigma Variations of the text, the critic is still envisaged as seeing, with St Paul, *per speculum in aenigmate*, still staring into the cabbalistic mirror of enigmas. Derridianism hooks back to link up with the cabbalists, with Pico della Mirandola and his kind, the keen-eyed neo-Platonistic presiders over recessive meanings, infinitudes of symbolics, and allegorical truths, and with all the devious and canny rabbis and other Midrashics across the ages. Eco calls this post-Scriptural or pseudo-Scriptural criticism 'Paranoid Criticism'. It's a hermeneutics skidding perilously about on what he labels 'Hermetic Drift'. Fear of this interpretative paranoia – *suspicious* reading carried to the point of insanity – has prompted Eco to call latterly for *limits* to our views of what interpretation can do.[54]

Troping as Onto-Theology

Eco appears to believe that the syndrome by which 'a text becomes sacred for a certain culture' and so 'becomes subject to the processes of suspicious reading and therefore to an excess of interpretation' can be modified and contained, even if not absolutely cured. Paranoia can give way to sanity; Augustinian excesses of allegorization and abundances of 'spiritual' senses can be controlled by a Thomist faith in the 'literal sense'. Few would argue with Eco's honest-broker advocacy of some sort of dialectic between Augustine and Aquinas – I certainly wouldn't: something like that wish is a theme of this book. The declaration that 'any act of interpretation is a dialectic between openness and form, initiative on the part of the interpreter and contextual pressure', looks to me like very good sense.[55] But whether the historically persistent parasitical relation between books and the Big Book, between *écriture* and Scripture, between secular and sacred hermeneutics, which has been so peculiarly dramatized in post-modernist theory and practice, can ever be dodged is much more open to dispute. Eco seems to hanker after a great secularizing leap forward, out of sacred Augustinian paranoia into secular Thomist sanity. But so far – and Eco's own criticism and fiction tell mightily against him – the desired *coupure* or break, a great repressive hermeneutical shift as it would be, has not occurred. What's more, and crucially, any attempt at it would have, and has, to cope with the transcendentalism implicit in all rhetorical acts of speech or writing. For what is at issue are what appear to be the onto-theological implications of all rhetoric *per se*. As deconstructionist hostility to logocentrism has endlessly avowed, all our linguistic practices, our poetics, our rhetorics, are, whether we like it or not, inescapably metaphysical through and through. 'La métaphysique – relève de la métaphore.' However one reads this enigmatic Derridian slogan – and Derrida's English translator has us hovering tantalizingly between a relation of outright cancellation and one of skewed preservation – the necessary implication of a symbiotic interdependence between metaphor and metaphysics is clear, even if its acceptance by Derrida comes riven by a sense of tragedy and despair cohabiting in this particular piece of parasitic feeding.[56]

Take *prosopopoeia*. It's the trope by which things, ideas, non-persons, are given a *persona*, an actor's mask, are granted a face and a personality. It's also the poetic manoeuvre that has, ever since Ruskin, been rather sneered at as 'the pathetic fallacy'. Despite Ruskin's suspicions, prosopopoeia is utterly fundamental to fiction, and arguably to all writing. Prosopopoeia instigates and undergirds *apostrophe*, the rhetorical activity of addressing persons and things which otherwise have no perceivable existence. And as ancient rhetoric recognized, apostrophe and prosopopoeia are the key tropes by which the gods are invoked or made present.

All of which is vividly apparent in the Old Testament. As Herbert Marks has nicely put it, the prophetic oracle of the Old Testament is 'a hyperbolic prosopopoeia'.[57] And Ruskin's famous worried skirmish with prosopopoeia in that chapter of his *Modern Painters* (III. 12) entitled 'Of the Pathetic Fallacy' is based in at least two clear counts of this trope's offence to rationalism. The first is the utter dependence of the existence of God in the Old Testament upon what Philip Sidney in 1595 in the *Defence of Poesie* (in a passage where he was defending poetry against Puritans with the argument that the Biblical Psalms were 'a heavenly poesie') praised as the Psalmist's 'notable *Prosopopoeias*' ('when he maketh you as it were see God comming in his maiestie'). These tropes may be aweing, Ruskin concedes, in prophetic hands. He's prepared to allow that the 'presence of the Deity' can only be registered in such 'great astonishment' as 'The mountains and the hills shall break forth before you into singing, and all the trees of the field shall clap their hands'. But this is a kind of verbal ecstasy that mere poets must avoid. It's ungoverned and perhaps ungovernable: 'feverish and wild fancy'. 'Even in the most inspired prophet it is a sign of the incapacity of his human sight or thought to bear what has been revealed to it.' The second, and fundamental, offence, according to Ruskin, is the glaringly anti-empirical, non-scientific, metaphysical nature and tendency of all prosopopoeias. The great poet perceives the primrose 'rightly in spite of his feelings'. For him 'the primrose is for ever nothing else than itself – a little flower apprehended in the very plain and leafy fact of it, whatever and how many soever the associations and passions may be that crowd around it'. The root problem of prosopopoeia for Ruskin is the suggestions of transcendence always implicit in it. Donald Davie agrees with Ruskin's perception, but from the opposite point of view. His Bateson Memorial Lecture on 'Personification' is not only a general defence of prosopopoeia and of the poetry of the eighteenth century which is so remarkably full of the trope against Ruskin (who is, though, never named in the lecture); it is also keen to praise the metaphysical consequences that follow when 'Nature' is personified in the habitual eighteenth-century way: 'personification, far from being a device that we may or may not avail ourselves of as we please, implies one rather alarming image of what sort of world it is that we live in. Either that world is by and large "up to us"; or else it is not. And personification implies that it is not.'[58] And if prosopopeia lets the transcendent leak busily into writing, apostrophe is, of course, the fundamental trope of prayer.

Can These Dry Bones Live?

According to Quintilian, prosopopoeia was anciently not only the means of bringing the gods down from heaven; it was also the way the dead were raised. The idea that the dead, or somebody not actually present – an author, for instance, or a fictional character or narrator, indeed anybody whose words are on the paper in front of you though they are not otherwise present – might speak, nonetheless, to us is a wager that most writing and reading and literary criticism are built on. 'He being dead, yet speaketh': this is the faith of writing; and it's not accidental that this faith should be expressed thus vividly in the famous chapter on Faith in the Biblical Letter to the Hebrews (11: 14) in the matter of the perdurably eloquent faith in God of the dead patriarch Abel.

'Lazare, veni foras': Lazarus, come forth! Thus Christ apostrophizes the dead Lazarus (John 11: 43), and by this apostrophe the dead man is raised. For Maurice Blanchot, this is the essence of the 'miracle' of reading, the liberation of life, presence, meaning, from within the tomb of the text, so that 'we converse with Lazarus, dead for three days'.[59] With sure appropriateness T. S. Eliot too appropriates this Biblical encounter as the model for what reading is about in the prosopopoetic encounter between reader and text, and between present reading and writing and the texts of the canon or tradition. Were conditions to be right for him, J. Alfred Prufrock might bring himself to say that he was Lazarus come back from the dead – that he was a reanimation of the person animated by the apostrophe of Christ, the one thereafter latent in the Biblical text for subsequent reanimations by readers. Eliot said that he was thinking at this point in 'The Love Song of J. Alfred Prufrock' of that extraordinary moment in Dostoevsky's *Crime and Punishment* (IV. 4) when the prostitute Sonia Marmeladov seeks to bring the killer Raskolnikov back from sinful unbelief to belief by reading to him, straight, the Fourth Gospel's story of the raising of Lazarus. So in his poem, in a rich layering of prosopopoeias, Eliot would raise the prospect of raising Lazarus again, with multivalent intent: seeking to reanimate the texts of the past, St John's and Dostoevsky's, to revive the theological claim for life after death made in the story of Lazarus's raising in the Biblical text, and also to resurrect the combined textual and theological meanings presented by the attempted re-resurrection – both a textual and moral, theological resurrection – of the Biblical Lazarus by Dostoevsky's fallen-woman reader. What, then, Eliot's poem's encounter with Lazarus brings home is that readers and re-readers, all those engaged with the tradition through its texts, are resurrection men (and women). The question of presence, of what is made really present or not, in writing and reading, is, as Eliot knew and as George Steiner's *Real Presences* keeps insisting, of course theological and Biblical. It is some version of the question that Eliot's *The Waste Land* appropriated from Ezekiel (37: 4): 'Son of man, can these bones live?' The issue is, in the end, sacramental. The table at which the literary parasite sits looks oddly akin to a eucharistic one.

But recognizing this paramount fact about poetics and hermeneutics, which is in my contention the big ideological key to (post)modernist critical theory and writing practice, by no means provides a way out of the paradox of the 'Two Interpretations of Interpretation'. For we have, I think, to follow Derrida (and Jabès) in a critical-historical recognition that the Two – tantalizingly opposed, dauntingly parergonic – Interpretations of Interpretation are both located within the Judaeo-Christian idea of the text, the book, and reading. Here, as at most points, deconstruction is utterly parasitic upon the Biblical. The Mosaic Breaking of the Tables is, as Derrida's commentary on Jabès spells it out, fundamental for all parties. 'Rabbi' and 'poet' – that is, on the one hand, the interpreter who seeks final signifieds and original truths and, on the other, the interpreter who eschews final truths for mere delight in the play of signifiers – both stand among the fragments of an original divine writing, both of them commanded, though diversely so, by 'the necessity of exegesis, the interpretative imperative': 'The original opening of interpretation essentially signifies that there will always be rabbis and poets. And two interpretations of interpretation.'

And the Judaeo-Christian tradition has never lost sight of this rupture, 'a rupture within God as the origin of history', and so within writing and inter-pretation, as articulated by the breaking of the tables of the Law.[60] Alongside the idea of the revelatoriness of the Open Book, the Light of Scripture, the historicism and referentialism of the Word, alongside the claim to true teleo-logy and to the reality of God and the real presence of Christ in the Writings, in history, and within the sacrament, there has always functioned a counter-set of equally felt realities: the dark side of the Deity, the mystery of the absence of God and the averted divine face (the de-facing of God, as it were – the antithesis of prosopopoeia), the troubling silence of the heavens, the founding wilderness experience, the daunting caginess of hermeticism and closed meanings – indeed, the occasional but persistent sheer uninterpretability of the Scripture.

It's a double bind which helps make Judaeo-Christianity so existentially tragic and, naturally, turns the scene of twentieth-century existentialism into a tragedy. In their various, but connected, ways Kafka and Beckett are in this tight Biblicist mew or impasse, impelled, with that Beckett character who is named – after Jahweh – Innommable, the Unnameable, to go on – living, interpreting, speaking, explaining – but unable to go on. It's the impasse at the very heart of Derrida's deconstruction, at the centre of what he believes is the essence of all post-Graeco-Judaeo-Christian text-making, a cruel dilemma traceable all the way back, beyond even Sinai and the Breaking of the Tables, to the founding confusion at Babel, that confounding of speech which mirrored even more movingly for Derrida than Sinai did, a tragedy in the very name of God – and so an impasse in all the divine naming, textualizing, and work. It's a dilemma over which God himself weeps in a passage in which Derrida's tone becomes quite majestically Beckettian:

> The original is the first debtor, the first petitioner; it begins by lacking and by pleading for translation. This demand is not only on the side of the con-structors of the tower who want to make a name for themselves and to found a universal tongue translating itself by itself; it also constrains the deconstructor of the tower: in giving his name, God also appealed to translation, not only

between the tongues that had suddenly become multiple and confused, but first *of his name*, of the name he had proclaimed, given, and which should be translated as confusion to be understood, hence to let it be understood that it is difficult to translate and so to understand. At the moment when he imposes and opposes his law to that of the tribe, he is also a petitioner for translation. He is also indebted. He has not finished pleading for the translation of his name even though he forbids it. For Babel is untranslatable. God weeps over his name. His text is the most sacred, the most poetic, the most originary, since he creates a name and gives it to himself, but he is left no less destitute in his force and even in his wealth; he pleads for a translator. As in *La folie du jour* by Maurice Blanchot, the law does not command without demanding to be read, deciphered, translated. It demands transference (Übertragung and Übersetzung and Überleben). The *double bind* is in the law. Even in God, and it is necessary to follow rigorously the consequence: *in his name*.[61]

In his well-known comments on Wordsworth's *Essay upon Epitaphs*, Paul de Man dwelt rather impressively on the mortality latent within the resurrection work of prosopopoeia – 'the latent threat that inhabits prosopopoeia, namely that by making the dead speak, the symmetrical structure of the trope implies, by the same token, that the living are struck dumb, frozen in their own death'. Commenting on this passage, Herbert Marks wants to generalize de Man's claim. This is a rhetorical commonplace: *eidolopoeia*, the specific function of raising the dead, 'may also refer to the petrifying impact the trope can have on the audience'; but it's also a commonplace within the Judaeo-Christian prophetic tradition. Prophecy turns you to stone, knocks you cold, paralyses you, by its obscurities.[62] And something of such deadliness – silence, blankness, absence – is widely recognized within Judaeo-Christian hermeneutics as the corollary of prosopopoeia's life-force. Lazarus, for instance, comes forth from the tomb. The utterance of Christ the Logos is a performative one. The apostrophe produces the man. A living *prosopon* emerges from the grave. But, famously, he says nothing, and there is no book of his experiences, remembrances, sayings. He's the type, then, of the resurrected Christ in every way, including his mysterious silence. D. H. Lawrence, provoked by the large blanknesses of Christ's alleged resurrection time on earth, rushed in to supply missing details in *The Man Who Died* (1931). The Gospel itself, though, remains provokingly silent. 'And there were also many other things which Jesus did, the which, if they should be written every one, I suppose that even the world itself could not contain the books that should be written' (John 21: 25). But these books were not written.

T. S. Eliot's 'Prufrock' is provoked by the multiple cases of this kind of silence that frame the Lazarus story. The dumbness of Mary and Martha's brother is afforced by the restraint that Father Abraham imposes on the other

Lazarus of the Gospels – who also hangs around Prufrock as a kind of possible model – the poor man who sat at the gate of Dives. In that story of Jesus, Abraham refuses to allow this Lazarus to return from the dead to warn the rich man's brothers: 'If they hear not Moses and the prophets, neither will they be persuaded, though one rose from the dead' (Luke 16: 31). And the Lazarus who will not speak and the Lazarus whose message would not be listened to even were he allowed to return to utter it are part of the impressive cast-list of dead prophets and dumb advisers who provide Prufrock with glumly negative models of anti-eloquent selfhood: the prophet John the Baptist, his severed head on a platter; the Fool in *Hamlet*, an empty skull tossed up from a hole in the ground by a rebukingly garrulous grave-digger; Dante's Guido de Montefeltro, in the poem's epigraph, who only spoke out in *Inferno*, canto xxviii, because he believed that Dante would never get out of Hell to repeat his words. These potential prophetic models are stammering prophets, shaky examples. And Prufrock stammers even as he raises the possibility of stepping into their shoes: 'I am no prophet'; 'No! I am not Prince Hamlet . . . Am . . . At times, indeed, almost ridiculous – Almost, at times, the Fool'. Only almost. And he never actually says 'I am Lazarus', only raises the possibility of doing so ('would . . . after all . . . if . . .'). So Lazarus does not come back from the dead to any good purpose, then, in the person of Prufrock. There's no real resurrection in the text, no actual word of promise 'to tell you all', only stammering hints of that possibility. Much like in *Crime and Punishment*, then, after all.

Sonia Marmeladov reads the Lazarus story at great length in hopes that Raskolnikov, 'blinded and unbelieving' like the Jews in the Gospel account, 'will hear it now, and he, too, will believe'. But when she ends her reading, nothing happens. 'That is all there is about the raising of Lazarus.' Raskolnikov appears to be moved by the narrative, but after five minutes' silence he returns to other matters. There's no conversion, no modern miracle, no re-raising of Lazarus from the dead. In effect, the null effect upon the killer reproduces the traditional silence of Christ's Gospel client. It also anticipates *Prufrock*'s later aggregation of stammerings: Dostoevsky's potential Lazarus, like Eliot's might-be Lazarus, Baptist, Hamlet, and Yorick, remains locked up in mere possibility. A Biblical silence reigns. If there be resurrection here, it's a resurrection of negative reminders, negative moments in a tradition of deadly silences.

In the Wilderness

But it is still a *Biblical* silence. For silence, puzzle, *aporia*, absence, blankness, stuttering, are as much part of Biblical theology, of Scriptural logocentrism, as are their opposites. George Steiner writes eloquently of the 'heresy' of 'absolute tragedy' – the black condition of deconstructionist agonistic 'negative ontology' that was given terrible expression in our time by 'the phenomenology of Auschwitz'. A mature theology, he declares, has to confront this absence: 'Where theology and metaphysics, be they of a Judaic or of a Christian source, aim to be adult in the face of the strident facts and provocations of the inhuman, of the radically damned, as they inform our recent history, they must make themselves freely accessible to the hypothesis of despair. If this hypothesis is a heresy, it is one which now lies at the centre.'[63] But, of course, as the texts that Steiner cites continually reveal, this hypothesis has never been far from the centre of the Judaeo-Christian. The hints and provocations of 'absolute tragedy', the utter defacement of God, arise in the texts of Shakespeare and Beckett, Freud and Kafka, Kierkegaard and Karl Barth, from within, rather than from outside, the Judaeo-Christian tradition. The 'unsparing humiliation' of the negativity Steiner anticipates is *already* 'inside theology itself'. It was, for instance, the cabbalists themselves who imagined God's 'abstention from a flawed creation'. 'No man knows who he is': Borges quotes the turn-of-the century cabbalist Léon Bloy, and adds that 'No one could illustrate that intimate ignorance better than he'. Intimate ignorance: it isn't only in modern times that negative or 'absurd' theology has been on the Judaeo-Christian stage.[64]

What Kafka focuses, as Albert Camus recognized both in Kafka and in Kierkegaard, is the complete enfolding of the Judaeo-Christian hope by manifest absurdism. 'They embrace the God that consumes them.' This faith – Job's faith: 'Though he slay me, yet will I trust in him' (Job 13: 15) – is, as Martin Buber explained it, the essential paradox of the wilderness wandering of the Jews, where trust, perseverance, *Emunah*, are called for, and actually developed, within 'the course of the world . . . depicted in more gloomy colors than ever before'.[65] It's *diaspora* doctrine that is central to the Biblical theology of redemption. 'My God, my God, why hast thou forsaken me?' The question, preserved in the Aramaic in most manuscripts of the Gospel texts of Mark 25: 34 and Matthew 27: 46 – 'Eli, Eli (or Eloi Eloi), lama sabachthani?' – strikingly refers back to the Hebrew of Psalm 22: 1, seemingly via some colloquial Aramaic paraphrase of that text. The most solemn moment of redemptive Christological suffering is enacted, thus, in a momentous intertextual engagement with a voice from the traditional Jewish wilderness agony, from the ancient encounter with God's absence or silence, with the 'infinite distance of the Other' that makes the Jewish consciousness so 'unhappy' and Jabès so arresting for Derrida.[66] It comes, then, as no surprise at all to see that St Luke is moved to add to the crucifixion story that 'there was darkness over all the earth' (Luke 23: 44).

That darkness in Luke's Gospel coincided with the tearing of the veil of the Temple which in the other narratives followed the words about foresakenness. That veil, the shroud over the Holy of Holies in the Jewish Temple, was thus 'removed' for Christians. The tearing was dramatically allegorized by the writer to the Hebrews as an emblem of the opening to Gentiles of the way to God through the broken body of the crucified Christ − 'through the veil, that is to say, his flesh' (Hebrews 10: 20) − as well as being associated with the 'vail' over the Jewish mind in its reading of the Old Testament, a version of the veil which Moses put on over his face when he came down from Mount Sinai and his meetings with God out of which came the Tables of the Law (a version, too, of the veiled, curtained Torah which animates *voile*-obsessed De-Rideau). 'Which veil is done away in Christ', St Paul went on (2 Cointhians 3: 14). Nonetheless, this Mosaic veil, declared to have been done away with, remains in place: 'even unto this day, when Moses is read, the vail is upon their heart.' Still, if Jews will 'turn to the Lord, the vail shall be taken away'. Just as, St Paul claims, it has been for Christians: who 'all with open face' behold 'as in a glass the glory of the Lord' (2 Corinthians 3: 15–18). But for all that, 'we' Christians still 'see through a glass darkly' (1 Corinthians 13: 12). So this piece of spry Midrashic reading and re-reading is a very dance of several veils, now in place, now removed, all as variously interpretable as the suggested purpose of Moses' veiling in the first Biblical place. Was that done because the 'glory of his countenance' was too intense to be looked at 'steadfastly' (2 Corinthians 3: 7)? Or done so that they might not notice when the glory faded (verse 13)? No wonder Biblical commentary has danced in some consternation about this (un)veiling. No wonder, either, and especially in the light of my historical allegations in this chapter, that the deconstructionist should find such pronounced, if negative, stimulation in this veiling as textual parable − as Hillis Miller and his editors do in reading Hawthorne's story 'The Minister's Black Veil'.[67]

John Bunyan's great text *Come, & Welcome, to Jesus Christ* (1678), in commenting on 2 Corinthians 3: 17–18, can only repeat the Pauline dualism − now Christ's Glory is unveiled, now it is still veiled. Just so, in Bunyan's *The Pilgrim's Progress* we find the pilgrims still 'as yet' unable 'with open face' to behold the Celestial City.[68] Seeking, as ever to unveil the precious, saving meanings of the Word, this great and representative Protestant interpreter necessarily finds himslef again and again confronting the daunting habit its meanings have of remaining imperiously veiled within it. And this is important to stress because of those commentators on deconstruction who try, wrongly I think, to drive a massive wedge between Judaism and Christianity, describing the former as based *Ur*-Derridianly in endless, fluid, Midrashic Scripturality ('the home of the Jews is a sacred text in the middle of commentaries') and the latter as triumphalistically resolving this rabbinical difference-deferment of meaning because of the claimed intervening person of Christ the Logos. 'Paul and the Church Fathers after him replaced the prolonged Rabbinic meditation on and mediation of the Text with the pure unmediated presence of Jesus, who resolves all oppositions, stabilizes meaning, provides ultimate identity, and collapses differentiation'. This is Susan Handelman's influential argument – it has influenced Jürgen Habermas for one – but it's a summary of the New Testament and the subsequent Christian commentary tradition that bears scant relation to the actuality. What, I wonder, would Lancelot Andrewes have made of being dismissed as one not meditating on the text in prolonged ways or of accepting the a-textually 'unmediated presence of Jesus'!

Revealingly, Ms Handelman calls 2 Corinthians 3: 14–17 in aid as proof that Paul is 'anti-textual'. 'He is impatient and frustrated with the Jews because they cling to the "letter"; that is, they will not read the text Christocentrically.' But this quite ignores the complex textual play of veilings within this very passage of St Paul and also within the undoubtedly rather aporetic tradition of later Christian commentary upon it.[69] The whole Christian tradition reveals there's a distinct degree of veiling hereabouts for the Christian as well as for Moses. Of veiling or, indeed, of prophylaxis: which is the Scriptural problematic (and a general Biblical, not just a Jewish, one) that Derrida announces in that excited place in *La Carte postale* where the *Dictionary* suddenly reveals to him the etymological connection between *prophylaxis* and *phylacteries*: '*phulaktèrion* . . . lieu pour garder, *poste*, corps de garde . . . préservatif . . . talisman, amulette, chez les Juifs, *pancarte* qu'on portait suspendue au cou et où étaient inscrits des versets de la loi mosaïque.'[70] Obsessed by the prophylactic, condomized aspects of communication by words, postcards, letters, the post (the headgear of the writer portrayed in Derrida's inspirational Bodley postcard is, as we saw earlier in chapter 5, shaped like a used condom), this latter-day rabbi is delighted ('j'ai bondi à lire cette définition dans mon dictionnaire') to see how traditionally Judaic the deconstructionist condomization of the Word might be. In the phylactery, Scripture is treasured up, guarded, preserved; but it's also preserved – perhaps – as in a *préservatif*; that is, rendered, so to say, impotent, unproductive, Shandyanly phimotic.

Phylacteries developed slowly, we're told, in Jewish religious practice, and seem not have become universal much before the end of the second century AD.[71] But their implications are of the oldest theological date. What Derrida finds pronounced in Jabès is the ancient idea that the writing of God which must be meditated on day and night is not only legible but also illegible – because God is a cack-handed writer, cacographic, divinely dyslexic. The deconstructionist notion of 'radical illegibility' – an 'original illegibility' – basic to 'the book', thus begins in a Jewish sense of divine illegibility that's basic to the book as it is to The Books.[72] For Derrida the question of the 'non-existence' of 'writing' is, then, the same question as that of the existence or not of God; the one question is parasitical upon the other, the logocentric upon the onto-theologocentric. And as Derrida's explication of this para-siting suggests (if I read him aright), the whole exemplary deconstructionist rhetoric and lexicon of parasite-work continually invokes, at least as a dynamic subtext, this parasiting of the writing question upon the 'serious' Cartes-ian 'question concerning the proof of the existence of God'.[73] No wonder the drift of deconstructionist hermeneutic in general, and of Derrida's powerful illustrative lexicon in particular, has suggested a theology, even if a 'negative theology'.

Even as Derrida seeks to deny that he is a negative theologian, he's com-pelled to admit that he does sound uncommonly like one:

> Suppose, by a provisional hypothesis, that negative theology consists of con-sidering that every predicative language is inadequate to the essence, in truth to the hyperessentiality (the being beyond Being) of God; consequently, only a negative ('apophatic') attribution can claim to approach God, and to prepare us for a silent intuition of God. By a more or less tenable analogy, one would thus recognize some traits, the family resemblance of negative theology, in every discourse that seems to return in a regular and insistent manner to this rhetoric of negative determination, endlessly mutiplying the defenses and the apophatic warnings: this, which is called X (for example, text, writing, the trace, différance, the hymen, the supplement, the pharmakon, the parergon, etc.) 'is' neither this nor that, neither sensible nor intelligible, neither positive nor negative, neither inside nor outside, neither superior nor inferior, neither active nor passive, neither present nor absent, nor even neutral, not even subject to a dialectic with a third moment, without any possible sublation ('Aufhebung'). Despite appearances, then, this X is neither a concept nor even a name; it does *lend itself* to a series of names, but calls for another syntax, and exceeds even the order and the structure of predicative discourse. It 'is' not and does not say what 'is'. It is written completely otherwise.[74]

And, of course, as indicated by the way Derrida inspects 'negative theology' (not to mention the work of enthusiastic 'Christian' negative theologians such as Mark C. Taylor, wild, riddling, babbling, stammering[75]), this is a negative theological stress that is not simply Jewish. If Jewish Lazarus, 'come back from the dead', stayed silent, then Christ, the Christian Logos, the paramount Word within the Christian Word, never for his part left any writings behind. When he did, on one rare occasion, write someting, it was in the ephemeral dust, and the Gospel writer doesn't disclose what it was. In any case, this episode occurs in a much disputed passage (John 8) that most of the manuscripts mark as doubtful or leave out altogether (in token of which *The New English Bible*, for instance, banished it to a marginal position at the end of that Gospel text).

Hupogrammatics

But, then, this is surely only in keeping with the radical New Testament suggestion elsewhere that Christ, the *Alpha* and the *Omega*, the beginning and end of all alphabeticism, is a *hupogrammos*. 'Christ also suffered for us, leaving us an example, that ye should follow his steps' (1 Peter 2: 21), and 'example' there is *hupogrammos* (Kafka's *Schönschrift*), that exemplary line of textual stuff written out by Greek pedagogues at the top of the schoolboy's wax writing tablet to provide him with copy for handwriting practice. Characteristically the *hupogrammos* included all the letters of the Greek alphabet. In this metaphor, then, Christ is, of course, envisaged as embracing all of language's potentia, the whole A to Z. He's the ultimate authoritative origin of the Christian experience as text, and of text – the Logos precisely as the centre of logocentrism in the common view of that term. But, most arrestingly, the matter doesn't stop there. For the *hupogrammos* was also frequently a nonce-sentence concocted by the schoolmaster not for the sake of sense but for mere practice in the formation of letters, and, what's more, this sentence commonly contained nonsense words. So that here the Logos as ultimate *telos*, the ground of all meaning, the followable example, is also the Logos as non-referential, mere language stuff, a self-enclosed, riddling, even nonsensical sentence or (fairly) random collocation of language bits.

Here the Biblical Christ is indeed exemplary. The way that the *hupogrammos* opens itself to two interpretations – the darkly hermetic parasitical upon the clearly followable, and vice versa – is revealing in several directions. This is a clear example of the Judaeo-Christian doubleness that has provoked exegetes at every stage of the tradition. The Logos is indeed, as Lancelot Andrewes put it in his Christmas Day sermon of 1618, 'a sign to wonder at', a sign 'able to amaze any': for it was the '*Verbum infans*, the Word without a word; the eternal Word unable to speak a word'. The Word, centre of a sign-system of astonishing versatility, as explicated here and elsewhere with such critical dexterity and intellectual suppleness by Andrewes: but still swaddled in silence. This sign, guarantor of the eloquence of signs, proof of the contention that ' "signs have their speech" ', this so very much not-dumb sign ('this is no dumb sign'): yet still a dumb sign. As a new-born babe, Christ 'speaks, and out of His crib, as pulpit, this day preaches to us'; and 'yet He cannot speak as a new-born babe'. The paradox – the deconstructionist paradox, no less – is one that the unregenerate Eliot could not quite grasp, as is evident from his adulteration of Andrewes' words in his poem *Gerontion*, where 'the Word without a word' is bowdlerized as 'The word within a word'. Only after his conversion to Christianity, in its Anglican version, was Eliot able to condone or grasp the fullness of Andrewes' amazement. In *Ash Wednesday*, part IV, 'The silent sister' 'bent her head and signed but spoke no word', and the bird sings of the dream that's 'The token of the word unheard, unspoken'. By the time of *Four Quartets* the inaudibility of the Word – the eloquent silence, the 'music heard so deeply / That it is not heard at all' – has been accepted as the very essence of the faith, which consists of hints and guesses afforced by 'prayer, observance, discipline, thought and action'. And, as the reliance on Lancelot Andrewes for this paradox of belief and of the believer indicates, this is not some twentieth-century dilution of belief, a late diminishment of a once unwavering logocentrism, but rather an ancient essence of Christianity and of the Judaeo-Christian tradition.

Touching the Torpedo-Fish

Which is why the historic dualism of the *hupogrammos* and the ancient bivalence of the Scriptures are so exemplary for the literary critic and the literary historian now, in our time. For this Biblical logocentricity is already deconstructionist. And in being so, the logocentric is, of course, the great analogue of, and indeed programmer of, the deconstructionist. The (post)modernist is indeed the parasite at the eucharistic feast. But once again, as ever, the logic of parasite-feeding applies. Deconstructionism is not some awful spectre to be banished if possible from the Table of the Lord. Theology needs the reminders of deconstruction as much as deconstruction depends on theology's. But, of course, as Derrida is foremost in recognizing, theology has never, ever, not dealt in the aporetic, the desert experience, the *via negativa*.[76] Aporia infects the very ecstasy of the believer. It's what the mystery of the faith includes; it's always been at the very heart of the mystical 'marriage' of Christ and the believer:

> There is therefore now no sentence of death against those that are in Christ Jesus. Of what, then, have we been speaking? Of religion as a human possibility – or of that freedom in God which is ours beyond all human possibility? Of sin – or of righteousness? Of death – or of life? What sort of a man is this man, who is able to apprehend – as we have apprehended – the frontier, the

meaning, the reality, of religion? Whence has he come? Whence does he observe? Whence does he know? Who tells him that he is – man? Once these questions are asked – formulated indeed before we have asked them – we become like the interlocutors of Socrates: we have touched the torpedo-fish and are benumbed.

That's from Karl Barth's Commentary on the Epistle to the Romans. The torpedo-fish allusion is to Plato's *Meno* (80A–C), where Meno says that Socrates is like a torpedo-fish, a *narke*, because his arguments have narcotic, numbing, cramping effects on his victims' minds, bringing them to a state of *aporia*. Three times at this place in the *Meno* the word *aporia* occurs. And Socrates' interlocutor is said to be in *aporia* because Socrates is: the great man induces *aporia* ('doubt' – the Loeb translation; *Verwirrung*: confusion, muddle, be-wilderment – Schleiermacher's translation) because he is in *aporia* himself. It's an extraordinarily arresting place for one of the most powerful twentieth-century apologists for Christian belief to find himself as he reads the Christianly triumphalist eighth chapter of Romans – in an aporia which comes from God himself and which is, by implication, of the very nature of God-in-Christ himself.[77]

At a certain point in his *Real Presences* argument George Steiner's defences against negativity cave in:

> *On its own terms and planes of argument*, terms by no means trivial if only in respect of their bracing acceptance of ephemerality and self-dissolution, the challenge of deconstruction does seem to me irrefutable. It embodies, it ironizes into eloquence, the underlying nihilistic findings of literacy, or understanding or rather in-comprehension, as these *must* be stated and faced in the time of epilogue.

But as Steiner's book keeps showing, deconstruction has in effect no terms or planes of argument of its own. From the beginning, from Babel onwards, or from the time when Moses the prophet returned stuttering from en-countering the tautologous Deity of the Burning Bush, the 'I Am that I Am', 'the challenge of deconstruction' has been the challenge of theology. And, of course, vice versa.[78]

NOTES

1 By George Steiner I mean, of course, the arguments in his *Real Presences* (Faber, London, 1989). Amusingly, Steiner seems to have become known, after this book, in Germany as Pfarrer – Pastor, Preacher, the Reverend – George. The onto-theological idea comes from Heidegger: see e.g. Richard Rorty,

'Nineteenth-Century Idealism and Twentieth-Century Textualism', in *Consequences of Pragmatism (Essays: 1972–80)* (Harvester, Brighton, 1982), *c*.140. Cf. Roger Poole, 'The Yale School as a Theological Enterprise', *Renaissance and Modern Studies*, 27 (1983), 1–29; *Idem*, 'Generating Believable Entities: Post-Marxism as a Theological Enterprise', in *Comparative Criticism*, ed. E. S. Shaffer (Cambridge University Press) 7, (1985), 49–71.

2   See Linda Hutcheon, *A Poetics of Postmodernism: History, Theory, Fiction* (Routledge and Kegan Paul, London, 1988), not least 'Historicizing the Postmodern: The Problematizing of History', 87 –101.

3   Louis-Jean Calvet, *Roland Barthes 1915–1980* (Flammarion, Paris, 1990), 285.

4   Michel Serres, *The Parasite*, trans. Lawrence R. Schehr (John Hopkins University Press, Baltimore and London, 1982), Translator's Preface, vii.

5   Jacques Derrida, *La Vérité en peinture* (Flammarion, Paris, 1978), 60 – 6; *The Truth in Painting*, trans. G. Bennington and Ian McLeod (Chicago University Press, Chicago and London, 1987), 53–6. Immanuel Kant, *Die Religion innerhalb der Grenzen der blossen Vernunft*, ed. Rudolf Mauter (Reclam, Stuttgart, 1974), 66–8. Jacques Lacan, 'The Empty Word and the Full Word', in *The Language of the Self: The Function of Language in Psychoanalysis*, trans. and ed. Anthony Wilden (John Hopkins University Press, Baltimore and London, 1968), 25, added in June 1966: 'Pascal's wager . . . still intact . . . what it conceals . . . inestimable for psychoanalysis – at this date . . . still in reserve. . . .'

6   Derrida, *La Vérité en peinture*, 77–8.

7   Derrida, 'Ellipsis', in *Writing and Difference*, trans. Alan Bass (Routledge and Kegan Paul, London, 1981), 300.

8   'I too am called Elijah . . . the name of the prophet present at *all* circumcisions . . . the patron . . . of circumcisions. The chair on which the new-born baby boy is held is called "Elijah's chair". This name should be given to all the "chairs" of Joycean studies': *Ulysses Gramophone*, in *Jacques Derrida: Acts of Literature*, ed. D. Attridge (Routledge, New York and London, 1992), 284–5. Cf. 'Wasn't I about to act . . . like Elijah': 'The Principle of Reason: The University in the Eyes of its Pupils', *diacritics*, 13 (Fall 1983), 5. *'Mon nom secret, Elie'*: 'Circonfession' – i.e. Circumcision-Confession, in *Jacques Derrida par Geoffrey Bennington et Jacques Derrida* (Seuil, Paris, 1991), 85. This is the outcome of a long projected *Livre d'Elie*, a book 'sur la circoncision', ibid., 84ff. *Derrière les rideaux* : *Glas* (Galilée, Paris, 1974), 268–9b. For discussion, see Susan Handelman, 'Jacques Derrida and the Heretic Hermeneutic', in *Displacement: Derrida and After*, ed. Mark Krupnick (Indiana University Press, Bloomington, 1983), 98ff.; and Susan Handelman, *The Slayers of Moses: The Emergence of Rabbinic Interpretation in Modern Literary Theory* (State University of New York Press, Albany, N.Y., 1982). (Christopher Norris, *Spinoza and the Origins of Modern Critical Theory* (Blackwell, Oxford, 1991), esp. ch. 5, 'From Scriptural Hermeneutics to Secular Critique', is vaguely pertinent.) For discussion of Derrida's self-namings – Reb Rida and Reb Derissa (*Écriture et Différance*), De Rideau (*La Carte postale*) – and *fort-da*, veils and curtains, see John Llewellyn, *Derrida on the Threshold of Sense* (Macmillan, London, 1986), 70ff. (Llewellyn's 'Jack Derippa' suggestion should be taken as

an affectionate Aussie tribute: in Australia 'a ripper' is a fine performance or performer.)

9   Harold Bloom, *Ruin the Sacred Truths: Poetry and Belief from the Bible to the Present*
(Harvard University Press, Cambridge, Mass., and London, 1989), 8.

10   Roland Barthes, 'The Struggle with the Angel: Textual Analysis of Genesis 32:
23–33', in *Structural Analysis and Biblical Exegesis: Interpretational Essays*, trans.
Alfred M. Johnson (Pickwick Press, Pittsburgh, Penn., 1974), 21–33; in R.
Barthes, *Image-Music-Text*, ed. and trans. Stephen Heath (Fontana, London, 1977);
and in R. Barthes, *The Semiotic Challenge*, trans. Richard Howard (Blackwell,
Oxford, 1988), 246–60. *Idem*, 'A Structural Analysis of a Narrative from Acts
x–xi', in *Structuralism and Biblical Hermeneutics*, ed. and trans. Alfred M. Johnson
(Pickwick Press, Pittsburgh, Penn., 1979), 109–43; and as 'The Structural
Analysis of Narrative: Apropos of Acts 10–11', in *Semiotic Challenge*, 217–45.

11   Jean-François Lyotard, *The Differend: Phrases in Dispute*, trans. Georges Van Den
Abbeele (Manchester University Press, 1988), para. 144, p. 83.

12   Michel de Certeau, *Heterologies: Discourse on the Other*, trans. Brian Massumi,
Foreword by Wlad Godzich, Theory and History of Literature, 17 (Manchester
University Press, 1986), 58–9.

13   Hillis Miller's point in *Hawthorn and History: Defacing* It (Blackwell, Oxford,
1991), 134, that there is a plurality of 'deconstructionisms', is well made.

14   The phrase 'Interpretive Community' appeared first, it seems, in Josiah Royce's
Problem of Christianity: see Samuel Weber, Introduction to *Demarcating the
Disciplines*, *Glyph* Textual Studies, 1 (University of Minnesota Press, Minneapolis,
1986), xi. Weber is perturbed by the link and by Fish's (implied) messianism.

15   R. Barthes, 'Structural Analysis of Narrative', *Semiotic Challenge*, 241–2.

16   'After three J writers, as it were – the great original J, Jeremiah, and the author
of Job – I conclude with a brief coda on a fourth J writer, the author of the
humorous and belated Book of Jonah': Bloom, *Ruin the Sacred Truths*, 22. N.B.
also *The Book of J*, trans. David Rosenberg, interpreted by H. Bloom (Faber,
London, 1990). Dan Jacobson is author of *The Story of the Stories: The Chosen
People and its God* (Secker and Warburg, London, 1982); Gabriel Josipovici of
The Book of God: A Response to the Bible (Yale University Press, New Haven and
London 1988). For other evidence of the Biblicism phenomenon see *The Literary
Guide to the Bible* (Collins, London, 1987), edited by two leaders in this field,
Robert Alter and Frank Kermode, as well as the discussion and bibliography of
ch. 7: 'Literary Study of the Bible', in Robert Morgan and John Barton, *Biblical
Interpretation* (Oxford University Press, 1988). But the movement is currently
unstoppable: see e.g. Martin Warner (ed.), *The Bible as Rhetoric: Studies in
Biblical Persuasion and Credibility* (Routledge, London, 1990); Regina Schwarz
(ed.), *The Book and the Text: The Bible and Literary Theory*, (Blackwell, Oxford,
1990); Stephen Prickett (ed.), *Reading the Text: Biblical Criticism and Literary
Theory* (Blackwell, Oxford, 1991). For fair summaries of some recent approaches,
see T. R. Wright, *Theology and Literature* (Blackwell, Oxford, 1988), ch. 2: 'On
Reading the Bible as Literature', 41ff. The reference to Lancelot Andrewes is to
his Easter sermon of 20 April 1617 on Matthew 12: 39–40, 'The sign of the

prophet Jonas': 'Among the Jews it goes for current – the Rabbins take it up one after another, that this Jonas was the widow of Sarepta's son': Lancelot Andrewes, *Ninety-Six Sermons* vol. 2 (John Henry Parker, Oxford, 1841; AMS reprint edn, New York, 1967), 392.

17 Herself, yes; though, as a matter of fact, the main critical wrestlers in my story of Jacob *redivivus* are male; and among the attractions offered male critics by consciously Old Testament, rabbinical, Midrashic, and other variously Judaeo-Christian models for criticism are, it seems to me, precisely their patriarchalism.

18 Harold Bloom, 'Wrestling Sigmund: Three Paradigms for Poetic Originality', in *The Breaking of the Vessels* (Chicago University Press, Chicago and London, 1982), 47ff. See also *idem, Ruin the Sacred Truths*, ch. 1: 'The Hebrew Bible', and *The Book of J*.

19 Geoffrey M. Hartman, 'The Struggle for the Text', in *Midrash and Literature*, ed. Hartman and Sandford Budick (Yale University Press, New Haven and London, 1986), 3–18. Cf. Hartman's discussion of his increasing attraction towards Jewish traditions of Biblical interpretation and his Jewish Scriptural heritage, in Imré Salusinszky (ed.), *Criticism in Society* (Methuen, New York and London 1987), esp. 86–7.

20 See the discussion in John Paul Russo, *I. A. Richards, His Life and Work* (Routledge, London, 1989), 143–4.

21 Cf. Hugh Kenner, *Ulysses* (George Allen and Unwin, London, 1980), ch. 10: 'Maelstrom, Reflux', 93ff.

22 Jacques Derrida, 'Two Words for Joyce', in *Post-Structuralist Joyce : Essays from the French*, ed. Derek Attridge and Daniel Ferrer (Cambridge University Press, 1984), 145–59; *idem*, 'Des tours de Babel', trans. Joseph F. Graham, in *Difference in Translation*, ed. Joseph F. Graham (Cornell University Press, Ithaca and London, 1985), 170; *idem, La Carte Postale* (1980), 257–8.

23 The charge of heretical rivalry between, and extension of, orthodox (Jewish) Biblicism's interpretative postures is spelled out in e.g. Susan Handelman's 'Jacques Derrida and the Heretic Hermeneutic', in *Displacement and After*, ed., M. Krupnick (Indiana University Press, Bloomington, 1983), 98–129.

24 Walter Redfern, *Puns* (Blackwell, Oxford, 1984), 18.

25 See ibid., 36–7, and Bloom, *Breaking of the Vessels*, 53. *Jacob*, Heb. Ya'ªqōb, *he clutches*, or *he clutched*. cf. ya'ªqōb-il: *may God protect*. Root 'qb also gives verb *to take by the heel* (i.e. to supplant, trip up, or overtake).

26 D. H. L. to Edward Garnett, 5 June 1914, in *The Letters of D. H. Lawrence*, vol. 2: *1913 –16*, ed. George J. Zytaruk and James T. Boulton (Cambridge University Press, 1981), 182–3.

27 D. H. Lawrence, *Apocalypse*, ch. 10, in *Apocalypse and the Writings on Revelation*, ed. Mara Kalnins (Cambridge University Press, 1980), 101.

28 D. H. Lawrence, 'The Novel', in *Phoenix II: Uncollected, Unpublished and Other Prose Works*, ed. Warren Roberts and Harry T. Moore (Heinemann, London, 1968), 416–17.

29 For the Great War and modernist aesthetics of violence, see ch. 3: 'Destructive

Elements', in Valentine Cunningham, *British Writers of the Thirties* (Oxford University Press, 1988), 36ff.

30 See e.g. Carolyn Dean, 'Law and Sacrifice: Bataille, Lacan, and the Critique of the Subject', *Representations*, 13 (Winter 1986), 42–62.

31 See e.g. Elaine Scarry, *The Body in Pain: The Making and Unmaking of the World* (Oxford University Press, New York, 1985), and *idem* (ed.), *Literature and the Body: Essays on Populations and Persons, Selected Papers from the English Institute, 1986*, n.s. 12 (Johns Hopkins University Press, Baltimore and London, 1988). A quick glance at, say, the journal *Representations* tells this particular story of somatic stress and distress: e.g. Wolfgang Kemp, 'Death at Work: A Case Study on Constitutive Blanks in Nineteenth-Century Painting', 10 (Spring 1985), 102–23; Joseph Leo Koerner, 'The Mortification of the Image: Death as a Hermeneutic in Hans Baldung Grien', 10 (Spring 1985), 52–101; Julia L. Epstein, 'Writing the Unspeakable: Fanny Burney's Mastectomy and the Fictive Body', 16 (Fall 1986), 131–66; Frances Ferguson, 'Rape and the Rise of the Novel', 20 (Fall 1987), 88–112. See also the essays in the forum 'Séance and Suicide: The Media of Somatic History', 22 (Spring 1988); Page du Bois, *Torture and Truth* (Routledge, New York and London, 1991); and Michael Feher, Ramona Nadaff, and Nadia Tazi ed., *Fragments for a History of the Human Body*, 3 vols (*Zone*, nos 3–5), (Urzone, New York, 1989).

32 Jacques Derrida, *La Carte postale* (Flammarion, Paris, 1980), 270, 271.

33 See e.g. Derrida, 'Violence and Metaphysics, An Essay on the Thought of Emmanuel Levinas', in *Writing and Difference* (Routledge and Kegan Paul London, 1978), 79–152.

34 Derrida, 'Edmond Jabès and the Question of the Book', in *Writing and Difference*, 67.

35 Derrida, 'Des tours de Babel', 170.

36 Jacques Lacan, 'The Freudian Unconscious and Ours', in *The Four Fundamental Concepts of Psychoanalysis*, ed. Jacques-Alain Miller, trans. Alan Sheridan (Peregrine, Harmondsworth, 1986), 17–28. Charmingly, but also repressively, Pontius Pilate becomes *Pontius Pilot* in this translation.

37 Sigmund Freud, *Die Traumdeutung* (Fischer Verlag, Munich 1977), 309–12; *The Interpretation of Dreams*, trans. James Strachey, Pelican Freud Library, vol. 4 (1976), 493–8; Jacques Derrida, 'The Flowers of Rhetoric', in the 'White Mythology: Metaphor in the Text of Philosophy' section of *Margins of Philosophy*, trans. and ed. Alan Bass (Harvester, Brighton, 1982), 245ff. Cf. René Girard: 'As the evidence of what I say becomes compelling [about the Biblical master trope of the Scapegoat], attempts will be made to rearrange it in a manner more compatible with the self-esteem of an intelligentsia, whose sole common ground and binding theme – *religio* – has become the systematic expulsion of everything biblical, our last sacrificial operation in the grand manner' ('Interview', originally in *diacritics*, 8 (1978); repr. in Girard, *'To Double Business Bound': Essays on Literature, Mimesis, and Anthropology* (Johns Hopkins University Press, Baltimore and London, 1978), 227.

38   Jeffrey Mehlman, 'Writing and Deference: The Politics of Literary Adulation', *Representations*, 15 (Summer 1986), 1–14. *On the Origin of Language: Jean Jacques Rousseau, Essay on the Origin of Language; Johann Gottfried Herder, Essay on the Origin of Languages*, trans. with afterwords by John H. Moran and Alexander Gode (Frederick Ungar Publishing Co., New York, 1966). John Milton, *De Doctrina Christiana, Complete Prose Works*, VI (Yale University Press, New Haven and London, 1973), Translator's Preface by John Carey, xiii–xvi. J. Hillis Miller singled out the Mehlman piece as the reason for handing the *Representations* people the black spot in his MLA presidential address: 'and, on the left, Jeffrey Mehlman, [and] the editors of *Representation* who ran an essay of his as the lead piece' (*Theory Now and Then* (Harvester Wheatsheaf, Hemel Hempstead, 1991), 315).

39   J. Hillis Miller, *Hawthorne and History: Defacing It*, The Bucknell Lectures in Literary Theory (Blackwell, Oxford, 1991), 147 – 8; 162 – 3; 171, n. 3. How multiplexly ironic that Hillis Miller should go out of his way to warn us that 'to find out what Freud really said one must read him in German': 'Constructions in Criticism', *Theory Now and Then*, 261, n. 5.

40   Walter Benjamin, 'Die Aufgabe des Übersetzers', in *Illuminationen: Ausgewählte Schriften* [1955] (Suhrkamp Verlag, Frankfurt am Main, 1969), 69.

41   Derrida, 'Des tours de Babel', 205.

42   Ibid., 204.

43   Paul de Man, 'Conclusions: Walter Benjamin's "The Task of the Translator"', edited transcript of a 1983 lecture, with discussion, in *The Resistance to Theory*, ed. Wlad Godzich (Manchester University Press, 1986), 73 – 105. The Luther information is on 105, n. 8. De Man no doubt thought, as Hillis Miller reports, 'that religious questions are the most important ones' (Interview, in *Criticism in Society*, ed. Imré Salusinszky (Methuen, London, 1987), 232); but he was keen to magick them all down to a self-negatingly deconstructed impasse in some version of his *Dasselbe bei Gott / ohne Dasselbe* formulation. See e.g. 'The Timid God: A Reading of Rousseau's *Profession de foi du vicaire savoyard*', *Georgia Review*, 29, no. 3 (Fall 1975), 533–58; and 'Pascal's Allegory of Persuasion', in *Allegory and Representation, Selected Papers from the English Institute, 1979–80*, ed. Stephen Greenblatt (Johns Hopkins University Press, Baltimore and London, 1981), 1–25.

44   Derrida, 'Edmond Jabès', 68.

45   Franz Kafka, *In the Penal Settlement: Tales and Short Prose Works*, trans. Ernst Kaiser and Eithne Wilkins (Secker and Warburg, London, 1949; repr. 1973), 196 –7; Kafka, *Gesammelte Werke, Erzählungen* (Fischer Taschenbuch Verlag, Frankfurt am Main, 1983), 159 – 61.

46   Derrida, 'Edmond Jabès', 68, 65. For more of Derrida on Kafka, see 'Before the Law', a meditation on Kafka's story 'Vor dem Gesetz'/'Before the Law', where the question What is Literature? is strikingly cast in terms of a Talmudic questioning (rabbinical, Pauline, Kafkaesque) of the Law, the Old Testament Law, and of texts of standing before the Law (a rabbinical sequence that Derek Attridge's commentary is scarcely interested in at all): 'Before the Law', in

Jacques Derrida: Acts of Literature, ed. D. Attridge (Routledge, New York and London, 1992), 181ff.

47 Hartman, *Midrash and Literature*, 8.

48 Conrad, letter to Marguerite Poradowska (1? February 1891), in *Collected Letters of Joseph Conrad* ed. Frederik R. Karl and Laurence Davies, vol. 1: *1861–1897*, (Cambridge University Press, 1983), 67–8, n. 1.

49 Bloom, *Breaking of the Vessels*, 63ff.

50 Freud, *Die Traumdeutung*, ch. 7a, 419; Penguin trans., 658.

51 Jorge Luis Borges, 'The Mirror of Enigmas', in *Labyrinths*, ed. Donald A. Yates and James E. Irby (Penguin, Harmondsworth, 1971), 246–7. Cf. 'The God's Script', where the divine sentence, revealed in 'the tireless labyrinth of dreams', would be a single word of 'absolute fullness', because produced by 'an absolute mind' (ibid. 205, 206).

52 Borges, 'The Kabbalah', in *Seven Nights*, trans. Eliot Weinberger (Faber, London, 1984), 95ff.

53 See, 'Revolution of the Word', *Transition*, no. 16–17 (June 1929), 11ff; and Eugene Jolas, 'The Revolution of Language and James Joyce', in Samuel Beckett et al., *Our Exagmination Round His Factification for Incamination of Work in Progress* (Paris, 1929), (Faber, London, 1936).

54 Umberto Eco, 'After Secret Knowledge', *TLS* (22–8 June 1990), 666, 678; *idem*, 'Some Paranoid Readings', *TLS* (29 June – 5 July 1990), 694, 706; *idem*, *The Limits of Interpretation* (Indiana University Press, Bloomington and Indianapolis, 1990), esp. ch. 1: 'Two Models of Interpretation', and ch. 2: 'Unlimited Semiosis and Drift'.

55 Eco, *Limits of Interpretation*, 21.

56 Jacques Derrida, *Margins of Philosophy*, trans. Alan Bass (Harvester, Brighton, 1982), translator's note on *relève* (and *Aufhebung*), 258.

57 Herbert Marks, 'On Prophetic Stammering', in *The Book and the Text*, ed. Regina M. Schwarz, 74–5, 77.

58 John Ruskin, *Works*, Library Edition, ed. E. T. Cook and Alexander Wedderburn, vol. 5 (1904); *Modern Painters*, vol. III, (1856), Part IV; *Of Many Things*, ch. 12; 'Of The Pathetic Fallacy', 201–20. Donald Davie, 'Personification', *Essays in Criticism*, 31 no. 2 (April 1981), 103.

59 Maurice Blanchot, 'Reading', in *The Space of Literature*, trans. with an introduction by Ann Smock (University of Nebraska Press, Lincoln, 1982), 194–6.

60 Derrida, 'Edmond Jabès', 67, and Translator's Note 3, 311.

61 Derrida, 'Des tours de Babel', 184. Cf. the discussion of Beckett in Attridge's interview with Derrida: 'This is an author to whom I feel very close . . . but also too close'. 'He is nihilist and he is not nihilist': *Jacques Derrida: Acts of Literature*, ed. Attridge, 60, 61.

62 Herbert Marks, 'On Prophetic Stammering', 74–5; Paul de Man, 'Autobiography as DeFacement', in *The Rhetoric of Romanticism* (Columbia University Press, New York, 1984), 75–6, 78.

63 George Steiner, 'A Note on Absolute Tragedy', *Journal of Literature and Theology*, 4, no. 2 (July 1990), 147–56.

64   Borges, 'Mirror of Enigmas', 247.
65   Albert Camus, 'Hope and the Absurd in the Work of Franz Kafka', in *The Myth of Sisyphus* (1955), and Martin Buber, 'Kafka and Judaism', in *Two Types of Faith* (1951); both in *Kafka: A Collection of Critical Essays (Twentieth Century Views)*, ed. Ronald Gray (Prentice-Hall Inc., Englewood Cliffs, N.J., 1962), 147–62.
66   Derrida, 'Edmond Jabès', 68, 69.
67   Hillis Miller, *Hawthorne and History*, 38, 46ff. See my chapter 2: 'Textual Stuff'.
68   See my discussion of the passage and similar ones in 'Glossing and Glozing: Bunyan and Allegory', in *John Bunyan: Conventicle and Parnassus: Tercentenary Essays*, ed. N. H. Keeble (Oxford University Press, 1988), e.g. 231–2.
69   Susan Handelman, 'Jacques Derrida and the Heretic Hermeneutic', in *Displacement and After*, ed. M. Krupnick (Indiana University Press, Bloomington, 1983), 106 *et passim*. Jürgen Habermas, *The Philosophical Discourse of Modernity*, trans. Frederick Lawrence (Polity, Cambridge, 1987), Lecture VII: 'Beyond a Temporalized Philosophy of Origins: Jacques Derrida's Critique of Phonocentrism', 160–84 and 406–7, n. 46.
70   Derrida, *La Carte postale*, 91.
71   'Phylacteries', in *The New Bible Dictionary*, ed. J. D. Douglas (Inter-Varsity Press, London, 1975), 995.
72   Derrida, 'Edmond Jabès', 77–8.
73   Jacques Derrida, 'Limited Inc abc . . .', *Glyph*, 2 (1977), 223ff.
74   Jacques Derrida, 'How to Avoid Speaking: Denials', in *Languages of the Unsayable: The Play of Negativity in Literature and Literary Theory*, ed. Sanford Budick and Wolfgang Iser (Columbia University Press, New York, 1989), 4; repr. in *Derrida and Negative Theology*, ed. Harold Coward and Toby Fashay (State University of New York Press, Albany, 1992), 73–142.
75   Mark C. Taylor, *Erring: A Postmodern A/Theology* (University of Chicago Press, 1984); and 'Non-Negative Negative Atheology', *diacritics*, 20, no. 4 (Winter 1990), 2–16; and 'nO nOt nO', in *Derrida and Negative Theology*, 167–98. Cf. Kevin Hart, *The Trespass of the Sign: Deconstruction, Theology, and Philosophy* (Cambridge University Press, 1989).
76   See Derrida, 'Post-Scriptum: Aporias, Ways and Voices', in *Derrida and Negative Theology*, 283–323.
77   Karl Barth, *The Epistle to the Romans*, trans. from the 6th edn by Edwyn C. Hoskins (Oxford University Press, 1933), 271. The Loeb Plato, *Laches, Protagoras, Meno, Euthydemus*, ed. W. R. M. Lamb (Heinemann, London; Harvard University Press, Cambridge, Mass., 1962), 296–7. *Platons Werke*, von Friedrich Schleiermacher, Teil 2, Band i, 3rd Auflage (Georg Reimer Verlag, Berlin, 1856), 245.
78   Steiner, *Real Presences*, 132, 112.

Index